Canada
Concept Map

Review ● Chapters 1, 2, 3

● Chapters 4, 5

● Chapters 6, 7, 8, 9, 10

● Chapters 11, 12, 13

Section   I   II   III   IV

History Concepts

Change

Regionalism

Power

Identity

Co-operation/
Conflict

Section Structure

Section Story
Chapter Visual Overview
Chapter Focus
Chapter Preview/Prediction
Chapter Content
Chapter Review

Assessment
Understanding Concepts
Developing Research Skills
Developing Communication Skills
Applying Concepts
Challenge Plus

Jordana Sherman
8A 3/8H3

Canada Revisited

Confederation, The Development of Western Canada, A Changing Society

Phyllis A. Arnold

Penney Clark

Ken Westerlund

ARNOLD PUBLISHING LTD.

For more information contact
Nelson
1120 Birchmount Road
Scarborough, Ontario
M1K 5G4

Or you can visit our Internet site at
http://www.nelson.com

Authors

Phyllis A. Arnold, Penney Clark, Ken Westerlund

Canadian Cataloguing in Publication Data

Arnold, Phyllis A.
    Canada revisited 8

Includes index.
ISBN 0-919913-49-0

1. Canada—History—Juvenile literature. I. Clark, Penney, 1950– II. Westerlund, Ken, 1936– III. Title. IV. Title: Canada revisited eight.
FC172.A76 2000   971   C00-910278-7
F1008.2.A76 2000

Arnold Publishing Project Team

Editor-in-Chief: Karen Iversen
Senior Editor: Betty Gibbs
Project Managers: Nancy Marcotte, Betty Gibbs
Project Co-ordinators: Judi Hanson, Christina Barabash
Educational Editor: Phyllis A. Arnold
Editors: Nancy Marcotte, Christina Barabash
Design: Linda Tremblay, Marcey Andrews
Production: Marcey Andrews, Judy Bauer, Colette Howie,
                Zenna Liber, Leslie Stewart,
                Linda Tremblay
Proofreaders: Christina Barabash, Dianne Smyth
Cover Design: Marcey Andrews

Assisted by

Illustration: Marcey Andrews, Claudia Bordeleau,
                Claudette MacLean
Maps: Johnson Cartographics Inc., Wendy Johnson

Printed and bound in Canada
4 5 05

Support Materials
Canada Revisited 8 Teacher's Resource Package
ISBN 0-919913-63-6

Canadian Historical Images ClipArt CD-ROM
Macintosh, ISBN 0-919913-41-5
Windows, ISBN 0-919913-71-7

The following is referred to throughout this book:
Ordinary People in Canada's Past, Second Edition, by Nancy Sellars Marcotte, published by Arnold Publishing Ltd., ISBN 0-919913-46-6

Throughout this book you will be provided with a number of website addresses. These are provided to you as a resource list only. Due to the changing nature of internet resources, Arnold Publishing Ltd. does not warrant that these websites will continue to exist, nor does Arnold Publishing Ltd. warrant or endorse the content of these websites and any websites linked to these references. You will want to discuss these references with your teacher in order to ensure that they continue to be appropriate.

Cover Photographs

Front: tl This publication includes images from *Corel Professional Photos* CD-ROMs which are protected by the copyright laws of the US, Canada, and elsewhere. Used under license. The photographic images may not be copied, are only to be used for viewing purposes.; tc Phyllis A. Arnold, Photographer. Site: Fort Edmonton Park, Edmonton, Alberta; tr ml Paul Punyi, Actor, *An Interview With History*, Edmonton, Alberta. Roth and Ramberg Photography; mr bl International Movie Services Ltd. (www.internationalmovie. com); mc Maureen Rooney, Actor, *An Interview With History*, Edmonton, Alberta. Roth and Ramberg Photography; br CP Picture Archive/Ken Gigliotti; bc Kennedy Jenson, Edmonton, Alberta.

Back: tl Digital imagery® copyright 1999 PhotoDisc, Inc.; tc Phyllis A. Arnold; tr Steam train at Heritage Park Historical Village, Calgary, Alberta (www.heritagepark.ab.ca); br Courtesy Betty Peters, © Betty Peters; bc Photo Courtesy of Lower Fort Garry National Historic Site (W. Lynch); bl Brad Gibson & Sara Taylor Gibson, *Eureka Theatre Company*, Barkerville, British Columbia. © Studio Grandell Photography, Photographer, Leif Grandell; ml Canadian War Museum, Victoria Cross; mc International Movie Services Ltd. (www.internationalmovie.com).

Acknowledgements

We would like to acknowledge the contributions of the talented production team at Arnold Publishing. They are indeed a remarkable group: Karen Iversen, editor-in-chief, Betty Gibbs, senior editor, and Linda Tremblay, lead designer, dedicated many extra hours of their time to help bring this book to completion; Nancy Marcotte, Marcey Andrews, Christina Barabash, Judy Bauer, Judi Hanson, Zenna Liber, Leslie Stewart, and Colette Howie worked efficiently and cheerfully under pressure. To them a very special thank you. Thanks also to Wendy Johnson for her excellent maps, Claudette MacLean, and Claudia Bordeleau for their wonderful illustrations.

Penney and Ken would like to thank Phyllis for inviting us to participate in this demanding, but very worthwhile project.

A special thank you to Jeffrey L. McNairn, John Smith, and Olive Dickason, who worked with meticulous care to assist us with historical accuracy.

Each of us would like to thank our families (Arnie, Ian, Emily, and Lois) for their patience and support.

As teachers all, we hope that this textbook will excite its readers about the history of their country and awaken an interest in exploring it further. We hope that they take pride in their country, and possess the ability to make thoughtful judgements about people and events in its history. We would like students to understand how Canada developed to the place we are today, and be able to consider how we may change in the future.

Phyllis A. Arnold
Penney Clark
Ken Westerlund

Validators

ABORIGINAL CONTENT VALIDATOR
Olive Patricia Dickason
Adjunct Professor
Department of History
University of Ottawa
Ottawa, Ontario

HISTORICAL VALIDATOR
Jeffrey L. McNairn
Postdoctoral Fellow
Department of History
York University
Toronto, Ontario

EDUCATIONAL VALIDATORS
Annetta Apostoli-Casati
Teacher
Corpus Christi Catholic Elementary School
Richmond Hill, Ontario

Sharon Willan
Principal, Retired
York Catholic District School Board
Aurora, Ontario

Bias Reviewer
John M. Smith
Principal
Green Glade Senior Public School
Mississauga, Ontario

Special Thanks
Jill Baird
Curator of Education
Museum of Anthropology
University of British Columbia
Vancouver, British Columbia

David J. Rees
Department of Modern Languages and Cultural Studies
University of Alberta
Edmonton, Alberta

Bernie Rubinstein
Program Advisor
Social, Canadian and World Studies
Toronto District School Board
Toronto, Ontario

Glenbow Archives
Calgary, Alberta

National Archives of Canada
Ottawa, Ontario

Pan Productions
Victoria, British Columbia

Rogers Communications, Inc.
(Confederation Life Gallery of Canadian History)
Toronto, Ontario

Dedication
This book is dedicated to the students who will be making history as they shape our country in the twenty-first century.

We acknowledge the financial support of the Government of Canada through the Book Publishing Industry Development Program for our publishing activities.

Canada

Table of Contents

To the Student

By looking at history we can often examine the roots of events and issues of today. Methods of preventing problems or facing today's issues may be built upon ideas and methods used in our past. People in history faced situations that relate to those of today. Many fascinating individuals who had impact on the history of Canada appear throughout this text.

Canada Revisited 8 begins with a brief review of Canadian History before 1850. The remaining four sections trace Canada's history from just prior to Confederation to 1920, just after World War I. Most information is arranged chronologically, in the order in which events in Canada's history happened.

An understanding of history can prepare you for addressing and resolving with more confidence the issues that we face today.

Canada Revisited 8 focuses on the way you learn. Activities for "revisiting" times and places in Canadian history are provided in the textbook before discussion of major political changes. Predicting outcomes, then reading further to confirm your prediction and add to your knowledge, will help you learn.

You will be involved in building thinking and learning skills as you increase your knowledge of Canada's past. Photo essays, works of art, narratives (stories), and excerpts from historical documents will give you the feeling of "revisiting Canadian history." Role-plays, simulations, debates, critical thinking exercises, and decision-making exercises will draw you into historical situations.

Problem-solving, research projects, and Review activities encourage you to apply and extend your skills and knowledge of Canadian history. Many types of activities are provided to suit your interests and learning style. Challenge yourself by selecting a range of different activities.

An understanding of the way you learn can allow you to become more confident, involved, and responsible for your own learning.

The pages that follow provide more detail about the features of this text and how you can best use them to understand and experience Canada's past.

Have fun and enjoy revisiting Canada's past!

About the Text

The more involved you become in reliving history through *Canada Revisited 8*, the more meaningful and enjoyable your study can be.

Icons

The five History concepts used in *Canada Revisited 8* follow. Wherever an icon appears the concept is a focus of that section. When the History Concept Icons appear in colour in the Chapter Focus they show which concepts are the main focus of the chapter. History icons are also found at the beginning of sections of content and in activities.

Change
The icon for change represents the process of something becoming different. Eight agents of change are examined.

Regionalism
The icon for regionalism is a highlighted square in a grid, set apart from its surroundings by boundaries. Five regions in Canada are examined.

Power
The icon used for power shows a bull. When seeing this icon ask: Who held (holds) the power? Does the country/region/group have control over its own internal affairs? Does it have control over its own external affairs?

Identity
In the icon for identity, the outlined square represents characteristics that are shared in common. The triangles represent the forces from within and from outside that shape our particular identity. When seeing this icon ask: How do Canadians see and describe themselves? How are we seen and described in other countries?

Co-operation/Conflict
On the icon for co-operation/conflict, the two parallel arrows represent co-operation and the two opposing arrows represent conflict.

This icon suggests using the internet to do further research.

Preview

Section stories relate to students' lives and introduce the section theme. See page 22 for an example. Each section has an activity relating to the theme of the section and the chapters within that section.

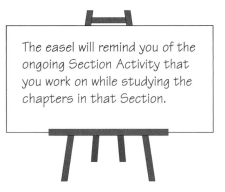

The easel will remind you of the ongoing Section Activity that you work on while studying the chapters in that Section.

The **Ongoing Project Icon** signals continuing projects. For example, the Section I Activity is introduced on page 31 and continued on pages 50, 53, 70, 73, and 86.

An **Overview** at the beginning of each chapter shows the main ideas of the chapter. See page 30 for an example.

The **Chapter Focus** points out which of the five History concepts (described on pages 24, 25, 28, and 29) will be emphasized. See page 31 for an example.

A **Chapter Preview/Prediction** activity helps you make predictions about the main ideas to be covered in that chapter. See page 31 for an example.

Visual Cues and Features

This textbook has been designed in ways that assist you to understand, organize, and remember information.

Graphics present information in visual ways. Read the illustrations, charts, maps, and graphs for information. (See example page 95.)

Titles in each chapter are coded by size and colour so you can tell when a new idea begins. As the title size decreases, the idea is explained in more detail. There are four main heading sizes.

Narratives have a coloured border and a row of dots along the top of the page. Section stories introduce a theme of the chapter. Other narratives portray fictional people in stories based on actual events. See page 38 for an example.

Focus On sections appear on a tabbed divider page with a tan background colour. They offer more detailed information about people, places, and events. See page 37 for an example.

Quotations from documents (usually primary sources) are written in a contrasting type style. (See pages 97 and 105.)

Biographies highlight individuals who are recognized as having contributed to events in Canada's past. A photograph or illustration is provided where available. See page 37 for examples.

Vocabulary words or expressions in **bold** print are explained at the bottom of that page. They also appear in the glossary at the end of the text (pages 372 to 377).

Footnotes marked by asterisks (*) signal that something on the page is explained in more detail at the bottom of the page. See page 42 for example.

Political Acts show changes made to government  throughout our history. The symbol on the left indicates a Proclamation or Parliamentary Act. See an example on page 130.

Sidebars are portions of important text that are emphasized by coloured background with a ragged edge.

Canada Revisited sections highlight and revisit historic sites, people, and events as they relate to today. (See page 40.)

Timelines are a visual way of showing a series of events in chronological order. (See pages 5 and 54 for examples.)

Numbered dots relate visual and textual information to each other. (See page 3.)

The **Inside Back Cover** provides a mini-atlas and charts to which you may wish to refer regularly.

The **Inside Front Cover** is a concept map. It summarizes the organization of the book and the icons used in it. (The History icons are described on page vii.)

Activities

Critical Thinking activities ask you to think about various points of view. Some are identified with the heading Point of View. See page 49 for an example. Others are indicated with a heading like the example below.

Decision-making activities require you to make a choice related to an historical event. These are indicated with a heading like the example below. See page 119 for an example of a decision-making activity.

Problem Solving activities ask you to become involved in an historic event by solving a related problem.

Simulations are meant to help you experience life as a person in a particular time period would. See page 102 for an example.

Research Projects ask you to find and present materials related to history. See page 90 for an example.

Many of the special projects include opportunities for you to share what you have learned with others (parents, classmates). See page 137 for an example.

Role-play activities ask you to place yourself in the situation of one of the individuals you are studying. See questions 9 and 10 on page 51 for examples.

Learning Skills

The **Learning How to Learn (SKIMM™) Appendix** is on pages 348 to 371. When working on exercises and Review activities, the icons are your cue to turn to the Appendix for ideas to help you complete the activity.

Additional ideas on **Learning How to Learn (SKIMM™)** are found on the *Canada Revisited 8* web page.

For Your Notebook questions ask you to understand and work with information you have read.

 **Exploring Further** questions ask you to extend your learning beyond the information in the chapter.

A **Review** section is found at the end of each chapter. This includes a chance to check the predictions you made at the beginning of the chapter. Review questions and activities are designed to help you understand concepts and develop research and communication skills (reading, writing, listening and speaking, viewing, and presenting). You can also apply and extend what you have learned in Applying Concepts and Challenge Plus activities. See page 50 for an example of a Review.

Concept Map

A Concept Map to *Canada Revisited 8* is included inside the front cover. It is a visual summary of the organization and features of the book. The coloured rings show the four Sections of the book. Chapters found within each Section are also identified. For example, Section II (blue ring) contains Chapters 4 and 5. The Section Structure box on the lower right page lists regular features of each Section and Chapter. Icons (pictorial representations) on the far bottom right are cues to material throughout the textbook that focuses on these five History concepts. The icons on the left page are cues to learning strategies used in the book. (See Appendix pages 348 to 371.)

A Research Model

Research means using an organized procedure to locate useful information on a topic. In various activities in *Canada Revisited 8* you are asked to do research and solve problems or make decisions about issues. The research model shown below is provided to help you. You may modify the model or design your own research model to suit your needs.

This model divides research into three parts: Gathering Information, Examining and Organizing Information, and Communicating the Information.

Gathering Information

 1. Understanding what you are to do

 2. Planning the project

 3. Locating the information

 4. Recording the information

Examining and Organizing Information

 5. Examining the information

 6. Organizing the information

Communicating the Information

 7. Preparing the presentation

 8. Sharing the presentation

 9. Assessing what you've done

Gathering Information

1. **Understanding what you are to do**
   Focus on the topic you are researching.
   - Read your topic several times and think about what you are being asked to do.
   - Examine the topic by asking what, why, which, where, when, who, and how.
   - Rewrite the topic in your own words or explain the topic to another student.

2. **Planning the project**
   Make a list of what you need to know and do before you start solving the problem.
   - Develop questions to guide your research:
     –What type of information is needed?
     –What key terms do you have to define?
     –What are possible sources of information?
   - Decide on the steps to follow to locate your information.
   - Think about the **criteria** you will use to assess your project. Decide how best to meet the requirements. See Appendix page 368 for self-assessment ideas.
   - Decide on an action plan to outline how you are going to do your research.

Action Plan

1. Date of Presentation...
2. Describe what you want your part of the presentation to look like and/or sound like.
   ....
   ....
   ....
3. Plan on paper what tasks have to be done. Assign a completion date for each task.

Task/Person	Completion Date	Done
1. _____	_____	_____
2. _____	_____	_____
3. _____	_____	_____

(add to this list as needed)

Criteria—standards by which something is judged or categorized

- Set target dates for stages of completion.
- Remember your plan of action must be flexible. Review it often and revise it if it isn't working.
- Think about how you will present your research project later on.

3. **Locating the information**
Use a variety of information sources:

–almanacs	–maps
–charts and graphic organizers	–monuments
–cartoons	–museum displays and artifacts
–CD-ROMS	–newspapers and magazines
–data bases	
–diaries and journals	–photographs
–dictionaries	–posters and banners
–encyclopedias	–radio and television programs
–fiction and non-fiction material	
–government records	–re-enactments
–graphs (circle, bar, line)	–reference books
	–scrapbooks
–reconstructed historical sites	–scripts and transcripts
	–songs
–internet	–speeches
–interviews and surveys	–statistics
–legal documents	–textbooks
	–videos and films

- Do surveys.
- Interview a variety of people about your topic.
- Contact experts.
- Skim read; use the table of contents, the index, the glossary.
- Keep a record of reference materials you use by following this format: author's last name, first name, book title, place of publication, date of publication (e.g., Marcotte, Nancy Sellars, ***Ordinary People in Canada's Past***, Second Edition, Edmonton, AB, Arnold Publishing Ltd., 1997).

4. **Recording the information**
Record only information related to your project.

- Use one of the following or a combination:
  –make graphic organizers and notes (see Appendix pages 349 and 362–364)
  –draw pictures, maps, and create graphs
  –make diagrams and charts
- Record definitions that relate to your topic.
- Write the information in your own words.

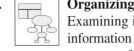
Examining and Organizing Information

5. **Examining the Information**

6. **Organizing the Information**
Examining information and organizing information are difficult to separate. These steps are often done at the same time.

- Go through all the information you have collected. Organize it into groups of similar types of information using graphic organizers such as charts, webs, diagrams, and maps. (See Appendix pages 349 and 362–364.)
- Decide if you need to do more research.
- Decide on an answer or a conclusion to end your project.

Communicating the Information

7. **Preparing the presentation***

- Ask yourself if you really have done what you were assigned to do.
- Decide how you wish to communicate your research findings to others. Choose a presentation idea from the Appendix on page 365.
- Prepare your presentation.

8. **Sharing the presentation**
   - Practise sharing your presentation.
   - Show it to a friend before you share it with others.

9. **Assessing what you've done**

- Judge your project based on the criteria you determined when planning it. See Appendix page 368 for self-assessment ideas.
- Record in your History Journal what you would do differently next time. Record what you would do the same.

---

*Presentation, as used in this book, refers to communicating information in visual, oral, or written forms.

Our History to 1850

The Review chapter summarizes what you studied in Grade 6 Social Studies and Grade 7 History. Pictures, maps, and other visuals on pages 3 to 20 are labelled with circled numbers that relate to the text material marked with the same number.

The First Nations

Chapter Activity

1. A review of the history of our country before 1850 is presented using timelines and related information. The timelines in this chapter are divided into time periods. The time periods often begin or end at turning points in our country's history.
   a) Preview the chapter. The coloured bars and triangles beside some headings relate to the timelines found within the chapter. Make a historical timeline of the chapter using the time periods and event points given.

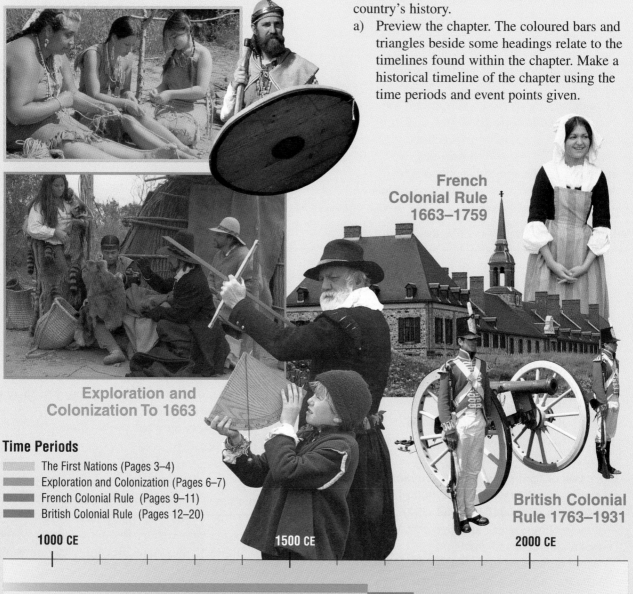

French Colonial Rule 1663–1759

Exploration and Colonization To 1663

British Colonial Rule 1763–1931

Time Periods

- The First Nations (Pages 3–4)
- Exploration and Colonization (Pages 6–7)
- French Colonial Rule (Pages 9–11)
- British Colonial Rule (Pages 12–20)

1000 CE   1500 CE   2000 CE

The First Nations

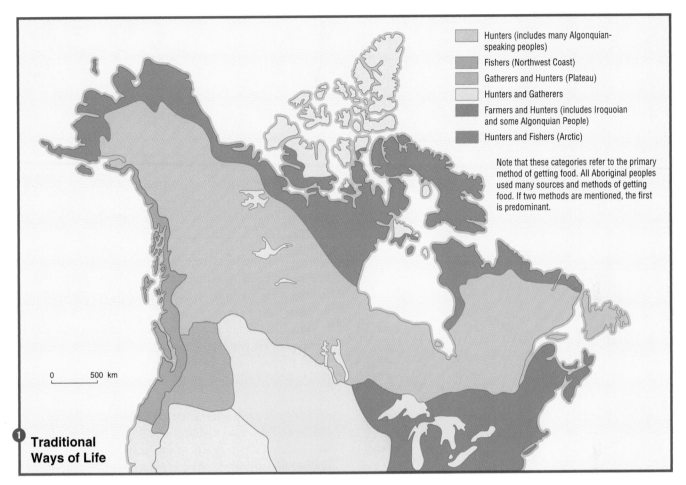

Legend:

- Hunters (includes many Algonquian-speaking peoples)
- Fishers (Northwest Coast)
- Gatherers and Hunters (Plateau)
- Hunters and Gatherers
- Farmers and Hunters (includes Iroquoian and some Algonquian People)
- Hunters and Fishers (Arctic)

Note that these categories refer to the primary method of getting food. All Aboriginal peoples used many sources and methods of getting food. If two methods are mentioned, the first is predominant.

0   500 km

① Traditional Ways of Life

❶ In the **pre-Contact** period, Aboriginal people lived all over what is now Canada. Groups of people were related in some ways, yet distinct. Groups can be described by the language spoken, or by their traditional way of life. The traditional way of life was the way they met their basic needs. The categories in the map refer to the primary method of getting food. All peoples used many sources and methods of getting food. If two methods are listed in the legend, the first is the more important.

❷ Unity and harmony between humans and nature were important to the First Nations. The land and all living things were respected. Needs were met from the environment. Food, clothing, shelter, and tools came from natural resources. The vegetation, climate, and land and water animals of a place influenced how a culture developed. The environment influenced the people, and the people interacted with and changed the environment.

Pre-Contact—before an Aboriginal people came into contact with European explorers; contact with Europeans happened earlier for people who lived near the Atlantic Ocean.

③

④

related extended families. Some were matrilineal: they traced their relationships through their mothers. Other nations were patrilineal: they traced their relationships through their fathers.

Wealth was not usually based on owning material goods, but on personal qualities. For a man, this meant being a good hunter or warrior. Women were respected for their skills in making food and clothing, and raising children.

Elders were highly respected. Male and female elders ensured that traditions, customs, and history were passed down orally to the next generation. Co-operation was valued. Making decisions by consensus was important. Survival often required co-operation. Food, often scarce, was shared.

The spirit world and human world were not separate for most First Nations peoples. Existing in a close relationship with nature was also a spiritual belief.

Harmony in groups was important, but differences did arise. There was plenty of space for all, so people who disagreed could move away and form their own communities. There could also be, and were, hostilities between different First Nations.

This chapter has been written in the past tense, because the generalizations refer to the historical period before 1850. However, many Native people today still hold the beliefs and values described.

For Your Notebook

1. Prepare a concept poster representing environmental interaction and/or balance. Concept posters are explained on page 350.

③ The cultures of First Nations were similar in some ways but not the same. It is important not to over-generalize about their ways of life.

④ The family was the basic unit of society. First Nations cultures were based on a family unit and **kinship**. Most had clans, which were large groups of

---

Kinship—having some of the same ancestors or being related by marriage

Timeline
Exploration and Colonization to 1663

The First Nations

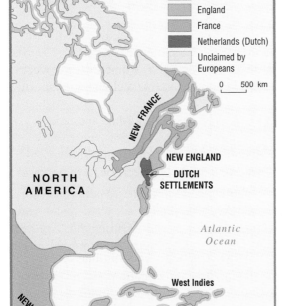

Map legend:
- Spain
- England
- France
- Netherlands (Dutch)
- Unclaimed by Europeans

0   500 km

NEW FRANCE

NEW ENGLAND
DUTCH SETTLEMENTS

NORTH AMERICA

Atlantic Ocean

West Indies

NEW SPAIN

CENTRAL AMERICA

SOUTH AMERICA

Territorial Claims

Time Periods

The First Nations

Early Asian and European Exploration About 500–1100

Age of European Exploration 1450–1600

French Colonization of New France 1604–1663

Early Asian and European Exploration About 500–1100

- possible visits to the West Coast of North America from Asia
- possible visits to the East Coast of North America from Europe
- archaeological evidence proves voyages by Vikings in this period

Age of European Exploration 1450–1600

- Europeans crossing the Atlantic, searching for a sea route to Asia
- Europeans searching for a Northwest Passage to Asia
- lands explored and claimed for various European mother countries

French Colonization of New France 1604–1663

- theory of mercantilism was a major reason behind exploration and colonization
- colony at Quebec established by Champlain in 1608; fur trade developed
- New France controlled by French colonial government

Timeline scale (right margin): 500, 600, 700, 800, 900, 1000, 1100, 1200, 1300, 1400, 1500, 1600

Exploration and Colonization to 1663

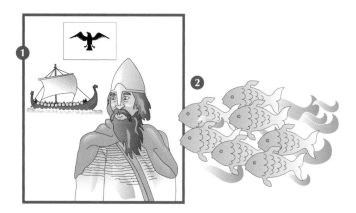

Early Asian and European Exploration

1 There are legends about first sightings of North America by Asian and European explorers, but little concrete proof. Norse sagas describe voyages to the Atlantic coast of North America. Archeological evidence verifies that, between 900 and 1000 CE, the Vikings came to North America and established several settlements.

2 There is some evidence that Portuguese, Basque, Spanish, French, and English expeditions visited North America in the early 1400s. They fished along the Atlantic coast. Some trading with Aboriginal people also occurred.

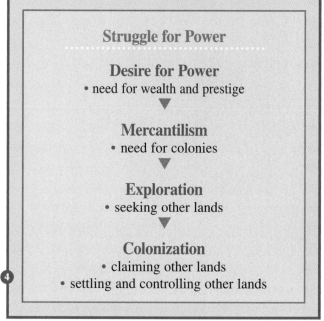

Struggle for Power

Desire for Power
• need for wealth and prestige
▼

Mercantilism
• need for colonies
▼

Exploration
• seeking other lands
▼

Colonization
• claiming other lands
• settling and controlling other lands

Age of European Exploration

3 During the later 1400s, explorers from many European countries searched for new water routes to Asia. They sought goods such as silks and spices, and to find out more about the world. During the "Age of Exploration" (1450–1600) Europeans explored lands in the Americas. Some European explorers were Columbus, Caboto, Cartier, Frobisher, Davis, Hudson, and Champlain.

Explorers claimed ownership over lands in the Americas on behalf of European rulers. Europeans believed that they had the right to control trade in the areas they claimed, even though Aboriginal people had lived there for thousands of years. Some also believed their control extended beyond the land and its resources to include the people.

4 During the 1500s and 1600s, many European countries aggressively sought wealth and power. Monarchs and merchants encouraged overseas exploration. They wanted colonies established to support trade. European countries obtained raw materials from colonies and sold finished goods there. Missionary efforts among Aboriginal people were also promoted.

French Colonization of New France

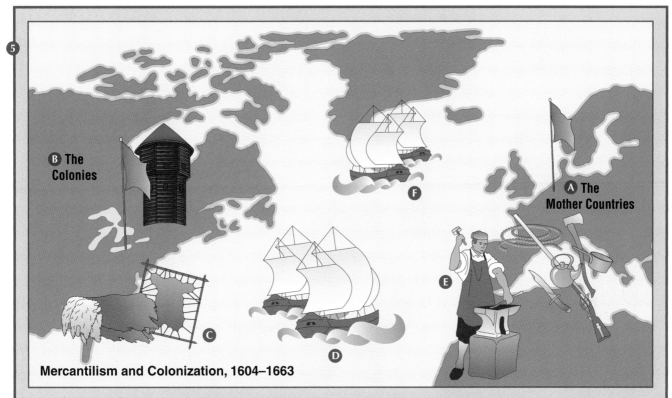

Mercantilism and Colonization, 1604–1663

The letters in the text correspond to the letters on the diagram.

Ⓐ Countries in Europe (the mother countries) started colonies in North America, Africa, and Asia.

The mother country had direct control over how the colonies were run. The mother country decided on the type of government for the colony. Europeans believed their way of life was superior to the ways of First Nations. Many thought that everyone in the claimed land should share the culture of the mother country.

Ⓑ Europeans needed to explore lands before they could establish colonies.

Ⓒ Settlers in the colony were expected to work with First Nations people to provide raw materials to the mother country. Workers were needed to collect, process, and transport raw materials.

Ⓓ The raw materials were then shipped to the mother country in Europe.

Ⓔ Raw materials were made into finished products in the mother country.

Ⓕ Profits were made by selling finished goods to other nations and colonies.

⑤ As the above chart shows, **mercantilism**, exploration, and colonization were closely related. In 1608 Champlain founded the colony of Quebec for France. He had a habitation (fort) built there. The fur trade became the main economic activity, and remained so for two centuries.

Contributions of the First Nations were critical to European exploration and the fur trade. First Nations people acted as guides and interpreters. They shared their knowledge about trapping, hunting, snowshoeing,

and canoeing. Food, shelter, and clothing were provided to the Europeans and survival skills were taught to them. In exchange, Europeans offered goods such as metal tools, firearms, and cooking utensils.

For Your Notebook

1. Continue with the timeline you started on page 2.

2. Prepare a concept poster that uses a different means of presenting the information in the chart Struggle for Power (page 6) or the diagram Mercantilism and Colonization 1604–1663 on this page.

Mercantilism—economic theory that called for a country to accumulate wealth in gold and silver; this was done, in part, by developing colonies as sources of raw materials and markets for finished goods.

Timeline
France and Great Britain

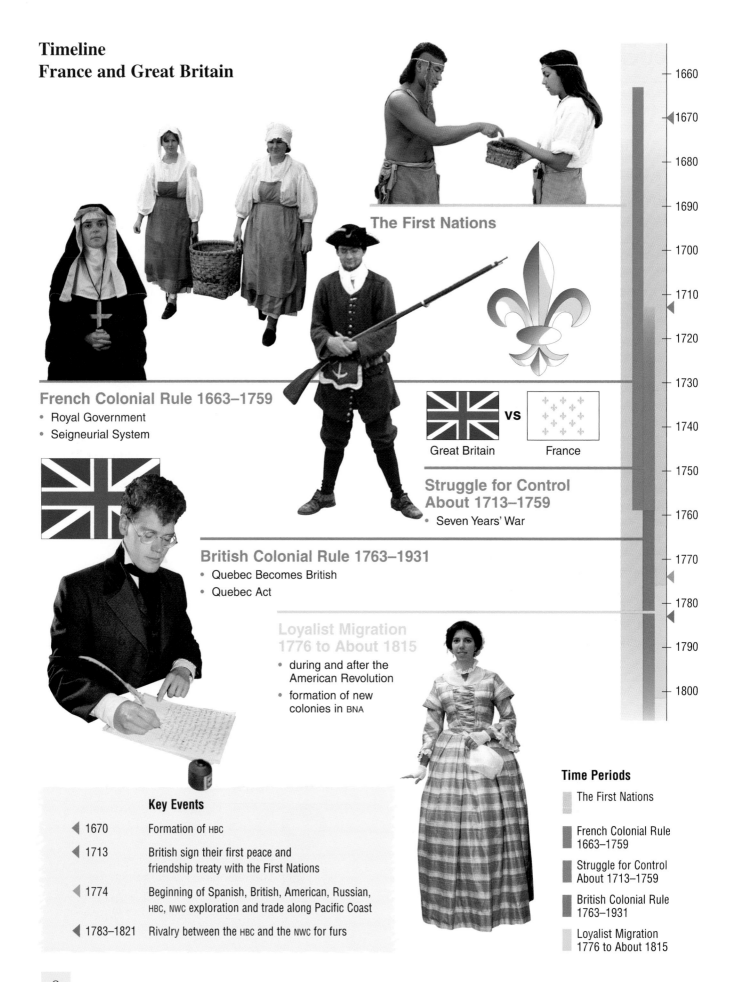

The First Nations

French Colonial Rule 1663–1759
- Royal Government
- Seigneurial System

Great Britain   vs   **France**

Struggle for Control
About 1713–1759
- Seven Years' War

British Colonial Rule 1763–1931
- Quebec Becomes British
- Quebec Act

Loyalist Migration
1776 to About 1815
- during and after the American Revolution
- formation of new colonies in BNA

1660
1670
1680
1690
1700
1710
1720
1730
1740
1750
1760
1770
1780
1790
1800

Key Events

◄ 1670	Formation of HBC
◄ 1713	British sign their first peace and friendship treaty with the First Nations
◄ 1774	Beginning of Spanish, British, American, Russian, HBC, NWC exploration and trade along Pacific Coast
◄ 1783–1821	Rivalry between the HBC and the NWC for furs

Time Periods

- The First Nations
- French Colonial Rule 1663–1759
- Struggle for Control About 1713–1759
- British Colonial Rule 1763–1931
- Loyalist Migration 1776 to About 1815

8

French Colonial Rule 1663–1759

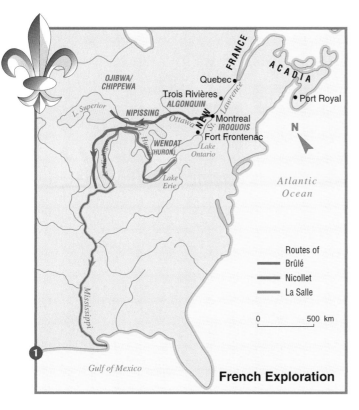

French Exploration

Routes of
— Brûlé
— Nicollet
— La Salle

0   500 km

Royal Government ▌

❶ The French began a settlement in Acadia, where farming was the major occupation. In the later settlements and along the St. Lawrence, most people were involved in farming and the fur trade. French exploration expanded westward and southward.

❷ In 1663, New France became a Royal Colony under the control of Louis XIV of France. The colony of New France was administered by a governor general, an intendant, and a bishop. The king's orders from France took so long to arrive by ship that decisions were most often made by these three men.

❸ New France grew along the banks of the St. Lawrence River. The French king granted land to seigneurs. The seigneurs divided the land into long narrow river lots and brought settlers called habitants from France to farm them.

❹ The Roman Catholic Church played a very important part in New France. The church provided religious teachings, schools, and hospitals, and influenced many decisions.

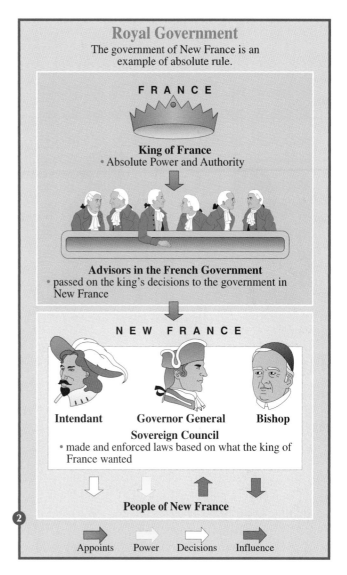

Royal Government
The government of New France is an example of absolute rule.

F R A N C E

King of France
• Absolute Power and Authority

Advisors in the French Government
• passed on the king's decisions to the government in New France

N E W   F R A N C E

Intendant   Governor General   Bishop
Sovereign Council
• made and enforced laws based on what the king of France wanted

People of New France

Appoints   Power   Decisions   Influence

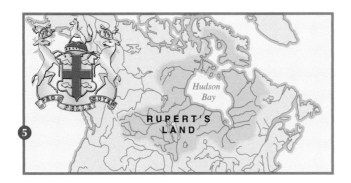

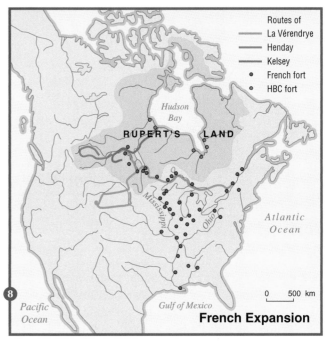

Routes of
La Vérendrye
Henday
Kelsey
• French fort
• HBC fort

Hudson
Bay

RUPERT'S   LAND

Mississippi

Ohio

Atlantic
Ocean

0   500 km

Pacific
Ocean

Gulf of Mexico

French Expansion

Hudson's Bay Company

1670 ◀

5 The English, like the French, were interested in obtaining wealth through the fur trade. In 1670 King Charles II of England granted a charter to the Hudson's Bay Company (HBC). This charter gave the Hudson's Bay Company a monopoly for trading on all lands draining into Hudson Bay. This territory was called Rupert's Land. The Hudson's Bay Company controlled Rupert's Land from 1670 until 1869. Then they sold their interests to Canada.

6 The Hudson's Bay Company made no attempt to colonize Rupert's Land. They built forts at the mouths of main rivers flowing north into Hudson Bay. First Nations traders acted as go-betweens with Nations of the interior. They brought furs by canoe to the forts and traded for British goods. The Hudson's Bay Company was dependent on them for trade into the interior.

7 In 1690, the Hudson's Bay Company sent Henry Kelsey on an expedition inland. He was to encourage First Nations to bring their furs to the posts on Hudson Bay. The painting above shows Kelsey hunting buffalo with Nakota (Assiniboine) people on the plains. Kelsey was the first European to see large herds of buffalo grazing on the northern plains.

8 The French sent traders (like the La Vérendrye family) into the homelands of First Nations to build forts and trade. First Nations traders began taking their fur pelts to inland French forts rather than travelling the long distance to forts on Hudson Bay. The Hudson's Bay Company then sent Anthony Henday inland to persuade them to travel to the forts on Hudson Bay. Eventually, in 1774, the Hudson's Bay Company began to build their forts in the northern forests. Later they moved south and west to build forts on the interior plains.

Struggle for Control

8 The British* and the French continued to compete for control of the fur trade. They also struggled for political power (control) to strengthen their economic hold.

9 Control of the Atlantic coast of North America was a concern for both the French and the British. The French needed a fort at a **strategic** location to guard the entry to New France. They built a fortress at Louisbourg in 1720. (The reconstructed Louisbourg is shown above.) The British needed to defend the Atlantic coast to protect their colonies in Acadia and in New England. In 1749, the British built the fortress of Halifax. French-speaking Acadians were eventually expelled from Acadia because they would not swear loyalty to Britain.

10 The Seven Years' War between the British and the French was also fought in North America. In 1759, the French under General Louis-Joseph de Montcalm were defeated by British troops under General James Wolfe on the Plains of Abraham near Quebec.

11 Montreal surrendered to the British in 1760.

For Your Notebook

1.  Add information from pages 8 to 11 to the timeline you started.

Exploring Further

2. **Group Share** (homework plus one class period)
   Form groups of three to work together.
   a) Each person selects one of the following topics:
      - Royal Government in New France (page 9)
      - Hudson's Bay Company (page 10)
      - Struggle for Control (page 11)
      Become experts on your topics by reading and studying the information for homework. During your next class, share what you've learned within your group. You may use your textbook as a reference.
   b) OPTIONAL: Make game cards with questions on one side and answers on the other. Each question and correct answer earns the team two points. Where you have to look up the answer in this textbook, each question and correct answer earns the team one point. (Ideas for making games are on page 354.)

---

*In 1707, England and Scotland united and took the name Great Britain.
Strategic—valuable for military or naval purposes

British Colonial Rule 1763–1931

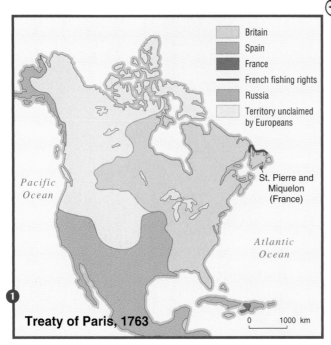

Treaty of Paris, 1763

- Britain
- Spain
- France
- French fishing rights
- Russia
- Territory unclaimed by Europeans

St. Pierre and Miquelon (France)

Pacific Ocean

Atlantic Ocean

0   1000 km

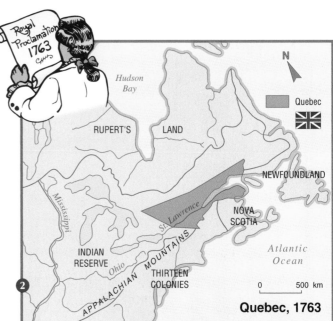

Quebec, 1763

Quebec

N

Hudson Bay

RUPERT'S LAND

NEWFOUNDLAND

NOVA SCOTIA

Mississippi

St. Lawrence

INDIAN RESERVE

Ohio

APPALACHIAN MOUNTAINS

THIRTEEN COLONIES

Atlantic Ocean

0   500 km

❶ Between 1759 and 1763, a temporary government was established in New France. This was known as the period of British Military Rule. The French people were concerned about what would happen to them and their way of life. Life in the colony changed little during this time.

The Seven Years' War concluded with the signing of the Treaty of Paris in 1763. Britain controlled most of North America (as the map shows). France was allowed to keep two tiny islands off the coast of Newfoundland and certain fishing rights.

The British Governor General Guy Carleton recognized that control of Quebec depended on the support of the large *Canadien* population. To ensure their loyalty, he encouraged Great Britain to allow the two cultures to exist side-by-side.

❷ In the Royal **Proclamation** of 1763, the British government addressed the governing of the French population of New France. The intent of the Proclamation was to make the people of Quebec British through assimilation. Use of British institutions, laws, customs, and the English language would be enforced in Quebec.

Assimilation

The process through which one culture is absorbed into another: Under British rule in Quebec, British laws were to be enforced and the (French) *Canadiens* and/or the Aboriginal peoples strongly encouraged to adopt British customs and religion, and the English language; British immigration would be encouraged to create an English-speaking majority.

The British believed that, in time, the French would adopt the British way of doing things.

Many people from the Thirteen Colonies had been moving west into the territory controlled by First Nations. The British government knew that the First Nations were not happy about it. The Proclamation of 1763 created a large "Indian Territory" (Indian Reserve) by limiting the boundaries of Quebec and the British colonies along the coast.

Canadiens—French-speaking people born in New France (Quebec); distinct from the French in Europe
Proclamation—a formal announcement issued to the public by the government

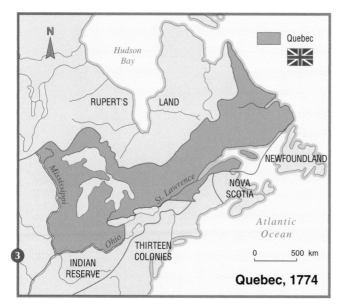

Quebec, 1774

The Quebec Act

British Government

Council

Appoints

Governor

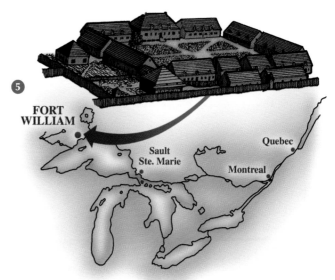

FORT WILLIAM

Sault Ste. Marie

Quebec

Montreal

❸ To gain the loyalty of the *Canadiens*, the British government changed its policy and passed the Quebec Act of 1774. The *Canadiens* would be allowed to maintain the French character of Quebec. The aim of the Quebec Act was to strengthen the British Empire by allowing Quebec to remain both British and French. The boundaries of Quebec were enlarged to include more rich fur-producing areas.

❹ The Quebec Act allowed the French language, the Roman Catholic religion, the seigneurial land holding system, and French civil law to continue. Quebec would be ruled by the British-appointed Governor and his appointed council.

❺ In 1783, large numbers of fur traders who were not working for the Hudson's Bay Company formed the North West Company. Their headquarters were in Montreal. Fort William was a meeting place for traders of the North West Company. Furs from the West were collected at Fort William before they were sent to Montreal. Between 1783 and 1821 there was intense rivalry between the HBC and NWC.

❻ Many Metis men served the fur trade as voyageurs (boatmen), interpreters, and buffalo hunters. Metis women made pemmican, the food the fur traders carried with them. First Nations people continued to be involved in the fur trade.

13

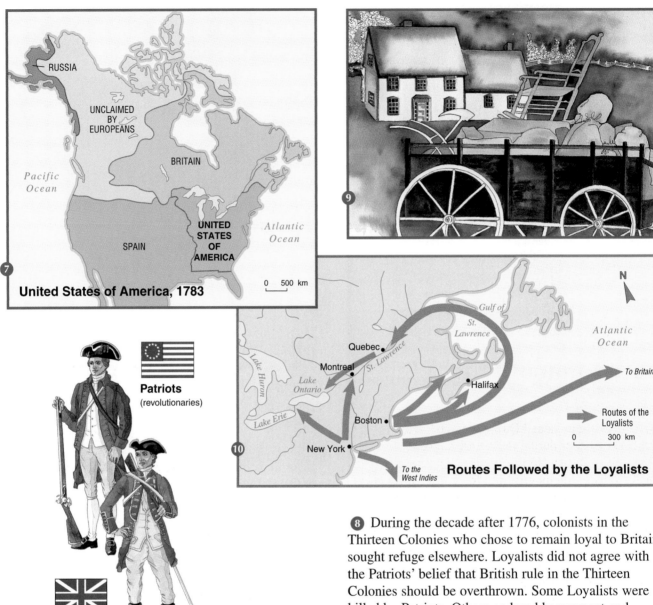

United States of America, 1783

Patriots
(revolutionaries)

Loyalists

Routes Followed by the Loyalists

Routes of the
Loyalists
0   300 km

The Loyalist Migration

7 In 1775, many people in the Thirteen Colonies (see map page 13) rebelled against Great Britain. The American Revolution (or War of Independence) ended with the Treaty of Paris of 1783. By the terms of the treaty, Great Britain surrendered the lands south of the Great Lakes and recognized the independence of the former Thirteen Colonies. The Thirteen Colonies became the United States of America.

8 During the decade after 1776, colonists in the Thirteen Colonies who chose to remain loyal to Britain sought refuge elsewhere. Loyalists did not agree with the Patriots' belief that British rule in the Thirteen Colonies should be overthrown. Some Loyalists were killed by Patriots. Others endured harassment and harm.

9 Many Loyalists moved to safer British territory. The British government helped the newcomers by giving them provisions and land acquired from First Nations by treaties. Over 100 000 Loyalists left the Thirteen Colonies.

10 Over 40 000 Loyalists chose to move to British territory north of the Thirteen Colonies. Loyalists made large changes to areas of lands where few people lived in the colony of Nova Scotia. In the colony of Quebec, Loyalists developed prosperous farming communities. Seven thousand Loyalists had arrived in Quebec by 1785.

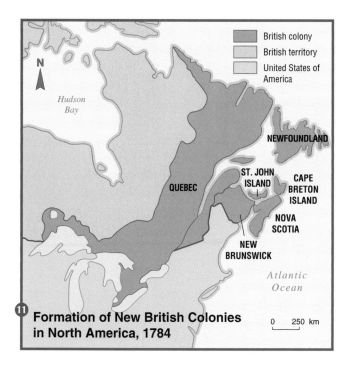

11 Formation of New British Colonies in North America, 1784

0   250 km

12

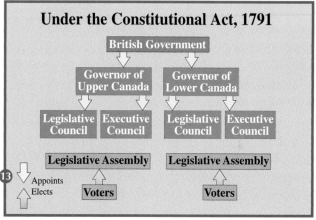

Under the Constitutional Act, 1791

British Government

Governor of Upper Canada | Governor of Lower Canada

Legislative Council | Executive Council | Legislative Council | Executive Council

Legislative Assembly | Legislative Assembly

13 Appoints / Elects

Voters | Voters

Formation of New Colonies

11 Great Britain gained Quebec in 1763, then lost the Thirteen Colonies during the American Revolution. By 1784, life in British North America was very different. The Loyalists who moved from the Thirteen Colonies to Quebec felt **alienated** in their new land. They wanted their familiar laws and democratic government structure. Because of Loyalist demands in the Atlantic region, in 1784 the British government created the colonies of New Brunswick and Cape Breton Island separate from Nova Scotia.

12 Thayendanegea (also known as Joseph Brant) was a Loyalist and a leader of the Iroquois Six Nations Confederacy. After the American Revolution, he led many Six Nations people to settle on a reserve (now called the Six Nations Reserve) in British North America. Many other members of the Iroquois Six Nations Confederacy remained south of the border, where their descendants live today.

13 In 1791, the British government passed the Constitutional Act. Governing a Quebec that was both English and French was still a problem. Quebec was divided into Upper Canada (Ontario) and Lower Canada (Quebec). Some of the terms of the Quebec Act continued to be applied (see map page 13). Upper Canada had an English-speaking majority and Lower

Alienated—isolated; feeling that laws and customs are foreign to them

Representative government—citizens elect people who represent them in their Legislative Assembly (decision-making body)

Canada a French-speaking majority. Each colony was given an elected Legislative Assembly. This meant they had a form of **representative government**.

For Your Notebook

1. 1800 1900 Add information from pages 8 to 15 to the timeline you started on page 2.

Exploring Further

2. **Group Share** (homework plus one class period) Form groups of three to work together.
   a) As a homework assignment, each member becomes an expert on one of the following topics:
      • British Colonial Rule (pages 12 to 13)
      • The Loyalists (page 14)
      • Formation of New Colonies (page 15)
      During your next class share what you've learned with your group. You may use your textbook as a reference.
   b) OPTIONAL: Make game cards, with questions on one side and answers on the other. Each question and correct answer earns a team two points. Where you have to look up the answer in this textbook, each question and correct answer earns the team one point.

Timeline
Conflict and Change 1812–1855

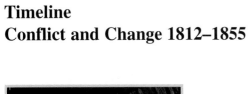

The First Nations and Metis

- 30 000 to 40 000 First Nations and Metis people lived between the Great Lakes and the Rocky Mountains

British Rule Continues

The Great Migration 1815–1850

- thousands of Irish, Scottish, and English immigrants
- much of the land cleared in Upper and Lower Canada, Nova Scotia, New Brunswick, and Prince Edward Island
- further development of farming, fishing, and the fur trade
- towns slowly built

Conflict and Change 1812–1855

- in both Upper Canada and Lower Canada, government controlled by small groups of powerful and conservative men appointed by the governor

	1800
	1810
	1820
	1830
	1840
	1850

Key Events

◀	1812	Red River colony established by Lord Selkirk; War of 1812
◁	1815	Conflict between the NWC, Metis, and settlers in the Red River settlement at Seven Oaks
◀	1821	HBC and NWC united, ending rivalry
◁	1837–1838	Rebellions in Lower Canada and Upper Canada
◀	1840s–1860s	Britain wished to become less involved in government of British North American colonies
◀	1841	Upper Canada and Lower Canada united, called the United Province of Canada

Time Periods

- The First Nations
- British Rule Continues
- The Great Migration 1815–1850
- Conflict and Change 1812–1855

16

VS

Upper and Lower Canada, 1791–1841

The War of 1812 ◀

❶ Between 1812 and 1814, the United States of America and Great Britain were at war. Many of the major battles were fought in Great Britain's colonies of Upper and Lower Canada. There was no clear winner of the war. It had several long-lasting effects on Canada, including the following three:

• American immigration to British North America was discouraged and immigration from Great Britain was encouraged.

• Feelings of pride and a sense of unity began to develop in Upper and Lower Canada.

• First Nations people played a major role in wars fought in British North American colonies. After the War of 1812, the services of First Nations people as military allies were no longer needed. The British government decided their former allies should now be assimilated.

❷ The fur trade continued. The ongoing participation of First Nations and Metis was essential in this activity.

The Great Migration ▌

❸ Between 1815 and 1850, many newcomers came to the British colonies. Almost all were from Great Britain; the largest percentage was Irish. The majority chose to settle in Upper Canada. A number settled in the eastern townships of Lower Canada south of the St. Lawrence River. This area had been set aside for English-speaking farmers. Many newcomers also settled in Montreal, and in the Atlantic colonies.

❹ While many people in Upper and Lower Canada viewed immigration from Great Britain as a threat to their way of life, most welcomed immigrants as a means to develop the resources of the colonies.

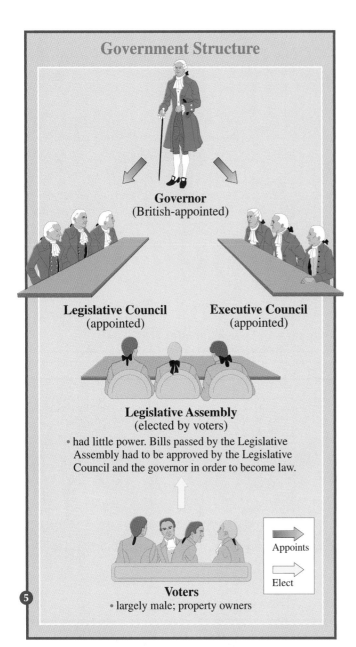

Government Structure

Governor
(British-appointed)

Legislative Council
(appointed)

Executive Council
(appointed)

Legislative Assembly
(elected by voters)

• had little power. Bills passed by the Legislative Assembly had to be approved by the Legislative Council and the governor in order to become law.

→ Appoints

⇨ Elect

Voters
• largely male; property owners

⑤

⑥

⑦

Conflict and Change ▮

⑤ In Lower Canada. The Legislative and Executive Councils (appointed) were controlled by the English-speaking merchants and government officials known as the Château Clique. Bills from the Legislative Assembly (elected) were not passed by the Legislative Council.

⑥ In Upper Canada. The government was controlled by a small group of officials known as the Family Compact. They opposed any changes to the structure of the government and gave privileges or property to friends or supporters. They were loyal to Britain.

In both Lower Canada and Upper Canada, many people whose interests were not represented by the Château Clique or the Family Compact were discontented. A **reform movement** began to appear. By the 1830s **radical** reformers were seeking to create a country modelled on the United States.

Rebellions ◁ 1837–1838

⑦ Rebellions of 1837 and 1838 in Lower Canada.
Rebellion broke out against the government in Lower Canada in 1837. The British quickly put down the rebellion. Louis-Joseph Papineau and other rebel leaders fled to the USA.

Rebellion of 1837 in Upper Canada. William Lyon Mackenzie and his radical supporters attempted to overthrow the government. However, those involved in the revolt in Upper Canada were quickly dispersed, and the rebellion ended.

Reform movement—group of people who want to change government and society
Radical—holding extreme opinions; wanting fundamental social, economic, and political changes

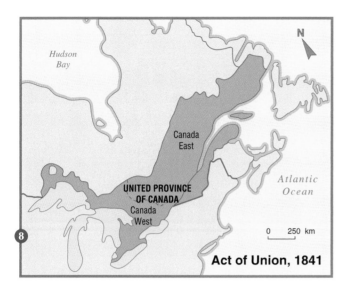

Act of Union, 1841

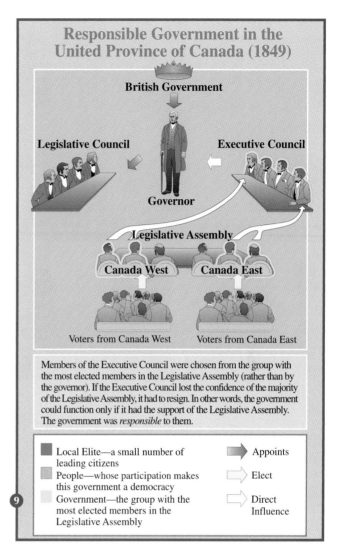

Responsible Government in the United Province of Canada (1849)

British Government

Legislative Council

Governor

Executive Council

Legislative Assembly

Canada West

Canada East

Voters from Canada West

Voters from Canada East

Members of the Executive Council were chosen from the group with the most elected members in the Legislative Assembly (rather than by the governor). If the Executive Council lost the confidence of the majority of the Legislative Assembly, it had to resign. In other words, the government could function only if it had the support of the Legislative Assembly. The government was *responsible* to them.

- Local Elite—a small number of leading citizens
- People—whose participation makes this government a democracy
- Government—the group with the most elected members in the Legislative Assembly

- Appoints
- Elect
- Direct Influence

Act of Union ◀ 1841

⑧ Durham Report and the Act of Union. Great Britain appointed Lord Durham to investigate the rebellions. Durham's report recommended uniting the two Canadas and granting responsible government to the British North American colonies.

In 1841, the Act of Union created the United Province of Canada—a single government with equal representation from Canada West (formerly Upper Canada) and Canada East (formerly Lower Canada).

⑨ In the 1840s, the British government began to rethink its costly colonial policies. To reduce the cost of food in Britain, the government adopted free trade. They abandoned the special trading protection given to their colonies. The British government felt that the problems of the colonies and the demands of reformers would be best addressed by the colonies' governments. In 1847, Nova Scotia was granted responsible government. Canada West and Canada East were granted responsible government the next year.

⑩ The Rebellion Losses Bill of 1849 was a major test of local self-government. The people of Canada East demanded repayment for the losses they had suffered during the rebellions. Repayment had been granted to the people of Canada West. There was angry debate from those who opposed repayment to rebels. However, the Rebellion Losses Bill was passed by the Legislative Assembly and Legislative Council. Lord Elgin, the governor, signed it, although he did not personally agree with the bill. English-speaking Tories were angered, and some proposed Canada join the United States. The Parliament Buildings in Montreal were burned to the ground in protest.

Rebellion Losses Bill

Legislative Assembly

Establishing Responsible Government	
Nova Scotia	1847
Prince Edward Island	1851
New Brunswick	1854
Newfoundland	1855

11 The Act of Union (1841) enabled Canada West and Canada East to work together to build railways, expand industry, and increase growth in farming and forestry.

12 However, in the 1850s the government of the United Province of Canada became ineffective. Equal representation of Canada West and Canada East in the Legislative Assembly resulted in political deadlock. French–English conflict over culture, particularly religion and education, remained. People in Canada West became angry over the failure to introduce representation by population after their population grew larger than Canada East's. They wanted the number of elected members (the representatives) in the Legislative Assembly to be based on the number of voters (the population). This is often abbreviated as "rep by pop."

13 Maritime political development was more stable. In the Maritime colonies the focus was on economic expansion—primarily fishing, agriculture, shipping, and timber. Here, radical political change did not end in rebellion. The movement for reform focused on issues like wanting the Legislative Assembly to control government spending. Reformers also wanted to end **patronage** and the control of land-granting by small groups of appointed officials. They sought responsible government. In Prince Edward Island, the settlers wanted to own their own farms rather than rent from absentee landlords. Joseph Howe became the most prominent reformer in the Atlantic region.

14 **Responsible Government.** In the 1840s and 1850s, all four Atlantic colonies achieved responsible government. The Executive Council of each colony was chosen from the group with the most elected members in the Legislative Assembly. Each Executive Council could stay in power only as long as it had the support of that colony's Legislative Assembly.

For Your Notebook

1. Add information from pages 16 to 20 to the timeline you started.

Exploring Further

2. **Group Share** (homework plus one class period) Form groups of five to work together.
   a) Each group member becomes an expert on one of the following topics:
      • The War of 1812 (page 17)
      • The Great Migration (page 17)
      • Rebellions of 1837 and 1838 (page 18)
      • Act of Union (page 19)
      • Responsible Government (pages 19 and 20)
   b) During the next class, share what you've learned within your group.

Patronage—the power to give favours or jobs in return for political support

Review

Understanding Concepts

1. Using one of the methods for recording vocabulary, add these words to the Word-Book section of your notebook. (See Appendix page 369.)

   - mercantilism
   - colonization
   - colonial government
   - assimilation
   - representative government
   - rebellion
   - responsible government
   - political deadlock
   - political change

2. Complete the timeline you started on page 2. Add illustrations, notes, and colour to help you remember the sequence of events in Canada's history.

3. Review and compare the maps in the Review chapter, including the one on this page. Write three generalizations about changes that took place in territorial boundaries up to the early 1850s. Comparison strategies are found on page 349.

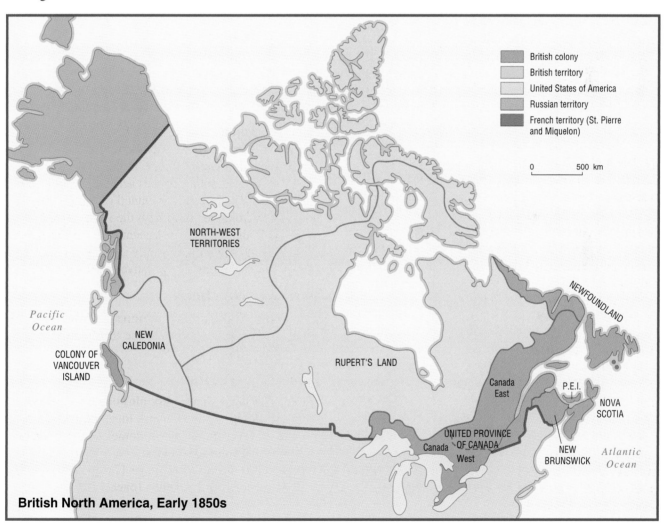

British North America, Early 1850s

Legend:
- British colony
- British territory
- United States of America
- Russian territory
- French territory (St. Pierre and Miquelon)

0   500 km

Pacific Ocean

NORTH-WEST TERRITORIES

NEW CALEDONIA

COLONY OF VANCOUVER ISLAND

RUPERT'S LAND

NEWFOUNDLAND

Canada East

P.E.I.

NOVA SCOTIA

UNITED PROVINCE OF CANADA

Canada West

NEW BRUNSWICK

Atlantic Ocean

It was the first day of school. Haley Morris picked up her shoulder satchel and slipped into her shoes. "I can't believe I haven't seen my three best friends for the entire summer," she said over her shoulder to her mother. "Darin was visiting his cousins in Quebec, Lee was travelling in Europe, and Susan was out West—I feel like my social life disappeared. Now things can get back to normal!"

"Hurry up please, dear!" Haley's mother said as she came into the hallway. "I have to leave for work, and I'd like to lock up. A good thing you packed your lunch last night!" Haley held the door for her mother, who was looking in her pockets for her keys.

"Haley, why don't you take Miss Rodine some sweet peas from the backyard? I remember always taking flowers the first day."

Haley groaned, "M-om! I'm not in kindergarten. Nobody does that stuff any more! I would be totally embarrassed!"

Her mother shook her head. "Kids sure have changed!"

Haley took her usual, familiar route to Lethburn Community School, eight blocks from her home. The huge maple trees along these streets had provided shade for generations of students walking to the old red brick school. Haley's own mother had played under them. The trunks were too big to get your arms around now. The community had seen many changes, but the trees changed very slowly.

The trees were a reminder of continuity amid the changes that had occurred over the years. Haley thought about the changes to the community. The house on the

Section I
British North America
Prior to Confederation

● ● ● ● ● ● ● ● ● ● ● ● ● ● ●

corner of the block, for instance, had once been her grandparents' farm home. A long time ago this area had been fields.

Haley glanced up at the front porch to see if Grandma was out drinking her morning cup of tea.

"Oh, Haley, have you got a minute?" Haley's grandmother was calling to her so she turned up the sidewalk. Haley heard something about "pickles I just made yesterday."

". . . Miss Rodine always said I made the town's best dill pickles. She told me at the grocery store she was looking forward to teaching one more Morris before she retires next year."

"Grandma, you know what?" Haley asked. "I'm afraid the glass jar might break in my bag. Why don't you have Miss Rodine over for tea and give her the pickles yourself?"

"Why, what a nice idea, Haley." Grandma and Miss Rodine had been girlhood friends.

Continuing on her way, Haley thought about the changes in Grandma's life. She and Grandpa had stayed in their farm home after the town council had

purchased the land from them for expansion. Haley's mother worried about Grandma. Grandpa had died a few years ago and she wondered if Grandma should sell her old house and move in with them. Haley's mom said there was a great market for these old "heritage houses."

But Grandma wanted to be independent as long as possible. She liked her big garden, which was all that remained from the original farm. She grew her own apples, raspberries, and vegetables. She also liked her neighbours on the street. There was a family from Barbados on one side and several families along the street who had originally come from India. Grandma said the food at the block parties was wonderful. Her apple pies were as popular as the spicy food of her neighbours.

Haley thought her Grandma had seen a lot of changes. She was glad that her own life mostly stayed the same. She liked going to the same red brick school and walking under the same trees that her mother had.

Haley's mother had been a hospital nurse once, but now she

worked in a clinic so she had regular hours. She liked to be home when Haley was, and she made Haley's friends welcome. Haley's grandparents had helped with after-school care when Haley was small. Now Haley often helped her grandmother instead of being "looked after."

Swinging her bag to the ground, Haley leaned against the cool, rough trunk of a maple tree at the last intersection. She waited there for her three best friends from last year—Susan Osaka, Lee Polischuk, and Darin Fortier—to appear. "Even though I will be getting different teachers," she thought, "and a different class-room, and new subjects, at least I'll keep the same friends."

After school that day, Haley met Darin and Lee in a booth at the Retro. The owners of the coffee shop had bought a bakery that had closed soon after the new supermarket opened. They remod-eled it in 50s-style, and it had become a gathering place for the youth of the community.

Haley sighed, "What a long day! So many changes. First Susan wasn't back, then a new teacher for history. I can't believe Miss Rodine retired! At least you guys are still here! But Darin! Your hair! It's so blond! I can't get used to it."

Darin grinned. "Cool eh? My cousin did it for me. We did his too!"

"Maybe you can colour mine," said Lee. "Lots of guys in Europe had their hair dyed. I wonder who started the fad first? My dad says style changes mostly start in Europe, but I think more come from the USA."

"Who knows—maybe it started here? Canada's not necessarily behind the times! Lethburn—fashion capital of the world!"

Questions for Small Group Discussion

1. What changes have occurred in the lives of the characters in the story? In the town?
2. What things do not seem to have substantially changed? Why do some things change while other things remain constant?
3. How important in our lives are changes? constants?
4. What general conclusions can you make about the **concept** of change?

Questions for Class Discussion

1. Within the story, to what extent do attitudes and tradi-tions seem to have changed? What values seem to be constant?
2. Share some things that have changed/stayed the same in your community, in your school. Why do you think some have different reactions to change than others?

Questions to Ask an Adult

1. Compare your childhood with that of today's children. What are the three most significant changes you have seen? What do you think caused each of these changes?
2. Why is the rate of change today so rapid? What are some results of this rapid change?

Concept—a general idea or thought

3. In what ways might change lead to misunderstandings?
4. Is change viewed the same way by different generations? Why? Why not?

Notebook Organization

 Start a binder for your notes on Canadian history. A loose-leaf binder will make it easy to insert pages. Create a title page for Section I "British North America Prior to Confedera-tion" and place it at the front of your binder.

Prepare the following dividers and sections for your binder:

a) A section called Activities, for your notes, activities, maps, and illustrations, with section/chapter title pages.

b) A section to record vocabulary called WordBook.

c) A section for your thoughts, ideas, and feelings on history called History Journal.

d) A section called Learning How to Learn for information on how to learn and think.

Ideas for notebook organization are found on page 364.

History Concepts

Five main concepts are emphasized throughout *Canada Revisited 8*. They are change, regionalism, power, identity, and co-operation/conflict. These concepts are explained on pages 24, 25, 28, and 29.

Change

 The icon for change represents the process of something becoming different. **Change is a continuous process that occurs unevenly within a culture.** A culture is always in transition.

Some people accept new ideas more easily than others do. Some ideas may change quickly within one generation, while others may change slowly. Changes can be temporary or permanent.

Some aspects of a culture are more enduring than others. Some aspects of culture remain constant (unchanged) from one generation to the next, or for hundreds of years. This is known as cultural retention.

Cultural change happens as the result of internal and external influences. Internal influences come from within a country. External influences come from outside the country. Internal and external influences that cause change are known as agents of change. Agents of change are factors contributing to change. Eight agents of change follow.

Agents of Change

Geographic Isolation

Isolation, the lack of contact with other peoples, can affect the ways a culture changes. When a cultural group has very little contact with other peoples, it often develops customs, beliefs, and values that are different from other cultures living nearby.

Changes in Population

Changes in population (the number of people living in a city, region, or country), such as immigration, can cause changes in how people live. Population increases can make it difficult for people to find adequate food, housing, water, and means of living, such as jobs. People may have to move to new locations to find jobs. Decreases can influence marriage, family organization, and work. Changes in where people live can also affect culture. Changes in population can be an internal or external influence on the way of life.

Changes in Government

The different ways people choose to govern themselves can have significant effects on culture. A change of government can cause changes in a culture. Education, housing, religion, roles, and work may change. Change of government is usually an internal influence.

Sir John A. Macdonald (Conservative) 1867–1873 **Alexander Mackenzie** (Liberal) 1873–1878 **Sir John A. Macdonald** (Conservative) 1878–1891 **Sir Wilfrid Laurier** (Liberal) 1896–1911 **Sir Robert Borden** (Conservative) 1911–1920

Contact with Other Cultures

Ideas, customs, and technology are often exchanged between cultures. Trade is an important means of cultural contact. Contact with other cultures and countries is an external influence.

Interaction with the Environment

The ways people meet their basic needs in different environments are important parts of their culture. Changes in the environment can produce changes in a culture. The ways people make a living are affected when the environment changes. Interaction with the environment can be both an internal and external influence.

War

War often produces great changes in the way people live. After a war, ideas about family organization, marriage, food, housing, religion, work, and education can change. War can be both an internal and an external influence on cultural change.

New Knowledge/Technology

Sometimes cultural changes happen because of new knowledge and changes to existing technology.

People continually invent new tools and ways of doing things and improve old tools and methods. New technology can change transportation, jobs, how people communicate, where people live, and what people eat. Over time, new knowledge may affect one's values, beliefs, customs, and even a country's traditions. New knowledge can be both an internal and an external influence.

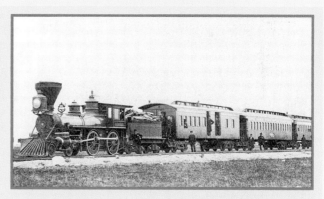

Changes in Economic Conditions

Changes in economic conditions can change how people live. Economic conditions describe how well people are able to meet their needs. Poor economic conditions mean that people have a difficult time providing food, shelter, and clothing for their families. In times when economic conditions are good, people are able to satisfy these basic needs for their families. Better education, housing, transportation, food, and health care are available. Changing economic conditions may be the result of internal or external influences.

1.

Use the information on pages 24 and 25 to make a web to record your notes on the characteristics of cultural change. Include the eight agents of change. Refer to page 363 in the Appendix.

2. Refer back to the story on pages 22 and 23.

a) Find examples of change agents in the story.

b) Give examples of temporary and permanent changes in the story and in your life.

c) List examples of change leading to more change in the story.

d) Does change always mean progress? Explain.

Connecting with Change

Ms Pozzi was passing out the new history textbooks. "Here's something to think about, class," she was saying. "By age 12, you have spent more time in front of your TV than you've spent in school."

"Excellent!" said Benjamin. "TV's more interesting anyhow. It's more exciting."

"Exactly! That's what I just read in a history journal article. It seems we are more 'connected' with TV. Why do most of you know more about how Americans live than how Canadians in other provinces live, for instance?"

"I think I know." said Haley. "Is it because we see so many American TV shows?"

"You're right! When *do* you see other parts of Canada?"

"Sometimes on the news," said the new student, Jasmine, rather shyly. "When I moved from Jamaica, I only knew Toronto and Lethburn. My mom made me watch the 6 o'clock news to learn about Canada. I really want to see the Rocky Mountains, and Niagara Falls, and . . . even Anne of Green Gables' house in Prince Edward Island." Jasmine looked down at her desk, embarrassed.

"You probably will, Jasmine. What you are doing is making connections with your new country through what you see on TV. Did anyone see the summer replay of the movie *Ben Hur*?"

"I think I saw part of it," said Darin from the back. "Was that the story with the great chariot race?"

"It was. Darin remembers something about Roman history that he saw on TV. He is connecting with the past through TV. Jasmine is connecting with Canada."

Haley wondered what point her teacher was making.

Ms Pozzi continued, "Sometimes we'll use videos in the classroom to help you make some connections with real people who lived before you and who helped make Canada the country it is today. Our textbook will also give a lot of information and visuals, as well as activities and guideposts for learning." Ms Pozzi used her computer to display the words Change, Regionalism, Power, Identity, and Co-operation/Conflict on the

large classroom monitor. Each word had an icon beside it.

"Some of these concepts are fairly complicated. Let me tell you a little story to help you understand them."

"As you can guess from my name, I am Italian–Canadian. One day a long time ago, my Grandpa Pozzi looked across the table in their house in Italy and announced, 'We will go to Canada.' Grandma cried at first. She didn't know any English, for one thing. But Grandpa explained his dream of having a vegetable shop in Canada where there would be more opportunities for their two boys, so she began to pack. They moved to Toronto to a neighbourhood where many other Italians had come. The boys worked in the shop after school. Grandpa and Grandma made their own pasta and they sold some of it in the vegetable shop. Grandma still wore long skirts at first, and her black shawl. Finally, she bought a new modern dress to wear to church. Their lives had many changes over the years. When Grandma was 75, she got her first microwave! I speak less Italian than my father does, just enough to talk to Grandma when I visit her."

"Now, in my story, who had 'Power'?"

Ben put up his hand. "Your grandpa! He's the guy who told everyone to leave!"

"Absolutely. After some 'conflict,' because she was afraid, Grandma went along. She still 'co-operates' with Grandpa today in the family business. Now what 'regions' did I mention in my story?"

"You talked about Italy and Canada and the Italian district and Toronto," answered Haley.

"Right. A lot of Italians moved into one neighbourhood. They brought many old ways with them, but was it the same?"

"No way! It was Toronto."

"Of course. Toronto was in a new region. Central Canada was very different from Italy.

"And the Italian district was a new sub-region—part of Toronto but with special characteristics. I think of myself as Canadian but also Italian. That is part of my 'Identity.' You'll understand these terms better as we study history this year.

"Let's go back to connections. Jasmine, you're a new Canadian. I know that my Grandma is a lot older than you, but do you have anything in common with her? Can you connect with her experience?"

"Well," Jasmine hesitated, "I guess we were both afraid. I can speak English, but I was afraid people would laugh at my accent."

"I can make a connection!" interrupted Leonard. "I bet they both eat some foods from their original home and some from Canada!"

"That's quite likely," said Ms Pozzi with a smile. "Now, to wrap up . . . Each one of you in this class is making history. Every day. When you make choices, like what styles of clothes to buy, you might be helping to create a fad, or to influence the fashion industry. When you attend a hit movie, you become part of a statistic. That's making history. The ways you save or spend your money affects the Canadian economy and the industries that make up the economy.

When you elect your student government, you may be electing a future prime minister!

"Some day in the future, Grade 8 students will be trying to make connections with your experiences in the year 2000. How could they best go about it?"

Several students had opinions. Ms Pozzi wrote some of the ideas on the overhead:

"Ask us about it."

"Look at pictures."

"See videos about us."

"Look up stuff in the library."

"Check the internet."

"Look at old letters, or magazines and newspapers."

"Make plays about some things that happened."

'Super ideas, class,' Ms Pozzi agreed. "We will be trying some of your suggestions to connect with some of the people in Canada's past. I think it could be quite exciting."

For Your Notebook

1. In Section I of your study of Grade 8 History you will be connecting new learnings to prior ones. Chapters 1, 2, and 3 contain a combination of connections from former grades and new materials relating to Grade 8 History. These three chapters will provide you with a basic understanding of what British North America was like just prior to Confederation—when the Dominion of Canada was created.
   a) Record your personal expectations for Section I in your journal. You might begin, "In Section I we'll be learning about . . ."

2. Ms Pozzi has told the students that five main concepts will guide their study of Canada. What are those concepts? Draw the five icons in your notebook, label them, and colour them. Define each concept in your own words. Refer to the inside front cover for models to copy.
3. Find examples of each concept in the story on pages 22, 23, 26, and 27.
4. With the help of your teacher, brainstorm other examples of each of the concepts.

Section I Focus

While all of the book's five concepts will be examined, the three chapters in Section I will focus on change, regionalism, and power. For each chapter you will be expected to find information to answer each of the questions on the easel that follows.

What Were We Like?

1. What factors (agents of change) contributed to change among each group of people?
2. What interests, if any, were shared by the people living in this region?
3.  Which groups held more power and influence in making decisions?

27

History Concepts

Regionalism

The icon for regionalism is a highlighted square in a grid, set apart from its surroundings by boundaries. Canada is a nation of many regions. Regions are areas with similar characteristics. We will refer to physical regions, economic regions, and political regions.

Each region (part) of what is now Canada has had its own special concerns at different times. These regional concerns sometimes differ from the concerns of the country as a whole. People within each region have points of view about how the region should develop or remain the same. These are their regional interests. Some ideas are held in common by most people. In other ways, different groups in the region disagree. Regionalism is about contrasting the needs of one region with the needs of the country as a whole.

Some ideas to consider when looking at regionalism:
- There are many regional differences within Canada. Each region has its own special needs and concerns.
- Canadians have a sense of national identity. They also have regional identities. Sometimes regional and national identities are very different. This can be a source of conflict.
- Regionalism is a source of federal/provincial conflict.

Canada Revisited 8 divides Canada into five regions: Atlantic Canada, Central Canada, the Prairie Provinces, the Pacific Coast, and the North.

Atlantic Canada
Central Canada
Prairie Provinces
Pacific Coast
The North

0   500 km

Regions of Canada

Power

The icon used for power shows a bull. The bull is an international icon for power. Power means
- commanding people's obedience with or without their agreement
- deciding who gets what
- giving or refusing to give rewards
- using superior strength and authority

There is another way to look at power. People give power to others because they trust them to use it well. They believe that they will use the power given to them to make life better or easier, or that they will use it to benefit society in general.

When looking at political power in a country ask the following questions:
- Who held (holds) the power?
- Who controls the internal affairs (control of the land within its border)? Who makes the laws? Who controls the police force and/or army?
- Who controls the external affairs? Who makes treaties with other nations?
- Who decides about the flag, money, stamps, and passports?
- Is the country recognized by other countries? Does it have embassies in other countries?

THOSE COLONIAL CUBS

Identity

 In the icon for identity, the outlined square represents characteristics that are shared in common. The triangles represent the forces from within and from outside that shape our particular identity.

When you answer the question "Who am I?" you are defining your identity. Identity is the way you perceive (see) yourself. What characteristics do you have that make you distinctive? Various groups of people within Canada have distinct group identities. Regions have regional identities. Countries also have national identities. These are general descriptions of the people who live there and their qualities that make them different from people from other countries.

Under the concept of identity, you will examine information on the ways various individuals and groups of people (Aboriginal, British, French, and groups who have immigrated to Canada) have identified themselves. You will look at contributions they have made to Canada's national identity. Canada is a young country. Our national identity is still evolving.

When examining Canadian identity ask:
- How do Canadians see and describe themselves?
- How are we seen and described internationally?

The items that make up Canada's Coat of Arms tell us about our country's history and identity.

Co-operation/Conflict

 On the icon for co-operation/conflict, the two parallel arrows represent co-operation and the two opposing arrows represent conflict.

 Co-operation means

- working with other people to achieve a common goal
- sharing thoughts and then building upon these ideas
- using the strengths of different individuals to complement each other
- trusting each other
- understanding that the team matters, as well as the individual
- agreeing that not everyone gets the same thing or does the same thing

 Conflict is natural since people often disagree. It can lead to open protest or rebellion. Conflict is

- a struggle between opposing forces
- a clash between individuals, groups, or societies holding opposing ideas, interests, or ways of life
- a battle or a war
- a tense situation

Canada has experienced both co-operation and conflict in the course of its history. When examining co-operation/conflict in Canada ask:
- What part does co-operation play in national unity?
- What part does conflict play in national unity?

For Your Notebook

1. Make a mind map on each of the textbook's main concepts: regionalism, power, identity, and co-operation/conflict. (See page 363 in the Appendix for ideas on how to make a mind map.)

Exploring Further

2. Create a collage to illustrate each of the textbook's five main concepts. Use a large sheet of poster paper, dividing it into five sections. Label each section with one of the five concepts. Find pictures in magazines or create pictures for each of the concepts, grouping them in the correct sections of the poster paper. Share your collages with your classmates.

Chapter 1
The Pacific Coast
Prior to Confederation

O v e r v i e w
Use this Overview to predict what you will read in this chapter.

2 Explorers and Fur Traders

The British had claimed the Pacific Coast following exploration during the late 1700s and early 1800s. Fur traders came to the west coast by sea and overland. The British came into contact with First Nations of the Pacific Coast through the fur trade.

1 The Nuu-chah-nulth

Plentiful resources and travel by water were the bases of the way of life of the peoples of the Pacific Coast.

5 1858

The British Colony of British Columbia

The mainland (New Caledonia) became a British colony.

4 1858

Gold Rush in the British Territory of New Caledonia

Many gold miners were from the United States of America.

New Caledonia (British Territory)

Colony of Vancouver Island

3 1849

The British Colony of Vancouver Island

Vancouver Island became a British colony. The mainland territory was called New Caledonia. European settlement there consisted of Hudson's Bay Company fur forts.

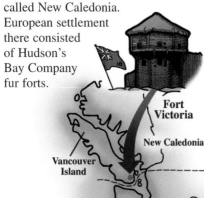

Fort Victoria

New Caledonia

Vancouver Island

6 Changes and Regional Interests

Thousands of gold miners and business people brought many changes.

Chapter 1 Focus

In Chapter 1, you will read a case study about the traditional culture of the Nuu-chah-nulth* people. You will also read about changes to the lives of people living on the Pacific Coast of British North America that resulted when explorers, fur traders, British government officials, gold miners, and business people came there. While the concept of co-operation/conflict will be examined, the focus in this chapter is on change, regionalism (regional interests), and power.

| Change | Regionalism | Power | Identity | Co-operation/ Conflict |

Other Concepts and Main Topics

- environmental interaction and balance
- trade
- cultural contact
- colony

Learning How to Learn

 Critical Thinking

Note Making

 Cause and Effect

  Understanding Chronology

Chapter Preview/Prediction

1. In pairs or small groups, use the overview on the previous page to preview the six major topics in the chapter.
   a) Scan the chapter to locate each of the six Level 1 titles. What colour are Level 1 titles?
   b) Locate the sub-headings (Levels 2 and 3).
   c) What are the differences between major headings and sub-headings?
2. Use the overview and the chapter's titles to make a web of events in this region and time period.
3. Discuss with a partner what you think the chapter is about.

---

*known as Nootka in some references
A blackline master of this chart is in the *Canada Revisited 8 Teacher's Resource Package* and on the **Canada Revisited 8 web page.

An ongoing section activity will be introduced in this chapter. Instructions follow.

Section I Activity

 Throughout your study of Section I, you will work on an ongoing activity that focuses on change, regionalism, and power. In Chapters 1, 2, and 3 you will be studying the concerns and points of view of some of the groups of people living in various regions of British North America.

In groups of four, use this chapter as a source of information to locate relevant information about 1., the agents of change; 2., the regional interests; and 3., power of the groups on the chart below.

Pacific Coast Retrieval Chart**

1. What factors contributed to change among each group of people (agents of change)?	
Nuu-chah-nulth along the Pacific Coast	
Traders at fur trade forts	
British government officials	
Miners and business people in the gold fields	

2. What interests, if any, were shared by these different groups of people living along the Pacific Coast?

3. Which groups would have held more power and influence in making political decisions?

31

Nuu-chah-nulth

The Nuu-chah-nulth of the Pacific Coast inhabited an area of ocean, mountains, and rain forests.

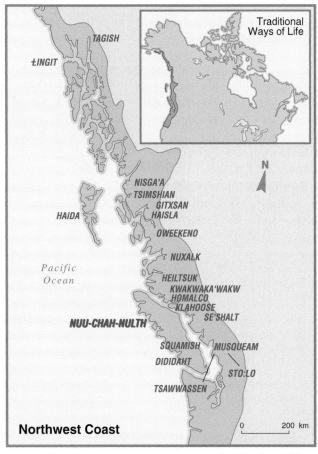

Many different First Nations live along the Pacific Coast. The map uses the names that the First Nations prefer to call themselves. Spellings may be different in other books. For information on the map insert see page 3. The peoples of the Pacific Coast belong to many different language families. Their traditional ways of life had many similarities and some differences.

Environmental Interaction

 The Nuu-chah-nulth lived on the west coast of what is now Vancouver Island. Their way of life was adapted to the land, climate, and vegetation where they lived. They kept their environment mainly as they found it and were careful not to upset the balance of nature. They knew they were just one of the many interdependent parts existing in a sacred relationship with nature. Spiritual rituals were centred on their relationship with the ocean and land.

The Nuu-chah-nulth were among the most skillful canoe-makers of the Pacific Coast. The huge, sea-going canoes were built from red cedar logs. The log was hollowed out with fire and carved with stone and bone tools (see below). When metal tools became available they were highly prized by these canoe-makers.

The amount of rainfall in the area affected the type of clothing and housing the Nuu-chah-nulth made. Cedar bark, goat hair, and dog hair were used to make clothing. Woven cone-shaped hats kept off the rain.

A typical village consisted of 30 cedar houses in a sheltered inlet or cove along the coast. Several families lived in each house. Each family had its own area and cooking fire. Raised wooden platforms for sleeping and storage extended around inside the walls. Containers for storage were made from split cedar boards and usually carved or painted, or baskets were woven from grasses.

The Nuu-chah-nulth found it easier to obtain food from the ocean, where it was abundant, than by hunting in the dense rain forest along the coast. They were also very successful whale-hunters.

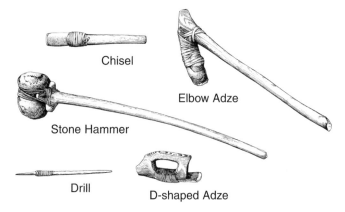

Available resources such as stone, bone, wood, and animal hides were used to make tools.

The Nuu-chah-nulth paddled canoes out to the open ocean in their search for whales.

In winter the Nuu-chah-nulth lived in large houses constructed of cedar planks. Several related families would share a house. Each family had its own sleeping area. As many as 30 houses might be built together in one seashore village with up to 1000 inhabitants.

The teams of paddlers handled their large canoes with great skill on these dangerous expeditions. A whale could provide food, whale oil, whale bone, and other products for many people. To supplement their diets the Nuu-chah-nulth obtained some products from the forest. They regularly traded products with other First Nations groups of the Pacific Coast.

All people and all things in nature had their place and their purpose. Men and women from the elderly to children had specific roles. Everyone respected the contributions made by others, including the plants and animals that provided their basic needs. In this way harmony and balance were maintained.

The most important way of sharing good fortune and establishing rank was to give a **potlatch**. (The word comes from a Nuu-chah-nulth word *patshatl*, which means "giving.") These gatherings lasted for days. People from other villages were invited to eat, tell stories, sing, dance, and receive gifts. The amount of wealth that the host of the potlatch gave away established his importance. Each person who received gifts was expected to host a potlatch in return and give away even more valuable gifts.

Wealthy families were responsible for feeding and sometimes providing homes for the poor, or women and children who had no families. This is another example of the importance of generosity in their culture.

Nuu-chah-nulth artists created and decorated beautiful objects. Many had powerful spiritual qualities. Carvers created ceremonial face masks, canoe prows, wooden chests, and bowls. A totem pole, carved from the trunk of a cedar tree, often stood at the front of a house and depicted the history of the families living in the house. Music was important to the Nuu-chah-nulth. Teams of hunters sang as they paddled in search of a whale. Singing was also used in ceremonies.

Like the Nuu-chah-nulth, the other First Nations along the Pacific Coast based their way of life on the ocean, the rivers, and the rainforest.

For Your Notebook

1. a) Reread the characteristics of co-operation on page 29.
    b) List examples of co-operation among the Nuu-chah-nulth people.
    c) Explain how important co-operation is in one of the following: in your classroom, among your friends, in your family, on a sports team, or in an organization to which you belong.

Exploring Further

2. Work with a partner to answer the following:
    a) Define environmental interaction.
    b) Find examples of this concept in this description of the Nuu-chah-nulth people.

Potlatch—large gathering or celebration where gifts are given

Explorers and Fur Traders

   When British Captain James Cook first came into contact with the Nuu-chah-nulth in 1778 he found that they were already familiar with iron and its uses. Europeans from Russia and Spain had explored parts of the Northwest Coast and done some trading with First Nations groups. The area was later developed through the fur trade. The coastal trade in sea otter furs reduced the sea otter population of the coast until its survival was threatened. European and American traders and First Nations competed for a share of this source of wealth. British, French, and Aboriginal traders also came from the interior to trade with the coastal peoples for a variety of furs. (For more information see pages 9 to 13, 16, and 17.)

The Hudson's Bay Company

In 1821, when the North West Company joined the Hudson's Bay Company, George Simpson was made governor of the Northern Department. In 1826 he became governor-in-chief of Rupert's Land.

HBC Post, Fort Vancouver

 One of Governor Simpson's early duties was to develop trade in the Pacific region in order to compete with Russian and American traders. Simpson thought that trade in the Pacific region could eventually "yield double the profit that any other part of North America does." He believed that the two districts, New Caledonia and Columbia, should be managed as one unit, along with the fur trade in inland areas.

There already were Hudson's Bay Company forts in the region. Simpson decided to abandon Fort Astoria (also called Fort George) and build a new post called Fort Vancouver,* on the north side of the Columbia River about 130 kilometres from its mouth. After 1825, furs in the Pacific region interior were transported down the Columbia River to Fort Vancouver. Fort Vancouver became the largest HBC fort on the Pacific Coast and headquarters of the Hudson's Bay Company's Columbia District. Dr. John McLoughlin was the chief factor there.

*Note that Fort Vancouver is near the present-day city of Portland, Oregon, in the United States, not the Canadian city of Vancouver.

The Hudson's Bay Company fur post at Fort Vancouver was built near the mouth of the Columbia River to protect British interests along the Pacific Coast.

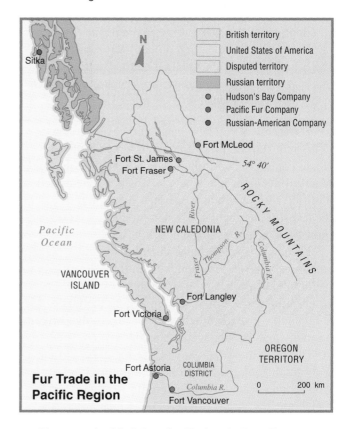

Fur Trade in the Pacific Region

Simpson decided that the Hudson's Bay Company forts should become more self-sufficient. The residents should get their food from the area by hunting local animals and planting gardens, rather than by importing food from Great Britain. Gradually, more people moved to the area around the HBC forts, living nearby and providing services to the forts.

HBC Post, Fort Victoria

Great Britain and the United States were in dispute about control of the Columbia valley, where Fort Vancouver was located. It seemed the United States would probably get control of the territory. Governor Simpson decided that the Hudson's Bay Company needed a new headquarters in undisputed British territory. He sent James Douglas north to build one on Vancouver Island. Douglas described his choice of the site for Fort Victoria: "The place itself appears a perfect 'Eden' in the midst of the Northwest Coast, and so different in its general aspect, from the wooded, rugged regions around, that one might be pardoned for supposing it had dropped from the clouds into its present position."

Fort Victoria was built in 1843 as a HBC trading post.

With the help of his men and some Nuu-chah-nulth people living there, in 1843 Douglas built Fort Victoria on the southeastern tip of Vancouver Island.

In 1846, the Treaty of Washington established the boundary between American and British territory west of the Rocky Mountains. The British were to have Vancouver Island and the area north of 49° North latitude (the 49th parallel). The United States was to have the area to the south. As a result of this treaty, Fort Vancouver belonged to the United States. Fort Victoria, located in British territory, became the Pacific headquarters of the Hudson's Bay Company. The Hudson's Bay Company dominated the fur trade north of the 49th parallel along the Pacific Coast and in the interior. Russian trading continued along the Alaska coast, and the Americans took control south of the 49th parallel.

For Your Notebook

1. a) Reread the characteristics of conflict on page 29 and list examples of conflict from pages 34 and 35.
   b) Explain what "disputed territory" means.
2. a) Why was Fort Vancouver built? What difference did it make to the HBC to have a fort on the north shore of the Columbia River rather than the south? Why was Fort Victoria built?
   b) Diagram an example of cause and effect in relation to Hudson's Bay Company forts and the 1846 Treaty of Washington. (Review Cause and Effect on page 348.)

Fort Victoria was built in British territory in anticipation of the 1846 Treaty of Washington, which gave Fort Vancouver and the Columbia district south of the 49th parallel to the United States.

The British Colony of Vancouver Island

James Douglas and colleagues discuss plans for colonizing Vancouver Island, 1849.

  In 1849 Vancouver Island became a British colony. Richard Blanshard, who arrived from Britain in 1850, was its first governor. In 1851 James Douglas, Chief Factor of the Hudson's Bay Company post, took his place. There were fewer than 1000 settlers living on the island at the time. On the British mainland territory, known as New Caledonia, settlement consisted of only a few fur forts. New Caledonia was administered by the colonial government in Fort Victoria because it was considered to be too sparsely settled to need its own government.

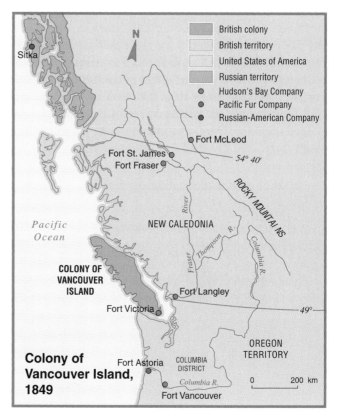

Colony of Vancouver Island, 1849

For Your Notebook

1. Refer back to the map of British North America on page 21. List the British colonies located in British North America.

Fort Victoria, in the British colony of Vancouver Island

Richard Blanshard
1817–1894

Richard Blanshard arrived from England in March 1850 to become the first governor of the colony of Vancouver Island. He had no experience in administering a colony.

Blanshard was surprised by the situation in the colony. The land grant he had expected did not exist and no home had been prepared for him in Fort Victoria. He had to live on the ship that had brought him until space could be found in the fort. He had accepted the position with no salary, but expected to be paid before too long out of the income of the colony. Unfortunately, the colony did not have a lot of income at the time. Income was to come from land sales and coal royalties. Land was not selling because there was better, less expensive land available in the Oregon Territory (in the United States). Coal mining was not yet successful. Therefore Governor Blanshard was not paid.

Before very long, it became apparent to Blanshard that James Douglas, the chief factor of the Hudson's Bay Company, held all the power in the colony. Blanshard became very discouraged, and suffered from ill health throughout the time he was on Vancouver Island.

Ten months after his arrival, Blanshard sent his resignation to England. The British government took almost a year to respond. While in the post, Blanshard acted on a request of the few settlers in the colony who were not connected to the Hudson's Bay Company. In 1851 he established the colony's first legislative council. It consisted of three men. James Douglas, the HBC factor, was appointed as its head.

James Douglas
1803–1877

 James Douglas was born in British Guiana, South America. His father was Scottish, and his mother was of African descent. Douglas came to British North America from Scotland in 1819 to work for the North West Company. After the Hudson's Bay Company and the North West Company united in 1821 Douglas moved west to work for the HBC. He was chief factor at Fort Victoria, and in 1851 he was appointed as the second governor of the Colony of Vancouver Island.

Douglas's great accomplishment was that he was able to keep law and order in the colony, even during the gold rush. In 1858, when Douglas saw the large numbers of American miners entering the colony, he was concerned that the American government would soon want to **annex** the area. Although he was not governor of the mainland at that time, he decided to establish control over New Caledonia on behalf of the British government. He collected fees from the miners to build the Harrison–Lillooet Trail and the Cariboo Wagon Road. These routes improved access to the Cariboo gold fields.

James Douglas is known as the Father of British Columbia. Douglas was granted a knighthood upon his retirement in 1864.

Amelia Douglas
1812–1890

Amelia Connolly was the daughter of the Hudson's Bay Company's chief factor in New Caledonia, William Connolly, and his Cree wife, Suzanne Pas-de-Nom. Amelia became the wife of James Douglas. When James Douglas was knighted in 1864, Amelia became Lady Douglas. She did not participate actively in the social life of Fort Victoria. This was partly because her English was not fluent. It was also partly due to the **discrimination** she faced, as some British-born people did not consider her social standing to be as high as theirs because her mother was Cree.

Annex—join one territory to another
Discrimination—an attitude of hostility directed against an individual, group, or race, which limits them unfairly compared with other groups

Charley McKay

Fictional Narrative

by Nancy Sellars Marcotte

The first thing that made me angry about William Hunnicutt was that he said that his mother was going to plant apple trees. Apple trees! At Fort Victoria! As if we would still be there long enough for the trees to grow and have fruit. I told him a wise man would go out and pick blueberries, and we had our first fight.

William was straight off the ship from England. He didn't think much of Fort Victoria, at least not as it was then, but he thought he could improve it, just by bringing ideas from England. Like a school. And maybe race horses. And supper parties. And a colonial government.

I wasn't so sure that I wanted to be in Fort Victoria. I was born in Rupert's Land, like my mother, but I grew up in the Oregon territory. My mother died and was buried there, a long way from her people, the Cree.

Her people used to go to Fort Cumberland once a year to trade furs for blankets and guns and tea. My father, Big Charley McKay, came to Fort Cumberland from his home in the Orkney

Islands across the Atlantic Ocean by ship, across Hudson Bay, and then by canoe along the rivers to Fort Cumberland.

I was eight when my father brought me from Fort Vancouver to Fort Victoria. We came north on the Hudson's Bay Company ship with Mr. Douglas. The head men of the Hudson's Bay Company, people who lived in England, were afraid that the Columbia District and Fort Vancouver with it would become part of the United States. They wanted a fort on the Pacific Ocean that would remain in British territory. We were with Mr. Douglas when he sailed into the bay on Vancouver Island and saw the flat plain where Nuu-chah-nulth women were picking wild plants. We never would have got the fort built if the Nuu-chah-nulth men hadn't shown us how

to strip the bark off the cedar trees and lay it on the roof to keep the rain out. That was in 1843.

My father had been born in England and he went to school there. He came to Fort Victoria because he thought it was important to remain British. Part of his job with the Hudson's Bay Company was to help settlers get farms from the Puget's Sound Agriculture Company. My father liked to talk to these people about what had been happening in London and Edinburgh and Glasgow. As for me, the best city I could imagine was San Francisco.

Just about the time that the Reverend and Mrs. Staines decided that the children of Fort Victoria needed a school, my father decided that I needed to learn more about reading and figuring and history and geography. It was handy for him to send me to live in that bare, rat-infested school room over the bachelors' hall in the fort. That meant I wouldn't be left alone when he had to take people to look for farms.

That's where I met William. We didn't say much. I was too busy looking at the tweed trousers and white shirt and hard leather London shoes he was wearing. I think that he was

Southwest bastion at Fort Victoria.

actually sniffing at me, as though I might smell of smoke or the tanned deerskin of my moccasins.

William and I slept on hard little cots in the school room. Well, we couldn't exactly sleep, not until the bachelors downstairs had finished their dinner and stopped singing. Sometimes we would peek through the cracks in the floor to watch Mr. Douglas's servant, a man from the Hawaiian Islands, serve dinner. As long as Mr. Douglas was there, the conversation was serious—the importance of the British Empire, or whether Vancouver Island would be made a colony.

It reminded me of our history lessons, where we learned about governments and battles that seemed too far away and too long ago to matter. Only when we read about Captain James Cook and Captain George Vancouver sailing up the Pacific Coast did I realize that British history had happened right here on Vancouver Island— and still was happening!

William thought Vancouver Island becoming a colony was a good idea. "Then we would be equal to the other British colonies in North America," he said.

"What other British colonies?" I asked. Then I wished I hadn't, because there was nothing William liked better than to show me that he knew something that I didn't.

"Newfoundland," he said. "And those other ones. Nova Scotia, and Prince Edward Island, and . . . and New Brunswick. And Canada."

"Isn't that where Montreal is?" I said, doing a little showing off of my own.

"Ye-es." William didn't sound entirely sure.

"That will never matter to us," I said. "Do you know how far it is to Montreal?" William didn't answer. "First you have to ride a boat to New Caledonia on the mainland, to Fort Langley. Then you have to go up the rivers, over the mountains, and then some other mountains. Then you'll be in Rupert's Land. You have to go all the way across Rupert's Land, past the Red River, and to Fort William. Then you have to go by canoe through five huge lakes and down an enormous river before you get to Montreal. Only the strongest of the fur trading paddling crews can do that. It would take you all summer to get there."

"Perhaps so," said William. "But I went all the way around South America and past Mexico and California. And that was after I crossed the Atlantic Ocean to get here from England."

⬩

The next day we had some spare time. I headed out of the fort toward the house where Mr. and Mrs. Douglas lived with their family. Mrs. Douglas reminded me of my mother, and she baked bannock like my mother used to make. As I sat on her steps, she asked me in Cree, "Are you learning good things at school?"

"I'd rather be travelling with my father," I said. I looked up, and there was William. He had followed me!

"What was she saying to you?" William asked. I said, "She asked me if I am still the strongest boy in Fort Victoria. I told her yes."

Vancouver Island did become a colony, at last, in 1849, but it didn't seem to make any difference. They sent Mr. Blanshard from England to be governor, but most people didn't pay much attention to him. Mr. Douglas was still in charge.

That year my father decided that I needed to learn history and geography and figuring in ways that he thought could only be taught in a school in Britain. That was how I ended up on a paddle-wheeler steaming out of the harbour, wishing I could stay in Fort Victoria, while William stood on the dock waving me off, wishing that *he* could travel to school in London.

For Your Notebook

1. What political, economic, and social changes were occurring in the settlement at Victoria? Relate each to an agent of change.
2. What environmental changes do you think were occurring at the same time?
3. Identify the different groups of people in this story that have different interests and concerns about how the region should change or remain the same in the time to come. What are their points of view?

The British Territory of New Caledonia

  Most of the people living in the British territory of New Caledonia were from First Nations. Small numbers of British, Russian, and American fur traders lived there in isolated forts. There were so few of them the British colonial leaders felt they could administer New Caledonia from their headquarters on Vancouver Island. New Caledonia was not made a colony in 1849 when Vancouver Island was. It remained a British territory. Development and change in the territory came about through the fur trade and then the discovery of gold.

The Fur Trade

Fort Langley

Fort Langley was built on the Fraser River in 1827 as the Pacific Northwestern headquarters of the Hudson's Bay Company. (See map page 34.) Living quarters and a storehouse were enclosed within the palisade of the original fort.

The headquarters of the Hudson's Bay Company was later moved to Fort Victoria. Fort Langley became a major supply depot on the Pacific Coast. The Sto:lo First Nation* traded salmon, hazelnuts, and cranberries to the fort for export. Wheat, barley, oats, potatoes, and peas were grown in the fields of the fertile lower valley of the Fraser River. Pigs and cattle were also raised near the fort at Langley Farm. All these products, in addition to skins from beaver and other small animals, were exported to Europe, the Hawaiian Islands, and California.

A scene from the historical Fort Langley

---

*See map page 32. The Sto:lo (also known as Coast Salish) people belonged to the Salish language family.

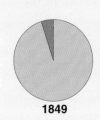

Population

☐ First Nations people (95%)
■ Other (5%)

The vast majority of people in the British colony of Vancouver Island and the territory of New Caledonia belonged to First Nations.

1849

Canada Revisited

Fort Langley

Visitors to British Columbia can take a trip back in time to the 1850s. Fort Langley, 40 km south of Vancouver, has been reconstructed. Once you enter the gate in the wooden palisade, you are back in the days of the fur trade.

Unlike today, the blacksmiths and carpenters in the 1850s would have seen few visitors, and they would not have had time to stop and chat. The residents would have been busy with chores— baking, berry picking, gardening, moving bales of fur, and packing barrels of dried salmon. They would not have had time to stop and enjoy the fresh-baked bread that was a treat for fur traders tired of their usual diet of dried salmon and pemmican.

Part of Fort Langley has been restored and may be visited as a tourist attraction.

Gold

On the Lower Fraser River

The Sto:lo people of the Fraser River Valley had been mining **placer** gold for years. They traded it at Hudson's Bay Company forts for European goods. By 1858 the Hudson's Bay Company had purchased over 20 kilograms of gold. The gold was taken on the Hudson's Bay Company's ship *Otter* to the United States mint in San Francisco to be weighed, analysed, and made into coins.

The story quickly spread throughout California. The big gold rush in California had almost ended. To many, the stories of gold in the British territory in the north seemed like an opportunity to finally find riches.

The first big strike of **paydirt** below the rapids on the Fraser River was made by a small group who had come up from California. Word about the gold in the Hill's Bar area soon spread. Miners came from all over. Doctors, farmers, thieves, bankers, prospectors, store clerks, and many more came to strike it rich, to see the country, or to be part of the adventure of the search for gold. Jobs, homes, and families were left behind, as thousands of miners swarmed into the lower Fraser Valley.

Changes to Fort Victoria

The influx of miners brought changes to Vancouver Island and New Caledonia. Before the gold rush Fort Victoria was a peaceful little village of about 800 people. Sunday, April 25, 1858, just as the townspeople were leaving church, 450 miners arrived aboard the paddlewheel steamer *Commodore* from San Francisco. Before nightfall Fort Victoria was transformed into a bustling tent city full of men on their way to the goldfields on the mainland.

Victoria Harbour, 1858

Placer—deposit of gravel or sand, usually in a streambed, that contains valuable minerals such as gold
Paydirt—earth or ore that contains enough gold to be worth mining

Changes in the Fraser Valley

By the middle of August there were about 30 000 more people in the lower Fraser Valley than had been there the previous year. With all these miners arriving, the lower Fraser Valley changed. The river banks were soon covered with miners. Some were digging the sand; others were working at their rockers, others using sluices to extract between five dollars and one hundred dollars worth of gold a day. (These mining methods are described on page 45.)

Soon the area all around Hope had been **claimed**. Miners moved northward to search in unclaimed areas. Not all found gold. By the end of the year many unsuccessful miners had left, convinced that the Fraser River gold rush was a hoax. Activity in the lower Fraser Valley declined. Luckily for the miners, gamblers, businessmen, and merchants, gold was discovered in the Cariboo region of the interior.

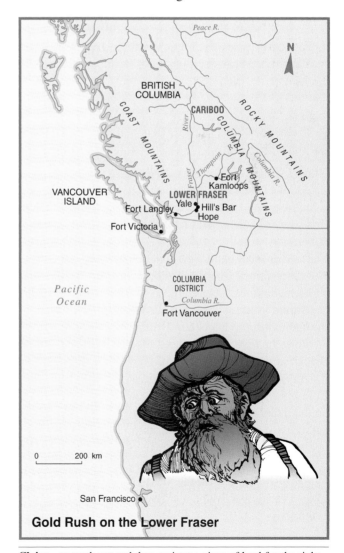

Gold Rush on the Lower Fraser

Claim—to mark out and then register a piece of land for the right to remove minerals from it

41

The British Colony of British Columbia

Treaties

Between 1851 and 1854, Governor James Douglas negotiated 14 small treaties with First Nations on Vancouver Island. Douglas tried to deal fairly with First Nations. Most nations were not covered by treaties.* Each nation that agreed to give up its traditional lands for European settlement was given a small sum of money. Most First Nations people had no contact with fur traders, miners, and government officials.

The First Nations of the east side of Vancouver Island and the lower Fraser Valley were Sto:lo, a Salish-speaking people. They were fishers and hunters whose way of life was based on salmon fishing. The Sto:lo of the lower Fraser Valley used nets and weirs to catch spawning salmon for their own use and for trade with other First Nations and with the Hudson's Bay Company.

A New Colony

  The 1858 gold rush on the lower Fraser River brought over 30 000 miners to New Caledonia. Many of these miners came from the United States. The British were concerned that the Americans would try to annex Vancouver Island and New Caledonia. Governor James Douglas had heard about lawlessness during the California gold rush. He did not want the same thing to happen in British territory. In 1858 he convinced the British to make the territory of New Caledonia into the colony of British Columbia. As governor of the colony on the mainland, Douglas had the authority to maintain control and to punish lawbreakers.

From 1858 to 1866, there were two British colonies on the West Coast: Vancouver Island and British Columbia.

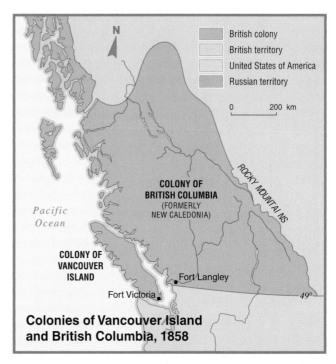

Colonies of Vancouver Island and British Columbia, 1858

British colony
British territory
United States of America
Russian territory

0   200 km

Pacific Ocean

COLONY OF BRITISH COLUMBIA (FORMERLY NEW CALEDONIA)

ROCKY MOUNTAINS

COLONY OF VANCOUVER ISLAND

Fort Langley

Fort Victoria

49°

Fort Langley was the capital of the new mainland colony of British Columbia. It was here that British Columbia was proclaimed a British colony in 1858. The illustration shows James Douglas leaving Fort Langley after becoming governor of British Columbia.

*Treaties had been negotiated in the eastern part of British North America between the British Crown and various First Nations for over 100 years.

Gold Rush in the Cariboo

 As the banks of the lower Fraser River yielded smaller amounts of gold, most of the fortune seekers left. In 1859, some of the hardier, more hopeful prospectors ventured northward up the Fraser River to the Quesnel River in the Cariboo Mountains region. From there they branched out into Keithley Creek, Antler Creek, Lightning Creek, and Williams Creek. They found many rich sand bars, which they worked with good results.

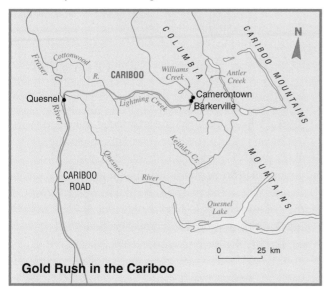

Gold Rush in the Cariboo

In 1861, the richest gold deposits ever discovered in the Cariboo region were found at Williams Creek. Many claims were made along this creek. Some claims paid their owners from $20 000 to $60 000 a year. One man, John Cameron, left the country after a year's work with $150 000 in gold dust. Most miners were not this fortunate.

Camerontown in the Cariboo

These miners are bringing gold out of a tunnel mined by the Neversweat Mine in the Cariboo, 1868.

A Few Facts About Gold

- Gold is one of the most sought-after metals. (First Nations people did not particularly value gold, except for ceremonial uses.)
- Gold is one of the heaviest metals known. When disturbed by movement it settles to the bottom of a stream, or into cracks and crevices, or into the bottom of a gold pan or sluice box.
- Gold in streambeds is found as dust (flour), flakes, or nuggets; gold ore in rock is found in veins.

Location of Gold

1. **In Lode Deposits**—Veins of gold found in rock called lode deposits are often referred to as "mother lode." In British Columbia the mother lode was found in the Cariboo area east of Quesnel, around Barkerville.

2. **In Placer Deposits**—Deposits of gold found in wet or dry riverbeds, sandbars, or streambeds are placer gold. They have been washed away from the mother lode by water or wind. The dust or nuggets mixed with gravel are carried downstream. In British Columbia gold was washed away from the mother lode in the Barkerville area and carried down the Fraser River. In the lower Fraser Valley the river abruptly flattens out and slows down. Heavier materials being carried by the water are deposited there.

Barkerville

Billy Barker

 Billy Barker arrived at Williams Creek during the summer of 1862 to find thousands of miners busy working at their claims. Many seemed to be striking it rich. Barker selected a location back from the river, away from all the other successful claims. He and his partners sank a crude mine shaft. The other miners questioned his thinking because they knew gold was always found by the creek, not where Barker was digging. He convinced his partners to ignore the other miners and continue digging. At about 17 metres they struck an old river channel. A shovel full of gravel was sent up from the shaft and panned in the creek. It revealed $5 worth of gold. A bucket was next filled to the top with gravel and panned. It yielded $1000 worth of gold. This was the richest paydirt in the Cariboo. It yielded Barker and his partners a fortune of $600 000.

A town soon grew up around Barker's mine. The miners named it Barkerville in honour of Billy Barker. The ten general stores in Barkerville carried almost everything a miner might need. Food, hardware, clothes, fabric, button shoes, cooking utensils, saddles, and horses' harnesses were sold in these stores. Prices were high. In 1862 flour sold for $1.25 a pound. Beans, bacon, and dried apples cost $1.00 a pound.

Many Chinese men took part in all of British Columbia's gold rushes. They made up about a third of the town of Barkerville. They worked as miners and gardeners, and in the commercial areas of town.

The main street of Barkerville in the 1800s: buildings were built on stilts along a long, narrow, and usually very muddy street.

Matthew Baillie Begbie, 1819–1894

 Judge Begbie was described as "a fine, tall fellow of 6 feet, well made and powerful, magnificent head, hair scanty and nearly white, with nearly black mustache and beard." He was sent by the British government to be the first judge in the Colony of British Columbia in 1858. He held trials all over the colony, sitting in front of his tent dressed in his traditional robes, wig, and black cap.

Begbie had to be tough to travel through the gold fields. Many who were there were used to carrying weapons and men were often quick to show their anger. To the Americans he said, "In those countries over which the British flag flies there is no necessity for carrying or using offensive weapons." One day as he was resting on the balcony of his second-floor hotel room, he heard some men below discussing a plan to murder him. He calmly emptied the contents of his chamber pot over their heads and then returned to his rest.

Begbie did not hesitate to express his opinion when he did not agree with a jury's verdict. On one occasion when a jury did not convict a man of attacking another man, he told the accused, "You can go, and I devoutly hope the next man you sandbag will be one of the jury."

Begbie often stood up for the rights of First Nations peoples. When amendments to the Indian Act in 1884 outlawed the potlatch ceremony, he refused to approve a law that would bring the legislation into force.*

Begbie was knighted by Queen Victoria in 1874 as a reward for his efforts to keep British Columbia orderly during its early days as a colony.

*Later the law was enforced and the potlatch was outlawed.

Placer gold mining methods depended on the fact that gold is heavier than most other materials. Common tools used for mining gold were the gold pan, the rocker, and the sluice box. A gold pan was used to sift small amounts of paydirt. The rocker and sluice box separated gold from paydirt brought up in larger amounts from the mines and tunnels. The hydraulic method used water under pressure to move earth.

Rocker

A rocker consisted of a small wooden tray with holes in the bottom, sitting on top of one end of a larger wooden tray. Paydirt and water were poured through the small tray. A handle was moved to rock the tray. Large chunks stayed above the holes and could be thrown away. Water and lighter particles of dirt, gravel, and clay were washed out the end of the larger tray. Gold, being heavier, was trapped in the bottom of the larger tray.

Sluice Box

When water and paydirt were dumped into the top of the long wooden troughs of a sluice box, the water, sand, clay, and gravel ran downhill and out the end of the sluice, leaving particles of gold trapped in the bottom of the sluice.

Mines and Tunnels

In the Barkerville area, gold was found deep in the ground. Vertical shafts and horizontal tunnels were used to get at it.

The shaft mines of Barkerville could not be operated by individual miners. Waterwheels and shaft mines were too expensive for one person to build. Instead groups combined their money to finance these more expensive methods.

A waterwheel was used to pump water out of underground shafts and to hoist buckets of paydirt to the surface. Once the gold-bearing gravel reached the surface, it was put through a sluice box to separate out the gold.

Hydraulic Method

Hydraulic (water) pressure was used to wash away the gravel bank of the river to get at a gold vein. Water under a great deal of pressure was aimed through a metal pipe at a gravel bank. Great amounts of gravel and gold could be moved this way. The water, gravel, and gold mixture was diverted through a sluice box to separate the gold from the gravel.

The Cariboo Road

 Travelling the Fraser River was a major hardship for many miners going to the Cariboo region, especially if they went during a time when the river was flooded. Canoes and rafts were often upset going through the rapids and their passengers drowned. Many miners rode the steamboat as far as Yale and then went on foot, mule, or horse. For hundreds of miles they followed the narrow zig-zag paths over mountainous terrain, swamps, bogs, and creeks. The northern section of the Fraser Canyon was especially dangerous. Men and animals clung to the cliffs while the Fraser River raged far below.

The cost of shipping meant prices along the route were high. Food selection was limited so meals were monotonous. Only hardy individuals who weren't easily discouraged travelled to the Cariboo.

The problems of getting people and supplies in and out of the Cariboo was so great that Governor Douglas undertook the task of having a road built. He felt that such a route would also be useful for getting law-enforcement troops into the Cariboo quickly should they be needed.

The Cariboo Road, nearly six metres wide, was blasted through rock and bridged across rivers and gaps. It covered about 800 kilometres from Yale to Barkerville. (See map page 41.)

With the completion of the Cariboo Road in 1865, travel to the Cariboo was easier and safer. Supplies could be brought in much faster, so prices went down. Mule trains, oxen teams, and even camels were used as transportation on the Cariboo Road. A variety of stern-wheeler and sidewheel steamers travelled across the Strait of Georgia and up and down the Fraser River between Victoria and Yale.

On the Cariboo Road, at Great Bluff, 130 kilometres above Yale

Focus On: The Overlanders

Travel to the goldfields from the coast was difficult, especially before the building of the Cariboo Wagon Road. However, few goldseekers experienced the hardships of the group of people known as the Overlanders.

The Overlanders chose to travel by land to British Columbia in pursuit of gold instead of up the west coast by sea, as many people did. Two hundred and twenty Overlanders began their journey in 1862. They travelled by various means, including railroad, steamboat, and stagecoach from eastern Canada, the United States, and elsewhere. They met at Fort Garry, at the junction of the Red and Assiniboine Rivers. They left there in early June, travelling by Red River carts to Fort Edmonton. From there 125 people left on foot to cross the Rockies, with First Nations guides. Eventually all of the horses and cattle who had not already perished were abandoned or killed for food because the journey was too difficult for them. The Overlanders floated down the North Thompson and Fraser rivers on rafts to reach Fort Kamloops in October.

Catherine Schubert
1835–1918

Six Overlanders died in the dangerous rapids of the Fraser River. Catherine Schubert, her husband, and three children were among the survivors. Schubert had been pregnant throughout the perils and hardships of the journey. She gave birth to her fourth child, Rose, on the day she arrived in Fort Kamloops in October. The baby was delivered by a woman from the Shuswap First Nation living in the area. Rose was the first Euro-Canadian child to be born in the colony of British Columbia.

Focus On: Obtaining Information from Historical Photographs and Other Sources

For Your Notebook

1. a) Look at Yale in photograph ❶ and describe the location of the town. On what river is Yale located?

    b) This was the last stop for the steamboats. Upriver from Yale transportation became much more difficult. Why? You may have to refer to the maps on pages 42 and 43 or an atlas for this answer.

2. a) What was the name of the road in photograph ❷? What problems would there have been in building it?

    b) What changes have been made in this environment?

Describe several uses to which the vegetation has been put.

    c) Barkerville is located on this creek. Billy Barker's mine was 17 metres deep. Why would it have been difficult to dig?

3. a) In photograph ❸ there are at least five men working on this claim. Why wouldn't they each work on a separate claim? What would be the advantages of working together? Disadvantages?

    b) What personal qualities would a miner need? Were these men entrepreneurs?

Why or why not?

4. a) Would you like to have lived in the town of Richfield, photograph ❹? Why or why not?

    b) What was the attitude of most Cariboo miners to conservation? On what observations do you base your answer?

5. Look at all of the photographs to answer these two questions:

    a) What businesses or services would be started up to serve a gold rush mining community?

    b) Which of them would remain in the region when the gold was gone?

Yale, British Columbia

Williams Creek

Cameron and Company Staff, 1863, Camerontown, British Columbia

Richfield

Change

  Economic, social, political, and environmental changes in a region have effects on the ways of life of the groups of people living there. Changes of any kind often bring about other changes that may not have been planned. Changes like a government's political decision to establish a colony are controlled by a few people who have power. However, other groups are affected by them. Accidental changes, like the discovery of gold, may have many effects that are difficult for anyone to control.

There were two major uprisings by First Nations in the Colony of British Columbia because of the gold rush. Gold miners invaded regions where only First Nations had lived. Many did not respect their lands, homes, grave sites, and other special places.

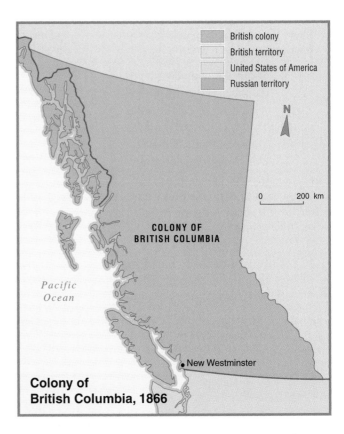

Colony of British Columbia, 1866

In addition to fur trade and gold mining, forestry became an important industry in British Columbia. John Muir's lumber mill at Sooke, Vancouver Island (about 1867–70), is shown above.

This group of First Nations chiefs from different parts of the lower mainland were photographed in New Westminster. First Nations of mainland British Columbia did not sign treaties surrendering their lands at this time. However, changes in the region affected their ways of life and homelands.

In 1866, the colonies of Vancouver Island and British Columbia were united under the name British Columbia. The capital of the united colony was New Westminster.

For Your Notebook

Work in small groups to do the following questions.

1. a) Use the information from this chapter to make a list of changes that occurred on Vancouver Island and in British Columbia during this time period.

    b) Reread pages 24–25 in this textbook on change. Identify the agents of change responsible for each of the changes you listed in a).

    c) Organize the initial list of changes into causes and effects using a cause and effect chart. (See page 348 for ideas.)

2. Identify the point of view held by each of the fictitious people on page 49 about the future of the British colonies on the Pacific Coast. Are they in favour of change or against it?

An Exercise in Critical Thinking

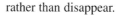

Points of View

By the early 1860s, there were many groups in British colonies on the Pacific Coast. Each had differing interests and points of view about the future of the colonies in the region.

As a government leader I talk with many people in the colony. People are beginning to consider the economic advantages that could be gained by joining with the British colonies in the east. I agree with this direction for our colony. We are too small and have too many financial difficulties. We must join with the other British colonies in North America.

I've been in the area since I came here from Britain as a young man with the Hudson's Bay Company. I've seen many changes occur. Too many people have come for the gold who don't care about the region. I would like our ties with Britain to continue. We are a British colony and a British colony we shall remain. We need help from the British government to prevent lawlessness and possible takeover from the United States.

I was educated at the fort and now I work for one of the businesses there. I am saddened at what I see happening to my people. Many have died from diseases brought here by the newcomers. Many of my people live partly in the world of our ancestors and partly in the world of the newcomers. I hope that change occurs slowly so my people can adapt

rather than disappear.

I came from California to the Cariboo at the start of the gold rush. I was one of the fortunate ones and didn't lose my life savings. I want to stay here and I want the area to become part of the United States. We have more things in common with each other than with Easterners. That is the only future British Columbia has.

About 50 Chinese people came here about 70 years ago to build fur trade posts. Many more of us have come from China and San Francisco to prospect for gold. There are as many as 7000 of us in these two British colonies. Many hope to return to China with great wealth. However, I will keep my business importing food. It is a good living too.

Exploring Further

Imagine it is 1862. Select one from the following activities on change and regionalism.

1. You are a British newspaper reporter on assignment. You will travel to the British colonies of Vancouver Island and British Columbia to research the region and the people living there.
   - Write five journal entries of your experiences and observations.
   - Write an article for your newspaper.
2. Create brief character sketches of four people from the west coast with different points of view about regional interests. Add sketches or clip art as visual reminders of the individuals.

Review

The icons are your cue to refer to the Learning How to Learn Appendix (pages 348–371) for ideas on how to complete these activities.

1. Complete a self-assessment for one assignment from this chapter (see Self-assessment on page 368.)

Understanding Concepts

2. Use one of the methods for recording vocabulary (see page 369) to add any words from this chapter you don't know to the WordBook section of your History notes.

3. Here are some of the main ideas from the chapter:
   - environmental interaction and balance
   - fur traders of the Pacific Coast
   - establishing the British colony of Vancouver Island
   - individuals
   - gold miners bring changes
   - establishing the colony of British Columbia
   - changes to British Columbia at the end of the gold rush

   Do either a) or b)

   a) Create a concept poster about one of these ideas (see page 350). Present your poster to the class.

   b) Use a web, mind map, outline, or chart (see pages 362 and 349) to create a permanent set of notes about one of the above ideas. Use colour and drawings wherever possible. Explain your work to a classmate.

4. Refer to page 23 for ideas on Notebook Organization. Organize your notes. Compare your notebook to that of a partner. Check to see that items are not missing and are in the correct order.

5. Add any dates from this chapter you feel are important to the timeline you started on page 2. (Timeline suggestions are on page 350.)

Developing Research Skills

6.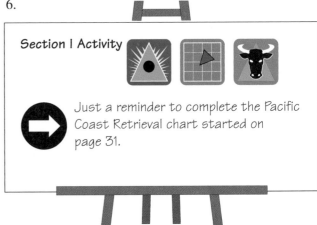

Section I Activity

Just a reminder to complete the Pacific Coast Retrieval chart started on page 31.

Developing Communication Skills

Writing

7. Pretend you are going north to Barkerville to visit your father, who is a miner. Write a story about your trip from Yale to the Cariboo region. Select any of the transportation methods used, including walking. Describe the things you would see along the way, the friends you might make, the problems you would encounter, and some of the experiences you might have.

8. Write a story about one or several of the following topics:
   - A Nuu-chah-nulth boy goes on his first whale-hunting trip.
   - First Nations people bring gold nuggets to the traders at the Hudson's Bay Company post at Fort Kamloops.
   - Miners in California try to decide whether they should leave the goldfields of California and go to the goldfields up north.
   - Gold is discovered at Hill's Bar.
   - A servant in England tries to convince her husband that they should leave their home and go to New Caledonia to find gold.
   - A hotel manager in Victoria sees the paddle-wheel steamer *Commodore* arriving from San Francisco with 450 miners aboard.
   - A disappointed miner who has just returned to California from the Fraser talks to his or her friends.

Listening and Speaking

9. Role-play in small groups one or all of the scenes from number 10. You may wish to write a script beforehand. Decide which part each person is to play.

10. Role-play the following situation:
Date—1863
Setting—England
A letter has just arrived in the mail. It is the first letter that your family has ever received, for letters are very expensive to send. Your father and older brother left two years ago to go to the goldfields of California to try their luck. The letter brings good news to your family. Your father has struck it rich, earning $125 000 (worth about $1 million today). You and your mother, three brothers, and three sisters think back over the years of poverty and begin to dream of the future. Role-play the conversation that would probably take place in your home and the plans you might make for the future.

11. Make up a song to sing around the campfire or at a music hall. Individually or as a group sing it to the class. Learn some steps from the cancan or make up a dance to perform for the rest of your classmates.

Viewing and Representing

12. Create a variety show to perform in the Theatre Royal. Acts on your program might include songs, dances, musical numbers, jokes, jugglers, poems, and skits related to the time period of this chapter.

13. Use the graph to obtain the answers for the following questions.
   a) Put the names of the mines in sequence from the one that produced the smallest amount of gold to the one that produced the most.
   b) How much more gold was produced by:
   • the Aurora than the Adams claim?
   • the Neversweat than the Prairie Flower claim?
   • the Steele than the 12 ft. Davis claim?
   • the Caledonia than the Adams claim?
   • the Cunningham than the Diller claim?

Applying Concepts

14. List the eight agents of change from pages 24 and 25. Working with several other people, find two examples from Chapter 1 of each agent of change. Share your examples with another group.

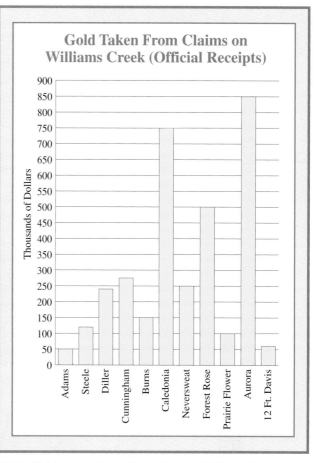

Gold Taken From Claims on Williams Creek (Official Receipts)

Thousands of Dollars (y-axis, 0 to 900)

Mines (x-axis): Adams, Steele, Diller, Cunningham, Burns, Caledonia, Neversweat, Forest Rose, Prairie Flower, Aurora, 12 Ft. Davis

Total official output from all the mines on Williams Creek was $19 000 000; unofficial output was about $50 000 000.

Canada Revisited

This modern-day diorama of Billy Barker striking it rich is found in Barkerville, British Columbia.

For more information go to http://www.heritage.gov.bc.ca/index.htm and click on link called Barkerville Town.

Chapter 2
In Rupert's Land
Prior to Confederation

Overview
Use this Overview to predict what you will read in this chapter.

❶ First Nations

Before European settlement, approximately 30 000 to 40 000 First Nations people lived between the Great Lakes and the Rocky Mountains. Two First Nations will be studied in this chapter, the Woodland Cree and the Siksika.

❷ The Woodland Cree

The Woodland Cree lived in small family groups in northern woodlands. They met all of their needs from the environment.

❸ The Siksika

The culture of the Siksika was based on following migrating herds of buffalo across the broad plains.

❹ Contact with Fur Traders

Contact with the fur traders of the HBC and the NWC influenced the ways of life of the Woodland Cree and the Siksika.

Red River Settlement

❺ 1812

Lord Selkirk was given a land grant known as Assiniboia.

❻ 1840s

About 4000 Metis lived in the Red River area. Metis are people of mixed First Nation and European ancestry.

Chapter 2 Focus

Chapter 2 focuses on the ways of life of several different groups of people living in Rupert's Land. You will first read about the traditional lifestyles of two First Nations in Rupert's Land, and then consider the changes that newcomers (such as the Hudson's Bay Company traders and the Red River settlers) brought to these First Nations and the Metis at Red River. All the book's concepts will be examined in this chapter.

Change   Regionalism   Power   Identity   Co-operation/Conflict

Other Concepts and Main Topics

- environmental interaction and balance
- trade
- cultural contact
- Metis
- Red River Settlement

Learning How to Learn

 Cause and Effect

 Chronology

 Critical Thinking

 Note Making

 Research

Chapter Preview/Prediction

1. In pairs or small groups, use the overview on the previous page and the titles in the chapter to predict what major topics you will read about in the chapter.

   a) Using the information in the overview and the chapter's titles, make a web of the historical topics and events to be covered.

Section I Activity
(continued from pages 27 and 31)

Different groups of people living in Rupert's Land had their own special concerns and their own points of view about development and change in the region. This activity is similar to the one you did in Chapter 1.

Using this chapter as a source of information, locate relevant information about 1., agents of change; 2., the regional interests of the groups; and 3., power. Use a chart similar to the following.

Rupert's Land Retrieval Chart*

1.  What factors contributed to change among each group of people (agents of change)?

Woodland Cree in the Northern Woodlands	
Siksika on the Prairies	
Metis at Red River	
Fur Traders and Settlers at Red River	

2. What interests, if any, were shared by these different groups of people living in Rupert's Land?

3. Which groups would have held more power and influence in making political decisions?

---

*A blackline master of this chart is in the *Canada Revisited 8 Teacher's Resource Package* and on the **Canada Revisited 8** web page.

Canada Revisited

In 1982, the Constitution Act gave an official definition of Aboriginal. As the web below shows, in modern-day terms Aboriginal includes Indian, Inuit, and Metis peoples of Canada. This textbook uses First Nations (when referring to Indian people), Metis, and Inuit. It uses Aboriginal (and sometimes Native) when referring to two or more different groups. Indian is used in most primary sources written by previous generations and in many government documents.

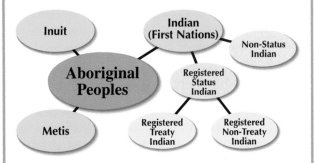

Mohawk composer John Kim Bell started the National Aboriginal Achievement Awards program.

Architect Douglas Cardinal, of Metis ancestry, designed the Museum of Civilization building, shown above.

Timeline
Rupert's Land 1760–1866

- 1760
- 1770
- 1780
- 1790
- 1800
- 1810
- 1820
- 1830
- 1840
- 1850
- 1860
- 1870

Time Periods

The First Nations

Struggle for Control

Key Events

◀ 1774   Cumberland House built by the HBC to counter competition from independent fur traders from Montreal

◀ 1783   Formation of the North West Company (NWC)

◁ 1812   Red River Settlement started by Lord Selkirk

◁ 1816   Seven Oaks Incident

◁ 1821   The HBC and the NWC united under the name Hudson's Bay Company

◁ 1843   Population at Red River increased to 5000 (4000 Metis, 1000 Euro-Canadians)

Cultural Contact

When people from two cultures meet, they affect each other. The people often exchange objects or ideas with one another. Often one culture has a stronger influence on the other. Conflict can occur.

Cultural Contact

 Rupert's Land was a large northern territory that had been granted to the Hudson's Bay Company by King Charles II of England in 1670. From 1670 to 1869, the Hudson's Bay Company's charter gave the company the right to control trading north and west of the Great Lakes. The area was also known to Europeans as "the North-West." Aboriginal peoples living there included Inuit and hundreds of First Nations. Two First Nations groups that were important in the fur trade and in the settlement of the west were the Woodland Cree and the Siksika.

In the late 1700s and early 1800s in the area now known as Western Canada, there were few Europeans compared to the number living in the eastern colonies. Some First Nations people had no direct contact with Europeans. Still, their lives were affected by European goods acquired through trade, and by the demands by Europeans for land and other resources.

Changes in the environment and contact with other groups were two agents of changes that affected the ways of life of all groups who lived in Rupert's Land. European fur traders, settlers, business people, and government officials had to learn new skills and knowledge, and acquire new technology in order to survive and succeed in the Rupert's Land environment which was unfamiliar to them. The Inuit and First Nations peoples were affected by the Europeans' desire for many furs and the introduction of new products and tools.

Early European explorers and fur traders found survival in North America difficult. They constantly feared injury, starvation, freezing, drowning, or being killed by animals. First Nations people understood their environment. They shared information about trapping, the environment, and travel routes with the Europeans. They supplied most of the food for the fur forts.

First Nations guides showed explorers and fur traders the best trails and canoe routes.

Aboriginal people were also the principal labour force for the fur trade. In exchange for helping Europeans survive, First Nations people received European goods such as guns, blankets, and metal containers. Metal goods were valued and traded between First Nations groups all across the continent. Access to European goods changed long-standing trade patterns between First Nations.

Some European fur traders married First Nations and Metis women. Some learned to speak their Aboriginal languages. Some of these women learned to speak the European languages of their husbands and acted as interpreters. Those who knew the travelling routes of Western Canada sometimes also served as guides. They taught the newcomers how to live comfortably by wearing skin and fur clothing.

Women also made clothing that traders needed to keep them warm in winter, and snowshoes that they needed to travel over snow.

First Nations and Metis women made pemmican, a traditional food they supplied to fur traders to carry with them on their long trips.

Woodland Cree

The homelands of Algonquian-speaking* peoples, shown on the maps, extended from the Atlantic Coast to the Plains. For information on map inset see page 12.

Traditional Ways of Life

ATHABASCAN-SPEAKING

ALGONQUIAN-SPEAKING

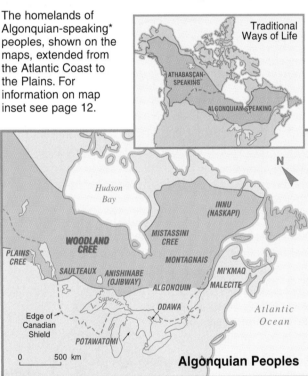

Hudson Bay

WOODLAND CREE

PLAINS CREE

SAULTEAUX

ANISHINABE (OJIBWAY)

ALGONQUIN

INNU (NASKAPI)

MISTASSINI CREE

MONTAGNAIS

MI'KMAQ

MALECITE

ODAWA

L. Superior

Edge of Canadian Shield

POTAWATOMI

Atlantic Ocean

N

0   500 km

Algonquian Peoples

Environmental Interaction

The Woodland Cree are an Algonquian-speaking people. They lived in a land of forests, rock, muskeg, many lakes, rivers, and streams. Like all Aboriginal peoples, they were greatly influenced by their environment. They believed in the interconnectedness of all things and lived in harmony with nature. Their way of life helped maintain the balance of nature. Traditionally, they were big game hunters. The moose, woodland caribou, deer, and bear that the Woodland Cree hunted lived spread out in the forest. Because the small numbers of animals in any

*Numerous First Nations groups with related languages

area could not support large groups of humans, the Woodland Cree lived in small family groups. They did not live in permanent villages, and families moved often to find new food sources. All the members of a group worked to provide for their basic needs. Men hunted ducks and geese as well as big game. Women and children snared rabbits and fished. Women gathered plants for food and medicines. Women made clothing from hides which they prepared and tanned. Homes were temporary structures made of hides or bark stretched over a frame.

The lives of the Woodland Cree were closely tied to the seasons. In winter, they lived in small, isolated groups of 25 to 30 people. Everyone in the extended family group was related through kinship or marriage. In summer, groups formed larger communities for activities such as duck hunting and fishing. At these times, they made decisions that affected them all. They also visited and held celebrations and ceremonies.

Hunting moose was a co-operative activity that needed the skills and strength of a group.

56

Spirituality was part of everyday life for the Woodland Cree.* Their spiritual practices related to practical needs of life, such as hunting. Elders taught that all parts of Earth and all forms of life had been made by the Creator. All were **sacred** and had a place within the Sacred Circle—rocks, lakes, rivers, trees, animals, the moon, thunder, the spirits, and people. If one part was injured, everything would be affected. People, the natural world, and the world of spirits were interconnected.

Elders were respected for what they had learned in life and for their special relationship with Mother Earth and all living things. Traditionally, Elders had an important role in teaching children the stories, history, and values of the people. Elders also acted as advisors to adults. They taught trust, loving others, honesty, sharing, kindness, obedience, and respect for all living things.

"KEEPERS of NATURE" —D. B. Pawis

In observing the changes in seasons, Woodland Cree noticed phases of the moon, length of days, growth of plants, migrations of birds, and many other recurring events. Knowledge of these events was essential to the careful planning of their seasonal activities and central to their spiritual life.

---

*Many of these beliefs are still held today. Because spiritual practices are difficult to fully understand out of their context, the sacred ideas and practices of First Nations will not be discussed in detail in this textbook.
Sacred—holy; having high spiritual value and given great respect

The Woodland Cree were active traders. They built fine canoes for travel on the swift rivers and many lakes. The trading season was in the summer when the waterways were open. Trading groups might travel many hundreds of kilometres in a summer before rejoining their community. Traditionally, the Woodland Cree traded for products that were not available in their environment, such as corn, tobacco, birchbark, wild rice, and maple sugar. They mainly traded surplus furs they had trapped and prepared during the winter for these products.

When the Hudson's Bay Company first established posts at the mouths of rivers flowing into Hudson Bay, the Woodland Cree were among the first groups they encountered. The Woodland Cree acted as go-betweens for the fur trade. They exchanged furs for European goods, then traded the goods to inland First Nations for more furs. Traditional trading patterns were disrupted and new patterns established. The Woodland Cree and other groups around Hudson Bay and James Bay controlled this flow of European goods until the Hudson's Bay Company moved its trading posts inland to better compete with the North West Company.

European goods made some differences to the way of life of the Woodland Cree, but most of the people continued to live a traditional lifestyle and meet most of their needs from the environment for many more generations. At that time, Europeans did not want their lands for settlement or farmland. Mining and hydro-electric projects would bring many changes, but not until the next century.

Paul Kane, *Indian Encampment on Lake Huron*, c. 1845–50, Art Gallery of Ontario

Summer camps were usually near a lake for fishing and canoe travel.

For Your Notebook

1. With a partner, reread the pages about the Woodland Cree. Find and record examples of environmental interaction and co-operation among the Woodland Cree.

The Siksika

The maps show where the Siksika lived before the arrival of the Europeans. For information on map inset, see page 12.

The Western Plains

Environmental Interaction

The Siksika speak an Algonquian language related to Woodland Cree, but their traditional way of life was different in many ways. The Siksika culture was based on following the migrating herds of buffalo on the plains. The Siksika were buffalo hunters and skilled hunters of antelope and deer.

Because they travelled great distances following the buffalo, the Siksika needed homes and possessions that were light enough to move from place to place. During the winter they lived in small family groups in sheltered river valleys or in the foothills of the Rocky Mountains. When spring came they moved out onto the prairie, where they were joined by other family groups.

In summer, the Siksika came together in large groups for the buffalo hunt. They needed to co-operate to hunt such large animals, particularly in pre-Contact times before they had horses. They would chase buffalo over cliffs, or into an area enclosed by bushes called a pound. The hunters then killed the buffalo with bows and arrows or spears. The Siksika were careful to treat the buffalo with respect and tried to waste no parts of them. However, wastage could occur, especially at buffalo jumps, where it was impossible to control the number of animals killed.

After the buffalo were killed and skinned, the women dried the meat. Most of the dried meat was ground into powder. It was mixed with melted fat and berries to make pemmican.

Every Part of the Buffalo Was Used

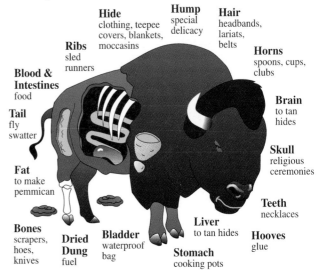

Hide
clothing, teepee covers, blankets, moccasins

Hump
special delicacy

Hair
headbands, lariats, belts

Ribs
sled runners

Horns
spoons, cups, clubs

Blood & Intestines
food

Tail
fly swatter

Brain
to tan hides

Skull
religious ceremonies

Fat
to make pemmican

Teeth
necklaces

Bones
scrapers, hoes, knives

Dried Dung
fuel

Bladder
waterproof bag

Liver
to tan hides

Stomach
cooking pots

Hooves
glue

58

Teepees were made from deer or buffalo hides stretched over a frame of poles. These wooden poles were obtained in the foothills, where lodgepole pines were plentiful. Teepees were taken down when the Siksika moved to a new area. The people took the poles and hides with them. A travois pulled by horses was used to carry some burdens.

The Siksika wore clothing made of animal skins, usually deer or buffalo sewn with thread made from sinew. Warm robes and mittens for winter were made from buffalo hides.

The Siksika used resources that they found in the environment to make tools and other products. Materials such as stone, bone, wood, and hide were used. The knowledge and skills for making tools were passed from one generation to the next. The introduction of metal tools and guns changed the way Siksika interacted with the environment, as well as their trading patterns with other groups.

The Siksika did not believe in private ownership of land. They believed the land had been made by the Creator or Great Spirit for all to use. They believed that everything on earth was sacred and should be respected. The Siksika believed strongly in the importance of sharing, since their survival depended on co-operation. Everyone, from the elderly to children, was expected to make a contribution. Women and men had specific roles to perform and jobs to do. Girls and boys learned knowledge and skills from their parents and other adults. The main roles of young men were those of hunter and warrior. They trained from boyhood to acquire skills and a high level of physical fitness. These were needed both to hunt large game and for defence.

The Siksika believed all living things were interconnected. They treated nature with respect, living on the land mainly as they found it, and being careful not to upset the balance of nature.

The circle was an important sacred symbol, representing the cycle of life. Circles were used in ceremonies and on objects like sacred drums and shields. Children were an important part of the cycle of life. They spent a lot of time with their grandparents and Elders learning about their culture.

Elders were highly respected for their advice and for their knowledge of the group's history and customs. Some Elders led ceremonies and some gave spiritual guidance to their people.

The Siksika followed a consensus model of decision-making. In consensus, no action is taken until all people involved agree with it. Group decisions made by the Siksika were respected by everyone. Chiefs did not rule their bands, but rather spoke for them at gatherings. At annual gatherings, decisions about trade or war were made by consensus on behalf of the entire nation.

The way the Siksika lived showed their belief in co-operation with each other and the environment.

The Siksika followed a consensus model of decision-making.

One of the Great Spirit's gifts was sweetgrass, which was used in many ceremonies.

For Your Notebook

1. With a partner, reread the pages about the Siksika. Find and record examples of environmental interaction and co-operation amongst the Siksika.

The Metis

Origins of the Metis

 As a distinct people, the Metis of the North-West had their roots in marriages of English, Scottish, or French men with First Nations women, many of Cree origin. They had varied backgrounds, with skills, knowledge, and customs from the cultures of all their ancestors. Most of them spoke either English or French and at least one First Nations language. Some of the boys were educated in the cities of British North America, or in France or Great Britain. Most of the girls learned the ways of their First Nation ancestors. Most Metis honoured the spiritual beliefs of both their parents. Metis who were of French background were usually Roman Catholic, and those from English or Scottish background were usually Protestant.

Not all Metis children were part of the Metis culture. Many were assimilated into the culture of one of their parents. The distinct culture of the Metis developed as Metis intermarried and passed on their way of life. The fur trade and the buffalo hunt were key parts of the Metis way of life in Red River.

At Red River

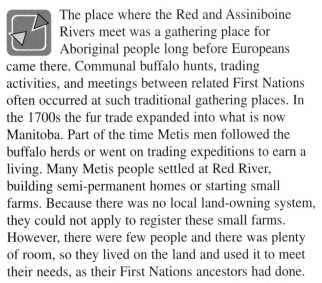 The place where the Red and Assiniboine Rivers meet was a gathering place for Aboriginal people long before Europeans came there. Communal buffalo hunts, trading activities, and meetings between related First Nations often occurred at such traditional gathering places. In the 1700s the fur trade expanded into what is now Manitoba. Part of the time Metis men followed the buffalo herds or went on trading expeditions to earn a living. Many Metis people settled at Red River, building semi-permanent homes or starting small farms. Because there was no local land-owning system, they could not apply to register these small farms. However, there were few people and there was plenty of room, so they lived on the land and used it to meet their needs, as their First Nations ancestors had done.

Both the Hudson's Bay Company and North West Company established fur trade posts at Red River. The region had a central location, abundant resources, and a local supply of workers. The Metis population expanded and the people developed a distinct identity and pride in their community.

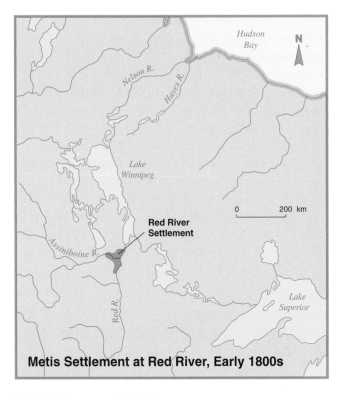

Metis Settlement at Red River, Early 1800s

Making a Living

The Metis at Red River supported themselves in different ways.

- Many worked at the fur trade posts as labourers, interpreters, and company clerks.
- Others worked for the fur trading companies as hunters or trappers, or on the York boats that transported trade goods and furs to and from the fur forts, or as freighters in brigades of Red River carts.
- Many Metis women worked to supply the fur trade companies with pemmican.
- Other Metis chose to trap furs and hunt buffalo independently instead of working for the large fur trade companies.
- Still others preferred to stay in the Red River Settlement and farm for most of the year.
- Some early Metis lived in teepees; others lived in or near the fur trade posts. During winter they lived in log cabins; however, summers took them away from Red River on buffalo hunts.

Annual Buffalo Hunt

The annual buffalo hunt was an important part of Metis life and a major source of food. The hunters rode horses and families travelled in Red River carts until a buffalo herd was sighted. When "running the buffalo," hunters rode amongst the herd. Each man would kill from two to five buffalo on each run as the buffalo stampeded past. Following the hunt, the women skinned the buffalo and cut them up. Meat that was not eaten immediately was dried to make pemmican. Surplus pemmican was traded at the fur trade posts for other items.

The illustration on pages 62 and 63 shows a running buffalo hunt and families processing the meat.

Metis Farms

The Metis did not use the block method of dividing land that was used in Canada West. Metis farms (and those of the later Scottish settlers) were usually in three-kilometre-long strips. They often had a 100-metre frontage on the rivers, allowing access to water transportation, as roads were not common.

In gardens near their log cabins, the Metis of the early 1800s grew barley and root vegetables, such as potatoes, onions, and prairie turnips. In addition to their horses, they often kept oxen.

On a quiet day in the Red River Settlement, the squeaking of the unoiled wheels of a Red River cart announced the passing of travellers.

tam

decorative beadwork

capote

sash pouch

blanket or buckskin coat

moccasin

plaid shawl

cotton or woolen dress

Clothing

The Metis usually wore a combination of European and First Nations clothing. Leather and fabric were both used as materials. Home-spinning and home-weaving were common. The men wore capotes (wool coats with hoods) or coats made from buffalo robes, woven trousers, and shirts, which they often bought at trading posts. The women wore woven cotton or wool dresses. In cold weather they wore heavy shawls over their dresses. Footwear was usually moccasins. Metis clothing was decorated with beadwork, embroidery, and bright woven sashes. Men often carried brightly beaded bags over their shoulders.

For Your Notebook

1. After reading the pages on the Metis and studying the painting on pages 62 and 63, record
   a) ways environment influenced the way Metis people lived
   b) ways Metis changed the environment
   c) examples of cultural contact
   d) examples of co-operation
   e) examples of cultural change (relate to the Agents of Change on pages 24 and 25)

2. Select one of the activities in the painting on pages 62 and 63. In the role of one of the people, write a story about your day.

Exploring Further

3. 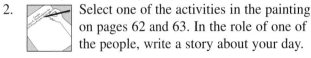 Research other types of buffalo hunts (surround, pounds, individual stalking, and jumps).

Metis Buffalo Hunt

LARISA SEMBALIUK-CHELADYN

The Red River Settlement

Lord Selkirk

 A Scottish nobleman, the Earl of Selkirk, wanted to help **crofters** of Scotland who had been forced off their small rented farms by landowners who wanted to put the land to a different use. Wool was fetching a high price, so the landowners thought they would make more money by raising sheep on the land.

Lord Selkirk asked the British government for a land grant in the Red River Valley in Rupert's Land. The British government had given the Hudson's Bay Company a monopoly for fur trading on that land. Lord Selkirk was refused, but he was very determined. He and Sir Alexander Mackenzie, the explorer of northwestern North America, bought enough shares in the Hudson's Bay Company to gain control of the company. This position of power allowed Selkirk to be able to get a land grant of 300 000 square kilometres in Rupert's Land, in the valley of the Red and Assiniboine Rivers. The area also stretched south into what is now the United States. Selkirk's land grant, Assiniboia, is shown on the map below.

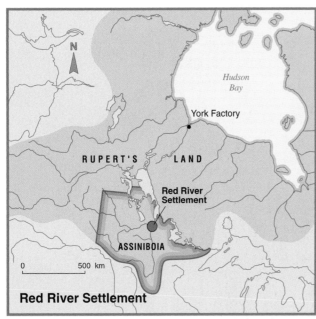

Red River Settlement

The part of Rupert's Land granted to Lord Selkirk was called Assiniboia. The Red River Settlement was located in Assiniboia along the Assiniboine and Red Rivers.

As part-owner of the Hudson's Bay Company, Selkirk also wanted to stop the North West Company from competing for furs in the region. The Nor'Westers (people who worked for the North West Company) relied on the Metis of the Red River area to provide them with pemmican and other provisions. The route the Nor'Westers used when taking furs to Montreal also ran through the Red River region. (See also pages 13, 16, and 17.)

Selkirk's First Settlers

Late in 1811, Selkirk's first group of about 80 Scottish settlers arrived at York Factory, a Hudson's Bay Company fur trade post. They spent a difficult winter, enduring homesickness, cold, poor food, and scurvy. In spring they set out on the 420-kilometre journey to the Red River Valley. They arrived in August of 1812, too late to plant crops. Since no special preparations had been made for their arrival, another difficult winter followed. The settlers survived mainly because of the help they received from the Saulteaux First Nation* and because they were able to obtain food from the local Metis.

Selkirk's Second Settlers

In the spring of 1813 Lord Selkirk sent another group of settlers from Scotland. They also endured many hardships. This party of settlers included the first group of European women to settle in the West. There were 18 women over the age of 15, one girl, and 11 children under the age of eight. One woman gave birth to a child while on ship, during a furious storm in Hudson Bay.

Scottish settlers arriving at the Red River, Manitoba

Crofter—a Scottish person who cultivates a small farm
*The Saulteaux are an Algonquian-speaking people. At that time they were hunters, trappers, and traders living in the woodlands. See maps pages 56 and 58.

Lord Selkirk
1771–1820

Thomas Douglas, fifth Earl of Selkirk, was the seventh son of a Scottish Earl. Because he had six older brothers, he did not expect to inherit the family estate, so he went to university to prepare to be a lawyer. While there he became interested in **social problems**, especially the poor Scottish farmers who were being displaced from their lands. Some of them ended up living in the poor districts of Britain's industrial cities and looking for work in the new factories. Others were leaving Britain and moving to the United States. When Selkirk inherited his father's estate after the unexpected deaths of his brothers, he decided to help these people. He used his own money to help poor farmers settle in Prince Edward Island in 1803 and Upper Canada in 1804. In 1812, he established the Red River Settlement. Selkirk spent his final years in legal battles with opponents of the Red River Settlement.

Isabel Gunn

Isabel Gunn, from the Orkney Islands off the northeast coast of Scotland, lived in Rupert's Land from 1806 until 1809. She travelled on a Hudson's Bay Company ship and worked in the fur trade disguised as a man, using the name John Fubbister. She would not have been allowed to live and work with the men if anyone had known she was a woman. According to the journal of the fur trader Alexander Henry, she gave birth to "a fine boy" on December 29, 1807, at the trading post at the mouth of the Pembina River. She and her son returned to Scotland on the annual ship in 1809.

Marie-Anne Lagemodière

Marie-Anne Lagemodière is often referred to as the first non-Aboriginal woman in the West. She was born in Quebec, where she married a fur trader, Jean Baptiste Lagemodière. Marie-Anne and her husband travelled by the fur traders' route from the St. Lawrence, a journey of over 3000 kilometres, to come west in 1807. Their first child was born in a wigwam near the bank of the Pembina River on January 6, 1807. Julie, the second youngest of Marie-Anne's children, was to become the mother of Louis Riel.

Catherine McPherson

Among the women in the second group of Selkirk settlers was Catherine McPherson. She risked her own health to care for those who were ill during the long journey from Hudson's Bay to the Red River Settlement. She was always positive and encouraged the others. A young man named Alexander Sutherland, in the same group of settlers, admired her courage and strength. The two were married shortly after their arrival in the Red River Settlement.

Social problems—problems concerning life in a community, problems between people that arise in day-to-day living

Many Red River Metis were descended from Scottish fur traders and First Nations women. These two Metis women were Caroline Sinclair (née Pruden) and Maggie Stewart (née Mowat).

Conflict

 Assiniboia was formed from the lands granted to the Hudson's Bay Company. However, it was on the transportation route and in the midst of the trading territory used by the North West Company. The Nor'Westers thought that the Hudson's Bay Company was trying to block their supplies of pemmican from reaching the fur trading posts. Losing their source of supplies would disrupt their trading practices.

The Selkirk settlers met with considerable opposition. The Metis and First Nations people were afraid that the settlers, who were farmers, would interfere with their hunting of buffalo. The Nor'Westers feared that food, especially pemmican, would become scarce if the Metis could no longer hunt buffalo. Also, many of the Metis were farmers. They had no legal rights or title to the land even though they had farmed it for generations. The Nor'Westers warned the Metis that in the future they could lose their land to the settlers, who would likely receive legal title.

Conditions for the Red River settlers were harsh. The governor of Red River, Miles Macdonell, was worried that the Selkirk settlers would starve. In January of 1814, he issued a law called the "Pemmican Proclamation." It stated that, for the next year, no food could be taken

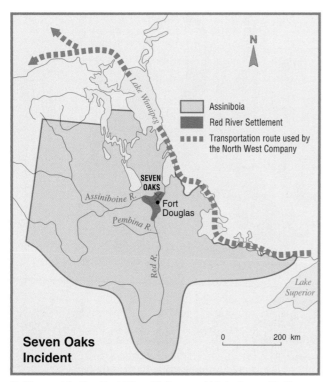

Seven Oaks Incident

Settlement in the Red River Valley could interfere with the North West Company's fur trade route.

from Assiniboia without a licence. Only he, acting as governor, could issue licences. This affected the Metis because they made pemmican to sell to fur traders for their long trips to the North-West. The Metis were greatly angered because sale of pemmican and buffalo meat was an important source of income for them. They felt that Governor Macdonell had no right to pass laws in their land. A very tense situation developed.

The Metis began to destroy the settlers' crops. They attacked Fort Douglas in the Red River Settlement and burned some of its buildings. By 1815, only 60 settlers remained, many having fled to Upper Canada.

Incident at Seven Oaks

A young Metis named Cuthbert Grant was one of four captains of the Metis. Beginning in 1814, Grant took an active role in the campaign to drive settlers out of the area. On June 19, 1816, Grant and a group of Metis met the new governor, Robert Semple, and his men near a grove of trees called Seven Oaks. Historians do not agree about which side fired the first shot, but at the end of the encounter, one Metis and 21 settlers, including Governor Semple, were dead.

Following the incident at Seven Oaks, the remaining settlers abandoned the settlement to the Metis. However, the following year Lord Selkirk himself arrived in the colony, bringing with him about 90 Swiss and German soldiers called the de Meurons, to take control. Many settlers returned to the Red River Settlement, especially after the merger of the Hudson's Bay Company and North West Company in 1821.

Merger of HBC and NWC

 The merger of the two fur trade companies brought many changes in the Red River region. The Metis people were particularly affected. The HBC and NWC were no longer competing against each other, so in places where each had built a fort, one was closed. Fewer workers were needed, so men were out of work. Fewer provisions were needed to feed them, so the pemmican trade declined. For some years buffalo meat and pemmican helped feed the colonists but soon their farms filled most of that need. The Hudson's Bay Company had a trading monopoly in the region, so they could pay lower prices for furs. All of these changes affected the Metis people's way of life.

Cuthbert Grant led the Metis in the incident at Seven Oaks.

Cuthbert Grant
1793–1854

Cuthbert Grant was the son of a North West Company trader and a Cree woman. He went to school in Montreal and Scotland. When he returned to the Red River area in 1815, he was elected the captain-general of the Metis. He was the leader of the Metis at Seven Oaks in 1816, after the incident. Grant made sure that the remaining Selkirk settlers were allowed to leave the Red River safely.

Grant was later arrested and sent to Montreal to be tried for his part at Seven Oaks. He came back to the Red River before his trial and never returned to Montreal to be tried. In 1821, when the Hudson's Bay Company and the North West Company merged into one company under the name Hudson's Bay Company, Cuthbert Grant began working for the Hudson's Bay Company.

In 1824, Grant led a group of Metis families to begin farming at Grantown, west of the Red River. There he built a mill to make it easier for the Metis to grind their wheat into flour. In 1828, Grant was made Warden of the Plains. This meant that he and his Metis followers were responsible for controlling illegal fur trading.

Cuthbert Grant's education may have included some medical training. He often visited the sick and provided medicine for such diseases as smallpox and measles.

Cuthbert Grant died at Grantown in 1854.

Pierre Falcon
1793–1876

The best known composer of Metis songs in the 1800s was Pierre Falcon. Falcon's father was a North West Company trader and his mother was Cree. Although he went to school in Montreal, Falcon lived most of his life in what is now Manitoba. He was married to Cuthbert Grant's sister.

Falcon worked for the fur trade companies, then was a farmer at Grantown. By the end of his life he was a magistrate. He composed many songs about Metis events.

The Battle of Seven Oaks

Would you like to hear me sing
Of a true and recent thing?
It was June 18, the band of
  Bois-Brûlés
Arrived that day,
Oh, the brave warriors they!

. . .

Well, we were just about to
  unhorse
When we heard two of us give,
  give voice.
Two of our men cried, "Hey?
  Look back, look back!
The Anglo-Sack
Coming for to attack."

. . .

You should have seen those
  Englishmen—
Bois-Brûlés chasing them,
  chasing them.
From bluff to bluff they
  stumbled that day
While the Bois-Brûlés
Shouted "Hurray!"

For Your Notebook

The following questions and activities are based on pages 60 to 67.

1. a) What role did Lord Selkirk play in developing the Red River Settlement?
    b) How did the Hudson's Bay Company and the North West Company each view the Selkirk settlers? What was the importance of the Red River area?
    c) What words would you use to describe how the Saulteaux treated the settlers? Why was their help important?
    d) After the many difficulties between the Hudson's Bay Company and the North West Company, what was the result?

2. Diagram an example of cause and effect in relation to the Metis, the Red River settlers, the fur trade companies, and the Canadian government.

3. Add events from these pages to the timeline you have started.

Change

An Exercise in Critical Thinking

 By the early 1860s, there were many groups in Rupert's Land. Each had differing interests and points of view of the changes occurring there.

Work in small groups to do the following activities.

1. a) Use the visuals in this chapter, your notes, and the comments on this page to make a list of changes that are occurring in Rupert's Land.*
    b) Categorize the above changes based on the Agents of Change on page 24.
2. Add information from this page to the chart you started on page 53.

Woodland Cree

Many of my people have been involved in trading with the men at HBC posts. Their trade goods have brought some changes to my people's way of life. We work with them as guides and interpreters. We wish to be able to continue our traditional way of life.

Siksika

My people have their own identity. We see ourselves as a nation. We have traded for many years with other First Nations and with the Europeans to get products like iron tools and guns. I see our way of life changing as more and more people are moving onto the plains.

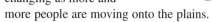

Hudson's Bay Company Officials at Red River

By moving our traders inland from Hudson Bay we were able to work with many First Nations trading partners. We want the First Nations and Metis to sell their furs only to our company. I'm concerned that many of the First Nations and Metis people trade with the Americans farther south.

The Metis at Red River

My people provide workers, services, and food to the fur trade. With more European settlers arriving the land is being made into farms. Buffalo are being killed to feed more people. Our traditional way of life is threatened. The Hudson's Bay Company calls our free trade with the Americans to the south illegal. The Metis people see themselves as a new nation—distinct from the Europeans and the First Nations. We don't want to be told who we should trade with.

Red River Settlers

My people have come a long way to establish a new life. There is no place for us back in Scotland. It may be difficult here but we will stay. We want to create farms and businesses to make this settlement succeed. We like this new land and we are starting to identify with it but we still think of

*Note: The viewpoints on this page are from imaginary people.

68

Metis Identity

Before the events of 1814–1816 in Assiniboia, the Metis had been traders, hunters, and employees of the North West Company. Many families were interrelated by blood and marriage, and they lived in communities in the same geographic area. As a result of events in the Red River Settlement, they began to consider themselves a new nation. They felt united as a people, separate from the First Nations and the Europeans. They had their own leaders, and were the largest group in the Red River region. As the fur trade declined they sought to control (or at least have influence on) how the Red River Settlement developed.

This strong sense of identity was to play a large part in the coming events of 1869 and 1870.

Population of Red River Settlement

- French Metis (50%)
- English Metis (30%)
- Selkirk Settlers (mostly Scottish, 10%)
- First Nations (10%)

1843

In 1843 there were approximately 5000 people in the Red River Settlement.

Canada Revisited

Metis People Today

Metis people contribute to all parts of Canadian culture today. Many individuals are well known for their achievements and contributions.* Until recent decades, the Metis traditional culture was in danger of being entirely assimilated into Canadian culture. Metis groups and individuals now seek to reclaim and preserve the unique elements of their traditional culture. Young Metis are being taught the history of their people as well as the dances, music, symbols, and stories. Skills such as sash-weaving, traditional embroidery, and outdoor cooking are taught. Competitions in fur trade activities like back-packing take place at large community celebrations. In Metis communities across Canada, there is a growing sense of pride in their important place in the history of Canada.

Metis traditional dances such as the Red River jig feature quick footwork in complicated patterns.

Population of Canada

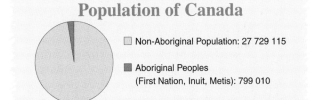

- Non-Aboriginal Population: 27 729 115
- Aboriginal Peoples (First Nation, Inuit, Metis): 799 010

1996

Aboriginal Population (1996)	
First Nations	554 290
Inuit	41 080
Metis	210 190
Total	**799 010****
Non-Aboriginal Population	27 729 115
Total Population of Canada	28 528 125

The emblem on the Metis flag is the eternity symbol. The background may be either red or blue.

---

* Students, visit the Arnold Publishing website to read about Aboriginal people who are making a difference. Send us more names to add to our list!

**This total is slightly less than the numbers of First Nation, Inuit, and Metis people added together. This is because some people told the census they belong to more than one group.

Review

The icons are your cue to refer to the Learning How to Learn Appendix (pages 348–371) for ideas on how to complete these activities.

 This icon is a reminder to turn to the Research Model on pages x and xi.

1. Complete a self-assessment for one assignment from this chapter. (See Self-assessment on page 368.)

Understanding Concepts

2. Examine the web you did from the chapter Preview/Prediction on page 53. Working with a partner, identify two things about each heading that you learned from this chapter. Add them to the web.

3. Using one of the methods for recording vocabulary, add any words you don't know to the WordBook section of your History notes.

4. Do either a) or b)
   Here are some of the main ideas from the chapter:
   - environmental interaction and balance
   - cultural contact between Metis and Red River settlers
   - everyday life of the Metis
   - individuals

   a) Create a concept poster about one of these ideas. Present your poster to the class.

   b) Use a web, mind map, outline, or chart to create a permanent set of notes about one of the above ideas. Use colour and drawings wherever possible. Explain your work to a classmate.

5. Add any dates you feel are important to the timeline you started on page 2.

6. Reread the definition of identity on page 29. Review all of the examples of identity that are found in this chapter. Work with a partner to draw a mind map that organizes all of these examples on one sheet of paper. Use simple line drawings and at least three colours. (Mind maps are explained on page 363.)

7. Refer to page 23 for ideas on Notebook Organization. Compare your notebook to that of a partner. Check to see that items are not missing and are in the correct order.

Developing Research Skills

8.

Section I Activity

If you haven't done so already, complete the Rupert's Land Retrieval Chart on page 53.

9. Carry out research to find out what happened when the Metis moved farther West. What influence did this have on the fur trade, the First Nations people, and the natural resources?

10. Read more about the situation in Great Britain in the early 1800s that made Lord Selkirk decide to establish a settlement for poor Scottish farmers in Rupert's Land. Use your research as background information for a newspaper article describing the situation.

Developing Communication Skills

Reading

11. a) Read one of the stories "Alex MacBeth" by Ted Stone, "LaLouise Letendre," or "Madeline Nolin," by Alice Lee Setka in **Ordinary People in Canada's Past**, by Nancy Sellars Marcotte, published by Arnold Publishing. Make a list of points about the Red River Settlement found in these stories that you did not read in this textbook.

   b) What jobs for men and women are described in the story? Provide several pieces of evidence to indicate this work is extremely hard.

c) Find examples of identity in the story you read.

Writing

12.   Pretend you are a reporter for a Scottish newspaper. You will be spending the next year in the Red River Settlement. Your readers are especially interested in the changes that are occurring in the region and the interests of the people living there. In role
    • write five journal entries of your experiences and observations.
    • write an article for your newspaper.

13.   Create a brief character sketch of four people in the Red River Settlement and surrounding area. Present their point-of-view on regional interests. You may wish to draw or use clip-art of the person you are presenting.

14.   Create a brief character sketch of four Metis people. Write a story that expresses feelings of Metis identity.

15. In the History Journal section of your notebook, tell which person from this chapter you would have liked to have met. Tell why you find this person interesting.

16.   Write a story from the point of view of a young Selkirk settler who has just arrived in the settlement. Write about your hopes for the future.

Listening and Speaking

17. Listen to modern-day Celtic music and music from a First Nations group. Notice the rhythms. Then listen to some Metis music. In chart form, compare their rhythms, melodies, words, and subject matters.

18. Select a story about a First Nations group that lived in Rupert's Land, the Metis people, or the Selkirk settlers and prepare it for oral reading to the class.

19.   Prepare and present a speech defending your homeland. You may write this from the point of view of (one of) a member of a First Nation in the area, a Selkirk settler, or a Metis person.

20. Prepare and sing one of Pierre Falcon's songs. Carry out research to find music of other Metis musicians.

21. Invite a First Nations or Metis person to speak to your class on how his/her family tries to keep their Aboriginal identity in today's world.

Viewing and Representing

22. Research media or interactive resources to find out more about the art, music, poetry, and stories of the Metis people.

23. In a small group, prepare a series of **tableaux** showing life among (one of) the Woodland Cree, the Siksika, the Selkirk settlers, or the Metis. Your tableau may represent a picture or description of a scene or a story found in this chapter.

24. Prepare a game about the regional interests of either the Metis or the Selkirk settlers. It may be a board game, card game, role-play game, or computer game. (Ideas for making games are found on page 354.)

Applying Concepts

25. Find examples in the newspaper showing achievements and/or identity concerns of First Nations and Metis people.

26. Check out this website to find Aboriginal people who are making a difference.
    • http://www.westindies.cibc.com/aboriginal/ 99recipients.html

---

Tableaux—participants represent a scene by taking a position and not moving. This can be based on a picture, story, or idea.

Chapter 3
Central and Atlantic Colonies

Prior to Confederation

Overview

Use this Overview to predict what you will read in this chapter.

❶ British Colonial Policy

Most of the BNA colonies had prospered under the protective economic policy of mercantilism. In 1846 Great Britain introduced free trade, resulting in economic hard times in the colonies, especially in Atlantic Canada. The Reciprocity Treaty removed tariffs between the BNA colonies and the USA. The 1850s were a time of prosperity in British North America.

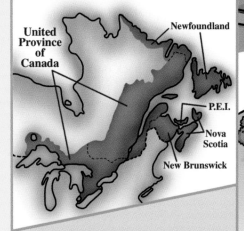

❷ United Province of Canada

Most of the people in the United Province of Canada (Canada West and Canada East) were farmers. Recent immigrants from Great Britain (especially Ireland) changed the ethnic diversity, especially in Canada West. Most people in Canada East were French-speaking.

❸ Colony of Nova Scotia

Mostly British people lived in the colony of Nova Scotia. Fishing, farming, ship-building, and ocean trade were the main industries.

❹ Colony of New Brunswick

British people and French-speaking Acadians were the European population of the colony of New Brunswick. Fishing, farming, and shipbuilding were important ways of making a living.

❺ Colony of Prince Edward Island

Most of the people in the colony of Prince Edward Island had British ancestors. Fishing and farming were the main industries. Over half of the farmers were tenant farmers.

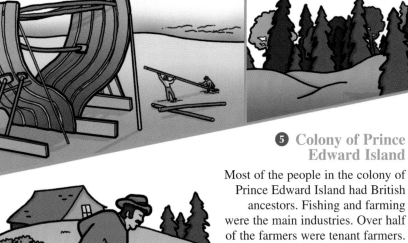

❻ Colony of Newfoundland

Most people in the colony of Newfoundland had British ancestors. Fishing was the main industry.

Chapter 3 Focus

Chapter 3 focuses on changes and the regional interests of the people in the central and Atlantic colonies of British North America during the 1850s. The main focus in this chapter is on change, regionalism (regional interests), and power.

| Change | Regionalism | Power | Identity | Co-operation/Conflict |

Other Concepts and Main Topics

- British Empire
- British colonial policy
- mercantilism
- free trade
- reciprocity
- economic situation
- responsible government
- political deadlock
- alliance

Learning How to Learn

 Critical Thinking

 Chart Making

 Presentation

 Note Making

 Chronology

Chapter Preview/Prediction

1. Use information in the overview and the chapter's titles to make a web of the historical topics and events covered.

2. Predict what major topics will be covered in this chapter. What do you think will be regional interests of the Central and Atlantic colonies?

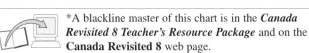
*A blackline master of this chart is in the *Canada Revisited 8 Teacher's Resource Package* and on the **Canada Revisited 8** web page.

Section I Activity

This chapter will continue the activity started in Chapters 1 and 2 on change, regionalism, and power. This activity is in three parts.

Part One

 In Part One record on a chart like the one below,* information about agents of change, common interests of the people in the colonies, and groups holding power in the colony.

Part Two follows on page 74 and Part Three on page 86. The Section I Activity is concluded on page 87 in the Section I Review.

Central and Atlantic Canada Retrieval Chart*

1. 	What factors contributed to change among each group of people (agents of change)?
The colony of the United Province of Canada	
The colony of Nova Scotia	
The colony of New Brunswick	
The colony of Prince Edward Island	
The colony of Newfoundland	
2.	What interests, if any, were shared by the people living in the Central colonies? Atlantic colonies?
3.	Which groups would have held more power and influence in making political decisions? (Identify the colony where each group lived.)

Section I Activity

Part Two

a) Form five groups based on the five colonies of British North America studied in this chapter.
- United Province of Canada: 16 students (may be sub-divided into 8 students for Canada West and 8 for Canada East)
- Nova Scotia: 6 students
- New Brunswick: 6 students
- Prince Edward Island: 2 students
- Newfoundland: 2 students

(Note: The number of students in each colony group is proportional to the colony's actual population in 1861.)

b) Each group is to research its colony by studying the material in this chapter. Group members may also want to do additional research in the library or on the internet. Find information about the colony in the areas of:
- history
- population, cities
- environmental interaction (ways of making a living)
- transportation
- links and relationships with other colonies and countries
- regional interests (special needs and concerns)

c)   As a group, present the information on your colony by making a group display or a large wall chart.

Note

Store/file the display and/or charts. You will use the display and/or charts again for the Confederation Simulation on page 102.

Timeline
Trade 1840–1870

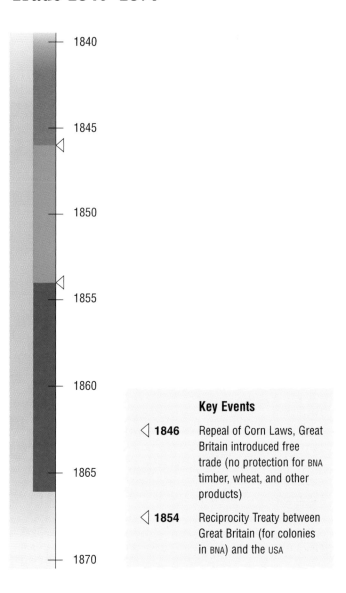

- 1840
- 1845
- 1850
- 1855
- 1860
- 1865
- 1870

Key Events

◁ **1846** Repeal of Corn Laws, Great Britain introduced free trade (no protection for BNA timber, wheat, and other products)

◁ **1854** Reciprocity Treaty between Great Britain (for colonies in BNA) and the USA

Time Periods

Mercantilism To 1846
BNA colonies received special protective trading status (lower tariffs) when most of their products entered Great Britain.

Repeal of Corn Laws 1846–1854
With the repeal of the Corn Laws, Great Britain changed its economic policies and favoured free trade rather than protectionism. (They withdrew the laws protecting the British grain industry.) Tariffs were removed on certain items traded between BNA colonies and Great Britain. Economic hard times in BNA Colonies resulted.

Reciprocity Treaty: Period of Free Trade on certain products 1854–1866
Certain natural resources could be traded between the BNA colonies and the USA without tariffs (taxes). Economic situation in BNA colonies improved.

British Colonial Policy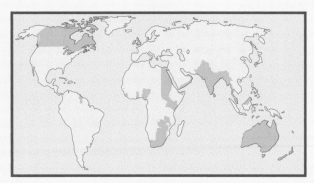

The British Empire

The British Empire began with English overseas exploration and colonization in the sixteenth century. It grew as the English established colonies throughout the world. The map shows the British Empire in 1901, at its greatest extent. At that time, the Empire included Canada, Australia, India, New Zealand, and parts of Africa. The Commonwealth was established in 1931 in place of the British Empire. Canada is still a member of the Commonwealth.

"The sun never sets on the British Empire."

Changes in Trade Policies

Mercantile System

Under the British mercantile system, colonies were considered to be sources of raw materials and markets for manufactured goods made in Great Britain. This meant that goods such as timber or wheat from the British North American colonies were sold in Britain with lower **tariffs** than goods from other countries. The lower prices encouraged British manufacturers to buy raw materials from British colonies rather than from other countries. In return, colonies bought manufactured goods from Great Britain. The mercantile system contributed to the prosperity of those in the colonies who were involved in the export of raw materials. The British North American colonies became prosperous.

Repeal of Corn Laws

 From 1791 to 1846, tariffs on grains imported into Britain were set according to a part of the mercantile system called the Corn Laws. ("Corn" was the British word for grain.) Under the Corn Laws, wheat and flour from the British North American colonies were imported to Britain with lower tariffs than wheat and flour from other countries. This ready market for wheat from their farms contributed to a time of prosperity for the British North American colonies.

The Corn Laws made the price of bread high in Great Britain. In 1846 the British repealed the Corn Laws. They adopted a policy of **free trade** so their manufacturers could buy wheat and other raw materials from wherever they could get it most cheaply. The British North American colonies lost their guaranteed market for their wheat and other raw materials.

Reciprocity Treaty

 In 1854 Britain signed the **Reciprocity** Treaty with the United States. This allowed the British North American colonies to trade in raw materials and agricultural products with the United States without tariffs being charged on these goods. The Reciprocity Treaty contributed to a period of renewed prosperity for the colonies from 1854 to 1866.

The lack of reliable transportation between the British North American colonies made trade difficult. Also, manufactured goods were available from the United States and Britain but very few from other colonies. Therefore, the colonies traded more with the United States than with each other.

For Your Notebook

1. Add definitions for British Empire, reciprocity, tariff, mercantilism, and free trade to your WordBook.
2. Explain the meaning of the statement "The sun never sets on the British Empire."

Tariff—tax paid on goods brought into a colony or country; tariffs protect internal production by raising the price on imported products and raise revenue for the government
Free trade—trade between countries without tariffs on imports and exports

---

Reciprocity—a mutual arrangement between two or more, in which each side gives the other similar advantages; an agreement for limited free trade between two countries

United Province of Canada

History

 The United Province of Canada was created in 1841 by uniting Canada West and Canada East. Canada West and Canada East were part of the same political unit, but their populations were quite different. Each group of people had its own needs and concerns. The following viewpoints show some of these concerns.

Canada West*

 My people have lived on the land the Europeans call Canada West since long before anyone can remember. Other First Nations groups came north from the United States as Loyalists. The British want us all to live on special lands they call reserves. We cannot move to find better hunting. Diseases have reduced our own numbers. It is difficult to carry on our traditional way of life.

My family came here many generations ago as Loyalists after the American Revolution. There are now over 30 000 African-Canadians in Canada West. We have small farms or we work in the towns. We are loyal to Britain.

My ancestors came here as Loyalists. They wished to continue living in British territory. After the War of 1812 American settlers were not welcome to settle in British territory. Immigration from Britain helped to keep the culture British.

My ancestors are English-speaking Irish Protestants. They came here during the Great Migration. Most of us settled in rural areas. Many became farmers, but by the 1850s good available farmland in Canada West was becoming scarce. We also worked as servants, labourers on canals and railways, in the forest industry, or at whatever jobs were available.

Canada East*

 My ancestors came here in 1663, when King Louis XIV of France established a Royal Colony in New France. We settled and prospered along the banks of the St. Lawrence River as farmers. We have been in this country longer than any other European group. We wish to carry on our French traditions and language.

A small group of British merchants moved into Montreal after the war ended in 1763. My ancestors were among this group. This is a British colony and we have continued our British traditions. It is not always comfortable living in an area where the majority of the people speak another language. We would like more British immigration.

As a result of the American Revolution, people like myself who were loyal to Britain moved northward into Quebec. Some people called us Loyalists. We transformed huge areas of land not settled by the *Canadiens* into prosperous farming communities.

 Here in Canada East, as in Canada West, powerful and conservative men control the government. The ordinary people, such as myself, have little influence in the government. It is difficult to get changes made that benefit ordinary people if powerful people oppose it.

---

*Viewpoints on this page are from imaginary people based on real situations.

Population

In Canada West

During the 1850s many immigrants settled in Canada West. Most of the Euro-Canadian population was of British descent. Settlement extended inland along the Great Lakes–St. Lawrence corridor and west from the Ottawa River to Lake Huron. The Toronto–Hamilton–London triangle was becoming the economic centre of Canada West.

Population—1 396 000 (1861 census)

Major Cities in Canada West, 1851
Toronto—over 30 000
Kingston—11 700
Hamilton—14 100
Bytown*—7800

By the 1850s, Toronto was the transportation and industrial centre of Canada West.

Hamilton, shown here in 1862, was one of the fastest-growing cities in Canada West.

In Canada East

The majority of the Euro-Canadian population in Canada East was of French descent. Most lived in the lowlands along the St. Lawrence River. The population of Canada East increased greatly during the first part of the 19th century due to a high birth rate. British and Irish immigrants settled in the Eastern Townships and in Montreal.

Population—1 112 000 (1861 census)

Major Cities in Canada East, 1851
Montreal—107 225
Quebec City—59 700

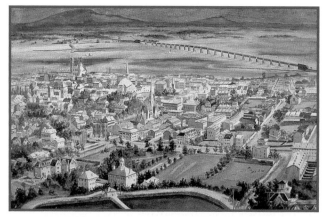

In the mid-1800s, Montreal was the dominant commercial centre for the United Province of Canada.

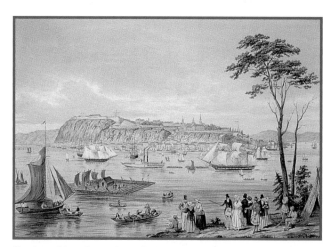

Quebec City, shown here in 1844, was divided into the Lower Town on the shore of the St. Lawrence River, and an Upper Town high on the cliffs.

*Bytown was renamed Ottawa in 1855.

Environmental Interaction

In Canada West

Primary Industry
* Farmers raised livestock and grew crops such as wheat.
* Forestry industries produced square timber and sawn lumber. A forestry by-product was potash, used for making soap and glass, sold locally and exported.

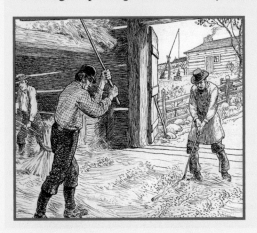

Secondary Industry
* Mills ground grain and sawed timber.
* Some examples of small industries were weaving, brewing, carpentry, saddle-making, blacksmithing, printing, baking, dressmaking, and tailoring.

Tertiary (Service) Industry
* Labourers built roads, canals, and railways.
* Some examples of services were those provided by clerks, hotel-keepers and their staffs, bankers, preachers, teachers, professionals, merchants, tradespeople, and servants for the wealthy.
* The military, including the navy, and government activities involved both skilled and unskilled workers.

In Canada East

Primary Industry
* Farmers raised livestock and grew crops on the long narrow river front farms. (Note: Wheat had to be imported from Canada West.)
* Forestry industries produced square timber and sawn lumber for local use and for export.

Secondary Industry
* Industrial development was common in the urban centres of Montreal and Quebec City.
* Local industries made timber into lumber. Wood products were manufactured: door-frames, windows, furniture, and shingles. Other factories made footwear. Woolen mills were common, as were flour mills and sugar refineries. Craftspeople produced furniture, clothing, and other products for local use. Iron and steel foundries made steam locomotives and railway rails, nails, and spikes.

Tertiary (Service) Industry
* Labourers built roads, canals, and railways.
* Some examples of services were those provided by merchants, professional people, hotel-keepers and their staffs, bankers, clergy, tradespeople, and servants for the wealthy.
* Military and government activities involved both skilled and unskilled workers.

Links and Relationships

Roads and streets were poor in both Canada West and Canada East. Often they were nothing better than wide, muddy footpaths. In the larger cities some streets were paved with cobblestones. In the countryside logs were laid side-by-side on the ground to form corduroy roads. Vehicles were horse-drawn wagons or stage coaches in summer and sleighs in winter.

Steamboats carrying passengers and cargo were a common sight on the rivers and lakes. Canals provided links between natural bodies of water. The business people in Canada West and Canada East wanted to improve canals, harbours, and roads to make it easier to transport wheat and timber to Britain. Money to pay for these improvements came from tariff revenue on goods imported into the colony.

During the 1850s, the United Province of Canada went through a railway-building boom. Railways made it possible to get farm crops and manufactured goods to market quickly and cheaply, even in winter, when rivers and lakes were frozen.

The Grand Trunk Railway was the first major railway in British North America. The people of Canada West and Canada East could travel by rail from Rivière-du-Loup in the East to Sarnia in the West. However, the railway could expand no farther because the owners were close to being bankrupt.

(Refer to the timeline on page 74 while reading the following.)

In 1846, as a result of Great Britain's introduction of free trade, Canada West and Canada East lost their special trading status with Britain. This led to the loss of many markets because the colonies had to compete with other countries. Some countries could provide timber and wheat more cheaply, because they were nearer to Great Britain. Although Canada was unable to compete in most British markets without protection, Canadian wheat exports were affected very little by free trade.

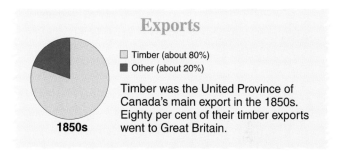

Exports

☐ Timber (about 80%)
■ Other (about 20%)

1850s

Timber was the United Province of Canada's main export in the 1850s. Eighty per cent of their timber exports went to Great Britain.

In 1854, the economic situation in Canada West and Canada East improved as a result of the Reciprocity Treaty. Natural resources from British North America, especially timber and wheat, could now be exported to the United States without tariffs. The Reciprocity Treaty improved the economic situation in British North America. However, in spite of the Reciprocity Treaty, Great Britain continued to be Canada's main trading partner.

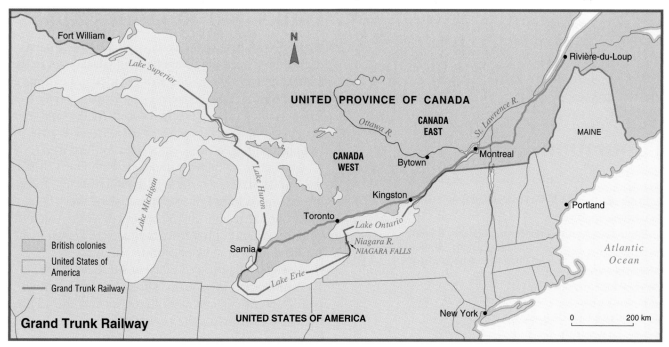

Grand Trunk Railway

British colonies
United States of America
Grand Trunk Railway

Colony of Nova Scotia

History

My ancestors, the Mi'kmaq and Maliseet people, have lived here for thousands of years. Basques and French came here to fish in the early 1500s. Merchants, traders, and colonists followed. Too many people live here now for my people to follow their traditional lifestyle.

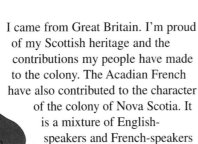

Our numbers are small compared to the British, but we have lived here for hundreds of years as farmers and fishermen. We are Roman Catholic and speak Acadian French.

I came from Great Britain. I'm proud of my Scottish heritage and the contributions my people have made to the colony. The Acadian French have also contributed to the character of the colony of Nova Scotia. It is a mixture of English-speakers and French-speakers and their traditions.

Population

Population—331 000 (1861 census)

Capital—Halifax

Populated Areas—Halifax (population 29 580), Shelbourne, Sydney, Lunenburg, Digby, Yarmouth, Antigonish, Pictou, and numerous small rural and coastal communities.

Environmental Interaction

Primary Industry

The Atlantic Ocean provided abundant fishing. Cod was the main trade product. Forestry served the shipbuilding industry. There was some farming, especially in the Annapolis Valley. Coal mining was also important.

Secondary Industry

Shipbuilding was an important industry, based on plentiful timber and good harbours.

Tertiary (Service) Industry

Merchants, bankers, professional people, government officials, artisans, and servants provided services. Workers and services involved in harbours and shipping and other tradespeople were important.

Links and Relationships

Because some Nova Scotia ports were not frozen during the winter, they were busy all year round. In the 1840s, Samuel Cunard of Halifax started a steamship line. Travelling time between Great Britain and the Atlantic colonies was greatly reduced. Mail to and from Britain could be delivered in 14 days. Horse-drawn wagons and stagecoaches were used for land travel.

Most of Nova Scotia's trade was with Great Britain, the United States, and the West Indies, although food was imported from Prince Edward Island. Very little trade was carried on with other British North American colonies. Ships built in Nova Scotia were known in all the main ports around the world.

Nova Scotia produced salted and dried cod; the West Indies produced sugar. These items were traded with Great Britain and other European countries. These exchanges formed a trade circuit known as the Golden Triangle.

By the 1860s, industrial activity was declining and people were forced to leave Nova Scotia to find work.

Colony of New Brunswick

History

My French ancestors came to Acadia as farmers in the mid-1600s. Most of them were deported by the British in 1755. My great-grandparents returned and we have been living in this area ever since.

My ancestors came to New Brunswick as Loyalists from the United States. It was just after Nova Scotia was divided and New Brunswick was created as a separate colony. Most of our friends are British, with very old ties to Great Britain.

My sailing ships carry timber from New Brunswick to Britain. On the return trip, the empty timber ships are usually filled with immigrants on their way to Canada West.

Population

Population—252 000 (1861 census)

Capital—Fredericton

Populated Areas—Saint John (population 28 805), Fredericton

Environmental Interaction

Primary Industry

Forestry and fishing were major industries in New Brunswick. Trees were cut in inland forests and the logs floated downstream to sawmills. Thousands of people were employed in the lumber industry. Inlets and bays provided shelter for hundreds of fishing vessels. Salted cod from New Brunswick was in great demand in the West Indies.

Farming was important, especially in the Saint John River valley. Dairy products, potatoes and other root vegetables, apples, and maple syrup were major products. They were produced mostly for local use or sold to feed the thousands of people working in the lumber industry or on sailing ships.

Secondary Industry

New Brunswick became one of the world's major builders of wooden sailing ships in the early 19th century. Many skilled workers, like ship's carpenters and sail-makers, worked in the industry. Craftspeople produced furniture, clothing, and other goods for local use.

Tertiary (Service) Industry

Several ports in New Brunswick were used as trading centres between Europe, the United States, and the islands of the West Indies. Services were provided by merchants, clergy, teachers, doctors, lawyers, bankers, tradespeople, government officials, and servants.

Links and Relationships

Because ports in the Bay of Fundy were not frozen during the winter months, they were busy all year. Stagecoaches were used for land travel.

Saint John, New Brunswick, prior to Confederation.

Most of New Brunswick's trade was with Great Britain, the United States, and the West Indies. There was little trade with other British North American colonies. In 1854, as a result of the Reciprocity Treaty, New Brunswick began to replace its British markets with American markets. But by the 1860s, little secondary industry had developed in the colony of New Brunswick. Many people left to seek work elsewhere.

Colony of Prince Edward Island

History

The majority of people in the colony of Prince Edward Island are from Great Britain. Scots make up a large majority, and most of us are fishermen or farmers. We remain loyal to Britain.

Population

Population—80 000 (1861 census)

Capital—Charlottetown

Populated Areas—Charlottetown (population 7000)

Environmental Interaction

Primary Industry

Farming was the main industry in Prince Edward Island. Potatoes and other root vegetables, apples, and vegetable crops grew well in the rich red soil. Livestock was also raised. Food products were produced for local use and export. Some Prince Edward Islanders made their living by fishing. The island has few natural harbours for large vessels, but many sandy coves provide shelter for small fishing craft.

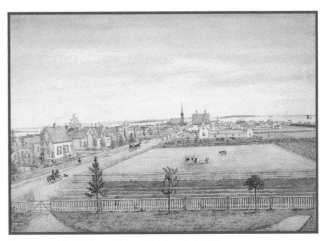

Summerside, Prince Edward Island, 1880

Secondary Industry

Some ships were built for export. Craftspeople produced necessary products for local sale, such as clothing, furniture, and candles.

Tertiary (Service) Industry

Merchants, professional people, bankers, government officials, tradespeople, and servants provided services to Prince Edward Islanders.

Links and Relationships

Railway bridges linking the island and the mainland were impossible to build at that time, and the island was small. The people had relatively little interest in building a railway. During the winter months, Prince Edward Island was isolated from the mainland. Horse-drawn wagons and stagecoaches were used on the island.

Surplus food was exported by ship to Nova Scotia, New Brunswick, Newfoundland, Great Britain, or the American New England states. By the early 1860s the colony of Prince Edward Island was prosperous. However, 60% of the farmers were tenants who paid rent to landlords who lived in Great Britain. Because they could not buy the land they had cleared and farmed, some farmers left the colony of Prince Edward Island.

Like other colonists in British North America, Prince Edward Islanders were confident that the British navy would protect them from any attempted attack by the United States.

Charlottetown, Prince Edward Island, 1843

Colony of Newfoundland

History

My ancestors from England have been fishing the Grand Banks since John Cabot claimed Newfoundland for England in 1497. Many Irish also moved here to live. Most of us make our living from the sea as fishermen.

St. John's, Newfoundland, 1831

Population

Population—125 000 (1861 census)

Capital—St. John's

Populated Areas—St. John's (population 20 941 in 1845)

Environmental Interaction

Primary Industry

Nearly all of the people in Newfoundland lived along the coast, either in the city of St. John's or in tiny outports. Fishing was by far the largest industry. Codfish caught on the Grand Banks were dried or salted, then sold in Great Britain or the West Indies. There was also a seal hunt every spring. Whales were caught during summer off the coast of Labrador and their oil extracted.

Secondary Industry

Secondary industry in Newfoundland consisted mostly of industries that supported fishing, such as shipbuilding, net making, and sail making. Craftspeople produced products for local use, such as clothing and furniture.

Tertiary (Service) Industry

The service industry in Newfoundland consisted mostly of merchant suppliers. They served the needs of the fishermen and their families. Merchants often served as the business link, shipping fish overseas and selling it there. Bankers, professional people (teachers, doctors, nurses), government officials, and tradespeople also provided services.

Links and Relationships

It was difficult to travel from the isolated outport communities to Newfoundland's only city, St. John's. As the picture on the left shows, most transportation was carried on from harbour to harbour by sailing ship or boat. Roads across and around the island were few.

Newfoundland had almost no trade with the other colonies in British North America. The exception was food imported from Prince Edward Island. Most links were with Great Britain and the West Indies.

Keeping Our British Customs Alive

Fictional Narrative

—by Sandra Kuelz

"Isobel."

I stopped.

"Isobel of Murray Lane
Sings when walking in the . . ."

Nobody in Saint John knew that rhyme. It had to be someone from Belfast. I scanned the fronts of the grey stone buildings.

"Michael Burns. What are you doing in New Brunswick? You said you'd never leave Ireland, never go to the colonies."

Michael was a terrible tease but he had been my neighbour. I was almost teary-eyed at the sight of him, but I could not let it show. After all, we were both fourteen that year—1856.

"Circumstances change." He looked a little sheepish. "I have a position on a trading ship that transports lumber to New York."

New York. Mrs. Foulis had travelled to New York and bought herself a beautiful tweed coat. Aunt Abigail tells me to keep envy in its place—and to remember mine. I am "the other pair of hands" in the Foulis household.

Right now I had errands to run and Michael had an impatient captain. I watched as the wind blew him down the steep street toward the harbour. His ship was to sail the next morning. That turned into a very bad day. October can dish up a nasty storm.

Aunt Abigail was watching for me when I hurried up the wooden sidewalk. Tea was to be taken in to Mrs. Foulis. "We must keep our British customs alive even if we live on the far side of a broad and fierce ocean," Mrs. Foulis would say. She always had afternoon tea in the parlour. If she was alone, she would sometimes pour tea for me from her silver pot into a real china cup.

While we sipped our tea, Mrs. Foulis might ask me to read aloud a few paragraphs from the London newspaper—that was if a London ship had brought newspapers to Saint John recently. Or, while she embroidered a tablecloth, I worked my lace. It was on account of my reading and lacemaking skills that Aunt Abigail was able to persuade Mrs. Foulis to place me in her employ. Otherwise I would have been placed with the other poor Irish orphans to work in the fever hospital on Partridge Island.

Partridge Island juts out of the Bay of Fundy at the edge of Saint John harbour. It is the quarantine station where the sick are landed from immigrant ships. Mrs. Foulis said that eight years ago the fever sheds were overflowing and patients were put into tents. Many poor Irish perished there. She told of their friend Dr. Collins, who cared for them until he caught typhus and died.

Today there would be no time for making lace. Mr. Foulis had invited some of the finest of Saint John for dinner. I had vegetables to prepare.

Later, when the last pot was washed and I climbed the stairs to go to bed, I was dog tired. My room was under the eaves and not so well finished as the rest of the house. I shivered as I looked out the window. I could see some of the shipbuilding yards, a little slice of harbour, and the masts of a few ships riding anchor. The moon was full but the wind was picking up and there was a bank of clouds on the horizon. I didn't know it, but that was a prelude to disaster.

When I served breakfast to Mr. and Mrs. Foulis, Mr. Foulis was more irritated than I had ever seen him. Mrs. Foulis was the audience but she wasn't the cause.

"My dear," he said. "I tried to tell them at dinner that the world is changing. Saint John is a great shipbuilding city. Our *Marco Polo* is the fastest sailing ship in the world. But we build wooden ships that are powered by wind. The new ships will be steel and powered by steam. Our city is enjoying good times, thanks to trade with the United States, so no one is in the mood to listen to my stories of changes to come."

When Mr. Foulis left for work, the wind blew rain right into the front hall. That had never happened before. I got a bucket and some rags to clean it up.

"Isobel." Aunt Abigail was speaking. I was looking out the pantry window. "I sent you for the soup pot. Have you forgotten?"

"I can hardly see the neighbours' house. Do you think any ship would sail on a day like this?"

"There are good captains and bad," was the reply. "Money motivates some, the safety of their seamen motivates others."

Michael's captain would receive a bonus if the ship reached New York early. As it was, it never made it at all.

Mr. Foulis burst into the house before lunch and called to Mrs. Foulis, "A ship bound for New York is aground on Partridge Island. It is being pounded by heavy seas."

"Aunt Abigail, I know someone on that ship." I had not told of meeting Michael because a servant girl employed in a good home should not be seen with a sailor if she wants to keep her position. "He was our neighbour from Belfast."

Mr. Foulis was going to the wharf as soon as he had his soup. When he heard my story, he said

I should go with him. Aunt Abigail would do my afternoon chores. Mr. Foulis was very kind. Hired help are not supposed to have feelings or, at the very least, not to let them show.

I wrapped a shawl around my shoulders. Mrs. Foulis gave me another. My teeth still chattered as I hurried behind Mr. Foulis along King Street, past the shops to where a crowd was gathering. The wind had dropped and the first rescue boat was pulling for shore. There were more bodies aboard than men. Michael wasn't among them. The drowned sailors were laid out and covered with tarps.

Mr. Foulis was muttering about the need to warn ships when visibility was poor. "A lighthouse works when the weather is clear, but what about foggy times like this? We need some kind of horn."

I had to wipe tears from my eyes as I returned home. "Aunt Abigail, they didn't find him." I was given tea and allowed to go to my room.

I woke to a knock at my door. It was dark. I guessed I was needed to serve dinner.

"Isobel. Isobel, I have news for you." I was on my feet.

"They have found Michael Burns. He was holding a man on a rock ledge. Mr. Foulis has seen Michael. He was very cold but he is getting good care."

I am seventeen now. I have just finished the dishes after a big dinner. Mr. and Mrs. Foulis were celebrating the installation of the first fog horn. It is on Partridge Island and is powered by steam. Mr. Foulis is very pleased with his invention and hopes that steam-powered foghorns will soon be in use around the world. He was right about steamships. We are seeing more and more in the harbour.

Other changes are coming too. Mr. Tilley, the druggist on King Street, is a member of the New Brunswick legislature. He dines here on occasion. He is talking about the colonies of British North America and their need to unite. Mr. Tilley would like to see a railway link to Saint John. A lot of people are ready for that. We shall see what the future brings.

Michael Burns and I have plans for next year, but I'll tell you about that another day.

Review

The icons are your cue to refer to the Learning How to Learn Appendix (pages 348–371) for ideas on how to complete these activities.

 This icon is a reminder to turn to the Research Model (pages x–xi).

1. Complete a self-assessment for one assignment from this chapter.

Understanding Concepts

2. At the beginning of this chapter (see page 73, Chapter Preview/Prediction), you made some predictions on what you thought would be the regional interests of each of the central and Atlantic colonies. Discuss these predictions with a partner. Were your predictions correct?

3. Use one of the methods for recording vocabulary to add words from this chapter to the WordBook section of your notebook.

4. Here are some of the main ideas from the chapter:
   • British colonial policy
   • mercantilism
   • free trade with Great Britain
   • Reciprocity Treaty with the United States
   • primary, secondary, and tertiary industries
   Do either a) or b)
   a) Create a concept poster about one of these ideas. Present your poster to the class.
   b) Use a web, mind map, outline, or chart to create a permanent set of notes about one of the above ideas. Use colour and drawings wherever possible. Explain your work to a classmate.

5. Organize your notes. Compare your notebook to that of a partner. Check to see that items are not missing and are in the correct order.

6. Add any dates from this chapter you feel are important to the timeline you started earlier.

Developing Research Skills

7.

Section I Activity

Part Three
If you haven't done so already, complete the Central and Atlantic Canada Retrieval Chart you started on page 73.

Developing Communication Skills

Select from the following:

8. Form into groups of five—one from each of the colonies studied in this chapter. Share information on your colony with the other people in your group (e.g., history, environmental interaction, regional interests).

9. Sketch a map of the colony you selected. Indicate visually as much information as you can about the colony; for example, population centres, land use, resources, trade links, transportation. Be sure to include a legend with your map.

10. Imagine you are a British reporter visiting the central and Atlantic colonies of British North America. Your readers want to know about the regional interests of the people living there.
    a) Write five journal entries of your experiences and observations when visiting one of the colonies. Use your journal entries to write the article for your newspaper.

Applying Concepts

11. Research to find out about the British Commonwealth of Nations. What is its relationship to the British Empire? (See page 75.) On a world map show which modern-day countries belong to the Commonwealth.

Section I Review

For Your Notebook

On pages 26 and 27 you were introduced to the Section I Focus. The activities on this page will help you review what you learned about change, regionalism, and power.

The Section I Activity Focused On

Change   Regionalism   Power

You may want to review these concepts on pages 24, 25, 28, and 29 while doing this review. Your retrieval charts from each chapter should also be especially useful.

Questions for Class Discussion

1. Based on what you learned in Chapters 1, 2, and 3 discuss each of the questions on the easel on page 27.

For Your Notebook

Do numbers 1 to 3.

1. a) Review pages 24 and 25 on change.

   b) Use your History notes as a reference. Do a think-pair-share to identify examples of changes brought about by at least six of the agents of change from Section I (Chapters 2, 3, and 4).

   c) Create a wall poster to illustrate what you learned.

2. a) Select from among the following regional interest groups of British North America.
   * colony of British Columbia
   * the Red River Settlement
   * one of the First Nations studied in Chapters 1 and 2
   * the United Province of Canada
   * the colony of New Brunswick
   * the colony of Nova Scotia
   * the colony of Prince Edward Island
   * the colony of Newfoundland

   b)   In groups create a concept poster based on the regional interests of the group you selected in a). Share your understanding of regionalism with the rest of the class. (Concept posters are explained on page 350.)

3. Who held the most power and influence in making political decisions in the colonies of British North America?

For several weeks, Ms Pozzi's class had been researching the history of Canada before Confederation. Using their ideas from the earlier class about making connections with history, some students had visited the local museum and library. Others used the internet. Darin found a speech by Joseph Howe of Nova Scotia and delivered it in fine style wearing a frock coat and top hat. Several students invited a First Nations Elder to talk to the class. Three other students had created a video, dramatizing the struggles of three prospectors panning for gold in the interior of British Columbia. Another group had designed the front page of a newspaper depicting Metis identity in Red River. Antonio's collage of "Who's Who in Canada's History?" with his archival photos of George-Étienne Cartier, John A. Macdonald, and other leaders had been reproduced in the *Lethburn Gazette.*

Ms Pozzi was so pleased with her students' work that she submitted some of their research projects to the selection committee of the Canadian Youth Educational Project. The committee was planning a youth conference, "Youth Shaping Canada's Future." They were accepting teacher nominations of Grade 8 students from across the country. A train that started in British Columbia would pick up the successful student delegates along its way. The conference was to be held in Charlottetown, so the train was called the Confederation Train. At the conference, students would be challenged to discuss issues they felt would be important to Canada in the twenty-first Century. This

Section II
Confederation
1860–1867

project was to be partially funded by the Canadian government. Ms Pozzi mentioned the conference to her class but warned the students not to get their hopes too high. In fact, she nearly forgot about it herself. Then one day she was called to the principal's office for a phone call. Three of her students had been selected.

"I have great news," Ms Pozzi announced. "Several of our students have been chosen to go to Charlottetown, and I will be going too as one of the chaperones. Antonio, Jasmine, and Haley —congratulations!" For a few minutes there was excited chaos in the classroom. Once everyone had calmed down, Ms Pozzi went on to explain that the students would need to raise some funds to cover the remaining costs not covered by the government.

Darin could not hide his disappointment. He raised his hand. "No offence, Ms Pozzi, but what about the rest of us? I thought I had a pretty good project. How come we have to raise funds when we're not even going?"

Ms Pozzi smiled. "Good point, Darin. I do understand. It

doesn't seem fair. However, this is like an election. Many excellent candidates do not get elected, because only a certain number can be chosen. Those who are chosen represent the interests and concerns of the rest. This is very important in a democracy! However, for each student chosen, we will also receive one computer for our history classroom. Think of what we can do with three new computers! They will allow us to make even more connections."

"All right!" said Tara. "So how can we raise all that money?"

"Now slow down, Tara," laughed Ms Pozzi. "Let's do some planning here. What we need is a committee to organize our fundraising. Let's see . . ."

Ms Pozzi divided the class into six groups so that everyone would be involved. The class would have six different plans to raise funds. The next week, the groups were ready to present their fundraising plans to the class.

Haley, Darin, Lee, Jasmine, and Ben were in one group. Haley's group had elected her as leader. Things were *not* going well.

"Okay," said Haley, "we have to decide. Jasmine wants a huge bake sale. Lee wants a garage sale. Darin thinks we should hold a talent show. So, Ben, do *you* have any ideas?" Haley said. "You weren't even at the meeting we had at my house on Saturday night. What happened anyway?"

"I had to help my dad at the shop," Ben explained.

The students hadn't noticed Ms Pozzi until she pulled up a chair. "You guys sound like the government in the United Province of Canada in 1859. Noisy and frustrated! What you need is consensus."

"Consensus? What's that?" chorused the five voices.

"That's complete agreement." Ms Pozzi repled. "Or, at least try to give in a little to one another—that's compromise!"

"But three people only want their ideas!" protested Haley.

"Don't expect instant success, Haley. Sometimes people need more time," answered their teacher. "Try to work on agreeing. I heard 'garage sale,' 'bake sale,' and 'talent show.' You might think of combining those ideas. A bake sale and a garage sale could be combined into one big sale. That way you might make more money! At least think about it. Now I must go help the other groups."

Everybody sat silent for a few minutes. At last Ben spoke. "My mom owns a small warehouse. She is going to rent it for storage space, but if we ask I think we could use it for our sale first. We could put tables for baking at the front. Other families in the class could drop off their stuff for the garage sale the week before."

"Do we all agree that this would work?" Haley asked.

Everybody was in favour of asking Ben's mother.

By the time Ms Pozzi ended the meetings, the group had made some plans. Ben would let them know tonight what his mother said. Jasmine and Haley said their parents would help to get baking from all the families. Darin said that he would recycle his cans and bottles to get change for the cash box. Lee promised to print flyers requesting donations of used goods they could sell. Maybe their group, which they named the Famous Five, would have a good project after all!

"Good," said Ms Pozzi. "Now all of the groups are ready. Remember now—we are united by our common goal. Together we can succeed. Good luck, everyone!"

Section II Focus

The two chapters in Section II will focus on co-operation. In each chapter you will be expected to find information to answer the question on the easel that follows.

How Did We Become a Country?

1. How did the people work together to achieve a common goal?

 Make a title page for Section II: Confederation

Questions for Class Discussion

1. When Haley's group ran into conflict, how did they solve their disagreements?
2. What was the class's common goal? How could Haley's group be more successful by working together?

Section II Activity

 Throughout your study of Section II, you will be working on an ongoing activity that will focus on co-operation.

1. Use a cardboard box or make a cardboard cube to display what you've learned about Confederation. Consider each side of the box/cube as a mini-bulletin board; add pictures you have made or use clip-art. Make your cube attractive and interesting with colours, titles, and images.

Confederation Cube

Side 1. Reasons for Confederation
Side 2. Key Personalities
Side 3. Key Events
Side 4. Names and Dates of Canada's Provinces
Side 5. Map of Canada in 1867

The Memory Box

"What's in the box, Ms Pozzi? It looks really old," Amir asked, as Ms Pozzi walked into the class. Ms Pozzi made her way between the students and placed the box on her desk. Amir was right behind her. Before she could answer him the rest of the class had gathered around them.

Ms Pozzi had a look of pride on her face as she unlocked the old box. "It's my Grandma Pozzi's memory box. It's full of a lifetime of memories and treasures. It's her story."

The students were curious as Ms Pozzi took out a bundle of old letters tied with a ribbon. They watched as she unfolded a large official document. It was brightly coloured and gave the name, date, and birthplace of Ms Pozzi's grandmother in Naples, Italy. There were dozens of old photographs, a steamship ticket from Naples to Montreal, a CPR ticket to Toronto, and a yellowed and very frayed newspaper clipping.

They leaned closer as Ms Pozzi took a very old locket from the box, a pressed red rose, and what could have been a decoration from the top of a wedding cake.

They all wanted to see more but Ms Pozzi asked everyone to sit down so she could tell them about the major research project she wanted them to work on in history this year.

"I want each of you to make a memory box," she said. She turned on her computer. Four men's faces looked down at the students from the classroom monitor.

"Hey, I've seen those guys before." Haley quickly opened her history textbook to page 24. "They're prime ministers! Macdonald, Mackenzie, Laurier, and Borden."

"Correct," laughed Ms Pozzi. "And each of you is going to create a memory box of one of their lifetimes."

A Prime Minister's Memory Box

The research model shown on pages x and xi may be used to guide you through the steps for completing this project.

Steps for Planning

1. **As a class, brainstorm for ideas of what to include in your prime minister's memory box.** Since you can't get the actual items to put into the memory box, you'll have to create them. This project will include two parts:
   - researching the historical facts
   - using the information you researched and turning it into a product (such as a birth certificate, letter, newspaper clipping)

Your final products—the items in the memory box—will be a combination of fact and fiction. The fiction should be based on historical facts. (In other words, you can't have Prime Minister Macdonald drive a sports car on the 401 or e-mail his wife while he's on a business trip.) You will have to make the items in the memory box as authentic as possible.

Some items you could include:
- journal
- personal letters
- business letters
- poem
- inspirational verses
- job application
- newspaper articles
- photo album
- recipes
- samples of art work
- scrapbook
- birth certificate
- speeches
- diary

2.   **Decide on criteria for assessing the products that go into the memory box.**

The final assessment will include the memory box and the items inside. Items should include the person's personal life and their political life.

As a class, brainstorm some ideas for assessment of this project. Each of you will be responsible for working with your teacher and creating your own assessment criteria for this project. Ideas for self-assessment are found in the Appendix on page 368.

3. You may wish to complete an Action Plan once you have an understanding of what you are expected to do.

Action Plan

1. Date project due: ....

2. Describe what you want to include in the memory box. (This may change.)

3. Plan on paper what tasks have to be done. Assign a completion date for each task.

Task	Completion Date	Done
1. _____	_____	_____

(add to this list as needed)

Researching the Project

It is very important that you read all of pages 90 and 91 before starting the project.

Gathering Information

1. Understanding what you are to do
(See steps on page x.)

2. Planning the project
(See steps on page x.)

3. Locating the information
(See steps on page xi.)

It is too early to create the items that go into the memory box. At this stage you are gathering information on the prime minister you have selected. Start with this textbook and read about the person you are researching. Then, refer to the list on page xi for ideas on where else to look for information.

4. Recording the information

In this part of your research you should be recording information related to your project. For ideas, see page xi and the following websites.

- Sir John A. Macdonald,
  http://cnet.unb.ca/achn/pme/jamcb.htm

- Alexander Mackenzie,
  http://cnet.unb.ca/achn/pme/amcb.htm
- Sir Wilfrid Laurier,
  http://cnet.unb.ca/achn/pme/wlcb.htm
- Sir Robert Borden,
  http://cnet.unb.ca/achn/pme/rlbcb.htm

Examining and Organizing Information

5. Examining the information

6. Organizing the information
Examining the information and organizing the information are often done at the same time.

- Go through the information you have collected. Separate it into two groups: personal information and information relating to their political career.
- Decide if you need to do more research.
- Check your assessment criteria.

Communicating the Information

You will be communicating the information through the memory box.

7. Preparing the presentation
In this step you will take your research information and change it into items that will go into the memory box. Be creative! Try to make the items look as authentic as possible. Check the assessment criteria established earlier.

8. Sharing the presentation
Your teacher will explain how your memory box will be shared with the other students in the class.

9. Assessing what you've done
Try to make the prime minister come alive through your memory box. You will be helping each other make connections with history.

Chapter 4

Reasons for Confederation

1860–1866

O v e r v i e w

Use this Overview to predict what you will read in this chapter.

2 1857–1864

Political deadlock occurred frequently in the Legislative Assembly in the United Province of Canada, making it difficult to pass important laws.

Legislative Assembly

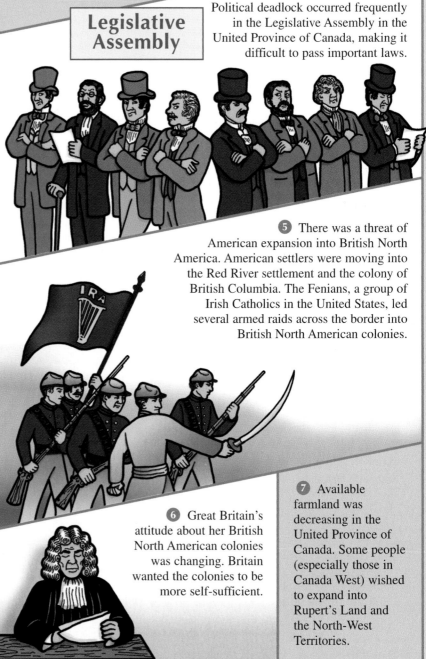

1 The colonies in British North America began to think about joining together to form a new country. This process was called Confederation.

5 There was a threat of American expansion into British North America. American settlers were moving into the Red River settlement and the colony of British Columbia. The Fenians, a group of Irish Catholics in the United States, led several armed raids across the border into British North American colonies.

3 An intercolonial railway was needed to increase trade and improve transportation and communication. If the colonies joined together they could share in the costs.

6 Great Britain's attitude about her British North American colonies was changing. Britain wanted the colonies to be more self-sufficient.

7 Available farmland was decreasing in the United Province of Canada. Some people (especially those in Canada West) wished to expand into Rupert's Land and the North-West Territories.

4 Trade with the USA was no longer protected under the advantages of the Reciprocity Treaty. If the colonies joined together and traded among themselves, economic prosperity might continue.

Chapter 4 Focus

In Section I of this textbook you examined changes that were occurring in the regions of British North America. This chapter introduces Section II, Confederation. In Section II you will read how the changes discussed in Section I led to plans for union among the British North American colonies. You will examine the leadership role that key individuals played in building the Dominion of Canada. A variety of internal and external pressures encouraged the people of the British North American colonies to consider co-operation within a larger political union. All five concepts are the focus of this chapter, with co-operation being the most important.

| Change | Regionalism | Power | Identity | Co-operation |

Other Concepts and Main Topics

- compromise
- Reciprocity Treaty
- federal union (Confederation)
- free trade
- tariffs
- Maritime union
- "Rep by Pop"
- intercolonial railway

Learning How to Learn

  Chronology

 Decision-making

 Critical Thinking

Role-playing

Section II Activity

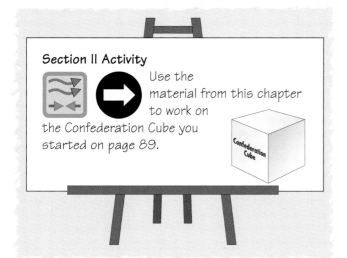

Use the material from this chapter to work on the Confederation Cube you started on page 89.

Chapter Preview/Prediction

1. Examine the overview found on the previous page, the visuals, and the titles in this chapter.
   a) Based on these, discuss with a partner what you think this chapter is about.
   b) Predict answers to the questions in the Prediction Chart. Put your predictions in the "My Predictions" column.*

Prediction Chart—What Do You Think?		
Questions	**My Predictions** (fill out now)	**What I Found Out** (fill out after you have read Chapter 4)
1. What is the meaning of Confederation?		
2. Why did Confederation come about?		
3. Which British North American colonies joined Confederation?		
4. How might the First Nations have felt about Confederation?		
5. How does Confederation relate to you? to our country today?		
6. What would you like to learn about Confederation?		

The Dominion of Canada, 1867

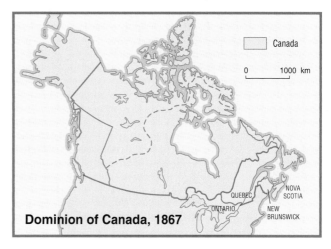

Dominion of Canada, 1867

 *Your teacher may provide you with a full-sized working copy of the Prediction Chart. This chart is available as a blackline master in *Canada Revisited 8, Teacher's Resource Package* and on the **Canada Revisited 8** web page.

Confederation

   During the early 1860s, people in the colonies of British North America did not think of themselves as one nation. The colonies were quite different geographically, and very far apart.

However, by the mid-1860s there was concern in each colony that the economic prosperity that had come from free trade with the United States was ending. People began to wonder whether uniting the British North American colonies would allow them to build transportation links and regain their prosperity. Many people felt a strong loyalty to Britain. They hoped to build a country that could resist joining the United States and would remain loyal to Britain.

For Your Notebook

1. Using one of the vocabulary strategies on page 369 define Confederation.

Exploring Further

2. Use the map on page 93 and a map of the physical features of Canada in an atlas to answer the following:
   a) What physical features (lakes, rivers, mountains, and plains) in our country made political union a challenge?
   b) How do you think Canada's size affected political union?

Confederation

In 1867, the British North American colonies of the United Province of Canada (Canada West and Canada East), New Brunswick, and Nova Scotia agreed to join together in a federal union. They joined in Confederation as four provinces: Ontario, Quebec, Nova Scotia, and New Brunswick. Each member in this union retained some power over its own affairs and turned some powers over to a more powerful central government. This central government, located in Ottawa, is Canada's federal government.

Reasons for Confederation

    During the 1850s and early 1860s, there were many changes that affected the colonies in British North America. Some of these changes were internal. Other changes occurred in Great Britain or the United States. By 1867, these changes had led to a federal union (Confederation). There were six main reasons why some politicians and citizens of the 1860s were in favour of Confederation. These reasons will be examined on the next six pages.

For Your Notebook

1. After studying pages 96 to 101, create a concept poster showing the six reasons for Confederation. Present it to the class.

❶ Political deadlock led to the Great Coalition in the United Province of Canada.

❷ A railway linking the colonies was needed to increase trade and to move troops.

❸ Cancellation of the Reciprocity Treaty by the United States in 1865 ended limited free trade between British North America and the United States.

❹ There was a threat of American expansion into British North America.

❺ Great Britain wanted her colonies to be more self-sufficient.

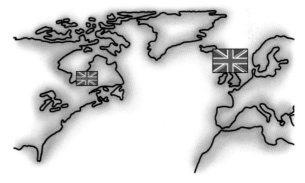

❻ Some people (especially in Canada West) wanted to expand settlement into Rupert's Land and the North-West Territories.

95

Reason

Political deadlock led to the Great Coalition in the United Province of Canada.

  In 1841, Canada West and Canada East were part of the United Province of Canada. Each region had an equal number of seats in their joint Legislative Assembly. This made it possible for one group to stop legislation that the other group wanted to pass. Disagreements in the government were common. The English-speaking majority of Canada West and the French-speaking majority of Canada East were often on opposing sides over issues.

There were four parties in the Legislative Assembly—two from Canada West and two from Canada East, as the following chart shows. To form a government with a majority, at least one party from each section had to co-operate in a **coalition**. In the 1860s, the coalition between the Liberal-Conservatives in Canada West and *le Parti bleu* in Canada East was closely balanced by the coalition of the Reform Party of Canada West and *le Parti rouge* of Canada East. The coalition government in power had a difficult time getting a strong enough majority to pass legislation. This led to political deadlock and frequent elections and changes of government. The fact that the leaders in Canada West, George Brown and John A. Macdonald, were bitter enemies made the situation worse.

Canada West	Canada East
Liberal-Conservative Party (*Tories*) (John A. Macdonald)	**le Parti bleu** (conservatives) (George-Étienne Cartier)
vs	**vs**
Reform Party (*Clear Grits*) (George Brown)	**le Parti rouge** (reform party) (Antoine-Aimé Dorion)

Canada West
Population 1861
1 393 000
Mainly English-speaking and Protestant

Canada East
Population 1861
1 112 000
Mainly French-speaking and Roman Catholic

0   250 km

United Province of Canada

Coalition—a temporary joining together of two or more political parties

The Great Coalition

 In 1864, George Brown made a courageous move. He stood up in the Legislative Assembly and announced that he was willing to work with his political enemies, John A. Macdonald and George-Étienne Cartier. This co-operation was called the Great Coalition.

Liberal-Conservative Party (*Tories*) (John A. Macdonald) + Reform Party (*Clear Grits*) (George Brown) + *le Parti bleu* (conservatives) (George-Étienne Cartier)	**vs**	*le Parti rouge* (reform party) (Antoine-Aimé Dorion)

Under the Great Coalition, three of the four parties in the Legislative Assembly of the United Province of Canada agreed to work together. The new political alliance is shown above.

The members of the Great Coalition were willing to work together because they knew that they had to break the political deadlock. The United Province of Canada needed a strong government that could stay in power long enough to pass laws and make improvements, such as building railways.

The politicians involved in the Great Coalition wanted to form a federal union. This would allow Canada West and Canada East each to have its own provincial government for its own affairs, such as language, religion, and educational matters. They would share a central government that would deal with matters that concerned both Canada West and Canada East. The seats of the central government would be divided on the basis of Representation by Population ("Rep by Pop").

The politicians of the Great Coalition government of the United Province of Canada began to wonder whether the Atlantic colonies (Nova Scotia, New Brunswick, Prince Edward Island, and Newfoundland) would join them in a federal union. (A federal union is a political union with two levels of government. The members of a federal union have certain powers over their own affairs, and certain powers are turned over to a central government.)

For Your Notebook

1. How did conflict between the French-speaking and English-speaking members of the government eventually contribute to Confederation?

Reason 2

A railway linking the colonies was needed to increase trade and to move troops.

 By 1860, each of Canada West, Canada East, Nova Scotia, and New Brunswick had its own railway. However, no railway joined the colonies. The United Province of Canada was separated from the Atlantic colonies by the mountains in Gaspé and the northern part of the state of Maine. The St. Lawrence River froze each winter, stopping water transportation between the colonies. An **intercolonial** railway would overcome these obstacles. The distance between the colonies would seem much shorter. An intercolonial railway would increase trade among the colonies and speed up mail delivery. In case of war, especially attack by the United States, a railway would move troops quickly from one colony to another.

Unfortunately, by 1860 the Grand Trunk Railway, which ran from Sarnia in Canada West to Rivière-du-Loup in Canada East, was bankrupt. The Great Western Railway, which ran from the Niagara River to Windsor, also developed financial trouble. Railway building in the British North American colonies came to a halt. However, some politicians and businessmen were beginning to dream of a new country united by a railway.

. . . Montreal is at this moment competing with New York for the trade of the great West. Build the road and Halifax will soon become one of the great emporiums of the world. All the great resources of the west will come over the immense railways of Canada to . . . your harbor. . . .

—from a speech by John A. Macdonald,
September 12, 1864

. . . Some other scheme had to be concocted for bringing aid and relief to the unfortunate Grand Trunk—and the Confederation of all the British North American Provinces naturally suggested itself to the Grand Trunk officials as the surest means of bringing with it the construction of the Intercolonial Railway. Such was the origin of the Confederation scheme. The Grand Trunk people are at the bottom of it . . .

from a speech by A.A. Dorion,
Confederation Debates,
February 16, 1865

For Your Notebook

1. What were the advantages for the colonies of British North America of an intercolonial railway? What were the disadvantages?
2. Why would the need for an intercolonial railway be a reason for federal union (Confederation)?

This is the Great Western station at London, Ontario, in 1858. The large building in the background is Tecumseh House, the largest hotel in British North America at this time. Railways enabled quicker movement of mail, goods, and people throughout the colonies.

Intercolonial—joining the various colonies

Reason 3

Cancellation of the Reciprocity Treaty by the United States in 1865 ended free trade between BNA and the US.

 From 1854 to 1865, there was free trade between the British North American colonies and the United States under the Reciprocity Treaty. This allowed agricultural products and raw materials to be sold across the border without high tariffs being paid. The colonies had stronger trade links with the United States than with each other.

In 1865, the United States ended the Reciprocity Treaty. People in the colonies of British North America began to think of joining together so they could trade among themselves with no tariffs. They hoped that this would increase their economic prosperity.

For Your Notebook

1. Use your History Notes for Chapter 3 and/or reread pages 74 and 75 before answering the following:
   a) Describe the trade situation in British North America prior to 1846.
   b) How did Britain's repeal of the Corn Laws in 1846 change trade in British North America?
   c) What effect did the 1854 Reciprocity Treaty have on trade in British North America?
2. What were the advantages of free trade and reciprocity to the colonies of British North America? What were the disadvantages?

Pemmican and buffalo hides were two products traded from the Red River Settlement to the United States.

3. Using the graph on this page, explain the changes in the economic situation in British North America as a result of the Reciprocity Treaty of 1854.
4. In 1865 the Americans decided to end the Reciprocity Treaty. How did this become a reason for federal union (Confederation) in the colonies of British North America?

Exploring Further

5. Carry out research on modern-day trade agreements between Canada and the United States. Share your findings with your class in an oral presentation or in a concept poster.

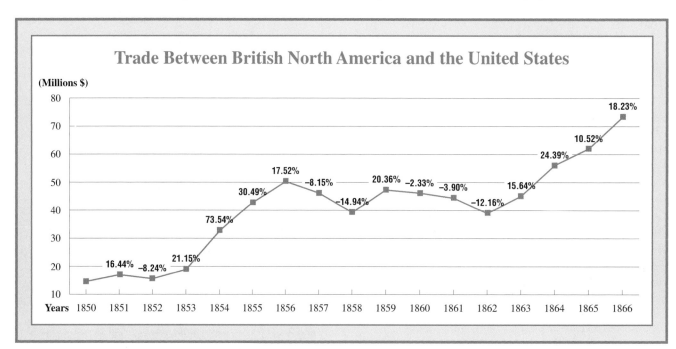

The figures on the points of the graph show the percentage the value has changed since the previous year.

Reason ④

There was a threat of American expansion into British North America.

 The British North American colonies were concerned about a possible American invasion. People thought that if the colonies united they would be better able to defend themselves.

During the 1860s the Northern and Southern states fought each other in the American Civil War. Southern raiders used Canadian territory as a base from which to attack Northern states. In 1865, at the end of the Civil War, the Northern states accused the British colonies of helping Southerners who were fleeing from Northern troops. The relationship between the British North American colonies and the United States was also uneasy because the British government had supported the South in the conflict. This made people in the British North American colonies afraid that the Americans would try to expand into their territory.

These fears seemed to become reality in 1866. Fenians from the United States made several armed raids across the border into British North American colonies. The Fenians were a group of Irish Catholics in the United States who wanted to end British rule over Ireland. Since they could not attack Britain directly, they decided to attack her North American colonies.

> . . . For myself, I have no belief that the Americans have the slightest thought of attacking us. . . . But . . . there is no better mode of warding off war when it is threatened, than to be prepared for it if it comes. The Americans are now a warlike people. They have large armies, a powerful navy, an unlimited supply of warlike munitions, . . . and unless we are willing to live at the mercy of our neighbours, we, too, must put our country in a state of efficient preparation. War or no war—the necessity of placing these provinces in a thorough state of defence can no longer be postponed.
>
> —George Brown from *Confederation Debates,*
> February 8, 1865

After the Civil War, Americans continued to move westward, following their belief in **Manifest Destiny**. They had already obtained lands formerly controlled by Spain, Mexico, France, and Great Britain. British North Americans were concerned about Americans taking over western lands in British North America.* Would Americans try to buy land in British North America from Great Britain? Would they invade British North America as they had during the American Revolution, the War of 1812, and recently during the Fenian border raids? Would so many Americans migrate into the North-West that they would be a majority and then demand that the United States annex the territory?

This painting depicts a battle between the Fenians and British soldiers that took place in 1866 at Ridgeway near Niagara. The Fenians wore green and carried a green flag with a gold harp. The British wore red.

Manifest Destiny—a policy of expansion based on the belief that all of the North American continent should belong to the USA
*See map page 100. Most of these lands were held under charter to the Hudson's Bay Company (see page 10).

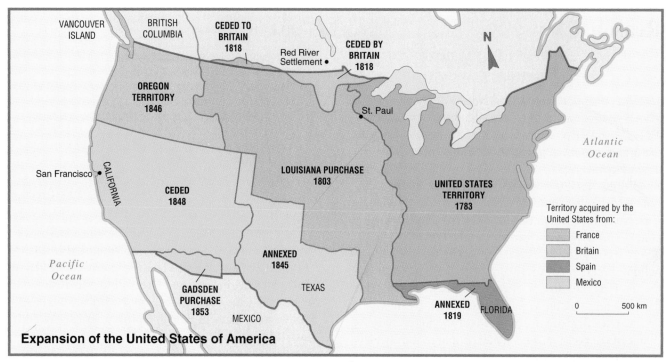

Expansion of the United States of America

Map legend: Territory acquired by the United States from:
- France
- Britain
- Spain
- Mexico

Labels on map: VANCOUVER ISLAND, BRITISH COLUMBIA, CEDED TO BRITAIN 1818, Red River Settlement, CEDED BY BRITAIN 1818, OREGON TERRITORY 1846, St. Paul, Atlantic Ocean, CALIFORNIA, San Francisco, LOUISIANA PURCHASE 1803, UNITED STATES TERRITORY 1783, CEDED 1848, Pacific Ocean, ANNEXED 1845, GADSDEN PURCHASE 1853, TEXAS, MEXICO, ANNEXED 1819, FLORIDA, N, 0 500 km

. . . They [the United States] coveted Florida, and seized it; they coveted Louisiana, and purchased it; they coveted Texas and stole it; and then they picked a quarrel with Mexico, which ended by their getting California . . . had we not the strong arm of England over us, we would not now have had a separate existence. . . .

—D'Arcy McGee from *Confederation Debates*, February 9, 1865

The Americans in the Red River Settlement wanted to join the United States. There was already a great deal of trade going on between Red River and the American community of St. Paul, Minnesota.

There was also a danger that the colony of British Columbia would be taken over by the United States. Many American miners who had come to the area during the gold rush in the late 1850s and early 1860s had settled there. There was quite a bit of trade between British Columbia and the American port of San Francisco. Many British Columbians felt they had more in common with California than with eastern British North America.

 Many people in the British North American colonies were concerned about the threat of American takeover. These people thought that if the British North American colonies united, they would be better able to defend themselves.

In 1803 Louisiana was purchased from France. In 1819 the United States expanded south to include Florida. In 1845 Texas was annexed after war with Mexico. In 1848 California was acquired by the United States after gold was discovered there.

For Your Notebook

1. Why were Americans interested in expansion northward?
2. What evidence was there that Americans might expand into British North America?
3. What areas of British North America seemed most vulnerable to American expansion?
4. In what ways was the threat of American expansion into British North America a reason for federal union (Confederation)?

Exploring Further

5. a) Review what the term Manifest Destiny means, and when it was used.

   b) Do you think the people in the colonies of British North America had reason to fear the Americans' belief in Manifest Destiny?

   c) If a policy of Manifest Destiny had been carried out by the United States through expanding northward, how do you think Canadian history would have been different? Sketch a map of how you think North America would look today.

Reason 5

Great Britain wanted her colonies to be more self-sufficient.

 In the mid-1860s, Great Britain's attitude toward her colonies in North America began to change. Opinion was divided as to whether the colonies were a benefit to Great Britain.

Some British politicians wanted to keep the colonies. Since the repeal of the Corn Laws in 1846, the policies of mercantilism were no longer in effect. However, some people in Great Britain still thought of the colonies as a source of raw materials and a market for manufactured goods. These people thought the colonies could still provide huge profits.

Another argument in favour of Great Britain keeping the colonies was to provide opportunity for British people to **emigrate**. If they moved to a British colony they could remain British citizens. In the event of war, the colonies could provide Britain with soldiers and military bases.

Some British politicians felt that the world-wide colonies were a burden on British taxpayers. These politicians wanted the colonies to become independent so they could pay for their own government and defence.

A federal union of the British North American colonies was seen as the best way for them to become more self-sufficient. By co-operating in a federal union (Confederation), they would be able to share the costs of government, railway building, and defence.

Great Britain's decision to encourage union was very important because many British North Americans were still intensely loyal to Britain. They were also aware they needed Britain's support. If Great Britain wanted Confederation, these loyal people would view Confederation more favourably. The British governors in the colonies in British North America were told to encourage Confederation.

For Your Notebook

1. Why did Great Britain have colonies in North America?
2. What change occurred in Great Britain's attitude toward its colonies in the mid-1860s?
3. Explain why some British politicians thought it would be good for Great Britain to keep the colonies.
4. Explain why other British politicians thought it would be good for Great Britain if the colonies became more self-sufficient and eventually independent.
5. How was Great Britain's new attitude a reason for Confederation?

Reason 6

Some people (especially in Canada West) wanted to expand settlement into Rupert's Land and the North-West Territories.

 The supply of good, available farmland in Canada West was dwindling. Many people in Canada West looked to the lands to the west (present-day Manitoba, Saskatchewan, and Alberta) as possible areas of settlement. But Americans were also thinking about moving into these western lands! If the colonies of British North America were to join together and annex these western lands, they could settle the land before Americans did.

For Your Notebook

1. How did the shortage of good farmland contribute to the desire for federal union (Confederation)?

Chapter Preview/Prediction

1. Reread the predictions you made on page 93 for questions 1 and 2. Fill in the "What I Found Out" column of the Prediction Chart.
2. On a large sheet of paper make a web or mind map of the reasons for Confederation.

Emigrate—to leave one country to move to another

Confederation Simulation

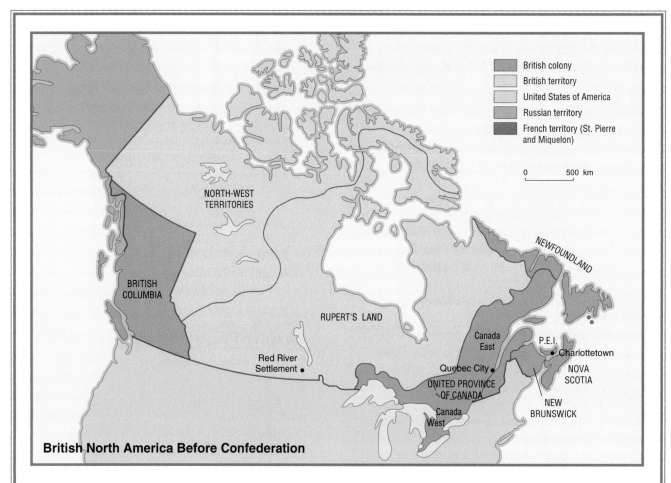

British North America Before Confederation

 August 1864—
Representatives from
the colonies of Nova
Scotia, New Brunswick, and Prince Edward Island
are planning to meet to discuss a union of the
Atlantic colonies. Representatives from the United
Province of Canada (Canada East and Canada West)
have asked to join the discussion. Since there are
representatives from four colonies at this meeting,
your class will divide into four groups: the United
Province of Canada (made up of Canada West and
Canada East), Nova Scotia, New Brunswick, and
Prince Edward Island. (Newfoundland did not attend
this conference so role descriptions are not included
for the colony of Newfoundland.) The four groups
move to different parts of the classroom.

Groups will perform a number of tasks. Later you
will meet as a large group and carry out a role-play
activity.

Establishing the Groups

- **United Province of Canada**: 17 students (Canada
  West: George Brown, John A. Macdonald, plus 7
  citizens); (Canada East: George-Étienne Cartier,
  Thomas D'Arcy McGee, Antoine-Aimé Dorion,
  plus 5 citizens)
  (Note: Because Canada West and Canada East
  are both part of the government of the colony of
  the United Province of Canada, they must work
  together to get bills passed.)
- **Nova Scotia**: 7 students (Dr. Charles Tupper,
  Joseph Howe, plus 5 citizens)
- **New Brunswick**: 5 students (Samuel Leonard
  Tilley, A.J. Smith, plus 3 citizens)
- **Prince Edward Island**: 3 students (John
  Hamilton Gray—chair of the Charlottetown
  Conference, plus 2 citizens)

Each group selects a group leader, a spokesperson, and a scribe to record information.

Role Descriptions

On pages 105 to 114, you will find role descriptions.* The first role descriptions at the beginning of each colony are the politicians for that colony. You will recognize these as real people because their pictures are photographs, not illustrations. The other role descriptions are imaginary citizens of that colony. The pictures of these imaginary people have been drawn by an artist.

As you hold your discussions, remember that some of the roles are for people who would not actually have had a chance to speak at the Charlottetown Conference. In 1864 women did not vote or hold political office. Only men who owned property could vote. In the real world of 1864, some of these people would have been able to express their opinions only to their friends and family.

Part One

Task 1—Find out what your colony was like in 1864. Post the presentation material your class prepared in Chapter 3 (page 74) on the wall to use as research material. Also use the information in Chapters 1, 2, and 3 and this chapter. Be sure your group leader directs the discussion and your scribe (recorder) keeps a record of it.

a) A description of your colony and the feelings of its people about the possibility of Confederation is provided on the following pages for you to read. To help you imagine that this is really 1864 and the Confederation debates are happening now, this section is written in the present tense. You may also want to refer to information on the colonial charts your class prepared in Chapter 3.

b) Each person in your group should choose one of the people on pages 105 to 114 from the appropriate colony. Choose either an imaginary character or an historical figure, and read the description of that person. (The group leader, spokesperson, and scribe also each choose a role to play.)

Part Two

You will be involved in a role-play activity that requires a decision on the following issue: **Should your colony join Confederation?**

*Note: This simulation is based on a class of 32 students; add or subtract roles as size of class varies.

Charlottetown Conference 1864 Chart

Colony Name Ⓐ _____

Issue: Should your colony join Confederation?

Positive Consequences Ⓒ	Factors (Reasons for Confederation) Ⓑ	Negative Consequences Ⓓ
	1.	
	2.	
	3.	
	4.	
	5.	
	6.	

Your Colony's Decision Ⓔ _____

Ⓕ Number of people in favour of Confederation _____
Number of people opposed to Confederation _____

SAMPLE

Task 1—The members of your colony (your group) have mixed feelings about the idea of political union. Some of you are in favour of union and some are against it. In character (as described in the role descriptions on pages 105 to 114), brainstorm with your group your opinions about having your colony join with the other colonies of British North America. The scribe should write the ideas from brainstorming on chart paper.

• What problems is your colony facing?
• Is it to your advantage to have your colony join with the other colonies? What will your colony gain?
• What will your colony lose?
• What type of government do you want in order to meet your colony's special needs and protect your interests?

Task 2—Use the ideas you accumulated from brainstorming to make a list on a large chart of all the factors your colony should consider when deciding whether you should join Confederation. Remember when you make up your list of factors that you must consider the wishes of everyone in your colony. (Just make up a list—do not discuss or evaluate any of the factors. Before you start, make sure everyone in your group understands what you are to do.)

Task 3—Refer to your group's list from Task 2 to prioritize up to six factors that are the most important for your colony. In your notes, make a chart like the Charlottetown Conference 1864 Chart on the previous page.* Fill in the information in Ⓐ and Ⓑ for your colony.

Task 4—As a group, review the factors your colony should consider if it is to become part of Confederation. Examine the positive and negative consequences of each factor (both short-term and long-term). Decide how these factors will affect you personally (as the character in your role description) and how they will affect the other people in your colony. Fill in the appropriate part of the Charlottetown Conference 1864 Chart with as many positive consequences Ⓒ and negative consequences Ⓓ for each factor as you can think of.

Task 5—In character, make a personal decision about the issue: Should your colony join Confederation? Consider all the factors and the consequences of each factor that your group listed on the Charlottetown Conference 1864 Chart. As a group, decide what your colony should do. Record it in the space, "Your Colony's Decision" Ⓔ . Record how many are in favour of Confederation and how many are against it Ⓕ .

Task 6—Thinking About Thinking: take some quiet time to reflect upon the procedures your colony/group went through while doing the tasks in Part Two. Record these procedures in your Learning How to Learn Journal.

Part Three

Task 1—Considering other people's points of view is an important critical thinking exercise. Think about why people saw the issue of federal union (Confederation) differently. If someone sees an issue differently than you do, does this mean that his or her way of thinking is the wrong way? Record your ideas in your Learning How to Learn Journal.

Task 2—As a group discuss why some of the people in your colony thought their way was the best way.

Task 3—Critical thinkers sometimes change their decisions because of new evidence. There is nothing wrong with this. As a group, think critically about and then discuss whether your decision really solves the issue. Do this by referring to the factors and consequences that were noted on the Charlottetown

*Masters for Charlottetown Conference 1864 Chart are located in the *Teacher's Resource Package* and on the **Canada Revisited 8** web page for Chapter 4.

Conference 1864 Chart, and by brainstorming the following questions: How does the decision you reached solve the issue? What other solutions can you think of? What are the advantages and disadvantages of the other solutions? Do you wish to change your solution?

When the groups working on the colonies of Nova Scotia, New Brunswick, and Prince Edward Island finish Parts 1 to 3, they should carry out the following tasks to prepare for the debate the class will be doing in Part 5. (The students from the United Province of Canada will probably need more time to finish Parts 1 to 3.)

Students from Nova Scotia: Plan and organize the debate (e.g., write the agenda, order of speakers, time allotted). Research how debates work. Start by checking the information on debates in the Appendix.

Students from New Brunswick and Prince Edward Island: Work together to create criteria for assessing the debate. Your teacher can help you with this. (See page 368 for ideas.)

Part Four

Task 1—Your colony's leader and other key representatives will meet with the leaders of the other colonies to debate the issue of Confederation in your next history class. If your colony decided to join the other colonies, help your leader prepare for this debate by making sure the special concerns of your colony are not lost in the proceedings. If your colony decided not to join the other colonies, help your leader prepare arguments against joining Confederation.

Part Five

Task 1—It is September 1, 1864. Your colonial leader is sitting in one of the chairs around the "Confederation table" at Charlottetown, Prince Edward Island. Debate whether your colony should join the other colonies of British North America, forming the new Dominion of Canada. Ideas for how to carry out a debate are in the Appendix on page 354.

At the conclusion of the debate, a vote should be taken in response to the issue. Record the results of the vote.

> Later in history class you will find out what actually happened at the Charlottetown Conference of 1864.

The Colony of the United Province of Canada

In June 1864, in spite of their differences, some of the politicians in the United Province of Canada have decided to join together. The politicians in this Great Coalition government want to create a federal union in the United Province of Canada. In fact, they are seeking a larger union with the other eastern British North American colonies: Nova Scotia, New Brunswick, Prince Edward Island, and Newfoundland. Members hope that eventually the colonies of Vancouver Island and British Columbia, as well as the North-West Territories and the Red River Settlement, will become part of the proposed union.

There is talk that the United States wants to end the Reciprocity Treaty. Many people in Canada West worry about the United States putting heavy tariffs on products going into the United States from the United Province of Canada. They are afraid tariffs will cause trade with the United States to decrease. The economy of the United Province of Canada will suffer. The dwindling of British markets also means it is important to develop new markets with the other British North American colonies. Farmers and business people need these new markets to prosper.

There is talk of the Americans invading British North America. There is also concern that the Americans will convince the people of the Red River Settlement, the colony of British Columbia, and the colony of Vancouver Island to join the United States.

With the huge growth in population, good farmland in Canada West is becoming scarce. Many people want the government of the United Province of Canada to buy Rupert's Land from the Hudson's Bay Company. They want these lands opened up for farming. Those favouring expansion of Canada include George Brown of the Clear Grit Party and George-Étienne Cartier of *le Parti bleu*. Opposition to the plan to purchase Rupert's Land is coming from some of the representatives of Canada East.

The people of Canada West are particularly eager to join with the other colonies of British North America. They think they will have stronger defence and better business opportunities.

Main Political Leaders

Canada West

John A. Macdonald—leader of the Liberal-Conservative (Tory) Party
George Brown—leader of the Reform (Clear Grit) Party

Canada East

George-Étienne Cartier—Leader of *le Parti bleu* (conservatives)
Antoine-Aimé Dorion—Leader of *le Parti rouge* (reformers)
Thomas D'Arcy McGee—Irish Catholic Conservative cabinet member

Canada West

George Brown

- leader of Reform (Clear Grit) Party
- wanted to acquire Rupert's Land
- in favour of Confederation—as long as Canada West and Canada East don't have to work together as one province and get "Rep by Pop"

You are the editor of the Toronto *Globe* newspaper. You believe in the British parliamentary system of government. Because Canada West now has a large population, you would like each colony's number of seats in the government to be based on "Rep by Pop."

This spring you decided to join with your political opponents, George-Étienne Cartier and John A. Macdonald, to form a Great Coalition government in the United Province of Canada. Together you are working for a federal union in British North America.

> . . . I go heartily for the union, because it will throw down the barriers of trade and give us the control of a market of four millions of people . . . . I am in favour of a union of the provinces . . . because it will make us the third maritime state of the world [after Great Britain and the United States of America]. . .
>
> —George Brown from *Confederation Debates,* February 8, 1865

John A. Macdonald

- leader of Liberal-Conservative (Tory) Party
- interested in economic development
- in favour of Confederation

You are a lawyer from Kingston, Canada West. You have been active in politics for 20 years. A strong believer in the British parliamentary system, you would like to see co-operation between French-speaking and English-speaking Canadians. You have recently decided you are willing to work with your political opponent, George Brown, in a coalition government. Together with George Brown and your traditional political ally George-Étienne Cartier, you will work for federal union.

> . . . If we wish to be a great people, if we wish to form . . . a great nationality commanding the respect of the world, able to hold our own against all opponents and to defend those institutions we prize: if we wish to have one system of government, and to establish a commercial union with restricted free trade, between people of the five provinces, belonging as they do, to the same nation . . . this can only be by a union.

—John A. Macdonald,
from *Parliamentary Debates on
the Subject of Confederation*

Role Descriptions for People from Canada West

Benjamin

- 40-year-old factory owner
- in favour of Confederation

You are a businessman whose many factories manufacture iron products such as stoves, plows, and other household products needed by farmers. You currently sell only to the people in Canada West. You would like to expand your market eastward to the Atlantic colonies. Perhaps someday you will even sell to the farmers in the Red River Settlement. You believe Confederation will help support an intercolonial railway, so you favour federal union.

Bertha

- 50-year-old wealthy widow
- in favour of Confederation

You are managing your husband's investments after his death. His vast business empire consisted of investments in the Grand Trunk Railway and numerous shipping and lumbering companies. Your investments have done well from trade with Great Britain and the United States. You are concerned that if the Reciprocity Treaty with the United States ends, you will lose your fortune. You believe that if the colonies join together and remove the tariffs between them, the resulting trade will bring prosperity.

However, as a woman you will have no voice in the decision.

Ezra

- 50-year-old colonel in the British army
- fears US invasion, but feels British army will protect Canada West
- opposes Confederation

As a member of the British military stationed at Kingston, you feel it is just a matter of time before Americans invade parts of British North America. There is currently a great deal of trade going on between the Red River area and the American trading centre of St. Paul. You are also concerned that the western colonies of Vancouver Island and British Columbia could be taken over by the United States. Your cousin has just returned from Barkerville. She has told you of large numbers of Americans currently living in the goldfields. These Americans trade at the American port of San Francisco. Soon, she feels, British Columbia could become part of the United States. But you feel the British army will be able to protect the Central and Atlantic colonies just as they have always done. A union of colonies is not necessary!

Charles

- 45-year-old carpenter
- wants to move west to become a farmer
- in favour of Confederation

You are a carpenter with four grown sons. One of your sons is married. He and his wife live with you because they cannot afford their own home. You would like to move your whole family out west. There is no good farmland available near your home in Canada West. Every day you hear of more settlers moving west because all the good farmland in Canada West has been taken up. If your entire family moved west you could all get good land at a cheaper price. You are anxious for the colonies to join together so they can purchase Rupert's Land.

Richard

- 40-year-old wealthy farmer
- wants "Rep by Pop"
- opposed to Confederation

You are a member of the Reform (Clear Grit) Party. You object to what you call the French domination of the United Province of Canada. You would like the government changed. Right now Canada East has the same number of representatives in the Legislative Assembly as Canada West. You would like to see representation by population introduced. Then Canada West would have more representatives because its population is larger. You believe this would be fairer. You know it would reduce the political power of the French. You believe that this political change would allow Canada West to make the economic changes it wants. Canals, harbours, and roads are what you want, not Confederation. You are opposed to the idea of federal union because it would be unnecessary if Canada West could control the Legislative Assembly of the United Province of Canada.

Edward

- 50-year-old businessman
- in favour of Confederation

You are a member of the Liberal-Conservative (Tory) Party. You believe the United States will take over the British colonies if something isn't done to change the government. You grew up hearing your father tell stories of Americans invading Canada West during the War of 1812. Now the American states are fighting each other in the Civil War. Britain has supported the South. This makes you afraid some of the Northern states might attack British North America.

You want federal union. Then a railway could be built between the colonies of British North America, which would speed troop movements between the colonies. If the railway were expanded to the West, it would help open up Rupert's Land for farming.

George

- 40-year-old lawyer
- supports British government policies
- in favour of Confederation

You consider yourself to be loyal to Great Britain and you support its decisions. You are aware that defending its vast Empire is very expensive for the government of Great Britain. You feel that the Liberal-Conservatives (Tories) and *le Parti bleu* should work together to promote the idea of federal union. You believe all of British North America would be stronger if the colonies were united. You are aware of the changing colonial policies of the British government. You know Britain believes the colonies should unite and pay the cost of their own defence and government. It's time for the colonies to stand together and stand on their own feet.

Canada East

George-Étienne Cartier

- leader of *le Parti bleu* (conservatives)
- in favour of Confederation

You are a *Canadien* lawyer, businessman, and poet. The survival of your French culture is very important to you. You are in favour of economic development through annexing the West and by building railways. You believe this can best be done if the colonies of British North America unite. Canada East would become a predominantly French province in this union. You believe the French *Canadiens* need to co-operate with the English Canadians for the sake of ensuring their economic way of life. You have co-operated in the Assembly with Macdonald's Liberal-Conservatives since 1854. Now you would like to see the colonies of British North America united under a British parliamentary system of government.

> When I think of the nation we would compose if all our provinces were organized under a single government, I seem to see the rise of a great British American power. The provinces of New Brunswick and Nova Scotia are like the arms of the national body able to embrace Atlantic trade. . . . And Canada will be the very trunk of this vast creation. The two Canadas, stretching far out towards the West, will bring to confederation a huge part of the western territories.

> —George-Étienne Cartier, from *Discours de Sir Georges Cartier*

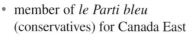

Thomas D'Arcy McGee

- member of *le Parti bleu* (conservatives) for Canada East
- in favour of Confederation
- in favour of annexation of Rupert's Land

As a young Irish Catholic man, you fought to free Ireland from British rule. Then you lived in the United States. Now you live in Montreal, where you have founded a newspaper called the *New Era*.

When you were first elected to the Assembly you were a reformer, but now you are a conservative. You have warned the Canadians of the threat of Fenian invasion. You feel an enlarged militia will be needed to help protect the colonies. You feel that there could be a great future for British North America if the colonies united.

Antoine-Aimé Dorion

- leader of *le Parti rouge* (reformers)
- opposed to Confederation

You are a member of the Legislative Assembly of the United Province of Canada and opposed to the Great Coalition. While you might be able to accept some form of federal union, you are not happy with the form that is being discussed at Charlottetown. You are afraid that the provinces will lose their powers to the central government if there is Confederation. The French will be a minority in the federal union. They might lose their rights to their language and culture.

Although you want to uphold French language and culture, you think the Roman Catholic Church should have less power in government.

Role Descriptions for People from Canada East

Jacques

- 30-year-old lawyer
- opposed to influence of Roman Catholic church on government
- Confederation not a priority

You are a professional man, a lawyer who was recently elected to the government of the United Province of Canada. You are a member of *le Parti rouge*. The working people in the cities of Montreal and Quebec City are your supporters. You believe in the right of the *Canadiens* to have the French language and culture protected. You are against the power the Roman Catholic Church exerts on the government. You do not think federal union will solve the problems you see in Canada East, so Confederation is not an important issue for you.

René

- 40-year-old businessman
- doesn't want expensive railway
- opposed to Confederation

As a small businessman you are not in favour of federal union. You buy squared timber from the hundreds of loggers cutting trees during the winter months. These squared timbers are floated down the St. Lawrence River during the spring floods. Your sawmills turn the logs into sawed lumber. You are just starting to open up markets in Portland, Maine. You transport your timber on American railways and find this arrangement to be very satisfactory. You feel federal union of the colonies would not help your business, so you are against it. You are not in favour of an all-Canadian railway route to markets in Nova Scotia. Building such a railway would be very expensive and in your mind not worth the huge costs!

Father Lucien

- priest
- opposed to Confederation

You have recently become interested in politics. As with many of the people in your parish, you are concerned with the way English-speaking merchants seem to be taking over the government. They get laws passed that put large amounts of tax money from your parishioners into the improving of canals, harbours, and roads. None of these improvements help the farmers in your parish. You are against federal union. You feel the *Canadiens* would lose their French language, their special schools, their civil laws, and their religion. They might lose this by joining the union. Although your bishop supports Confederation, you think that it would not benefit your parishioners.

Étienne

- 50-year-old lawyer
- wants Roman Catholic rights guaranteed
- supports Confederation

As a professional man, a lawyer, you speak for the French-speaking people in Canada East. You feel it is your duty to help promote French rights and preserve the *Canadien* way of life, the French language, and the Roman Catholic religion. You have joined *le Parti bleu*, a political party that believes *Canadiens* need to co-operate with English Canadians in order to ensure the survival of the French culture and maintain the power of the Roman Catholic Church. You want those rights guaranteed in writing in the constitution of a federal government.

Stephane

- 60-year-old male landowner/businessman
- wants religion and culture of *Canadiens* defended
- supports Confederation

You are powerful in the community. You agree with Cartier and favour a federal union. This will end the Union of 1841 and create a province of Quebec. In Quebec, *Canadiens* will be in the majority. *Canadien* civil laws, language, and education will be protected.

Your businesses are many and varied and involve exporting goods from Canada East to Europe and the United States. As a member of *le Parti bleu*, you use your political power to get the government to pay for improvements like harbours, canals, and roads, and to assist the Grand Trunk Railway. You would like them to build an intercolonial railway that would stretch from the Atlantic Coast to the Pacific Coast. You had hoped that the Reciprocity Treaty would go on forever. Now that there is talk of it ending you are concerned about American markets for your products.

You would support a federal union among Canada East, Canada West, Prince Edward Island, Nova Scotia, New Brunswick, and Newfoundland for the sake of better trade with the other colonies.

The Colony of Nova Scotia

The mountains in Gaspé and northern Maine and the ice that closes the St. Lawrence River each winter separate the colony of Nova Scotia from the United Province of Canada. This makes it difficult to move goods between the colonies. Travel by water is slow and in the winter the rivers freeze. Only ocean ports like Halifax stay open in winter. Railways within the colony have improved transportation. Now some people want to see Halifax linked by railway to the United Province of Canada. Such a railway would help industrial development in Nova Scotia. Goods produced there could be sold in the other colonies.

Parts of the colony are facing problems. Industrial development is slowing down. As a result, fewer immigrants are coming to the colony. Many people are leaving to seek work elsewhere.

Rumours say that the United States will end the Reciprocity Treaty. Many Nova Scotians fear the United States putting heavy tariffs on products from Nova Scotia that compete with American products. Trade to the United States will decline and the economy will suffer. People feel that new markets should be developed with the other British North American colonies. New Brunswick, Newfoundland, Prince Edward Island, and the United Province of Canada might be good markets.

If the colonies of British North America join together, the tariffs between the colonies might be removed. Then economic prosperity would return. The idea of uniting the colonies has been discussed in Nova Scotia for years.

Many Nova Scotians are concerned about American expansion. They are worried about the continuing threat of the Fenians. Large numbers of British soldiers and sailors are stationed at the fortress of Halifax. Still, Nova Scotians feel they would be better protected if the colonies co-operated.

Many of the people are proud of being part of the British Empire. They will not be interested in joining the other British North American colonies unless Great Britain wants them to do so.

Main Political Leaders

Joseph Howe—Liberal
Charles Tupper—Conservative

Joseph Howe

- former leader of the government of the colony of Nova Scotia
- opposed to Confederation

Your newspaper the *Novascotian* is the leading paper in Nova Scotia. You are known for your blunt comments about local politicians. Once you even fought a duel over remarks you made about a judge. (You deliberately did not shoot your opponent.)

You are against the British North American colonies joining together to form a federal union (Confederation). You believe Nova Scotians have closer trade ties with Great Britain and even the United States than they do with the other colonies in British North America. You are a representative of the Reform Party in the Assembly. In the 1850s, you tried to get the governments of Great Britain, New Brunswick, and the United Province of Canada to work together on an intercolonial railway. From 1860 to 1863, you were premier of Nova Scotia. By the 1860s you were opposed to Confederation. You would rather strengthen Nova Scotia's ties with Great Britain.

> Is this [Canada] the country for Nova Scotia to unite with, and to whose entire control we should turn over the management of our affairs? Here we have peace and order . . . . If border wars break out arising from raids upon a people with whom we ought to be at peace, . . . let those who provoke these controversies fight them out. . . .
>
> —from *The Speeches and Public Letters of Joseph Howe*

Dr. Charles Tupper

- medical doctor who became premier of the colony of Nova Scotia in 1864
- in favour of Confederation

You are a pro-Confederation premier in a province that is mostly opposed to Confederation. You have been serving as a Conservative member of the Nova Scotia Assembly since 1855.

You are known for your bluntness and your determination to support Confederation.

Role Descriptions for People from Nova Scotia

Josiah

- 50-year-old banker
- supports Confederation

As a banker in Halifax, you are in favour of **Maritime union**. You also favour a larger union with the United Province of Canada. If a larger union occurred you believe the eastern link of the intercolonial railway would terminate at Halifax. You believe that Nova Scotia's cultural, political, trade, naval, and military ties with Great Britain, the United States, and the British West Indies will continue if union occurs.

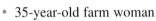

Genevieve

- 35-year-old farm woman
- opposed to Confederation

Your farming family has lived in Nova Scotia for hundreds of years. You love the land and feel pride in your Acadian heritage. You are against union with the other British colonies. You fear that you will lose your Acadian French culture and language. Besides, you feel you would have to compete for markets for your farm products should Nova Scotia unite with the other Maritime colonies.

Because you are a woman, you would not have an opportunity to influence the decision by voting should there be an election on the issue.

Samuel

- 45-year-old fisherman
- supports Confederation

You are in favour of federal union (Confederation). You make your living as a fisherman. You have six sons who are fishermen as well. In your younger years you travelled a great deal on merchant ships and have travelled to the United States. There you saw the positive changes that union of the states made

to the economy. You feel that if Nova Scotia joined with the other British colonies, Nova Scotia would continue to be wealthy.

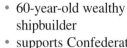

Ernest

- 60-year-old wealthy shipbuilder
- supports Confederation

You are in favour of Confederation. As owner of a large shipbuilding business you know that the day will come when wooden ships built in your colony will be replaced by metal ships powered by steam. The people who buy your ships are involved in world trade. They do not see their future as tied to British colonies. You want your colony to be strong when economic changes occur. Confederation might provide support that Great Britain is withdrawing.

Alexander

- 65-year-old wealthy businessman
- against Confederation

To your way of thinking, Nova Scotia's future is connected with the sea. It always has been and, in your opinion, always will be. Your sons are all a part of your worldwide business empire. Ships from your company sail around the world. They carry Nova Scotian cod to the West Indies and to the United States, wool from Australia to Europe, coal from England to the Far East, and European immigrants to lands around the world. You trade very little with the United Province of Canada and the other Atlantic colonies. If Nova Scotia were to join a federal union your business would not necessarily increase. In fact, you might lose business if goods are shipped by rail to Montreal. Why should Nova Scotia give up its independence to become a small part of a federal union?

Maritime union—union of the Atlantic colonies (except Newfoundland) based on their common interests as a maritime (ocean) region

The Colony of Prince Edward Island

 By the early 1860s the people of the British colony of Prince Edward Island are very concerned about the landholding system. Some hope that money will be provided through union to buy out the absentee landlords who own most of the Island. Absentee landlords take money from their tenants but they don't do anything to improve the colony. If the politicians from the other colonies are willing to help island farmers buy their farms from the absentee landlords, then support for Confederation will be strong.

Being on a small island, the people have no interest in building a railway connecting Nova Scotia to the United Province of Canada via New Brunswick. The railway won't go through Prince Edward Island.

Prince Edward Islanders do not share a border with the United States. They have no concern about the Americans as an enemy. Should war occur, the Prince Edward Islanders feel the British navy would protect them.

Prince Edward Island has recently acquired responsible government. The current political situation is not very stable. Different governments are continually coming to power. But the people believe that, because of their small population, they would have few representatives in any type of federal union (Confederation). This would give them little influence on decisions of the federal government. Prince Edward Islanders feel pride in being part of the British Empire. They see no reason for joining with the other British North American colonies, although some feel there might be benefits in a Maritime union (union of Prince Edward Island, New Brunswick, and Nova Scotia).

John Hamilton Gray

- Conservative premier of Prince Edward Island
- pro-Confederation

As premier of Prince Edward Island, you will host the Charlottetown Conference. You were born and educated in Prince Edward Island, but spent 20 years in the British army, serving in India and South Africa. You have served in the Prince Edward Island Assembly since 1858. You are strongly in favour of Confederation.

Role Descriptions for People from Prince Edward Island

Frederick

- 60-year-old wealthy landowner and businessman
- opposes Confederation

You are a well-known landowner in the colony of Prince Edward Island. You are against Maritime union and federal union (Confederation). As you look around, you see prosperity in the colony of Prince Edward Island. You would consider federal union only if money were provided to buy out absentee landlords and get the land into the hands of the families who farm it.

Henry

- member of Prince Edward Island's government
- opposed to Confederation

As a representative on the Prince Edward Island government, you are against Maritime union and definitely against union of all the colonies of British North America. The new federal government, if it were based on representation by population, would have few representatives from Prince Edward Island. The island would have little influence on federal government affairs. You and most of the people on the island feel a government centre in the United Province of Canada would be too far away. It would not be part of your world or concerns. You just want things to go on the way they are now.

Main Political Leaders

John Hamilton Gray—Conservative

The Colony of New Brunswick

 The British governor in New Brunswick has told the people they should unite with the other British North American colonies to form a federal union (Confederation). In spite of this there is not much enthusiasm in the colony of New Brunswick for the idea of federal union. Most New Brunswickers don't even want Maritime union (the union of Nova Scotia, New Brunswick, and Prince Edward Island).

The economy of New Brunswick is doing well. Most people do not think Confederation will help their economy. The United Province of Canada (Canada East and Canada West) is so far away. The people of New Brunswick have little interest in their internal politics or in the desire in Canada West for westward expansion. Many in New Brunswick feel that problems at home should be solved first. Then they can become involved in the problems of the other colonies. Because of the small population in New Brunswick, they do not want a federal union where the government would be chosen on the basis of "Rep by Pop." New Brunswickers feel they would have little say in the federal government if they were to join together with the other British North American colonies.

Samuel Tilley sits in the New Brunswick legislature as premier of the colony of New Brunswick. He is outspoken about New Brunswick joining Confederation. Tilley is in favour of both railway building and federal union (Confederation). He wants a railway to connect the Atlantic colonies with the Province of Canada. He receives some support on the subject of the railway, but his ideas of Confederation are receiving very little support. In fact, in 1865 A.J. Smith breaks with Tilley and splits the Liberal Party over the Quebec Seventy-Two Resolutions.

Main Political Leaders

Samuel Leonard Tilley—Liberal
A.J. Smith—Liberal

Sir Samuel Leonard Tilley

- Liberal premier of the colony of New Brunswick (defeated by A.J. Smith in 1865 but returned to office in 1866)
- in favour of Confederation

You have served several times as a Liberal in the New Brunswick assembly. You are known for your strong stand against alcohol; in fact, you are part of a group called "the Smashers" who have tried to have alcohol prohibited in New Brunswick.

More recently, you have become a strong supporter of the idea of an intercolonial railway.

A.J. Smith

- former leader of the government of the colony of New Brunswick (1865–1866)
- opposed to Confederation

You are a lawyer from a small fishing town in northern New Brunswick. You are considered an authority in marine law and are often consulted on legal matters concerning the ocean. You have been known to be impatient with wealthy people. You are quick-tempered, and have had at least two fights in the Legislative Assembly.

You have served several times as a Liberal in the New Brunswick Legislative Assembly. For a while in 1865–1866 you were premier. Like your former party leader, Samuel Tilley, you are a "Smasher." You might have liked some forms of federal union, but you don't trust ideas that come from politicians from the United Province of Canada. You will be opposed to the terms that are drafted at the Quebec Conference.

Role Descriptions for People from New Brunswick

William

- 40-year-old bank manager
- supports Confederation

You would prefer that the colony of New Brunswick join the other colonies in a Maritime union but you support a large federal union as well. For decades your bank has served the local sawmill owners, merchants, shipbuilders, and their families. You lent them money when they needed it and helped them prosper. You believe that union will bring continued prosperity.

Oliver

- 50-year-old wealthy businessman
- opposed to Confederation

You are against Maritime union and federal union (Confederation). Your shipping business is doing well and as you look around you, you see a lot of prosperity in the colony. You favour free trade, and you believe that tariffs (taxes) would increase the costs of imported goods if union comes about. In your opinion, it's best for New Brunswick to continue just as it is. You also worry about the small population of New Brunswick. There is talk of the proposed federal government being based on "Rep by Pop." If the colony of New Brunswick joined the other colonies, the opinions of New Brunswickers might not be heard if the government were based on representation by population.

Nell

- 50-year-old grandmother
- supports Confederation

You are an innkeeper. You have repeatedly heard talk that Americans, and especially the Irish Fenians, will invade New Brunswick. These threats of invasion are becoming more frequent and frightening. You believe that New Brunswick should join with other colonies of British North America in some type of Maritime union or union that includes the United Province of Canada. Then your colony would be better protected. Besides, you think that the British North American colonies could together afford to build a railway joining the Atlantic colonies and the Province of Canada. Such a railway would provide protection against invasion from the United States. It would also increase trade and help the economy of New Brunswick.

As a woman, you will not be able to vote on the issue. However, you have made it clear to your sons and your son-in-law that you expect them to vote for pro-Confederation politicians in the upcoming New Brunswick election.

Review

The icons are your cue to refer to the Learning How to Learn Appendix (pages 348–371) for ideas on how to complete these activities.

 This icon is a reminder to turn to the Research Model (pages x–xi).

1. Complete a self-assessment for one assignment from this chapter.

Understanding Concepts

2. Complete the "What I Found Out" column of the Prediction Chart you started on page 93 if you haven't done so already.

3. Here are some main concepts and ideas from the chapter:
   - Confederation
   - the reasons for Confederation
   - free trade, tariffs, and Reciprocity Treaty with the USA
   - Maritime union
   - intercolonial railway
   - "Rep by Pop"

   Do either a) or b).

   a) Create a concept poster for one of these ideas. Present it to the class.

   b) Use a web, mind map, or chart to create a permanent set of notes about one of these ideas. Explain your work to a classmate.

4. Add entries for this chapter to your timeline.

Developing Research Skills

5.

Section II Activity

 Work on Side I: Reasons for Confederation on the Confederation Cube you started on page 89.

Developing Communication Skills

Select from the following.

6. Imagine that you are John A. Macdonald, one of the politicians mentioned in this chapter. Write a series of diary entries in which you provide information about the following questions. You may wish to illustrate each entry with pictures and maps.
   - In what way would an intercolonial railway help the eastern colonies? the United Province of Canada?
   - In what way(s) would an intercolonial railway help bring about federal union (Confederation)?

7. You live in one of the eastern colonies in British North America. Write a letter to a friend or family member in Great Britain on either a) or b).
   a) Describe relations between British North America and the United States.
   b) What influence do you think the building of an intercolonial railway would have in protecting the West from American takeover?

8. Select any character (fictional and/or real) in this chapter, and compose five questions and answers to demonstrate his or her special contributions to Canada.

9. Select any significant incident and/or character in this chapter. Dramatically re-create the incident or something the character said or did. You will need to do research for additional facts to enhance your re-creation.

Chapter 5

Pathway to Confederation

1864–1867

O v e r v i e w

Use this Overview to predict what you will read in this chapter.

❶ 1864

Some leaders in the maritime region wanted a union of three Atlantic colonies (New Brunswick, Nova Scotia, and Prince Edward Island).

MARITIME UNION!

❷ 1864

Charlottetown Conference

In September, representatives from New Brunswick, Nova Scotia, and Prince Edward Island met to discuss Maritime union. They were joined by delegates from the United Province of Canada, who put forward the idea of union of all four colonies.

❸ 1864

Quebec Conference (October): the Seventy-Two Resolutions were adopted.

72 Resolutions

❹ 1866

The British North America Act was drafted at the London Conference.

British North America Act

❺ 1867

On July 1, the British colonies of Nova Scotia, New Brunswick, and the United Province of Canada joined together to form the Dominion of Canada.

CONFEDERATION

Quebec

Ontario

New Brunswick

Nova Scotia

Chapter 5 Focus

Chapter 4 examined some of the reasons why the colonies of British North America considered forming Confederation (a federal union). This chapter will study the stages that the colonies went through to bring about Confederation. You will take part in decision-making activities and a major project in this chapter. This chapter will focus on all five concepts.

Change   Regionalism   Power   Identity   Co-operation/Conflict

Other Concepts and Main Ideas

- colony
- nation
- Maritime union
- Confederation
- conference
- resolution
- reaction
- pro-Confederation
- anti-Confederation
- federalism

- constitution
- federal government
- provincial government
- executive branch
- legislative branch
- judiciary branch
- parliament
- House of Commons
- Senate
- prime minister

Learning How to Learn

 Research Skills

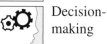 Decision-making

 Role-playing

 Critical Thinking

 Newspaper Writing

Chapter Preview/Prediction

Examine the Overview on the previous page and the chapter's titles and visuals. In pairs or small groups, use this information and what you already know to make the following predictions:
- What might the major events be?
- Who might some of the major participants (people) be?
- What might some examples of co-operation be?

---

*Chart available as blackline master in **Canada Revisited 8 Teacher's Resource Package** and on the **Canada Revisited 8** web page. See page ii for more information.
Visible minorities—people whose ancestry seems obvious from their appearance

Chapter Activity

 Read about the concept of power on page 28 before answering these questions.

1. Who held power in British North America before Confederation?
2. Make a copy of the chart below, or get one from your teacher.* As you study this chapter check (✔) the appropriate category to indicate the level of involvement in Confederation.

Who	Involved	Minimal Involvement	Not Involved
Colony of the United Province of Canada			
Colony of Nova Scotia			
Colony of New Brunswick			
Colony of Prince Edward Island			
Colony of Newfoundland			
Settlement of Red River			
Colony of Vancouver Island			
Colony of British Columbia			
Women			
Aboriginal People			
Visible Minorities			

3. What groups of people were not involved in the process leading to Confederation? Why were they excluded? Was this fair? How would these groups be included today?
4. Who held the power after Confederation?

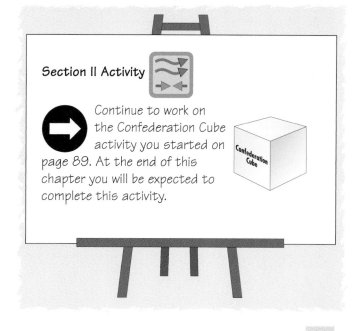

Section II Activity

Continue to work on the Confederation Cube activity you started on page 89. At the end of this chapter you will be expected to complete this activity.

Maritime Union

Charlottetown Conference

 The colonies of New Brunswick, Nova Scotia, and Prince Edward Island were considering uniting under a central government. They decided to meet in Charlottetown, Prince Edward Island, to discuss a Maritime union based on their common interests as a maritime region. Newfoundland was thought not to be interested, so delegates were not invited to attend. The United Province of Canada (Canada East and Canada West) decided to take advantage of this meeting to try to convince the Atlantic colonies to join with them in a larger union. They asked if they could join the conference. The official representative of Great Britain, Governor General Lord Monck, had to give approval for this meeting.

Eight representatives from the coalition government of the United Province of Canada attended the September 1, 1864, meeting in Charlottetown. John A. Macdonald and George-Étienne Cartier acted as leaders. All eight representatives argued in favour of broadening the idea of Maritime union into a British North American union.

The representatives from the Atlantic colonies had mixed feelings about Confederation. Representatives from Nova Scotia and New Brunswick were interested in discussing the idea, but they were divided. Some were in favour and some against. Representatives from Prince Edward Island were mostly opposed to or not interested in the idea.

The United Province of Canada promised that the government of the new union would build a railway connecting Canada and the Atlantic colonies. George Brown from Canada West promised

> . . . our farmers and manufacturers and mechanics shall carry their wares into every village of the Maritime Provinces and that they shall with equal freedom bring their fish, and their coal, and their . . . produce to our three millions of inhabitants.

By the end of the conference the decision had been made to spend more time considering a larger union— a Confederation of the British North American colonies. A second meeting would be held in a month's time in Quebec to work out terms.

The Fathers of Confederation, by Rex Woods. Delegates met in Charlottetown in 1864 to discuss the formation of a united Canada.

Conference Activities

George Brown from Canada West wrote to his wife, Anne, about some of the activities associated with the conference.

[At the close of the first day of the conference we had a fine dinner] of oysters, lobsters and champagne and other island luxuries. This killed the day and we spent the beautiful moonlight evening in walking, driving or boating, as the mood was on us. I sat on . . . [the] balcony looking out on the sea in all its glory.

Cartier and I made eloquent speeches . . . .

On the final night of the Charlottetown Conference people celebrated at a grand dance.

An Exercise in Decision-Making

1. You may carry out the following activity in the same group and role that you had in the Chapter 4 Confederation Simulation on page 102, or you may select new groups.

   a) Imagine that it is September 15, 1864. One of you is a representative from "your" colony who is reporting back from Charlottetown. Role-play the resulting conversation. Present your point of view of what happened in Charlottetown. Include whether you are in favour of or against this proposed union of the colonies of British North America (as outlined in your role description from the Chapter 4 Confederation Simulation).

2. Still in role, write a letter to a newspaper stating your opinion of the proposed federal union.

Canada Revisited

Site of the Charlottetown Conference

Province House, a National Historic Site, was the location of the Charlottetown Conference in 1864. Province House is the oldest existing British colonial parliament building in the world today.

Confederation room in Charlottetown, Prince Edward Island, where the delegates met for five days in 1864. The original tables, chairs, and gas light fixture have been restored and appear in this photo.

Quebec Conference

 Delegates met again in October 1864, this time in Quebec City. There were representatives from the United Province of Canada and all of the maritime (Atlantic) colonies. Newfoundland, which had not attended the Charlottetown Conference, attended the Quebec Conference.

The Quebec Conference lasted for over two weeks. The result was a list called the Seventy-Two **Resolutions**. The new country of Canada would be built on the basis of the Seventy-Two Resolutions. Highlights appear to the right.

The Quebec Conference was held in the temporary Parliament Building at Montmorency–Laval in Quebec.

Seventy-Two Resolutions

At the Quebec Conference, seventy-two resolutions were drawn up. Seven of the major ideas follow:

- A strong central government (federal government) would handle common affairs, notably economic development and defence.
- The central (federal) government was to **legislate** for "peace, order and good government."
- Provinces would have defined powers to handle local affairs, and social and cultural issues.
- The United Province of Canada would be split into Ontario and Quebec.
- A federal Parliament would be composed of two law-making houses. The lower house would be known as the House of Commons. The upper house would be known as the Senate.
- Members of the House of Commons would be elected according to representation by population.
- Members of the Senate would be appointed by the governor general. Quebec, Ontario, and Atlantic Canada (Nova Scotia, New Brunswick, and Prince Edward Island) would each be considered a region. Each region would have 24 members. (If Newfoundland joined, it would be given four additional seats in the Senate.)

This photograph, taken on October 27, 1864, the last day of the Quebec Conference, shows delegates from five colonies of British North America: the United Province of Canada, New Brunswick, Nova Scotia, Prince Edward Island, and Newfoundland.

Resolution—a formal statement of intention
Legislate—make laws

120

An Exercise in Decision-Making

1. In the roles used in the Confederation Simulation in Chapter 4 (page 102), or in new groups, carry out the following activity. On large paper make a chart similar to the one below.

   a) Using the information on pages 122 to 124, record how your colony reacted to the Seventy-Two Resolutions. Record the reactions on the chart under **A**. Note: It is important that the United Province of Canada be represented as two groups: Canada West and Canada East.

   b) Discuss the following two questions.
   - What economic factors influenced your colony before Confederation was proposed?
   - In what ways would Confederation help the economic situation in your colony? In what ways would Confederation either not affect your colony or harm your colony? Record your colony's information under **B** and **C**.

   c) Take a vote now in your colony. Under **D** and **E** record how many in your group were in favour and how many were against Confederation.

   d) What alternatives will be open to your colony if Confederation fails to pass in the Legislature? Add your answer to **F**.

Do one of the following.

2. Have someone from your colony give a speech to the class on your colony's reaction to the Seventy-Two Resolutions. A second person may want to give a speech from a contradictory point of view. Be prepared to defend your arguments.

3. As a group, create a colonial newspaper (dated 1865 or 1866). Prepare fictitious newspaper articles or write letters to the editor expressing your point of view on the Seventy-Two Resolutions and/or the idea of Confederation.

4. In role, react to the Seventy-Two Resolutions. Express this reaction through one of the types of writing on pages 370 and 371. For example:
   - storytelling—diary or journal, friendly letter, hard news story, historical story
   - persuading—editorial, letter to the editor, speech
   - reporting—news report, magazine/newspaper feature article, interview

---

Should Your Colony Accept the Seventy-Two Resolutions?

Colony of _____

A Reactions to Seventy-Two Resolutions

B Your colony's economic factors

C Confederation and the economy

D Number in favour of Confederation _____

F If Confederation fails to pass in the Legislature, our options are

E Number against Confederation _____

Reaction to the Seventy-Two Resolutions

Before the Seventy-Two Resolutions could be approved in Great Britain they had to be approved by the colonial governments. The job of the delegates who attended the Quebec Conference was to go home and debate the ideas put forward in the Seventy-Two Resolutions.

In the colonies, approval did not come easily.* There were many powerful people who were against the ideas that had been put forward. It took almost three years before three colonies agreed in 1867 to unite as the Dominion of Canada. The United Province of Canada, Nova Scotia, and New Brunswick formed a union. Prince Edward Island and Newfoundland decided not to join at that time.

The Confederation Debates included intense discussions of serious disagreements.

In the United Province of Canada

In the United Province of Canada the debate in the Legislature continued for six weeks. In the end the Great Coalition had an overwhelming majority in favour of Confederation. The vote in the Legislative Assembly was 91 to 33. A slim majority of the legislators from Canada East approved Confederation. Those against Confederation were concerned that their French language and culture would not survive in a country with more English-speaking people than French.

*Except in Canada West. The people there had a lot to gain from Confederation, so most were in favour of it.

Here follows an imaginary conversation that might have taken place among some of the members of the Legislative Assembly after the vote:

I voted for Confederation because if we are united we will be able to defend ourselves better against the Americans. Britain does not want to keep paying to defend us, so we must help ourselves. Besides, Britain seems to be in favour of a union of the colonies here.

That is perfectly true, my friend. However, more importantly, trade will improve within the British North American colonies. We will send our manufactured goods and our farm products to the Atlantic colonies. We will receive their goods in return.

As a *Canadien* and a representative of my people, I am interested in protecting the *Canadien* way of life. I think that a separate provincial government for Canada East will do that. I will vote for Confederation.

I am also a *Canadien*, but I do not share your feelings. I think if we join Confederation our way of life will be threatened. The central government will be too strong and will be run by English-speaking people. We *Canadiens* will have to stand up for ourselves at every turn in the future.

I am opposed to Confederation, even though I am not a *Canadien*. What good are the Atlantic colonies to the United Province of Canada? We don't need to unite with them in order to trade with them.

You nay-sayers are forgetting that Confederation might allow us to build a transcontinental railway. Then we will be able to unite with the colonies and territories to the west. We will become a nation from sea to sea. Look at all the good farmland we'll be able to acquire for the younger generations.

Reaction in the Atlantic Colonies

There was strong opposition in the Atlantic colonies to the Seventy-Two Resolutions. Some people opposed federal union on any terms. They thought that their colonies were doing fine on their own. They could see no reason to join the United Province of Canada and take on its problems. People in the fishing, lumbering, and shipbuilding industries felt that they had little in common with farmers of the United Province of Canada.

All in the Family. This 1865 cartoon from *Le Perroquet* shows Canada West and Canada East arranging to marry Nova Scotia and New Brunswick. They plan to adopt little Prince Edward Island. The USA is not invited to the wedding.

To briefly summarize what happened in the Atlantic colonies: New Brunswick and Nova Scotia reluctantly reversed their initial opposition to Confederation. Prince Edward Island and Newfoundland rejected the idea of Confederation. More details about the debates in each of the Atlantic colonies follow.

In New Brunswick

In 1865 Premier Tilley's New Brunswick government was in favour of Confederation. However, in the 1865 election, Tilley's opponents stressed that New Brunswick would lose control over its own affairs in Confederation. The people believed the opposition. Tilley's pro-Confederation party lost the election.

In 1866 the lieutenant-governor, appointed by Great Britain, was instructed to promote Confederation in New Brunswick. He pressured the anti-Confederation government into resigning. Then he appointed a pro-Confederation government and called another election.

Tilley was re-elected and the new assembly voted for Confederation. This seems like a surprising turnaround, but circumstances had changed in the time between the two elections.

- Fenian raids across the border had reawakened the fear of an American invasion. People felt that New Brunswick could better afford the cost of defence if it was shared with Great Britain and the other colonies.
- Great Britain announced that it supported the idea of union. People who were worried about breaking ties with Great Britain were reassured that some links would remain.
- In 1865 the United States announced that free trade through Reciprocity would not be continued. This made it very important to the people of New Brunswick to have a tariff-free market in the other colonies of British North America. Many people began to think Confederation would bring economic benefits.
- People thought union would mean more money for railway construction. This would mean more jobs in the colony. Railways would open up forested land for settlement.
- Tilley's campaign was supported financially by shipping, timber, and railway interests, which were pro-Confederation. The government of the United Province of Canada also contributed to his campaign.

In Nova Scotia

Nova Scotian politicians were largely responsible for initiating the Charlottetown Conference of 1864. People in Nova Scotia were interested in a union of the maritime colonies. Both New Brunswick and Prince Edward Island had previously been part of Nova Scotia in the early days of British North America.

In the minds of the pro-Confederation people in Nova Scotia, Confederation was tied to railway building. They wanted to see Halifax linked by railway to the United Province of Canada. Access to Canadian markets would greatly help industrial development in Nova Scotia. The reaction of communities in Nova Scotia to the idea of Confederation often depended on their nearness to the proposed railway. People farther away were less interested.

Many anti-Confederates, led by Joseph Howe, were concerned that a small province like Nova Scotia would have little influence in Confederation. They also worried that higher taxes would be needed to support railway development. They worried about losing ties with Great Britain.

Nova Scotia Premier Charles Tupper was pro-Confederation. He watched the pro-Confederation candidates in New Brunswick lose the 1865 election. He decided not to call an election or to put the Seventy-Two Resolutions to a vote in Nova Scotia.

A new pro-Confederation lieutenant-governor was appointed in Nova Scotia. Sir Fenwick Williams was well-liked because he had been born in the colony. He had been a hero in the British navy. With his help, Premier Tupper was able to win the support of the Legislative Assembly for the proposed union.

By 1867 Halifax was an important port and military centre.

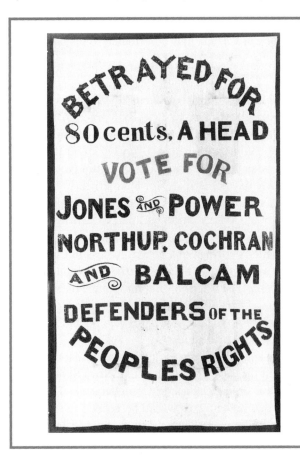

Many of the people of Nova Scotia felt they had been betrayed by their leaders.

Nova Scotia is standing at a crossroads, facing a **dilemma**.

In Prince Edward Island

In Prince Edward Island there was widespread opposition to Confederation. People were concerned that the island's five representatives in the new Canadian government would have little power.

Prince Edward Islanders had hoped that the new Canadian government would guarantee a £200 000 loan to buy out the absentee landlords who owned most of the island. When this was refused, many Islanders lost interest in Confederation. The island's government revenues came almost entirely from tariffs on trade with other colonies. Prince Edward Islanders saw no advantage in a tariff-free union, which would cause them to lose revenue.

In Newfoundland

The people of Newfoundland were not interested in Confederation. They felt that they had little in common with the people of the United Province of Canada. When they heard about the anti-Confederation resistance in the other Atlantic colonies, they decided to take no further part in Confederation discussions.

Dilemma—a difficult choice between equal options, each with good and bad consequences

Pro-Confederation

**John A. Macdonald
1815–1891**

John A. Macdonald was probably the most enthusiastic supporter of Confederation. He became the first prime minister of the new Dominion of Canada. (His biography is on page 129.)

**George Brown
1818–1880**

All right! Confederation through at six o'clock this evening—constitution adopted . . . a complete reform of all the abuses and injustices we have complained of! Is it not wonderful?

—from Brown's letter to his wife, Anne Brown

George Brown was called by journalist M.O. Hammond, "a steam engine in trousers, and had he lived in more recent times, he would no doubt be called a human dynamo."

George Brown was born in Scotland and immigrated to New York at the age of twenty. He moved to Toronto, where he founded *The Globe* newspaper. He was leader of the Reform (Clear Grit) Party in the Legislative Assembly of the United Province of Canada. He advocated representation by population. He also argued for the annexation of the Hudson's Bay Company's lands by the United Province of Canada.

In 1862, Brown visited Scotland. There he met and married Anne Nelson. Some historians have credited her with convincing him to form the Great Coalition.

In 1864 Brown stood up in the Legislative Assembly and crossed the floor to shake the hand of John A. Macdonald, leader of Conservatives. He indicated that he would work with Macdonald and George-Étienne Cartier instead of simply promoting his own party's interests. Brown, Macdonald, and Cartier formed the Great Coalition to break political deadlock in the Legislative Assembly of the United Province of Canada.

Brown retired from the Coalition cabinet in December 1865, saying that "party leadership and the conducting of a great journal [*The Globe*] do not harmonize." He was defeated in the 1867 elections. In 1873 he was made a senator. He continued to publish his newspaper until 1880, when he was killed by an unhappy employee.

**George-Étienne Cartier
1814–1873**

O Canada, my own beloved land!

—A line in a song composed by George-Étienne Cartier when he was a student in Montreal.*

"Frank and Without Deceit" was the motto George-Étienne Cartier chose when he was knighted in 1868.

Cartier was born and educated in Lower Canada. He began practising as a lawyer in Montreal in 1835. His interest in politics was evident when he took part in the 1837 Rebellion of Lower Canada under the leadership of Louis-Joseph Papineau.

Cartier married Hortense Fabre in 1846. They had three daughters, two of whom died before their parents.

He became a member of the Legislative Assembly of the United Province of Canada in 1848. Cartier held posts as provincial secretary, attorney general, and then leader of Canada East. When members from Canada West argued for "Rep by Pop" in the Legislative Assembly, Cartier argued for an equal number of representatives for Canada East.

Cartier was an ardent supporter of Confederation. In June 1864, as leader of *le Parti bleu*, Cartier, John A. Macdonald, and George Brown formed the Great Coalition. This was the first step toward achieving Confederation. He attended both Confederation conferences. It was largely because of Cartier's assurances that the people of Canada East would keep their language, culture, and religion that they agreed to join a federal union.

Cartier filled in as prime minister for four months in 1870 when John A. Macdonald was ill. Cartier

*Canada in Cartier's song referred only to Quebec (Canada East) not to the United Province of Canada.

negotiated British Columbia's entry into Confederation during this time, then sailed for England, where he died in 1873.

Thomas D'Arcy McGee
1825–1868

D'Arcy McGee was born in Ireland. He came to America in 1842, returned to Ireland, then left again because of his involvement in an Irish rebellion against Great Britain in 1848. When first in the United States, McGee supported violence against Great Britain. However, after moving to Canada in 1857, he spoke out for loyalty to Great Britain. This angered the Fenians, who hated Great Britain.

McGee first worked as a journalist, but soon turned to politics, representing the riding of Montreal West. He was very concerned about the threat of the American belief in Manifest Destiny. He saw Confederation as the only way for the British North American colonies to protect themselves. He said

Rest assured, if we remain long as fragments, we shall be lost; but let us be united, and we shall be as a rock which, unmoved itself, flings back the waves that may be dashed upon it by the storm.

D'Arcy McGee is remembered for his passion for this country, and for his untimely death at the hands of an **assassin** on April 7, 1868. Lady Macdonald described how she heard the news of his death:

[I was almost half asleep] when I was roused by a low, rapid knocking on the front door. In an instant, a great fear came upon me. Springing up, I threw on a wrapper . . . just in time to see John throw up the window & hear him call out "Is there anything the matter?" The answer came up fearfully clear & hard . . . "McGee is murdered—lying in the streets—shot thro' the head." The words fell like the blow of a bar of iron across my heart—it was too dreadful.

A young Fenian sympathizer, Patrick James Whelan, was convicted and hanged for the crime.* He never admitted to it, although he said that he knew who had done the killing.

Alexander Galt
1817–1893

Alexander Galt was born in Great Britain. He came to Canada at age 18 to work for the British American Land Company, which his father had helped set up. Galt was first elected to the Legislative Assembly of the United Province of Canada as a Liberal in 1849. He later became a Conservative in the Great Coalition Cabinet. Galt was an early supporter of Confederation.

Galt attended the Quebec Conference in 1864 and was a Canadian delegate to the London Conference in the winter of 1866–1867. He served briefly as the first finance minister of the new Dominion of Canada.

Samuel Leonard Tilley
1818–1896

Samuel Leonard Tilley was born to Loyalist parents who came north after the American Revolution. He had a profitable medical supply business before entering politics. He represented New Brunswick at both the Charlottetown and Quebec Conferences. He led the fight to convince the people of New Brunswick to join Confederation.

Following Confederation Tilley joined John A. Macdonald's Conservative government, first as minister of customs, then as minister of finance. In 1885 he became lieutenant-governor of New Brunswick.

Charles Tupper
1821–1915

Tupper was a third-generation Nova Scotian. He was a doctor and became the first president of the Canadian Medical Association.

Assassin—killer, especially one motivated by political or religious beliefs
*This was the last public hanging to take place in Canada.

In 1864 Tupper became the premier of Nova Scotia. He attended the Charlottetown and Quebec Conferences that year. He is given credit for his province's entry into Confederation. After Confederation, Tupper held many Cabinet posts in Canada's federal government. He was minister of railways and canals from 1870 to 1884, while the Canadian Pacific Railway was being built. He replaced Sir Mackenzie Bowell as prime minister in May 1896. After the Conservatives were defeated by Wilfrid Laurier's Liberals on July 8, he resigned. He led the Official Opposition for another four years before retiring from politics.

Opposed to Confederation

Joseph Howe
1804–1873

Joseph Howe tried to get the governments of Nova Scotia, the United Province of Canada, and Great Britain to co-operate in building a railway from Halifax to Quebec in the 1850s. This idea failed. In the 1860s, Howe led the fight against Confederation in Nova Scotia. His 12 "Botheration Letters" were printed in the *Halifax Morning Chronicle* from January to March, 1865. This is an example of what he said:

> Comparing Confederation to a piece of cloth, it is a weak and poorly planned piece of material. Is it a good idea to put new wine [Nova Scotia] in an old bottle [United Province of Canada] or to attach new cloth to an old item of clothing? Is union strong when a wise man, doing a steady business, is tricked into joining a gambler? Was Samson stronger when combined with Delilah, who tied him with ropes and cut off his hair?

After Confederation, Howe tried to arrange for Nova Scotia to withdraw. However, by 1869 he had accepted Confederation. He became a cabinet minister in the federal government.

A. A. Dorion
1818–1891

Dorion led *le Parti rouge* in the Legislative Assembly of the United Province of Canada before Confederation. He and his party opposed Confederation. They were concerned that the strong powers given to the proposed federal government in the Seventy-Two Resolutions would be a threat to the French-speaking people of Canada East.

In 1873, when Prime Minister Alexander Mackenzie's Liberal government came to power, Dorion was appointed minister of justice.

Joined a Few Years Later

James Colledge Pope
1826–1885

Before entering politics, Pope was a successful businessman. He became Prince Edward Island's largest shipowner of the nineteenth

century. He was premier of the island when it joined Confederation in 1873. Following Confederation, Pope became one of Prince Edward Island's first federal members of Parliament.

Couldn't Persuade His Colony to Join

F.B.T. Carter
1819–1900

Carter was first elected to the Newfoundland House of Assembly as a Conservative in 1855. He was pro-Confederation and was a Newfoundland representative to the Quebec Conference of 1864. Following the conference, he could not raise much support for the Seventy-Two Resolutions in Newfoundland. He became prime minister of Newfoundland in 1865. In 1869 his government ran for re-election on a pro-Confederation platform and was defeated. Carter was re-elected in 1874, but he did not raise the issue of Confederation again.

The London Conference

   Sixteen delegates from the United Province of Canada, Nova Scotia, and New Brunswick sailed to London in 1866 to present the Seventy-Two Resolutions to British officials. During the meetings in London, the delegates from Nova Scotia and New Brunswick were able to make some changes that were to their benefit. New Brunswick got assurances that the intercolonial railway would be built. The Atlantic colonies would be connected with the United Province of Canada. **Subsidies** to the provincial government were increased.

On February 12, 1867, the bill containing the modified Seventy-Two Resolutions, known as the British North America Act, was introduced in the British Parliament. It passed through the House of Commons and House of Lords quickly. On May 22, 1867, Queen Victoria proclaimed that the Dominion of Canada would be created.

For Your Notebook

1. Why did the delegates go to London in 1866 to present the Seventy-Two Resolutions to British officials?

Exploring Further

2. Imagine you were one of the delegates in London when Queen Victoria proclaimed that the Dominion of Canada would be created. React in role through one of the types of writing on pages 370 to 371. For example:
   • storytelling—diary or journal, friendly letter, hard news story, historical story
   • persuading—editorial, letter to the editor, speech
   • reporting—news report, magazine/newspaper feature article, interview

The London Conference, by J.D. Kelly. The London Conference lasted from December 1866 to February 1867.

Subsidy—a grant; an amount of money that the government contributes or sets aside from a given year's budget, usually for a specific project

Personal Summary

John Alexander Macdonald was born in Glasgow, Scotland. He came to Canada as a young boy. He later said that he did not have a boyhood because he left school at the age of 14 and went to work in a law office at 15. By the time he was 19 he had started his own law practice. He served in the militia, helping to defeat the Rebellion of 1837 in Upper Canada.

In 1843 Macdonald married Isabella Clark. Their first son died in 1848. Their second son, Hugh John, would serve briefly as premier of Manitoba in 1899–1900. Isabella was ill most of her married life and died in 1857.

In 1867 Macdonald married Susan Agnes Bernard, in London during the London Conference. She was very interested in Macdonald's political career and often sat in the gallery of the House of Commons to watch him. When she accompanied him on a trip to British Columbia by train in 1886, she rode part of the way on the cowcatcher (a metal framework at the front of the train) to better enjoy the scenery. Macdonald's second marriage, like his first, was tinged with sadness. Their only child, Mary, was born severely handicapped. However, John A. believed in making the best of things. Lady Macdonald once wrote:

> Oftentimes he comes in with a very moody brow, tired and oppressed, his voice weak, his step slow; and ten minutes after he is making very clever jokes and laughing like any schoolboy with his hands in his pockets and his head thrown back. . . . I tell him his good heart and amiable temper are the great secrets of his success.

At the time of Confederation Macdonald was knighted by Queen Victoria for his work, and thereafter was called Sir John A. Macdonald.

Political Summary

John A. Macdonald helped create the Liberal-Conservative Party in Canada West in 1854. In 1856 he became leader of the government of Canada West (in the Legislative Assembly of the United Province of Canada). In 1867 he became the first prime minister of the Dominion of Canada.

Sir John A. Macdonald
1815–1891

Dates as Prime Minister—1867–1873,
1878–1891
Party—Conservative

• • • • • • • •

Macdonald presided over the union and expansion of Canada. The first provinces joined together in 1867 (Confederation). In 1869 the North-West Territories were brought into Confederation and in 1870 the province of Manitoba came into being. In 1871, British Columbia entered Confederation, and in 1873, Prince Edward Island joined. In 1880 the British government transferred the Arctic Islands to Canada.

Macdonald once said that he would be quite willing to not have Canadians settle the Prairie West for the next half century, but he was afraid to leave it unsettled because of the threat of American takeover. Large numbers of settlers loyal to Canada were needed to fill the West. Macdonald presided over the building of the Canadian Pacific Railway, which made the settlement possible.

The Pacific Scandal, which caused Macdonald and his Conservative Party to resign from office in 1873, was related to the building of the railway. In 1872 the Conservatives received a large campaign contribution from Sir Hugh Allan, the man who had been awarded the contract to build the railway. Macdonald and his Conservatives won the election, although with a reduced majority. The Opposition accused them of accepting bribes from Allan and his company. The Conservatives resigned in 1873 and lost the election of 1874. However, they returned to office with a majority in the election of 1878.

Wilfrid Laurier, a Liberal opponent of Macdonald and later prime minister, summed up Macdonald's accomplishments after Macdonald's death in 1891:

> It may be said, without any exaggeration whatever, that the life of Sir John Macdonald, from the day he entered Parliament, is the history of Canada, for he was connected and associated with all the events, all the facts which brought Canada from the position it then occupied—the position of two small provinces, having nothing in common but their common allegiance, united by a bond of paper and united by nothing else—to the . . . state of development which Canada has reached.

The British North America Act 1867

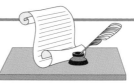

Introduction

  The British North America Act (BNA Act) created the Dominion of Canada in 1867. It stated the powers of the provincial and federal governments, outlined the way in which the government would be structured, and guaranteed protection for minority groups. The BNA Act was the first Canadian constitution.*

Aim: to create a federal union (Confederation) of the colonies of British North America, associated with Great Britain.

Dominion of Canada, 1867

The proclamation of the Dominion of Canada was made at Windsor Castle in Great Britain on May 22, 1867. The Dominion of Canada was to consist of the provinces of Ontario, Quebec, Nova Scotia, and New Brunswick. Provision was made for other provinces to join later.

*Just as you cannot play hockey without rules, you cannot govern a country without rules. The rules that govern a country are called a constitution. There are basically two types of constitutions: written and unwritten. The United States has a written constitution. Great Britain has an unwritten constitution. In 1982, the BNA Act was renamed the Constitution Act, 1867. Canada's constitution is written in some areas and unwritten in other areas. The 1982 Constitution moved Canada closer to a written constitution and farther from reliance on knowledge of custom and tradition. See page 140.

Federalism

 The most important question that the writers of the British North America Act, 1867, had to settle was whether there should be two levels of government (national and provincial) or just a national level. Two levels of government exist under federalism. John A. Macdonald and others had not wanted provincial governments. However, *Canadiens* felt that if Quebec didn't have a provincial government, it would lose its identity: its French language, culture, traditions, and its civil laws. Many people in the provinces of New Brunswick and Nova Scotia were also anxious to have their own provincial governments.

A system of federalism resulted. The Dominion of Canada would have two levels of government: federal (national/central) and provincial. The federal government would handle matters affecting the Dominion as a whole. Each provincial government would handle matters affecting only the people within its boundaries. The federal government would have more powers than the provincial governments.**

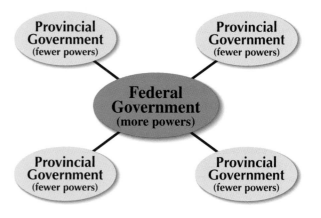

**In 1982, changes were made to the Canadian Constitution giving the provinces additional powers.

A Strong Central Government

 The federal (or central) government was to be very strong. The American Civil War (1861–1865), in which the states fought each other, was still fresh in the minds of the Fathers of Confederation. They were afraid that if the provinces were too powerful, they might conflict with each other instead of working together.

The federal government in Canada was given three important powers:

1. authority over matters of general (national) concern, including everything not specifically given to the provinces
2. the power to veto (to reject) any provincial law within one year of its passage
3. the power to appoint each province's lieutenant-governor

Federal Powers Specified in the 1867 Constitution

Among the 29 items that were specifically stated as powers of the federal (central) government were

- trade and commerce
- raising money by taxation
- money (currency and banking)
- postal service
- armed forces and defence
- fisheries
- Aboriginal peoples and lands reserved for them
- divorce
- criminal law
- penitentiaries

Some powers are covered by the POGG clause—Peace, Order, and Good Government. "The federal government shall make laws for the peace, order, and good government of Canada in regard to all subjects not specifically given to the provinces . . . ." The POGG clause potentially made the federal government very powerful.

Provincial Governments

 While matters of national economic interest were to be legislated by the federal government, matters of a particular or local interest were the responsibility of the four provincial governments (Ontario, Quebec, New Brunswick, and Nova Scotia).*

Provincial Powers Specified in the 1867 Constitution

- direct taxation within the province
- management and sale of public lands and natural resources belonging to the province
- provincial prisons
- hospitals and asylums
- local works and projects
- education (with exceptions)**
- administration of justice and provincial courts
- issuing licenses to shops, saloons, taverns, and other businesses
- property and civil law

Canadian Federalism

Federal Government		Provincial Government
public debt and property; defence; regulation of trade and commerce; taxation; post office; census; shipping; money and banking; interest; bankruptcy; copyrights and patents; Aboriginal peoples; criminal law; fisheries; foreign affairs	agriculture, immigration, education	direct taxes and debt; local affairs; labour laws; credit unions; licensing; justice; health and welfare; natural resources; municipalities; language and culture

Shared Powers in the BNA Act of 1867

Some powers, such as immigration and agriculture, are shared by the federal (central) government and the provincial governments.

---

*As the years went by, these powers often overlapped and blurred. The division of powers is no longer easy to explain and continues to be an issue between governments.

**Education was technically a shared power in regard to minority rights (as per Section 93). This area will be studied later.

Branches of Government

The Canadian constitution (BNA Act, 1867) established three branches (or parts) of government, as the following chart shows.

1. **Legislative Branch**—Parliament (the law-making body of government), composed of an elected House of Commons and an appointed Senate

2. **Executive Branch**—headed by a Governor General acting in the name of the British monarch

3. **Judiciary Branch**—the system of courts and Supreme Court

Canada's System of Central Government
(as outlined in the BNA Act, 1867)

Monarch

1. LEGISLATIVE BRANCH—Parliament
- makes laws and votes on taxes and other sources of revenue

2. EXECUTIVE BRANCH—policy-making body
- approves the proposed legislation before it goes to the House of Commons and Senate, where it is debated

Governor General—British-appointed
- officially appoints the Cabinet from the majority party upon the recommendation of the prime minister and the political party in power

Senate—appointed
- members, called senators, appointed for life

SPEAKER

PRIME MINISTER

House of Commons—elected
"the people's representatives"
- elected representatives called Members of Parliament

The Cabinet—chosen by the prime minister
- prime minister and cabinet ministers
- the leader of the political party holding the majority of seats in the house is the prime minister

Legend

Crown	Voters
The political party with the second largest representation in the House of Commons becomes the Official Opposition.	The political party with the most elected members in the House of Commons is asked to form the government.

Appoints   **Elects**   **Advises**

Voters

3. JUDICIAL BRANCH
Court System
- interprets the laws and carries out justice through the courts

132

Celebrating July 1 Project

   For more information check

http://canada.gc.ca/canadiana/cdaind_e.html and http://national.gallery.ca

Exploring Further

1. Why is it important to celebrate birthdays? How do you celebrate Canada Day? How does your community celebrate Canada Day? Is it important to celebrate national events? Why or why not?

2. Survey your parents and grandparents to find out how they celebrated these special Canadian events in the past. Make a chart of the survey results.
   1967—Centennial, 100 years
   1992—Canada was 125 years old
   2000—Canada entering the 21st century

3. a) Make a list of images suggested by the following words or phrases:
   - an RCMP officer in uniform
   - the Canadian flag
   - the Rocky Mountains
   - the Prairies
   - Central Canada
   - the *fleur-de-lis*
   - Toronto
   - Atlantic Canada

4. a) What symbols and songs identify Canada?
   b) Start collecting pictures of symbols and examples that show Canadian identity. Arrange them on a large collage.

5. a) What is identity?
   b) How are image and identity related?
   c) What aspects of Canadian identity can you personally change? Which can you not change?

6. Create a poster to let people know about the July 1, 1867 celebrations. Celebrations occurred in Ottawa and throughout the four provinces of Ontario, Quebec, Nova Scotia, and New Brunswick.

Newspapers on July 1, 1867, described celebrations that took place.

Dominion of Canada.

CONFEDERATION DAY.

1st JULY, 1867.

Programme of Celebration.

At 10 o'clock a. m., a grand Review of Her Majesty's Troops, regulars and volunteers, will take place on the Bathurst Street Commons.

At 3 o'clock; provided pending arrangements can be consummated with parties in New York, a grand Balloon Ascension will take place from the Queen's Park.

By the kind permission of Lieut.-Col. Brunel and Major James Stephenson, the Bands of the 10th Royal Regiment and the Grand Trunk Brigade will give a Grand Promenade Concert in the Queen's Park commencing at 7 o'clock p. m; open to all, to be accompanied by the most magnificent display of Fireworks ever exhibited in Canada.

The Ground of the Park will be beautifully illuminated and decorated during the evening.

GOD SAVE THE QUEEN !

GEO. D'ARCY BOULTON,
Chairman Select Com. on Celebration
JOHN BOXALL,
Chairman Decoration Committee.

June 25.   5331 5t

The Globe.

TORONTO, MONDAY, JULY 1.

Confederation Day.—As the city clock struck midnight, and the Dominion of Canada began its legal existence, the bells of St. James' Cathedral, under the charge of Mr. Rawlinson, sent forth a merry peal. Bonfires were lighted in various parts of the city. Small arms went off as rapidly as pop-guns and a foretaste was taken of the general rejoicings of the day. Crowds of citizens paraded the streets from midnight, and various companies of seranaders marched in different directions singing loyal and patriotic anthems.

Confederation Celebrations

On Monday, July 1, 1867, a Toronto newspaper announced: "A united British North America takes its place among the nations of the world." There were fireworks, cheering crowds, fine speeches, parades, and gun salutes to celebrate the occasion.

Right: The Confederation Medal was ordered by John A. Macdonald in 1867 to commemorate Confederation.

BY THE QUEEN!

A PROCLAMATION

For Uniting the Provinces of Canada, Nova Scotia, and New Brunswick, into one Dominion, under the name of CANADA.

VICTORIA R.

Above: On Monday, July 1, 1867, market squares and open places in front of public buildings were packed with people eager to hear the reading of Queen Victoria's proclamation that the United Province of Canada, Nova Scotia, and New Brunswick had been united into one Dominion under the name of Canada.

Above: One of Canada's early postage stamps shows a profile of Queen Victoria. In 1868 it cost 3 cents to send a letter within Canada, 6 cents to the United States, and 12.5 cents to Great Britain.

Above: This crowd gathered in Kingston's Market Square on July 1, 1867, to hear the proclamation announcing Confederation.

Left: Viscount Monck was Governor of British North America from 1861 and Canada's first Governor General until 1868.

Left: At the time of Confederation, Canada's flag was the Union Jack of Great Britain.

Left: John A. Macdonald worked hard to bring the first four provinces together into Confederation. He became the first Prime Minister of Canada.

Above: This photograph of Queen Victoria was taken during Canada's Confederation year, 1867.

Below: The unofficial coat of arms was based on the arms of the four original provinces.

Right: The Parliamentary Library was photographed by Samuel McLaughlin about 1865. The library was the only part of the Parliament Buildings to survive the fire of 1916.

Confederation Newspapers
Primary Source Materials

The Globe.

TORONTO, MONDAY, JULY 1.

CONFEDERATION DAY!

The Union of the Provinces of Canada, Nova Scotia and New Brunswick, under the new Constitution, takes effect to-day. We heartily congratulate our readers on the event, and fervently pray that all the blessings anticipated from the measure, by its promoters, may be fully realized.

So far as the people of Upper Canada are concerned, the inauguration of the new Constitution may well be heartily rejoiced over as the brightest day in their calendar. The Constitution of 1867 will be famous in the historical annals of Upper Canada, not only bec———

ritory, but because it relieved the inhabitants of Western Canada from a system of injustice and demoralization under which they had suffered for a long series of years.

The unanimity and cordiality with which all sections of the people of Canada accept the new Constitution, gives the happiest omen of its successful operation. And, assuredly, if the people of the United Provinces are true to themselves and exercise a persistent and careful control over all public proceedings, there is not a shadow of doubt as to success. The only danger that threatens us is, lest the same men who have so long misgoverned us, should continue to misgovern us still, and the same reckless prodigality exhibited in past years should be continued in the future; but this we do not fear. We firmly believe that from this day, Canada enters a new and happier career, and

The Ottawa Citizen.

I. B. TAYLOR, PROPRIETOR.

FRIDAY, JULY 12, 1867.

CONFEDERATION DAY appears to have been generally well-observed throughout the Dominion. But in Nova Scotia, the stronghold of Anti-Unionism, the day passed over without jubilation. This, of course, is no more than we might have predicted, for, weeks ago, Mr. Howe and the anti-Confederate journals recommended that the day should be devoted to fastings and humiliations. The recommendation of Mr. Howe was followed by at least one Quebec Rouge—a Mr. LABERGE—who, as Mayor of Dorchester, withheld his sanction and authority for the holding of a celebration. When asked to convene a public meeting to take into consideration the celebration of the day he refused to do so on the ground that he believed Confederation to be a public misfortune, and that, before rejoicing, the people should wait at least one year to see how the Union should work. We have reason to believe that the Mayor of Dorchester is not the only Rouge who is still unfriendly to the Union and disposed to do all in his power to make Confederation a "public misfortune." Mr. DORION, although he has quite recently publicly addressed his constituency, has not accepted Confederation in

The Globe.

TORONTO, MONDAY, JULY 1, 1867.

CONFEDERATION DAY.

The Dominion of Canada.

HISTORICAL NOTES

HOW CONFEDERATION HAS BEEN BROUGHT ABOUT.

With the first dawn of this gladsome midsummer morn, we hail the birthday of a new nationality. A united British America, with its four millions of people, takes its place this day among the nations of the world. Stamped with a familiar name, which in the past has borne a record sufficiently honourable to entitle it to be perpetuated with a more comprehensive import, the DOMINION OF CANADA, on this First day of July, in the year of grace, eighteen hundred and sixty-seven, enters on a new career of national existence. Old things have passed away. The history of old Canada, with its contracted bounds, and limited divisions of Upper and Lower, East and West, has been completed, and this day a new volume is opened, New Brunswick and Nova Scotia uniting with Ontario and Quebec to make the history of a greater Canada, already extending from the ocean to the head waters of the great lakes, and destined ere long to embrace the larger half of this North American continent from the Atlantic to the Pacific.

Let us gratefully acknowledge the hand of the Almighty Disposer of Events in bringing about this result, pregnant with so important an influence on the condition and destinies of the inhabitants of these Provinces, and of the teeming millions who in ages to come will people the Dominion of Canada from ocean to ocean, and give it its character in the annals of time. Let us acknowledge, too, the sagacity, the patriotism, the forgetfulness of selfish and partisan considerations, on the part of our statesmen, to which under Providence are due the inception of the project of a British American Confederation and the carrying it to a successful issue. Without much patient labour, a disposition to make mutual concessions, and an earnest large-minded willingness to subordinate all party interests to the attainment of what would be for the lasting weal of the whole people of British America, the result we celebrate this day would never have been achieved. It has taken just three years to accomplish—not certainly an unreasonable space of time for a work of such magnitude. Three years ago, Mr. Brown, Mr. Mowat, and Mr. McDougall, as representing the Reformers of Upper Canada, joined Mr. John A. Macdonald, Mr. Cartier, and their political associates, in forming a Government whose single and sole mission it should be to aim at the establishment for these Provinces of a new state of political existence, in which we should be rid of the peculiar evils and grievances which had hitherto obstructed our progress, and enter on a happier and brighter era. That Government was formed on the 30th June, 1864. On the 1st July, 1867, we witness the fruition of what was then undertaken. The public men of the Maritime Provinces joined in the good work, the sympathy and support

La Minerve

LUNDI MATIN, 1er JUILLET, 1867.

Dépêche Privée à La Minerve.

Nous assistons, aujourd'hui, à l'inauguration d'un nouveau système politique qui doit nous remplir d'un légitime orgueil pour notre influence dans le passé, et d'une grande confiance dans l'avenir.

Le Canada est maintenant une Puissance, non-seulement dans son titre, mais encore dans sa force, dans sa population, dans ses richesses, dans ses moyens d'avenir.

Sujets d'une grande puissance, possesseurs de vastes ressources, jouissant du meilleur système politique, protégés par des institutions éminemment favorables au progrès et à la prospérité des nations, nous avons en nous tous les éléments d'un grand et glorieux avenir.

Si nous voulons remplir les devoirs que nous impose notre nouvelle position, si nous sommes fermes au poste que nous assignent l'honneur et le patriotisme, nous réaliserons les vœux des plus sincères et des plus dévoués amis de notre pays. Que nous faut-il pour arriver à ce succès, si fort ambitionné ? Des hommes, du travail, du talent, du dévouement.

For Your Notebook

1. Newspapers on July 1, 1867, described local feelings about Confederation. Why were newspapers so important in the 1860s as a source of information? (Hint: What information sources exist today that were not in existence in the 1860s?)

Project
Writing a Confederation Newspaper

 Divide your class into four groups to represent the four original provinces (Ontario, Quebec, Nova Scotia, New Brunswick). Each group will write a newspaper discussing the issues that surrounded that province's entry into Confederation, and events that occurred at Confederation. This newspaper should be a reflection of the time period. It should include columns making arguments for the province to join, as well as those making arguments against. It should also include news articles describing everyday events.*

Step One

a) Each group's newspaper should include writing and drawings and have the following features:**

- an editorial
- columns
- feature articles
- news articles
- want ads (classifieds)
- weather
- announcements
- leisure section
- business section
- political cartoons

b) Check a local newspaper to see if there are other features you would like to include.

c) In addition to writers, you will require an editor, copy editors, a layout artist, and possibly someone to do the final word processing. Each person in the group will need to complete two or more tasks.

Step Two

Work in pairs: Choose one feature from Step One a) and find a sample of that feature in a local newspaper. Work together to list the criteria for that feature on chart paper. For instance, a list of criteria for an effective editorial might include:

- discusses an issue of concern to the newspaper's readers
- takes a position on the issue
- clearly states a position
- provides facts to support its position

A list of criteria for an effective article might include:

- begins with the most important information— who, what, where, when, why, and how
- itemized specific details
- has a catchy but brief headline

Step Three

Read your criteria to other members of the group. Ask for their comments. Add and delete items to improve your list. Post the lists on a bulletin board so that your group members can refer to them as you work on your newspaper.

Step Four

a) Choose an editor. This person will take a leadership role in the writing and production of your newspaper. First, list the responsibilities you think the editor should assume. Then, consider which group member could best carry out these responsibilities.

b) Decide how the other tasks will be divided. Remember that this may need to be altered later as you see that some tasks require more (or less) work than you expected.

Step Five

a) Work as a group to develop a mind map of the various issues around Confederation and events that occurred at your colony's entry into Confederation.

b) Identify additional information that you will require to complete your task.

Step Six

a) Conduct research to locate the additional information needed.

b) Write a draft of your piece. Edit your work.

Step Seven

Ask another student in the group to edit your work a second time.

Step Eight

Go through the editing suggestions and incorporate those that are appropriate. Write a new draft.

Step Nine

Have copy editors do a final edit on each segment. Incorporate any corrections.

Step Ten

Choose a name for your newspaper.

Step Eleven

Work together under the leadership of the student you have designated as layout artist to decide on the appearance of the newspaper.

Step Twelve

Print copies for other class members or make a bulletin board display of the newspapers.

---

*  For more information check http://www.pch.gc.ca/ceremonial-symb/english/day_can.html

---

**Newspapers of the 1860s did not yet have the technology to include photographs. Drawings were used instead.

In 1867

In the Dominion of Canada
Political Divisions

 The Dominion of Canada had four provinces in 1867; Ontario, Quebec, Nova Scotia, and New Brunswick. The people in the new Dominion of Canada had not yet begun to develop a national identity.

Rural and Urban Population

Rural (80%)
Urban (20%)

One in five (20%) of Canada's population lived in a town or city. The other four of five (80%) lived in rural areas.

1867

In rural areas people produced almost everything they needed. Animals provided the power necessary to make work easier and provided most of the transportation.

By 1867 the north shore of Lake Ontario was settled from Kingston to Niagara Falls. In 1867, large cities like Montreal, Toronto, Quebec City, and Halifax were developing the appearance and services of modern cities.

Origins

British (60.5%)
French (31%)
Other (8.5%)

1867

In 1867 Canada was predominantly a British country with British customs and traditions.

Social Classes

Canada's social classes ranged from wealthy property and business owners, to well-off middle class people, to the working-class, and the poor.

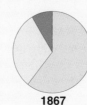

The wealthy lived in mansions (or large houses). Their luxurious lifestyle often included keeping servants.

Workers in industries such as this copper mine usually worked long hours under dangerous and unhealthy conditions.

Elsewhere in British North America

In addition to the four provinces in Canada, there were three colonies and two territories of British North America that were not involved in the process of Confederation in 1867. (See the map on page 130.) All of these areas will be studied more closely in the next section and chapters of this textbook.

- the colony of Prince Edward Island
- the colony of Newfoundland
- the colony of British Columbia
- the territory of Rupert's Land
- the Red River Settlement (part of Rupert's Land)

In the Colonies

After Confederation, life in the Atlantic colonies of Prince Edward Island and Newfoundland continued much as it had for decades. Agriculture in Prince Edward Island and fishing in Newfoundland were the basis of the economy. The sea was the most important transportation route for both colonies.

By 1865, the gold boom in the colony of British Columbia had neared its end. The colonies of Vancouver Island and British Columbia were in a financial crisis. Since it was especially expensive to maintain two separate governments, the two colonies joined in 1866 under the name of British Columbia. The capital was at New Westminster, Frederick Seymour was the governor. In 1867, the United States completed its purchase of the Alaska Panhandle from Russia. The territory along the coast both north and south of the colony of British Columbia was American.

The fur trade was still an important part of the economy in the colony of British Columbia.

These people from the colony of Prince Edward Island are hauling their boats across the frozen Northumberland Strait.

In Red River

The Red River Settlement was an active trading centre with a growing population. The Hudson's Bay Company trading monopoly was a source of conflict with the large Metis population. The colony's political future was unclear. The different groups disagreed about what they wanted.

Tsuu T'ina (Sarcee) living on the prairies in Rupert's Land still had a traditional way of life, but the buffalo herds were shrinking because of commercial hunting in the western United States.

Canada Revisited

Recent Developments in Confederation

These two pages will start you on a process of analysing and describing current, modern-day issues and their potential impact on Confederation today.

Exploring Further

1. As a class brainstorm and start a list of current issues that affect Confederation. Add to this list in the months ahead.

Constitutional Change

  Ever since 1867, changes to the constitution have been discussed. The most important changes were made in the Constitution Act. The Meech Lake **Accord** and the Charlottetown Accord proposed other changes. Also, in Quebec, the people voted on two proposals (called referendums) to give their province more power and the right to re-negotiate Confederation.

Constitution Act 1982

In April 1982, the British North America Act, which created Canada in 1867, was renamed the Constitution Act of 1867 and revised. The British North America Act had been an Act of the Parliament of Great Britain. It was replaced by the Constitution Act, which was an act of the British Parliament making it possible for Canada to change its Constitution without approval by Great Britain. The Constitution Act 1982 included a Canadian Charter of Rights and Freedoms for all Canadians. It recognized that Canada had become a **multicultural** country. The Constitution Act also declared that the country's provinces would receive federal grants of money for education, health, and welfare. The provincial government in Quebec was the only province to refuse to accept the Constitution Act. It said that the Constitution Act did not recognize Quebec's special place in Confederation.

Meech Lake Accord 1987

In April 1987 at Meech Lake (Quebec), the prime minister and the premiers met. The Meech Lake Accord proposed changes in the interpretation of provincial powers and how the constitution could be modified based on recognizing the **cultural distinctiveness** of Quebec. The agreement also proposed to give more power to the Senate and the Supreme Court. In June 1990, the Manitoba legislature did not approve the Meech Lake Accord because it recognized only Quebec's distinctiveness and not that of Canada's Aboriginal peoples. Since all provinces had to approve it, the Meech Lake Accord failed.

Elijah Harper, Member of the Manitoba Legislative Assembly, refused to approve the Meech Lake Accord.

Prime Minister Pierre Trudeau watches as Queen Elizabeth II signs the Constitution Proclamation on April 17, 1982.

Accord—an agreement
Multicultural—including cultural elements (language, religion, customs) from many different groups
Cultural distinctiveness—having unique cultural characteristics

Canada Revisited

Charlottetown Accord 1992

The prime minister and the premiers met at Charlottetown to discuss a new accord called the Charlottetown Accord. The Charlottetown Accord called for the recognition of Quebec's distinctiveness. It also proposed to protect the rights of the Aboriginal peoples. Representatives at the Charlottetown Accord discussed creating an elected Senate and reforming the House of Commons. In October 1992, Canadian voters were asked to approve the Charlottetown Accord. About 55% of voters in Quebec and 70% of voters in Western Canada rejected the accord. Voters in Ontario and Atlantic Canada narrowly approved it. More than 54% of Canadian voters rejected the Charlottetown Accord. The amendments to the Constitution were not approved.

Quebec Referendum 1995

A few years after Canadian voters rejected the Charlottetown Accord, voters in Quebec elected the *Parti Quebecois*. The *Parti Quebecois* was committed to establishing Quebec as an independent country in an economic partnership with the rest of Canada.

In October 1995, voters in Quebec were asked to support their government in establishing their province as a separate country with ties to Canada. Quebec voters narrowly defeated their government's proposal to declare Quebec independent from Canada.

Enthusiastic *"Oui"* (Yes) supporters

  Many people in the province of Quebec are opposed to Quebec independence. However, not all groups want the same future for their province. Many First Nations living in northern Quebec are opposed to separation, as are many English-speaking people and recent immigrants. French-speaking residents are also divided about what they think is best for the province.

Supreme Court Decision 1998

In August 1998, the Supreme Court declared that Quebec did not have the right to become an independent country without talking to the governments of the other provinces. The Supreme Court also stated that the other provinces could not stop Quebec from becoming a separate country if a majority of the province's population wanted it.

A march from Ottawa to Montreal in October 1995 of people opposed to separation

Review

The icons are your cue to refer to the Learning How to Learn Appendix (pages 348–371) for ideas on how to complete these activities.

 This icon is a reminder to turn to the Research Model (pages x–xi).

1. Complete a self-assessment for one assignment from this chapter.

Understanding Concepts

2. At the beginning of this chapter you made some predictions on what the chapter was about. Check your predictions to see how accurate you were.

3. Use one of the suggested methods for recording vocabulary to add new words from this chapter to the WordBook section of your notes.

4. a) Canada has a federal system of government. Explain what this means.
   b) Which had the most power in 1867, the federal government or the provincial government? What future problems might this cause for the new Dominion of Canada?

5. Add entries for this chapter to your timeline.

Developing Research Skills

6.

Section II Activity

Complete the Confederation Cube you started on page 89.

7. In a small group discuss and then research:

   a) What qualities do you think a leader, such as a class/school president or a prime minister, should have? You may wish to get suggestions from your parents and other adults, or phone the office of your provincial or federal representative for ideas.
   b) Combine your list with those of several other groups and discuss the following questions.
      • Is it possible for one person to have all these qualities?
      • How many of the qualities on your list did Sir John A. Macdonald, Canada's first prime minister, have?
   c) How many of these qualities does Canada's current prime minister have? Provide examples of behaviour to back up your opinion.

Developing Communication Skills

Select from the following.

Writing

8. Put yourself in the place of one of the people mentioned in this chapter. Write a journal entry or entries describing at least one of the events leading to Confederation (Charlottetown Conference, Quebec Conference, or London Conference) and your opinion of it.

Listening and Speaking

9. Select any significant incident in the chapter and dramatically re-create it. You will need to research additional facts to enhance your re-creation.

Viewing and Representing

10. Create a game showing how co-operation helped to bring about the formation of the Dominion of Canada. Your game should include:
    • major factors (reasons for Confederation)
    • key personalities
    • significant events
    • regional interests
    (Ideas for games are found on page 354.)

Section II Review

The activities on this page will help you review what you have learned about Confederation. First review the concept of co-operation on page 29 and the Section II focus on pages 88 and 89.

The Section II Activity Focused On

Co-operation

For Your Notebook

1. Using material from Chapters 4 and 5, the internet, and your library, find answers to the following questions. Select one of the presentation ideas on page 365 to present the answers.

   a) When did Canada become a country?
   b) Who was Canada's first Prime Minister?
   c) Where is Canada's capital located?
   d) Name the four original provinces of Canada.
   e) Name the other six provinces of Canada and the date each one joined Confederation.
   f) Name Canada's territories. When was the newest territory formed?
   g) To what political party did Canada's first prime minister belong?
   h) Name three Fathers of Confederation.
   i) Who is Canada's current prime minister?
   j) What do you think and feel about Canada continuing as a country in the future?
   k) What do you think will happen to the rest of Canada if Quebec withdraws?

Questions for Class Discussion

2. Based on what you learned in Chapters 4 and 5, discuss the question on the easel on page 89.

For Your Notebook
Select one from the following

3. Individually or in small groups, prepare a TV script and present a talk show that is being taped in Ottawa on July 1, 1867. (The idea of a television show in 1867 is imaginary.) Your talk show will review the events and people that led to Confederation. Co-operation should be your theme. Your guests represent the various people who helped bring about Confederation.

4. Imagine you have been given the responsibility of selecting five historical pictures to be part of an historical Confederation museum located in Ottawa. Your pictures should reflect accurate images of Canadian life around 1867. Prepare the art collection by using resource materials, the internet, or personal artwork.

5. Review all of the examples of co-operation that are found in this section (Chapters 4 and 5). Do either a) or b) to show how co-operation was used in forming the Dominion of Canada.

   a) Draw a mind map to organize the examples on paper. Use simple line drawings and at least three colours.
   b) In groups create a concept poster.

6. The strong anti-Confederation movement in Nova Scotia was an example of federal/provincial conflict. Check newspapers and other media daily for a period of two weeks. List examples of federal/provincial conflict that you find. Display the information in a chart to share with others.

7. What rights of minorities were guaranteed in the British North America Act of 1867? Check the newspaper and other media to find examples of how governments protect the rights of minorities today. Tell a classmate about what you found or create a bulletin board using newspaper clippings, opinions, and other resources.

"**A**agh!" Haley looked with horror through the oven door. Her cake was flatter than a no-topping pizza. "Mom! I give up! Can't we just buy some cakes?"

"Wait a minute!" Haley's mother was already looking through the cupboard. "Look here! One angel food mix and one brownie mix coming up!"

Haley was experiencing challenges. The goal of a trip to Charlottetown sounded so exciting, but it would not be reached easily or quickly.

Just then the phone rang. In a raspy voice, Ben reported to Haley that he had a sore throat. He was too sick to work Friday or Saturday night. However, lots of stuff was being dropped off for the garage sale, and Ben's father would be there to help set up on Friday. Ben would have the signs ready for them.

Haley, Lee, Darin, Jasmine, and their families worked until 10:30 Friday night getting the sale ready. Haley had never been so tired in her life. When Ben's father finally said, "Looks good, folks!" Haley could have hugged him.

It was raining when Ms Pozzi got to the garage at 8:00 AM. Who would come to a garage sale in the rain?

Haley and Jasmine were sitting by the cash box. "Hi, Ms Pozzi. No one's coming."

"Well, it's early yet," she answered. "People sleep in on rainy Saturdays. You've advertised well with your door-to-door leaflets and got your signs up early. Here's what I'll do. I'll call the radio station. We'll get you more publicity!"

By noon, the rain had stopped and business was brisk. Ben's

Section III
Challenges to the New Dominion
1867–1905

• • • • • • • • • • • • • • • •

mother said they could keep the warehouse open Sunday too if they needed to. Late Saturday afternoon, the manager of the local thrift shop came by. He offered Ben's father a lump sum for all the items not sold by the end of the day on Sunday. That sounded like a great offer to the tired crew. Ben came over in the afternoon. When he saw the over-flowing cash box he croaked, "Wow! I hope all of the other fundraising teams did as well as we did!"

On Monday, Ms Pozzi greeted the class. "You've had a busy weekend! Let's talk about some of your challenges in working towards your goal."

Amir raised his hand. "Our car wash got caught in the rain. By noon we had only done three cars. Charles and I felt like we were wasting our time, but then the sun came out and we had so much business I had to phone my sister to come and help. My dad says we can use his service station as a location for the next three Saturdays."

"How about Eric's group?" asked Ms Pozzi. "Mr. McKee said there was a good turnout at your dance in the gym. Did you have any problems?"

"Mostly just the sound system," reported Antonio. "It died after the first two songs! But Eric's mom checked all the connections, and she and Eric got it going again. The Grade 7s bought lots of soft drinks and popcorn too."

Ms Pozzi was pleased. "It sounds like you've been meeting your challenges and solving your problems. Remember our slogan: Together we can reach our goal! The chart on the board is to keep track of our funds. I'm not listing the groups because I want everyone to focus on the group's total goal. We work together!"

Everyone checked the fundraising chart after every weekend. Ms Pozzi encouraged each group. The day the class reached their goal Ms Pozzi wrote across the board "CONGRATULATIONS!" Underneath it she printed, "TO CHARLOTTETOWN!"

A Research Model to Meet Challenges

"Your groups all faced challenges as you worked towards your common goal," Ms Pozzi said, starting the class. "In the next section we will be studying about challenges—challenges the new Dominion of Canada faced between 1867 and 1905. Let's go through the chart I've displayed on the classroom monitor. You'll be using it to record information from the next five chapters. Each of you has a similar chart on your desk.

"Let's use your fundraising situation for the Youth Shaping Canada's Future Conference in Charlottetown to help you understand the chart. Under number ❶, Goal, write what our class's goal was and why it was important."

She paused. "Darin, will you read what you've written?"

"Our goal was to raise enough money to send three representatives to Charlottetown. I guess it's important because it will cost a lot of money, so we all pitched in to help. Besides, our class will get three computers," replied Darin.

"Okay." Ms Pozzi pointed to number ❷, Challenges. "I prefer to think of challenges rather than problems that you encountered. Challenges seem attainable—problems often seem too big an obstacle! So for your group's money-raising project, what did you do that moved you towards your goal? Write these on the left. Then write what hindered you from reaching your goal on the right side.

"Let's try to think of solutions you undertook that helped you move closer towards your goal.

Record these under number ❸, Solutions."

Ms Pozzi waited while the groups filled in the information. Next she pointed to section ❹ and added, "Examine the first four solutions you've listed. Write them on the ladder, putting the most important at the top.

"In number ❺, briefly add what you did to carry out your plan. Now that we've completed the project it is important to reflect on the process you used. Record this in number ❻."

Questions for Discussion

1. What are some of the advantages of using A Model to Meet Challenges to help you solve a problem or an issue?

A Model to Meet Challenges

❷ CHALLENGES
From point of view of _____

| What is moving you towards your goal? | **GOAL** ❶ **What?** **Why is it important?** | What is hindering you from reaching your goal? |

❸ SOLUTIONS
To move you towards your goal
- _____
- _____
- _____
- _____

❹ PRIORITIZE SOLUTIONS

❺ ACTION PLAN

❻ REFLECTION
Was your plan successful? Why or why not?

On the Train

The Saturday morning that Antonio, Jasmine, and Haley caught the Confederation Train was a pleasant blur of noisy good-byes from classmates, hugging parents, bulging luggage, a crowded station platform, and local reporters. A sea of strange faces stared at them from the train windows.

The train had pulled out of Vancouver several days ago. It had travelled through the Rockies, across the Prairies, and around Lake Superior. Delegates from the western provinces, Yukon, Northwest Territories, and northern Ontario had boarded along the way. There were two special railway coaches nearly filled with excited Grade 8 students and their chaperones.

Haley, Antonio, and Jasmine sat near Ms Pozzi. Everyone else seemed to know each other. Haley noticed several nearby students wearing ski toques. She asked one of them and was told that the BC students had chosen the toques to identify their home province. There had already been some swapping—several Alberta students were sporting toques, while BC students were wearing Alberta pins with oil derricks on them. The Northwest Territories students had brought small flags with polar bears on them. Many of these were now attached to sweaters, jeans, and baseball caps on students from both coaches.

The countryside sped by. Haley decided to ask the group across the aisle from her if she could join their card game. "*Mais oui!*" exclaimed a dark-haired boy. "I'm Jean Paul from Gravelbourg, Saskatchewan. This is Ravi from Saskatoon, and Marie from Regina."

"Don't worry," laughed Marie. "Jean speaks English. He's just bragging because he's bilingual and can be a conference translator if any French-speaking delegates need one."

"Don't listen to her. She's just jealous," said Jean, grinning.

Haley was feeling more comfortable. These people had been strangers to each other until a couple of days ago. She would make new friends.

Antonio and Jasmine wandered into the second coach where there was a noisy but good-natured free-for-all. "You have to admit that BC has the best scenery. And the mountains! Some of us get skiing as a school sport," said a girl from Nelson.

A boy with an oil derrick pin on his Haida First Nation baseball jacket teased the girl across from him, "And then there's good old Saskatchewan, which goes on forever, completely flat!"

"I like the Prairies," said Mr. Singh, one of the chaperones, who was teaching in Brandon, Manitoba. "You seemed quite impressed yesterday when I was describing a buffalo stampede—how there were once herds so big they were like a rumbling sea of animals."

Regional discussions surfaced again and again on the journey, especially after the Quebec and Nunavut students boarded the train. Much of the teasing seemed to arise from curiosity, or comments that students had picked up from the media.

"Do the French in Quebec really want to separate from Canada?" asked a quiet girl from Nunavut.

"Not necessarily. Most people just want to be sure we keep our own culture, not be assimilated," answered a girl from Chicoutimi. "Hey, I heard that no one in Nunavut has dogsleds any more. Is that true?"

"Not too many people use them for travelling or hunting," Emily answered. "But lots of people still keep dogs, especially for competitions at festivals. We are trying to keep a balance between new technology that is really useful, like snowmobiles, and traditions that are still important to us."

By the time the train stopped in Moncton, New Brunswick, to make the connection to PEI, the students and adults were a well-mixed group. Most people had got along well. "I thought we would have to referee behaviour," Ms Pozzi commented to Mr. Singh, "but they adapted well to each others' differences. Our jobs have been quite enjoyable."

"It will be interesting to see what kinds of issues are raised at the Conference," said Mr. Singh. "Will regional differences be a larger factor then, do you think?"

"I guess we'll see." said Ms Pozzi, as she stepped off the train.

Questions for Small Group Discussion

1. What interests were shared by the students on the train?
2. What are some of the challenges faced by the delegates on the train trip?
3. In what ways did students express their regional identities?

Questions for Class Discussion

1. What challenges do you think the students will have at the Youth Shaping Canada's Future Conference?
2. Between 1867 and 1905 Canada increased from four to nine provinces. Predict what challenges you think the new Dominion of Canada had between 1867 and 1905. (Record these on a chart for future reference.)

For Your Notebook

1. Examine the maps on the endsheets of the back cover of this textbook. Which regions added new provinces between 1867 and 1905?
2. Reread page 28 and/or your History notes on regionalism. Discuss the meaning of regionalism with a friend. Predict how you think regionalism will affect the new Dominion of Canada.
3. Make a title page for Section III: Challenges of the New Dominion.

Section III Focus

While all of the book's five concepts will be examined, the five chapters in Section III will focus on change, regionalism, and co-operation/conflict.

What challenges did we face as a new Dominion?

1.  How did Canada change? What challenges did change bring?

2. What needs and concerns did each region have? Did regionalism lead to conflict?

3. What part did co-operation play in moving Canada towards its goal of a country from sea to sea? How did conflict hinder Canada from its goal?

Section III Activity

 In the five chapters within Section III, *Challenges of the New Dominion (1867–1905)*, you will be applying A Model to Meet Challenges (page 145) for specific issues covered within each chapter.

Most of the information you will need is found within the chapter and in your History notes. Some issues will require additional research.

The Section III activity starts in Chapter 6.

Chapter 6
Manitoba Becomes a Province
1867–1870

O v e r v i e w
Use this Overview to predict what you will read in this chapter.

2 1860s

There were 30 000 to 40 000 First Nations people living in the area between the Great Lakes and the Rocky Mountains.

1 Provincial rights and minority rights became issues soon after Confederation. Nova Scotia threatened to withdraw from Confederation.

3 1860s

About 10 000 Metis lived in the Red River area.

5 1869

Rupert's Land was purchased from the HBC by the Canadian government and renamed the North-West Territories. The government sent surveyors to the Red River area in 1868 and 1869.

4 The Canadian government was interested in Rupert's Land because it wanted to expand from "sea to sea" and also needed more farmland. It did not want the area to be taken over by the United States. Prime Minister Macdonald wanted Rupert's Land to join Canada, but saw no reason to grant it provincial status.

6 1869–1870

Louis Riel became leader of the Metis. The Red River Resistance occurred.

7 1870

Manitoba became a province in the Dominion of Canada.

CONFEDERATION

Chapter 6 Focus

Chapter 5 described the union of the United Province of Canada, Nova Scotia, and New Brunswick to form the Dominion of Canada in 1867. In Section III (the next five chapters) you will explore the growth and development of the Canadian West. The focus will be on how different groups and individuals contributed to this development. Between 1867 and 1905, five more provinces became part of the Dominion of Canada. In this chapter you will read about how part of Rupert's Land became Canada's fifth province, Manitoba, in 1870. The concepts of change, regionalism, power, and conflict are the special focus for this chapter.

Change   Regionalism   Power   Identity   Conflict

Other Concepts and Main Topics

- provincial rights
- minority rights
- separate schools
- federal/provincial conflict
- separatist movement
- provisional government

- compromise
- annexation
- resistance
- Bill of Rights
- insubordination
- crown lands
- controversy

Learning How to Learn

 Critical Thinking

 Decision-making

 Cartoon Analysis

 Writing

Chapter Preview/Prediction

1. Examine the Overview on the previous page, the maps on this page, and the titles in this chapter. In pairs or small groups, use this information and what you already know about Canada's history to list at least five questions for which you would like to find answers as you study the chapter. These questions should be about major topics or ideas rather than specific details.

2. Examine the two maps on the right. What major change occurred in 1870?

The Growth of Canada, 1867–1870

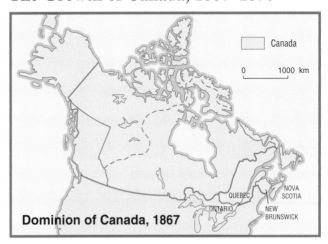

Dominion of Canada, 1867

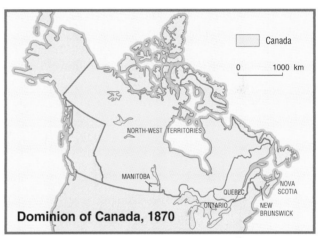

Dominion of Canada, 1870

Section III Activity

The goal of John A. Macdonald's government was to make the North-West Territories part of Canada as a step toward the goal of expanding the Dominion from sea to sea. In Chapter 6 you will be looking at the challenges involved in carrying this out.

Part One

Take the role of Prime Minister Macdonald and fill out ❶ of the chart A Model to Meet Challenges (page 145).

This activity is continued on page 160.

The Years After Confederation

Minority Rights

The British North America Act of 1867* protected French civil laws and the status of the English minority in Quebec, as well as the use of the French language in federal institutions. **Separate schools** in each province at the time of Confederation were to retain their rights.

Certain minority education rights for Catholics and for provinces were guaranteed in the BNA Act of 1867. The rights of other minorities in Canada were not. In most cases, minorities were expected to live by the will of the provincial or national majority. There would be an attempt to assimilate Aboriginal peoples into the dominant Canadian culture. They would be strongly encouraged to give up their customs, traditions, languages, and religions. They were expected to become like Canadians of British or French background.

Assimilation
Assimilation occurs when one culture is absorbed into another. In Canada in 1867 assimilation meant enforcing Canadian laws and encouraging acceptance of the majority culture by minority peoples.

The BNA Act of 1867 has only one direct reference to Aboriginal peoples: Section 91 (24) gives the Parliament of Canada exclusive authority over "Indians and lands reserved for the Indians." (The Inuit and Metis were not mentioned in the Act.) Aboriginal peoples did not have any input in the Confederation negotiations or in policies affecting them. Great Britain (and the United Province of Canada) had already

worked out its Aboriginal policy. When the new government of Canada had to make decisions regarding Aboriginal peoples, they adopted the policy already in effect:
- Lands of First Nations were to be acquired by treaty.
- The people were to be settled on reserves.
- A federal government department was to be created to manage how First Nations were to live. When treaties were completed, First Nations received reserves and services such as education and health care. Many First Nations believe that what they gave up was not matched by what they received.

Federal/Provincial Conflict

Provincial rights are powers held by the provincial governments. They usually involve cultural, social, and local matters. The Fathers of Confederation believed that the division of powers between federal and provincial governments would not be a cause of tension. However, provincial rights almost immediately became an issue in Atlantic Canada.

In Nova Scotia

Not everyone in the new Dominion of Canada wanted to celebrate on July 1, 1867. Most of the people in Nova Scotia were against Confederation. The July 1st *Halifax Morning Chronicle* newspaper appeared edged in black like an **obituary**. It declared that "the free and intelligent Province of Nova Scotia" had "died last night at twelve o'clock." In Yarmouth, Nova Scotia, pro-Confederation politicians were burned in **effigy**, along with a dead rat.

The anti-Confederation feeling in Nova Scotia became evident to the rest of Canada after the September elections of 1867. In the first federal election held in Nova Scotia, 18 anti-Confederation candidates and only one pro-Confederation candidate were elected. In the Nova Scotia provincial election held on the same day, the anti-Confederates won 36 of the 38 seats.

Separatist Movement

Following Canada's first federal election, the Nova Scotian members of Parliament were led by Joseph Howe. He was known for his opposition to Confederation. The Nova Scotians

---

*The British North America Act of 1867 was renamed the Constitution Act of 1867 when the BNA Act was transferred from Great Britain to Canada in 1982.
Separate schools—publicly funded schools intended for Roman Catholic students in provinces other than Quebec

---

Obituary—notice of a person's death
Effigy—an imitation of a person

presented a motion in the House of Commons in Ottawa. It stated that Nova Scotia should be released from Confederation. The motion was rejected by the powerful Conservative majority in the House of Commons.

In Nova Scotia, the public showed their discontent with Confederation. They wrote petitions, argued in the provincial Legislature, and contacted the British government. Howe and members of the Nova Scotian anti-Confederation group again went to London. They asked the British government to allow Nova Scotia to withdraw from Confederation. They were told that they would not be released. Any complaints about Confederation should be taken up with the government of Canada.

Some members of the anti-Confederation group began to talk of joining the United States. However, Howe and most of the group's members remained loyal to Britain.

Howe returned to Nova Scotia from London. He had decided to **compromise**. He wanted to "accept the situation, repair the mischief, and make the best of a bad business." Nova Scotia would stay in Confederation and try to arrange a better agreement with the Canadian government.

Prime Minister Macdonald was worried about the **separatist** movement in Nova Scotia. He decided to offer better terms to the province. The yearly grants from the federal government to the provinces were increased by $20 000. Macdonald also asked Howe to become a member of the federal Cabinet.

When Howe accepted the position of federal Cabinet minister, the anti-Confederation movement in Nova Scotia was left without a leader. The movement weakened and was no longer a threat to a united Canada.

In Ontario, Quebec, and New Brunswick

Most people in Ontario, Quebec, and New Brunswick seemed satisfied with Confederation. The Confederation agreements had passed with only a small majority among French members of the United Province of Canada Legislative Assembly. However, English-speaking members from Canada East had been overwhelmingly in favour of Confederation. So were members from Canada West. No strong anti-Confederation movements like the one in Nova Scotia arose in the other provinces.

Compromise—an agreement in which each side gives up some of its demands

Separatist—trying to withdraw from a political union and set up a separate state

Possibility of American Annexation

 The possibility that the United States might annex British Columbia and the North-West Territories continued to concern Great Britain and Canada. The threat of Manifest Destiny influenced Canada's political choices, such as the eventual decision to make Manitoba a province.

The political cartoon on this page appeared in the *Canadian Illustrated News* in June 1870. It shows Mother Britannia and Uncle Sam standing by the child Canada and marvelling that he can stand on his own. The Americans did not think that they would necessarily have to use force to establish control over British Columbia and the North-West. They thought that these areas might simply fall into their hands, in the same way that the baby in the cartoon could be expected to fall eventually.

MOTHER BRITANNIA.—*"See! Why, the dear child can stand alone!"*
UNCLE SAM.—*"Of course he can! Let go of him, Granny; if he falls I'll catch him!"*

For Your Notebook

1. What minority rights were guaranteed in the BNA Act of 1867?
2. Why was Nova Scotia dissatisfied with Confederation? Why were Ontario, Quebec, and New Brunswick relatively satisfied with Confederation?
3. Define: annexation, Manifest Destiny.
4. In the cartoon, whom do Mother Britannia and Uncle Sam represent?
5. Identify three challenges faced by the new Dominion of Canada in its first three years. How were these challenges met?

Inventions

In the years after Confederation, the greatest changes in technology occurred in the areas of communication and transportation. Steamship lines, railways, the telegraph, and the telephone were all signs of a shrinking world. The transatlantic telegraph cable was completed in July 1866. Vast changes in communication and transportation technology would come in the 20th century. They were just beginning at the time of Confederation.

Above: Completion of the Atlantic Telegraph Cable in July 1866. Over 2500 miles of cable were laid under the Atlantic Ocean between Ireland and Newfoundland. Sending a twenty-word message cost the equivalent of $100. In spite of the high cost, 2700 messages were sent by the end of September.

Left: 1876—The first long-distance phone call took place between Alexander Graham Bell in Brantford, Ontario, and his father, 12 kilometres away in Paris, Ontario. The call lasted for three hours, consisting mostly of singing. The first telephone exchange in the British Empire opened in Hamilton, Ontario, in July 1878.

Education

Education was a provincial responsibility under the BNA Act. School attendance was made **universal** and **compulsory** in Ontario in 1871, and in most other provinces by the 1890s.

School children and their teachers at a one-room school in Oxford County, Ontario. Teachers were usually young, unmarried women. Children of all ages attended such schools. The older children helped the younger.

Universal—for everyone
Compulsory—required

Work

At the time of Confederation most Canadian workers were employed in primary industries. Farming, forestry, fishing, and mining were still major industries. Farming was the largest sector of the economy in settled regions. Working conditions were generally poor and there was little job security.

This 1867 photograph shows women workers sorting ore at the Huntington copper mine near Bolton, Quebec.

Workers were often laid off or their wages were reduced in winter. There was no **employment insurance**. During times of unemployment people found it difficult to buy fuel and other things they needed. Distribution of firewood to the needy became an annual event.

Leisure Activities

The well-to-do middle-class and the wealthy of the 1860s and 1870s took part in leisure activities such as dancing and attending theatrical productions. Working class people worked very long hours. They did not often have time, energy, or money to spend on leisure pursuits.

People of every class enjoyed outdoor activities of all kinds, winter and summer, when time was available. In the winter, ice-skating, tobogganing, and sleigh rides were popular activities. In the summer people enjoyed picnics and games such as croquet.

Above: Organized hockey began in Montreal in 1875.

Left: Ice-skating was a popular winter activity.

Employment insurance—money given by the government to people who have lost their jobs

153

Rupert's Land

The vast 7 770 000-square-kilometre area known as Rupert's Land lay to the north and west of the Dominion of Canada. This area had been under the control of the Hudson's Bay Company for 200 years. Eventually the area to the north and west also came to be called "the North-West" or the North-West Territories. However, it was still technically "Rupert's Land."

First Nations

The peoples living in Rupert's Land were spread over a huge area. First Nations lived mainly as hunters. They also trapped, fished, and gathered products from the environment. The Dene, Anishinabe (Ojibwa), Cree, Tsuu T'ina (Sarcee), Nakota (Assiniboine), and Siksika had large populations in Rupert's Land. (See maps pages 56 and 58.)

Population

In 1870, there were 30 000 to 40 000 First Nations people living in the area between the Great Lakes and the Rocky Mountains. Because an accurate census was not taken, these figures are approximate. Metis people, other fur trade employees, and Red River settlers also lived in the area.

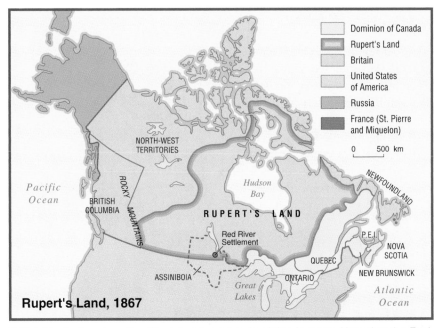

Rupert's Land, 1867

British North America after Canada became a dominion in 1867. Note that the Red River Settlement and Assiniboia (the land granted to Lord Selkirk) were located within Rupert's Land, the land controlled by the Hudson's Bay Company.

A Metis hunter

The above photograph shows Cree people in the North-West Territories.

Below: The Hudson's Bay Company built Fort Garry in 1835 at the junction of the Red River and the Assiniboine River to provide a base for governing Assiniboia. This painting of Fort Garry was done by Ernest J. Hutchins in 1872.

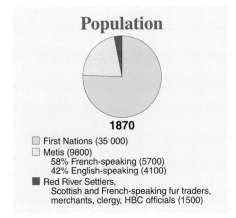

Population

1870

☐ First Nations (35 000)
☐ Metis (9800)
   58% French-speaking (5700)
   42% English-speaking (4100)
■ Red River Settlers,
   Scottish and French-speaking fur traders,
   merchants, clergy, HBC officials (1500)

154

The Red River Settlement, 1869

The Metis of the Red River Settlement were farmers, Hudson's Bay Company employees, and self-employed fur traders and trappers.

Over half of the Metis at the Red River area were descendants of people who had come from Quebec. Many had ties with family still living there. French was the main language of the settlement. Most of the missionaries were from Quebec. The French Metis and Scottish Metis people of the Red River Settlement had developed a distinct culture and identity over the years. They had little contact with the people of Ontario. The non-Metis people were either Roman Catholic missionaries, Scottish farmers, Hudson's Bay Company employees, or English-speaking Protestants from Ontario or the United States. Some of them were merchants and **land speculators**.

Metis hunters and traders photographed on the plains by the Boundary Commission in the early 1870s

The Red River Settlement did not have the status of a separate colony. It was governed by a governor and a council appointed by the Hudson's Bay Company.

Fort Garry was located at the present-day site of Winnipeg. It was built in 1835 to serve as the main Hudson's Bay Company post in the region, and became the centre of government.

The paddlewheeler *Dakota* on the Red River at Fort Garry

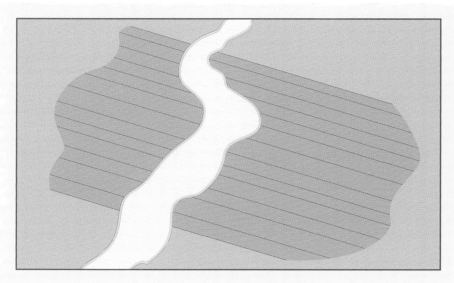

River Lot Farms

Settlers at Red River built farms along the riverbanks. Long, narrow lots ran back from the water after the style used in Quebec. Most farmers did not hold land titles to their land, which was unsurveyed. They had simply settled down and begun working them. This kind of ownership was recognized as valid by the community.

Land speculator—someone who buys land intending to sell it and make a quick profit, rather than live on it

Canada's Interest in Rupert's Land

 The government of Canada was interested in Rupert's Land for several reasons. There was very little good farmland left to settle in Ontario. People who wanted to be farmers were starting to look farther west. The Canadian government's goal was to expand Canada from the Atlantic Ocean to the Pacific Ocean. This was part of John A. Macdonald's Conservative government's policy of *A Mari usque ad Mare*—"From Sea to Sea." For the government to achieve that goal, the North-West Territories would have to become part of Canada.

The Canadian government felt that if they did not move quickly and take over Rupert's Land, the Americans would. Some American settlers had already moved into the area. The state of Minnesota (south of the Red River Settlement) had a population of 300 000 by 1865. Trade between the Red River Settlement and St. Paul, the capital of Minnesota, was already established.

This cartoon appeared in the *Canadian Illustrated News* on January 29, 1870. What are the choices facing the Red River Settlement? What impression of the Red River Settlement does the cartoonist present to the viewer?

Sale of Rupert's Land, 1868

The government of Canada decided to buy Rupert's Land from the Hudson's Bay Company. The Hudson's Bay Company would keep its fur forts and some large land grants amounting to about 1/20 of the total land area or about three million hectares. It would also receive $1 500 000 for Rupert's Land.

In 1868, the British government approved the terms of this sale and arranged for the transfer of the land to the government of Canada. The transfer was to take place on December 1, 1869. After gaining control of the area, the Canadian government named it the North-West Territories. At this time they did not plan to make any part of the area into a province.

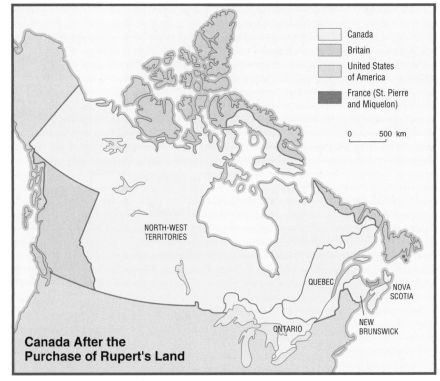

Canada After the Purchase of Rupert's Land

In 1869, Rupert's Land, the land on which the Hudson's Bay Company held the fur-trade monopoly, was transferred to the government of Canada.

An Exercise in Critical Thinking

Points of View

In the fall of 1869, several different groups were involved in the Canadian government's proposed takeover of Rupert's Land. The following are some points of view on the issue.

The Canadian Government

The settlement of the North-West was necessary to fulfil Cartier and Macdonald's dream of a Canada that stretched from sea to sea. The government saw the North-West as a place for new settlers to go. Good Ontario farmland was mostly settled. They were also concerned about a possible American takeover of the area. The people of the North-West were not consulted in the decision to make the area part of Canada. Macdonald assumed that they would go along with the union of the North-West and Canada. He did not think there was any need to grant the North-West provincial status. He felt that Ottawa should initially govern the area like a colony.

The British Government

The British government had approved the sale of the Hudson's Bay Company lands to the Dominion of Canada in 1869. The British felt it was now Canada's responsibility to govern Rupert's Land.

Hudson's Bay Company

William Mactavish was governor of the Hudson's Bay Company at Fort Garry. He felt that the authority of the Hudson's Bay Company over Rupert's Land had ended, since the transfer to Canada was to take place on December 1, 1869.

(The fact that the governor was unwell may have been part of the reason he did not want to become involved in the events in the Red River Settlement at this time.)

Settlers

A group of people at Red River were urging the Canadian government to make the Red River Settlement a province of Canada. They were known as the Canada Party. Many of the English-speaking Protestants from Ontario belonged to the Canada Party, which was led by Dr. John Christian Schultz. Schultz owned a store in the Red River Settlement and published a newspaper. Members of the Canada Party wanted the English-speaking Protestants from Ontario to govern the area. Schultz campaigned for the Canada Party in his newspaper, *The Nor'Wester*, promoting union with Canada. The settlers were bitterly disappointed that Rupert's Land would not have an elected government when it was taken over by Canada. They hoped that this would be temporary.

Metis

The Metis were uncertain about the Canadian government's plans for their homeland. They were concerned that the English-speaking newcomers might take over their lands. The Roman Catholic French-speaking Metis also wanted their culture to be respected, especially religious and language rights. All of the Metis were angry that their opinions were not sought in regard to union with Canada.

For Your Notebook

1. Explain why the Canadian government wanted to gain control of Rupert's Land.
2. Why did the Metis people feel threatened by the action of the Canadian government regarding Rupert's Land?
3. Identify the issue debated on this page. Relate it to the Canadian government's purchase of Rupert's Land.
4. With which point of view would you have agreed? Give reasons for your answer.
5. Why is it important to look at an issue from various points of view?
6. Predict some problems that may have resulted because of the points of view expressed here.

Red River Resistance

Government Surveyors

 The Canadian government decided to begin surveying for roads and boundaries for townships before the official transfer of Rupert's Land on December 1, 1869. A survey crew was sent to the Red River area in the autumn of 1868. A second crew arrived in the summer of 1869. The surveyors began dividing the land into large squares similar to the block system used by the people in Ontario.

The people of the Red River Settlement, both the settlers and the Metis, were surprised to see the surveyors. No one from Ottawa had been sent out to inform them of the government's plans.

The Metis decided to stop the surveying by taking away the chains that were being used by the surveyors for measuring. The surveyors gave up and left.

The government of Canada decided to appoint William McDougall as lieutenant-governor of the North-West Territories. This also angered the Metis of Red River. McDougall was known as a federal minister who strongly favoured the westward expansion of Canada. McDougall had been responsible for sending the road and land surveyors.

Louis Riel

 At this time Louis Riel emerged as a leader of the Metis. Riel was well educated. He had been born in the Red River Settlement, but was sent to Montreal to study for the priesthood. He was a persuasive speaker who was fluent in both French and English. Oscar Malmros, an American consul at Red River, described Riel:

> . . . ambitious, quick of perception, though not profound, of indomitable energy, daring, excessively suspicious of others and of a pleasing and rather dignified address [speech].

Riel helped to set up *Le Comité National des Métis* (the Metis National Committee). He was the secretary and John Bruce the president. The purpose of the committee was to determine the future of the Metis people and to negotiate with the Canadian government on their behalf.

Riel and the National Metis Committee, 1869. Riel is third from the left, in the centre row.

William McDougall

One of the first acts of the Metis National Committee was to stop the newly appointed lieutenant-governor, William McDougall, from entering the Red River Settlement. On November 2, 1869, McDougall's way was blocked by 14 armed Metis when he tried to enter the settlement. They gave him a message from the Metis National Committee telling him not to enter until he had permission from the inhabitants. The Metis wanted to negotiate their status before allowing the Canadian government to officially take over. In fact, Prime Minister Macdonald had sent McDougall instructions not to officially take over Rupert's Land until he was told to do so. McDougall, however, was not aware of Macdonald's instructions because he had not yet received them.*

Upper Fort Garry Seized

On the same day, the Metis National Committee seized Upper Fort Garry (the headquarters of the Hudson's Bay Company in Red River) without firing a shot. The fort contained cannons, guns, and enough pemmican to feed a large group for the winter. The approaching winter would prevent outside military forces from reaching the settlement for at least six months. These two factors meant that the Metis were able to negotiate from a position of military strength.

Provisional Government

It was important for all groups in the Red River Settlement to present a united front to the Canadian government. On November 16 at Fort Garry, Riel met with a convention of 12 French-speaking and 12 English-speaking representatives from the Red River Settlement. They discussed the possibility of forming a provisional government. A provisional government is a temporary government set up until a more permanent one can be established. At this time Riel had the support of the majority of both English-speaking and French-speaking people in the community.

Macdonald did not want the Red River Settlement to become part of Canada until calm had been restored. The Hudson's Bay Company officials did not want to step in because they were no longer in authority. As a result, there was no official government in the North-West. McDougall waited until December 1, 1869, the day that Rupert's Land was to be officially transferred to the Canadian government. On that day he crossed the border, read his proclamation claiming Rupert's Land for Canada, and then left again.

The Canada Party wanted English-speakers of European ancestry to control Red River. On December 7, Riel and his Metis followers surrounded the store owned by Dr. John Schultz, leader of the Canada Party. The Metis claimed the large supply of government pork stored there. They put the 50 people who had been guarding the store and its contents into the cells at Fort Garry. On December 8, Riel and his followers set up a provisional government. Their government's goal was to maintain order in the colony during this transition period and to determine the future of union with Canada. The provisional government drew up a **Metis Bill of Rights**. They asked the convention of 12 English-speaking and 12 French-speaking representatives to examine it.

Exercises in Critical Thinking

1. Were the Metis justified in seizing Fort Garry? Write two paragraphs—one describing the event from the Metis point of view, and one describing the event from the Canadian government's point of view.

2. Work in groups to write a list of the rights and responsibilities you think teenagers attending school should have. Each group records its list on chart paper, and one student in the group reads it to the rest of the class. As a class, make a list of the 10 most important rights. (You may want to send a student council delegation to discuss the list with your school's principal. He or she may be able to point out implications that you may not have considered.)

3. In groups, brainstorm to predict what you think the Metis would have listed in their Bill of Rights regarding their conditions for joining with Canada.

---

*Many historians believe McDougall used poor judgement in attempting to enter the North-West before it had officially become part of Canada. His reputation suffered as a result of his actions.

Metis Bill of Rights—a list of conditions that the Metis demanded the Canadian government recognize and abide by

The Bill of Rights

In mid-December of 1869, Lieutenant-Governor McDougall gave up and went back to Canada. In late December, Prime Minister Macdonald sent Donald Smith, a senior officer of the HBC, to speak to the people of Red River. Smith had two jobs. One was to explain to the Metis the Canadian government's plans for the Red River. The other was to find out and report back on the Metis concerns.

Riel was forced to let Smith speak to the people. In spite of the cold, over 1000 people, mainly Metis, attended an outdoor meeting at Fort Garry. Smith told them about the establishment of a territorial council. He also said that Canada would acknowledge land titles. Riel then formed a convention of 40 English-speaking and French-speaking people from the community. They drew up a revised Bill of Rights. Finally, the executive of the provisional government created a third version. Three members of the community, an English-speaking judge, a French-speaking Roman Catholic priest, and an English-speaking saloonkeeper, then travelled to Ottawa, taking this revised Bill of Rights with them.

When in Ottawa, the members also demanded two publicly funded school systems—Roman Catholic and Protestant. It is not known if the executive had approved this demand.

The Metis Bill of Rights included these items

- that the territories of Rupert's Land and the North-West enter the Dominion of Canada as a province
- the right to elect their own Legislative Assembly, with the power to pass all local laws
- the right to approve or reject any federal government laws affecting the Red River area
- the right to elect local officials such as sheriffs and constables
- the right to have land set aside for schools, roads, and public buildings
- the right to have Fort Garry connected by railway to Lake Superior
- that the federal government pay all expenses involved in governing the new province for the first four years
- that any military forces stationed in the Red River area be made up of Red River residents
- that treaties be signed between the federal government and First Nations in the area
- that both French and English be used in the provincial legislature and courts, and in all provincial government documents and acts
- that every male householder aged 21 or over be entitled to vote
- that all existing customs, rights, and privileges remain after joining Canada
- that **amnesty** be granted for actions occurring during the Resistance

An Exercise in Decision-Making

1. a) Divide into small groups. Each group takes three or four different items from the list shown above right. Groups analyse each item from the point of view of the Canadian government, then accept or discard it. Discuss each item until consensus is reached about whether it should be accepted or discarded.

   b) As a class compile a list of the items each group discarded. Compare the list to the Bill of Rights. Discuss why the Metis and the Canadian government would have different ideas about the rights of the people of Assiniboia. Explain your small group's reasons for accepting or discarding items.

Exploring Further

1. If you were a Metis living in Red River at this time, would you have added any other points to the Bill of Rights? If yes, what would you add and why? If no, why not?

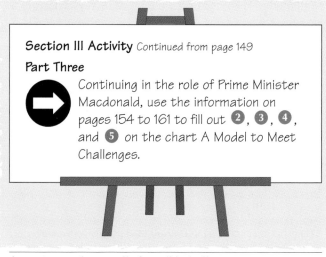

Section III Activity Continued from page 149

Part Three

Continuing in the role of Prime Minister Macdonald, use the information on pages 154 to 161 to fill out ❷, ❸, ❹, and ❺ on the chart A Model to Meet Challenges.

Amnesty—pardon, usually for political offences

Thomas Scott

 Thomas Scott was a 28-year-old labourer from Ontario. Upon arriving in Red River he joined "the Canadians." These English-speaking Protestants were working to make the North-West part of Canada. They believed that English Protestants should control the North-West. They were not interested in the rights of the Metis.

When the Metis took over Fort Garry on November 2, 1869, they put some members of the Canada Party, including Thomas Scott, in jail. While in jail Scott insulted and attacked the guards. He also threatened to escape and kill Louis Riel. In January, he and two other prisoners did escape from the fort. They were recaptured in March. At that time Scott continued to show his contempt for the Metis. He was tried for insubordination—disobedience to a lawful authority. He was convicted and sentenced to death. Scott was executed by a Metis firing squad on March 4, 1870.

The execution of Thomas Scott caused many of the English-speaking people in the settlement to withdraw their support from Riel. Many people in Quebec and Ontario also reacted strongly to the execution. Many English-speaking Ontario Protestants called Riel a murderer. They demanded that Prime Minister Macdonald send an army to the Red River Settlement to capture Riel and bring him to Canada for punishment. They also thought the army might be needed to protect supporters of the Canada Party in the Red River area and to restore order.

Many French-speaking Roman Catholics in Quebec saw Riel as a man who stood up for French rights. They were alarmed at the anti-Catholic and anti-French reaction in Ontario.

The reaction to the execution of Thomas Scott put the Conservative government of Sir John A. Macdonald in Ottawa in a difficult position. The Conservative government did not want to lose the support of either Quebec or Ontario, but it was very difficult to keep the majority of people in both provinces happy.

The Manitoba Act, 1870

 After several months of consideration, the Canadian government agreed that the area surrounding the Red River Settlement should become a province. The government had originally planned to leave it as a territory. A province had much greater control over its own affairs than did a territory. That is why the Metis were negotiating to be a province.

On July 15, 1870, the Manitoba Act went into effect. Through this act Canada's fifth province, Manitoba, came into being. Manitoba was known as the "postage stamp" province. It was much smaller than it is today, only 224 kilometres wide and 176 kilometres long. The rest of Rupert's Land continued to be part of the North-West Territories.

Many of the points from the Metis Bill of Rights became part of the Manitoba Act. For instance, French and English were both to be official languages. There would be two publicly funded school systems—Roman Catholic and Protestant. However, the federal government retained control of **crown lands** and natural resources. The government did not pardon the Metis for their actions during the Red River Resistance, as requested in the Bill of Rights.

Canada
Britain
United States of America
France (St. Pierre and Miquelon)

0   500 km

NORTH-WEST TERRITORIES

MANITOBA

QUEBEC

ONTARIO

NOVA SCOTIA

NEW BRUNSWICK

Dominion of Canada, 1870

In 1870, Manitoba became the fifth province in the Dominion of Canada.

Crown lands—lands belonging to the government. When the BNA Act was passed, Crown lands in the first four provinces were transferred to the provinces.

Wolseley in Red River

Prime Minister Macdonald decided to send troops to the Red River Settlement. He was concerned about the continued unrest in the area. People in Ontario were demanding punishment for those who were considered rebels and murderers. Macdonald wanted to satisfy their demands. Finally, he wanted to send a message to the Americans that Canada had control over the area.

An expedition under Colonel Wolseley was dispatched and arrived in Red River on August 23, 1870. Angry at not finding Riel, some of Wolseley's troops attacked two of Riel's followers, Elzear Goulet and André Nault. Goulet, a member of Thomas Scott's firing squad, drowned while trying to escape. Nault, Riel's uncle, was badly beaten. Fearing for his life, Riel fled to the United States. (This was not the end of Louis Riel's role in the history of Canada. You will read about his return to the North-West in 1884 in Chapter 9.)

For Your Notebook

1. What was the result of Scott's execution?
2. Why did Prime Minister Macdonald send troops to Manitoba?

The Red River Expedition, 1870. Colonel Garnet Wolseley led 1200 men on the difficult journey from Toronto to Fort Garry.

Louis Riel
1844–1885

Louis David Riel was born at Red River on October 22, 1844. He was the eldest of Louis Riel and Julie Lagemodière's eleven children. Louis Riel's father was a leader of the Metis. He helped to lead the protest against the Hudson's Bay Company's monopoly on trade in the 1840s. Riel's mother was the daughter of the first European woman to come from Canada to the North-West.

In 1858, Bishop Taché sent Louis Riel to Montreal to study for the priesthood. In 1865, having decided that the priesthood was not for him, Riel left school. He studied in a law office for a short time before moving back west.

By the summer of 1868 Riel was back in the Red River Settlement. There, his fluency in both French and English, his education, and his pride in the Metis people made him a natural leader. Riel is known as the Father of Manitoba because of his work to make Manitoba a province of Canada in 1869 and 1870.

During the Red River Resistance of 1869–1870, Riel and his followers executed Thomas Scott, a Canadian who opposed them. Riel fled to the United States following the events of 1870. He returned to Red River and was twice elected Member of Parliament. However, when he travelled to Ottawa, he was unable to take his parliamentary seat because the Ontario government had offered a $5000 award for the arrest and conviction of Thomas Scott's "murderers." In 1875 he was granted an amnesty if he stayed out of Canada for an additional five years. He spent two years secretly receiving treatment in mental institutions in Quebec. Following his release from hospital in 1878, he took a teaching position at a Jesuit mission in Montana. There he married and had two children.

In 1884, Riel returned to Canada to champion Metis rights once again, this time in what is now Saskatchewan. For his part in the 1885 Resistance, Riel was hanged. His sentence remains controversial to this day.

An Exercise in Decision-Making

Should Louis Riel be considered a Father of Confederation?

Points of View

Louis Riel was the head of the provisional government that the Metis set up in Red River in 1870. This government negotiated with Ottawa the terms under which Manitoba became a province. Because of this, some people think Louis Riel should be considered a Father of Confederation. The following are some points of view on the issue.

1 "The Hudson's Bay Company had no right to transfer our land to Canada without our consent. Riel led a temporary government to maintain law and order and to negotiate terms with Canada that we could accept."

2 "We had little information about the negotiations between the HBC and Canada. Canada sent road and land surveyors as if they already controlled the settlement. Would Canada respect our property rights? How would our economy and way of life be affected by annexation to Canada?"

3 "Riel's actions made sure our concerns were heard in Ottawa. Because we prevented McDougall from taking control, we ensured that the Red River settlement entered Confederation as a province under terms accepted by its people."

4 "The Metis people should have governed the new province of Manitoba. The execution of Thomas Scott, and, later, of Louis Riel, left the reputation of Metis as community leaders under a shadow. They suffered as a people for over a century. Metis identity had to be rebuilt and reclaimed in the twentieth century because of that shadow."

5 "The administration by the Hudson's Bay Company collapsed because of the illegal, revolutionary action of Riel and his supporters. This affected the settlement's means of support and survival as well as leaving it without government."

6 "McDougall should have been allowed to enter the territory. He would have made Canada's intentions clear. Negotiations to protect the interests of all parties at Red River could then have taken place. There was no need for Riel to take matters into his own hands or use physical force. Who gave him the right to arrest people or to declare a provisional government? He acted outside the law."

7 "Even without Riel or the uprising, the Red River settlement would have been made into a province eventually. Because of Riel's actions, some eastern Canadians became suspicious of the loyalty and political intentions of Metis and western First Nations people."

For Your Notebook

1. Identify the issue debated on this page.
2. With which points of view do you agree? Give reasons for your answer.
3. Why is it important to look at an issue from various points of view?
4. Write a paragraph giving your position. Support your position with reasons.

Review

The icons are your cue to refer to the Learning How to Learn Appendix (pages 348–371) for ideas on how to complete these activities.

 This icon is a reminder to turn to the Research Model (pages x–xi).

1. Complete a self-assessment for one assignment from this chapter.

Understanding Concepts

2. Provide answers to the five questions you wrote for the Chapter Preview/Prediction on page 149.

3. a) Here are some main concepts and ideas from the chapter. Enter definitions for any unfamiliar words in your WordBook.
   - minority rights
   - separate schools
   - federal/provincial conflict
   - separatist movement
   - compromise
   - annexation
   - Red River Resistance
   - bill of rights
   - provisional government
   - insubordination
   - crown lands
   - controversy

   Do either b) or c).

   b) Create a concept poster for one of these concepts or ideas. Present it to the class.

   c) Use a web, mind map, or chart to create a permanent set of notes about one of these concepts or ideas. Explain your work to a classmate.

4. Add entries for this chapter to your timeline.

5. Organize your notes. Compare your notebook to that of a partner. Check to see that items are not missing and are in the correct order.

Developing Research Skills

6.

Section III Activity
Continued from page 160

 Now that you have studied this chapter, consider what challenges the new Dominion of Canada faced under the leadership of John A. Macdonald. List these in your History Notes. In role as Prime Minister Macdonald, fill in part on the chart A Model to Meet Challenges that you started on page 149.

Part Three

As a class discuss

a) the challenges faced by Prime Minister Macdonald and how they were met

b) whether we would solve these challenges in the same way today.

7.  Research and write a position paper on the following topic:

Should the events in Red River in 1869 and 1870 be classified as a rebellion?

Some historians have called the events in Red River in 1869 and 1870 the Red River Rebellion or the First Riel Rebellion. The term rebellion is used when people attempt to overthrow a government that is legally in power. However, some historians raise the question as to whether there was a government in power in Red River.

The government of Canada would not take control of Red River until December 1, 1869. When Prime Minister Macdonald heard about the troubles there he told Lieutenant-Governor McDougall not to enter the area until the problems were resolved. The Hudson's Bay Company considered its authority to have ended, since the agreement to transfer Rupert's Land had already been signed. (See Essay Writing on page 358 in the Appendix for information about writing a position paper.)

Developing Communication Skills

Do number 8 and then select one from numbers 9 to 15:

Writing

8. In Chapter 5 you created a Confederation newspaper for Ontario, Quebec, New Brunswick, or Nova Scotia. Create a Confederation newspaper for Manitoba. See page 137 for ideas on how to do this.

9. a) Imagine that you are John A. Macdonald. Write a series of diary entries in which you provide information about the following. You may wish to illustrate each entry with pictures and maps.
   - events in the Red River settlement from 1869 leading up to the Manitoba Act, 1870
   - deciding whether you should send troops to the Red River Settlement

   b) Write about the same events as in 9a) but write the diary entry from the point of view of Louis Riel.

10. a) Take the point of view of a Metis farmer living in the Red River area in 1869. Describe your thoughts as you see the surveyors walking over your land.

    b) Create a column written by Dr. Schultz in his newspaper, *The Nor'Wester*, promoting the union of the Red River Settlement with the rest of Canada.

11. Select any person in this chapter, and compose five questions and answers to demonstrate his or her special contributions to Canada.

12. In your opinion, what is the most memorable event from this chapter? Explain why.

Listening and Speaking

13. Select any significant incident or character in this chapter. Dramatically re-create the incident or something the character said or did. You will need to do research for additional facts to enhance your re-creation.

14. Research an invention or an organized sport that was introduced in the 1860s or 1870s. Prepare a presentation using visuals.

15. Hold a debate between Joseph Howe and Sir John A. Macdonald on the subject of Nova Scotia's withdrawal from Confederation (see page 150, Federal/Provincial Conflict). Debates are explained in the Appendix on page 354.

Applying Concepts

16. This chapter discusses a separatist movement in the province of Nova Scotia after Confederation in 1867 (see pages 150 and 151). Watch the newspapers and other media for information about the separatist movement in Quebec today. Draw imaginary people and write statements that could depict a conversation between someone who is a separatist and someone who is against the Quebec separatist movement.

Challenge Plus

17. a) What challenges did the new Dominion of Canada face in the first three years?

    b) What was the result of these challenges?

    c) Were these challenges a serious concern regarding Canadian unity? Give reasons for your answer.

18. 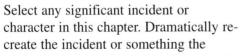 One of the goals of the Metis living in the Red River Settlement was to keep their culture and identity. Use the chart A Model to Meet Challenges (on page 145) to organize the events on pages 154 to 163. Fill out the chart from the point of view of the Metis people.

Chapter 7
From Sea to Sea
1871–1873

O v e r v i e w

Use this Overview to predict what you will read in this chapter.

1 **1871**

Prime Minister John A. Macdonald negotiated the Treaty of Washington as a British rather than a Canadian representative. The treaty allowed free navigation of American vessels in the St. Lawrence. The USA also purchased 10 years of fishing rights.

Treaty of Washington

2 By the late 1860s the gold rush in the colony of British Columbia was almost over. Other industries included lumbering, the fur trade, farming, ranching, and fishing.

3 Heavily in debt, the colony of British Columbia considered the advantages of
- joining with the Dominion of Canada, or
- joining the United States, or
- remaining a British colony.

4 **1871**

With the promise of a transcontinental railway, British Columbia became the sixth province in the Dominion of Canada.

5 **1873**

Prince Edward Island became the seventh province in the Dominion of Canada.

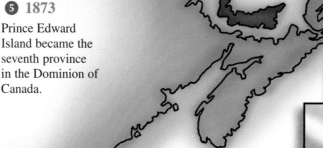

Deed
$

Chapter 7 Focus

In 1867 the new Dominion of Canada contained only four provinces: Ontario, Quebec, Nova Scotia, and New Brunswick. Between 1867 and 1905, the Dominion of Canada added five new provinces. You studied about Manitoba becoming a province in the last chapter. Chapter 7 provides the history of British Columbia and Prince Edward Island joining the Dominion of Canada. While all the book's concepts will be examined, the focus in this chapter is on concepts of change, regionalism, identity, and co-operation.

Change   Regionalism   Power   Identity   Co-operation

Other Concepts and Main Topics

- fishing rights
- commission
- political necessity
- economic necessity
- annexation
- petition
- negotiation
- westward expansion
- tenant farmers
- absentee landlords
- industrialization

Learning How to Learn

 Decision-making

 Critical Thinking

 Writing

 Cause and Effect

Chapter Preview/Prediction

1. a) Examine the Overview on the previous page, the maps on this page, and the titles in this chapter. In pairs or small groups, use this information and what you already know about Canada's history to make a web or mind map of the chapter.

   b) Examine the two maps on page 149 and the two above right. What major differences are shown in 1871 and in 1873?

The Growth of Canada, 1867–1873

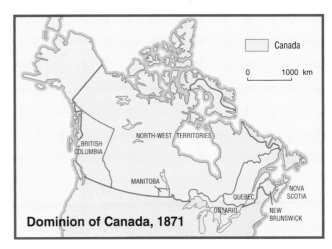

Dominion of Canada, 1871

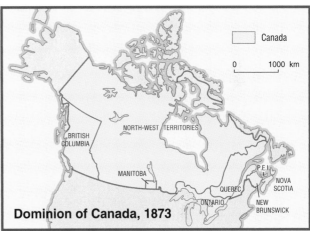

Dominion of Canada, 1873

Section III Activity

 The goal of John A. Macdonald's government was to expand the Dominion from sea to sea. In Chapter 7 you will be carrying out an activity similar to the one you did in the last chapter.

Part One

 Assume the role of Prime Minister Macdonald to examine the process by which British Columbia became a province. Fill out ❶ of the chart A Model to Meet Challenges (page 145).

This activity is continued on page 175 and 181.

Canadian–American Issues

Political issues between Great Britain and the United States affected Canada. During the American Civil War (1861–1865), Britain was suspected of supporting the Confederate (Southern) states. After the Union (Northern) victory, there was tension between the United States and Britain. This affected Britain's colony, Canada. In 1871, four years after Confederation, the United States still posed a threat to Canada. Prime Minister Sir John A. Macdonald knew that if the Americans ever decided to invade, Canada would not be able to defend its borders. The British had sent their troops back to Britain, except for some who were stationed in Halifax.

The problem came to a head over American fishing rights in Canadian waters. Canada charged a licence fee for this right, but Americans refused to pay it. To enforce the rule, British ships seized about 400 American ships fishing illegally in Canadian waters. As Lady Macdonald put it in her journal: "I think this American fishery question bothers Sir John. I suppose it is ticklish business as Brother Sam may show fight."

A second issue involved damage inflicted on Northern ports by Confederate ships during the American Civil War. The Americans demanded payment to compensate them for the damage because some Confederate ships had been built in British ports.

Other issues between Canada and the United States were navigation of the St. Lawrence River, some unsettled boundary disputes, and Canadian claims that the Americans should compensate them for Fenian raids.

Treaty of Washington, 1871

A British–American **commission** was established to deal with these issues and improve relations between Great Britain and the United States. Prime Minister Macdonald was invited to be one of the three British delegates. He went to Washington for meetings. After the Treaty of Washington, both sides agreed to

- allow American ships to navigate the St. Lawrence River
- allow fish from Canada to enter American markets without tariffs being paid
- allow American fishery vessels in Canadian Atlantic fisheries for ten years after payment of a lump sum to Canada

- pay $15.5 million for damages during the Civil War
- settle boundary disputes under terms of the treaty. For example, San Juan Islands, between Vancouver Island and the United States, became American.

A later commission awarded Canada $5.5 million for extended American fishing rights. The Americans refused to discuss Canadian claims to be paid for damage caused by the Fenian raids. Eventually the British compensated Canada for these raids.

Significance

The Treaty of Washington marked the first time that a politician from one of the colonies (John A. Macdonald) was included in a British delegation to negotiate an international treaty. This was a step forward, but Canada was still not recognized as an independent nation. Canada was a member of the British Empire; therefore, Great Britain negotiated on Canada's behalf.* Canadian Prime Minister Macdonald went as a British, not a Canadian, representative.

For Your Notebook

1. Who were Lady Macdonald and Brother Sam? What does the statement "Brother Sam may show fight" mean? What were the Fenian raids?

2. a) What issues involving the Americans did Canada face in the early 1870s?
   b) Select one of these issues and make a chart to show the points of view of the Canadians, British, and Americans.

Issue	
Individuals/ Groups Involved	Goals (What they wanted)
Decision	

3. Why couldn't Prime Minister Macdonald make his own decisions on foreign matters relating to Canada? Why were final decisions made by Great Britain?

4. Why is the identity icon an appropriate one to show on this page?

Commission—a group of people given specific tasks to perform or issues to consider; usually government-appointed

*Canada was granted formal independence from Great Britain in the Statute of Westminster, 1931.

In the Colony of British Columbia

By the end of the 1860s, the British Columbia economy was in a slump. The amount of gold being mined had declined and many of the miners had left the colony. When the miners left, so did the market for products such as beef, salmon, lumber for homes and stores, and services such as shipping. To succeed, it was thought by the colony's leaders that British Columbia needed a larger permanent population. Farmers were needed because agriculture would support the colony while industry developed. People in the colony of British Columbia began to consider the economic advantages that could be gained by joining Canada or the United States.

Industries

Exports from Colony of British Columbia

- ☐ Gold (75%)   ☐ Lumber (10%)
- ■ Fur (10%)   ■ Other (5%)

Gold mining, fur trading, lumbering, fishing, ranching, and farming were the main industries in British Columbia.

late 1860s

Trees of this size were common in the early years of logging.

Gold Mining

Although the amount of gold being found was less, gold still accounted for 75 percent of British Columbia's exports at this time. (You read about the importance of gold to the British Columbia economy on pages 41 to 46.)

Fur Trading

The importance of the fur trade had also declined in British Columbia. In fact, by the beginning of the gold rush in 1858, the fur trade had depleted the fur-bearing animal populations in many areas. The sea otter was nearly extinct. The marten population had dwindled alarmingly. By this time, hunters and trappers were operating primarily in the northern interior part of the province. In the central and southern parts of the province, other industries such as lumbering and mining had become more important.

Lumbering

At the time of British Columbia's entry into Confederation in 1871, lumbering was still in its infancy as an industry. Few could have predicted that it would be the most important industry in the province during much of the twentieth century. The first sawmill had opened near Fort Victoria in 1848. It exported sawn timber to San Francisco to meet the demand created by the California gold rush. In the late 1860s two large mills had been built on Burrard Inlet. These mills had been immediately successful. There was a demand for wood for building materials in the colony itself. The state of California was also a ready market for cedar used in the making of shakes and shingles.

The first sawmill on Vancouver Island was built at Victoria in 1848. By 1849 logging operations like this one were providing logs for the mills to saw and export to San Francisco.

Fishing

The fishing industry in the 1860s and 1870s was based on salmon. Salmon had been an important food for First Nations people in British Columbia long before the arrival of Europeans. It was also an important part of the diet of early European fur traders. It was supplied by the Sto:lo and dried at Fort Langley, a fur fort on the Fraser River, and sent to other Hudson's Bay Company posts, as well as to the gold-mining centres and to Hawaii.

British Columbia's fishing industry became more important to the economy after the invention of canning in the late 1860s. Canning made it possible to export food products over greater distances. In 1877, 55 000 cases of salmon were exported from British Columbia, most going to Great Britain. Canneries operated on a seasonal basis, for about two months of each year. Many of the cannery workers were of Chinese or First Nations ancestry.

Ranching and Farming

Some of the cowboys in the Okanagan were from First Nations.

Dairy and mixed farming were found in British Columbia in the late 1860s and 1870s. These farms were located in the lower Fraser Valley and the southern end of Vancouver Island. They provided food for the main settlements.

More than 7000 cattle were imported from the United States between 1860 and 1864. Beef from ranches in the Okanagan and Cariboo regions was sent to Barkerville to feed the miners. Later it was needed to feed the men building the Canadian Pacific Railway.

Until the late 1880s land could be had in the interior of the province for $1 for 0.4 hectare (one acre). Grazing land could be leased at an annual rent of six cents for 0.4 hectare. In the 1870s ranchers began to take over huge parcels of land.

Canada Revisited

O'Keefe Ranch

In 1867, Cornelius O'Keefe and his partner, Thomas Greenhow, drove cattle north through the Okanagan Valley to the goldfields to sell the beef to miners. They liked the land they saw in the Okanagan Valley and decided to stay. They each settled on 65 hectares (160 acres) of good grazing land and began cattle ranching.

Until the 1960s the O'Keefe Ranch was still owned and operated by the O'Keefe family. In 1967 Cornelius O'Keefe's son Tierney opened it as an historic site. He later sold it to a nonprofit organization.

Today the O'Keefe Ranch is a popular tourist site. The original buildings have been made available for visitors to tour.

British Columbia Becomes a Province

  By 1868, the colony of British Columbia was heavily in debt. Roads and other expensive services had been needed during the gold rush. With the gold rush over, there was little money left to pay for these services. The colony was spending more money importing goods they needed than they were making from exporting goods. Much less gold was now being exported than during the gold rush. Far fewer furs were being exported as well. Lumbering, fishing, farming, and ranching were not yet as profitable as they would be in later years. Coal mining would not develop as an industry until the 1880s.

People in the colony of British Columbia began to consider the economic advantages that could be gained by joining Canada. There were some people in the area who wanted British Columbia to remain a British colony. There was also growing pressure, both from within the colony and outside, for annexation by the United States. Great Britain concluded that British Columbia should be joined to Canada as the best way to preserve its link with the British Empire.

For Your Notebook

1. Read the following dialogue for three characters. Record in your notes what three options were available for the colony of British Columbia in 1869.

Scene: Hotel, Barkerville
Time: Fall 1869

Jeffrey: Gentlemen, my name is Ralph Jeffrey. I'm with the *Globe* newspaper in Toronto. We've been hearing a lot of talk in the East about how the gold rush days are almost over out here. My newspaper sent me out to interview some of the miners. They want me to go to the source to get the most accurate information I possibly can.

Moore: Well, you certainly have come to the right bunch. I'm James Moore. I'm not a miner but maybe I can help you. I had several packers leading pack animals along the trail, so I made more money than most of the miners! What we needed was a proper road. Fortunately, because of the gold rush, British Columbia had lots of money. Governor Douglas had the Cariboo Road built, and a regular stagecoach

service started operating. I bought into a freight wagon outfit and did all right.

Brown: After the fire in Barkerville last fall, things changed. The miners left here by the thousands. The excitement that was in the air is gone. The Cariboo's days are over.

Jeffrey: Over? What do you mean?

Brown: The Cariboo region has had its big gold rush, and now it's dying out. In a few years, these booming towns will be ghost towns. I saw it happen in California. Places boomed over night, when gold was discovered—and they died almost as quickly. It will happen here too. Just you wait and see!

Jeffrey: You mean to say that you think that British Columbia will go back to the way it was before the gold rush? Wasn't gold good for British Columbia?

Moore: Yes, it *was* good for British Columbia—but not now. Financially, British Columbia is in real bad shape. There's no money to be found anywhere.

Brown: He's right, young fellow. The gold rush is finished, and British Columbia with it!

Moore: If it wasn't for my freighting business, I would leave too, but I'm still making a fair living by moving goods. Mind you, not as much as I made during the gold rush, but at least this is steady. There are a few miners up here, and I haul in supplies for them.

Brown: Yep, things are pretty bad. British Columbia is fighting for her very life. A few years ago Vancouver Island and British Columbia united in the hope of staying British. Now I bet they will join the United States.

Jeffrey: There's talk in the East of having British Columbia join with Canada. They say they'll build a railway clear across the continent.

Brown: They'll never do it. It would be impossible to build, and it would cost too much money!

Moore: You're right, Brown. What British Columbia needs is to join with the United States of America. That is the only way we will have any future. Most of us are Americans anyway. And besides Canada's too far away!

An Exercise in Decision-Making

Towards the end of the 1860s the people of the colony of British Columbia had the following three choices in regard to their political future.

Choice One: They could remain a British colony and hope to have a government in which they had more influence in the future. A small but powerful British group of Hudson's Bay Company and government officials supported this position.

Choice Two: They could become part of the United States. This appealed to the Americans who had arrived in the colony during the gold rush. The United States completed the purchase of the Alaska Panhandle from Russia in 1867. The United States then controlled the areas both south and north of British Columbia. California was a good market for British Columbian goods, and the American trading centre of San Francisco was much nearer than the Canadian trading centres of Toronto and Montreal.

Choice Three: They could join Canada. The British government favoured the choice of connecting the British North American colonies together. Some people in the colony of British Columbia felt threatened by the United States. They thought they might be forced to become part of the United States against their will if they did not have the protection of being part of Canada. Also, if they became a province in Canada they could ask the Canadian government to pay the colony's debts.*

Your Task:

1. In groups make a timeline of events in the colony of British Columbia from 1867 to 1871. Use documents 1 to 8 on pages 172–174 as reference.

2. Use a decision-making chart to decide which choice you would have made had you lived in the colony of British Columbia in the 1860s. Consider all eight documents on pages 172–174 before making your decision. Ideas for decision-making are found on page 356.

---

*The decision-makers in Ottawa did not ask the minority peoples of British Columbia their opinions. The First Nations people and Chinese were not consulted.

Document 1

Resolution passed by the Legislative Council of British Columbia regarding Confederation

Monday, the 18 day of March 1867

. . . Resolved, That this Council is of opinion that . . . it is very desirable that his Excellency be respectfully requested to take such steps, without delay, as may be deemed by him best adapted to insure the admission of British Columbia into the Confederation on fair and equitable terms, this Council being confident that in advising this step they are expressing the views of the colonists generally.

Document 2

Message from Governor Seymour of British Columbia to Great Britain

September 24, 1867

My Lord Duke,

I TELEGRAPHED to your Grace's predecessor, on the 11th of March -

"Can provision be made in the Bill before Parliament for the ultimate admission of British Columbia to Canadian confederation?"

2. I have the honour to enclose copy of a resolution passed by the Legislative Council in favour of negotiations being entered into for the union of this colony with the Eastern Provinces of North America.

3. I have made some remarks on this subject in a separate Despatch of even date.

I have, &c.
(signed) Frederick Seymour

Document 3

Message sent by British Colonial Secretary to the Governor General of Canada, Viscount Monck

Downing-Street, 13 April 1868

My Lord,

I HAVE the honour to acknowledge the receipt of your Despatch, . . . however willing Her Majesty's Government may be to promote that union, the practical consideration of the question must at all events await the time when the intervening territory now under the control of the Hudson's Bay Company shall have been incorporated with the confederation.**

I have, &c.
(signed) Buckingham and Chandos

**The British Colonial Secretary is suggesting that they cannot advise the colony of British Columbia about being admitted to Canadian Confederation until Rupert's Land is purchased by Canada and made part of confederation. This was done in 1869.

Document 4

1868: An imaginary conversation between Dr. John Helmcken and Amor de Cosmos about whether British Columbia should become a province in the Dominion of Canada.

Dr. Helmcken was a doctor in Victoria. He was the first president of the British Columbia Medical Society. Dr. Helmcken was strongly in favour of British Columbia remaining a colony of Great Britain; he changed his position on Confederation later. Amor de Cosmos was a newspaper editor and a strong advocate of Confederation. Dr. Helmcken ran against de Cosmos for a seat in the legislative council in 1868 and won. Start by reading a statement by Dr. Helmcken. Then read what Amor de Cosmos says directly across the page.

Dr. John Helmcken

Mr. de Cosmos, you are wrong to try to convince the people of the colony of British Columbia that we should join the Dominion of Canada. Confederation is only an experiment so far. Why should we ally ourselves with something that has not yet been proved to be workable?

Rupert's Land, with its vast area, is between us and the Dominion of Canada. There is no road or railway to join us. If we unite with Canada, the other four provinces that are near one another geographically will make decisions that benefit themselves. They are not going to worry about British Columbians. We are 2000 kilometres away and would have few representatives in the country's government.

The American trading centre of San Francisco is much nearer to us than the Canadian trading centres of Montreal and Toronto. California is a good market for British Columbian goods. We have no control over what the Canadian government does about trade policy. The Canadian government could hurt our economy by forcing us to trade with the rest of Canada instead of with the United States.

My loyalty cannot be bought. I won't agree to join the Dominion of Canada just so our debts will be paid. As for your point about government, the British will probably grant us a government where the voters have more influence. There is no reason to join Canada just to get better government.

Amor de Cosmos

My dear Dr. Helmcken, the people of Ontario, Quebec, Nova Scotia, and New Brunswick put a lot of thought into their decision to join together to form the Dominion of Canada. Confederation has been successful so far and will continue to be successful.

If British Columbia becomes part of Canada, the other provinces will have to consider what we want. Eventually Canada will be one nation that stretches from the Atlantic Ocean to the Pacific Ocean. There will be a railway to link the provinces and transport goods from one province to another.

You must remember, Dr. Helmcken, that our colony is in debt. We are importing more goods than we are exporting. If we join the Dominion of Canada, the Canadian government will pay our debts and we will have a fresh start. Also, the Canadian government may grant us a responsible type of government. We want the decision-makers in our government to represent the voters.

I suppose that remains to be seen. Please keep in mind that Britain wants us to join Canada. Also, by joining a Dominion within the British Empire, rather than remaining a small colony, we will have more say in the empire itself. Joining Canada is also the best way to protect ourselves against American Manifest Destiny. I hope, Dr. Helmcken, that one day you will come to see the advantages for British Columbia of joining the Dominion of Canada.

Document 5

Excerpts from a letter to the editor, *The British Columbian*, April 30, 1869.

Note: The government of Canada and the government of Great Britain were negotiating about British Columbia becoming a province. However, a certain group in British Columbia was not in favour of having British Columbia join with Canada. Their position is given in Document 5.

With a depleted treasury, revenue falling off, and the Colony suffering from a depression beyond all precedent, with no prospect, either present or remote, of immigration, what are we to do? . . . .

Were the inhabitants of British Columbia a thriving community, the question of annexation would not be popular; for the people are loyal and patriotic. The force of circumstances alone compels them to advocate a change of nationality. . . .

I am a loyal Briton, and would prefer living under the institutions of my own country, were it practicable. But I, like the rest of the world of which we are each an atom, would prefer the flag and institutions of the United States with prosperity, to remaining as we are, with no prospect of succeeding as a British colony.

Document 6

Excerpts from an annexation petition sent in 1869 from the colony of British Columbia to the president of the United States (43 signatures were attached).*

To

His Excellency, the President of the United States of America:

. . . we are residents of the Colony of British Columbia—many of us british subjects and all deeply interested in the welfare and progress of our adopted country.

. . . That this Colony is now suffering great depression, owing to its isolation, a scarcity of population and other causes too numerous to mention.

That we view with feelings of alarm the avowed intention of Her Majesty's Government to confederate this Colony with the Dominion of Canada . . .

That confederation cannot give us protection against internal enemies or foreign foes, owing to the distance of this Colony from Ottawa.

That it cannot open to us a market for the produce of our lands, our forest, our mines or our waters.

That it cannot bring us population (our greatest need) as the Dominion itself is suffering from lack of it. . . .

---

*In the fall of 1870 a supplementary list containing 61 names in favour of annexation was forwarded to the United States government. This was a very small percentage of the non-Aboriginal population.

. . . The only remedy for the evils which beset us, we believe to be in a close union with the adjoining States and Territories. . . .

For these reasons we earnestly desire the ACQUISITION of this Colony by the United States. . . .

Document 7

After the death of Governor Seymour, Anthony Musgrave was appointed governor of the colony of British Columbia. His instructions from the British Government were to bring British Columbia into Confederation.

On May 10, 1870, three leaders of the colony of British Columbia left for Ottawa to negotiate with the Canadian government suitable terms for the entry of British Columbia into the newly-formed Dominion of Canada. They were: J.W. Trutch, R.W. Carrall, and J.S. Helmcken.

Since transportation facilities from British Columbia to Ottawa through Canadian territory were very inadequate, the three men travelled to Ottawa through the United States—from Victoria to San Francisco, across the United States by train, and then to Ottawa.

Excerpt from one of the proposals presented to this group by the Canadian government.

May 1870

8. . . . the Dominion shall, within three years from the date of Union, construct . . . . the initial sections of such Railway from the Seaboard of British Columbia, to connect with the Railway system of Canada.

Document 8

Excerpts from one of the sections of the 1871 confederation negotiations

Section 11. The Government of the Dominion undertake to secure the commencement simultaneously, within two years from the date of the Union, of the construction of a Railway from the Pacific towards the Rocky Mountains, and from such point as may be selected, east of the Rocky Mountains, towards the Pacific, to connect the seaboard of British Columbia with the railway system of Canada, and further, to secure the completion of such Railway within ten years from the date of the Union.

Just a reminder to complete the Decision-making activity you started on page 172.

The British Columbia Act, 1871

Confederation Negotiations

 The Canadian government was anxious to extend the Dominion of Canada to the Pacific Coast. Dr. Helmcken changed his anti-Confederation position and became a supporter. He was one of the representatives who went to Ottawa in 1870 to discuss British Columbia becoming a province of Canada. The decision-makers did not ask the First Nations and minority peoples of British Columbia their opinions.

In return for BC joining Confederation, the Canadian government promised the following:

- a railway joining British Columbia to Canada, to be begun within two years of the date of union (July 20, 1871) and to be finished within 10 years
- payment of the colony's debt of over $1 000 000
- an annual subsidy to the province of $35 000 and a yearly grant of 80¢ per person until the population reached 400 000
- British Columbia to have control of government-owned public land (crown lands), as in the four original provinces*

Legend:
- Canada
- Britain
- United States of America
- France (St. Pierre and Miquelon)

0   500 km

BRITISH COLUMBIA · NORTH-WEST TERRITORIES · MANITOBA · ONTARIO · QUEBEC · NOVA SCOTIA · NEW BRUNSWICK

Dominion of Canada, 1871

In 1871 British Columbia became the sixth province in the Dominion of Canada.

Sir Anthony Musgrave 1828–1888

 Anthony Musgrave was appointed governor of British Columbia in 1869. He had been the governor of Newfoundland since 1864. Musgrave was given instructions by the British government to negotiate British Columbia's entry into the Canadian Confederation. Once the colony became a province of Canada his term ended.

Section III Activity

Part Two

 Use the information on pages 169 to 175 to fill out ❷, ❸, ❹, ❺, and ❻ on the chart A Model to Meet Challenges (page 145).

---

*Crown lands are lands belonging to the government. When the BNA Act was passed, crown lands were transferred to the provinces. Manitoba did not gain control of its crown lands when it became a province in 1870. When British Columbia became a province in 1871, it kept control of the crown lands.

Focus On: Scenes from British Columbia at the Time it Became a Province

Left: Nanaimo, Vancouver Island, about 1870

Below: Siseanjute, First Nations Chief (centre) and band members from Bonaparte Creek at Lytton, British Columbia

Above: Wharf Street in Victoria, about 1871

Above: Part of the British Pacific Fleet in Esquimalt Harbour, in the colony of British Columbia, 1867–70

Above: Newitta Village, British Columbia Coast, 1881

The North-West Territories

Dominion Lands Act, 1872

  The Dominion Lands Act gave settlers about 65 hectares (referred to as a quarter section) of land. However, they were required to pay a $10 registration fee. They also had to live on the land and work it for three years.

This Act was intended to encourage people to settle on and cultivate the prairie grasslands of the North-West Territories. This was to serve several purposes. Settlement by people loyal to the British Crown would discourage Americans from coming north and settling in the area. Settlement would provide more reason for the Canadian Pacific Railway to be completed. Farmers would need a way to transport their agricultural products to the East. Settlement in the North-West would also provide markets for goods produced in Central and Atlantic Canada.

Townships and Sections

Preparations were required for the expected influx of settlers to the West. The government first had to have the land surveyed. The western lands were divided into squares called townships. Each township contained 36 sections of land, with each section containing 260 hectares (640 acres). The sections were divided into quarter sections of 65 hectares (160 acres) each. A prairie homestead was a quarter section in size. Land was also reserved for the Crown (government lands), schools, the Hudson's Bay Company, and the Canadian Pacific Railway.

N
9.7 kilometres (6 miles)

9.7 kilometres (6 miles)

W   **E**

31	32	33	34	35	36
30	29	28	27	26	25
19	20	21	22	23	24
18	17	16	15	14	13
7	8	9	10	11	12
6	5	4	3	2	1

S

Prairie farmlands were surveyed into townships 9.7 kilometres square. The shaded portion is the southeast quarter of section 20. The legal description for this homestead was SE 20 4725. In the number, 47 stands for township and 25 for range, which aren't shown on the diagram.

Between 1872 and 1874 the Royal Engineers surveyed the International Boundary between the Lake of the Woods and the Rocky Mountains. During the 1870s several parties surveyed the North-West Territories to prepare the area for settlement.

An Exercise in Decision-Making

Prairie Homesteads

 By the early 1870s most of the good farmland in Central Canada had already been cleared and settled. Farmers began to look to the United States and to the North-West Territories for land. There was plenty of good farmland in the West but there were several issues and/or concerns that had to be solved before settlement could begin.

1. Work in groups of four or five. Imagine it is 1873. You are listening to a conversation in a small farming community in rural Ontario.

   a) Read the following points of view and make notes on what issues and/or concerns the people had about opening the West to settlement.

   b) Predict what you think should be done before settlement could occur.

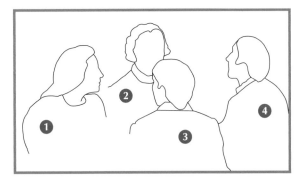

1 "We have four sons in our family. We lost our small farm because we couldn't make the mortgage payments. We've heard that the government bought Rupert's Land from the Hudson's Bay Company so there is plenty of land available. How do we get some of it?"

2 "The Dominion Lands Act was recently passed by Macdonald's Conservatives. Once the West is surveyed settlers such as your husband or adult sons can get a quarter section* of free land, but you have to pay a 10-dollar registration fee."

1 "Ten dollars! That's all?"

2 "Yes, but they also have to live on the land and work it for three years. All four of your sons can get land and so can you and your husband. Unfortunately there are many things that have to be done in preparation for settlers."

3 "You can't move west yet. There are land claim issues with the Aboriginal people living in the North-West Territories that the government has to solve. A few treaties have been signed, and their people have started to move onto the reserves. But more treaties need to be signed so farmers like you and your sons can move onto the western lands."

4 "Aren't the First Nations and Metis people against the settlers coming into the West? What about the rebellion that occurred in the Red River colony? I wouldn't take my family there. There might be more uprisings!"

2 "I had heard the land was unsuitable for farming but the government sent an expedition to check this out. They found that some areas are poor but most have good soil. There is a concern over the weather, however. You might be fortunate enough to get a crop to grow, only to have it freeze with an early snowfall in September. I suppose the government will have to convince settlers to go there rather than to the United States."

3 "I've heard stories that whiskey traders from the United States have moved northward and are trading whiskey for furs. I am reluctant to take my family out there until there is a means of keeping law and order. It sounds dangerous."

4 "Besides, how will settlers get there? Once the Canadian Pacific Railway is built there will at least be a way for people to get to the West and transport the products they grow to the markets in Ontario."

1 "Building a future is never any easy task! We have to balance the challenges against the opportunities. I want my sons to be able to own their own land."

*About 65 hectares

Getting the West Ready
for Settlers

 The chart below provides a summary of the changes that led to the settling of the West. These points are explored in more detail in the chapters that follow.

 The chart is designed to show cause and effect. Read the sections of the chart from left to right.

Issue/Concern	Solution	Result
1. HBC owned Rupert's Land.	1868: Rupert's Land was sold to Canada.	Land was available for settlement in NWT once First Nations signed treaties (see number 6).
2. A transcontinental railway was needed to bring people to the NWT and to ship products to the East.	1871: The Canadian government in Ottawa agreed to start construction of a railway across the continent. This railway was to be completed by 1881.	The Canadian Pacific Railway was completed in 1885. This made it easier and faster for settlers to go to the West and for western products to go to markets in the East.
3. NWT was not surveyed and prepared for settlers. There were few roads and towns.	1872: Dominion Lands Act was passed.	Preparations to encourage settlement started; land surveyed; free homestead land granted (65 hectares); $10 registration fee.
4. Settlers feared lawlessness in the NWT.	1873: North West Mounted Police (NWMP) formed.	Law and order established in the West.
5. The NWT had no government of its own.	1875: North-West Territories Act was passed.	Gradual implementation of representative government was provided for.
6. First Nations people were living on the land wanted for new settlers.	The Canadian government signed Numbered Treaties 1, 2, and 3 with First Nations living in the NWT between 1871 and 1873.	First Nations moved onto reserves (lands set aside for their use only); vast amounts of western lands were freed for farms and settlement.
7. Autumn frosts in the West killed crops. Existing ploughs were difficult to use on prairie grasslands.	Advances in science and technology: • Hardy types of wheat (Red Fife and Marquis) were developed. • Steel tipped ploughshares and specialized farm machinery were developed.	Western farmers had less fear of early autumn frosts. Equipment to meet western farming conditions—for example, to break new land for agriculture—became available.

Prince Edward Island Becomes a Province

Before Confederation

Prince Edward Island rejected the idea of joining Confederation in 1867. They decided they would be better off continuing as a British colony.

Land Ownership

Most of the land in Prince Edward Island was owned by absentee landlords. The majority of those landlords lived in Great Britain. They rented the land to **tenant farmers**. Over time, the fact that the tenant farmers of Prince Edward Island could not own their own land caused much unrest. In 1864, politicians from colonies in favour of Confederation promised to deal with the land crisis on the Island. However, at the Quebec Conference in 1864, Prince Edward Island delegates were refused financial support for buying out the absentee landlords. This decision caused many who had been pro-Confederation to lose interest. They argued that if Confederation would not provide a solution to their land ownership problems, then it would not be a help to Prince Edward Island.

Islanders decided to take matters into their own hands. Many either joined, or at least supported, the Tenant League, which was formed in 1864. The Tenant League recommended they protest their lack of land ownership by refusing to pay the rents. Members of the Tenant League even stood up to troops sent by the British government in 1865. Following this confrontation, some of the absentee landlords began to sell their property to the tenant farmers.

Government

Islanders had achieved responsible government in 1851. They were satisfied with being a self-governing British colony. In the opinion of the majority they had more independence as a colony of Great Britain than they would have as a very small province of Canada. For example, if they joined the Dominion of Canada they would have only five representatives in the 200-member Canadian House of Commons. This was not enough to have any say in how their area would be governed.

The Economy

Prince Edward Island was prosperous in the 1860s. Islanders could see no financial benefits to becoming part of Canada. Island shipyards were building over 100 ships a year. Harvests were excellent and Great Britain purchased most of their products. As a result of a successful free trade arrangement, the United States was also an important trading partner.

By joining the Dominion of Canada, Prince Edward Island could have free trade with Canada. However, residents were not particularly interested in this benefit because so little of their trade was with Canada. As one member of the legislative assembly said, "Our imports from that colony are almost entirely of flour, and we export nothing to it save a few quintals* of fish and some barrels of oysters."

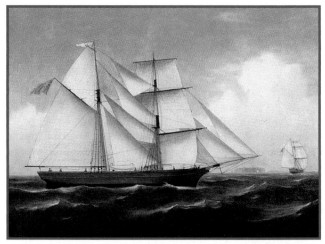

The *Fanny Bailey* was built after 1856, when wooden ships were still in demand and the shipyards of Prince Edward Island were still prosperous. By 1873 the economy was declining. Wooden sailing ships were being replaced by steam powered ships.

For Your Notebook

1. In a retrieval chart, list points for and against Prince Edward Island joining the Dominion of Canada in 1867.

Tenant farmers—farmers who rent, rather than own, their land

*A quintal equalled about 50 kilograms.

Reasons for Joining the Dominion

 In the end, economic concerns caused Prince Edward Islanders to seriously consider joining Canada. The economy had declined in the six years since Prince Edward Island had rejected Confederation. Island exports declined more every year.

By the early 1870s, much of the colony's revenue was being spent in an effort to buy land from the absentee landlords. This was difficult, in view of the colony's financial situation. By 1873, the colony was on the verge of bankruptcy. The decision to build a railway on the island had contributed greatly to the debt. In 1871 residents had found themselves caught up in railway fever. They had thought that a railway would employ hundreds of people, help farmers get their produce to markets, promote industry, and attract tourists. These benefits would improve the ability of the island to resist Confederation. Unfortunately, there was not enough money available to make the railway a success. By 1873, railway construction had stopped because the builders feared they would never be paid. No banks would extend the loans needed to continue construction.

 Joining Canada offered people from Prince Edward Island a way out of their financial difficulties. Canada offered to take over the railway debt and to increase the legislature's provincial subsidy. Canada also offered to assist in purchasing the land from the absentee landlords.

Another key condition was that the federal government would maintain an official year-round steamer service to the island.

Lord Dufferin was governor general of Canada at the time. He commented that Islanders seemed to feel "it is the Dominion that has been annexed to Prince Edward Island."

Exploring Further

1. William Henry Pope was the editor of a newspaper called the *Islander*, a member of the Executive Council, and provincial secretary. He was a strong advocate of Confederation. Write an editorial that he might have written in 1873, trying to convince the people of Prince Edward Island to join Canada.
2. What do you think Lord Dufferin meant in the above quote?

Section III Activity

Part Three

  Continue in role as Prime Minister Macdonald to examine Prince Edward Island's becoming a province. Fill out ❶ to ❻ of the chart A Model to Meet Challenges (see page 145). Use the map on page 182 and the information on pages 180 to 182.

Winter mail service, Prince Edward Island. This painting shows how difficult it was to deliver mail during the winter months. A railway would greatly improve communications in Prince Edward Island but would not give the residents stronger links with the mainland.

Prince Edward Island Act, 1873

 On July 1, 1873, Prince Edward Island became a province. There was not a great deal of celebration or even interest in the event at the time. Islanders considered the decision to be more a matter of necessity than choice. A local newspaper described the interest shown in the reading of the Union Proclamation on July 1, 1873 as follows: "The audience within hearing consisted of three persons, and even they did not appear to be very attentive."

In return for joining Confederation, the Canadian government gave Prince Edward Island an $800 000 loan, which was to be used to buy land from the absentee landlords. The Canadian government agreed to pay all the railway debts, and to provide a $50 grant for every person living on the island. Year-round ferry and telegraph service would be provided between Prince Edward Island and the mainland.

Prince Edward Island became the seventh province of Canada. The first four provinces—Ontario, Quebec, Nova Scotia, and New Brunswick—were created in 1867. Manitoba became a province in 1870 and British Columbia in 1871. In 1873, when Prince Edward Island became a province, the future provinces of Alberta and Saskatchewan were still part of the North-West Territories. The future province of Newfoundland was still a British colony.

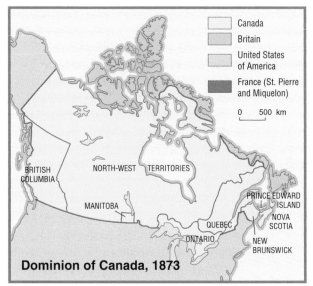

Dominion of Canada, 1873

In 1873, Prince Edward Island became the seventh province of the Dominion of Canada.

Charlottetown became the capital of the province of Prince Edward Island.

The Colony of Newfoundland

 The colony of Newfoundland had not been invited to the Charlottetown Conference in 1864. Newfoundland's delegates did attend the Quebec Conference and supported the Seventy-Two Resolutions. Two important sections of the Newfoundland population were strongly anti-Confederation, the business community and the Irish Roman Catholics. The people of Newfoundland had few dealings with Canada. They exported salt fish to Europe, the West Indies, and Brazil. They imported food and manufactured goods from the United States. They were against political changes that might increase their taxes or restrict their freedom to choose their own trading partners.

The Irish Roman Catholics had several reasons for opposing Confederation. They were afraid of losing their government-funded separate schools. They were pleased that Newfoundland had been granted responsible government by Great Britain in 1855. Most did not wish to give power to a distant government upon which they would have little influence. Many people thought Newfoundland had many resources that had not yet been found. They saw responsible government as a means to future prosperity.

There was another reason for the lack of support for Confederation among Irish Catholics. Confederation reminded some of them of the Act of Union of 1801, by which Britain and Ireland had been joined together. They saw that event as a tragedy for Ireland. They did not want to see it repeated in North America.

The sea off Newfoundland was a rich source of cod. Here, fishermen are having their dried cod weighed.

In 1874, the Conservatives returned to power in Newfoundland. Even though members of this party tended to favour union, they made it clear to the voters that Confederation would not be forced on them. They proceeded with a program of railway building. They hoped railways would help to develop the colony's rich resources. They saw a railway as a way to bring investment dollars into the colony. Money would help to develop mining, forestry, and agriculture. At this time, there was still not strong enough support to push for negotiating to become a province.

There were several further attempts to renegotiate entry into Confederation but it wasn't until 1949 that Newfoundland actually became a province.

Anti-Confederation Song

Hurrah for our own native isle, Newfoundland!
Not a stranger shall hold one inch of its strand!
Her face turns to Britain, her back to the Gulf,
Come near at your peril, Canadian Wolf!

Ye brave Newfoundlanders who plough the salt sea
With hearts like the eagle so bold and so free,
The time is at hand when you'll all have to say
If Confederation will carry the day.

Cheap tea and molasses they say they will give,
All taxes take off that the poor man may live;
Cheap nails and cheap lumber our coffins to make,
And homespun to mend our old clothes when they break.

If they take off the taxes how then will they meet
The heavy expense on the country's upkeep?
Just give them the chance to get us in the scrape
And they'll chain us like slaves with pen, ink, and red tape.

Would you barter the rights that your fathers have won,
Your freedom transmitted from father to son?
For a few thousand dollars of Canadian gold,
Don't let it be said that your birthright was sold.

For Your Notebook

1. What argument is used in the anti-Confederation song to convince Newfoundlanders to vote against Confederation? What image is used for Canada? How does the song picture Newfoundlanders who would be willing to join Confederation?
2. Why did the people of Newfoundland still not support becoming a province in the 1870s?

Industrialization

 Industry in Canada before the 1890s was mainly related to producing or processing primary resources. Sawmills and fish packing plants were important early secondary industries in Canada. The population was still largely rural or living in small towns. The economy depended on exports to Great Britain (and to her colonies). Exports consisted mainly of raw materials (wheat, fish, furs, timber, and minerals) and food products. Imports were mainly manufactured goods from Great Britain. Smaller amounts of trading were done with the United States.

Manufacturing (secondary industry) gradually grew in importance. Factories were established especially in Central Canada to produce goods for use in Canada and to export to Britain and the United States. **Industrialization** spread slowly. Factories were built, more people were employed as factory workers, and towns grew larger.

   Industries in Canada were seen as one way to bring about national unity for the new dominion. The vastness of the country, the variety of physical landforms, climates, and vegetation, and the limited transportation and communication systems were barriers to national unity. These factors con-tributed to regionalism and diversity rather than helping to bring about a national industrial policy. Strong ties between Great Britain and Canada con-tinued to influence Canada's economic policies. For example, Canadian factories were modelled on the factory system used in Great Britain. Goods were produced to suit British markets.

Industrialization in Canada will be referred to in various chapters in this textbook. Different regions industrialized at different rates and at different times.

Rural and Urban Population

☐ Rural (about 80%)
■ Urban (about 20%)

Canada was mainly a rural, agricultural country during the 1870s.

1870

Industrialization—the growth of larger industries as an important part of a region, employing a large number of people

Trade Union Movement

 The beginnings of industrialization in Canada brought many changes. As people moved to live near the factory sites, overcrowded living conditions resulted. Working conditions were usually not very satisfactory. Lack of safety regulations, long hours, and low pay were usual.

 The trade union movement first started in Great Britain and spread to the United States and Canada. Workers found that if many workers joined together into organizations called unions they had more power than if they approached their employers individually or in small groups. The expression "Power in Solidarity" became a union slogan. Labour unions tried to bring about better working conditions—higher wages, job security, greater on-the-job safety, and shorter hours.

The unions represented only a small proportion of the work force, mostly only skilled workers. There had been a number of strikes and demonstrations during the mid-1800s, but they increased in number as Canada industrialized.

Steel-workers in Hamilton demanding the nine-hour working day marched in a demonstration in May 1872. Number of hours worked per day was the main issue for trade unions in the 1870s.

Review

The icons are your cue to refer to the Learning How to Learn Appendix (pages 348–371) for ideas on how to complete these activities.

This icon is a reminder to turn to the Research Model (pages x–xi).

1. Complete a self-assessment for one assignment from this chapter.

Understanding Concepts

2. Examine the web or mind map you did for the Chapter Preview/Prediction on page 167. Working with a partner, identify two things about each heading you learned from this chapter. Add them to your web or mind map.

3. Use one of the suggested methods for recording vocabulary to add new words from this chapter to the WordBook section of your notes.

4. a) Select any one of the chapter's concepts or main topics listed on page 167.
   Do either b) or c).
   b) Create a concept poster for one of these ideas. Present it to the class.
   c) Use a web, mind map, or chart to create a permanent set of notes about one of these ideas. Explain your work to a classmate.

5.
   Refer to the Chapter 7 Focus on page 167. Notice that the concepts of change, regionalism, identity, and co-operation have been the focus of this chapter. Create a web to show examples found in this chapter of each of these concepts.

6. Add entries for this chapter to your timeline.

7. On page 171 you read three points of view about the colony of British Columbia becoming a province. The First Nations and Chinese people living in the colony were not consulted. Choose one or the other of these groups and list concerns about Confederation that they might have had. Put your in a letter to Governor Musgrave. (He's featured on page 175.)

8. What was the Dominion Lands Act (1872)? Why did the government pass it?

Developing Research Skills

9.

Section III Activity

Part Four

Work in small groups for the Section III Activity.

1. Using the chart A Model to Meet Challenges you made in Chapters 6 and 7 as a source of data, discuss which challenges Prime Minister Macdonald and his Conservative government faced between 1867 and 1873?

2. Using your History notes as reference and/or this textbook make a list of other challenges the new Dominion of Canada faced.

Developing Communication Skills

10. In Chapter 5 you made a Confederation newspaper for Ontario, Quebec, New Brunswick, or Nova Scotia. Make another Confederation newspaper for British Columbia or Prince Edward Island. See page 137 for ideas on how to do this.

11. Debate the statement: British Columbia would be better off today if it had joined the United States rather than Canada.

12. Select three people from this chapter and list what admirable qualities you think they had. If you were one of these people, of what accomplishment would you be the most proud?

13. In your opinion, what is the most memorable event from this chapter? Explain why.

Chapter 8
Strengthening the Dominion
1873–1878

O v e r v i e w

Use this Overview to predict what you will read in this chapter.

1 **1873–1878**

In 1873, the Pacific Scandal toppled John A. Macdonald's Conservative government. Alexander Mackenzie and the Liberals governed Canada.

2 A number of influential political and economic events took place during Mackenzie's Liberal administration.

1873

NWMP was formed.

1874

Royal Military College of Canada was established in Kingston, Ontario.

1875

Supreme Court of Canada was created.

1875

The North-West Territories Act was passed. It provided for the gradual implementation of representative government.

1878

First election to use the secret ballot took place.

The North-West Territories Act

3 **1873**

Canadian Labour Union (CLU) was formed. It lasted until 1878.

4 **1876**

The Indian Act was passed. Several treaties were signed in the West.

5 **1876**

Intercolonial railway was completed. It connected the Atlantic provinces to Quebec.

Chapter 8 Focus

Chapters 6 and 7 dealt with the period immediately following Confederation (1867–1873), the formation of three new provinces (Manitoba, British Columbia, and Prince Edward Island) and the Conservative government of Prime Minister John A. Macdonald. This chapter covers the period 1873–1878, when Alexander Mackenzie and the Liberals were in power. Further changes occurred in the North-West Territories. The North West Mounted Police force was formed to enforce law and order in the North-West. The concepts of change, power, and co-operation are the focus of Chapter 8.

| Change | Regionalism | Power | Identity | Co-operation |

Other Concepts and Main Topics

- Pacific Scandal
- bribe
- secret ballot
- political donation
- ethics of business contracts
- Supreme Court of Canada
- recession
- provincial rights movement
- intercolonial railway
- North West Mounted Police
- treaties

Learning How to Learn

 Critical Thinking

 Research

 Role-playing

 Cause and Effect

Decision-making

Cartoon Analysis

Chapter Preview/Prediction Chart

In pairs or small groups, examine and discuss the Overview on the previous page. Read the Chapter Focus above. Look through the chapter and examine the titles and visuals. Think about what you already know about the topics discussed in this chapter. Use all of this information to answer the questions on the Prediction Chart in the next column. Put your predictions in the "My Predictions" column.

Prediction Chart—What Do You Think?		
Questions	My Predictions (fill out now)	What I Found Out (fill out at end of chapter)
How did Canada change under the federal government of Alexander Mackenzie?		
Give examples of how the government used its power.		
Give examples of political, economic, and social co-operation during this period.		

SAMPLE

Section III Activity

    In this chapter you will study the challenges Alexander Mackenzie and the Liberals faced in their goal of strengthening the Dominion from sea to sea.

Part One

1. Select one of the following goals that Mackenzie and the Liberals tried to accomplish:
   a) to bring the country out of economic recession (pages 192 to 195)
   b) to have the Canadian government establish law and order in the NWT (pages 196 to 205)
   c) to sign treaties with the First Nations and move their people onto reserves (pages 207 to 209)

2. Approach this activity by assuming the role of Prime Minister Alexander Mackenzie. Use the chart A Model to Meet Challenges to record your notes on the item you selected (see page 145). Fill in number ❶.

This activity is continued on page 213.

187

Timeline
Challenges of the New Dominion
1867–1880

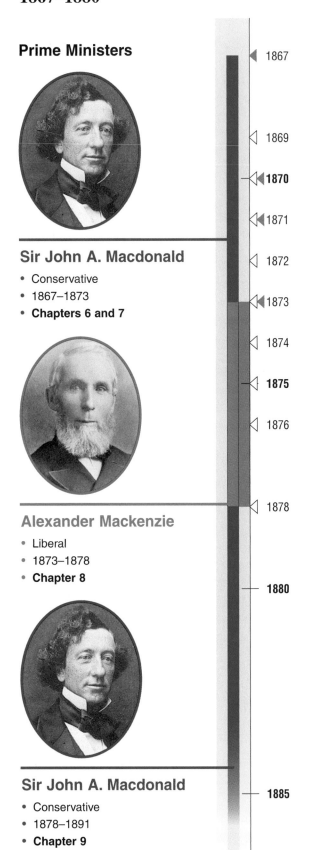

Prime Ministers

Sir John A. Macdonald
- Conservative
- 1867–1873
- **Chapters 6 and 7**

Alexander Mackenzie
- Liberal
- 1873–1878
- **Chapter 8**

Sir John A. Macdonald
- Conservative
- 1878–1891
- **Chapter 9**

◀	1867
◁	1869
◀◁	**1870**
◀◁	1871
◁	1872
◀◁	1873
◁	1874
◁	**1875**
◁	1876
◁	1878
—	**1880**
—	**1885**

Key Events

- ◀ **1867** • **Confederation (Ontario, Quebec, Nova Scotia, and New Brunswick are the first four provinces of Dominion of Canada)**
- ◁ 1869 • Rupert's Land transferred from the Hudson's Bay Company to Canada
- ◁ 1870 • Red River Resistance
- ◀ **1870** • **Manitoba becomes a province**
- ◁ 1870 • Butler sent by Canadian government to investigate unlawfulness in the West; Robertson-Ross sent in 1873
- ◀ **1871** • **British Columbia becomes a province**
- ◁ 1871 • First numbered treaties in the North-West between the Dominion of Canada and First Nations
- ◁ 1872 • Dominion Lands Act
- ◀ **1873** • **Prince Edward Island becomes a province**
- ◁ 1873 • Pacific Scandal results in change of government
  • Establishment of NWMP
  • Canadian Labour Union formed
- ◁ 1874 • Establishment of Royal Military College of Canada at Kingston
- ◁ 1875 • Supreme Court of Canada created
  • North-West Territories Act
- ◁ 1876 • Indian Act
  • Completion of Intercolonial Railway in Atlantic Canada
- ◁ 1878 • First election to use secret ballot

Time Periods

■ Conservative Leadership

■ Liberal Leadership

■ World-wide recession (1873–1878)

The Pacific Scandal

 You read in the last chapter that the Conservative government of Sir John A. Macdonald planned to build a railway from sea to sea. The contract for the Canadian Pacific Company was awarded to Sir Hugh Allan. A secret raid on Sir Hugh Allan's lawyer's office revealed a telegram sent to him by Macdonald during the 1872 election campaign. It said, "I must have another ten thousand. Will be the last time of asking. Do not fail me." It soon became public knowledge that Allan had donated $350 000* to the Conservative Party during the 1872 election campaign. Macdonald's Conservative government was accused of accepting a **bribe** in exchange for giving the railway contract to Allan. In the resulting uproar, this action was called the Pacific Scandal.

"WE IN CANADA SEEM TO HAVE LOST ALL IDEA OF JUSTICE, HONOR AND INTEGRITY."—THE MAIL, 26TH SEPTEMBER

This cartoon was published in the weekly **satirical** magazine, *Grip*, in September, 1873.

On the evening of November 3, 1873, Macdonald made a four-and-a-half hour speech, defending his actions and arguing that he had done nothing illegal. Lady Dufferin, the wife of the governor general,

described it as a "splendid speech" that produced "a continuous chorus of admiration." However, in spite of this enthusiasm Macdonald was forced to submit his resignation two days later. Even though the Conservatives had won the 1872 election, the Liberals were asked to form a new government. Alexander Mackenzie became prime minister. Then an election was called, the Conservatives lost, and Mackenzie was returned as Liberal prime minister.

The Liberal government promised to improve the way in which elections were run. This was a positive outcome of the Pacific Scandal. The Liberals kept this promise by bringing in the practice of voting by secret ballot and other reforms to election practices. They also began the practice of candidates being required to file a statement of how much they had spent on their campaigns.

For Your Notebook

1. In pairs or triads, discuss the following questions. Each of you is responsible for making your own notes.

   a) Who was Sir Hugh Allan? Why did Macdonald ask him for $10 000?

   b) Macdonald's Conservative government was accused of accepting a bribe in exchange for giving the railway contract to Allan. In your opinion, was Macdonald rightly or wrongly accused of accepting a bribe? Provide reasons. When is money a donation and when is it a bribe?

   c) Why did Macdonald resign? Who became Prime Minister?

2.
   a) Who are the men in the cartoon?

   b) On what issue is the cartoonist focusing?

   c) If you were to draw a cartoon representing the point of view opposite to that shown, what would you draw?

Exploring Further

3. Find newspaper articles or carry out research to find modern-day examples within the last 20 years where there were problems or questions involving campaign donations or bribes at any level of government in Canada.

---

*This was an enormous amount at the time. The prime minister earned $8000 a year.
Bribe—a gift, usually money, given in order to get someone to do something wrong or against his/her intention
Satirical—holding someone or something up to ridicule in order to bring about change

Liberal Administration

Personal Summary

Alexander Mackenzie was born in Scotland in January 1822. He had only a limited education because he had to leave school at 13 to help support his widowed mother and six brothers. In 1842, at the age of 20, he followed his girlfriend Helen Neil to Canada. She and her family settled on a farm near Kingston in Canada West. Mackenzie found work as a stonemason and the two were married in 1845. Helen died seven years later at the age of twenty-five. Two of their three children also died while very young. Mackenzie married Jane Sym in 1852. They did not have any children, but she became mother to Mackenzie's five-year-old daughter. Following the Liberal party defeat in the election of 1878, Mackenzie and his family moved to Toronto. He became the first president of the North American Life Assurance Company in 1881, while continuing as a Member of Parliament.

Political Summary

In the early 1850s Mackenzie edited a Reform* newspaper called the *Lambton Shield* in Sarnia. He was elected to the Legislative Assembly of the United Province of Canada in 1861. In 1867 he won a seat in the first Canadian House of Commons. In 1872 he was chosen as Liberal leader. In 1873, when Macdonald's government fell as a result of the Pacific Scandal, the Liberals were asked to form a government. Alexander Mackenzie became Canada's second prime minister.

Lady Dufferin, wife of the governor general, described Mackenzie as "very straight-forward, and very Scotch, in accent and looks." Mackenzie described himself as "Clear Grit—pure sand without

Alexander Mackenzie
1822–1892

Dates as Prime Minister—1873–1878
Party—Liberal

• • • • • • • •

a particle of dirt in it." He was known for his honesty and fair dealings with people. He refused a knighthood from the British.

Alexander Mackenzie and his Liberal Party had a difficult time governing Canada. The country's economy was hurt by a worldwide recession, which caused prices to fall and reduced markets for Canadian products. There were crop failures because of plagues of insects. Canadians were buying goods made in the United States because they cost less than many of the goods made in Canada. Lack of sales caused many Canadian workers to be laid off from their jobs. Some companies went bankrupt. The Liberals had to cut back on projects, which caused more loss of jobs. The Liberals were unable to meet the promise to British Columbia that it would have a railway within ten years of entering Confederation. The survey work for the Canadian Pacific Railway was completed, but the railway itself was not completed. This angered British Columbians. The difficult economic situation caused the Liberals to lose the election of 1878.

While the Liberals were in office under Mackenzie, they established several important new institutions. The North West Mounted Police was established in the West. The Supreme Court of Canada, the Royal Military College at Kingston, the practice of voting by secret ballot and other election reforms, and the North-West Territories Act were all initiated by Mackenzie's Liberals.

The government began the practice of publishing the debates of the House of Commons in *Hansard*, so a permanent record was kept and was available to the public.

Mackenzie stayed on as Liberal party leader after the Liberal defeat in the election of 1878. He resigned as leader in 1880, but continued as a Member of Parliament until his death in 1892.

*Before Confederation (1867) the Liberals were called the Grits or Reform Party. After Confederation they were called the Liberals, but the nickname Grits was still used.

Mackenzie's Accomplishments

The Liberal party under Mackenzie brought in several important changes during its five years in power.

Royal Military College

Mackenzie saw the need to increase Canadian military strength after British troops left Central Canada in 1871. He oversaw the opening of the Royal Military College. It was built in Kingston, Ontario, in 1874. Graduates of this college made their mark during World War I, when twenty-eight of them served as officers in the British army. A number of graduates earned honours in this war.

The entrance to the Royal Military College today

Supreme Court of Canada

The British North America Act had provided for a Supreme Court, but it had not been established during Macdonald's term as prime minister. One of Prime Minister Mackenzie's accomplishments was to establish the Supreme Court of Canada as a court of appeal. Appeals still had to be referred to the Judicial Committee of the Privy Council in London.*

Changes to Election Practices

Mackenzie made a number of changes to the way elections were held. Before the secret ballot was introduced, a man (all voters were male) voted by publicly stating his choice. This practice left elections open to abuse, since people with power could control the way others voted. For instance, an employer could insist his employees vote for his favourite candidate.

*The Judicial Committee of the Privy Council continued to be the highest court of appeal for Canadians until 1949, when the Supreme Court of Canada took its place as the highest court.

Mackenzie also ordered taverns to close on election day. As well, men who did not own land received the right to vote. (Aboriginal people and women still did not have the right to vote.)

Before Mackenzie's changes, the prime minister could decide the order in which ridings (districts) voted. This gave him a great deal of control over the outcome. He could have the ridings that he knew would vote for his party vote first. This created momentum for his party. As voters in later ridings heard about the way the vote was going, many would vote the same way in order to be on the winning side. Today, ridings all vote on the same day.

Provincial Rights

Sir Oliver Mowat, Premier of Ontario, 1872–1896

You read in Chapter 5 how the British North America Act (1867) set out federal and provincial powers. The provinces and the federal government interpreted the articles of the BNA Act differently. The provinces wanted more control over their own affairs. The fight for provincial rights was led by Oliver Mowat, premier of Ontario. The Liberal government was more sympathetic with the fight for provincial rights than Macdonald's Conservative government had been.

For Your Notebook

1. Why was the building of the Royal Military College at Kingston so important?
2. In your opinion what was Mackenzie's greatest accomplishment? Explain your choice.
3. What was the highest level of appeal through the courts at this time? Find an example on this page to show that Canada was not a fully independent nation at this time.
4. Describe elections in Canada before and after Mackenzie's changes.

Mackenzie's Challenges

Recession

 During the 1870s Canada was mainly an agricultural nation. Other primary industries included fishing, fur trading, logging, and mining. Industries based on natural resources, such as sawmills and packing plants, were found in many regions. Canada's economy was based on exporting raw materials to countries that were more advanced industrially. Canada imported goods manufactured in countries such as Great Britain and the United States.

Slowly industrial production developed, mainly in Central Canada. In the new factories being built some **mass production** techniques were introduced, based on those used in Great Britain. Manufacturing was not yet a major part of Canada's economy.

As the graph shows, a recession in Canada occurred during the mid-1870s. The percentage change is shown for each date. A recession is a sharp drop in levels of production and employment. Because the recession was international, manufacturers in the USA were also affected. Sometimes they were forced to reduce their **inventories** by selling their goods at less than their cost. They often chose to sell these goods far below cost in Canada. These low-cost imports competed against Canadian-made products. New, less-developed Canadian industries suffered financially. They could not reduce the costs of production sufficiently to compete with the cheap imports.

In the depth of the recession the *Canadian Illustrated News* published this cartoon on Christmas Day. It shows a sad Santa Claus thinking about the fact that only the rich could afford to celebrate the season with feasting and gaiety.

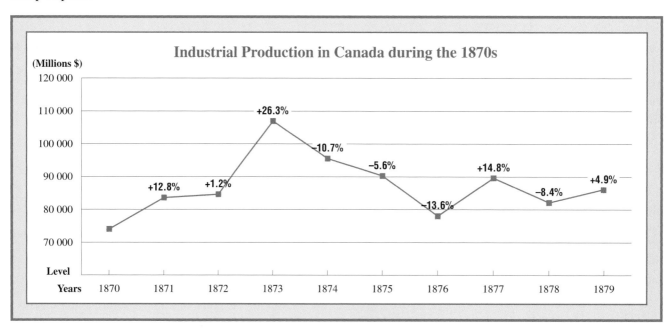

Mass production—producing many identical articles, usually in a factory

Inventory—the collection of unsold goods belonging to a business

The Issue of Trade

The Liberals wanted limited free trade. They thought that goods should be able to travel across the Canadian–American border with low tariffs. They believed some tariffs should be imposed because they were the government's chief source of income. There was no income tax at this time. However, the Liberals viewed competition as healthy. They did not want to raise tariffs to the point where they protected Canadian industry against all competition.

The Liberal Party's refusal to protect industry with increased tariffs did not contribute to their popularity as a government. Industry owners and investors who wanted this protection turned to the Conservatives.

Protective Tariffs

Canadian manufacturers wanted the Canadian government to introduce tariffs to protect them from competition from American industries and farm products. The following comments are from imaginary people discussing tariffs.

Why not buy what we need from the United States? Goods made in Canada cost more than goods made in the United States. Why should we pay more for Canadian-made goods?

Where's your loyalty to Canada? I'll **lobby** my Member of Parliament, and if necessary talk to Prime Minister Mackenzie. I'll demand that the government increase tariffs on American products coming into Canada. When you add tariffs to the cost of the product, Canadian buyers won't pay the higher American price! The government can get revenue from the tariffs, and we'll get our railway. It will also increase employment.

Canadians should trade with other Canadians instead of with Americans. Tariffs on American goods will encourage that. We don't need the Americans! We'll build more Canadian industries and protect them while they get established. Canadian manufacturers and farmers will flourish and more employment will be created in our country!

Trade Unions

Strikes in 1872 (see page 184) had not achieved the trade unions' immediate goal of a nine-hour work day. However, union leaders realized that there was power in solidarity. In September 1873, union leaders formed the Canadian Labour Union (CLU) to promote co-operation among the unions that joined. Because of the recession, the momentum created by the formation of the CLU did not continue through the rest of the 1870s. Workers did not wish to risk losing their jobs during these years. By 1878, the Canadian Labour Union had disbanded. However, union leaders had learned some important lessons that they were able to apply later in the century.

For Your Notebook

1. Discuss the economic situation in Canada during the 1870s. Were Canadian businesses the only ones suffering economically?
2. a) What is the difference between an economy protected by tariffs and one that operates under free trade?
   b) Which political party favoured which policy in the 1870s?
3. In what ways did the economic situation in Canada contribute to the unpopularity of the Liberals?

Exploring Further

4. For homework, find out which political parties in Canada today favour tariffs and which advocate free trade.
5. If you were to draw a cartoon representing the point of view of the Canadian government today on free trade, what would you draw?
6. Working with a partner, discuss this question: Do the ideas expressed in the 1870s on protective tariffs still apply today? Should free trade today continue?

Lobby—represent a special interest to the government; a lobbyist tries to get lawmakers to introduce or vote for measures favourable to the lobbyist's special interest.

Changing Technology

 Wind, water, and animals had been used as power sources in the past. By the mid-1800s wood and coal were also used as a power source in steam engines. Wood, brick, and stone were the basic construction materials. Gradually iron and steel came into use as construction materials.

Farm Implements

Farming was hard physical work. Improvements in farm implements increased efficiency. The drawing below of an early type of seed drill was done by artist C.W. Jefferys. The illustration and photo below show prairie farmers stooking grain and stacking bundles to be transported to the threshing machine on a horse-drawn wagon.

For Your Notebook

1. Using all the information on this page, determine in what ways the Massey Manufacturing Company would have made use of the changing technology.

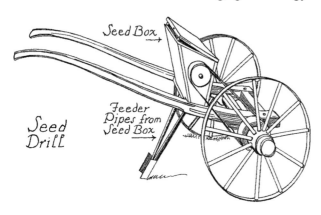

Hart Massey
1823–1896

One firm that flourished during the recession of the 1870s was the Massey Manufacturing Company. The company was started in 1847 by Daniel Massey as a blacksmith shop called Massey Agricultural Works. Daniel's son, Hart, brought them international fame with his farm machinery designs. In 1867, at the Paris International Exposition, the company won the first grand prize and two gold medals. They were congratulated by the French Emperor, Napoleon III.

In 1870, Hart Massey formed the Massey Manufacturing Company. He was president and his 23-year-old son Charles was vice-president and superintendent. In 1876 the company earned $100 000, an immense sum for the times.

In 1891, the company merged with its rival, the Harris Company of Brantford, to become the Massey-Harris Company. It was the largest company of its kind in the British Empire. In 1953 Massey-Harris joined with Harry Ferguson Ltd. of England. It became known as Massey-Ferguson Ltd. That company was bought in 1994 by AGCO, an American farm machinery company.

A Massey-Harris mower

Railway Building

Railways had three important advantages as means of transport. Steam locomotives were faster than horses and wagons. Trains could carry heavier, bulkier loads. They also ran year-round, unlike shipping by water, which was disrupted by freeze-up each year. Railways were key to industrial development. They carried raw materials to factories and carried finished goods to other centres or to ports for international export. Canada focused on two major railways at this time—the intercolonial and the transcontinental.

The Intercolonial Railway

An intercolonial railway would link the Atlantic provinces with Central Canada. Three goals prompted the building of the intercolonial railway. One was to promote unity among the provinces. Another goal was to provide a way to deal with a possible American invasion. The main goal was to promote industrialization, link markets, and create jobs.

When the Fathers of Confederation met at Quebec in 1864 to draft the Seventy-Two Resolutions, one resolution was for the intercolonial railway to be completed immediately. When the British parliament passed the British North America Act, it authorized a $12 million **loan guarantee**. However, railway construction had to begin within six months of Confederation and be completed without delay.

Sandford Fleming was asked to supervise the building of the intercolonial railroad. He was the former chief engineer of Toronto's Northern Railway and later the inventor of standard time zones. When the intercolonial railway was completed on July 1, 1876, the ninth anniversary of Confederation, Fleming called it "the full consummation of the Union of the British Provinces in North America."

A Transcontinental Railway

The colony of British Columbia was separated from the provinces of Canada by thousands of kilometres. Shipping products to and from Central and Atlantic Canada and the Prairies was slow and costly. The route around the tip of South America and the route across the continent were long and expensive. A transcontinental railway would change this.*

Loan guarantee—promise to pay debt if the borrower is unable to; this helped the region raise money

*You will read more about this in Chapter 9.

British Columbia in a Pet

UNCLE ALECK:—Don't frown so, my dear, you'll have your railway by-and-bye. MISS B. COLUMBIA:—I want it now. You promised I should have it, and if I don't, I'll complain to Ma.

For Your Notebook

1. The political cartoon above appeared in the *Canadian Illustrated News* in September 1876. It depicts British Columbia's disappointment at the limited progress of the Canadian Pacific Railway. The Premier of British Columbia travelled to Ottawa and then to Great Britain to express his concerns.
   a) Who do the people in the cartoon represent? Who is "Ma"? Why would "Ma" be involved?
   b) When and why was the colony of British Columbia promised a railway?

Exploring Further

2. 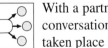 With a partner, role-play the conversation that could have taken place between "Uncle Aleck" and "Miss B. Columbia" in the above cartoon.

The North West Mounted Police

The Situation in the West

 In the years following the transfer of Rupert's Land to Canada by the Hudson's Bay Company in 1869, law and order were difficult to administer in the huge territory. The First Nations kept order among their own people. The rest of the population was sparse and spread out. There was no authority keeping order among them in the West. American traders began to move into the area in great numbers.

The Hudson's Bay Company had no fur trading forts in the prairie regions of the Bow River, the Belly River, and the South Saskatchewan River. American traders of the I.G. Baker Company and T.C. Power and Company came north from Fort Benton in the United States. They gradually began to enter the territory of the Siksika and other First Nations of the plains. The American companies set up posts as far north as the Bow River. They traded products such as flour, salt, tea, knives, axes, beads, needles, thread, and metal pots to First Nations people for buffalo robes and furs. In addition to these products, American traders sold whiskey and repeating rifles. A missionary living among the Siksika during the 1860s described changes he saw. He said the Siksika changed from the most powerful nation on the prairies to a poverty-stricken people. They traded their possessions to American traders in exchange for liquor and repeating rifles.

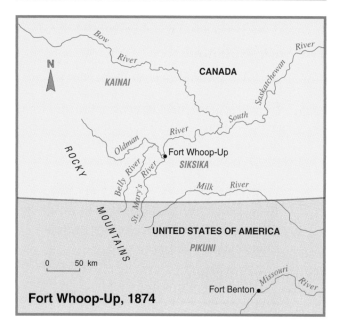

Fort Whoop-Up, 1874

American traders built their headquarters at the junction of the Oldman and St. Mary's Rivers near the present city of Lethbridge. They called it Fort Hamilton after its founder, but it became known as Fort Whoop-Up.

Trade Goods

. . . The trader stood at the wicket, a tub full of whiskey beside him and when an Indian pushed a buffalo robe to him through the hole, he handed out a tin cup full of the poisonous concoction. A quart of the stuff bought a fine pony. When spring came, wagon loads of the proceeds of the traffic were exported to Fort Benton in Montana, some 200 miles south of the border line.

Description by Colonel Steele of the North West Mounted Police

Trade	For
1 ordinary buffalo robe	2 cups whiskey
1 superior quality buffalo robe	1 blanket and 2 cups whiskey
1 horse	1 quart whiskey
furs equal to the height of a gun	1 repeating rifle

Kainai (Blood) people at Fort Whoop-Up, 1870s

Reports to the Government

The Dominion government at Ottawa was disturbed by reports of lawlessness they received from missionaries and the Hudson's Bay Company in the West. The Canadian government had hoped that settlers would make their homes on the Prairies. However, they knew that few people would risk taking their families into the West until law and order were established.

Captain Butler

In 1870, the federal government sent Captain Butler to investigate and report on affairs in the South Saskatchewan River valley.

. . . As matters at present rest, the region of the Saskatchewan is without law, order, or security for life or property; robbery and murder for years have gone unpunished . . . institutions are entirely unknown . . .

. . . Indians visiting the Rocky Mountain House during the fall of 1870 have spoken of the existence of a trading post of Americans from Fort Benton, upon the Belly River, sixty miles within the British boundary-line. . . . for the purpose of trading alcohol, whisky, and arms and ammunition. . . .

. . . I would recommend the following course for the consideration of Your Excellency . . . the organization of a well-equipped force of from 100 to 150 men, one-third to be mounted, specially recruited and engaged for service in the Saskatchewan; enlisting for two or three years service, and at expiration of that period to become military settlers, receiving grants of land, but still remaining as a reserve force should their services be required.

Excerpts from Butler's Report to the Canadian Government, 10 March 1871

Lt. Col. Robertson-Ross

As a result of Captain Butler's report, Lt. Col. Robertson-Ross was sent to study the situation on the prairie and to make suggestions to the Canadian government to improve conditions.

. . . The demoralization of the Indians, danger to the white inhabitants, and injury resulting to the country from this illicit trade is very great. . . .

. . . Year after year these unscrupulous traders continue to plunder our Indians of their Buffalo robes and valuable furs by extortion and fraud, and the shameful traffic causes certain bloodshed amongst the Indian tribes.

. . . It is indispensible for the peace of the country and welfare of the Indians that this smuggling and illicit traffic in spirits and firearms be no longer permitted.

[Recommendations]

. . . One regiment of mounted riflemen, 550 strong, including non-commissioned officers, divided into companies of fifty, would be a sufficient force to support Government in establishing law and order in the Saskatchewan, preserving the peace of the North-West Territory, and affording protection to the Surveyors, Contractors, and Railway Labourers about to undertake the great work of constructing the Dominion Pacific Railway . . .

Excerpts from Robertson-Ross' Report to the Federal Government, 17 March 1873

For Your Notebook

1. Who was responsible for law and order in the West before the arrival of the North West Mounted Police?
2. a) From where in the United States did the American traders come?
   b) What fort in Canada was the centre of operations for the American traders?
   c) In what types of activities were the traders at Fort Whoop-Up involved?
3. How did the Canadian government arrive at an accurate picture of the state of law and order in the West?
4. See page 198. While the Canadian government was deciding on the best solution for the West, an incident happened that caused the government to pass a bill immediately establishing the North West Mounted Police. What was it?

Exploring Further

5. It is 1872. You live in the NWT. Write a letter to the Canadian government explaining why there is a need for a police force in Western Canada.
6. What effect did the transfer of Rupert's Land to the Dominion of Canada have on law and order in the West?

Formation of the North West Mounted Police

 An incident in the Cypress Hills, in the southern part of modern-day Alberta and Saskatchewan, demonstrated the great need for a police force. In June 1873 a group of American and Canadian traders and trappers killed 36 Nakota people. News of this incident reached the Canadian government later in the summer. The Cypress Hills incident became a symbol of the lawlessness in the West.

In August 1873 Prime Minister Macdonald's Conservative government created a special police force for the West. This was the beginning of the North West Mounted Police (NWMP).

The scarlet jackets worn by the North West Mounted Police were distinctive. They reminded people of the jackets worn by soldiers in the British army.

The March West

There were only 300 men in the first group of NWMP sent to patrol the West. This was an amazingly small number to be given the task of patrolling the whole North-West Territories. However, by the early 1880s they were well respected by Canadians, the First Nations people, and the Americans for their ability to keep law and order in the Canadian West.

During the famous march to Western Canada in 1874, the force was under the command of Commissioner George French.

On July 8, 1874, the entire force of 300 set out from the small settlement of Dufferin on the Red River under the command of Commissioner George French. Their objective was Fort Whoop-Up in whiskey trader territory.

The long column of men was a spectacular sight.* The cavalcade consisted of over 100 Red River carts and about 70 wagons. There were two muzzle-loading field guns, two brass mortars, mowing machines, field kitchens, portable forges, and an ambulance hauled by either horses or oxen.** To supply some of their own food, the force took 93 cattle with them.

*The front cover of the textbook shows a photograph from a re-enactment of the March West.
**Field guns and mortars were large weapons on wheels, also known as artillery; a forge was a blacksmith's furnace for heating metal.

Day after day, the travel-weary group of North West Mounted Police pressed westward. Some of their experiences and hardships were recorded in the drawings and writings of Henri Julien, a French Canadian artist who accompanied them. Excerpts from Julien's diary follow on this page.

This long procession filed out of Dufferin in the afternoon of the 8th of July and camped about two miles out. Now we are in for it. Until now, it had been all plain sailing—fresh horses, plenty of rest, easy stages and untired bodies. But from this point, the real difficulties of the expedition became apparent. The very keeping together of so vast a caravan, with so many sluggard animals as oxen, cows, calves, through the untravelled country, was bound to be wearisome. Then there was the ride itself, over hundreds of miles, which, to the unhardy, was no trifling test of endurance. Add to this that the military regulations had to be severely enforced.

July 23rd—After leaving Souris River, we passed through a rather barren country and suffered a great deal from heat. Our skin felt as if on fire from the combined effects of hot winds, dust and mosquito bites. We were also frequently short of good water.

Julien's drawing shown on the right illustrates the NWMP meeting with a party of Dakota (Sioux) near Old Wives Lake on August 13, 1874.

After a few preliminaries one of the Dakota leaders shook hands with the mounted police. He then made a speech, which the guide, Leveille, interpreted. Leveille said the Dakota expressed trust in the British Queen, Victoria. They complained of the treatment their people were receiving in the United States. After the speech there was more shaking of hands. French then made a speech. It was recorded by Julien as follows:

The first meeting between First Nations and the North West Mounted Police

My brothers wish to know why we come this way. I will tell you. The white mother who lives beyond the great waters sent me. She heard the [Americans] came to kill you and give you bad whiskey. The white mother has white children, and red children, and black children. She loves them all alike. She sent these braves to punish those that kill them . . . We want to capture those who killed the white mother's red children. . . . We do not want the land of the Dakota nor any one else's. . . .

Fort Benton, USA

Inspector William Jarvis led part of the NWMP troop north to Fort Edmonton. On September 12, the main body of the NWMP, led by French, reached three deserted, broken-down, roofless log huts. They wondered if this was the famed Fort Whoop-Up they had travelled so far to capture, or an abandoned fur trade or whiskey fort.

Commissioner French was worried about the safety of his men. Winter would be arriving soon. Without proper food and shelter the horses and men would die. He decided to send the main body of the force to the Sweet Grass Hills just across the Canadian–American border. There they would find plenty of fresh water and grass for the horses. French, Assistant Commissioner James Macleod, and a small group of men then went south to Fort Benton in the United States for food, supplies, and horses.

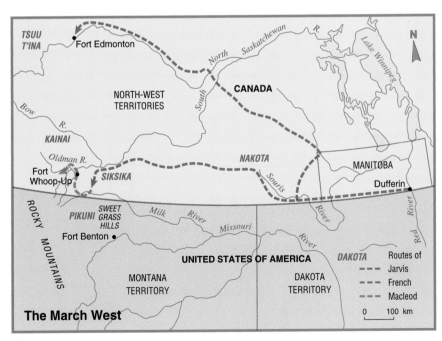

The March West

Fort Whoop-Up

Assistant Commissioner James Macleod

After the force reunited at the Sweet Grass Hills, it broke up. Troops D and E were going to Swan River and then back to Dufferin under the command of Commissioner French.

Troops B, C, and F were under the command of Assistant Commissioner Macleod. Guided by Jerry Potts, whom they had met in Fort Benton, Macleod set out in search of Fort Whoop-Up. Potts led them northward over the Fort Benton–Fort Whoop-Up Trail. On October 9, just as dusk was falling, he stopped. From high above the two rivers, the men gazed down on the junction of the Belly and St. Mary's Rivers. A flag fluttered in the wind over the wooden stockades and watch towers of Fort Whoop-Up. Otherwise there was no movement at all.

Macleod ordered the two nine-pounders and the two mortars* pointed towards the fort. Macleod and Potts then rode down the embankment and made their way towards the massive front gate. Darkness was fast-approaching. It was difficult to see exactly what was happening. Macleod knocked at the main gate and entered the fort. All was quiet within.

The buildings around all seemed to open onto the large centre square. Each building had loopholes in the walls for seeing out and aiming weapons. Was there an armed whiskey trader behind every loophole? A door opened and an older man slowly made his way towards Macleod, followed by a few First Nations people.

Macleod searched the entire fort. Not a whiskey trader nor a drop of whiskey was to be found. The whiskey traders had heard about the arrival of the "Red Coats." They had sold Fort Whoop-Up, packed their guns, whiskey, and other trade goods, and moved across the border to safety in the United States.

Fort Macleod

Macleod selected a spot on an island in the Oldman River, where the men built their headquarters. It was named Fort Macleod in honour of Assistant Commissioner James Macleod. There the small force of 150 men under Macleod's command began their first winter. They were completely isolated and without hope of reinforcements from the East if trouble started.

Fort Macleod, 1880: the first NWMP post later grew into a town in Alberta.

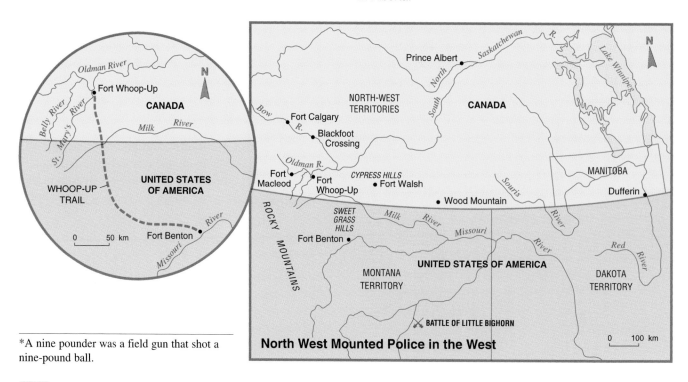

North West Mounted Police in the West

---

*A nine pounder was a field gun that shot a nine-pound ball.

Sam Steele
1849–1919

Sam Steele was a remarkable man who had an important role to play in many of the events that shaped Canada around the turn of the century. In 1866, he joined the Canadian militia in order to help protect Canada against Fenian raids from the United States. He served the Canadian government during both Metis Resistances. As a member of the newly formed North West Mounted Police, he took part in the March West. He was involved in negotiating treaties with First Nations on the prairies.

Later he was involved in maintaining order as the Canadian Pacific Railway was built through British Columbia. He was present at the CPR Last Spike ceremony at Craigellachie. Steele was the officer commanding the Mounted Police during the Klondike Gold Rush. He also went to the South African (Boer) War as commanding officer of the **cavalry** unit called Strathcona's Horse. During World War I he was in command of the second Canadian contingent to be sent overseas. (You will read about both of these wars later in this textbook.)

Sam Steele was present at virtually every important event in the Canadian West from the Red River Resistance in 1869 through to the Klondike gold rush. He also distinguished himself in the two international conflicts in which Canada was involved during his lifetime. He had a remarkable career.

Jerry Potts
1837–1898

Jerry Potts worked as a guide and translator for the NWMP for 25 years. He was a Metis whose mother was from the Kainai (Blood) First Nation. His father was a clerk for the American Fur Company.

On the famous March West, Potts led the NWMP to Fort Whoop-Up. He also selected the location for Fort Macleod on the Oldman River.

Potts once had a dream that cat skin would protect him, so he wore one under his shirt. He was never injured in battle.

Lieutenant-Colonel George French 1841–1921	Lieutenant-Colonel James Macleod 1836–1894	Lieutenant-Colonel A.G. Irvine 1837–1916	Major James Walsh 1840–1905
• Responsible for initial organization of the NWMP, and for its military character • First NWMP Commissioner, 1873–1876	• Second NWMP Commissioner, 1876–1880 • Founded Fort Macleod • Stopped American whiskey trade • Negotiated Treaty 7 • In 1887, was appointed a judge of the Supreme Court of the NWT	• Third NWMP Commissioner, 1880–1886 • Force grew to 500 men • Training depot set up • Headquarters moved to Regina	• Inspector in the NWMP, 1873–1883 • Came west on the first march • In charge of Fort Walsh • After a 14-year absence, returned to the NWMP because of the Klondike gold rush • Commissioner of Yukon District, 1897–1898

Cavalry—army units on horseback

Bringing About Law and Order

   C.E. Denny, one of the original North West Mounted Police, wrote of challenges and successes in the early years of the force:

> . . . That not one case of robbery or loss of this annuity money ever occurred shows, perhaps better than anything else, the respect for the law which had been established through the North West Mounted Police. Across the boundary line conditions were vastly different. Hardly a month passed that did not bring its tale of stage robbery, mine hold-up, or murder . . . crime was still prevalent and maintenance of law and order suffered greatly in comparison with what obtained in the Canadian North-West.
>
> Three years later the force was reduced from a thousand to seven hundred. . . .

For Your Notebook

1. Working in a group of four or five students take the role of members of a government committee responsible for deciding the objectives of the police force in the West.

   a) Make predictions on what challenges you think the NWMP will face in bringing about law and order in the North-West Territories.

   b) Make a list of the duties and responsibilities you think the police force should carry out.

2. The chart on pages 202 to 205 is designed to show cause and effect—how the NWMP met the objectives the Canadian government set out for them. Read the sections of the chart from left to right. Refer to the map on page 200 while reading the chart. Record the objectives the NWMP successfully carried out.

Objectives (Duties and Responsibilities)

1. To establish posts to house and protect the men and horses

Fort Walsh in the Cypress Hills

2. To track down people who broke the law and bring them to justice

Two NWMP corporals transporting a prisoner

Effect and Examples of Results

Fort Walsh

In the summer of 1875, B Troop, led by Inspector Walsh, constructed Fort Walsh in the Cypress Hills. The Cypress Hills was a major area of concern to the NWMP. There were many whiskey traders in the area. It was also the hunting ground for a number of First Nations. Conflicts between the various groups were common, as was horse stealing.

Fort Calgary

On August 18, 1875, 50 men of F troop under Inspector Brisebois set out from Fort Macleod to establish a post at the junction of the Bow and Elbow Rivers. The city of Calgary eventually grew up around this site.

Capturing Criminals

During 1883 and 1884 a great number of settlers entered the region. Crime was much more prevalent and the duties of the NWMP multiplied. Horse stealing had, by 1880, become almost a daily occurrence. Much of the time and energy of the NWMP was devoted to the capture of horse thieves.

Objective

3. **To collect customs dues; to track down illegal traders (to stop the liquor traffic between whiskey traders and First Nations)**

Police inspecting traders' carts (1874). Sketch by Henri Julien

4. **To help gain the respect and confidence of the First Nations**

Above: A group of Kainai (Blood) people at Fort Calgary, 1878.

Left: Chiefs of the Blackfoot Confederacy* at Fort Macleod, 1875, photographed here with Sergeant W. Piercy, NWMP. Chief Crowfoot is front-left and his secretary, J. L'Heureux, is behind him.

*The Blackfoot Confederacy included Siksika (Blackfoot), Tsuu T'ina (Sarcee), Kainai (Blood), and Pikuni (Peigan).

Effect and Examples of Results

In 1874, the Canadian government passed an act forbidding the importing, manufacture, and sale of liquor in the North-West Territories. In late October of the same year, the NWMP made their first successful whiskey raid. With the help of Jerry Potts, the police apprehended five whiskey traders.

Not all attempts by the North West Mounted Police to capture whiskey traders were successful. However, over the years they successfully managed to enforce the whiskey trading law.

> Fort Macleod—there are over three thousand Indians camped here at present, and more coming every day. There can be no doubt of the fact that they are very destitute—starving, in short, is about the only way to put it. There is not the sign of a buffalo, the season for berries is about over, and life cannot long be sustained on wild turnips and what other roots they can gather.
>
> They come to you and say 'We have had nothing to eat for two, three, or four days, and our children are crying with hunger; we do not care so much for ourselves but we do not like to see our children die.' . . .
>
> *Saskatchewan Herald*, November 3, 1879

As the *Saskatchewan Herald* primary source shows, the decline in buffalo was having devastating consequences for First Nations people. Many First Nations moved southward to the United States in an attempt to locate the few remaining buffalo herds. This caused conflicts over hunting grounds. The crowding together of First Nations, many of them old enemies, resulted in a situation that could lead to open warfare.

Those who remained in Canadian territory were forced to either starve or to eat anything they could find. Some turned to raiding ranchers' cattle to keep from starving. Supplies were sent by the Canadian government to the NWMP to assist the starving people.

Jerry Potts acted as a good will ambassador for the NWMP among the Siksika, explaining the motives of the police, as well as gaining their promises of co-operation.

Objective	Effect and Examples of Results

Objective

5. To police and protect the Dakota while they were in Canada

Chief Sitting Bull
Dakota (Sioux)

Inspector James Walsh
NWMP

6. To negotiate treaties with the First Nations

Chief Crowfoot
Siksika (Blackfoot)

Lieutenant James Macleod
NWMP

Treaty 7 with the Siksika, 1877, Blackfoot Crossing

Effect and Examples of Results

The late 1870s were critical years for the North West Mounted Police. During this time 6000 Dakota under the leadership of Sitting Bull sought refuge in Canada. (The Dakota lived on the western plains in the USA. In 1876 the Dakota, led by Sitting Bull and Chief Crazy Horse, had defeated General Custer's US cavalry at the Battle of Little Big Horn. Then they travelled northward into Canada to avoid the US army.)

Shortly after their arrival, Inspector Walsh, a sergeant, three constables, and two scouts paid Sitting Bull a visit in his camp in the Cypress Hills. Walsh explained the laws of Canada. He warned Sitting Bull that he was not to use Canada as a base from which to wage war on the Americans. Sitting Bull replied that his grievance was with the Americans, not the Canadians. Sitting Bull's men asked for ammunition. Walsh told them they would receive only enough for hunting purposes. An agreement was reached. If the Dakota behaved peacefully they would receive protection in Canada; if not, they would have to return to the United States.

One of the duties of the North West Mounted Police was to prepare First Nations for the treaty process and to assist in negotiations. The most famous treaty involving the NWMP was Treaty 7.

Negotiations for Treaty 7 took place in 1877 at Blackfoot Crossing on the Bow River. David Laird, Lieutenant-Governor of the North-West Territories, represented the Canadian government. Lieutenant Colonel James Macleod, 80 North West Mounted Police, and about 3000 Kainai (Blood), Pikuni (Peigan), Tsuu T'ina (Sarcee), Siksika (Blackfoot), and Nakoda (Stoney) people were present. In the painting at the bottom of the first column, Chief Crowfoot is speaking to Lieutenant-Governor Laird.

Under the terms of Treaty 7, reserves were established for First Nations people. The task of encouraging people to move to the reserves and to assist them in adapting to their new life fell to the North West Mounted Police. The transition was not an easy one. Centuries of living independently and following the migrations of the buffalo could not be changed in a few years to a life settled on the reserve.

You will learn more about these treaties and their effects on First Nations people later in the chapter.

Objective	Effect and Examples of Results

Objective

7. To keep law and order in the CPR construction camps

8. To give aid and advice to settlers

9. To perform all the duties of a police force

NWMP patrol guard the frontier during the North-West Resistance of 1885.

Effect and Examples of Results

Construction of the Canadian Pacific Railway began in 1875 and was completed in 1885. There were 4000 construction workers in the railroad camps. The NWMP kept law and order among them and settled disputes between railway workers and First Nations people. As the railway extended westward, towns grew up at various locations. The task of policing these towns also belonged to the NWMP.

Thousands of settlers took advantage of the protection provided by the NWMP to move westward once the railway was built. The police gave advice, helped settlers through difficult times, delivered mail, checked for smallpox, or just made friendly visits to remote areas.

> A traveller passing through the Territories at this time would have seen police engaged in fighting prairie fires, enforcing quarantine regulations, collecting customs dues, watching for smugglers, chasing horse thieves, conveying lunatics or prisoners, taking charge of mails on the Canadian Pacific Railway, and performing various other duties required by the several departments of the public service . . .
>
> —C.E. Denny, *The Law Marches West.*

On March 16, 1885, the NWMP at Regina received orders to march north to Prince Albert to protect the settlement. The North West Mounted Police played only a small part in the North-West Resistance of 1885. However, it was realized that a greater number of men was needed to police the North-West Territories. The size of the force was increased.

As part of their duties, the NWMP patrolled the North-West Territories. In 1896 gold was discovered in the Yukon. Since the Klondike gold strike was in Canadian territory, a larger presence of North West Mounted Police was needed to maintain law and order.

In the Twentieth Century

By the turn of the century the North West Mounted Police were becoming a familiar sight on the plains of Western Canada. In 1904 their name was changed to the Royal North West Mounted Police.

During World War I, many of the force entered the military. Two cavalry squadrons were formed for service in France and Siberia, Russia.

In 1920 the headquarters was transferred from Regina to Ottawa. During the same year the **jurisdiction** of the force was extended to the whole of Canada. Their name was changed again, this time to the Royal Canadian Mounted Police.

In 1928 the newly built police schooner, *St. Roch*, began patrol and supply duties in northern waters.

In 1940–1942, the *St. Roch* became the first vessel to navigate the Northwest Passage from west to east. The vessel successfully made the return trip from east to west in 1944.

Also in 1928, the Royal Canadian Mounted Police took over enforcement of provincial laws in Saskatchewan. It had previously been a solely federal police force.

Jurisdiction—area of authority and responsibility

In 1932 similar duties were assigned to them in Alberta, Manitoba, and the Maritimes. In the same year the Royal Canadian Mounted Police took on the duties of the Department of National Revenue and a Marine Section was started.

During World War II, the Royal Canadian Mounted Police contributed a company of soldiers, the No. 1 Provost Company, for service in Great Britain and Europe.

When Newfoundland became a province in 1949, the jurisdiction of the Royal Canadian Mounted Police was extended to include Canada's newest province. In 1950 the Royal Canadian Mounted Police assumed provincial duties in the province of British Columbia. Although the original force was all-male and mainly of British origin, women and people from visible minorities were included as full members of the RCMP in the 20th century.

The Royal Canadian Mounted Police is the law enforcement arm of the Canadian government. Its job is to enforce various federal laws and assist the departments of the Canadian government. The Royal Canadian Mounted Police are especially busy enforcing Customs and Excise laws. They attempt to stop smugglers from illegally bringing goods, especially drugs, into Canada. The Royal Canadian Mounted Police keeps a close watch on international drug traffic through offices in Washington and London and liaison with members of Interpol (International Criminal Police Organization). Other areas of responsibility include enforcement of the Income Tax Act and apprehending people making or circulating counterfeit money.

The RCMP are the police forces at parks and airports, Canadian embassies, and in other international contexts.

The Marine Division and the Air Division participate in rescue operations when necessary and cooperate with the land division. Services of the Air Division are especially valuable in northern Canada.

In less than 100 years the Royal Canadian Mounted Police successfully established itself as the sole police force in the vast regions of the Yukon and the North-West Territories, as well as the federal force from coast to coast in Canada.

Police work is complicated, difficult, sometimes monotonous, and often dangerous. There is little glamour in the work. Nevertheless, members of the Royal Canadian Mounted Police derive a great deal of satisfaction from living up to their motto—*Maintiens le Droit*—Uphold the Right.

In 1999, current and retired RCMP officers re-enacted the March West in order to mark its 125th anniversary. A photograph of this event is shown on the front cover of this textbook.

The Numbered Treaties

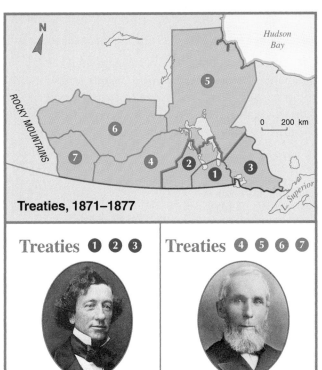

Treaties, 1871–1877

Treaties ❶ ❷ ❸

Conservative Government of
John A. Macdonald

Treaties ❹ ❺ ❻ ❼

Liberal Government of
Alexander Mackenzie

From 1871 to 1877, seven Numbered Treaties were signed between the Canadian government and First Nations living in the North-West Territories.

  Between 1860 and 1923, a total of 66 treaties were signed with First Nations for a number of reasons. Land-surrender treaties were the most significant. The Canadian government attempted to resolve First Nations land claims before settlers could move into the North-West Territories. This was done through a series of treaties known as the Numbered Treaties. From 1871 to 1877, seven Numbered Treaties were signed between the Canadian government and First Nations living between Lake Superior and the Rocky Mountains. Four more were signed between 1889 and 1921. Once treaties were signed, settlers began to move across Canada to occupy the lands where the First Nations had lived. (Numbered treaties continued to be signed into the 1950s.)

There is controversy about how the Canadian government and the First Nations people interpreted the treaties. Generally, in exchange for surrendering their lands, First Nations received the following: reserve lands to live on, a lump-sum payment, yearly payments, hunting, fishing, and mineral rights, and a school on reserves that requested one.

First Nations often received promises from the Canadian government that they would be given farm implements, tools, seeds, and the right to hunt, fish, and trap on crown land located throughout the treaty area.* Often these promises were not kept.

Many people have questioned whether First Nations had a choice about moving onto the reserves. Over time they had gradually lost their power. Towards the end of the 1700s and beginning of the 1800s, epidemics of smallpox, tuberculosis, and measles killed tens of thousands of people. Poverty resulting from the American whiskey trade weakened them as well. By the 1870s the herds of buffalo were few in number and a fraction of their former size. With their main source of food gone, First Nations were forced to accept treaties and help from the Canadian government.

The first Indian Act was passed in 1876. In the years that followed, the Canadian government controlled the lives of First Nations people more and more. The people who belonged to groups that signed treaties, and the descendants of these people, are legally known as "Status Indians." They are registered under the terms of the Indian Act. Those who did not sign treaties and their descendants, and descendants of people who lost or gave up their status are legally known as "Non-Status Indians" (see web page 54).

An Exercise in Decision-Making

1. Use pages 207 to 212 as reference, as well as carrying out additional research to answer the following: **Should the Indian Act be abolished? Or should it be revised?** (Consider historical need for the Act and modern day need, current impact on family life on reserves, effect on education, effect on personal freedoms, and effect on Aboriginal people's public image.)

Indian Act, 1876

Introduction

In 1876 the government of Canada passed the Indian Act.** This Act governs the First Nations people and their lands.

Aim: to set up a national administration for governing First Nations people and move the First Nations people onto reserves so the remaining lands could be used for settlement

- The purpose of the first Indian Act was to eventually assimilate First Nations people into Euro-Canadian culture.
- The Canadian government also introduced isolation policies. The First Nations people were put onto reserves, making the rest of the land available for settlement. Once on the reserves they were to be educated, "Christianized," and isolated from

harmful aspects of the Euro-Canadian society. The Indian Act treated First Nations people as minors (not legally adult). They were treated as wards of the government, whose lives needed to be controlled by a **benevolent**, parent-like government.

Assimilation (when a culture is absorbed into another): to require the Aboriginal peoples to accept the laws, customs, language, and religion of the culture of the people who hold the power in the country.

---

*Note: Crown land was held by the government of Canada to be used for settlement by non-Natives, but not yet sold.

**First Nations people were not consulted when this Act was drawn up. The Indian Act of 1876 has been revised many times. Some of the later amendments were very restrictive of First Nations

peoples' freedoms. The most recent change to the Indian Act was passed in 1988.

Benevolent—someone who wishes to help and do good for others; kind, caring

An Exercise in Critical Thinking

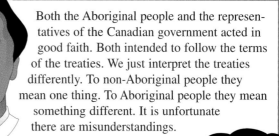

Critical thinkers realize there is more than one point of view on every issue. Read the following points of view presented by various modern-day Aboriginal people.* Identify the issues being discussed. Prepare arguments both for and against each issue. You may wish to do additional library research.

The land wasn't ours to give away. We did not surrender all our rights to the land. We gave some powers to the Canadian government in exchange for certain rights and privileges. As nations we retained use of the land and its resources. The land is ours to take care of—for all to use. We did not know that thousands of non-Aboriginal settlers would come here expecting to claim the lands as their exclusive private property. Our chiefs did not know they were giving up possession of our people's traditional lands.

We thought the treaties were intended to guarantee us our rights over lands that we traditionally occupied and used for thousands of years. When we signed the treaties we agreed to share the land with the newcomers. When the Canadian government signed, they recognized our Aboriginal rights and our claim to these lands. We entered into formal, political agreements with their country as nations. We formed a confederation, a political agreement with them.

The treaties are not fair! They are one-sided. They do not look after our interests. The treaties say the government will take care of us, teach us how to make a living like the Europeans. They haven't done this! Sure, we signed a treaty and got reserve land to live on. But according to the Indian Act, the Minister had control over the reserve lands. He decided what to do on the reserve—not us! We were told we could hunt on our reserves and get food from the crown lands. And now they won't let us! There are even some non-Aboriginal people farming on reserve lands!

Both the Aboriginal people and the representatives of the Canadian government acted in good faith. Both intended to follow the terms of the treaties. We just interpret the treaties differently. To non-Aboriginal people they mean one thing. To Aboriginal people they mean something different. It is unfortunate there are misunderstandings.

When we signed the treaties we did not give up our rights to govern ourselves. They took away our hereditary chief, whose ancestry went back 20 generations, and replaced him with an elected chief and council. The age-old rules for law and order were replaced by foreign laws of Canada. Often the Aboriginal people did not understand these Canadian laws.

We had no other choice. Our ancestors had to sign the treaties. At first we had enough land for our people. We had assistance from the government and promises of help and protection. Without that we would have all died. The buffalo were gone. Our people were starving. Many had died from smallpox. Before long we would all have been gone. We would have lost our land anyway to the settlers, who would have taken it from us. At least by signing the treaties we have a place to live on the reserves.

They outlawed our beliefs, our ceremonies, and our songs because they were different from theirs. We wanted to preserve our stories and legends, our traditional skills and arts, and our dances. The teachers in their schools told our children that our ways were wrong and not to be followed. When we spoke the language of our people we were punished. We had to speak English.

They took away our children for most of the year, taking them to residential schools. Why were non-Aboriginal children not treated the same way? When they took away our language and our culture, our children lost their connection with their history. In their school books they called us "savages." Our children lost pride in themselves and our culture when they read these books. They started to think the ways of the non-Aboriginal people were better than the ways of their own people.

*These are not actual quotations, but have been written after interviewing a large number of Aboriginal people.

You read about the potlatch on page 33 in Chapter 1. The potlatch was an elaborate give-away ceremony of many First Nations living along the Pacific Coast. There were dances, speeches, and feasting at a potlatch. Gifts were given to guests, and sometimes possessions were destroyed to impress them. Often, potlatch marked some special event, such as death, marriage, or the bestowing of an inherited name. It was also an opportunity to establish rank in the class system. People at the potlatch sat according to their rank. The quality of the gifts they received was also determined by rank.

The idea that people would give away or destroy all their most valuable possessions was viewed with disfavour by non-Aboriginal people. It went against their European goal of gaining material goods as a reward for hard work.

Euro-Canadian employers were not happy about the potlatch because First Nations workers would leave work for days or weeks at a time in order to attend. Christian missionaries were even more offended than other Europeans. Potlatch practices seemed like **pagan** ceremonies to them. Missionaries mistakenly thought that the ceremonial masks and totem poles were idols that the people worshipped.

In 1884, the Indian Act was changed to ban the potlatch. It threatened anyone who continued to take part in potlatches with imprisonment. The potlatch continued, but in secret. Some of the largest potlatches ever held took place in the years following the official ban. Over 20 Kwakwaka'wakw (Kwakiutl) were convicted and put in jail. Many of the gifts they had prepared were sent to the National Museum in Ottawa. A Kwakwaka'wakw person described what happened:

The scow came around from the cannery and put in at the village to pick up the big pile of masks and headdresses and belts and coppers— everything we had for potlatching . . . Our old people who watched the barge pull out from shore with all their masks on it said: "There is nothing left now. We might as well go home." When we say, "go home," it means to die.

Clellan S. Ford,
Smoke from Their Fires:
The Life of a Kwakiutl Chief.

Official approval to revive the potlatch custom was not given until changes were made to the Indian Act in 1951. The potlatch continues today in modified form. Factory-made clothing, dishes, blankets, and other items have replaced the carvings, masks, and other hand-made items of old. However, potlatches continue to be a way to strengthen social and cultural ties and to mark important events.

Exploring Further

1. Were government officials justified in taking First Nations possessions as museum **artifacts**? Should museums return artifacts to their former owners?

2.  You read in this chapter and Chapter 1 about the potlatch on the Pacific Coast and how it was banned under the Indian Act. Conduct research on the Sun Dance ceremony, which was part of the culture of some First Nations on the Prairies. How would some of the concerns that the government had about the potlatch also apply to the Sun Dance ceremony?

Royal British Columbia Museum, PN 1499

Potlatch gifts are arranged in front of the house at this 1905 potlatch at Quamichan, a Sto:lo (Coast Salish) village on Vancouver Island.

Pagan—not Christian

Artifact—an object or evidence of human life in the past

Canada Revisited

Aboriginal People Today

According to the 1996 Canadian census there were 28 528 125 people in Canada. Of this number, approximately 3%, or 799 010, were Aboriginal.

Population

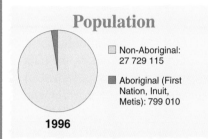

Non-Aboriginal: 27 729 115

Aboriginal (First Nation, Inuit, Metis): 799 010

1996

There are 608 First Nations in Canada. First Nations, Inuit, and Metis people today live in all parts of Canada. They live on reserves and off-reserve in rural areas. Others live in small towns and villages. In some places Aboriginal people are the majority of the population. Recently many more have moved to larger towns and cities. They are usually a minority in cities.

Treaties

Not all groups in Canada have signed treaties with the government. Not all parts of Canada have been covered by treaties. In the past, under the terms of treaties, First Nations groups agreed to share the land with settlers in return for certain treaty benefits.

After European colonization, Aboriginal people held little power to govern their own lives. They were governed by laws made by other governments. Their traditional leaders were not recognized. Groups had little control over their own security. They struggled to keep or to get back the lands they had once lived on and controlled.

During the last two decades of the twentieth century, Aboriginal groups have worked to bring about changes. Across Canada, thousands of demands are being brought to the law courts and government of Canada. Most have to do with self-government and land claims.

Land Claims

Land claims are issues about the ownership of land on which Aboriginal people originally lived or that they controlled. In some regions no treaty was ever signed with the government. Other land claims have involved settlements to meet treaty promises that a past government did not keep. Federal, provincial, territorial, and Aboriginal governments are involved in land claims. These disputes can take decades to settle. Not everyone agrees with the decisions.

The Nisga'a Treaty

Treaties were never signed for lands occupied by First Nations in mainland British Columbia while the province was being settled by Canadians, Europeans, and Americans. The Nisga'a chiefs from the Nass Valley in northwestern British Columbia asked the government in 1887 for title to their land. However, they were not given reserve lands.

Over the years, the Nisga'a continued to press the government for an agreement. After a long process, a settlement was reached in 1999. Land, money, and some powers of self-government were given to the Nisga'a First Nation. In return, the Nisga'a gave up title to much of the land they had originally controlled.

There are thousands of other negotiations for self-government and land claims under way. More arise each year.

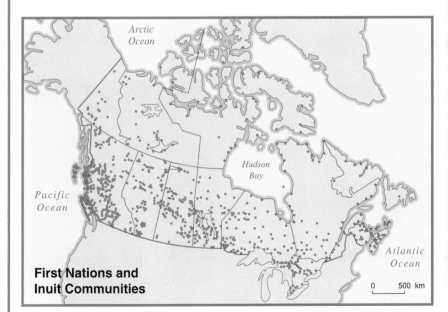

First Nations and Inuit Communities

0   500 km

There were 2406 reserves in Canada in 1997. As land claims are settled, these numbers will change.

Self-government

  Self-government is the power of the members of a group to govern the group. Self-government allows people to control their own affairs. Because of the Indian Act, First Nations governments had little power, except over local issues. Aboriginal groups are now seeking more power to govern themselves.

First Nations governments are taking control of more aspects of life on the reserve. A First Nation government, the government of Canada, and a province or territory share the costs of services on reserves and responsibilities for them. First Nations governments are made up of an elected chief and band council. Band councils control money taken in and how it is spent. Responsibilities include housing, education, health care, recreation, and local laws for the community.

Some First Nations have more income than others. They may get it from use of their land, natural resources, and local businesses. Other groups struggle with poverty and unemployment. These are often accompanied by social problems. They must find ways of meeting these challenges as their people attempt to meet their needs in the modern world and keep their identity.

The National Aboriginal Achievement Awards recognize the accomplishments of Aboriginal individuals each year. See their web page: http://www.westindies.cibc.com/aboriginal/community.html

The Metis

 The Metis are people who have both European and First Nations or Inuit ancestry and identify themselves as Metis. Many trace their ancestry to the time of the fur trade. They are recognized by the Canadian government as Aboriginal, but do not receive the legal benefits of Status Indians.

The Metis people struggled without success for many decades to get their own homeland. In Alberta in 1938, ten Metis settlements were established. Today most Metis people live scattered among the general population of towns and cities. In 1995, only about 6000 lived in the Metis settlements, a small fraction of the population of Canada.

It is difficult for Metis people to preserve their unique culture. Political events in Western Canada in the 1800s resulted in economic and social hardship for them.

Metis people are working to recover their traditional cultures, particularly in the Prairie region. Research and teaching of Metis history is one of the features of the Gabriel Dumont Institute in Saskatchewan. It is the first Metis-run college in Canada.

Through organizations such as the Metis National Council and provincial organizations, Metis people work together to achieve their goals and maintain their culture.

Inuit

 The Inuit are the people of Canada's North. Most of them live in the new territory of Nunavut, the Northwest Territories, northern Quebec, Labrador, and the Yukon Territory.

Nunavut

Capital	Iqaluit (formerly Frobisher Bay)
Population	27 219 (85% Inuit)
Languages	Inuktitut/English

©Canada Post Corporation, 1999. Reproduced with Permission.

After 30 years of political activity by Inuit leaders, the Inuit of the Eastern Arctic reached an agreement with the government of Canada. On April 1, 1999, Nunavut was officially created as a new political region of Canada. It has been called the largest land-claim agreement in Canadian history. It covers one-fifth of the land area of Canada. (See final map in the endsheet at the back of this textbook.) Nunavut means "Our Land" in Inuktitut. The agreement includes land, mineral rights, financial payments, and self-government.

The Inuit people have elected their first all-Aboriginal government. The legislature has 19 elected members. It operates under a consensus form of government.

The first Premier of Nunavut is an Inuit lawyer, Paul Okalik.

Review

The icons are your cue to refer to the Learning How to Learn Appendix (pages 348–371) for ideas on how to complete these activities.

1. Complete a self-assessment for one assignment from this chapter.

Understanding Concepts

2.

   a) As a class review the concepts that were the focus of Section III (see page 147).
   b) Discuss the three questions on the easel as they apply to Mackenzie's time as prime minister.

3. At the beginning of Chapter 8 (page 187) you made some predictions based on the Overview, your preview of the chapter, and what you already knew. Use what you have learned from reading the chapter to fill in the third column of the Prediction Chart, "What I Found Out."

4. Do either a) or b).

   a) Create a concept poster for one of the chapter's main ideas. Present your poster to the class.

   b) Use a web, mind map, outline, or chart to create a permanent set of notes about one of the ideas. Explain your work to a classmate.

5. Use one of the methods found in the Appendix for recording any new vocabulary in the WordBook section of your notes.

6. Add entries for this chapter in your timeline.

Developing Communication Skills

7. Imagine it is 1878. Write an editorial on Prime Minister Mackenzie's accomplishments.

8. In your History Journal tell of one person, place, idea, or event that you learned about, which you had never heard of before. Why do you think you have not learned about this until now? How can you relate this to your life now?

Developing Research Skills

9.

Section III Activity

 Part Two
Now that you have studied this chapter, consider what challenges the new Dominion of Canada faced under the leadership of Prime Minister Mackenzie. List these in your History notes. In role as Prime Minister Mackenzie, fill in parts ❷ to ❻ on the chart A Model to Meet Challenges for the topic you selected on page 187.

Part Three
As a class discuss
a) the challenges faced by Prime Minister Mackenzie and how they were met
b) whether we would solve these challenges in the same way today

Applying Concepts

10.  The biography of Mackenzie mentions that, after his party's defeat in 1878, he continued on as a Member of Parliament.

    a) What is a Member of Parliament? How does one get this position?
    b) Who is your Member of Parliament?
    c) Who is the leader of the Conservative Party in Canada today? The Liberals? Who are the other political party leaders in Canada today?
    d) Who is Canada's current Prime Minister? What political party does he or she represent?

11. Find examples in the media of modern-day treaties and/or land claims.

Chapter 9
The National Policy
1878–1896

O v e r v i e w
Use this Overview to predict what you will read in this chapter.

3 1885

The North-West Resistance was led by Louis Riel supported by Poundmaker, Big Bear, and Gabriel Dumont.

1 1878

Sir John A. Macdonald and the Conservatives were elected with a landslide victory. Macdonald won over the voters with his National Policy, which promoted protective tariffs, a transcontinental railway, and settlement of the West.

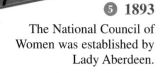

5 1893

The National Council of Women was established by Lady Aberdeen.

4 1891

After campaigning with the slogan: "The Old Flag, the Old Policy, the Old Leader," the Conservatives won the election.

2 1885

The Canadian Pacific Railway, a transcontinental railway, was completed on November 7th.

6 1892–1896

Canada had four prime ministers between 1892 and 1896: Sir John Abbott, Sir John Thompson, Sir Mackenzie Bowell, and Sir Charles Tupper.

Chapter 9 Focus

Chapter 8 described major events under the Liberal government led by Alexander Mackenzie between 1873 and 1878. Chapter 9 tells about Canada between 1878 and 1896 under a Conservative government. During this time, two of the three parts of Sir John A. Macdonald's National Policy were implemented. These were protective tariffs and the building of a transcontinental railway. Canada continued to change, as cities in Quebec and Ontario became more industrialized and the federal government prepared for settlement of the North-West Territories. The chapter also describes the North-West Resistance of 1885, led by Louis Riel. All of the book's concepts are focused on in this chapter.

| Change | Regionalism | Power | Identity | Co-operation/Conflict |

Concepts and Main Topics

- National Policy
- protective tariffs
- Canadian Pacific Railway
- industrialization
- factory system
- role of women
- changes to cities
- political necessity
- economic necessity
- North-West Resistance

Learning How to Learn

 Decision-making

 Critical Thinking

 Cause and Effect

 Cartoon Analysis

Chapter Preview/Prediction

Examine the Overview on page 214, read the Chapter 9 Focus, and briefly look through the chapter. Take note of headings and pictures. Use this information and what you already know about Canada during this period to predict what this chapter will be about. Create a three-column chart headed Know, Wonder, and Learn.

In the Know column, fill in everything you know about this chapter. Then think about what you would *like* to know. Add this to the Wonder column. At the end of this chapter, you will review your chart and summarize what you have learned in the Learn column.

Section III Activity

    In 1878 John A. Macdonald once again became prime minister of Canada. The following list contains some of the challenges Macdonald and the Conservatives faced.

Part One

Select one of the following goals Prime Minister Macdonald and the Conservatives tried to accomplish:

a) to bring about industrialization in Central Canada (pages 218 to 222)

b) to complete the Canadian Pacific Railway (pages 223 to 232)

c) to stop the North-West Resistance, 1885 (pages 233 to 240)

  Assume the role of Prime Minister Macdonald. Record your notes on the chart A Model to Meet Challenges (page 145).

This activity continues on page 243.

The building of a transcontinental railway was part of the National Policy.

The National Policy

 The Liberals, under the leadership of Alexander Mackenzie, had been governing Canada since 1873. During this time the country experienced economic problems. In the election of 1878 the Liberals under Mackenzie fought hard to stay in power. The Conservatives under Macdonald fought equally hard to regain power.

At this time, Canada was basically an agricultural country. Most of its population lived in rural areas in what is now Central and Atlantic Canada. Sir John A. Macdonald proposed a government policy called the National Policy. Its purpose was to strengthen and develop Canada as a nation from sea to sea. The National Policy had three parts: protective tariffs, a transcontinental railway, and settlement of the West. They are described in the chart below.

Arguments For the National Policy

The government and supporters of the National Policy believed it would strengthen the Dominion of Canada as a country. Trade among regions would strengthen the economy and help industries to develop. Canada would become more self-sufficient. Joining Canada from sea to sea with a railroad would promote political unity. Settling the West would be part of that link.

Arguments Against the National Policy

Some people were concerned about the effects of the National Policy. Some people in the Atlantic provinces argued that protective tariffs would favour industry in Toronto and Montreal. They worried cities in the Atlantic provinces would not be able to compete. People pointed out that higher prices would result from protective tariffs for manufactured goods. Goods from other countries would become more expensive than Canadian goods, and Canadian manufacturers would not be able to produce enough goods to make up for this. Farmers would have to pay more for farm equipment.

Some people were very worried that a transcontinental railway would be too expensive for Canada to undertake at this time.

The Result

The Canadian voters responded favourably to the ideas of Macdonald and his Conservative Party regarding the National Policy. In 1878 Sir John A. Macdonald became prime minister of Canada once again, after a landslide victory at the polls. The Conservative Party was returned to power.

You will be studying industrialization and protective tariffs next. The building of a transcontinental railway, the second part of the National Policy, will be studied later in the chapter. Chapter 10 will explore the period when settlers actually began to arrive in the West in large numbers.

For Your Notebook

1. Make a web or mind map of the National Policy. Add information as you study the chapter.

National Policy Overview

Sir John A. Macdonald's National Policy brought important changes to Canada.

1. **Protective Tariffs.** To protect Canadian manufacturers from foreign competition, high duties (taxes) called protective tariffs were to be put on foreign goods coming into Canada.

(pages 217 to 222)

2. **Transcontinental Railway.** The railway would take settlers to the West and bring their crops to the East. Also, an earlier Conservative government had promised British Columbia that a railway would join it to the rest of Canada within ten years of its joining Canadian Confederation.

(pages 223 to 232)

3. **Settlement of the West.** Macdonald planned to help immigrants from other countries settle in the Canadian West. These settlers would buy the products of Canadian industries and would grow wheat to be sold in Canadian cities and exported.

(Chapter 10)

An Exercise in Decision-Making

Protective Tariffs

If you had lived in Canada in 1878 when the Conservatives were re-elected, would you have been in favour of protective tariffs or against them? Use the information on this page to help you form an opinion. Imagine you are the editor of a Canadian newspaper (you pick the city). Write an editorial (see page 370 in the Appendix) expressing your opinion about protective tariffs.

  The Conservatives' **pro-manufacturing policy** had much more effect on some regions of Canada than others. It helped industry develop in Central Canada, especially in the city of Montreal in Quebec and in southwestern Ontario. The Atlantic provinces had difficulty competing against the cities of Central Canada. The policy did not promote manufacturing in the West, as there were few people living there. Canadians had mixed feelings about the Conservative party's policy of protective tariffs, as the following imaginary points of view show.

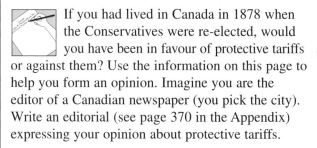

Canada is very dependent on the sale of products such as wheat, lumber, and fish to other countries. In the past when demand for these products went down, our Canadian economy slumped. Canada needs to become more independent of other countries. We need to sell more of our own raw materials to manufacturers inside this country. High tariffs will make goods from the United States very expensive. Canadians will then buy Canadian-made goods. With protective tariffs, the Canadian economy will improve and create more jobs.

Protective tariffs will give Canada's infant industries a chance to develop without competition from large manufacturers in Britain and the United States. Otherwise, American manufacturers will put our Canadian companies out of business. They won't get a fair chance to get established.

If we have protective tariffs to increase manufacturing in Canada we will have to accept the problems that come with growing cities and industrial development. We will have to build more factories in our cities.

All sorts of problems will result from many people moving into the cities to work in the new factories. The cities will become dirty and overcrowded. Outbreaks of disease will spread quickly. Some factories will use cheap child labour to make a great profit. Children who are working will grow up unhealthy and uneducated. It will make problems in the future.

Here in the Maritimes we are too far from the centres of large population which are the markets. Our costs will be higher. Our industries won't be able to compete with those in Montreal and Toronto. Before long they'll buy us out and control all manufacturing.

Pro-manufacturing policy—a government policy to promote the development of Canadian manufacturing industries

Industrialization

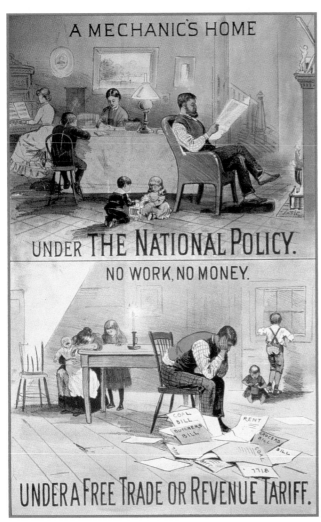

According to this campaign poster, the National Policy would bring happiness and prosperity to workers' lives.

Protective Tariffs

 Sir John A. Macdonald and the Conservatives announced that, as soon as they returned to power, higher tariff rates on goods coming into the country would be put into effect. The new tariffs were almost double what the previous ones had been.

Tariffs were placed on imported items such as woollen cloth, refined sugar, nails, and steam engines. These products competed with Canadian products. Imports threatened to prevent Canadian industries from making a profit. Tariffs made goods from other countries more expensive than Canadian goods. Canadian industries expected to sell more of their own manufactured goods.

Tariffs were also expected to bring in the tax revenues necessary to build the transcontinental railway. Although the tariffs were meant to benefit the majority, they actually caused them to pay more for manufactured goods. Manufacturers in Central Canadian cities benefitted more than those in the other regions.

A worldwide period of prosperity began soon after the Conservatives returned to power in 1878. Ontario and Montreal were Canada's centres of manufacturing. They enjoyed an increase in business. (See the Industrial Production graph on back cover endsheet.) It appeared that the National Policy had worked a miracle. However, the prosperity was mainly due to the worldwide business boom, a series of excellent grain crops, and the timber trade with the United States.

Changes

  Protective tariffs brought about population changes from rural to urban areas. In the factory system in Central and Atlantic Canada in the early 1880s, many labourers were gathered together in large factories. Industrial production was shifted out of people's homes or small shops into factories. Movement from the country to the cities increased.

Lady Aberdeen, wife of the governor general, described in her journal the conditions under which women factory employees worked:

. . . in factories, girls by the score earning only 2 dollars a week, afraid of giving up their work because there are hundreds of others ready to step in their places—afraid to join Protective Association—dismissed for attending meetings—fines, unsanitary conditions etc., & no women inspectors.

For Your Notebook

1. Is the election campaign poster in the left column for or against protective tariffs? In a few sentences, summarize the message of the poster.

2. Why were many Canadians pleased with the Conservative party's policy of Protective Tariffs? Why were many against it?

3. Make notes on pages 218 to 222.

In the factory system, each worker only completed one piece of the final product. For instance, one worker might sew the body of the shirt, a second the sleeves, a third the collar, and a fourth the buttons. All day long, each worker would do one piece of the shirts. Instead of one tailor producing two shirts in a day, now 50 factory workers might produce 2000 shirts in the same time, or the equivalent of 40 shirts each.

Changes to the Factory System

 The factory system involved many changes. Here are some to consider:

For Your Notebook

1. Overall, do you think the factory system was beneficial to Canadians? Tell why or why not.

Positive Changes

• Workers could produce as many as fifty times more products than they could produce by hand.

• Unskilled workers could find work easily. (When tasks in factories were broken down into steps, each step could be done without the specialized skill formerly required by a craftsperson, who made a product from beginning to end.)

• Factory owners wanted to hire unskilled workers because they could pay them lower wages than skilled craftspeople. Lower labour costs meant that people with money would start up factories, because they could make a profit.

• Factory-made goods were less expensive than those made by craftspeople. Therefore, more people could buy them. As a result, the standard of living in Canada went up between 1867 and 1896.

---

*Men and women were not treated equally in the new factories. Women were paid less for similar jobs, had fewer opportunities for promotion to better jobs, and often had to leave their jobs after marriage.

Negative Changes

• Workers worked long hours (60 to 70 per week), six days a week.

• Unskilled labour was often done by women and children at lower pay and in poor working conditions.* Unskilled male factory workers often could not earn enough to support their families. Therefore, women and children had to join the workforce.

• Workers who became ill could no longer support themselves. In a factory you had to work or you were not paid. Safety conditions were poor and accidents frequent. Workers usually lost their jobs when injured at work, with no compensation from their employer.

• Many people had to leave their homes in the country and start up again in the city. Often, they felt lonely and isolated without their extended family and friends.

• Local governments did not (or could not) provide the necessary services, such as water, sewage disposal, fire and police protection, for the many new arrivals. Cities were unsanitary and often dangerous places to live.

Changes to Canadian Cities

Some Canadian cities grew immensely during the 1878–1896 period when the Conservatives were in power. The graphs and charts indicate

- a population change from rural to urban areas (a result of protective tariffs to support growing industries in Ontario, Quebec, and the Atlantic provinces)
- slightly fewer people working in primary industries such as agriculture; more people working in secondary (manufacturing) and tertiary (service) industries.

People moved from farms to cities to work in the new factories. Shops and services that sprang up to serve the increased population also employed people. Cities also grew with immigration to Canada. Railways were another reason for the growth of cities at the end of the 1800s. Toronto was the hub of a huge network of railway lines connecting it to many other places. Most cities increased in size after 1881.

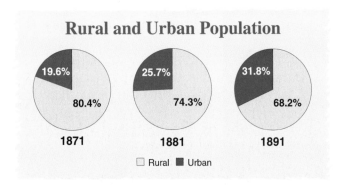

Rural and Urban Population

	1871	1881	1891
Urban	19.6%	25.7%	31.8%
Rural	80.4%	74.3%	68.2%

☐ Rural ■ Urban

Urban Population, 1881–1891		
	1881	**1891**
Vancouver	—	13 709
Calgary	—	3 876
Edmonton	—	—
Saskatoon	—	—
Regina	—	—
Winnipeg	7 985	25 639
Toronto	96 916	181 215
Montreal	155 238	219 616
Quebec City	62 446	63 090
Halifax	39 880	38 000
St. John	41 350	39 000

Some cities had impressive growth, while others hardly grew at all or declined.

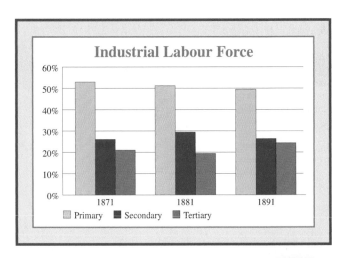

Industrial Labour Force

☐ Primary ■ Secondary ■ Tertiary

King Street, Toronto, in the early 1890s

City of Toronto Archives, SC478-19

For Your Notebook

1. Use the information in the bar graph Industrial Labour Force to create circle graphs comparing changes in types of work.

Changing Roles for Women

Married women were generally expected to remain at home, working for their families. Middle and upper class women often gave time to church and charity work. Only women who were as yet unmarried were likely to work outside the home. Working class households often could not manage without the wages from both the women and men.

While women working in the home were unpaid, their work was vital. In a time before electricity (and refrigeration), running water, and indoor plumbing, women spent long, hard hours preparing food, raising children, making and mending clothing, and doing laundry.

The majority of women in paid employment worked in domestic service. This meant that they worked in the homes of the well-to-do. Other working women worked in factories and mills. Factory jobs had one major advantage over domestic work. Workers had set hours and more personal freedom. They could live independently.

Women's wages in factories were generally about half that of men. A typical woman's wage was not sufficient to support a family alone. Single women usually lived with their parents and contributed their wages to a common household family fund. (Legally a husband was entitled to all money earned by his wife and children.)

Changes were just beginning to occur in this period. According to the Hamilton *Spectator* in December 1893, women were "exploring new worlds with cautious steps. They are subjects of a revolution none the less great because it is silent."

©Bettmann/CORBIS

A cartoonist's interpretation of domestic workers coming to Canada

A temperance parade in Toronto

Milestones

1874 Women's Christian **Temperance** Union is founded; fought for the prohibition of alcohol, as well as for women's **suffrage** and mothers' allowances.

1875 Grace Anne Lockhart receives a Bachelor of Science degree from Mount Allison University; possibly the first woman in the British Empire to receive a university degree.

1880s Typewriters begin to appear in offices. Women begin to be hired as secretaries and as clerks in city department stores.

1883 The Kingston Women's Medical College and the Women's Medical College in Toronto open.

1884 Ontario's Married Women's Property Act; married women allowed to own and control property.

1889 The Dominion Women's Enfranchisement Association formed to fight for women's suffrage.

1891 The Women's Christian Temperance Union endorses the vote for women at all levels of government.

1893 National Council of Women of Canada founded to fight for rights of women and children.

1895 Law Society of Upper Canada admits women; women can now practise law.

1897 Victorian Order of Nurses founded to provide nursing services to rural areas.

Temperance—moderation or total avoidance of alcohol

Suffrage—the right to vote

221

Lady Aberdeen
1857–1939

Lord and Lady Aberdeen, 1898

In 1893, Ishbel, the Countess of Aberdeen, arrived in Canada with her husband, the new governor general, Lord Aberdeen. They stayed until 1898. The Countess of Aberdeen had little patience for the social events that she and her husband were expected to organize and attend. Her interests lay with **social reform**, especially in the problems suffered by poor women and children. She could see that industrialization and the movement to the cities did not always benefit women and children. Lady Aberdeen made a visit to a group of women working for the Government Printing Bureau in Ottawa. A woman journalist reported on the event:

> A large room on the third floor is where the girls work. They stitch the leaves of the books together and then bind them. In this large room, the girls received Her Excellency . . . Piles of books were on the long tables and through rows of sewing machines, the visitors picked their way to the chairs prepared for them. . . .

> Her Excellency addressed the girls standing in groups before her. She spoke in a kind, affectionate manner. . . . of the nobleness of work, and of how much power for good lay in work and how much happier women were with it than without it. Her Excellency suggested that the girls of the Printing Bureau should form a benefit society among themselves, each member paying a small sum monthly and so ensure themselves from want in case of illness or want of work. A committee of four girls was appointed to confer with Lady Aberdeen at Government House on Monday at one o'clock. Before leaving, Her Excellency shook hands with every girl present.

National Council of Women

The National Council of Women was established by Lady Aberdeen in 1893 and has continued to the present day. Its membership grew to 250 000. It has fought for the rights of women and children in Canadian society for over a century.

Victorian Order of Nurses

The Victorian Order of Nurses (VON) was founded by Lady Aberdeen in 1897. Its purpose was to provide the services of visiting nurses to rural areas without hospitals or other medical facilities. Forty-four small hospitals were set up initially. These were eventually taken over by the government. Today the VON concentrates on providing home nursing services, particularly to the elderly.

For Your Notebook

1. Explain how women were "exploring new worlds" during this period.

Exploring Further

2. The National Council of Women, founded in 1893, and the Victorian Order of Nurses, founded in 1897, still exist. Find out more about one of these organizations and what it does today.

This 1898 photograph shows the leaders of the National Council of Women.

Social reform—improving the way people live by such means as education, health care, improved working conditions, wages, sanitation, and political power

The Canadian Pacific Railway

Canadian historians have written that the building of the Canadian Pacific Railway (CPR) was Canada's greatest achievement in the years between Confederation and the turn of the century. The CPR was part of the National Policy.

For Your Notebook

1. Work with several other students to create a concept poster about the reasons for building the CPR. Present your poster to another group.

Reasons for Building

The railway was a political necessity for Canada.

To a large extent, the success of Confederation depended on the building of a railway to the Pacific Coast.

- **An all-Canadian railway would meet the demand for an efficient transportation and communication system across Canada.** Canadian politicians did not want Canada to depend on transportation routes through the United States.

- **A railway would help unify Canada.** If the dream of a country from sea to sea was to succeed, a railway would be needed to unify widely separated areas of the country. A railway could transport people and products from the Atlantic Coast to the colony of British Columbia on the Pacific Coast and back.

- **The North-West Territories were sparsely populated. The CPR would open this area up for settlement by Canadian and European settlers rather than Americans.** The good lands of the American Midwest were rapidly being settled. The Red River area had close ties with the United States. There was concern that Americans would move northwards and make the North-West Territories part of the United States. Large numbers of American gold seekers had moved from the California goldfields into the colony of British Columbia. There was concern it would be annexed by the Pacific Northwest (California and Oregon). The United States acquired Alaska in 1867, and American expansion was feared because of the US policy of Manifest Destiny. Canadian politicians also feared American railways might extend their operations into Canada.

The railway was an economic necessity for Canada.

The railway was necessary to move goods and people across the new Canadian nation.

- **A railway would replace older, less efficient transportation methods.** Horse and wagon, ox cart, canoe, York boat, river steamers, and sail boats were either slow or restricted by winter freeze-up.

- **Trade between Canada and the United States declined with the end of the Reciprocity Treaty in 1866. The new provinces in Canada needed other markets.** Canadian businessmen reasoned that if other areas of British North America were settled, the settlers could become a market for goods made in Central Canada and in the Atlantic provinces. They needed to be connected by railroad to distribute goods efficiently.

- **A railway was needed so Canada could compete with the United States for trade with the Red River area and the colony of British Columbia.** Both the Red River area and British Columbia had economic ties with the United States. After the decline of the gold rush in British Columbia, new markets were needed to solve the colony's economic problems. The colony of British Columbia could not survive as an isolated outpost. A railway to both of these areas would be an economic benefit.

- **Available farmland in Ontario was scarce.** The good farmlands in Ontario were almost all taken. The North-West Territories offered new land. A railway would take settlers to the West. A railway would also bring the products of these farms, mainly wheat, to markets in Central and Atlantic Canada.

A Tremendous Challenge

  The building of the railway was part of Macdonald's National Policy. He dreamed of binding the country together from "sea to sea" (see page 216). A railway would fulfil the Canadian government's promise to British Columbia when it entered Confederation. It would also bring thousands of settlers to the North-West Territories.

> An American senator described the immensity of the task of building the Canadian Pacific Railway in these words:
>
> The story of the plans for, and the building of, the Canadian railways is epic in its bigness; in its vast hazard it has something of the heroic; it is unparalleled in history.

Immediately after being elected in 1878, Macdonald began working on getting the railway started. In 1880, the Canadian Pacific Railway Company was formed. The company was given the task of building a transcontinental railway from Montreal to the west coast of British Columbia. It would take over the rails already built from Montreal east to the Atlantic provinces. With a population of only 4 000 000, Canada managed to complete its transcontinental railway only a few years after the United States finished theirs. The United States had 10 times the population of Canada.

Cost of the Project

The CPR was extremely expensive to construct. Even though the builder was a private company (not government owned), it needed the financial help of the government. The government promised the CPR the following:

- $25 000 000
- 10 000 000 hectares of western land
- 1100 kilometres of railway lines that had already been built
- tariff-free railway building materials
- a 20-year monopoly over all rail traffic in the southern prairies

The $25 000 000 that was initially given to the CPR proved to be too little. The company went back to the government twice to get more money to continue building the railway. In 1885, officials from the CPR approached the government again to ask for more money. Many people said that a transcontinental railway was a crazy dream, which the country could not afford. They opposed the request for more money. However, when the North-West Resistance took place in the West that year, the president of the CPR, William Van Horne, transported soldiers to the West on the railway. It was still unfinished in some places. The Canadian public was impressed by the speed with which the soldiers reached the area of conflict by railway. As a result, the CPR received more money from the government for further construction.

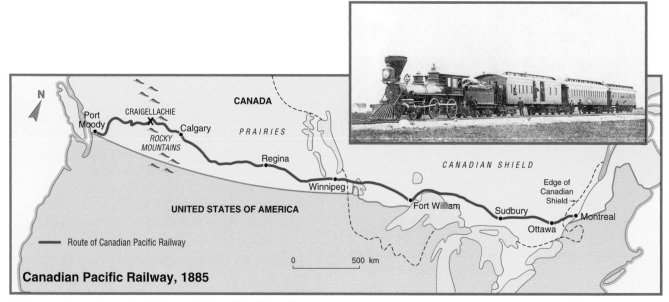

Canadian Pacific Railway, 1885

This map shows the route of the main line of the Canadian Pacific Railway. The railway line stretched 4660 kilometres from Port Moody, British Columbia, east to Montreal. The first train from Montreal arrived at the Pacific Coast in July 1886.

Building the Railway
On the Prairies

  William Van Horne, an American, was hired as general manager of the CPR in 1881. He began in the Prairies. Progress there would be quick because of the flat land. At Winnipeg 5000 men and 1700 teams of horses worked in order to fulfil Van Horne's promise of 800 kilometres of track laid in one year. The **navvies** worked all day at first. Later, they even worked at night. The rail moved across the Prairies at a rate of five or six kilometres a day.

On the Canadian Shield

Once construction on the Prairies was moving rapidly, Van Horne turned his attention to the Canadian Shield of Ontario. This was a much more difficult task. The route through the Canadian Shield was once described as "two hundred miles of engineering impossibility." The builders had to cope with rock and **muskeg**. The hard granite rock had to be blasted with dynamite, a new invention, in order to make a smooth path. The muskeg had to be filled in with tons of gravel to make a solid base. Otherwise, it would simply swallow up the track without a trace. (See map page 224 for the area of Canadian Shield.)

In the end it took seven years to complete the 700 kilometres from Lake Superior to Winnipeg. It would have been much easier and faster, therefore less expensive, to take a southerly route on American land. However, Prime Minister Macdonald insisted that the railway be built entirely on Canadian soil. He wanted it to be a truly Canadian railway.

Navvies—men who worked on the end of the railway line laying tracks
Muskeg—a bog or marsh

In the Rocky Mountains

The work in the Rockies was even slower than across the Canadian Shield. It was also very dangerous. As in the Canadian Shield, dynamite had to be used to blast a path through the mountains. Many men were killed when they couldn't get away from a blast in time. Some were caught in landslides caused by the blasts. Some simply fell from the sides of steep cliffs.

Canada Revisited

This monument at Craigellachie, British Columbia, commemorates the Last Spike of the Canadian Pacific Railway. The plaque reads: "Here was driven the last spike completing Canadian Pacific Railway from ocean to ocean November 7, 1885." When asked to make a speech at the ceremony on that day, General Manager William Van Horne, said, "All I can say is that the work has been done well in every way."

Leaders Involved in Railway Building	Personal Information

Sir William Cornelius Van Horne, 1843–1915

- General Manager, 1882–1888
- President of the CPR, 1888–1899
- Chairman, 1899–1910
- Completed the railway ahead of schedule in 1885, instead of the target date of 1891
- In the Last Spike photo on page 230, he is the man with the dark beard and mustache standing behind Donald Smith.

- Known for his amazing energy. While the railway was being built, he constantly rode back and forth along the line, sorting out problems and encouraging the men to work harder.
- A man of many talents; an excellent gardener, an amateur geologist. Loved to play chess, poker, and billiards

Sir Donald Smith, 1820–1914

- Formed a company with George Stephen and James Hill to finance the building of the CPR
- Pounded the last spike at Craigellachie, British Columbia
- In photo on page 230

- Came to Canada from Scotland at age 18 to work for the Hudson's Bay Company
- Became chief commissioner in Canada for the HBC
- Later known as Lord Strathcona; during South African War, personally paid to support Strathcona's Horse, a regiment of 500 mounted Canadian riflemen

Sir George Stephen, 1829–1921

- First President of CPR, 1880–1888
- Formed a company with James Hill and Donald Smith to finance the building of the CPR
- Was called "the greatest genius in the whole history of Canadian finance"

- Cousin of Donald Smith
- Came to Canada from Scotland at age 21
- President of the Bank of Montreal, 1876–1881
- Became wealthy through railway building
- A generous philanthropist who gave large gifts of money to hospitals in Montreal and England

Andrew Onderdonk, 1848–1905

- Hired by CPR in 1879 to supervise the building of the Fraser Canyon section
- Solved labour shortage by bringing in Chinese workers, first from Oregon and California and then directly from China

- An American engineer from a wealthy New York family
- Worked on railways and canals in Ontario after the completion of the CPR

Major A.B. Rogers, 1829–1889

- In 1882, discovered the pass that would allow the railway to travel through the Rocky Mountains. Rogers Pass was named after him.
- Given a bonus of $5000 for finding the pass; framed the cheque and proudly displayed it on a wall in his brother's house

- An American engineer and surveyor
- Had a reputation for travelling light. He could survive on very little food. Described as wearing "overalls with pockets behind, and a plug of tobacco in one pocket and a sea biscuit in the other, which was his idea of a season's provisions. . ."

**Sir Sandford Fleming
1827–1915**

 Sir Sandford Fleming was engineer-in-chief of the Canadian Pacific Company from 1871 to 1880. He was in charge of surveying the route. In 1872 he travelled across the continent to see the proposed route for himself and to check on the work of the surveyors.

Fleming was a man of many talents and accomplishments. He designed the United Province of Canada's first postage stamp, the Threepenny Beaver, which was issued on April 23, 1851.

Fleming's greatest achievement was the creation of Standard Time, which was adopted on New Year's Day, 1885. Before that, different places operated according to their own time systems. Standard Time and time zones made it possible to create train schedules and co-ordinate arrivals and departures.

Another of Fleming's accomplishments was the Pacific Cable, a telegraph line across the Pacific Ocean from Vancouver Island to New Zealand and Australia. The first message was sent over the Pacific Cable on October 3, 1902.

**Crowfoot
1830–1890**

 Crowfoot was a great chief of the Siksika (also called the Blackfoot) and a respected peacemaker. In order to help stop the conflict between the Siksika and the Cree, Crowfoot adopted the Cree chief, Poundmaker, as his son. He signed Treaty 7 on behalf of his people because he believed that he would gain more by co-operating with the Europeans than he would by conflict. Later, in 1885, Crowfoot convinced the Siksika people not to join Metis leader Louis Riel in his fight against the Canadian government. (You will read about the North-West Resistance of 1885 later in this chapter.)

The Siksika agreed to give up their traditional hunting grounds in exchange for a reserve under Treaty 7. They were angry to see railway construction workers' tents being put up in one corner of it. Father Lacombe, a Roman Catholic missionary (shown below), convinced Crowfoot and the Siksika Council that there was no point in forcing the railway workers off the reserve. Again, Crowfoot decided that negotiation rather than armed confrontation was the best approach. In exchange for allowing the railway to cross the reserve, the Siksika received some other lands.

Above: Father Lacombe

Left: 1879 Sir Sandford Fleming presenting the idea of Standard Time to the Canadian Institute for the Advancement of Scientific Knowledge in Toronto

227

Chinese Navvies

It was difficult to find enough railway workers in British Columbia. For one thing, not everyone was interested in such dangerous work. Much of the work involved the use of dynamite to blast rock out of the way. Many lives were being lost through blasting accidents. Most men in Canada who were available to work on railway construction were already employed east of the Rockies. The population of British Columbia was very small. The numbers of workers that were needed could not be be found there, so the railway began to employ Chinese workers. There were about 3000 Chinese in the province in 1878. The first Chinese men to be hired had already worked on railways in California. Many had come to British Columbia because of the gold rush. Even with these men, there was still not enough labour to meet the needs of constructing the railway.

By 1885, there were 15 000 Chinese workers employed on the railway. Workers came from China hoping to earn enough money to return to their homeland with some savings. They earned $1.00 per day, which was less than the $1.50 per day offered to other workers. The average wage in their home province in China was seven cents per day.

Railway workers were not paid during the harshest three winter months, when work came to a standstill. They also had to pay for clothes, tools, food, shelter, and taxes. The Chinese workers had to make payments to cover the steamboat trip from China. When the railway was completed, many of these men could not afford to return to China. About 5000 of the Chinese workers stayed in Canada after the railway was completed.*

Work on the railway was hard and dangerous. At least 600 Chinese workers died during the construction of the British Columbia portion of the railway. This was a cost of four men for every mile of track. Some died in dynamite explosions or accidents; others from scurvy and other diseases.

Historian Pierre Berton reported the following from a journal kept by Henry Cambie, a CPR employee in British Columbia:

August 13—A Chinese drilling on the ledge of a bluff near Alexandra Bar is killed when a stone falls from above and knocks him off.

August 19—A log rolls over an embankment and crushes a Chinese to death at the foot of a slope.

September 4—A Chinese is killed by a rock slide.

September 7—A boat upsets in the Fraser and a Chinese is drowned.

September 11—A Chinese is smothered to death in an earth cave-in.

Berton also reports that the *Inland Sentinel* newspaper announced on September 9th, that "there have been no deaths since the 15th of June."

For Your Notebook

1. What difficulties were encountered by the builders of the CPR?
2. In what ways were the Chinese navvies valuable to the CPR? How were they treated and why?

Exploring Further

3.  Why do you think that the *Inland Sentinel* reported on September 9th that there had been no deaths since the 15th of June, although several Chinese navvies had been killed?

---

*The Canadian government tried to discourage further Chinese immigration by imposing a $50 "head tax" on all new Chinese immigrants in 1886.

This photograph shows Chinese workers on the British Columbia section of the Canadian Pacific Railway.

Dong Yee

Fictional Narrative

—by Nancy Sellars Marcotte

I must go to the letter writer again soon. For a small sum of money he will write a letter to my wife and daughter across the sea in China to tell them that I am well. I have been on the Gold Mountain for two years now. I want to stay and continue to work on this railway. I want to save enough money to buy land for my family in China. But this railway is supposed to be finished next year, so my job will be over then. In two years I have earned $600. That is a lot of money, but I have only been able to send $80 to my family in China. All the rest has gone to pay for food, strong boots, and the shovel I need for this work. I will need to work for at least six more years to earn enough money for my family to buy a small farm in China.

The work here is dangerous. We have learned to be careful around the dynamite. But yesterday one of the Englishmen forgot and shook the ashes out of his pipe while he stood beside the dynamite. He was killed, and two of my Chinese friends died with him.

My job is to move the rocks that lie where they want to put the tracks. In order to build this railway we have had to move whole sections of mountains, and push tunnels right through other mountains. Other workers have built bridges to cross rivers and long bridges called trestles to go along the sides of mountains.

They tell me that on the east side of the mountains there is flat land where they might lay as much as eight kilometres of track each day.

Perhaps if I do not save enough money to buy my family land in China, I could bring my wife to live here in British Columbia, on the Gold Mountain. She would have to cross the Pacific Ocean like I did, deep in the hold of a ship. At Vancouver she would get on a paddle wheeler steamer and come up the Fraser River. Then she might ride the train on the part of the track that is already built.

But what would she do when she got here? Would she live in a tent the way the railway workers do? Would she eat rice and salmon and tea, and maybe get scurvy like some of the men?

And what about our daughter? She is two years old, and I have never seen her. Should we bring her to live in this country with so many mountains and lakes but hardly any people?

I must decide about the future of my family. Should I look for a job that will last after this railway is finished? Some of the men from my country are working as cooks or gardeners in the homes of wealthy people in the cities of Vancouver and Victoria. Others have started businesses in these strange mountain towns. They do the laundry for the workers, or they have restaurants where people can come to buy a meal. In this country my wife could help in that sort of business.

But there is talk of a tax that we must pay for every person who comes into Canada from China. I must pay $50 for my wife and $50 for my daughter to enter this country. I will have to work nearly three more years to save that much money. And I will also have to pay for them to ride on the ship.

But today I must move these rocks and be sure that no rocks from the mountain above roll down onto me. Tonight in my tent I will dream about my child in the land of my ancestors.

The Last Spike

On November 7, 1885, at a place called Craigellachie in British Columbia, Donald A. Smith drove in the last spike of the Canadian Pacific Railway. The railway line, completed under the leadership of William Cornelius Van Horne, ran 4660 kilometres from Montreal in the east to Port Moody, British Columbia, in the west.

—by Brenda Bellingham

Edward Mallandaine was only 17 when he pushed his way into Canada's most famous railway photograph.

The photograph, taken on November 7, 1885, shows one of the richest and most powerful men in Canada, Donald Smith (soon to be named Lord Strathcona), pounding in the last spike on the new Canadian Pacific Railway. In the photograph young Mallandaine stands in front of a group of bearded men. His right foot is planted on the rail, and he is peering around Smith. He seems determined to get into the picture. The young man is not related to anyone in this historic photograph, nor was he a railway worker. So who was he and how did he appear here, in this photograph?

Edward Mallandaine was born in Victoria, British Columbia, a place described at the time as a city "of tents, gullies and swamps, and the inhabitants were mostly

Donald Smith driving the symbolic Last Spike. Behind him is Edward Mallandaine.

miners." His father was an engineer and architect. His mother was a housewife. It seems likely that the boy's childhood was comfortable.

When the 1885 North-West Resistance broke out, Edward eagerly followed its progress in the newspapers. Patriotically, he decided to join up and fight against the rebels. This was easier said than done. To get off Vancouver Island, he had to take a ship to New Westminster, British Columbia. Then he made his way to Port Moody to catch a local train that connected with the new Canadian Pacific Railway line.

By the time he reached Golden, the North-West Resistance had been put down at Batoche, Saskatchewan, and most of the government troops had already been shipped out. Edward's

soldiering days were over before they had begun.

Disappointed and dejected, the boy turned around and headed back towards the coast. At Revelstoke (then called Farwell) he stopped to look around. Victoria was small, but Farwell just had one street with wooden shacks and a few log houses. The largest building was the Columbia Hotel, which was named for the nearby river.

It was not much to look at but it was a busy place. Between the mining at Big Bend and the railway construction with the CPR, Farwell's storekeepers were smiling.

There was talk of a new post office. In conversation, somebody suggested that maybe Edward would be interested in a delivery route. No wages were to be paid for the job; it was up to Edward to decide how to make things pay.

Each week he would make a mail run from Farwell to Eagle Pass. On the way, he picked up orders for papers or supplies. Then the following week, he'd make the deliveries, charging a service fee. At first he found the life of a business-person very hard.

His life on the road was never dull. Work on the new railway line was going full steam ahead. Some days, he would see as many as 50 men suspended over the cliffs at Summit Lake, drilling holes in the rock face to take the dynamite charges. Twice daily the huge blasts would roar through the pass, echoing like deep thunder off the mountain walls. Thousands of metres of material were moved by an army of labourers. Most of them arrived on crowded ships from the port of Hong Kong. This mighty railway machine, with its moving parts of human beings, could build a 100-metre truss bridge in one day.

The towns and work camps were lively too. Even after long hours of backbreaking work, workers found energy for entertainment, both in towns and in the camps. Medical people were kept busy attending to work accidents, accidents as a result of drinking, and injuries from fights. There was always something happening to satisfy the curiosity and need for excitement of a 17-year-old boy.

The rails starting in the West grew closer daily to the rails that had started in the East. The towns along the track, which had grown up almost overnight to house workers, began to shrink. Contractors, their projects over, let their

workers go. Some of those who were unemployed moved on. A few became "road agents" preying on their former work-mates, stealing their hard-earned wages. Some workers fought back, adding blood to the sweat on their Canadian railway dollars.

By the fall of 1885, delivery-man Edward Mallandaine found his route was taking him through deserted camps and ghost towns. Gone were the brawling crowds of men, the lights of the saloons, and the eager, smiling storekeepers.

The silent pass began to oppress Edward. Once in a while he would hear the eery shriek of a construction locomotive hauling flat-cars loaded with rails. The weather started to turn colder. It was time to close down the delivery business.

———◆———

There was one last moment of railway glory for Edward, one last, cold ride to Craigellachie to a place in Canada's history. In a *Victoria Colonist* interview in 1899 he described the trip:

On the afternoon of November 6 several of us left Farwell on a train consisting of an engine and tender and three flat cars loaded with rails—the last train to load rails for Craigellachie. A cold cheerless rough ride we had. Shortly after leaving Farwell, it began to snow. This made the rails slippery and when we reached the big gumbo slide or grade, we were unable to get over it, and after three attempts, in each of which the train would run back on itself, we were obliged to cut off one car. Then we managed to make it over the grade.

Far into the darkness of the night we travelled . . . Finally it came to an end. It was pitch dark and we were able to get off and after a great deal of difficulty we managed to snatch a

short sleep in a vacant box car. All through the night the rails were laid from both East and West and early the following morning, November 7, we were astir watching the rails gradually approaching each other.

Soon there remained but a single rail to be laid. The distance was measured: it was discovered that the rail was about three feet too long and while this was being shortened, Sir Donald Smith and his party came on the scene. They watched the proceedings in readiness to drive the last spike.

Then the rail was laid. The spectators numbering probably 50 outside of the workmen intently watched each spike as it was driven. Finally, there remained but one more spike to be driven. It was partly driven in and a hammer was given to Sir Donald Smith to drive it home.

Before doing so three photographs were taken by a photographer named Ross, of Ross Best & Co., Winnipeg; one when Sir Donald had the hammer over his shoulder, preparatory to striking; one with the hammer over his head, and one with the hammer on the nail head. Then he quickly and in a most workmanlike manner, drove the spike home. Everybody cheered; the locomotives whistled and shrieked; several short speeches were made; hands were shaken, and Major Rogers, the discoverer of the pass named after him, became so gleeful that he up-ended a huge tie and tried to mark the spot by the side of the track by sticking it in the ground.

Thus was the Dominion of Canada bound together by bands of steel reaching from the Atlantic to the Pacific . . .

As soon as the ceremony was over the last spike was extracted and hammered to bits, and the last piece of rail that was cut off was chipped, and the last tie was splintered and everyone who wanted it secured a memento of this memorable occasion.

For Your Notebook

1. Examine the photograph above and the one showing the Last Spike ceremony on page 230. (Refer to page 355, Interpreting Images, for help.)
    a) Tell what is happening in the two photographs.
    b) What features signal that an important event is occurring?
    c) What faces do you recognize in the first photo?
    d) Do you recognize anyone in the second photo?
    e) Why would there be recognizable faces in the first photo but not the second?
    f) Why do you think there were fewer labourers in the first, more famous photo?
    g) Why do you think the first photo has been included in many Canadian history books and the second one not?
    h) Who is missing from the labourers' photo?
    i) Who built the railway?
    j) What does this tell us about our perspectives on history?

2. Using the information on pages 223 to 231, make a mind map on the Canadian Pacific Railway. Mind maps are explained on page 363.
    a) Put CPR at the centre with the following branches—who, what, when, where, why.
    b) Where applicable, add challenges the people faced and solutions to these challenges.

3. In what way did the building of the CPR enhance Canada's identity?

Exploring Further

4. When Canada's politicians made their plans for a railway from sea to sea, Canada's First Nations people were not officially considered. What is your reaction to this statement?

5. Imagine you are a reporter accompanying Van Horne on his trip westward on the Canadian Pacific Railway. Prepare notes for three days of observations.

6. Imagine you were present during the Last Spike ceremony. Write a letter home describing the event.

7. Write a week's entries in the journal of a navvy.

8. Reread the accomplishments of Sir Sandford Fleming and Chief Crowfoot. Imagine you are each of them. Of which accomplishments are you the most proud? Explain why.

9. Locate a recording of the popular song "Canadian Railroad Trilogy," which was written in 1967 by Gordon Lightfoot. From whose point of view was it written?

The North-West Resistance 1885

The Manitoba Act of 1870, which you read about on page 161, set aside about 500 000 hectares for use by the Metis people who lived around the Red River settlement. However, the Canadian government was slow in distributing the promised land grants.*

In the meantime, more and more settlers were coming into Manitoba. Many military land grants were given in the area. The government wanted retired soldiers to settle there and be available as militia. Also the remaining buffalo were moving west.

Several thousand Metis decided that the only answer was to sell their land grants and move west into the North-West Territories. Many settled along the North and South Saskatchewan Rivers, which flow together east of Prince Albert (see map page 235).

Causes

❶ Land Ownership

When the Metis first settled on river lots in the North-West Territories in the 1870s, the area had not yet been surveyed. They settled along the river as they had done in the Red River settlement. Between 1872 and 1883 the Metis and other settlers of the North-West Territories sent a total of 15 petitions to various government authorities on the subject of land rights.

The Metis wished to be settled in a region where they were not crowded by European settlers. They became frustrated at the lack of response to their concerns by the government of John A. Macdonald. They had been overwhelmed by Canadian settlers in Red River and could see that the same thing was going to happen all over again. They knew that this meant that they would have to change their traditional way of life.

❷ Ability to Earn a Living

The Metis people's ability to earn a living was threatened by the changes in the environment and changes in technology. After 1878, the great buffalo herds were gone. They had been an important source of food. The Metis had also traded buffalo meat, pemmican, and robes for income or other products. Another way many Metis made their living was by transporting goods. They could see that the Canadian Pacific Railway, which was in the process of being built, and the new river steamboats would take over this job. Because buffalo hunting and transporting goods were disappearing as occupations, the Metis had to rely more on farming. Unfortunately, just as they were making this change, there was an economic recession and a fall in grain prices. They were unable to support themselves as farmers.

The decision for the CPR to travel through the more southern city of Regina (formerly Pile of Bones) instead of through Prince Albert was a disappointment as well. If the railway had gone through Prince Albert, there would have been a construction boom. This would have created many jobs for the people in the area.

❸ Louis Riel

On June 4, 1884, a four-man delegation went to Montana to ask Louis Riel to return with them to the North-West. Riel agreed to help them.

The return of Louis Riel as a leader focused the feelings of resistance of the Metis people. It may also have hardened the attitude of other Canadians against them. Canadians remembered Riel's role in the Red River Resistance.

In the North-West, Riel travelled around talking to people. He convinced them that the only way to protect their rights was armed resistance against the government, as had been done in Manitoba. Although Metis in other parts of the North-West had the same concerns as those in the Saskatchewan Valley, they did not have the leadership that Riel provided, and so did not join the movement.

---

*Eventually, the Metis received title to land on which they had settled, up to 65 ha each. They were also offered scrip. Scrip was a certificate or coupon entitling the holder to either cash or land. The majority chose money scrip.

Some people in the North-West were not pleased with the Conservative government in the early 1880s, as you can see from the points of view of the following imaginary people.

For Your Notebook

1. Use the information on the page as reference to list the groups of people in the North-West and the concerns that each had regarding the federal government prior to the North-West Resistance. Then use that information plus page 233 to make a web on the causes of the North-West Resistance.

Settlers

We are impatient that the government has been slow in completing the land survey and registering our land claims. Until these are done, we can not take possession of our land. We are anxious because the price of grain is falling. It is also very expensive to ship grain to eastern markets along the CPR route. And we are angry because we have to pay high prices for farm machinery that was manufactured in Central Canada. As part of his National Policy, Prime Minister Macdonald put tariffs on farm machinery coming from the USA. This makes it more expensive. It was to encourage people to buy Canadian products, but we would prefer to buy the cheaper American machinery.

The government set aside so much land for the Hudson's Bay Company and the CPR that now settlers have to compete for less land.

Furthermore, we were disappointed with the decision made by the CPR in 1881 to reroute the railway farther south than had been originally planned. This means that it will not run near the northern communities of Battleford, Prince Albert, and Batoche. As a result of this decision, the capital of the North-West Territories was moved from Battleford to Pile of Bones (later renamed Regina) in 1883. Many of us bought land in the northern area hoping to make money on it when the railway came through. Our hopes were dashed when the railway was rerouted to the south.

First Nations

Many of us signed treaties with the government and settled on reserves. We consider land as something to be shared, just as the air and the sunshine are shared. When we saw the settlers coming into the North-West we began to realize how much our lives were changing.

Many of us deeply miss our old way of life as buffalo hunters. Buffalo were always the main source of food for people living on the plains. Because of more people hunting buffalo using new weapons and methods, fewer and fewer are left. Many believe buffalo hunters from the United States were hired to kill off the buffalo in order to starve us into negotiating treaties. As a result of the dwindling supply of buffalo, some First Nations are facing starvation. The Canadian government has been slow to help us. Many of the agents from Indian Affairs did nothing to let the government know what needed to be done.

Metis

We Metis are also affected by the fact that there are fewer and fewer buffalo. We do not have reserve land on which to live. We are afraid of losing our river-lot farms, because the lots were not officially surveyed and registered. We do not have representation in the Canadian federal government in Ottawa. We have had to resort to letters and petitions. The federal government under John A. Macdonald has been very slow to respond to our concerns. This is extremely frustrating. It seems that no one in power cares what happens to us as a people.

Events Leading to the Resistance

After arriving back in Canada in the summer of 1884, Riel met with various groups living along the Saskatchewan River. The government had made considerable cutbacks in their treaty promises to First Nations. This had resulted in more distress and problems for them.

A final petition, drafted by Riel, was sent to Ottawa in December 1884. It included the concerns of the Metis, the First Nations, and the settlers. It also asked for responsible government for the North-West, control over the natural resources, representation in the federal Cabinet and Parliament, and provincial status for the District of Saskatchewan.

Letters were also sent to Ottawa. These were from local North-West government officials, the North West Mounted Police, missionaries, and others. These letters warned the federal government that there could be trouble if they did not respond to the complaints that had been outlined in the petition.

Prime Minister Macdonald did respond. A commission was formed to draw up a list of all the Metis who were eligible for compensation and land grants, and to register their river lot claims. Compensation was to be in the form of scrip, a certificate or coupon entitling the holder to a choice between cash or land.

The Metis were disappointed at Macdonald's response to their petition. They had expected more assistance. They asked Riel to stay in Canada to help them. Riel decided to stay. He believed that he was chosen as a prophet from God to lead the Metis people to get the land and rights they deserved.

Provisional Government at Batoche

In March 1885, Riel and his Metis followers seized arms and ammunition from a store in Batoche, and took several hostages. On March 19th, he set up a provisional (temporary) government, like the provisional government he had set up in Manitoba in 1869. Gabriel Dumont was appointed to be the military leader.

The settlers and English-speaking Metis along the Saskatchewan River did not wish to join the French-speaking Metis in an armed resistance. They were angry at the Canadian government, but most refused to follow Riel in violent resistance. Most First Nations also decided not to take up arms against the federal government. Two exceptions were the bands led by Poundmaker and Big Bear. However, the First Nations acted independently of the Metis.

An Armed Uprising

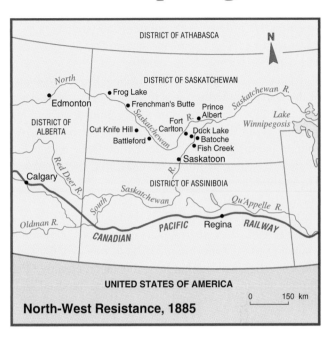

North-West Resistance, 1885

Duck Lake

The North-West Resistance began on March 26, 1885. At the small town of Duck Lake, Gabriel Dumont and a group of Metis attacked Superintendent Crozier of the North West Mounted Police and some of his men. The NWMP were on their way to remove guns and ammunition from a store in Duck Lake. Twelve of Crozier's men were killed and 11 wounded after a half-hour battle. Five Metis were killed.

Battleford

At the end of March, Chief Poundmaker travelled to Battleford to meet with the government agent to discuss getting more food for his people. When the townspeople heard that Poundmaker was coming, they fled to the safety of the fort. The town was deserted when he arrived and the government agent refused to come out of the fort to talk with him. Poundmaker's companions became frustrated and angry. They broke windows and took supplies.

Frog Lake

The most serious incident of the armed uprising occurred on April 2 at Frog Lake. Chief Big Bear's war chiefs, acting on their own, killed nine people, including the government agent, Thomas Quinn. Big Bear had wanted to negotiate.

Macdonald Sends Troops

Prime Minister Macdonald heard news of armed rebellion. He ordered 8000 soldiers and volunteers to travel west on the unfinished Canadian Pacific Railway. The trip took them only nine days.*

Major-General Frederick Middleton, the commander of the Canadian Militia, was in charge of battle operations. He divided his troops into three groups. He and his column set out for the Metis headquarters at Batoche. A column led by Colonel William Dillon Otter set out for Battleford, where he hoped to find Chief Poundmaker. The third column, led by Major-General Strange, set out after Chief Big Bear and his men.

Throughout the North-West Resistance of 1885, Riel was guided by his religious convictions. Dumont wanted to use hit-and-run guerrilla tactics to defend Batoche. Riel insisted that he had been ordered by God through visions to wait until Batoche was attacked and then defend it.

Fish Creek

On April 24, at Fish Creek, Gabriel Dumont's men attacked Middleton's column, using the hit-and-run and then hit again tactics that Dumont found so effective. Dumont was able to slow down Middleton's progress, but he did not stop him from reaching Batoche. Middleton arrived there on May 9.

The Battle of Batoche

The battle at Batoche lasted for four days, from May 9 to May 12. The 300 Metis and First Nations people had dug rifle pits from which they fired at their attackers. By the last day the defenders were out of ammunition. They fired stones and nails from their rifles. Finally Middleton's troops stormed the rifle pits and the battle was over. There were over 25 dead from both sides.

Cut Knife Hill

Both Riel and Dumont managed to escape. Riel gave himself up after a few days, but Dumont fled to the United States.

Colonel Otter located Chief Poundmaker and about 200 followers at Cut Knife Hill, near Poundmaker's reserve. Otter had hoped to make a surprise attack, but the Cree were ready for them and drove them off. Poundmaker's men had every opportunity to kill Otter's soldiers, but Poundmaker held them back and allowed the soldiers to return to Battleford. He saw no honour in killing an enemy who had already been defeated.

Poundmaker then decided to go to Batoche to help the Metis. On their way they heard the news of the Metis defeat. Realizing that there was no point in further resistance, Poundmaker surrendered to Middleton on May 26.

Frenchman's Butte

On May 28 Chief Big Bear and his men clashed with General Strange's soldiers at Frenchman's Butte. Strange withdrew at the end of the day, planning to fight again on the next. Big Bear and his men were low on ammunition. They took advantage of the lull in the action to escape while they could.

Both General Strange and General Middleton followed Chief Big Bear for the next few weeks. They never found him, but on July 2 he surrendered, accompanied only by his young son. His followers had either surrendered or gone elsewhere. Big Bear's surrender marked the end of the 99-day North-West Resistance.

Canadian government troops met the Metis forces at the Battle of Batoche, May 9 to 12, 1885.

*You read on page 224 about how Prime Minister Macdonald was able to get the money he needed to finish the railway after it transported soldiers so quickly to the troubled spot.

Poundmaker, 1842–1886

Poundmaker was a Cree chief and adopted son of Chief Crowfoot of the Siksika. Crowfoot adopted him in an effort to keep peace between their nations. Poundmaker got his name from his skill at driving buffalo into "pounds" or enclosures where they were trapped and then killed.

Poundmaker's people were having difficulty adjusting to a farming life after the hunting life they had known. They missed the freedom of following the buffalo. They were confined to a reserve with sandy soil that was not good for growing crops. They did not have enough to eat and grew more and more frustrated because the government would not listen to them.

This frustration found its expression in Battleford after the government agent refused to speak with the Cree delegation. Poundmaker's meeting with Colonel Otter and his soldiers at Cut Knife Hill is described on page 236.

After the North-West Resistance Poundmaker was sentenced to three years in prison, but was released after several months. He died while visiting Chief Crowfoot shortly after his release, and was buried in Crowfoot's camp. In 1967, his body was returned to his reserve and buried on the hill where the battle of Cut Knife took place.

Big Bear, 1825–1888

Chief Big Bear was unhappy with the federal government's treatment of First Nations people. He hoped that threats of a resistance would make the government take notice. However, he did not want to take part in a confrontation; he wanted to resist peacefully. His followers took up arms, so as their leader he took responsibility for their actions. He was sentenced to three years in prison for his part in the North-West Resistance. Like Poundmaker, he died shortly after his release.

Major-General Frederick Middleton, 1825–1898

Major-General Frederick Middleton was a British infantry officer who had served in Africa, India, and New Zealand. He came to Canada in 1884 and was placed in charge of the Canadian Militia. Middleton led his soldiers in the battles of Fish Creek and Batoche. Some historians believe that the storming of the Metis rifle pits by his troops on the fourth day at Batoche was not done under Middleton's orders. For his part in the North-West Resistance, Middleton received a medal and $20 000.

Gabriel Dumont, 1837–1906

Gabriel Dumont was one of the most respected men in the North-West. He was an excellent rider and marksman. He had come to the North-West in 1872 from Manitoba because he was unhappy with conditions there.

Dumont spoke French and six First Nations languages. He was a natural leader. He proved to be a skillful military strategist. He often argued with Riel about military plans. Dumont wanted to use guerrilla hit-and-run tactics on the Canadian troops. He knew that this was the only way their small forces could succeed against the far larger Canadian force. Riel insisted they meet the troops in an eye-to-eye battle at Batoche.

Following the North-West Resistance, Dumont fled to the United States. There, he joined "Buffalo Bill" Cody's travelling Wild West Show. He returned to Batoche after an official pardon (amnesty) was granted to those who had taken part in the North-West Resistance.

On Trial

 Louis Riel was put on trial in Regina for treason. He was found guilty by a jury of six Canadians. (There were no members of the Metis, Roman Catholic, or French-speaking communities on the jury.) The jury asked the judge for mercy, but the judge had no choice about the sentence. The automatic sentence for treason was execution.

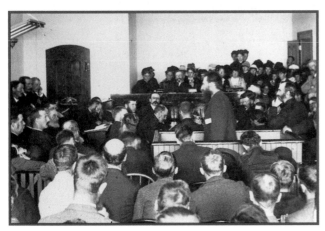

Louis Riel addressing the court at his trial, Regina, 1885

The decision to hang Riel caused a great reaction. Petitions were sent to Prime Minister Macdonald asking that Riel be pardoned, or that his sentence be changed from hanging to imprisonment. Queen Victoria ordered the governor general to ask that Riel not be hanged. The newspapers were full of articles on the subject. Some French Canadians thought Riel was insane. Some thought he had been convicted of treason because of Protestant Ontario anger against him for standing up for the rights of the French-speaking Catholic Metis. The debate was carried on in the House of Commons and in the Cabinet in Ottawa.

WHAT WILL HE DO WITH HIM?

Macdonald's dilemma over whether to have Riel hanged is depicted in this cartoon, which stereotypes the opposing forces of the two sides of the question.

Prime Minister Sir John A. Macdonald took two months to make up his mind. He had the power to step in and stop the hanging, but he did not. He knew that he would make some French Canadians very angry by not stopping it, and his Conservative Party would lose votes in Quebec. He knew that many people in Ontario were demanding a hanging, and he would lose votes in Ontario if he stopped it. Macdonald and his Cabinet decided that the hanging should go ahead. Riel was hanged on November 16, 1885.

Riel: Hero or Rebel?

   In his own time many Canadians viewed Riel as a lawless rebel. In recent years Riel has become a Canadian hero to some. Many see Riel as a symbol of Western Canada's ability to stand up to what they see as unfair treatment. He is also remembered as a defender of Metis and French Canadian minority rights in the West.

Many French Canadians feel Riel stood up for the rights of the French-speaking Metis in the North-West against what they believed was an uncaring federal government dominated by English-speaking Canadians.

In 1992, over 100 years after the North-West Resistance, the Canadian Parliament passed a resolution recognizing the contributions that Louis Riel made to Canada's growth as a nation.

For Your Notebook

1. Are uprisings like the North-West Resistance ever justified? Explain your answer.
2. What other methods might the Metis and the First Nations have used to solve their problems? How might Prime Minister Macdonald have avoided an armed conflict?
3. Do you think Riel received a fair trial? Provide reasons for your decision.

Challenge Plus

4. Using the readings and your personal opinion, was Macdonald's decision to execute Riel based upon politics or law?

Results of the North-West Resistance of 1885

❶ The Completion of the CPR

At the time of the North-West Resistance, the CPR had run out of funds. People were beginning to wonder if it would ever be finished. The government granted the CPR the money needed to complete the laying of track after seeing how quickly troops could be transported to the North-West on the railway.

❷ English–French Conflict

Riel's hanging caused great bitterness on the part of some French Canadians. They did not support Riel's choice of leading a resistance against the lawful government of Canada. However, they did not think Riel should have been hanged for it. Some believed that he was insane. Others felt that he was hanged because he was French-speaking and Roman Catholic. They saw this as a direct insult to all French Canadians.

The English Canadian reply was that if Riel had been English Canadian (or anything other than French Canadian) not a word of protest would have been heard from French Canadians. They said that French Canadians had no right to demand special treatment. Most English Canadians felt that Riel was sane and that he had committed treason by fighting against the government. Therefore, the only choice was to punish him according to the law.

The country was in an uproar. Newspapers across the country were full of the issue day after day. Petitions were sent to the government. Speeches were made both in and out of the House of Commons. Many French Canadians, and even some English Canadians, blamed John A. Macdonald's Conservative government for ignoring the concerns of the North-West for so long.

 **VS**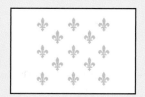

❸ Attitudes to Aboriginal People

Attitudes towards Aboriginal people hardened. A variety of repressive measures were introduced. The most notorious was the pass and permit system. The movement of Aboriginal people, mostly on the Prairies, was to be monitored and controlled. People wanted them confined to their reserves unless government Indian agents issued "passes" or gave permission to be absent. The system was also meant to "protect" Aboriginal people from being "corrupted" in the city or with alcohol. The repressions of the system were illegal. Government agents sometimes threatened to withhold rations to try to get the people to comply. However, the North West Mounted Police rarely co-operated in making the pass system effective. While technically in place until 1941 (and in some areas as late as the 1960s), the pass system failed to function as intended by the early 1890s.

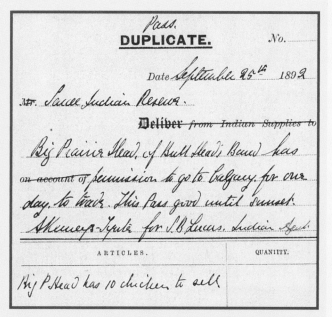

This pass allowed Big Prairie Head of Bull Head's Band to go to Calgary for one day to trade. The pass was good until sunset, September 25, 1892.

An Exercise in Decision-Making

Should Louis Riel Be Pardoned?

Some people today think that Louis Riel should be pardoned for his crime of treason. Several arguments on this issue follow:

For Your Notebook

1. Use the decision-making process outlined on page 357 to decide what you think about this issue.

2. Write a letter to your Member of Parliament giving your view and outlining your reasons for holding this view.

Yes, Louis Riel should be pardoned for his crime of treason.

1 He had a right to defend his people. The people of the West needed a spokesperson. The Metis people were losing their way of life. Westerners had tried many times to tell the government in Ottawa about their problems. Their nonviolent approaches had been ignored. Violence was the only way to get the government's attention. Future Prime Minister Wilfrid Laurier from Quebec remarked at the time, "Had I been born on the banks of the Saskatchewan, I would myself have shouldered a musket."

2 Metis law had been strictly followed in the trial and execution of Thomas Scott. By Metis law, Scott had committed treason.

3 Riel had an unfair trial. Riel was a French-speaking Roman Catholic. All six of his jurors were English-speaking Protestants. How could these men understand Louis Riel's point of view? Also, the presiding officer at the trial was a territorial magistrate, not a regular judge.

4 It is quite possible that Louis Riel was insane. Two priests testified at his trial that he was not responsible in matters of religion and politics. A young man who had been his secretary described some of Riel's strange behaviour. A doctor from an asylum where Riel had stayed said he was not responsible for his actions. If the trial had taken place today, he might have been declared insane, and therefore not guilty.

5 The punishment he received is something else to consider. Capital punishment is no longer used in Canada. If it is wrong now, then it was wrong in 1885. Riel should not have lost his life.

No, Riel should not be pardoned.

1 He was found guilty after a fair trial. Even Riel didn't deny that he and his followers had conducted an armed rebellion against the government of Canada. His lawyers tried to have him declared innocent by reason of insanity. But he stood up and argued against his lawyers, saying that he was not insane. Who was the jury to believe?

2 Some people today think he should not have been hanged. But, in 1885, hanging was still a penalty for serious crimes such as treason.

3 This was Riel's second offence. He had led a rebellion in Red River in 1869–1870. That time he had executed a Canadian civilian without a fair trial. He had been granted amnesty for these crimes, but he could not be forgiven again—not when 100 people had been killed.

4 It was not just the opinion of one judge and jury that he was guilty of treason as charged. His case was appealed all the way to the Judicial Committee of the Privy Council, the highest court in the British Empire. His own lawyer remarked, "It is impossible to pretend that Riel was unfairly tried."

5 What right do we have now to say that they were wrong to make that decision? If we say that Riel should have been declared innocent, then we are condemning our first prime minister, all those who were involved in the decision, and all the Canadians who supported the decision at the time. Is this a fair assessment of the situation?

Conservative Prime Ministers

Federal Election of 1891

This 1891 Conservative election poster aptly illustrates the campaign slogan at the bottom.

 In the election of 1891 Sir John A. Macdonald campaigned under the slogan on the poster above.

"The Old Flag," referred to loyalty to the mother country of Great Britain. Macdonald once declared, "A British subject I was born, a British subject I will die." Macdonald tried to link the Liberals to the movement that wanted Canada to join the United States.

"The Old Policy" referred to the National Policy. Two of its three pieces were in place. The CPR had been built and protective tariffs were in effect. The Liberals under Wilfrid Laurier were campaigning for reciprocity, a free trade agreement with the United States. They wanted tariffs on imported goods to be removed. But Macdonald stood by his policy of protective tariffs. The third piece of the National Policy, settlement of the West, was being promoted, although it had not yet been achieved.

"The Old Leader" was intended to appeal by suggesting Macdonald's personal popularity. There was a great deal of loyalty to him among Canadians. He was the prime minister who had achieved Confederation. Many people also found his colourful personality appealing. Macdonald and his Conservative party won the election, taking 121 seats. The Liberals won 94.

Macdonald Dies

"You'll never die, John A," crowds had shouted during the election campaign. Nevertheless, three months after winning the election, Sir John A. Macdonald was dead. He was mourned across the nation. His political rival and leader of the Liberals, Wilfrid Laurier, expressed it best when he said:

> The place of Sir John A. Macdonald in this country was so large and so absorbing that it is almost impossible to conceive that politics of this country . . . will continue without him. . . . the life of Sir John A. Macdonald, from the date he entered Parliament, is the history of Canada. . . .
>
> —*House of Commons Debates*, June 8, 1891

Four Conservative Prime Ministers

 After Sir John A. Macdonald's death there was a series of four Conservative prime ministers who were in power for brief periods.

Prime Minister	Time in Office
Sir John Joseph Caldwell Abbott	June 16, 1891–Nov. 24, 1892
Sir John Sparrow David Thompson	Dec. 5, 1892–Dec. 12, 1894
Sir Mackenzie Bowell	Dec. 21, 1894–Apr. 27, 1896
Sir Charles Tupper	May 1, 1896–July 8, 1896

For Your Notebook

1. Select a present day political leader and create a campaign poster for him or her.

2. Check the **Canada Revisited 8** web page for this chapter for more information on the four prime ministers listed above.

Many people in late nineteenth century Canada enjoyed watching and taking part in organized sports, just as people do today. Reading and home entertainment were common leisure pursuits.

Sports

The Canadian Cricket Association was formed in 1882 and still exists today. Like cricket, tennis has long been popular among middle and upper-class Canadians. Tennis clubs were formed in cities across Canada during the 1890s.

The first organized hockey team, the McGill University Hockey Club, was formed in 1879. In 1893, the Governor General, Lord Stanley, presented the Stanley Cup to the best amateur hockey team. Professional hockey teams were not formed until the early 1900s.

Baseball was popular, especially among working class people. Baseball was introduced into Ontario before 1900 and became popular in Western Canada after 1900.

Literature

Canadian poets Duncan Campbell Scott and Archibald Lampman began to publish their poetry during this period. They often took canoe trips to explore the wilderness around Ottawa where they lived. Scott and Lampman praised the power and beauty of the Canadian landscape through their poetry.

Leisure

Canadians enjoyed outdoor leisure activities such as ice-skating and tobogganing, just as they had in the earlier years of the century.

Most members of the working class had only Sundays off as a day of rest. Some were free on Saturday afternoon as well. Many people attended church services Sunday morning, then went to a public park in the afternoon. There they might listen to a band play, eat a picnic lunch of cold chicken and potato salad, and let the children wade in a cool pond.

On winter evenings, people entertained in their homes. They played cards, chatted, and often listened to someone sing, play a musical instrument, or recite a poem or speech which they had memorized. Children learned pieces to perform during family evenings and to entertain guests.

For Your Notebook

1. What sorts of things did Canadians like to do in their leisure time during the period between 1878 and 1896?

2. How did leisure and the arts help build a Canadian identity?

Exploring Further

3. What things do you enjoy doing in your leisure time that would not have been available to Canadians of your age in the late nineteenth century?

4. How has technology influenced the ways in which people spend their leisure time today?

The Montreal Amateur Athletic Association was the first winner of the Stanley Cup, in 1893.

Young women also enjoyed playing hockey at the end of the 19th Century.

Review

The icons are your cue to refer to the Learning How to Learn Appendix (pages 348–371) for ideas on how to complete these activities.

1. Complete a self-assessment for one assignment from this chapter.

Understanding Concepts

2. At the beginning of the chapter, you created a chart with three headings: Know, Wonder, and Learn. In the Know column you filled in everything you knew about this chapter. In the Wonder column you listed what you would like to know. Now, write what you have learned in the Learn column.

3. Use one of the suggested methods for recording vocabulary to add any new words from this chapter to the WordBook section of the notes.

4. Here are some of the main ideas from this chapter:

   - National Policy
   - protective tariffs
   - industrialization
   - Canadian Pacific Railway
   - role of women
   - factory system
   - changes to cities
   - political necessity
   - economic necessity
   - North-West Resistance

   Do either a) or b).

   a) Create a concept poster for one of these ideas. Present your poster to the class.

   b) Use a web, mind map, outline, or chart to create a permanent set of notes about one of the ideas. Explain your work to a classmate.

5. Prepare a wall chart to show how the National Policy of the Conservatives shaped the country from 1878–1896. Use examples from this chapter for Parts 1 and 2.

The National Policy	
Parts	**Example**
1.	
2.	

SAMPLE

6. Refer to the Chapter 9 Focus on page 215. Notice that all five History concepts have been the focus of this chapter. Select any three. Create three webs to represent examples of each of these concepts found in this chapter.

7. Add entries for this chapter in your timeline.

Developing Research Skills

8.   As a class, discuss the questions on the Section III Focus on page 147 as they apply to the National Policy, the topic of this chapter.

9.

Section III Activity

Part Two

1. Work in small groups for this activity. Work with people who selected a different challenge from page 215 than you did.

   a) Using the chart A Model to Meet Challenges as a source of data, discuss which challenges Prime Minister Macdonald and his Conservative government faced between 1878 and 1896.

   b) What solutions did Prime Minister Macdonald use? Do you agree or disagree with the methods he used? Provide reasons.

Developing Communication Skills

Do numbers 12, 13, 14, and select one other from the following.

Reading

10. Read "Angelique Dumas" by Jeannine Laboucane in *Ordinary People in Canada's Past*, by Nancy Sellars Marcotte (Arnold Publishing). Imagine you are

Gabriel Dumont and write an entry in his journal, describing his feelings as he hid from the soldiers.

11. Ask your librarian to recommend novels you can read that are set during this period.

Writing

12. Select three people from this chapter and list the admirable qualities you think they had. If you were one of these people, of what accomplishment would you be the most proud?

13. In your opinion, what is the most memorable event in this chapter? Explain why.

Listening and Speaking

14. Take the role of Prime Minister Macdonald. Prepare a speech to present to several friends:
    a) providing a brief overview on the National Policy
    b) convincing the voters of the benefits of protective tariffs
    c) giving the reasons why the Canadian Pacific Railway should be built

15. Wilfrid Laurier, a Liberal Member of Parliament and future Prime Minister, said of the 1885 Metis Resistance, "Had I been born on the banks of the Saskatchewan, I would myself have shouldered a musket to fight against the neglect of governments and the shameless greed of speculators." Laurier made this statement in Montreal on November 22, 1885, a week after the hanging of Louis Riel. He was speaking at a demonstration against Prime Minister Macdonald and his decision to allow the hanging. Write what Laurier might have said in the rest of this speech. Deliver the speech to the demonstrators (classmates).

Viewing and Representing

16. Cartoonists often use such devices as: symbolism (an image that actually represents something else), size (representing power or lack of power), caricature (distortion of features), and stereotyping (oversimplifying).
    a) Identify and explain which devices are used in the cartoon "Riding into Power."
    b) The title of this cartoon is "Riding into Power." Who was riding into power?
    c) What is the cartoonist saying about the strength of Macdonald's National Policy?
    d) What political party is represented by the people on the ground?

RIDING INTO POWER.

17. Do both a) and b).

    a) Assume the role of someone working on Macdonald's 1878 election. Create a campaign poster for him. Include his ideas on the National Policy.

    b) Assume the role of a college student working on the Mackenzie 1878 election team. You have just been given the job to critique Macdonald's National Policy. In a report to Mackenzie, point out the positive and negative features of the policy.

18. Refer to the cartoon on page 238 and then answer these questions.

    a) What are the points of view represented in the cartoon?

    b) How is each point of view presented in a stereotypical way?

    c) Discuss how the use of stereotyping can over-simplify or distort a situation.

    d) Explain how the device of size is used by the cartoonist.

    e) Explain how the situation represented here was more complex than it would seem. Use details from the cartoon to answer.

Applying Concepts

19. Choose an organization on the Milestones chart on page 221. Conduct research to discover what the organization's goals were and what it did to promote those goals. Create a visual timeline showing the steps it took to achieve its goals. If the organization had provincial branches, show their major activities as well. As you can see from the chart, women were beginning to realize that it was better to work co-operatively than individually to achieve their goals. In fact, by 1912 one in eight Canadian women belonged to a women's organization.

20. Skim a modern day national newspaper for one week and clip items related to issues concerned with French/English relations. Choose one issue and write an imaginary conversation about this issue between an English Canadian and a French Canadian.

21. Find out about protective tariffs on goods we import into Canada today. A source for this information is the Federal Department of Foreign Affairs and International Trade. The toll-free 1-800 phone number is in your local telephone book.

22. List the ways the building of the Canadian Pacific Railway benefitted Canada at the time and continues to benefit it today.

Challenge Plus

23. How did Macdonald's protective tariffs policy relate to regionalism?

24. The building of the CPR has been described in this chapter from the perspective of the railway builders. Describe the building of the CPR from the viewpoint of an Aboriginal person living in an area directly affected by the construction of the CPR. Think of the ways Aboriginal peoples had helped the Europeans in the past and the ways in which their lifestyle has been disrupted. You will need to do additional research in order to complete this task.

25. Reread the information about Lady Aberdeen that is given in this chapter and conduct other research to learn more about her. Use this information to decide if you consider Lady Aberdeen to be "meddlesome" or a "courageous crusader for social issues," or perhaps somewhere between. Write an essay providing arguments to support your point of view. (See Essay Writing on page 358 of the Appendix.)

Chapter 10

Settlement of the West

1896–1914

O v e r v i e w

Use this Overview to predict what you will read in this chapter.

① 1896–1911

Sir Wilfrid Laurier and the Liberals governed Canada.

② 1896–1899

The Klondike gold rush took place in the Yukon Territory.

③ 1900–1914

Almost three million immigrants came to Canada. Most moved to what is now Western Canada.

④ 1904

Charles Saunders developed Marquis Wheat. This led to prosperity in the Canadian West.

⑤ 1905

The provinces of Saskatchewan and Alberta were created.

CONFEDERATION

Alberta   Saskatchewan

Chapter 10 Focus

Chapter 9 described the first two parts of Sir John A. Macdonald's National Policy—protective tariffs and the building of the Canadian Pacific Railway. Chapter 10 continues the theme of protective tariffs and describes the third part of the national policy, settlement of the West. This settlement occurred mainly under Prime Minister Wilfrid Laurier and his Liberal government. This chapter also looks at the discovery of gold, the formation of the Yukon Territory, and the creation of Alberta and Saskatchewan as provinces in 1905. The concepts of change and regionalism are the special focus of this chapter.

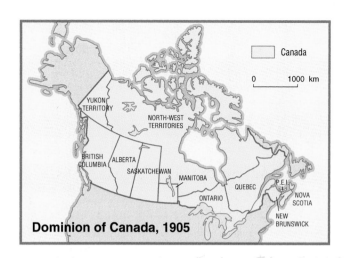

Dominion of Canada, 1905

Change   Regionalism   Power   Identity   Co-operation/Conflict

Other Concepts and Main Topics

- Klondike gold rush
- Settlement of the West
- creation of provinces of Alberta and Saskatchewan

Learning How to Learn

 Chronology

 Research

 Role-playing

 Writing

 Note Making

 Decision-making

Chapter Preview/Prediction

1. a) Examine the Overview on page 246. Read the column above, note the map above right, and briefly look through the chapter.

    Use the Level 1, 2, and 3 headings to make a set of outline notes of the chapter. (Outline notes are explained on page 362.)

   b) Working with a partner, talk about how each of the main topics above might have involved challenges, co-operation, critical thinking, and decision-making. Use the information in your notes from 1a) above and what you already know about Canada in this time period. Record your thoughts in note form beside each topic on the outline you just made.

Section III Activity

 In Chapter 10 you will be using A Model to Meet Challenges for your study of Western Settlement (page 145).

Part One

  Assume the role of Prime Minister Laurier. For years the goal of the Canadian government had been to get the North-West Territories ready for settlement (see chart page 179). Fill out number ❶ on the chart A Model to Meet Challenges from Laurier's point of view (page 145). This activity is continued on page 255.

Under the third part of the National Policy—settlement of the West—immigration was encouraged.

Liberal Administration 1896–1911

From Confederation until 1896 the Conservatives were in power, except during the years 1873–1878 when Alexander Mackenzie was a Liberal prime minister. It was an astounding victory for the Liberals when Wilfrid Laurier became prime minister in 1896. Laurier led Canada from 1896 to 1911.

Personal Summary

Laurier was born into a French-speaking Roman Catholic family at St. Lin, Quebec. He had a bicultural childhood. At the age of 10 he went to live with an Anglo-Protestant family. There he learned English and learned about the Protestant faith. Laurier obtained his law degree from McGill University in 1864. In 1868 Laurier married Zoe Lafontaine. They had no children.

Political Summary

Laurier practised law before winning a seat in the Legislative Assembly in Quebec. He first became a Member of Parliament in 1873, when Alexander Mackenzie's Liberals took over from John A. Macdonald's Conservatives. In 1896 Laurier became Canada's seventh prime minister, the first whose first language was French. He was prime minister for 15 years. This is the longest uninterrupted term that any prime minister of Canada has had.

Throughout his career, Laurier practised what he called his "sunny ways" approach. He always searched for a compromise, a middle path between French and English interests. He stressed that there was no single Canadian identity, but rather two identities, French and English, both of which had to be respected. He urged Canadians to be tolerant of **diversity**. One of the issues he dealt with was the Manitoba Schools Question: whether there should be two school systems in the Province of Manitoba. This was an issue of culture, religion, and federal/provincial rights. It was a challenge to Laurier's ability to negotiate. (You will read about it in Chapter 11.)

The new country of Canada changed rapidly during the time Laurier was prime minister. The

Sir Wilfrid Laurier
1841–1919

Dates as Prime Minister—1896–1911
Party—Liberal

• • • • • • • •

Klondike gold rush led to the creation of the Yukon Territory in 1898. Massive immigration to the Canadian West resulted in the creation of two new provinces, Alberta and Saskatchewan, in 1905.

Laurier was fortunate enough to be prime minister during a period of economic growth. European cities were demanding Canadian wheat. The development of hardy new strains of wheat made it possible to meet that demand. He encouraged large numbers of immigrants to settle in the West. The population increase caused a demand for new goods and services. Central Canada (Ontario and Quebec) was becoming more urban and many new industries were developing. Canadian businesspeople produced and marketed such products as steel, bread, cars, and farm machinery. British and American investment capital that was pouring into the country helped develop these new industries. Canada's new-found wealth inspired Laurier with such confidence that he said:

> . . . the twentieth century shall be the century of Canada and of Canadian development. For the next seventy-five years, nay for the next hundred years, Canada shall be the star towards which all men who love progress and freedom shall come.

Laurier lost the election of 1911 to Robert Borden and his Conservative Party. After Laurier lost, he worked to rebuild the Liberal Party. He continued to believe that Canada needed a Liberal government to maintain prosperity and unity. Above all, Wilfrid Laurier was a Canadian. He once said:

> Canada has been the inspiration of my life. I have had before me, as a pillar of fire by night, and a pillar of cloud by day, a policy of true Canadianism, of moderation, of conciliation.

Diversity—differences

Klondike Gold Rush 1896–1899

Canada was entering a time of economic growth. The Yukon gold rush provided some fortunate Canadians with a chance to be part of that growth.

Discovery of Gold

On August 16, 1896, George Washington Carmack, Skookum Jim, and Tagish Charlie made a major discovery of gold at Rabbit Creek (later called Bonanza Creek). Three months later nearly 500 claims had been staked in the area. Some of these claims made their owners rich beyond their wildest dreams. However, many of the people ended up with barely enough gold to pay their costs. Most of the claims that paid well were staked by prospectors who were already in the area at the time of the original discovery. There was not much left for the newcomers who were attracted by tales of wealth.

Getting there in the first place was an ordeal. Prospective miners had to bring in a year's supply of food or else the money to purchase it. Prices in the town of Dawson were extremely high. The photograph below shows miners bent over with the weight of the supplies they brought in. Local Chilkoot Tlingit people earned some income as packers and guides for the prospective miners. Otherwise, the gold rush provided few benefits to the Aboriginal people in the region.

Klondike Gold Rush, 1896–1899

Travellers had a choice of two passes into the Yukon: Chilkoot Pass and White Pass. It was a long, hard journey either way.

The Spell of the Yukon

—Robert Service

I wanted the gold, and I sought it;
    I scrabbled and mucked like a slave.
Was it famine or scurvy—I fought it;
    I hurled my youth into a grave.
I wanted the gold and I got it—
    Came out with a fortune last fall,—
Yet somehow life's not what I thought it,
    And somehow the gold isn't all.

Robert Service wrote many poems describing life in the Yukon during the Klondike gold rush. He actually did not arrive there until 1904, after the rush was over. His poems about it have inspired imaginations ever since.

Walking over the Chilkoot Pass was an ordeal. In 1898, over 25 000 made the trek. People carried their supplies either on their backs or on sleds. On page 251, Martha Black describes her trip over the Pass.

249

Dawson

The height of the Klondike gold rush was in 1898. By the end of the summer of that year, the town of Dawson, which had not existed before, had a population of over 20 000. Food was scarce and expensive. A turkey had been raffled off the previous winter for $174. Potatoes were $1.00 a pound, and flour $3.00. At this time, a labourer in Toronto made $1.25 a day.

This 1899 photo shows how busy Dawson was during the gold rush.

For a frontier gold rush town, Dawson was amazingly orderly and law-abiding. This was due to the work of the North West Mounted Police. They set up a checkpoint at the summit of the two passes into the Yukon and removed any pistols or revolvers from their owners. People who caught the eyes of the watchful Mounties could be ordered out of the Yukon without having been convicted of any crime. Murderers were hanged.

In three short years, by 1899, the Klondike gold rush was over. The change was dramatic. In fact, 8000 people left in one week after hearing about a gold strike at Nome, Alaska. The town of Dawson had a population of 20 000 at the height of the gold rush. Today it is down to 1000 people. Its economy relies on tourism. The Klondike gold rush is famous around the world. Many tourists visit Dawson to see its historic buildings and gold rush artifacts.

The Cremation of Sam McGee

—Robert Service

There are strange things done in the midnight sun
By the men who moil for gold;
The Arctic trails have their secret tales
That would make your blood run cold;
The Northern Lights have seen queer sights,
But the queerest they ever did see
Was that night on the marge of Lake Lebarge
I cremated Sam McGee.

For Your Notebook

1. Create a web or mind map to make notes on the gold rush. Discuss your ideas with another student before you begin.

Exploring Further

2. In a few sentences, summarize the meaning of the lines from Robert Service's poem, "The Spell of the Yukon," on page 249. Do you agree?
3. Develop a pictorial essay on the Klondike gold rush. This could be in the form of a photo album or a mural. Write a caption for each visual.

Gold seekers arriving at Dawson on the Yukon River are met by the NWMP, who were keeping order and giving aid, as needed.

Sam Steele, 1849–1919

On July 7, 1898, Sam Steele was appointed as Commanding Officer of the North West Mounted Police in the Yukon. His task was to bring to an end the lawlessness of the Klondike gold rush. He also became a member of the government of the North-West Territories.

When he first arrived, Steele called the town of Skagway "the roughest place in the world." However, he was so successful in keeping law and order that many people called him the "Lion of the Yukon." The people of Dawson were so satisfied with his work that they petitioned Ottawa to have him stay when he was transferred in September of 1899.

(See also page 201 for biography of Sam Steele.)

Martha Black, 1866–1957

Martha Black was an unusual and adventurous woman. In 1897, she travelled with her brother to the Yukon Territory to search for gold. Very few women travelled to the goldfields as prospectors.

In 1898, Martha Black crossed the Chilkoot Pass into the Klondike. She described her experience:

> . . . the last two miles into Lindeman was the most excruciating struggle of the whole trip. In my memory it will ever remain a hideous nightmare. The trail led through a scrub pine forest where we tripped over bare roots of trees that curled over and around rocks and boulders like great devilfishes. Rocks! Rocks! Rocks! Tearing boots to pieces. Hands bleeding with scratches, I can bear it no longer. In my agony, I beg the men to leave me—to let me lie in my tracks, and stay for the night.

Black returned to her home in Chicago the next summer, then in 1900 she went back to the Klondike. There she earned a living by staking goldmining claims and running a sawmill and a gold ore-crushing plant.

In 1935, Martha Black became the second woman elected to the Canadian House of Commons. She represented the Yukon Territory.

Yukon Territory

The Yukon Territory was formed in 1898. The Canadian government wished to establish control over the thousands of people entering the area to look for gold. The first territorial government consisted of a federally appointed commissioner (James Walsh of the North West Mounted Police) and an appointed council. The capital at the time was Dawson City.

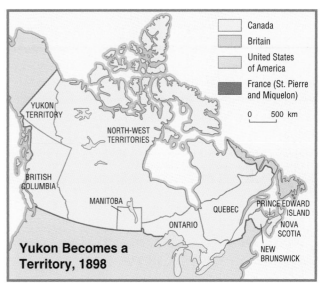

Canada
Britain
United States of America
France (St. Pierre and Miquelon)

0   500 km

YUKON TERRITORY

NORTH-WEST TERRITORIES

BRITISH COLUMBIA

MANITOBA

ONTARIO

QUEBEC

PRINCE EDWARD ISLAND

NOVA SCOTIA

NEW BRUNSWICK

Yukon Becomes a Territory, 1898

The Yukon Territory is separated from the North-West Territories by rugged mountains.

Martha Black hunting with her husband, George Black, a Yukon Member of Parliament

For Your Notebook

1. Compare the maps on pages 249 and 251. How and why are they different?

Exploring Further

2. Do you think that the Yukon should have been granted provincial rather than territorial status? Defend your point of view.

Industrialization

By 1901 Canada's economy was changing from agricultural to industrial. Different parts of the country were changing at different rates. Central Canada was more industrialized. The provinces of Atlantic Canada, Manitoba, British Columbia, and the vast North-West Territories were involved in primary industry. These included agriculture, fishing, forestry, mining, and trapping.

A new source of energy, steam power, was part of the process of industrialization. Steam transportation services such as riverboats and steam locomotives were key to industrial development. Using steam power in manufacturing processes meant certain goods could be produced faster and for less money. Factories were built to hold the new industries. A large number of workers were needed in the factories. This contributed to urbanization, as people moved to live near factories. The change-over from the agricultural age to the industrial age happened gradually. For many years, farmers used both horses and steam engines as sources of power, as the photo below shows.

In this period of transition, steam and animal power were used side by side.

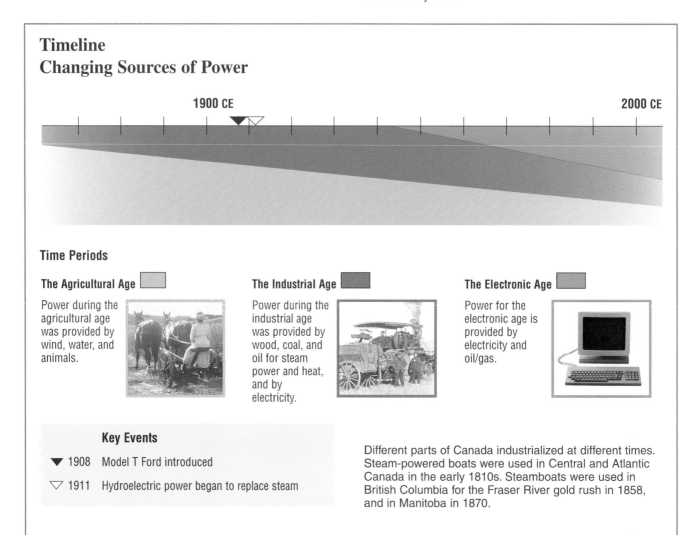

Timeline
Changing Sources of Power

1900 CE   2000 CE

Time Periods

The Agricultural Age

Power during the agricultural age was provided by wind, water, and animals.

The Industrial Age

Power during the industrial age was provided by wood, coal, and oil for steam power and heat, and by electricity.

The Electronic Age

Power for the electronic age is provided by electricity and oil/gas.

Key Events

▼ 1908   Model T Ford introduced

▽ 1911   Hydroelectric power began to replace steam

Different parts of Canada industrialized at different times. Steam-powered boats were used in Central and Atlantic Canada in the early 1810s. Steamboats were used in British Columbia for the Fraser River gold rush in 1858, and in Manitoba in 1870.

New Ideas and Inventions

Wheat

Early-maturing and high-yielding Marquis wheat was bred experimentally by Charles Saunders. It was tested carefully in Saskatchewan for two years before being released for general use. Marquis wheat was so successful it enabled the Canadian West to become the "breadbasket" of the world.

Historians H. Graham Rawlinson and J.L. Granatstein called Charles Saunders the most influential Canadian in the twentieth century for the economic benefits that he brought to Canada. Because of the new strain of wheat Saunders developed, Canadian wheat is valued around the world. When he died, London's *Daily Express* commented, "He added more wealth to his country than any other man." In 1934, he received a knighthood in Great Britain for his contributions to Canada.

Sir Charles Saunders
1867–1937

Many farmers on the Canadian prairies were being forced into bankruptcy when their wheat crops were destroyed by early frosts. Dr. Charles Saunders was searching for a wheat strain that would mature earlier than existing strains and would produce flour that would make good-tasting bread. In 1904, he produced Marquis by breeding Red Fife Wheat, a variety developed by David Fife in Ontario, and Hard Red Calcutta. Marquis wheat matured in about 115 days (seven to ten days earlier than other strains), was resistant to early frosts, and was hardy enough to withstand heavy winds. By 1920, 90 per cent of the 7 million hectares of wheat planted in Western Canada was Marquis wheat.

The Top Five Canadian Agricultural Exports in 1901	Canada's Five Leading Trading Partners in 1902
1. Cheese	1. United States
2. Pork, bacon, ham	2. Great Britain
3. Cattle	3. Germany
4. Wheat	4. France
5. Flour	5. West Indies

For Your Notebook

1. Review the chart on page 179 showing what had to be done to get the West ready for settlers. What role did Marquis wheat play in helping western settlement?
2. Did all farmers change to new technologies when they were introduced? Why was this so? (Use the photographs on page 252 as reference.)
3. The age you are reading about in this textbook can be called the industrial age and the age you live in is often called the electronic age. Make a collage that contrasts images from each age. Write a paragraph explaining why the images you have chosen are representative of each age.

Canada Revisited

In a living museum, a steam-powered tractor drives a threshing machine, using a long belt attached to a moving fly-wheel.

The threshing machine separates the grain from the straw.

253

Settling the West

Settlement of the West was the third part of Sir John A. Macdonald's National Policy. The first two parts, protective tariffs and the building of a national railway, were discussed in Chapter 9.

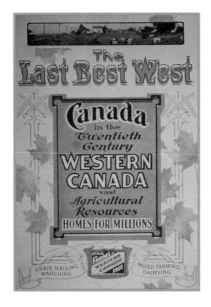

It was planned that the immigrants who would come from Europe and the United States to settle on the Canadian prairies also would use the Canadian Pacific Railway. They would buy Canadian-made goods, because high tariffs would be put on goods imported from the United States.

In spite of everything the Canadian government had done to encourage western settlement, new settlers were slow to move to the Prairies. It was not until much of the good land in the United States was taken that the Prairies of Canada also were settled.

Immigration to Canada, 1890–1914			
Years	**Numbers**	**Years**	**Numbers**
1890	75 067	1903	138 660
1891	82 165	1904	131 252
1892	30 996	1905	141 465
1893	29 633	1906	211 653
1894	20 829	1907	272 409
1895	18 790	1908	143 326
1896	16 835	1909	173 694
1897	21 716	1910	286 839
1898	31 900	1911	331 288
1899	44 543	1912	375 756
1900	41 681	1913	400 870
1901	55 747	1914	150 484
1902	89 102		

*The signing of Treaty 8 in 1899 opened up a large tract of land for settlement. See page 207 for a map of the main numbered treaties.

Between 1900 and 1914 (the start of World War I) almost three million people moved into the North-West Territories. Most of these people came from Ontario, Great Britain, and the United States. Others came from Europe.

There were several reasons why these people chose Western Canada as the place to settle. Six reasons are outlined below. Most of these reasons have been explored in earlier chapters.

Reasons for Coming to Western Canada

1. **Dominion Lands Act.** Changes to the Dominion Lands Act encouraged immigration. The settlers still had to pay a 10-dollar registration fee. Then they only had to reside on the homestead for three years before it was considered to be their land.
2. **The North West Mounted Police.** The NWMP had established law and order in the West, making it safe for settlers to move there.
3. **Treaties.** The Canadian government had signed treaties with many First Nations, creating reserves for them to live on.* This freed vast amounts of western lands for settlement.
4. **Canadian Pacific Railway.** In 1885, the Canadian Pacific Railway was completed. This meant that it was much easier and faster for settlers to travel to the West. Crops from the West could now be transported by railway to the markets of Eastern Canada.
5. **Marquis Wheat.** The farmland in Canada's West had to be viewed more positively by settlers than before. Marquis wheat, developed by Sir Charles Saunders, was fast-maturing and high-yielding. Western farmers had learned how to make the most of their prairie farms. Their costs were lower and they were getting higher prices for their crops. Canada developed a reputation as a major grain producer.
6. **"The Last Best West."** Good farmland near transportation routes was becoming scarce in Ontario. Many people believed that the same was true in the western United States. Canada took advantage of this and promoted its available western lands as "The Last Best West," as shown in the poster in the left column.

Advertising for Settlers

Clifford Sifton was the government minister in charge of immigration. He was largely responsible for bringing the settlers to the Canadian West through advertising and other means. Sifton placed advertisements in 6000 newspapers in the United States and Europe. He gave American newspaper journalists free guided tours of the Canadian Prairies so that they could see the inexpensive, fertile land for themselves. This advertising campaign was very successful. The chart on page 254 shows Canadian immigration from the years 1890 to 1914. Between 1897 and 1912, of the 2 491 031 settlers who immigrated to Canada, 785 137 were from the United States.

Initially, Sifton sent agents to Great Britain and the United States to promote settlement in the Canadian West. Later he decided to advertise heavily in central and eastern Europe. Exhibition vans travelled the countryside with displays of Canadian products and posters encouraging people to emigrate to Canada.

The government policy at the time was to encourage immigration from certain regions. Sifton felt some people were more likely to be successful settlers for the Canadian west than others.

There were many people in parts of Europe who would never have the chance to have a large farm of their own if they did not emigrate. They owned very small farms, often highly taxed, or they were tenants or labourers on the large farms of powerful landowners. Some wanted to leave Europe because they were being persecuted for their religious beliefs. Immigrants often sold most of what they owned to buy steamship tickets for their families and the supplies they would need on their homesteads in Canada.

Clifford Sifton 1861–1929

As minister of the interior, Sifton was responsible for immigration and for overseeing the vast western lands between the Ontario–Manitoba border and the Rocky Mountains, and north from the United States border to the Arctic Ocean. He was responsible for Aboriginal peoples, immigration, homesteads, railways, schools, forests, minerals, grazing lands, and national parks policy. Instead of waiting for immigrants to come to the West, he went out to get them. It was largely due to Sifton's advertising campaign that thousands of people came to settle in Western Canada.

For Your Notebook

1. Between 1900 and 1914 there was a flood of immigrants into the Canadian West.

    Create a concept poster to show the reasons why immigrants came to the Canadian West.

2. What part did advertising play in settling the West?

Canadian Government Emigration Offices in London advertised for settlers. Displays showed the quality of Canadian farm products.

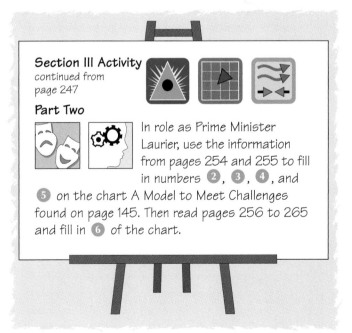

Section III Activity
continued from page 247

Part Two

In role as Prime Minister Laurier, use the information from pages 254 and 255 to fill in numbers ❷, ❸, ❹, and ❺ on the chart A Model to Meet Challenges found on page 145. Then read pages 256 to 265 and fill in ❻ of the chart.

With the introduction of Macdonald's National Policy, many immigrants from eastern and central Europe came to Canada. This section looks at groups of immigrants other than French, British, and Americans who came to Canada in the late 1800s and early 1900s. Pages 256 to 259 focus on the development of Canada as a multicultural country. A multicultural country is one that has people from many different cultural backgrounds. The term cultural backgrounds refers to the language, religion, traditions, music, art, and literature of a person's ancestral homeland.

In Canada, many people have retained parts of their homeland's culture. They often practise the religion of their country of origin and also teach their children the music, dances, and literature. Some live in communities where they are able to conduct much of their daily lives using the language of their country of origin.

German

Large numbers of Germans came to the Prairie Region during the 1870s and later, especially during the 1890s and the early years of the twentieth century. William Hespeler, himself a German immigrant, recruited German settlers from western Europe and Russia to immigrate to Manitoba. About 8000 Mennonite people came to

Canada from Russia and settled in Saskatchewan. By 1911 there were 403 417 Germans in Canada.

German immigrants, 1911

Ukrainian

Large numbers of Slavic immigrants came to Canada from Ukraine, Russia, and Poland in the late 1800s and at the turn of the century. Many of them settled in the West. They built farms or found work in industries, on the railroad, or in mines.

Left: A large number of settlers came to the Canadian west from the United States.

Below: These Canadians are wearing traditional Ukrainian clothing.

Major Immigrant Groups That Arrived 1896–1914	
Great Britain	1 200 000
United States	1 000 000
Germany, France, Norway, Sweden, and Iceland	800 000
Ukraine	171 000
Poland	116 000

Focus On: Turn-of-the-Century Immigrants

Many Ukrainians left their homelands to start a new life elsewhere because of shortages of land, compulsory military service, and religious persecution. The Canadian Prairie Region was a popular choice, since it was similar to the landscape of Ukraine. Once the new Canadians were established in their homes, they often encouraged and sometimes paid for family members and friends to come to Canada. The golden opportunities in Canada enticed more to come, especially the "free land" (the 65 hectares offered by Sifton's homestead system*). Ukrainians prospered in Canada and made many contributions to their new country.

They first settled in what is now the Province of Alberta, then in Manitoba, and later in what became Saskatchewan. They chose large bloc settlements along railway lines, close to their families and friends. From 1000 Ukrainian settlers in 1896, numbers rapidly increased to 27 000 in 1900, and about 200 000 in 1914.

A Slavic family

Immigrants from eastern Europe

Russian and Polish

Most Russian immigrants came in groups by special arrangement of the Canadian and Russian governments. In 1899, 7500 Doukhobor people emigrated from Russia to Canada and settled in rural communities. They left Russia in large groups looking for religious freedom. Several thousand Russian Jews came in the 1890s. Most settled in cities such as Montreal, Windsor, Toronto, Winnipeg, and Vancouver.

Between 1895 and 1913, 119 600 Polish people arrived in

Canada. Most were rural and small-town people from Austrian-occupied territories in eastern Europe. A large number became farmers in Manitoba, Saskatchewan, and Alberta.

Italian

Many Italian immigrants came to British North America to assist in the building of the Rideau Canal and the CPR. Others came to homesteads and ranches in the West. However, the largest numbers of Italians came to Canada after World War II. Many had urban backgrounds in Italy and they immigrated to cities in Canada.

This cowboy came to Canada from Italy in the early 1890s.

---

*While the land was "free" there was a ten dollar registration fee.

Jewish

The small numbers of Jewish people who came to British North America before Confederation were often wealthy merchant families who settled in Montreal. During the late 1800s many poor, working-class Jews left eastern Europe (particularly Russia) to settle in Canada. They settled mostly in Montreal, Toronto, and Winnipeg. (Since they were denied the right to own land in most European countries, they were not used to farming.) The 1901 census reported that there were 16 000 Jews in Canada. By 1911 the Jewish population in Canada had climbed to 76 000.

Japanese

In 1858, Japanese workers came to British Columbia to work in the goldfields. Their exact names were not documented. Manzo Nagano was the first recorded Japanese person to come to British North America. In 1877 he arrived and settled in Victoria. By 1894 there were approximately 1000 Japanese immigrants and by 1904 there were close to 7000. Most of them settled on the west coast of British Columbia to work in the fishing industry.

Above: Most Japanese Canadians are descended from people who arrived in Canada in the early 1900s.

Above: Most Jewish immigrants came to Canada from villages, towns, and cities in Europe.

Right: John and Mildred Ware. A former slave from the southern United States, Ware came to the area that is now southern Alberta in 1882. He worked as a cowboy, then bought a ranch.

Below: Immigrants from India on their way to Canada, 1906

South Asian

Sikhs and other groups from India started coming to Canada in the early 1900s. In 1908 the Canadian government passed a law forbidding their entry into Canada except under special circumstances. The *Komagata Maru* incident of 1914, which you will read about later, tested the government's **exclusionary** immigration policy.

Exclusionary—intentionally restrictive

African-American

When the Canadian government offered "free land" for settlers in the West, African-American settlers from Ontario and the United States moved west to become farmers and ranchers in present-day Alberta. In 1902 there were roughly 10 000 and in 1912 approximately 15 000 in Canada. Of the 300 000 African-Canadians today, approximately one quarter have emigrated from the West Indies since the 1960s.

Chinese

Large numbers of Chinese people (about 14 000) worked as labourers on the construction of the CPR. When the railway was completed in 1885, the Canadian government tried to force them to leave Canada. In 1886, restrictions were put on Chinese immigration to Canada. A 50-dollar "head tax" was imposed on all new Chinese immigrants. This tax was increased to $100 in 1900 and to $500 in 1904.*

At the beginning of the 1900s, many Chinese were working as household servants or in the service industries, running restaurants, laundries, or small shops. In 1907 they were subjected to racial riots and many of their homes and busi-

nesses were destroyed by English Canadians in British Columbia. Large numbers of Chinese families left British Columbia and moved to other parts of Canada.

Today, there are nearly half a million Canadians of Chinese ancestry.

Chinese children

Immigrants from Other Parts of Europe

- After exploration around 1000 CE, Scandinavians next arrived in the late 1800s. They settled primarily in the Western provinces.
- Portuguese explorers and fishers came in the late 1400s, but few Portuguese settlers stayed in Canada prior to 1912.
- Explorers and fishers came from Spain from the late 1400s. In the 1700s Spanish explorers went to the Pacific Coast. Few Spanish settlers stayed in Canada prior to 1912.
- French-speaking Swiss immigrants settled in New France first in the 1600s. Later they located on the Prairies and in British Columbia.

- Dutch people started coming to Canada in the 1800s, settling mostly on the Prairies and in Ontario.
- A small number of Greek immigrants came around 1900. Most settled in cities in Ontario and Quebec.
- Austrians came around 1900 and settled mostly on the Prairies.
- Belgians started coming to Canada in the 1900s and settled primarily in Manitoba, British Columbia, Quebec, Ontario, and Nova Scotia.
- Immigrants from Luxembourg have been immigrating to Canada since the early 1900s. They have settled in Manitoba, British Columbia, Quebec, Ontario, and Nova Scotia.

For Your Notebook

1. Why would people move to another country or region?

2. How might the people who live in an area feel about newcomers?

Exploring Further

3. Select one of the immigrant groups shown on pages 256 to 259.
   a) Carry out research to find out more about the reasons why this group came to Canada.
   b) Design a wall poster encouraging them to come to Canada.
   c) 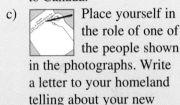 Place yourself in the role of one of the people shown in the photographs. Write a letter to your homeland telling about your new home.

4. Imagine you are a young adult from Europe arriving in the Canadian west in 1904. Write a letter to your family or to a friend describing the fertile farmland or one of the prairie towns, North West Mounted Police forts, reserves, or fur-trading forts you saw on your ride westward on the Canadian Pacific Railway, or any other event or situation you found especially fascinating.

*Because of a special agreement between the Canadian and Japanese governments, the Japanese did not pay a head tax upon entering Canada.

This photo essay shows rural life in the North-West Territories in the 1900s. The main economic activities were farming and ranching.

Rural and Urban Population

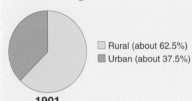

☐ Rural (about 62.5%)
☐ Urban (about 37.5%)

1901

At the beginning of the 1900s more than half of the people in Canada lived and worked in rural areas.

Above: When there were trees nearby, settlers built log cabins.

Above: These farm workers are stooking grain at harvest time near Wetaskiwin, North-West Territories (present-day Alberta).

Above: Pieces of sod from the prairie were cut and made into homes by prairie settlers where trees were scarce.

Below: Grain elevators along the railway stored the products of prairie farms until trains transported them to market.

Above: While the First Nations way of life changed on the reserves, some families continued to live in traditional homes.

Above: First
Nations women in
northern wood-
lands are preparing
a hide for tanning.

Above: Ranching
was suited to the
drier Prairie lands.

Above: As lumber became available log cabins
were replaced by wooden buildings.

Left: A settler's kitchen on a homestead

261

By the beginning of the 1900s, Western Canada had many busy towns and several cities.

Right: Edmonton, North-West Territories, 1902

Left: Main Street, Winnipeg, Manitoba, c. 1905, "Gateway to the West." Between 1896 and 1914, a million immigrants passed through Winnipeg on their way westward. Some stayed, making Winnipeg the sixth largest city in Canada in 1901. (See graph on page 277 showing the growth of Winnipeg.)

The general store was the source of most goods not grown or made by the settlers.

Main Street, Wetaskiwin, North-West Territories

Alberta and Saskatchewan Become Provinces 1905

An important issue between the federal government and the North-West Territories was whether the territories should be granted provincial status.* As leader of the Executive Council of the territories, Frederick Haultain urged the federal government to make the North-West Territories a province. The government argued that there were too few people living there. Also, since people in the North-West Territories could not agree on whether they should form one province or two, it was best not to do anything, at least for the time being.

Finally, in 1905, the disagreement was over. On September 1, 1905, the eighth and ninth provinces, Alberta and Saskatchewan, were created. The agreement between the federal government and Alberta and Saskatchewan covered the following points:

- Alberta and Saskatchewan received provincial status with control over all areas granted to provinces under the BNA Act, except for public lands.**
- They were promised more than $1 000 000.
- Money for public works and government expenses would be sent each year by the federal government.
- Taxes could be used to support separate Protestant and Roman Catholic schools.

The federal government had used "free" homestead land to encourage settlement in the Prairie provinces. Therefore, it kept control of public lands and natural resources.

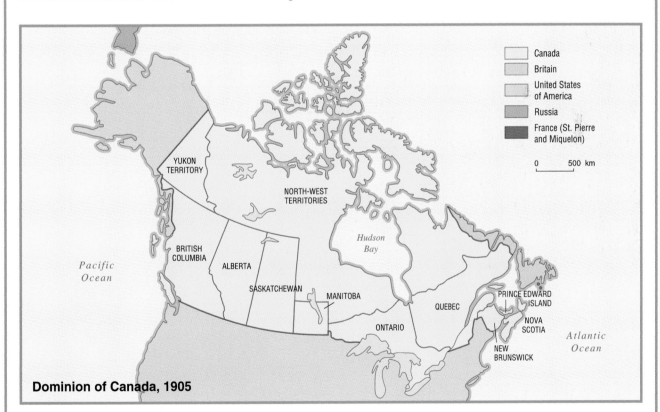

Dominion of Canada, 1905

Legend:
- Canada
- Britain
- United States of America
- Russia
- France (St. Pierre and Miquelon)

0   500 km

YUKON TERRITORY

NORTH-WEST TERRITORIES

BRITISH COLUMBIA

ALBERTA

SASKATCHEWAN

MANITOBA

Hudson Bay

Pacific Ocean

ONTARIO

QUEBEC

PRINCE EDWARD ISLAND

NOVA SCOTIA

NEW BRUNSWICK

Atlantic Ocean

---

* The Territories had won responsible government in 1897.
**Manitoba was not given control over crown lands when it became a province in 1870. Control of crown lands was turned over to the Prairie provinces in 1930, after most of the land that was suitable for farming had been settled.

Alberta

Calgary or Edmonton?

Several urban centres wanted their town or city to be Alberta's new capital. Edmonton and Calgary were major contenders. In 1905 Edmonton and Calgary each had populations of about 12 000. Residents of both cities had reasons why their city would be a more suitable capital of Alberta.

Edmonton was the geographic centre of the new province. Edmonton had been an early fur-trading post. It had also been the centre of activities in the northern part of the province for many years. On the other hand, Calgary was located on the main line of the Canadian Pacific Railway. Calgary was also the centre for the cattle industry.

In the end, Frank Oliver, member of parliament for Edmonton and minister of the interior in 1905, was asked to make the decision. He chose Edmonton to be the capital of Alberta.

Prime Minister Sir Wilfrid Laurier spoke at the Alberta Inaugural Day ceremonies in Edmonton on September 1, 1905.

Above: Jasper Avenue in Edmonton was decorated for the inauguration.

Below: The Alberta Legislative Buildings, showing the old Fort Edmonton.

Left: Alexander Cameron Rutherford was the first premier of Alberta.

Above: Prime Minister Sir Wilfrid Laurier (seated left) and Governor General Earl Grey (seated centre) attended inauguration ceremonies for the Province of Saskatchewan at Regina, 1905.

Left: Walter Scott was the first premier of Saskatchewan.

Saskatchewan

Prime Minister Sir Wilfrid Laurier and Governor General Earl Grey and their wives attended the inauguration day ceremonies for the Province of Saskatchewan on September 4, 1905.* There were crowds, bands, parades, speeches, the swearing-in of the lieutenant-governor of the new province, the musical ride of the Mounties, and a grand inaugural ball to celebrate the occasion.

As in the new Province of Alberta, different cities had wanted to become the provincial capital. However, in the case of Saskatchewan, there were six cities competing for the honour: Regina, Moose Jaw, Saskatoon, Prince Albert, Fort Qu'Appelle, and Battleford. Regina had been appointed the capital of the North-West Territories in 1883. It was the headquarters of the North West Mounted Police and the most important city on that part of the CPR line. Of the other cities, Saskatoon seemed particularly anxious to win this status. Members of boards of trade, newspaper editors, members of the Legislative Assembly, and other important people were invited to a lavish banquet. The hosts informed them of the benefits of Saskatoon as capital city, but in the end their efforts were unsuccessful. The Legislature voted 21 to 2 for Regina to become the capital of Saskatchewan.

For Your Notebook

1. How did Alberta and Saskatchewan benefit from becoming provinces?

2. On page 137 you made a Confederation newspaper for Ontario, Quebec, New Brunswick, or Nova Scotia. Make another Confederation newspaper for Alberta or Saskatchewan. See page 137 for ideas on how to do this.

Elaborate decorations were made to celebrate Saskatchewan's inauguration ceremonies in Regina on September 4 and 5, 1905.

---

*The province actually came into being on September 1, 1905, but Laurier and his party were in Edmonton inaugurating the Province of Alberta on that day.

Review

Understanding Concepts

1. At the beginning of this chapter, you recorded notes about how challenges, co-operation, critical thinking, and decision-making might be involved in each of the main topics of the chapter. Check the predictions that you made and then briefly record how each of these concepts was involved. Share your findings with a partner.

2. Record any new words in the WordBook section of your notes.

3. Here are some main ideas from the chapter:
   * Klondike gold rush
   * settlement of the West
   * the industrial age
   * new provinces of Alberta and Saskatchewan
   Do either a) or b):
   a) Create a concept poster for one of the chapter ideas and present it to the class.
   b) Use a web, mind map, outline or chart to create a permanent set of notes about one of the ideas. Explain your work to a classmate.

4. Add entries for this chapter to your timeline.

Developing Communication Skills

5. List jobs and chores a man living in a rural setting in 1901 would do in a day. List jobs or chores for his wife and one of the children. How are roles the same and different today? See page 349 for comparison strategies.

6. Select one of the people in the photographs on pages 256 to 259. Write a paragraph on what he or she might be thinking about just before arriving at a new home.

7. Analyse the success of the National Policy regarding settlement of the West. Write a newspaper editorial to explain your views.

8. Taking the point of view of a young man and his father, debate whether they should change their farming methods to use steam power rather than horses for their farm.

9. Taking the point of view of Sir Charles Saunders, explain to a friend why your new wheat, Marquis, is desirable for western farmers.

10. Work in groups of three: a writer, an artist, and a rhyme maker. Create a rhyming timeline to explain the three ages of technology: the agricultural, industrial, and electronic ages (page 252).

11. Assume the role of someone working in Clifford Sifton's Department of the Interior. You have been given the job of designing promotional materials on the Canadian West. Choose one of the following tasks:
    a) Write a slogan and make a poster or design a brochure that will encourage people living in western Europe, Russia, and/or the United States to immigrate to the Canadian west.
    b) Research and prepare a speech to present to the citizens of western Europe, Russia, and the United States. Tell them about the many wonderful opportunities that will exist for them should they choose to immigrate.
    In role, present your materials to the publicity department (your class), making it as interesting as you can.

12. Design and build a model of a typical log cabin, sod house, or part of a western town.

Applying Concepts

13. The large-scale immigration by which the West was settled was controversial. It changed the ethnic make-up of the population. Watch the media for a few days and list issues related to immigration that are controversial today. With a partner, choose one issue, and decide what position you take on it. Develop an action plan to resolve this issue. Present your action plan to the class.

Challenge Plus

14. Research and write an answer to the question: What effect did western settlement and the people travelling to the Yukon for the gold rush have on the peoples living in the area covered by Treaty 8?

Section III Review

On pages 144 to 147 you were introduced to the Section III focus. The activities on this page will help you review what you learned about change, regionalism, and co-operation/conflict.

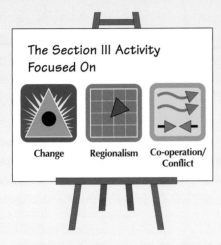

The Section III Activity Focused On

Change | Regionalism | Co-operation/Conflict

For Your Notebook

Complete the following activities using as resources your History notes, Section III (Chapters 6 to 10), and the exploration of the book's concepts on pages 24, 25, 28, and 29.

1. a) As a class, make a list of challenges Canada faced as a new Dominion (1867–1905).
   b) Work with a partner to draw a mind map that organizes all of these examples on one sheet of paper. Use simple line drawings and at least three colours. Show how the challenges Canada faced as a new Dominion were solved using co-operation. (Mind maps are explained on page 363.)

Questions for Class Discussion

2. As a class, discuss the three questions on the top easel on page 147.

For Your Notebook

3. Do a Think–Pair–Share to identify examples of change from Section III (Chapters 6 to 10). Use your History notes as reference. Identify at least one example of each agent of change. Select one of the presentation methods on page 365 to share what you learned about change.

4. Select one region from the ones identified on the map on page 28.

   a) Working individually or with a partner, find examples from Chapters 6 to 10 to show
   • needs and concerns felt in the region
   • how regionalism sometimes led to conflict.
   b) Use the information from a) to prepare a concept poster to share with your class.

5. Work in groups of two or three for the following activity. As a new Dominion, Canada faced new challenges, both from within and from outside. Some were met through co-operation, while others involved conflict. Make a chart similar to the one that follows. The first column lists some of the challenges Canada faced between 1867 and 1905, as it grew in size and gained confidence as a country. Write at least one example of each challenge in the second column. In the third column indicate whether the challenge involved co-operation, conflict, or both.

Challenges to the New Dominion

Challenge	Example, 1867–1905	Co-op.	Conflict	Both
Settling the North-West Territories				
Biculturalism				
Industrialization of Central Canada				
Social issues*				
Multiculturalism (many cultures within Canada)				
Red River Resistance and North-West Resistance of 1885				

*Social issues are problems concerning groups or communities. Some social issues are inequality, racism, crime, violence, and neglect or abuse of people who have less power by people who have more power.

Section IV
Emerging Canadian Identity
1896–1920

"I hope we're in the same group," Emily Tagoona was saying to Jasmine and Haley as they climbed the steps to the Conference Centre.

"Me, too!" said Chantal, one of the Prince Edward Island delegates. The girls had met Chantal the previous evening at the welcoming reception. They discovered that they were billeted at Chantal's home.

"You are so lucky," Chantal continued. "You had the whole train trip to get to know most of the other delegates. I only know you three, so far. Here's the registration desk. Let's pick up our conference packets."

The girls opened their conference packets together. Among other things, each found a delegate badge, the agenda, and a list of groups.

"Oh, no," Haley exclaimed. "We've been totally scrambled. Each group has 10 people, two from each region—Pacific Coast, Prairie Provinces, Central Canada, Atlantic Canada, and the North. I won't know a single person in my group."

Haley was placed in Mr. Leung's group. He was a history teacher from Newfoundland. She recognized a few of the students' faces, but didn't know them. Mr. Leung led the group in a fast, funny ice-breaking activity, then they had introductions before starting to work.

"Our first task," announced Mr. Leung, "is to decide exactly what it means to be a Canadian. In other words, what is Canadian identity?" As he spoke, Mr. Leung placed a large piece of paper and some felt markers at each end of the long table.

"When we planned this conference," he went on, "we agreed that before you students could plan the shaping of Canada's future, you needed to consider where we are now. To understand *where* we are, we should explore *who* we are."

Mr. Leung organized the students into two groups. He asked Haley to record notes for one group under the heading "How We Canadians See Ourselves." At the other end of the room Brian from Montreal recorded ideas for the other group under the heading "How Others See Canadians."

Mr. Leung made himself available to both groups, but mostly he let them brainstorm and write. When it was time to share ideas, Haley held up her group's list for everyone to see. Their list included the following ideas:

We see ourselves as people who share the following common features:
- Respect for multiculturalism
- Unique Canadian symbols like the flag, beaver, maple leaf, Canada goose
- The RCMP
- A national sport, hockey
- Free national healthcare
- Unique history
- Railroad from "sea to sea"
- A government different from the USA
- Close ties with the USA (e.g., media, trade, sports, movie stars)
- Our own national anthem
- Special heroes like Terry Fox and Wayne Gretzky
- Two main languages, English and French
- A Queen and British traditions
- Many famous innovators, artists, musicians, scientists, writers, and entrepreneurs
- Celebrities who are recognized outside Canada, like Michael J. Fox, Jim Carrey, Shania Twain, and Celine Dion
- Rights and freedoms that are protected by law

Everyone agreed that it was a good list. "Mr. Leung must have helped you more than he helped us," kidded Brian. "Your list is longer!" Brian held up his list to share his group's ideas:

How people outside of Canada see us:
- Peaceful and kind—peace-keepers for the world

268

- Helpful to the world's developing countries
- Living in a big country of ice and snow, inhabited by only a few people
- Polite and law-abiding
- Hard-working
- Cautious about new things and new ideas
- Quite influential for the size of our population
- Wealthy enough to live a good quality of life
- Having many natural resources
- Having lots of clean water
- Sort of a "kid brother" to the USA
- Living in a beautiful country with rugged mountains and vast empty spaces
- A fair and just people

"*Pret-ty* impressive lists!" exclaimed Mr. Leung. "You can see why the United Nations has named Canada the best place to live for several years now."

"Mr. Leung, I saw on TV that Canada has one fifth of the world's unpolluted water supply."

"You're absolutely right, Martina. That is an important fact to consider in the shaping of Canada's future. Now, how might this discussion of Canada's identity be helpful to you as you plan Canada's future?"

"I think it will help us set guidelines," said Carlos. "Like multiculturalism, for instance. We'll have to build that into our planning."

"We'll know our limitations," offered Janine. "I forgot about how small our population is, because I live in Winnipeg, which has a lot of people."

"Hey! Small can be mighty!" piped up Jeremy. "Like me!"

"Thanks for reminding us of that important idea," smiled Mr. Leung. "We must maximize our potential, as I remind my class back in St. John's."

"We should be able to!" This was from Brian. "I mean, Canada has such favourable conditions, like our geographical location, and a stable government. We're not having military revolutions every couple of years like some countries."

"You know," concluded Mr. Leung, "if you remember our 'tools,' too, like our wealth of resources, for instance, you should be able to plan wisely in the second part of our conference. As you mentioned in your lists, your planning should be guided by the values that have already shaped Canada into what it is today, values like human rights, for instance.'

Winding up the session, Mr. Leung stated, "I read in a recent poll that 80% of Canadians feel strongly loyal to Canada. What you have listed about Canada in this session tells us why."

Haley could hardly believe that the morning session was over. "My head hurts a little," she said to Brian at lunch, "but I'm excited about the recommendation our group will create when we meet again to talk about shaping Canada's future."

For Your Notebook
1. The characteristics that make you distinctive, your experiences, and your values and beliefs make up your identity. Countries also have identities. In Section IV of your study of History, you will be studying about Canada's emerging identity between 1896 and 1920. Review page 29 and your notes on identity.

2. Make a title page for Section IV: Emerging Canadian Identity.

Section IV Focus

While all of the book's five concepts will be examined, the three chapters in Section IV will focus on change, identity, and power. For each chapter you will be expected to find information to answer each of the questions on the easel that follows.

Who Are We?

1. What factors (agents of change) contributed to change in Canada between 1896–1920?

2. How did Canadians see and describe themselves between 1896 and 1920? How were we seen and described internationally?

3. Who held the power? Did we as a country have control over our external affairs? How did other countries recognize us?

Chapter 11
A New Era
1896–1914

Overview

Use this Overview to predict what you will read in this chapter.

① The "turn of the century" was a time of optimism about change. However, not all people shared the benefits of new ideas and technology.

② **Economic and Social Challenges**

Economic conditions and rapid growth of cities affected working and living conditions for many.

③ **1896–1911**

Sir Wilfrid Laurier and the Liberals governed Canada. Laurier's challenges included:

- balancing French and English concerns
- developing a stronger Canadian identity

④ **1911–1920**

Sir Robert Borden and the Conservatives governed Canada.

Borden and his government faced several political challenges such as

- the Naval Question
- the possibility of war in Europe

Chapter 11 Focus

This chapter focuses on key aspects of the administrations of two prime ministers:

- Sir Wilfrid Laurier, Liberal (the years between 1896 and 1911), and
- Sir Robert Borden, Conservative (the years between 1911 and 1914)

Laurier and Borden both favoured development of a stronger Canadian (national) identity. Both faced many challenges from political, economic, and social changes in urban Central Canada. The chapter examines life at the turn of the century—effects of technology on living and working conditions, and social reform.

Identity is a major concept for the chapter. The chapter will also focus on change, power, and co-operation. Compromise (agreement in which each side gives up some demands) will also be examined.

| Change | Regionalism | Power | Identity | Co-operation |

Other Concepts and Main Topics

- technology
- working conditions
- living conditions
- social reform
- biculturalism

- compromise
- controversy
- English-French relations
- ties with Great Britain

Learning How to Learn

 Critical Thinking

 Chart Making

 Role-playing

 Writing

 Research

 Note Making

Chapter Preview/Prediction

1. The Overview for Chapter 11, the visuals and the titles within the chapter highlight some of the events that occurred between 1896 and 1914. In pairs or small groups, use this information and what you already know about Canada's history to make a web or mind map of the chapter.

Section IV Activity
Writing Historical Fiction

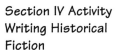

Part I

Throughout your study of Section IV you will be working on an ongoing activity that will focus on identity.

Select someone from the list on the next page. Repeats can be chosen after all individuals have been selected once. Select a name for your person, figure out their age in 1904, and decide the name of the town, city, or rural area in Canada in which they currently live. Your teacher will ensure your class represents individuals from all parts of Canada.

You will use this role in the Chapter 11 activity below and in the Chapter 12 and 13 activities. In Section IV you will be "seeing" Canadian history between 1904 and 1920 through the eyes of the person you create.

In Chapter 11

 In role for the person you selected (based on the information in this chapter), carry out the following:

 Create your character in your History Journal. The year is 1904. Describe "your character" as you see him or her; for example, height, approximate weight, hair and skin colour, likes, dislikes, education, hobbies, sports. Write something about your character and his or her family. (You may wish to create a photograph or drawing of yourself in the role.)

 Write about your character in a story or a letter to a friend. Write about a typical day in your life: it is the first Monday in April 1904. Describe your home, family, method of transportation, and what you would be doing. Write from the point of view of the person you select on page 272. Use the information from pages 273 to 276 to make your writing historically accurate.

Writing Historical Fiction

List of Individuals. Select one person from the following list of imaginary people. People are listed by birthdate, birthplace, family origin, sex, family, occupation. (If occupation is not given you are to make the decision yourself.) You can decide whether you want to be part of a family (e.g., oldest child) or a parent, depending on your age.

1. b. 1857, Ontario, German, F, family of 11, farmer
2. b. 1867, Ontario, English, M, family of 5, businessman
3. b. 1878, North-West Territories, German, F, family of 4, farmer
4. b. 1882, Great Britain, English, M, single, farmer
5. b. 1886, France, French, F, family of 8, nurse
6. b. 1887, United States, Norwegian, M, family of 6, farmer
7. b. 1891, Toronto, Irish, F, family of 4, mother is domestic (servant)
8. b. 1892, Great Britain, Scottish, M, family of 8, father is businessman
9. b. 1893, Russian Empire, Ukrainian, F, family of 8, father is factory worker
10. b. 1894, Russian Empire, Polish, M, family of 6, parents are factory workers
11. b. 1895, Ontario, First Nations, F, parents live on an Ontario reserve
12. b. 1896, Austro-Hungarian Empire, Ukrainian, F, family of 5, parents are farmers
13. b. 1897, Italy, Italian, M, family of 6, father is construction worker, mother is domestic (servant)
14. b. 1896, German Empire, German, F, family of 2, father is a farmer
15. b. 1867, China, Chinese, M, family of one, businessman
16. b. 1886, Ontario, Metis (First Nation/French), M, family of 5, packer
17. b. 1893, Norway, Norwegian, F, family of 8, father is a farmer
18. b. 1878, Russian Empire, Jewish, F, family of 6, factory worker
19. b. 1882, Ontario, African–Canadian, M, family of 4, farmer
20. b. 1894, Japan, Japanese, M, family of 4, father is a fisherman

Timeline
Laurier and Borden's Administrations 1896–1920

Key Events

◁	**1896**	Klondike gold rush
◁	**1896**	Resolution of Manitoba Schools Question
◁	**1897**	Imperial Council of British Colonies
◀	**1898**	**Yukon Territory is formed**
◁	**1899**	Signing of Treaty 8
◁	**1899–1902**	South African (Boer) War
◁	**1899–1903**	Alaska Boundary Dispute
◁	**1900**	Turn of the Century
◀	**1905**	**Alberta and Saskatchewan become provinces**
◁	**1909–1911**	Naval Question
◁	**1910–1911**	Consideration of Reciprocity Treaty with USA
◁	**1911**	Robert Borden (Conservative) becomes Prime Minister
◁	**1912**	Provincial boundary changes
◁	**1914–1918**	World War I

Conservative Prime Ministers After Macdonald (1891–1896):
Sir John Abbott, Sir John S.D. Thompson, Sir Mackenzie Bowell, Sir Charles Tupper

Sir Wilfrid Laurier
(Liberal)
1896–1911

Sir Robert Borden
(Conservative)
1911–1920

Time Periods

■ Conservative Prime Minister

■ Liberal Prime Minister

— 1890
— 1895
◁◁
◁
◀
◁◁◁
◁1900
◀1905
◁
◁1910
◁
◁
◁
— 1915
— 1920

In 1900

At the beginning of the twentieth century there were 5.4 million people in Canada.* Eighty-seven percent were Canadian born.

In 1900 Canada was predominantly rural, but urbanization was under way.

Rural and Urban Population

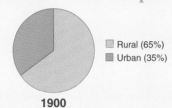

- Rural (65%)
- Urban (35%)

1900

Most Canadians lived on farms or in small communities. Rural and urban people's lives were different in some ways, although they still shared similar values. People of different social classes led very different lives in both the country and the city.

In 1900, most Canadians were still involved in primary resource industries, especially farming. However, manufacturing industries were being established.

This photograph shows threshing on a Prairie grain farm in the early twentieth century.

In 1900, Canada was a British Dominion, but it was also a country with many cultures. Two cultures were dominant, British and French. The situation was changing as new immigrants came in larger numbers.

City of Toronto Archives, SC478-19

Canada was a very British country.

In 1900, a shared Canadian identity had not been developed.

Prime Minister Laurier stressed there wasn't any single Canadian identity, but rather two identities— French and English. He urged Canadians to be tolerant of diversity.

In 1900, Canada had seven provinces.

- Canada
- Britain
- United States of America
- France (St. Pierre and Miquelon)

0   500   km

YUKON TERRITORY

NORTH-WEST TERRITORIES

BRITISH COLUMBIA

MANITOBA

ONTARIO

QUEBEC

PRINCE EDWARD ISLAND

NOVA SCOTIA

NEW BRUNSWICK

Dominion of Canada, 1900

*At the beginning of the twenty-first century the Canadian population was estimated at 30 million.

273

Change at the Turn of the Century

The Twentieth Century Belongs to Canada

Sir Wilfrid Laurier
(Liberal)
(1896–1911)

Prime Minister Wilfrid Laurier was proud of Canada and its accomplishments. In 1904 he announced that "the twentieth century shall be the century of Canada and of Canadian development."

I tell you nothing but what you know when I tell you that the nineteenth century has been the century of the United States development. The past hundred years has been filled with the pages of their history. Let me tell you, my fellow countrymen, that the twentieth century shall be the century of Canada and of Canadian development. For the next seventy-five years, nay for the next hundred years, Canada shall be the star towards which all men who love progress and freedom shall come. . . . and let your motto be: "Canada first, Canada last, and Canada always."

—Speech at Massey Hall, Toronto, October 14, 1904

The above poster shows a confident Canada entering a century of prosperity.

Technology

 As you learned on pages 24 and 25, cultural change is continuous but occurs unevenly. Changes in people's ways of life are often brought about by changes in technology. Some people in Canada in 1900 benefited from new ideas and inventions. Others could not share in these changes for various economic, social, and political reasons.

In Agriculture

Canada's wheat yield went from 18 million bushels a year in 1896 to 78 million in 1911. The major reasons for this rise was the development of hardier strains of wheat and more land under cultivation. Other inventions were also useful. The steam-powered tractor and the **threshing machine** became more widely used, although horse power was still common on farms. A tractor could pull a plough that could cut three furrows at once. A horse-drawn plough could cut only one furrow at a time.

A steam engine is providing power to a mechanical threshing machine to thresh wheat.

In Manufacturing

Although cost or lack of electricity in many homes prevented many consumers from buying them, all sorts of new consumer items were being produced in factories by 1910. Electric stoves, electric vacuum cleaners, and clothes washing machines were all manufactured. That same year, the first human-made fibre for weaving into cloth, a type of rayon, was produced.

Threshing machine—a harvesting machine used to separate grain from the hulls and straw

In Homes and Daily Life

Household tasks were time consuming, physically demanding, and tedious. Most people did laundry by hand on washboards, and then hung the wet wash up to dry. Ironing was done using irons heated on the top of a stove heated by wood or coal. In well-to-do and middle-class homes, meals were large and time-consuming to prepare. Bread and buns, cakes, pies, and cookies were baked at home. Dishes were washed by hand after each meal. There were no freezers. Many hot summer afternoons were spent in a steamy kitchen preserving foods by canning, because fresh fruits and vegetables were not available in winter.

Refrigeration of food had been invented at this time, but most people could not afford to have it in their homes. Middle-class people usually had ice delivered and kept perishable food in iceboxes. People without access to this service kept only as much fresh food as they could use, so it would not spoil.

Middle-class and upper-class homes in cities and towns had electricity by the turn-of-the-century. Working-class city homes and rural homes still relied on kerosene lamps for light. Heat came from wood stoves and coal furnaces. Middle-class homes in cities often had running water, but working-class ones often did not. There might be a backyard pump, and rain barrels were commonly used for collecting water. Outhouses were usual, rather than indoor toilets.

People who lived on farms produced most of their own food. They killed their own cattle for beef, milked cows, grew and preserved fruits and vegetables, churned butter, and picked berries for jam. It was not an easy life, and farmers on small farms had little money to spend. However, the farmers' diet was often better than that of factory workers in cities, who had to buy all their food with their low wages.

Labour-saving inventions such as electric vacuum cleaners did not replace human effort, even in homes of the well-to do. (A vacuum cleaner cost $25 in 1900, the equivalent of two weeks wage for a factory worker.) Middle-class and upper-class women often employed domestics to help with household tasks. These employees were either urban working girls or young farm girls who came to the city looking for a job. Working-class women did domestic tasks themselves, with only the help of their daughters who were old enough to lend a hand.

Maids were common in the homes of those who could afford them. These women are dressing a Winnipeg girl's hair.

Catalogue Shopping

People no longer had to make all their clothes as most had done in the past. In the cities, factory-made clothing was available in local stores. Rural dwellers could order clothing through mail-order catalogues. Department store catalogues such as Eaton's offered everything from underwear to tools. The first example shown is from the *Ladies' Home Journal* magazine, and the second is from the Sears catalogue.

In Transportation

For local transportation in cities, people relied on horse-drawn carriages, bicycles, or electric streetcars. Bicycles no longer had one large and one small wheel. They had two wheels of equal size, stronger tires, and were easier to steer. In 1899, a new bicycle might cost $40, a great deal of money at the time. However, it might be someone's principal means of transportation.

The electric streetcar was allowing cities to expand. People could commute to work on a streetcar, so they could move further from the city centre. Developers began to open up new areas of land and sell housing lots along the streetcar lines.

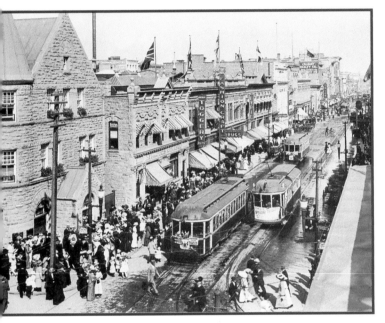

In 1910 electric trams (streetcars) were seen among the horse-drawn carriages on some Canadian city streets.

Cars were being manufactured in Canada, but they were not common in the early years of the twentieth century. By 1905, there were only about two dozen in the city of Toronto. They were too expensive for most people. Between 1900 and 1901, a car cost about $3000, as much as a male factory worker would earn in a decade. As well, people were not used to the speed of automobiles and felt they were dangerous. (Ontario established a 7 mile-per-hour speed limit in 1903.)

It was very annoying when automobiles broke down, because there were few garages where they could be repaired. Their tires were not as well made as car tires are today and punctures were frequent. Gas was bought in stores or livery stables and had to be carried in buckets in the car. This was both inconvenient and smelly. The first gas station in the country opened in Vancouver in 1908.

Canada is a huge country. The Canadian Pacific Railway, completed in 1885, could not handle all the people and products that needed to be transported from one part of the country to another. Two new transcontinental railways, the Canadian Northern and the Grand Trunk Pacific, were built during the Laurier years.

Inventions

1901   63 192 telephones in Canada, delivered 185 million messages.

1901   Guglielmo Marconi received the first transatlantic wireless message in Cabot Tower on Signal Hill, in St. John's, Newfoundland, on December 12th.

1902   First permanent movie house in Canada was opened in Vancouver.

1902   Trans-Pacific telegraph cable from Vancouver to Brisbane, Australia, was completed.

1906   First movie house in Toronto opened.

1909   J.A.D. McCurdy, age 22, made the first powered flight in Canada in his plane, the *Silver Dart*, at Baddeck, Nova Scotia.

For Your Notebook

1. Make a three-column chart. In the first column, list 10 household tasks such as washing dishes and making beds. In the second column, describe how this task was done at the turn of the century. In the third column, describe how this task is done today.

2. In Chapter 9 (1878–1896) women were described as in the process of "exploring new worlds." How did women continue to explore new worlds at the turn of the century?

3.

Section IV Activity: Writing Historical Fiction

In Your History Journal

In role, record your reaction to having just heard Prime Minister Laurier's speech (see page 274).

Economic and Social Challenges

Several economic and social challenges grew from industrialization and the growth of cities. The economy saw greater increases between 1905 and 1912 (see graph below). Industrial development and urban growth brought prosperity to many. However, not all social classes or regions of Canada benefited equally.

Economic Conditions

In 1912 signs of an economic slowdown appeared and unemployment increased. By 1913, there was a full world-wide depression, for which Canada was unprepared.

Western Canada especially felt the economic slowdown. Wheat prices dropped dramatically. Exports declined. The price of real estate declined, and many who had purchased land on credit saw their potential fortunes wiped out. Many villages and towns in the West were abandoned and simply disappeared. Although wheat prices and real estate declined, consumer prices remained high. People could afford to buy less and less with their income. For example, before 1909 a woman's blouse cost $1.15; after 1909 it cost $5.00.

The Eastern provinces felt the economic slowdown intensely. City dwellers in particular suffered. Unlike the farmer, they could not produce food for their families. The cities were unprepared for the demands from the unemployed for help. They had used up their funds meeting commitments to new industries and transportation projects. Many people turned to churches and social reformers for material and spiritual assistance if their families or friends could not help them.

Urban Growth

New immigrants continued to arrive in Canada. In 1913, a record 400 000 came to Canada. Earlier immigrants had been drawn to Canada's inexpensive farm lands. By 1900 most new immigrants were living in the larger cities, like Toronto, Montreal, Winnipeg, and Vancouver. Cities changed as they grew rapidly. City governments could not keep up with these changes. Cities experienced an increase in slums, poverty, disease, and pollution.

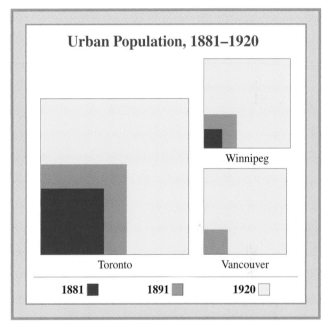

Urban Population, 1881–1920

Winnipeg

Toronto

Vancouver

| 1881 ■ | 1891 ▨ | 1920 ▢ |

Between 1891 and 1920 Toronto tripled in size, Winnipeg grew by 7 times, and Vancouver by 12 times. See the chart on page 220 for the populations of these cities in 1891.

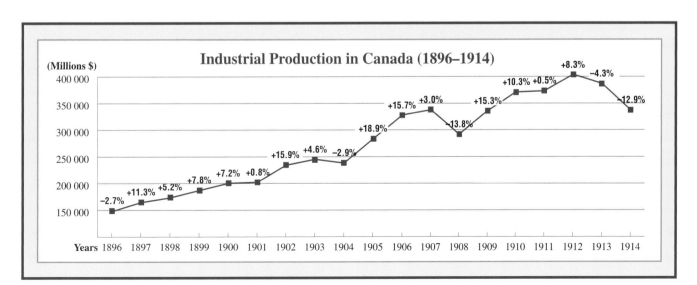

Industrial Production in Canada (1896–1914)

(Millions $)

-2.7% +11.3% +5.2% +7.8% +7.2% +0.8% +15.9% +4.6% -2.9% +18.9% +15.7% +3.0% -13.8% +15.3% +10.3% +0.5% +8.3% -4.3% -12.9%

Years 1896 1897 1898 1899 1900 1901 1902 1903 1904 1905 1906 1907 1908 1909 1910 1911 1912 1913 1914

Industrial Labour Force

- ■ Primary Industry (39.1%)
- ■ Secondary Industry (27.1%)
- □ Tertiary Industry (33.4%)

1911

Although it had been changing, Canada was still primarily an agricultural country. Most Canadians were involved in producing agricultural products or working in primary resource industries.

Exploring Further

1. **What responsibility should the government have for workers?**
   Write the numbers 1–13 down the left hand side of your notebook page. Then read each of the statements listed below. If you think *government* should have responsibility for (or pay for) an item, put a G beside the number; if you think *individuals* should be responsible, put an I; if you think the *employer* should, put an E. Tabulate your results.
   1. Pensions for workers injured at work
   2. Assurance that workers not be fired without reason or notice
   3. Job security for a worker who becomes ill or who is injured at work
   4. Assurance that workers can protest working conditions and ask for higher wages without losing their jobs
   5. Free medical treatment for workers who become ill
   6. Unemployment insurance payments for those unable to obtain jobs
   7. Dental care, eyeglasses, and medicines for workers
   8. Monthly pensions upon retirement
   9. Money for families to care for their children (These payments are called *baby bonuses* or *family allowances*.)
   10. Adequate living conditions for workers
   11. A set number of sick days per year for workers in case of illness
   12. Hot meals for sick workers or senior citizens who are unable to care for themselves at home
   13. Allowances for elderly widows, or mothers with young children

2. Class Discussion: What responsibility should the government have for workers?

Urban Working Conditions

  During the first decade of the twentieth century, Canadian industry grew rapidly and created employment for some of the thousands of young Canadian men and women coming from farms and immigrants entering the country.

Working conditions in factories were hard. Workers received no effective protection under the law. Employees worked long hours for low pay. Workers who arrived late, talked on the job, or broke equipment were treated harshly. They were sometimes slapped or beaten for working too slow or for not obeying orders. Although there were laws against these actions, few people would report such incidents for fear of being fired.

Most working-class people worked six days a week, usually between 9 and 10 hours a day. They often worked 52 weeks a year with no paid time off for vacations or sickness.

Most factories were dangerous places. They often did not have good lighting, heating, and ventilation. As a result, they were dark, noisy, and dirty. Toilets were few and unsanitary. Few factories had safety features. Many workers were hurt on the job because dangerous parts of equipment were not covered. Workers sometimes lost fingers and suffered more serious injuries like broken arms, legs, and ribs. Most factories did not provide protective clothing for workers when they worked with poisonous chemicals and materials. As a result, many became ill from exposure to dangerous chemicals. Every year thousands of Canadian workers died in work site accidents, such as mine cave-ins or explosions. Some companies had death benefits for widows and families of workers killed on the job, but such policies were not common. Widows left with children often found themselves in financial difficulties.

In the years before the World War I, workers rarely received financial help except their wages from their employers or the government. There was no government unemployment insurance, medical plans, hospitalization benefits, or pensions. Workers were expected to look after themselves. Sometimes an injured or older worker was kept on by the employer and given a less demanding job at a lower wage. Trade unions made efforts to improve conditions, but their progress was slow and difficult.

Despite harsh conditions in the cities, many thousands of immigrants and people from the rural areas continued to choose to live in the cities.

Women in the Labour Force

Labour Force

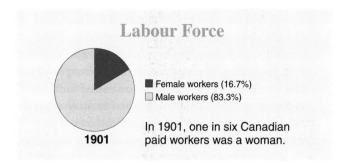

■ Female workers (16.7%)
□ Male workers (83.3%)

1901

In 1901, one in six Canadian paid workers was a woman.

 The majority of women in the labour force worked as domestics, teachers, nurses, factory workers, and sales clerks. In 1901, more women were employed in domestic service than in any other paid occupation. That same year, 22 percent of people who worked as clerks in offices were women. Lawyers, medical doctors, dentists, and clergy were almost all men.

Many young women from farms and immigrants newly arrived in the city worked as domestics. They lived with their employers, rather than looking for accommodation in an unfamiliar city.

Other women chose to work in textile mills, clothing factories, and food processing plants. Factory workers were paid higher wages, especially those who were skilled and quick. They also also had shorter hours and more freedom than domestics. Most women working in the factories were paid for **piecework**. Employers often set the rate for piecework on what the fastest worker could do. As a result, many earned less than they needed to survive. As well, there was no **pay equity**. A man earned double the wage of a woman for the same work.

In the manufacture of clothing, many women worked in crowded basements and attics, which were called "sweatshops." Their employers often lowered wages and increased the pace of work to make more profit.

Outside the factories, new work opportunities appeared for educated women. Teaching and nursing were two occupations open to women. A growing number of women were finding work as typists, book-keepers, and secretaries. Many found part-time employment as sales clerks in department stores and general stores. Despite changes in the labour force, very few women were managers in business or government.

Garment industry "sweat shops" were being replaced by machines (mechanized looms) in factories.

Piecework—pay for each item produced rather than a set wage
Pay equity—equal pay for equal work

Child Labour

At the turn of the twentieth century, if a family's income was very low they might depend on wages from the children to survive. As soon as a child was old enough, he or she was often sent to work in a factory or in some other job. Although schooling was compulsory, some children got very little education. Children worked alongside their parents on farms, and in factories and mines.

In 1903, the Ontario government gave money to schools to start trades shops and domestic science courses. Children were being encouraged to prepare for working in a more industrialized world.

Many child workers had terrible working conditions. In factories, children as young as 12 years old worked on dangerous equipment. Children were often punished for shouting, running, being late, or missing work. In the mines, many young boys faced the dangers of explosions and cave-ins. In other workplaces, young boys and girls worked as messengers, newspaper vendors, and cleaners. These jobs did not provide much income and workers had no assurance that they would not lose their jobs.

Children collected scattered pieces of coal for their families to burn if they could not afford to buy it.

These young girls are washing city steps for their employer.

Government Laws to Protect Children

Some of the first efforts to improve the lives of children in the labour force occurred in the 1880s. In 1888, the Ontario government passed the Children's Protection Act. Under this Act, neglected children could be sent to industrial schools or authorized homes until the age of 18 years. In 1893 the Ontario government formed the position of Superintendent of Neglected Children. John Kelso became the province's first Superintendent. Kelso was also the founder of the Children's Aid Society, which placed neglected children in foster homes. By 1905 children's aid societies had been formed across the country and several provinces passed legislation to protect children from neglect and abuse. Kelso remained Ontario's Superintendent of Neglected Children until 1934.

Left: This 14-year-old miner faces a dismal future. With little or no education, he will probably spend his life in the mines, where the danger of explosion and cave-in is ever present.

For Your Notebook

1. Use the information on pages 278 to 280 to record a permanent set of notes on working conditions in the early part of the twentieth century.

2. Who held the power in most workplaces and in relations between employers and workers?

3. In what way, if any, did the following factors, contribute to change in the early 1900s?

   • technology   • economic good times
   • immigration   • unions

Living Conditions of the Urban Working Class

Most working-class people in unskilled jobs in Canada's largest cities lived in miserable conditions. Few of them could afford to buy their own house. Single people lived with their parents or in boarding houses. Families often lived in tenement buildings. These were buildings with many small apartments of one or two rooms. There was little yard where children could play. Many of these buildings were poorly built. In winter, they were cold and drafty. In summer, they were hot and stuffy, with little ventilation. They usually did not have running water or indoor toilets.

Average Monthly Rents (Toronto)*

1900	1906	1911
$7.45	$14.00	$21.00**

*for a 4-room apartment
**average rent was $12.00/month for basement rooms.

Monthly rents took at least 25% of a worker's monthly wage.

Families often got their water for cooking and washing from a public tap outside or from a rain barrel. They shared an outdoor toilet with several other families. The toilet was often located behind the building, close to the water tap. People often fell ill from using polluted water. Diseases like cholera, typhoid, and diphtheria were common in these conditions. Infant death rates were also very high.

A family in Winnipeg living in small, crowded conditions

In 1911 the average male worker earned approximately $500 per year. The low wages of working-class families did not allow them to eat well. Most ate potatoes, bread, oatmeal, and milk, which were cheap. Meat, fish, fruit, vegetables, and desserts were too expensive for most working-class families to buy. Only on special occasions like weddings and on holidays would meat, fruit, and vegetables be eaten.

For many working-class families, losing a job was a constant worry. Many jobs were seasonal and layoffs were expected. When someone was out of work, the person had to live on savings until another job was found. There were no government unemployment insurance benefits to help an unemployed worker survive until he or she could find another job.

When the main earner of a working-class family was out of work, the family relied on credit at a local food store. When he found work and was earning a wage, he would try to repay the bill. For many working-class families, it was not possible to pay off the debt. Costs such as medical bills were beyond many families. Many people could not afford to see a doctor.

Wages were too low and the cost of necessities too high to permit most working-class families to save money. Some working-class families did save money for emergencies, but often this money was not enough.

Unmarried workers often lived in boarding houses rather than apartments or houses. They would rent a room and usually have meals with the owner and other boarders.

Section IV Activity

 In role based on the character you created on pages 271 and 272, write about your working and living conditions.

Movement for Social Reform

During this time there were no government medical plans to help pay medical bills, pensions when people got old, welfare or unemployment benefits if they could not work. Social reformers worked to change society. They worked to improve living and working conditions for people who were very poor, ill, or disadvantaged in some way. Social reformers strived to achieve long-term benefits. For example, rather than just providing food or clothing for poor people they worked to change government policies on minimum wages. Instead of just giving money to widowed or sick women, they worked to get women the vote. Social reformers began to urge that more attention be paid to providing services for needy people, especially children. Reformers wanted laws that would forbid employers from employing children in their workforce.

Church and volunteer groups gave aid and worked to improve conditions for children, the very poor, and others that needed it. Charitable organizations provided materials for schools, supported community health services, and the welfare of children generally. After 1893, Children's Aid Societies also worked for the protection of children.

Rapidly growing cities often failed to look after the needs of citizens, as industries continued to attract more workers. In Toronto, in 1904, it was reported that, "there is scarcely a vacant house fit to live in that is not inhabited, and in many cases by numerous families." Business and political leaders also called for improvements in the quality of life in cities and for changes in the living conditions of working-class people.

City of Toronto Archives, Board of Education, 92

Many women's organizations focused on visiting the poor to give help and advice. They also collected information about living conditions so they could lobby government and business to help those in need.

Members of the YWCA (Young Women's Christian Association) did volunteer work with prisoners and hospital patients, and worked with young single women in cities.

Milestones for Women

1897 The first Women's Institute formed by Adelaide Hoodless in Stoney Creek, Ontario. She wanted women to work together for mutual support and to learn the skills of good household management (domestic science). Soon there were branches in every province. These institutes lobbied for women's rights.

1900 The Imperial Order of the Daughters of the Empire (IODE) established to promote British imperialism by supporting Canada's involvement in the Boer War in South Africa.

1902 The Coloured Women's Club of Montreal formed by wives of African-Canadian railway workers. This group worked to make people aware of the problems, such as racial discrimination, faced by African-Canadian people in Montreal.

1909 Canadian Suffrage Association (formerly known as the Dominion Women's Enfranchisement Association) and the Women's Christian Temperance Union staged a massive demonstration for women's suffrage at the Ontario Legislature.

1910 National Council of Women endorsed suffrage for women.

1910 Alberta passed the Married Women's Relief Act, which entitled a widow to receive some of her husband's property if he had not left her anything in a will. Saskatchewan and Manitoba passed similar laws between 1910 and 1919.

Culture, sports, and inventions were all part of Canada's developing identity.

Canada was producing some world-class musicians, actors, artists, writers, and athletes. Most were English and French Canadian. Few Aboriginal people and new Canadians, unless they were part of English or French society, received recognition for their traditions and talents.

Most of the activities shown on these two pages were enjoyed by the wealthy and by the growing middle class.

Recreation

Many Canadians enjoyed sports, the arts, outdoor activities such as picnics in the summer and ice-skating in the winter, and entertaining friends in their homes.

A Sunday walk in the summer of 1905 on the suspension bridge across the Capilano Canyon near Vancouver

Three warmly-dressed young people going skating

The Boy Scouts movement was introduced to Canada in 1910.

Sports

Basketball, which was invented in 1891 by Canadian physical education teacher James Naismith, became popular in Canada and the United States. Hockey, baseball, and lacrosse were also popular team sports. The first Grey Cup football game was played in Toronto in 1909.

Tom Longboat was a long-distance runner who was an international athletic celebrity in the early twentieth century. He was born in 1887 on the Six Nations reserve near Brantford, Ontario.
Longboat enlisted during World War I and served as a runner carrying messages and orders between units. In 1998, he was chosen by *Maclean's* as Number 1 on their "Stars" list of the 100 Most Important Canadians in History. Longboat is seen as one of the finest Canadian athletes ever. He is in Canada's Sports Hall of Fame.

1909: The University of Toronto and the McGill University football teams in action during an intercampus match

283

Music

O Canada*

The Maple Leaf Forever

Some Hits from the 1890s

The Band Played On

A Bicycle Built for Two

Maple Leaf Rag

My Wild Irish Rose

The Sidewalks of New York

When You Were Sweet Sixteen

L.M. Montgomery was earning money from her writing by the 1890s. Her first novel was an instant best seller in 1908.

Pauline Johnson, the "Mohawk Princess," travelled across the country reciting her poetry, telling stories, and putting on brief plays.

Operas were popular. Emma Albani was the first Canadian-born musician to gain international fame.

Cinema

The movies were in black and white. Because there was no sound, a musician often provided background music on a piano in the theatre as the movie was shown.

*"O Canada" was adopted as Canada's national anthem in 1980. It had been sung as a patriotic song for many decades. See *Canada Revisited 8* on page 293.

Literature

Sometimes people went to theatres and auditoriums to see travelling actors and other performers. Often families would read aloud to one another on winter evenings after dinner. English literature by authors such as Charles Dickens or Jane Austen was a common choice. Canadians were beginning to appreciate Canadian literature of the time as well.

- Stephen Leacock is best known for his humorous writing. He was also an historian, a teacher, and a writer of economics and the science of politics.
- Lucy Maud Montgomery wrote the *Anne of Green Gables* novels and many other books. The "Anne" books, and television programs based on them, have been internationally popular.
- Robert W. Service, who has been called the "poet of the Yukon," wrote *Songs of a Sourdough* and other collections of poems while working for a bank in the Yukon.
- Pauline Johnson was a poet, Canadian nationalist, and an enthusiastic supporter of Aboriginal traditions.

Visual Arts

In the past, wealthy people had gone to Europe to appreciate and buy art. They were now beginning to be interested in the works of Canadian visual artists. Artists of this period used their canvasses to praise the beauty of the Canadian landscape. Painters such as George Reid and Homer Watson celebrated the fields and woods of Ontario in their landscape paintings.

Up until the twentieth century, sculpture in Canada had been done in traditional materials such as wood and stone. Materials such as bronze were being explored by sculptors like Louis-Philippe Hébert. He was the foremost sculptor of his generation in Quebec.

Section IV Activity

In role based on the character you created on pages 271 and 272, write about leisure and the arts for yourself, your friends, and/or family.

Laurier's Political Challenges

French-English Relations

   Canada's bicultural nature once again became an issue. Prime Minister Laurier had to deal with a number of situations where French and English Canadians had different views. Canadians today still struggle towards a balance between the rights of English and French citizens.

Biculturalism

In biculturalism, two cultures exist side by side in the same country or province.

In 1896, Canada had two dominant cultures (French and English) existing side by side.*

French Canadian Nationalism

  French Canadian nationalism refers to the feelings or desires of French Canadians to preserve their religion and traditions. Based on the British North America Act, French Canadians viewed Confederation as an agreement that guaranteed the equality of French and English.

Great numbers of immigrants arriving in Canada changed the situation. English Canada was changing its attitude to biculturalism. Some English Canadians did not want schools to be based on religion. They wanted all schools to be publicly funded and all children to attend together. In 1871, the provincial government of New Brunswick decided to stop supporting Roman Catholic schools. French Acadian and Irish Catholic people objected, but their objections were ignored. In 1890, the provincial government of Manitoba voted to replace its dual school system (Roman Catholic schools and public schools, both government funded), with a single system. You will read more about this issue on page 286.

The French Roman Catholics were afraid that English Canadian culture would overwhelm the French Canadian culture and that it would slowly disappear.

Many French Canadians wanted to see a bicultural nation in which the French and English cultures were of equal strength. Henri Bourassa, in his roles as journalist, Liberal, and later independent member of parliament, became a champion of the rights of the country's French Canadian minority. He said, "we do not have the right to make Canada an exclusively French country, any more than the Anglo-Canadians have the right to make it an English country." He argued that the French language and the Roman Catholic religion must be protected. He was against the multicultural immigration policy of the Liberals. He said, "I want selective immigration, so that we will not be swamped by the waves of [non-French-speaking settlers] . . . causing a decrease in the percentage of people of French origin . . ." He was also against the transcontinental railway because it used Quebec tax money and it brought too many English-speaking settlers. Bourassa and the French Canadian nationalists wanted to see a strong, independent Canada. They did not want to see increased political ties with Great Britain, and they definitely did not want to assist Great Britain should a war occur.

Henri Bourassa, shown here with his family, fought for the rights of Canada's French minority both as a journalist and as an independent member of Parliament.

---

*The government of Canada today officially recognizes that Canada is made up of many cultures (multiculturalism).

For Your Notebook

1. Define biculturalism, French Canadian nationalism, and dual school system.

2. What are some differences between biculturalism and multiculturalism?

3. a) Who was Henri Bourassa?
   b) What did Henri Bourassa believe? Prepare a concept poster on Bourassa's viewpoints.
   c) Explain why Henri Bourassa was against the Liberal Party's policy of encouraging immigration to Canada.

4. Find out more about Henri Bourassa. Write a brief biography about him. Remember to include information about both his personal and political life.

Manitoba Schools Question
Origins of the Issue

  The Manitoba Schools Question created a major controversy involving French-English relations. In 1870, when Manitoba joined Confederation, about half the population was French-speaking and Roman Catholic. Over the next 20 years of English Protestant immigration, French-speaking people became outnumbered. In 1890, the Manitoba legislature voted to set up a single public school system to replace the two publicly funded school systems (Roman Catholic and public) that were in place. This was a very controversial move. (Imaginary points of view on the Manitoba Schools Question appear below.)

The French Catholics appealed to Prime Minister Macdonald. He tried not to become involved. Politically, it was a dilemma for the Canadian government. If the government supported the French Catholics it would be seen as interfering in provincial affairs. If it did not support the Catholics, it would lose votes in Quebec.

Prime Minister Macdonald died three months after the election of 1891. Over the next five years, the leadership of the Conservative government changed four times (see page 241). In 1895, the Conservatives prepared a bill that would require public funding for public schools. But before the bill could become law an election was called.

English Protestant Points of View French Catholic Points of View

It will save a great deal of money to have one school system instead of two. We will have lower taxes!

It doesn't matter if money is saved. The British North America Act protects minority education rights that were established by law in 1867. It is against the law for Manitoba to set up a single school system.

More people in this country speak English than French. I know that the Constitution treats this as an issue of religion, not language. But if most of the children are French-speaking in a Catholic school, then instruction would be in French. They would learn the French culture. I think immigrants should learn to speak English. English is the language of the majority in the country.

It is important for French Roman Catholic children to attend school with children who are brought up the same way. These schools should be supported by public funds.

Laurier's Compromise

Wilfrid Laurier and his Liberal party won the election of 1896. Laurier compromised with provincial leaders. The provincially funded public school system remained in effect as the Manitoba government wished. A separate publicly-funded Roman Catholic school system was not restored. However, when there were enough students, religious teaching could take place in the last half-hour of the school day. Also, when there were 10 or more students who spoke a language other than English, they could be taught in that language and English. This did not, however, apply to First Nations languages.

Above: Schools were seen as a means to assimilate minorities. Immigration had brought together families from many cultures. Education was to make the next generation into Canadians.

Left: A typical one-room rural school in Manitoba; one teacher was usually responsible for teaching all grades. Students' ages ranged from about age 6 to 18. Few rural students got much education beyond Grade 8.

Laurier's "Sunny Ways Approach"

Laurier is well-known for his compromise tactics when he solved problems. He compromised between what the English wanted and what the French wanted. He tried to satisfy each side by giving them at least a part of what they wanted. He called this his "sunny ways approach." Often this had the opposite effect. Instead of making both sides happy it made them angry that the problem was not solved their way.

For Your Notebook

1. Define assimilation and compromise.
2. 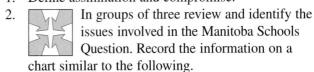 In groups of three review and identify the issues involved in the Manitoba Schools Question. Record the information on a chart similar to the following.

Event	Explain the Issue	English Position	French Position	Laurier's Compromise
Manitoba Schools Question				

3. Write a summary statement explaining how Laurier dealt with biculturalism in the school system.

Canadian Identity

 Laurier wanted to develop a stronger national identity. This meant that he wanted people in Canada to think of themselves as Canadians first and French Canadians or English Canadians second. During Laurier's time as prime minister several events occurred that caused Canadians to examine their changing role in the British Empire.

Canada's Changing Role in the Empire

 Canadians had different ideas about their role in the British Empire at the turn of the century. Three groups that had different points of view on the issues at this time are as follows:

The Imperialists

The imperialists were mainly English Protestants. They wanted Canada to become closer to Great Britain. They felt that close ties with Great Britain were in Canada's best interest. They wanted closer economic, political, and military alliances with Great Britain and the other dominions in the British Empire.

The French Canadian Nationalists

The French Canadian nationalists, led by Henri Bourassa (whom you read about on page 285), wanted their traditions and the Roman Catholic religion preserved in Canada. They wanted Canada's relationship with the British Empire to remain the same. They preferred Canada to be loosely associated with Great Britain, yet self-governing.

The Continentalists

The continentalists (a much smaller group) thought that Canada should be part of a single nation occupying the whole continent of North America. Many of the people in this group were Americans or people who traded with them.

An Exercise in Critical Thinking

Part One

Read the five issues following on pages 289 to 292. You'll see that Prime Minister Laurier was going to have a difficult time trying to please all Canadians. Choose one issue and examine it using the critical thinking strategies on pages 352–353.

Issue 1.
Ties with Great Britain

Issue 2.
The South African (Boer) War, 1899–1902

Issue 3.
Alaska Boundary Dispute, 1899–1903

Issue 4.
The Naval Question, 1909–1911

Issue 5.
Reciprocity, 1910–1911

Critical thinking usually involves looking at an issue from various points of view. In this activity you will be asked to examine the issue you chose from the perspective (point of view) of the imperialists, French Canadian nationalists, continentalists, and Prime Minister Laurier. You may wish to record your notes on a chart similar to the one below.

| The Issue | Points of View | | | |
	Imperialists	French Canadian Nationalists	Continentalists	Laurier
1.				
2.				
3.				
4.				
5.				

SAMPLE

Issue 1. Ties with Great Britain

The Diamond Jubilee Parade, London, England, 1897. Sir Wilfrid and Lady Laurier are in the carriage.

 In 1897, Laurier attended Queen Victoria's Diamond Jubilee in London, England. It celebrated Victoria's sixtieth year as Queen. Laurier was very well-liked in England. He was invited to many banquets and was granted honourary degrees from Oxford and Cambridge Universities. As a final honour, the Queen made him a knight. He was now Sir Wilfrid Laurier.

Joseph Chamberlain, the British **colonial secretary**, called a Colonial Conference during the Diamond Jubilee celebrations. Chamberlain had plans for making the British Empire stronger. He wanted to set up an imperial council. Britain and each of the self-governing dominions would be members. He thought the dominions could benefit from pooling expenses for naval defence and by increasing trade among themselves. He thought trade among the dominions would increase if tariffs were reduced or eliminated for all members.

At this time, Canada governed its own internal affairs but was still part of the British Empire. Its economic relations with other countries were independent of British control. However, external political decisions, such as signing a treaty with another country or declaring war, were still made by Great Britain.

Points of View

The imperialists wanted to remain part of the British Empire and to maintain very close, strong ties with Great Britain. While the imperialists did not want Great Britain to control everything in Canada, they did support efforts for common defence and trade. The French Canadian nationalists did not see a need to increase ties with Great Britain and would not support efforts to have more decisions made in Great Britain. The continentalists did not support closer ties to Great Britain. They felt Canada should join with the United States to deal with any issues of defence and trade.

Outcome

Laurier did not want to offend English Canadian voters or his British hosts. He saw the benefits to the present relationship between Canada and the Empire, but he did not want stronger ties with Great Britain.

Laurier rejected Chamberlain's proposal for a closer union of the colonies within the British Empire. However, to keep the imperialists happy, he made many positive remarks about Great Britain and said he was not trying to end Canada's role as part of the British Empire. Before returning home to Canada, Laurier visited France. There he made positive remarks about that country so French Canadians would not think that he only praised Great Britain.

This cartoon was printed after Laurier's return home from the Diamond Jubilee and Colonial Conference. It shows that both English and French were pleased with his performance.

Colonial secretary—the British Cabinet minister responsible for the colonies

Issue 2. The South African (Boer) War, 1899–1902

 In 1899, war broke out between British colonists and the **Boers** in South Africa. Great Britain expected Canada, as part of the British Empire, to send troops to help defend the British in South Africa (see map page 75).

Points of View

In English-speaking Canada, imperialists organized mass meetings, petitions, and newspaper editorials urging the government to send troops to South Africa to support Great Britain. An Ottawa columnist described the leave-taking of the 125 men of Company D, which was Ottawa's share of "Canada's offering to the Empire."

> The engines were puffing and blowing, bands were playing . . . the crowd, which some numbered at 15 000, simply surged into the station and neither the thick rope nor a guard of policemen, commanded by the chief in person were enough to hold it. . . . When the crowd grew wilder, I saw his Excellency [the governor-general] himself struggling in the midst of it like an ordinary citizen. . . . Some of the soldiers got into the train and put up the windows. There was a regular scrimmage to get near. Everyone wanted to shake hands, and above the din of bands and cheering, one often caught the words, 'God bless you boys.'

French Canadian nationalists could see no point in Canadian troops being sent off to the other side of the world to fight people who were not enemies of Canada. In fact, many French Canadian nationalists viewed the Boers in South Africa as a minority like themselves, trying to protect their culture in the face of British imperialists. They argued that Canada should not take part in Great Britain's wars unless it had a say in Great Britain's war councils.

Outcome

Laurier was in a difficult position. To please the British and the Canadian imperialists Laurier agreed to send about 1000 volunteer troops. Canada would pay for the costs of their equipment and travel. Many other Canadians went as individual volunteers. About 7000 Canadians in total went.

To please French Canadian nationalists, Laurier sent far fewer troops than the British and the imperialists wanted. He made it clear that, as volunteers, the troops became the responsibility of the British rather than the Canadian government once they arrived in South Africa. The costs of supplies and their pay of a shilling a day was to be paid by Great Britain. He made it known that although Canada had sent troops to this war it would not necessarily send troops to other wars in the future.

Imperialists were angry that so few troops had been sent to South Africa. French Canadian nationalists were angry that Canadians had taken part at all in a war that did not concern them directly. Henri Bourassa resigned from the Liberal party in protest and never rejoined.

Canadian soldiers fighting in the Boer War

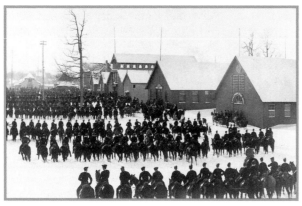

The Strathcona's Horse Regiment in Ottawa, March 1900, prior to leaving for the Boer War. Colonel Sam Steele of the North West Mounted Police was in command.

Boers—descendants of Dutch settlers in South Africa

Issue 3. Alaska Boundary Dispute, 1899–1903

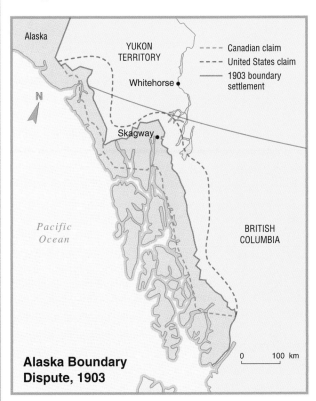

Alaska Boundary Dispute, 1903

In the Alaska Boundary dispute, Canada claimed the land in the Alaska Panhandle part way down the inlets.

  The Klondike gold rush turned the attention of both Canadians and Americans to the Alaska Panhandle. This is the long, narrow section of Alaska stretching southward along the Pacific Coast from the main body of Alaska. The shortest route to the goldfields in Canadian territory was through the Panhandle. Both the Canadians and the Americans were eager to control trade resulting from the gold rush. Although the boundary had first been drawn in 1825, the mountains and the indented coastline made it difficult to define. Its actual position was in dispute.

Points of View

Canada thought that the border should be moved so that the tops of the inlets were in Canada. This would also make the booming town of Skagway part of Canada. The Americans wanted the boundary to stay where it was. The continentalists thought that Canada should join the United States. If Canada did this, there would be no boundary dispute.

Outcome

Because Canada was still part of the British Empire, Great Britain played a major role in the negotiations. A joint commission was established by the United States and Great Britain to try to reach a settlement. Three Americans were appointed. Great Britain appointed two Canadian members and Lord Alverstone to the joint commission.

As it turned out, Lord Alverstone voted in favour of the American claim. As you can see from the map, the Americans did not get everything they wanted. However, the heads of the inlets and the town of Skagway stayed in American hands.

The imperialists were not pleased. They had expected Great Britain to put Canada's interests ahead of those of the United States because of the ties of the British Empire. French Canadian nationalists were not pleased with the commission's decision. They felt that the British had thought only of their own interests, not of Canada's.

In 1909, Canada and the United States formed a permanent Joint International High Commission to settle questions related to boundaries, rivers, and coastal waters. This commission has solved many concerns over the years and is still active today.

Issue 4. The Naval Question, 1909–1911

 The countries in Europe were enlarging their armies and navies. Concerned about the possibility of war, Great Britain decided to build more ships. In 1909 Great Britain asked the members of the Empire to contribute money to help build up its navy.

Points of View

The French Canadian nationalists and imperialists had different points of view. The issue was not of great concern to continentalists.

French Canadian nationalists did not want Canada to give money to the British navy. They were willing to spend money on building a Canadian navy, but not one to be used in a British war.

The imperialists argued that money would be better spent enlarging Britain's navy, which could protect Canada. They wanted Canada to give money to Great Britain immediately. They made fun of Canada's "tin pot navy." Laurier supported the establishment of a permanent Canadian navy controlled by the Canadian government.

Outcome

The Naval Service Bill was passed by the Canadian Parliament in 1910 but was not approved by the Senate before an election was called. Eleven million dollars was to be spent to build five cruisers and six destroyers for a Canadian navy. This navy would be sent to help if the British needed it. However, this help would be sent only in an emergency and the Canadians would decide what was or was not an emergency.

The naval question became one of the key issues in the 1911 election.

Issue 5. Reciprocity, 1910–1911

 For many years, some people in both Canada and the United States had made demands for freer trade between the two countries. The United States offered to lower tariffs on some Canadian manufactured goods and to put small or no tariffs on meat, cattle, dairy products, lumber, pulpwood, minerals, and fish from Canada. In return, they expected Canada to put lower tariffs on some manufactured goods from the United States, such as agricultural machinery and building materials. This proposed agreement of limited free trade was called reciprocity.

Points of View

Reciprocity was greeted by a storm of protests. Both imperialists and French Canadian nationalists were against it. They were afraid it could lead to the flooding of Canadian markets with lower-priced American manufactured goods. They also feared that the growth of north-south trade between Canada and the United States would result in less business between Central and Atlantic, and Western Canada. French Canadian nationalists had nothing to gain and everything to lose by a political union with the United States. Their French language and culture were unlikely to be recognized if such a union took place. Continentalists believed that reciprocity would lead to political union with the United States. They supported it.

As the photograph shows, Laurier supported reciprocity and the larger markets it would bring to Canadians.

Outcome

The issue of reciprocity was one of the key issues in the 1911 election (along with the Naval Service Bill). Laurier's campaign supported both reciprocity and the Naval Service Bill. Borden opposed both.

Borden and his Conservatives won the 1911 election with a majority. No reciprocity treaty was signed.

An Exercise in Critical Thinking

Part Two

1. Write a letter to Prime Minister Laurier stating your point of view on the issues you chose to study. Provide reasons to support your opinion.

Part Three

1. Individually, think about and write notes in your History Journal about one of the following:
   a) an issue that involved several points of view and how you compromised to solve it
   b) an issue that could better have been solved had you compromised.
   Record your findings.

The Legacy of Laurier

Sir Wilfrid Laurier
(Liberal)
1896–1911

After 15 years under Laurier, the government was turned over to Robert Borden, Laurier must have been proud of the accomplishments of his administration during the years some historians called "The Golden Years." The "brightest gem [Canada] in the Crown of the British Empire," as Laurier had boasted, still shone brightly.

- Internationally, Canada had gained some status and come to be viewed as a country with a promising future.
- Canada's population grew by over 34% in the first decade of the twentieth century, the greatest growth since Confederation. However, population increases also led to overcrowding, poor living conditions, and unemployment where cities were unable to absorb the changes so quickly.
- New cities, Regina, Saskatoon, Edmonton, and Calgary, rose in the new Prairie provinces. In British Columbia, Vancouver became a major port and industrial centre. In Central Canada, cities also experienced considerable growth. However, cities struggled to provide housing and services for rapidly growing populations. Montreal and Toronto had growth rates of over 80%. Halifax and St. John's populations also experienced remarkable growth.
- The times were generally prosperous. A booming economy had created a number of millionaires and produced an abundance of jobs. However, the workers available did not always match the jobs created. Unskilled workers had low pay, long hours, and poor working conditions. There were few options available to those who lost jobs or were unemployed. Some manufacturers became wealthy at the expense of their workers.
- Prosperity created a much larger middle class. Some were beginning to enjoy the new luxuries of technology—the telephone, radio, gramophone, and automobile. This group, in particular, felt confident and **optimistic** about Canada's prosperity. Most, however, could not afford these luxuries. When the economic slowdown began, workers suffered because costs did not decline with income.

- Canada's newcomers experienced little of the general prosperity of the period. However, although many faced poverty, disease, and prejudice, most continued to be hopeful of the future. They dreamed that their children and grandchildren would enjoy a prosperous future.

Canada Revisited

O Canada*

The official version of "O Canada," proclaimed as Canada's national anthem July 1, 1980, was based on a poem written by R. Stanley Wier in 1908. Judge Wier's poem captured the patriotic spirit of the times.

The music of our national anthem was composed in 1880 by Calixa Lavallée. The French lyrics that were written by Sir Adolphe-Basile Routhier at that time to accompany the music are still used today.

O Canada!
 Our home and native land!
True patriot love
 in all thy sons command.
With glowing hearts
 we see thee rise,
The True North
 strong and free!
From far and wide,
 O Canada,
We stand on guard
 for thee.
God keep our land
 glorious and free!
O Canada,
 we stand on guard for thee.
O Canada,
 we stand on guard for thee.

Ô Canada!
 Terre de nos aïeux,
Ton front est ceint
 de fleurons glorieux!.
Car ton bras
 sait porter l'épée,
Il sait porter
 la croix!
Ton histoire
 est une épopée
Des plus
 brillants exploits
Et ta valeur,
 de foi trempée,
Protégera nos foyers
et nos droits,
Protégera nos foyers
et nos droits,

Optimistic—expecting the future to be positive
*For information on Canadian symbols, check out this website:
http://www.pch.gc.ca/ceremonial-symb/english/index.html

Borden's Political Challenges

Robert Borden inherited the glowing legacy of the Laurier years. Canadians expected much from their new prime minister.

The task would not be easy. Borden also inherited a number of difficult problems. His economic challenge was to continue the growth and development of the country. There were, however, some early warning signs that a world economic slump was beginning.

Borden also faced the unresolved Naval Service Bill and the increasing possibility of a war in Europe. As a member of the British Empire, Canada would be expected to show its support should Great Britain become involved in a war. You will be introduced to Robert Borden's administration in this chapter. Chapters 12 and 13 will continue looking at events during Borden's time in office.

8th Prime Minister

Personal Summary

Robert Laird Borden was born on June 26, 1854, on a small farm at Grand Pré, Nova Scotia. His father was a farmer, then a railway agent. Robert Borden grew up in a reasonably comfortable household. His mother possessed a strong character, remarkable energy, high goals, and unusual ability. Both parents were enthusiastic readers, and Robert's home life centered on talk of literature and politics.

Robert's education gave him a strong understanding of Greek and Roman literature, but little else. By carefully planning his spare time between chores, Borden, an eager learner, began to educate himself. By the age of 14, he became assistant schoolmaster at his school. He taught there five years and another year in New Jersey.

Borden then returned to Halifax, where he became a law student. Entry into the legal profession was generally limited to the sons of the wealthy. Borden lived on a small salary, studying law at night. He passed the law examinations in first place.

Beginning as junior partner in a well-recognized law firm, he soon distinguished himself as a lawyer. He argued cases before the Supreme Court of Canada in Ottawa and the Judicial Committee of the Privy Council in London.

In 1889, he married Laura Bond, the daughter of a Halifax businessman.

Sir Robert Borden
1854–1937

Dates as Prime Minister—1911–1920
Party—Conservative

• • • • • • • •

By the 1890s, Borden's law practice was one of the largest in the Maritimes. It provided him with a good income, a fine home, and much prestige.

Political Summary

Borden's family were Liberals, but in the late 1890s, when Premier W.S. Fielding, a Liberal, threatened to pull Nova Scotia out of Confederation, Borden decided to become a Conservative. In 1896, Sir Charles Tupper asked him to be a Conservative candidate in the federal election.

The Liberals, led by Laurier, won the election. Borden was elected in his riding and was part of the Opposition. Borden quickly proved to be a good speaker and a knowledgeable member of the House of Commons.

In 1901, Tupper was defeated. He named Borden to succeed him as leader of the Conservative Party. Borden led the party through two unsuccessful elections in 1904 and 1908. In the election of 1911, they won a majority of seats, and Borden became the eighth prime minister of Canada. He was knighted by the King in 1914.

Borden's outstanding qualities were hard work, honesty, and sincerity. He guided Canada through nine difficult years, including World War I. The war years, in particular, seriously affected his health.

Borden resigned from the Office of Prime Minister in 1920. He continued to take an active role, representing Canada internationally and advocating for the formation of the League of Nations.

Naval Aid Bill

 Two election issues had contributed to Laurier's defeat, the Reciprocity Treaty with the United States and the Naval Service Bill. The majority of Canadians were against both. Laurier's Naval Service Bill did not pass in the Senate and did not become a law.

Prime Minister Borden (on the left) with Winston Churchill in London, England

Borden visited Great Britain to determine how serious the news of upcoming war in Europe was. Germany and Great Britain were involved in a race to expand their navies and control the seas. A war in Europe involving these two countries seemed possible. Great Britain asked for help from the larger members of the British Empire such as Canada.

Winston Churchill was the First Lord of the Admiralty, in charge of the British navy. He convinced Borden that the new German navy posed a threat to Great Britain and the British Empire, as well as to Europe. Churchill asked Canada to provide $35 million to Great Britain to build warships. Borden was persuaded by Churchill that the situation was a real emergency. Borden took the request for money to the Canadian Parliament as the Naval Aid Bill. It approached the naval question differently than Laurier's Naval Services Bill had.

Months of angry debate in Canada followed. The Liberals and French Canadian nationalists were against the Naval Aid Bill. Finally it was passed in the House of Commons but defeated in the Senate. Canada still had no naval policy.

Provincial Boundaries

  On May 15, 1912, the Borden government changed some political boundaries in Canada. Manitoba, Ontario, and Quebec were granted vast tracts of largely unsurveyed land.*

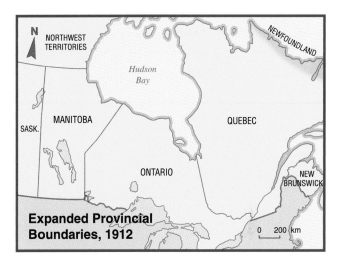

Expanded Provincial Boundaries, 1912

For Your Notebook

1. If you could have interviewed Prime Minister Borden, what three questions about his political career would you have asked him? What do you think he would have answered? (See Interviewing Techniques in Appendix, page 355.)
2. Compare the 1912 boundaries of Canada (above) with the map called Alberta and Saskatchewan Become Provinces, 1905, in the back endsheets.

Challenge Plus

3. Great Britain needed financial help to build a navy that would be larger than that of Germany. Laurier and Borden chose different solutions.
   a) Compare and contrast their solutions.
   b) Why do you think Laurier's solution was not well received by either English or French Canadians?
   c) Borden's solution was unacceptable to French Canadians. Why were English Canadians more satisfied with his solution?
   d) Should the unelected Senate have the power to reject bills passed by the elected House of Commons? Explain your answer.

---

*Treaty 9 with the First Nations of northern Ontario had been signed in 1905. Parts A and B of Treaty 5 for Manitoba were signed in 1875 and 1908. At the time of 1912 boundary changes, land surrender treaties had not been signed with First Nations in Northern Quebec. The James Bay and Northern Quebec Agreement was not signed until 1975.

Review

The icons are your cue to refer to the Learning how to Learn Appendix (pages 348–371) for ideas on how to complete these activities.

1. Complete a self-assessment for one assignment from this chapter.

Understanding Concepts

2. Do either a) or b).
   a) Create a concept poster for one of the chapter's main ideas. Present your poster to the class.
   b)   Use a web, mind map, outline, or chart to create a permanent set of notes about one of the ideas. Explain your work to a classmate.

3.   Use one of the methods found in the Appendix for recording any new vocabulary in the WordBook section of your notes.

4. Add entries for this chapter to your timeline.

Developing Research Skills

5.

Section IV Activity

Writing Historical Fiction
If you haven't done so already, complete the project you started on page 271 and added to on pages 276 and 284.

Part Two
Who Are We?
As a class, discuss the questions on the easel on page 269 that apply to Chapter 11 (the 1896–1914 time period).

Select from numbers 6 to 10.

6. You read that the first Grey Cup football game was played in Toronto in 1909. Conduct research on Grey Cup games and create a pictorial overview of the history of the Grey Cup. You might wish to use a timeline format with highlights of important players and statistics.

7. Carry out research to find out the history of basketball and its popularity during this time period.

8. Leisure time activities did not change very much during the period of 1896 to 1911. What inventions do you think caused such activities to change later in the twentieth century? Research one of these inventions and its impact on leisure activities of Canadians. Find historical photographs to illustrate your report.

9. Research the history of the scouting movement between 1896 and 1914.

10.   Research an invention from the 1890s to early 1900s. Find out where it originated or who discovered it, and how it was used. Demonstrate its impact using visuals or in a web.

Developing Communication Skills

Reading

11. Read a novel by Lucy Maud Montgomery.

Writing

12. Imagine you are a social reformer. Write a journal entry describing what you have observed that day in a factory, an office, or on the streets of a Canadian city.

13. To show how industrialization changed Canadian society select one of the following lifestyles. Describe in detail (or illustrate) a typical day about 1912. Use this chapter as reference.
   - a farmer living in the West
   - a professional or business person living in a city
   - a 15-year-old living in a city
   - a factory worker in a "sweatshop"

14. Pretend it is 1910. Assume the role of a child of 13 who has never gone to school. List all the things you might not be able to do because of your lack of education. (This may be done in the role you selected on the activity you started on page 271.)

15. Write a slogan for factory workers who want to set up a trade union. Create a poster using this slogan and listing their demands.

16. Select an event that occurred between 1896 and 1914. Write about the event from three points of view—a child from upper, middle, and working class families.

17. Design and prepare the entertainment and sports section for either a large city or small town newspaper.

18. Imagine you are Amaryllis, an Ottawa columnist reporting on social events during this period. Write a column that she could have written describing a dance or other social event. You will need to investigate the fashions that people wore at this time.

19. Choose one of the events involving inventions listed on page 276. Pretend you are a newspaper reporter and describe the event in an article for your newspaper.

Listening and Speaking

20. Pretend you are running for the position of mayor of a Canadian city at the turn of the century. Write a campaign speech you would make. Tell how you would make the city a better place to live.

21. If you had the opportunity to meet Tom Longboat, what three questions would you ask him? What do you think he would have answered? You will need to take his point of view to understand what he might have thought.

22. Listen to some of the music from the 1890s (see page 284). Explain to a friend why you like or dislike this music.

Viewing and Representing

23. You have probably seen the Heritage Minutes on television or in movie theatres. These are brief stories about people and events in Canadian history.
    a) Ask your teacher to let you see a few in class. (Possibilities include Guglielmo Marconi, Rural Teacher, and James Naismith.)
    b) Work with others to conduct research about one important person or event in this section of the text. Write a script for a scene that uses the information you have researched, then dramatize it.

c) Perform your "minute" for the rest of the class, or create a permanent record on video.

Applying Concepts

24. Why do you think that one of every eight adult Canadian women belonged to a women's organization during this period? Make a list of the benefits for individual women of belonging to such organizations.

25. Prime Minister Wilfrid Laurier predicted that "the twentieth century shall be the century of Canada." Was Laurier correct? Develop arguments in support of your point of view and present them to a group of other students.

26. Some of the issues faced by Laurier exist today. Choose one and conduct research to determine how it is similar or different today than in Laurier's time. You might consider French/English relations within Canada. Another choice would be to compare Prime Minister Brian Mulroney's 1988 free trade agreement with the United States with Laurier's goal for a reciprocity agreement in 1911.

Challenge Plus

27. a) What was the National Policy? Under what prime minister was it introduced? Of what three major parts did it consist?
    b) In what way were Canada's economic successes from 1880 to 1914 a result of the success of the National Policy?

28. Design a history magazine for Section IV: Emerging Canadian Identity (1896–1920). Decide how to show important people, places, events, and ideas in an interesting way, to assist other students to understand and appreciate Canadian history. Some items you could create include: fact files, visuals (e.g., maps, illustrations, diagrams), samples of students' work, chapter summaries, study guides and practice quizzes, and games. You might also include an interactive part, such as an opinion poll or survey (and tables and graphs to show the results), or a "write-in" question and answer column. Provide a list of related websites and resources.

Chapter 12
World War I
1914–1918

O v e r v i e w

Use this Overview to predict what you will read in this chapter.

❸ Hundreds of thousands of Canadian men fought and many died, mainly on the Western Front, but also at sea and in the air over Europe. The Canadian armed forces were greatly respected by the Allies and the Central Powers for their courage and determination.

❶ Causes of World War I

The political forces of imperialism, nationalism, and militarism led to war in Europe. Alliances created powerful opponents. An assassination in 1914 started the events of war in motion.

❶ *Imperialism*   **❷** *Nationalism*

World War I

❹ *The Assassination of Archduke Franz Ferdinand*   **❸** *Militarism*

❹ On the Homefront

Extraordinary efforts, especially by women, were needed in Canada to produce the weapons, food, and goods needed to fight the war.

1917 Military Service Act

❺ As the war continued, more soldiers were needed. Canada was divided politically over the conscription issue. In 1917, the Military Service Act was passed, bringing in conscription.

❷ Canada at War

The War Measures Act gave the Borden Cabinet authority to finance the war, expand the armed forces, and ensure internal security in Canada.

CANADA AT WAR

❻ Conclusion of World War I

Canada had a recognized place in the peace talks in Versailles after the war ended. The Treaty of Versailles set out the consequences for Germany for their responsibility in the war. The League of Nations and the International Labour Organization were also discussed at the peace talks.

Chapter 12 Focus

Chapter 12 focuses on the causes of World War I and Canada's involvement in the war in Europe and on the homefront. Participation in World War I contributed to an emerging Canadian identity. While all the book's concepts will be examined, the focus of this chapter is on power, identity, and conflict.

 Change
 Regionalism
 Power
 Identity
Conflict

Other Concepts and Main Topics

- political alliances
- imperialism
- nationalism
- militarism
- arms race
- enfranchise
- disenfranchise
- discrimination
- allies
- propaganda

- patriotism
- trench
- no man's land
- the front
- Vimy Ridge
- homefront
- conscription
- conscientious objector
- autonomous
- coalition

Learning How to Learn

 Critical Thinking

 Decision-making

 Role-playing

 Writing

Chapter Overview/Prediction

1. In pairs or small groups,
   a) use the chapter's titles, the overview, and the visuals in the chapter to fill out the following chart.
   b) Discuss what you think the chapter is about.

My prediction of what the chapter is about	Information from titles	Information from visuals
What I learned		

SAMPLE

Section IV Activity

Part One
Historical Fiction
In role, writing from the point of view of the character you represented on pages 271 and 272, write about how World War I affected you. For more information check out:

- http://www.vac-acc.gc.ca/general/sub.cfm?source=history/firstwar/canada
- http://www.civilization.ca/cwm/tour/trww1eng.html
- http://www.vac-acc.gc.ca

1. In your History Journal react to hearing about the start of the war and what caused it (pages 300–302).
2. Have your character become involved in the war
   a) through enlisting or volunteering; for example, as a soldier, nurse, doctor, ambulance driver, newspaper reporter, or war artist at the front lines (pages 303–315 and 319). Record at least three entries in your journal and/or letters, OR
   b) through efforts made on the homefront (pages 316–319)
3. In your History Journal, react to the Conscription Issue (pages 320–324). Record how you voted in 1917 (if you legally could).

THIS IS YOUR FLAG
IT STANDS FOR LIBERTY
FIGHT FOR IT
JOIN THE
OVERSEAS BATTALION
207
LT. Col. C. W. MACLEAN.
Officer Commanding
APPLY BASE RECRUITING OFFICE
SPARKS ST. OTTAWA

Recruiting posters appealed to feelings of patriotism and loyalty to symbols like the flag of Great Britain.

Causes of World War I

A Changing Europe

  In the first decades of the twentieth century, the countries of Europe were undergoing many political, economic, and social changes, just as Canada was.

Some countries in Europe had political and economic ties with each other that affected their policies. For example, Russia had an alliance with France and Great Britain. Russia also had historical connections with Serbia but no formal treaty. The German Empire was allied with Italy and with the Austro-Hungarian Empire. Belgium was politically neutral.

Three major factors (described on the next page) led to conflict in Europe. Imperialism, nationalism, and militarism in European countries created an unstable situation. A political assassination tipped the balance into war.

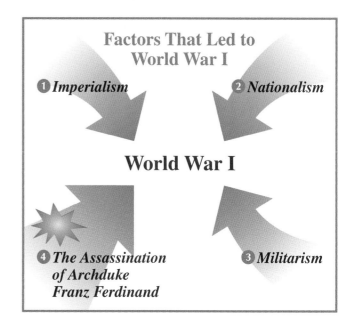

Factors That Led to World War I

❶ *Imperialism* ❷ *Nationalism*

World War I

❹ *The Assassination of Archduke Franz Ferdinand* ❸ *Militarism*

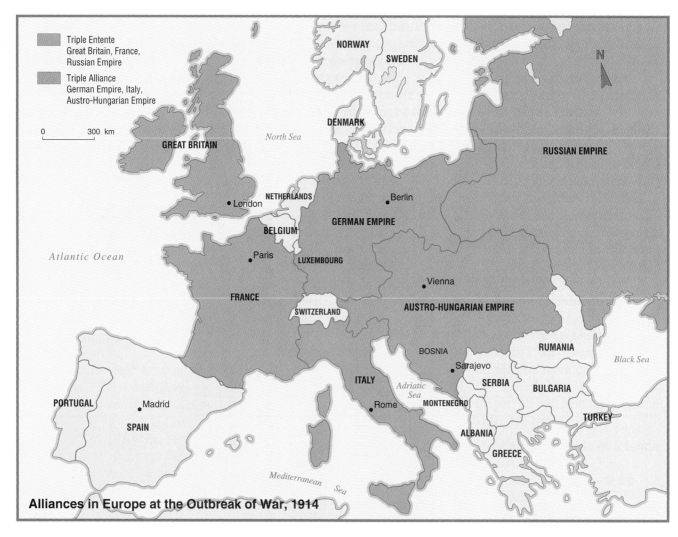

Triple Entente
Great Britain, France, Russian Empire

Triple Alliance
German Empire, Italy, Austro-Hungarian Empire

0   300 km

Alliances in Europe at the Outbreak of War, 1914

Causes of the War

The cause and effect chart below and the information on the next two pages can help you understand interrelationships among the factors of imperialism, nationalism, and militarism and their effects. Each effect brought about further changes. (See page 348 for more about cause and effect.)

Problem *cause*	Factors *event or situation*	Result *effect*
❶ **Imperialism** (the building of empires)	Many European countries extended their territories in the 19th century. Colonies were a source of raw materials and a market for goods. An empire gave a country prestige and economic power which could be used to increase military strength.	Frequent disagreements over colonies and annexed territories arose among the great powers of Europe. World peace was threatened.
❷ **Nationalism** (strong feelings of deep loyalty to one's people and homeland)	Nationalism drew people together, and a feeling of national pride became more evident in many countries.*	Nationalism strengthened the nation as an independent unit. Some people were willing to take any action to help their own nation, regardless of its effects.
❸ **Militarism** (the buildup of armies and navies)	The powerful countries had built up their military strength in an **arms race**. They had armies, navies, and arsenals of weapons available to use if they were needed.	European countries strengthened their alliances. Countries made political connections with other countries in order to be as strong as their opponents.

> Triple Entente **vs** Triple Alliance
> (Allied Powers   (Central
> or Allies)   Powers)

Widespread conflict had been building between the two old enemies, the German Empire and France. As each side tried to gain advantage, they drew other major European countries, their allies, into the conflict. By 1914, a war in Europe seemed inevitable.

Because of existing political alliances and historical relationships, Europe was divided into two main camps. On the German Empire's side stood the Austro–Hungarian Empire and Italy. During the war they were called the Central Powers (formerly, the Triple Alliance). They were soon joined by Turkey. On France's side were the Russian Empire and Great Britain. They were called the Allied Powers during the war (formerly known as the Triple Entente).

In an arms race in Europe, armies had been increased, modernized, and equipped with the latest in weapons. The German Empire and Great Britain were rebuilding their navies in a competition to control the seas. Larger, faster, and more powerful ships were built by both sides.

Meanwhile, another problem was developing. Austria had taken control of some lands in the Balkan region.** This expansion was seen as a threat to Serbian independence. Feelings of nationalism were growing in the Balkan states. These nationalist groups were encouraged by Russia, which had cultural ties with them.

---

*This was especially true in states that had been independent and were now part of another empire.
Arms race—a competition between countries to increase their weapons and fighting forces

---

**The area referred to as "the Balkans" is a mountainous region of many small states between the Adriatic Sea and the Black Sea.

The Event That Ignited World War I

④ *The Assassination of Archduke Franz Ferdinand*

On June 28, 1914, in the little-known town of Sarajevo in Bosnia, a young Serbian extreme-nationalist, Gavrilo Princip, assassinated the heir to the Austrian throne. Archduke Franz Ferdinand and his wife Sophie were shot and killed as they rode through the streets on a state visit to Sarajevo.

The Granger Collection/New York

Assassination of Archduke Franz Ferdinand

The assassination set off a series of events. Believing the Serbian government was behind the assassination, Austria-Hungary made a number of demands on Serbia. Serbia would not accept all of the demands. On August 1, 1914, Austria-Hungary declared war on Serbia. Germany, which was newly allied with Turkey, came to Austria-Hungary's aid. France and Russia began to prepare for war to support their ally Serbia. Germany ordered them to stop. They refused. Germany then declared war on Russia and the following day on France.

Germany attacked Belgium. Belgium, as a neutral country, did not expect to be attacked so it had no defences. Germany's military strategy was to take France by surprise, by attacking from the direction of Belgium.

Great Britain declared war on Germany on August 4, 1914, as a response to Germany's unprovoked attack on a neutral country.

The result was World War I, a war that everyone expected would be brief. It actually lasted four long years and cost hundreds of thousands of lives.

Declaration of War

 As a member of the British Empire, even without consultation, Canada and the other dominions were legally at war. However, the extent of their participation was up to them to decide. Canada made a large commitment to supporting Great Britain and opposing the Central Powers.

Canadians became aware of the war primarily through newspapers and radio. Some people in isolated areas did not know Canada was at war for days or weeks.

For Your Notebook

1. What were the major causes of World War I?
2. What action initiated the events that led to war?
3. In spite of not being in Europe, Canada went to war. Why?

Exploring Further

4. The area where the Archduke was assassinated is part of the Balkan region. Carry out research on the modern-day involvement of Canadian peacekeeping troops in the Balkans.

Canada at War

Canada Prepares for War

Great Britain's declaration of war on Germany brought Canada into World War I. Other dominions of the British Empire had made preparations for war much earlier. Canada was not prepared to fight a war. Its army consisted of just over 3000 men and a **militia** of 50 000. Its navy consisted of two ancient cruisers purchased from Great Britain in 1910, *H.M.C.S. Rainbow* and *H.M.C.S. Niobe*. The only major contribution Canada could send immediately was fighting men.

Prime Minister Borden moved quickly to make preparations for war. The War Measures Act was passed unanimously by Parliament (the House of Commons and the Senate).

> As to our duty, we are all agreed, we stand shoulder to shoulder with Britain and the other British Dominions in this quarrel.
>
> —Prime Minister Borden,
> August 18, 1914

War Measures Act

The 1914 War Measures Act gave the Cabinet extraordinary powers. They were given the power of **censorship**, the power to arrest, **intern**, and deport people, and the power to take over the nation's resources and use them for the war effort. Using these powers, the Cabinet took steps to finance the war. New taxes were placed on coffee, sugar, liquor, and tobacco. Over the next few years, others would follow, including a business tax in 1916 and a personal income tax in 1917. Travel outside of Canada was limited. Some **rationing** of food items was also introduced.

Canadian Expeditionary Force

The war was expected to be short, perhaps a few months long. Parliament decided Canada would provide Great Britain with 25 000 soldiers. Borden promised that compulsory service (conscription) would not be used: these soldiers would be volunteers. Throughout Canada there was enthusiasm for the war. Patriotism and belief in the need to protect democracy motivated both the troops and people on the homefront.

Militia—citizens who are not regular soldiers but undergo training for emergency duty
Censorship—examining communications for politically sensitive material and removing it; government control of publishing
Intern—to confine

Early Recruitment

**Sam Hughes
1853–1921**

Sam Hughes, minister of militia in the Borden government, called for 25 000 volunteers. Over 32 000 men showed up at recruiting stations across Canada. Most were urban men born in Great Britain or of British ancestry, but some French Canadians also volunteered. Lack of jobs due to the economic slowdown and a sense of adventure led many of the first recruits to join. Later, recruits more often went because of a sense of duty.

City of Toronto Archives, SC244-824

Volunteers who were recruited in 1914 expected the war to be brief. They left for the front enthusiastic about "seeing action."

The volunteers were immediately sent to Valcartier, near Quebec City, where Sam Hughes began their training with marches and drills. Some were afraid the war would end before Canadian troops reached Europe. On October 3, 1914, the First Canadian Division of the Canadian Expeditionary Force set sail for Europe with 32 100 men. They received additional training for combat in England. Hughes insisted that the Canadians not be used as reinforcements for British regular troops but remain together as one combat unit.

Rationing—controlling how much food or other products people can buy

Later Recruitment

As the conflict dragged on into 1915, Canada prepared for a much longer war. Over the next three years, Parliament approved the formation of other army divisions. The military college at Kingston trained many junior officers, although commanding officers all were British in the early years of the war. Increasingly, a broader range of Canada's ethnic population was encouraged to volunteer. Previously they had been discouraged from doing so. German and Ukrainian immigrants from places that had been made part of the German or Austro–Hungarian Empires volunteered. These men often changed their names to avoid being interned as "enemy aliens." Aboriginal, Asian, and African-Canadian men also volunteered, despite having experienced racial discrimination in Canada.

Every effort was made to encourage men between 18 and 24 to volunteer in the Canadian Expeditionary Force. Politicians, civic leaders, church ministers, and mothers whose sons had volunteered addressed rallies. Radio, newspapers, and posters played an important role. Those who chose not to volunteer were sometimes ridiculed and humiliated by others. Sometimes they were given a white feather, a symbol of cowardice.

The above photo shows Aboriginal soldiers from the North Bay area. Despite being discouraged from volunteering, close to 4000 Aboriginal soldiers served with the Canadian Expeditionary Force.

A recruiting sergeant visits young farmers on the Prairies. This 1915 painting entitled "Your Country Calls" is by Paul Wickson.

Canadian Troop Movements to Europe	
1914	30 999
1915	84 334
1916	165 553
1917	63 536
1918	73 630
Total	**418 052**

Internment Camps

Under the War Measures Act, steps were taken to protect the nation from what was considered to be "threats from within." Thousands of immigrants to Canada were classified as "enemy aliens" and required to report regularly to the police. This included thousands of Ukrainians from the German Empire or former Austro-Hungarian territories. **Internment camps** were set up across Canada for those considered to be a risk. A total of 8579 were interned during the war, over 5000 of them Ukrainian Canadians. Many were released before the war ended when they were no longer considered to be a threat to security.

This camp at Kapuskasing, Ontario, was built in an isolated area to confine men who were considered a security risk because of their country of origin.

For Your Notebook

1. a) What was the War Measures Act?
   b) Who passed it? Why?
   c) What special powers did it give the government?
2. Do you believe that in times of war the government should be allowed to pass and enforce acts like the War Measures Act? Provide reasons.

Internment camps—places where people are confined, often in isolated regions

Focus On: Poster Propaganda

 During World War I, the radio, newspapers, and posters were used to pass on information. Posters were especially popular, because not all Canadians owned radios or purchased newspapers. Hundreds of thousands of posters were placed in noticeable sites across Canada. They had dramatic illustrations and large type to attract attention and to appeal to the emotions of the readers.

Much of the information in the posters contained propaganda. Propaganda is the deliberate spreading of ideas, facts, or rumours to help one's own cause and to harm the opponent's cause. Through pictures and print, propaganda techniques were used to influence people. They urged people to agree with one side of an issue and to take action about it. Some propaganda techniques are described in the Appendix, page 359.

Some examples of propaganda posters are shown on this page. Other posters from World War I are found throughout this chapter.

For Your Notebook

1.   Select one of the posters from this chapter and/or from http://www.bcarchives.gov.bc.ca/exhibits/timemach/galler11/frames/poster.htm. Study the poster to determine what propaganda techniques are being used. (See page 359 in the Appendix). Share your findings with the class.

2. Advertisers use propaganda techniques to promote their products.
   a) Select product advertisements from modern-day newspapers or magazines and study them to see what propaganda techniques are being used.
   b) How does an understanding of propaganda techniques help you make wise purchasing decisions?

305

War in Europe
The War on Land

Germany's plan to defeat France depended on speed. The German army moved swiftly across Belgium into France. Great Britain was committed by treaty to support Belgium's neutrality. On August 4, 1914, Britain declared war on Germany and sent troops to help the French army slow the German advance. A battle on the Marne River east of Paris in mid-September ended Germany's plan for a quick victory in France. (Refer to the map on page 307.) Both sides dug trenches for protection and the armies faced one another across a narrow gap called no man's land.

On the Western Front

Over the next few years, trenches were dug from the English Channel to Switzerland in an almost-continuous line. This long strip of land where armies met and fought turned into a treeless wasteland of craters. It was called the Western Front. The major battles of World War I were fought along the northern-most 150 kilometres of trenches in north-eastern France and Belgium. The position of the front line changed little in the first three years of fighting, and there was a terrible cost in lives. These events are examined in more detail on pages 308 to 313.

The Allied Powers and the Central Powers used trench warfare on the Western Front.

On the Eastern Front

War was also waged in Eastern Europe. Germany's strategy was to hold back the slow-moving but huge Russian army with a small force while their main armies moved rapidly towards France. The Germans and Russians engaged in numerous battles on the Eastern Front. Both sides used cavalry in the early years of the war. Armies fought on horseback in several major battles. Each side gained some territory, then lost some. They fought a see-saw war which neither side could win decisively. There was much more movement of armies there than along the line of the Western Front. Trenches were used in places on the Eastern Front but not as extensively as on the Western Front.

Other Fronts

Although the most important battles of the war were fought on the Western Front, there was fighting between Allied and Central Powers in the Balkan region and on the border of Italy and Austria-Hungary. Most Canadian troops fought in northern France and Belgium.

Battlefronts in Europe

There were several changes to alliances and lands controlled by the different powers during the war. For example, Serbia was immediately overpowered by the Austro-Hungarian Empire. Italy and Portugal both joined the Allied Powers.

The Allied Forces

The Allied armies fighting on the Western Front were made up primarily of French, Belgian, British, Canadian, Newfoundlander, Australian, and South African divisions. The United States joined the Allies in 1917. This was principally because the German navy was sinking all ships it found in the north Atlantic Ocean, whether Allied or not.

 More than 400 000 Canadians fought in the Canadian Expeditionary Forces. Canadian divisions rapidly got a reputation for their bravery and determination. They were often used as "shock" or "storm" troops. These troops were sent towards the enemy lines first to spearhead an attack. When it was known that Canadians were in the trench opposite, the German troops fighting for the Central Powers took it as a sign that it would be a very tough attack.

The Final Year

In 1918, revolution in Russia brought down the government. The new government in Russia withdrew from the war. Russian soldiers on the Eastern Front went back to Russia. The army divisions of the Central Powers on the Eastern Front moved to reinforce their armies on other fronts. They hoped to reach France before the main American forces arrived there.

Canadian soldiers about to load ammunition

Advances by the Central Powers in March and May 1918 were halted by the Allies. When a large number of American troops arrived as reinforcements, the Allies began their own major advance in the Somme region of France. This drive was successful.

Military leaders of the Central Powers as well as soldiers in the trenches began to realize that the end of the war was near. Over the next few months the armies of Germany and the Austro-Hungarian Empire were pushed back, although they continued to fight. Morale began to sink. Some deserted their positions as the armies of the Central Powers fell to the Allied Powers. On November 11, 1918, at 11:00 AM, the **Armistice** was signed.

For Your Notebook

1. Who were the Allied Powers? Who remained neutral?
2. What were the major differences between the Western Front and the Eastern Front?
3. How did the abilities of the Canadian troops, as described on this page, lead to an emerging Canadian identity?

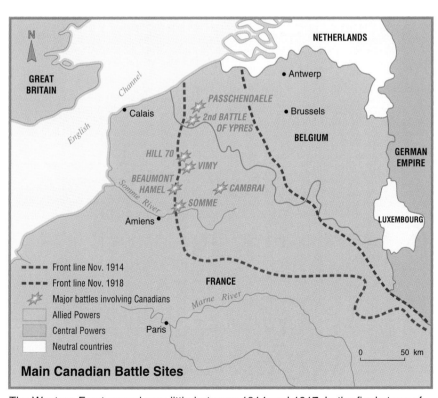

Main Canadian Battle Sites

Legend:
- - - - Front line Nov. 1914
- - - - Front line Nov. 1918
- ✫ Major battles involving Canadians
- Allied Powers
- Central Powers
- Neutral countries

0   50 km

The Western Front moved very little between 1914 and 1917. In the final stage of the war, the armies of the Central Powers were pushed back almost out of France.

Armistice—a formal agreement between countries to cease fighting

307

On both sides, soldiers ate, fought, and slept in trenches. During the day, some men were always on guard duty. The enemy could be as little as 25 metres away across no man's land. Others did necessary tasks like repair collapsing trench walls. In the spring and summer, they often worked in knee-deep water, sometimes filled with bodies. In the winter, they felt the cold of the snow and sleet. Soldiers had to move carefully, their heads always down to avoid becoming an enemy target. The noise and danger of shelling never stopped.

At night soldiers would climb out of their trenches to patrol no man's land and string or repair barbed-wire barriers. Surprise attacks often occurred during the night. Soldiers crept across no man's land to the enemy trenches to attack with hand grenades and rifle bayonets.

Trenches from the air

First aid was often given in the trenches.

Most major attacks occurred at dawn. At a signal, troops would go "over the top," charging toward the enemy trenches through cut barbed wire, mud, and shell craters.

Few made it. If possible, the dead, dying, and wounded would be carried back under gunfire. Sometimes they lay for days in no man's land.

Standing for hours in the cold mud and water caused "trench foot." Feet would swell and go numb. When the swelling went down pain was often severe. Those who got gangrene often had to have feet and legs amputated. Unable to bathe or change their clothes, most soldiers suffered from body lice. Disease from unclean water accounted for more men in hospital than wounds.

No man's land was a wasteland of shell craters, barbed wire, and mud.

Going "over the top"

A line of support trenches was dug behind the front line, connected to it by communications trenches. Food and ammunition were carried to the front line from the support trenches. Troops rotated between front line and support, doing several shifts of two days each. Then they had a short leave behind the lines to get clean and dry and to rest.

Life in the trenches was made more difficult by new weapons that were developed. In 1915, chemical warfare was introduced by the Germans. When the winds were right, clouds of toxic chlorine gas (later, mustard gas) were released from cylinders. The deadly gas was carried towards the Allied trenches. The choking gas burned and blistered the skin and lungs. Many died, and others would suffer for many years from the damage to their lungs.

The soldiers protected themselves any way they could. Allied Powers scientists raced to invent an effective protection. Dr. Cluny Macpherson, a Newfoundland doctor, developed the gas mask. Wearers breathed through an airline containing activated charcoal, which filtered the gas-filled air. By

the end of the war, the Allies were also using poisonous gases, particularly mustard gas, against the Central Powers.

The tank was another weapon developed for the Western Front. Great Britain produced these armoured vehicles to cross no man's land, crush down the barbed-wire defences, and attack the enemy line. In the wet and muddy winter season they often

got stuck in the mud of no man's land and had to be abandoned.

Airplanes were first used for observation. They provided photographs and information about enemy lines, and supply and troop movements. They were also used to drop grenades, bricks, and large darts on the men in the enemy trenches. Later, bombs of increasing size were dropped on trenches, bridges, factories, towns, and cities.

Gas was not a predictable weapon, particularly if the wind changed unexpectedly.

In 1916, Great Britain introduced the tank. Tanks were used to go over barbed-wire barricades to get to enemy lines.

Field hospitals at the front treated the wounded and sick. Some soldiers went back to the trenches. Some died, and others were sent to England or back to Canada for further treatment.

This field hospital near the front is staffed by Canadian nurses and doctors. Canada provided more than 1600 doctors and 2000 nurses to care for the wounded.

Focus On: Canadians Distinguish
Themselves in Battle

  Canadian soldiers distinguished themselves in a number of battles along the Western Front. Some of their most important battles were the Second Battle of Ypres, Somme, Vimy Ridge, and Passchendaele. Battle sites are shown on page 307.

Ypres, Belgium

In the Second Battle of Ypres, April 1915, Canadian troops were given the job of defending about 3.5 km of trench line. They came under heavy attack from German artillery. They held their position. Poisonous chlorine gas was released into the breeze blowing towards the Allied trenches. Many who breathed this new weapon of war choked, gagged, gasped, and died. Some Allied troops fled, but the Canadians did not. Using cloth soaked in urine as gas masks, the Canadians held on until they were relieved by reinforcements three days later. One-third of Canada's First Division soldiers were listed as killed in action, gassed, wounded, or missing. Six thousand died.

Somme, France

The Battle of Somme began July 1, 1916. Canadians fought as part of the British forces under General Douglas Haig. The first day of the battle proved disastrous. In spite of the Allied **artillery barrage** the German defences were strong. Thousands of Allied soldiers were killed by German machine gun fire crossing no man's land. By nightfall, British and Canadian casualties totalled over 57 000.

The Battle of Somme continued for another 141 days. During this time, troops from Great Britain, Canada, and the colony of Newfoundland, under orders, continued to attempt to advance towards the German trenches. In mid-July, 90% of the Royal Newfoundland Regiment was killed or wounded at a particularly strong part of the German line at Beaumont Hamel.

In September 1916, British tanks were used to break through the barbed wire and overtake the enemy trenches.

In the five months of the Battle of Somme, only 11 km were taken by the Allied forces. Casualties for both sides reached over 1 000 000. Canada suffered 24 000 casualties.

Artillery barrage—an intense attack using many large weapons of war, often used to break down enemy defenses before a ground attack by troops.

The packhorses in the photo above are transporting artillery ammunition to Canadian troops in France.

"The Taking of Vimy Ridge" by Richard Jack

Vimy Ridge, France

On April 9, 1917, the four divisions of the Canadian Corps under the command of British General Sir Julian Byng attacked the German-held Vimy Ridge. It was an area that the British and French had been unable to take. Careful preparations were made. Tunnels were dug to shelter the Canadians from German fire as they approached the front line. Artillery bombarded the German trenches to weaken their defences.

On April 12, Vimy Ridge was taken. It was an important victory for the Canadian army. Four Canadians won the Victoria Cross. The battle claimed the lives of 3598 Canadians. Another 7004 were wounded.

Passchendaele, Belgium

In the fall of 1917, for the first time in the war Canadian soldiers were under the leadership of a Canadian, General Arthur Currie. They were ordered by the British high command to capture targets outside the city of Passchendaele. Currie saw that the ground, once beneath the North Sea, was extremely marshy. Despite the difficulty of moving through the mud, Currie and the Canadian troops carried out their assignment. They reached the outskirts of Passchendaele, gaining 8 km of mud (which Germany regained within months). Canadian soldiers suffered extremely heavy casualties. After the battle, nine Canadians received the Victoria Cross.

Trenches could not be dug in the soft mud at Passchendaele, so there was little protection for the Canadians.

Vimy Ridge

Magazine Article

—by J.L. Granatstein and Norman Hillmer

Canada is a country with no military ambitions. Yet war has played a large part in our evolution as an independent nation. We won recognition and respect in two world wars, and peacekeeping gives us a distinctive role in the world.

The Canadians who went off to war in August, 1914, were mainly untrained soldiers. They had enlisted for many reasons, most honourable, some not. Many were patriots or adventurers, but there were also men fleeing their wives or evading the law. There were vastly more English-speakers than francophones, for this "British" war appealed more to some in Canada than others. Indeed, it appealed most to those who had been born in Britain itself—in fact, two-thirds of the first contingent to go overseas had been born there. Not until the end of the war did the Canadian-born composition of the Canadian Expeditionary Force exceed 50 per cent, and regretfully few were French-speaking.

But the war made all the soldiers who served into Canadians. The experience of the trenches helped erase the differences that separated the Nova Scotia fisherman from the Vancouver salesclerk. Even if he had been born in Edinburgh, the private in the 42nd Battalion discovered he was no longer British. He thought differently, he employed different fighting tactics, and he became closer to the man in the Canadian regiment next in the line than to his brother in the British Army.

Raising the Canadian Expeditionary Force and creating the Canadian Corps at the front was Canada's greatest achievement since Confederation. To recruit 650,000 men, equip and train them, and weld them into an effective fighting force took a massive national effort. To do this in the face of the huge casualties in the trenches made it even more challenging. But Canada did it—and in the process, Canada became a nation.

The key event occurred on Easter Monday, 1917. Fighting with four divisions together for the first time, the Canadian Corps launched a perfectly planned and executed assault on the German position on Vimy Ridge in the northern industrial area of France. The high ridge looked out over German-occupied France, and the enemy, seeing its value, had fortified the line so strongly that earlier assaults from the British and French had been hurled back.

Not this time. The Canadian artillery, using techniques developed by a McGill University engineering professor and lieutenant-colonel named Andy McNaughton, targeted German gun positions and destroyed them in the days before the assault. Using new tactics largely developed by the general commanding the First Division, a Victoria militiaman named Arthur Currie, the soldiers of the Corps had been trained to perfection, briefed on what they faced and instructed on how to overcome the enemy positions in front of them.

The Corps' early morning attack, 19,200 men in eight brigades,

directed by Lt.-Gen. Sir Julian Byng, their British commander, went in under cover of a creeping artillery barrage, and the Corps swept everything before it along most of the line. The Germans, their front-line soldiers unhinged by the explosions or killed in their dugouts, fell back, giving up their hitherto impregnable position.

In Britain, the United States and Canada, the victory was hailed as the greatest set-piece battle of the war. The Canadian Corps had done something the British and French could not do and, even if the 10,602 killed and wounded had been a terrible price to pay, the soldiers' pride was enormous. So, too, was Canada's. The headline on *The Globe* in Toronto on April 10 said it all: "Canadians lead in triumph." As *Maclean's* reader Roy Bartlett of Windsor, Ont., observed in response to the editors' request for suggestions for this July 1 issue, "Other nations suddenly took notice that this quiet, orderly country was for real."

The taking of Vimy Ridge led to no Allied breakthrough, however, and the war dragged on until Nov. 11, 1918. But soldiers at the time, and historians since, have argued that the victory on Easter Monday, 1917, was the key to making Canada a nation. Currie wrote that those who died in action had "no provincial prejudices and no racial suspicion in their heart . . . there was no Quebec and no Ontario . . . but one great country." If only it had remained so.

Reprinted from *Maclean's*, July 1, 1999, with the permission of the authors.

Canada Revisited

Vimy Ridge War Memorial

—by Glen BonBernard

 Vimy Ridge today looks like a well cared for park. Nowhere will you see deep shell holes filled with mud, water, the wounded, and the dead. Nowhere will you smell the odour of exploded shell or decomposed bodies. Nowhere will you hear the sounds of rifle, machine gun, artillery, or the screams of the wounded. What you will find today is an impressive memorial to the ordinary Canadians who went through a terrible ordeal in the name of Canada.*

The front line trenches were surprisingly close to each other. The Canadian trench is indicated by the flag in the background.

The remains of shell holes in the churned-up, treeless land are now covered with grass and trees. One tree was brought from Canada and planted for every Canadian who died at Vimy Ridge. (Compare this picture with page 308.)

The Vimy Ridge memorial was completed in 1936 on land given by France to Canada for the purpose.

Cemetery at Vimy Ridge

For Your Notebook

1. Review pages 306 to 313, The War on Land. Create a web of information about trench warfare in World War I.

2. Make a concept poster about the Battle of Vimy Ridge.

3. In your notes, identify examples of fact and opinion provided in the magazine article reprinted on Vimy Ridge on page 312. This article is an opinion piece in which authors take a stand. What is the stand they take?

*For more information, check this website: http://www.vac-acc.gc.ca/general/sub.cfm?source=history/firstwar/vimy

The War in the Air

The airplane was very new technology at the time of World War I.* However, the airplane came to play a role in World War I. At the beginning of the war, airplanes were used for surveying enemy territory. Pilots would report their findings of enemy movements so that the aim of artillery guns could be adjusted to be more effective.

Later, airplanes took on new roles. They were equipped for combat with other planes. Airplanes were also used to attack ground forces with machine guns and bombs. Some towns and cities were also bombed. The airplane was also used in anti-submarine warfare. Pilots spotted and tracked submarines. They reported their positions to war and merchant ships and bombed submarines that surfaced.

Canada did not have an air force of its own. A large number of Canadians chose to volunteer for the British Royal Flying Corps. At the beginning of the war, those who wanted to serve as pilots left Canada and trained in Great Britain. Later, pilots would receive some training at centres across Canada.

In this painting, Canadian pilot C.W.R. Nevinson is attacking three enemy aircraft.

*The Wright brothers' experimental airplane the *Kitty Hawk* had its first flight in 1903, and Douglas McCurdy first flew the *Silver Dart* in Nova Scotia in 1909.

Serving as a pilot was a dangerous job. The average life span of a pilot in active service was a few short weeks. Some flyers were more lucky and beat the odds. A pilot was considered an "ace" after shooting down five enemy aircraft.

Canadians played a major role in the British air force. Nearly one-third of Great Britain's air force was made up of Canadians.

The War at Sea

During the early war years, the British and German naval forces did not fight in open combat. In 1915, Germany began to use a new weapon, the submarine. Over the next two years, German submarines, called U-boats (undersea boats), sank a great number of British and Allied merchant and war ships. The sinkings included the British passenger liner, *Lusitania*, on May 7, 1915. Over 1198 people died, including 128 United States citizens.

Great Britain and the Allies depended heavily on food, war materials, and other supplies from world markets. German U-boats were a serious threat to these supply lines. Great Britain decided to further strengthen its navy. It leased some American destroyers and built submarines and more warships. Merchant ships needed protection, so Great Britain began to use warships to escort them. This convoy system proved to be somewhat effective in reducing the loss of merchant ships.

Canada's navy in 1914 consisted of only two ships, not intended for war purposes, manned by 350 men. By 1918, the navy had grown to 112 warships. These ships, under the command of a British Royal Navy officer, were manned by about 9000 men.

The main duty of the Canadian navy was to protect Canada's eastern and western coastlines. They particularly watched for German submarines. Some Canadians joined the Royal British Navy and were actively involved in combat at sea.

Germany's policy in the North Atlantic was to sink any ship that wasn't their own entering British waters, whether it was a passenger, merchant, or warship.

Many Canadians and Newfoundlanders were recognized for their contributions in World War I. Not all were involved in combat. The ones on this page are just a few examples.

Billy Bishop, an air "ace," was born in Owen Sound, Ontario. In 170 air battles, Bishop claimed 72 downed enemy aircraft. Bishop received the Victoria Cross for his single-handed dawn attack on a German airfield.

Roy Brown is often credited with shooting down Germany's leading "ace," Baron von Richthofen, the famous Red Baron.

Sixteen-year-old **Thomas Ricketts**, from the colony of Newfoundland, claimed to be eighteen and served in the Royal Newfoundland Regiment. For bravery in battle and saving the lives of many of his comrades, he was awarded the Victoria Cross.

Sir Arthur Currie was born in Napperton, Ontario. Currie completed his schooling there before moving to British Columbia to teach school, then run a real estate business. A longtime member of the Canadian militia, he became brigade commander of the first troops to go overseas. He saw action at Ypres, Somme, and Vimy Ridge before being given command of the Canadian Corps. His men distinguished themselves at Passchendaele and other battles in the final months of the war. Currie was knighted by King George V in France, June 1917. Between 1920 and 1930 he was principal of McGill University.

English-born **George Pearkes** emigrated to Canada, where he homesteaded on the Prairies before joining the Mounties in the Yukon. He volunteered for the army early in the war. For acts of bravery at Passchendaele he was awarded the Victoria Cross. He again served his country in World War II. Between 1957 and 1960, he was Canada's minister of defence. In 1960, he was appointed lieutenant-governor of British Columbia.

About 2500 Canadian women volunteered for gruelling and dangerous jobs overseas, serving as military nurses, assistant nurses, ambulance drivers, and doing other work. **Grace McPherson** was one of the first Vancouver women to own a car. After her brother and boyfriend were killed in the war, she volunteered overseas. In England, she was one of four Canadians to be selected as an ambulance driver. She was sent to Etaples, France, where she maintained her ambulance and worked shifts of 12 hours or more, driving wounded soldiers to hospitals.

Francis Pegahmagabow (no photo available) was an Ojibwa from Ontario who received more decorations than any other Aboriginal soldier. He received the Military Medal and two bars for bravery.

The Victoria Cross

The highest military decoration awarded by the British for bravery was the Victoria Cross. Seventy men serving in Canadian forces, or Canadians serving in other forces, in World War I were awarded the Victoria Cross. (The Victoria Cross is shown on the back cover of this textbook.)

On the Homefront

An All-out Effort

  Having so many of the young and able-bodied fighting in Europe made great demands on all other Canadians. Canadian women and men of all ages contributed to Canada's war effort.

To overcome the labour shortage, many older Canadians returned to work. Some took up full-time farming or became part of Canada's labour force, working in factories.

Women worked on farms, haying and harvesting, as part of the war effort.

In 1918, approximately 350 000 people, mainly women, were working in war factories. New factories were built to produce weapons, aircraft, and trucks for the war in Europe.

In most schools, young people were involved in many activities: knitting scarves and small squares which were pieced together to create blankets; planting vegetables in Victory Gardens; parading in cadet corps using broomstick guns; making and selling bazaar items to raise funds. Almost 12 000 boys between the ages of 15 and 19 enrolled in the Soldiers of the Land program. They worked on farms, doing a range of chores and helping produce food for the soldiers in Europe.

Women carried a large share of responsibility for supporting the war effort on the homefront. They often had jobs, while also looking after families and communities, usually without their husbands and other men.

As the men left to go overseas, women stepped in to take their jobs. They expected most of these jobs to be temporary, but many welcomed the opportunity to work outside the home. Over 30 000 women took on roles previously filled by men.* Women worked in machine shops, metal foundries, textile factories, munitions plants, aircraft factories, and shipyards. Women worked on buses, in police forces and the civil service, for banks, law offices, and insurance companies, as well as on farms.

Not all women worked outside the home. Some served the country by joining organizations that helped the men overseas. They did fundraising, knitted socks, scarves, and gloves, wrote letters, visited soldiers' families, and created food parcels. They hoped, prayed, and tried to remain optimistic, because morale was also important on the homefront.

Aboriginal communities actively contributed to the war effort. They made donations to relief and patriotic funds, sent parcels to men overseas, and were active in Canadian Red Cross Societies.

Groups like this one got together to knit for the armed forces. Trench warfare in the wet winter was terrible for the soldiers' feet, and warm, dry socks were greatly appreciated.

*Although women did the work of men they were often paid half the wage.

Women working in a munitions factory in Quebec. During the war women worked at jobs traditionally held by men. War-related industries needed more and more workers to keep up production of the weapons and ammunition needed at the front.

Industry

An enormous effort was made to manufacture products needed for the war. Weapons and ammunition, cloth for uniforms, and hundreds of other products had to be sent to Europe. It gave a huge boost to the Canadian economy (as the graph shows). However, it was funded by creating a large national debt.

Food was needed for the troops. Bread and meat were easiest to transport. Meat processing plants made millions of cans of tinned meat. At home, people were encouraged to eat more fish and vegetables. Posters like the one on page 305 appealed to people to use less food, so more would be available for the armed forces.

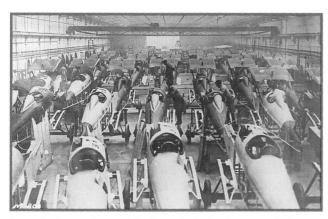

Many factories changed their products to those needed in wartime, such as bullets, shell cases, and airplane parts.

Increase in Canadian Exports

Beef	6755%
Cheese	300%
Pork	535%
Wheat	2183%

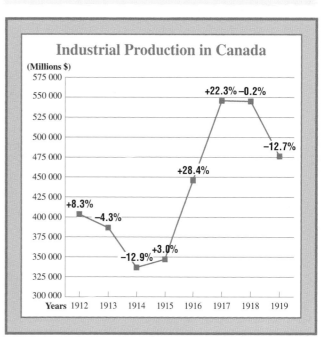

Industrial Production in Canada

(Millions $)

Years: 1912 (+8.3%), 1913 (−4.3%), 1914 (−12.9%), 1915 (+3.0%), 1916 (+28.4%), 1917 (+22.3%), 1918 (−0.2%), 1919 (−12.7%)

Financing the War

The people of Canada were expected to put the war effort before their own needs. Wasting anything, particularly food or money, was unpatriotic, and everyone was expected to contribute.

A considerable amount of money was needed to pay for the war. At first, Canada obtained loans from the United States and depended heavily on donations from organizations. Then Canada turned to its own citizens. Victory Bonds and Thrift Stamps brought in well over $600 million. Buying government bonds was like lending money to the government. Even children saved money by buying Thrift Stamps, which could be cashed in after the war. Over one billion dollars in war bonds were purchased. Canadian businesses also loaned money to the government. Canadians contributed $47 million to the Canadian Patriotic Fund.

The government set extra taxes. In 1917, they introduced income tax, which was supposed to be a temporary measure. The government also borrowed money directly from financial institutions in the United States. This created a "national debt" of over one billion dollars. This was money that the people of Canada would need to pay back. By 1918, the war was costing Canada over one million dollars per day. As of March of 1919, the total cost of the war had reached about 1.3 billion dollars.

The Halifax Explosion

Canadians on the homefront knew little first-hand about the horrors of battle. The Halifax explosion brought the war to their doorstep. On December 6, 1917, a French munitions vessel, the *Mont Blanc*, collided with the Belgium relief steamer, *Imo*, in the narrowest stretch of the Halifax harbour. Sparks from the collision ignited oil on the deck of the *Mont Blanc*. The fire spread to the holds below. Almost 3000 tons of explosive material, including TNT, was stored there.

The resulting explosion levelled a square mile of city along the city's north waterfront. It claimed the lives of 1630 people, injured thousands, and left 6000 of the city's 50 000 people homeless. Many of the city's industries were also demolished, including the naval dockyard, the railway station, and the sugar refinery. Wharves, breweries, printing houses, foundries, and warehouses were all flattened.

The devastation of the Halifax explosion had to be cleared away immediately, because the harbour and naval base were needed for the war effort.

For Your Notebook

1. Almost 12 000 boys between the ages of 15 and 19 enrolled in Soldiers of the Land.
   a) How did this activity help the war effort?
   b) What type of work did these boys do? Why?
   c) Create a visual poster encouraging boys to join this organization. (Boys were paid for this work. Those who gave three months of their time also received a bronze medal.)

2. a) Prior to World War I, women had traditional roles. What types of work did they do?
   b) How did the situation change during World War I? Provide reasons why.

3. a) The Canadian government raised money for the war through the sale of Victory Bonds. What were these?
   b) In an attempt to raise still more money, in 1917 the government introduced an income tax as a temporary measure. Was this tax temporary?
   c) Describe national debt. How would it be repaid?

The Halifax explosion was one of the worst disasters in Canadian history.

City of Toronto Archives, SC244-2450

Focus On: War Poetry, Songs, and Paintings

In Flanders Fields

In Flanders fields the poppies blow
Between the crosses, row on row,
That mark our place; and in the sky
The larks, still bravely singing, fly
Scarce heard amid the guns below.

We are the Dead. Short days ago
We lived, felt dawn, saw sunset glow,
Loved, and were loved, and now we lie
      In Flanders fields.

Take up our quarrel with the foe:
To you from failing hands we throw
The torch; be yours to hold it high.
If ye break faith with us who die
We shall not sleep, though poppies grow
      In Flanders fields.

—John McCrae
(Written during the second battle of Ypres)

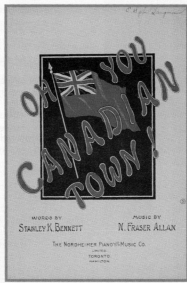

Many songs from World War I were either cheerful or sentimental. People did not wish to be reminded of the terrible losses of life that were occurring in Europe. They wished to believe that the war would be won, and those they loved would return home safely.

Artists

Artists who saw action in the battlefields painted some of the most powerful images that remain from that time.

1. Richard Jack (page 311)
2. Arthur Nantel
3. Alfred Bastien
4. Louis Keene
5. A.Y. Jackson
6. Frederick Varley
7. David Milne
8. Kenneth Forbes

John McCrae, born in Guelph, Ontario, was a doctor who enlisted in the Canadian Medical Corps. He wrote "In Flanders Fields" May 13, 1915, in the Ypres battlefield, after the death of a good friend. The poem has been read at Remembrance Day Services ever since World War I ended.

Song Hits From 1900–1920

Bill Bailey, Won't You Please Come Home

Give My Regards to Broadway

In the Good Old Summertime

In My Merry Oldsmobile

Wait Till the Sun Shines, Nellie

The Yankee Doodle Boy

Rock-a-Bye Your Baby With a Dixie Melody

How 'Ya Gonna Keep 'Em Down on the Farm (After They're Seen Paree?)

It's a Long, Long Way to Tipperary

Let Me Call You Sweetheart (I'm In Love With You)

Exploring Further

1. Use paintings, poetry, and songs from World War I as research sources. What did you learn about the war from these references? What feelings do the artists and poets portray?

- For information on John McCrae, contact Veteran Affairs: http://www.vac-acc.gc.ca/general/sub.cfm?source=history/firstwar/mccrae

- For WWI paintings at the Canadian War Museum contact: http://www.cmcc.muse.digital.ca/cwm/cwmeng/cwmeng.html

The Conscription Issue

  By late 1916, Canada had raised an army of nearly 500 000 volunteers. One-sixth of Canada's eligible men volunteered for the army. Thousands more volunteered to serve in the artillery, engineering, railway units, medical corps, Royal Flying Corps, Royal Canadian Navy, and the Royal British Navy. Some recent immigrants left Canada and returned to Great Britain to volunteer for the British army.

By 1917, sources of new volunteers began to dwindle. The number of volunteers was not keeping up to the number of Canadian men killed or wounded. Canadians were deeply divided about whether the government should introduce conscription. It was seen as a threat to national unity. Under conscription, able-bodied men who had not volunteered to join the army could legally be forced to do so. Exceptions could be made for individuals who could show they were indispensable at home or to the war effort in Canada.

For Your Notebook

1. Use a chart like the one on page 353 of the Appendix to make notes on the points of view in Quebec and elsewhere in Canada on the conscription issue (pages 320 to 324).

Points of View

In Quebec

At the beginning of the war, most English and French Canadians generally supported Canada's war effort. A smaller proportion of French-speaking Canadians volunteered to fight in Europe. One French-speaking regiment, the 22nd Battalion (known as the Vandoos), was raised entirely in Quebec. However, many French Canadians opposed the war, and their anti-war feelings were strong. Over the next few years, French Canadians, led by Henri Bourassa, began to oppose Canada's war efforts. There were a number of reasons for this:

- Many French Canadians viewed the war as a British war. They felt Canada was wrong in its whole-hearted response to supporting Great Britain. They felt the Central Powers were not a threat to Canada.
- Many French Canadian families had lived in Canada for several hundred years. They felt no strong ties to either Great Britain or France.
- Many French Canadians believed that English Canada did not respect them or their culture. They felt they had not been treated well since Confederation.

Autonomous—self-governing, able to act independently

- Sam Hughes, the minister of militia and defence, had created few Quebec regiments and appointed few French Canadian officers to important commands. He also made English the sole language of the army. Protestant clergy were used to recruit French Canadians in Quebec and to provide religious service to Roman Catholic soldiers serving in the war.

Elsewhere in Canada

Conscription was opposed by many English Canadians as well, but some felt it was necessary.

- Many Canadians felt that Canada had already contributed more soldiers in proportion to its population than either Great Britain or France, and no more should be sent.
- Many felt that the production of food and war materials was as important to the war effort as combat was, so more men could not be spared.
- Canadians were aware of the terrible losses of Canadian lives in European trenches. Some did not want further lives lost.
- The original reasons for going to war were still true for many: the patriotic need to support Great Britain and the need to oppose aggression against free democracies.
- Many Canadians felt that Canada could not reduce its commitment to the war in Europe because of the danger to the Canadians already fighting there, or in memory of those who had already died.
- Resentment grew because fewer volunteers came from French Canada.

Imperial Conference of 1917

 In early 1917, Great Britain's new prime minister, David Lloyd George, invited the dominions to attend an Imperial Conference. In a surprising move, he chose to consult with them and invited them to sit as full members of the British War Cabinet. The War Cabinet was responsible for decisions about running Great Britain's war effort. This invitation recognized the contribution the dominions were making.

At this conference, Canada's Prime Minister Sir Robert Borden proposed some important changes to the British Empire. He wanted the dominions to be recognized as **autonomous** nations and to have a voice in Great Britain's foreign policy. Great Britain did not object, but would not discuss the request at that time.

Following the conference, Borden visited Canadian soldiers in training and in hospitals in England. He also went to France, where he visited Canadian soldiers on the front lines. While there, Borden decided that conscription had to be introduced.

Military Service Act

On June 11, 1917, Borden introduced the Military Service Act to Canada's House of Commons. A short but angry debate followed. In his political party, only four French-speaking Conservatives failed to support Borden. Laurier strongly opposed conscription. The Military Service Act was passed by 102 votes to 44. On August 28, 1917, the Military Service Act became law. The Act made military service compulsory for all able-bodied male Canadians between the ages of 20 and 34. Some exceptions were made for those in essential war industries, **conscientious objectors**, and those whose families might experience great hardship if they were conscripted.

The issue of conscription not only divided the politicians, it divided the country. Some strongly opposed it. Some strongly supported it. Farmers generally opposed it. Conscription would take away more of their sons and hired men needed for their farms. Labour leaders opposed conscription. They felt factory workers were making an important contribution to the war. The loss of conscripted workers would severely limit Canada's production of food and wartime supplies. Labour leaders considered calling a general strike. Many farmers and labour leaders were English Canadians. The strongest opponents of conscription, however, were the French Canadians. They had little enthusiasm for World War I. In Montreal and other parts of Quebec, anti-conscription riots occurred during the summer of 1917. Quebec's less enthusiastic participation in the war effort was not understood by most English-speaking Canadians.

An anti-conscription march in Montreal on Victoria Day in 1917

Conscientious objectors—those who refuse to join the military because of their religious or moral beliefs
Rebuttal—argument that responds to and counters an opponent's argument

A Debate on Conscription

Review pages 320 to 323. The points of view on pages 322 and 323 are based on opinions of people at the time. (See also pages 353 and 354.) Debate the following issue:

The government of Canada should introduce conscription.

Step 1:
Your teacher will divide the class into three-person teams and organize them into pairs of opposing teams. In each pair one team will support the issue (Pro) and one oppose it (Con). The following format has been set for three-person teams, but may be adapted.

Step 2:
Each team reviews the material from pages 320 to 323 and makes notes on information that can be used to support their team's position on the issue. It is important to also anticipate what the opponents' arguments are likely to be so that you can rebut them (show why they are not right). **Rebuttal** is as important as argument. Plan your debate as a team so that you don't repeat each other and your team gives all the possible arguments for (or against) the issue.

Step 3:
Each pair of teams carries out its debate, following the rules of debating. One format is provided below:
1. First Pro Speaker—introduction; define terms; give opening argument
2. First Con Speaker—summarize opposing argument; give rebuttal; give your team's first argument
3. Second Pro Speaker—summarize previous Pro argument; rebut Con argument; give your team's second argument
4. Second Con Speaker—summarize debate points; rebut pro argument; give your team's second argument
5. Third Pro Speaker—summarize previous points; rebut Con arguments; conclude your team's arguments
6. Third Con Speaker—summarize previous points, rebut Pro Arguments; conclude your team's argument

Viewpoints on Conscription

Lucy

- a Regina mother of 3 sons (51)

The British Empire is a big family. When a member of the family is attacked by an outsider, I think it is only right to support them. It's hard to see our boys go but it's the right thing to do. My son, Jim, gave his life to preserve the Empire. I'm proud of him. If the Allies lose the war from lack of men, he will have died for nothing. We must win.

Martha

- a Toronto housewife (48)

This conscription law is not right. They shouldn't be able to just come in and take away our sons. My Robert is studying law at the university. In two more years he will finish his degree. His father worked long hours to build what we have, which one day will be Robert's. We can offer the government money for the war effort. I am doing considerable volunteer work. Shouldn't this be enough?

Claudette

- an Ontario French Canadian bus driver (25)

Canada has already sent more than 500 000 soldiers to be slaughtered. Will a few thousand more who are forced to go overseas make a big difference? If they choose to go, that is their right. Don't, however, force them. They won't make good soldiers.

Marcel

- an urban French Canadian (22)

I won't go! It's not our war. Canada should never have gotten involved in the first place. If the English Canadians want to fight that's their business. We French Canadians are not interested in fighting Britain's war. My friends and I plan to go up north where they won't be able to find us.

Johnson

- a Protestant clergy (52)

Borden is going to enact a just and necessary law. Granted, we do not wish to see our young go off to war. But, the fate of democracy is at stake. It is our duty to God and the King to come to Britain's assistance. Our boys have already gone, believing it to be the right thing to do. Now they need our help. Will we let them down? No! Canadians are not cowards. We will fight to enjoy a just victory.

Bill

- a Quebec construction worker (24)

My family left Europe only eight years ago. I guess if we had stayed there, I'd already be involved in the war. Probably as a soldier. I love this new country. As Papa says, it's been good to us. Now I have a good job. I guess I owe the country something in return, so I will support conscription if that is what the government wants.

Olaf

- a recent immigrant (49)

Our faith rejects war as a means of solving problems. We are forbidden to fight. We don't know what to do. If we declare ourselves conscientious objectors, my eldest son, Jacob and I lose the right to vote to defeat the government. If we don't make a declaration, Jacob can be forced to go. Governments shouldn't pass such laws. God wants men to live in peace, not to wage war.

Sarah

- a Manitoba farm wife (62)

It's about time they passed a conscription law. Now everyone will have to fight just like our boys. My sons joined up even though we needed them here on the farm. My husband is too sick to work in the fields, but the government cries out for wheat to feed the troops. I just want this war to be over.

Frank

• a Nova Scotia artist (30)

I got away from the continual unrest in Europe to come to a country that was peaceful. There are opportunities here that were not available to me there. Now Canada wants me to fight. No other dominion of the Empire has conscription, nor is planning it. What kind of a country is this anyway? It's a dictatorship; that's what it is.

Wilma

• retired; emigrated to Canada in 1910 (69)

The Americans had it right. They didn't enter the war until they felt themselves threatened. Had we waited instead of sending troops in 1914, Canada could have saved the lives of thousands of our men. Millions of dollars could have been saved if Canada had done like the Americans and offered only token support. We've already done more than enough.

Hilda

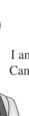

• a British Columbia secretary (31)

I can't say I support the idea of being part of the British Empire. I think Canada should be free of Great Britain. Yet, my parents still live there and if Germany wins the war, I guess we would become part of the German Empire. Will we be any more free then? No. I say, let's fight, then ask Great Britain for our total independence.

Charlie

• a Labour leader (38)

Borden promised us there would be no conscription. I believed him. He should not break his promises. Our men at home are supporting our men overseas and the Allied cause. The mines and factories at home require their labour. Without them our men overseas will not be able to do their jobs.

Pierre

• a French Canadian farmer (30)

I am French Canadian, but also I am Canadian. I know many French Canadians are most unhappy about conscription. I wouldn't want to say this out loud but I think they are wrong. This is a good country where French and English could live side by side and be friends. Both of our mother countries are suffering in Europe and we should help end it.

Tom

• an Alberta Metis soldier, serving overseas (19)

We need help. We are exhausted, and many who have had injuries or been sick are still here doing their duty. We believe we can and will succeed against the Central Powers but we need more fighting men to hold the line and push the enemy back. Don't let us down. Choose conscription.

Mary

• an Ontario factory worker (29)

Finally Borden got it right. It angers me to see all the younger men in the factory doing work that we are capable of doing. They claim they are necessary. Hah! They don't work any harder or faster then I do. Furthermore, we women are paid less. It's not a good enough excuse for them not to volunteer. So let conscription come—we women can handle the homefront.

Jeanette

• a French Canadian writer (40)

For Canada to succeed, French and English must understand each other. The English have never really attempted to understand us. They have always wanted to make Canada an English country. French Canadians must continue to demonstrate to the English that we are not interested in being involved in an European war. Attempts to force us to serve the English cause cannot and will not succeed.

The Election of 1917

Borden had to face an election in 1917. He expected the issue of conscription would play a major role in this election. To win the election, and to ensure conscription, he decided to form a coalition. He asked Laurier to join. Laurier refused, but Borden was able to attract some well-known Liberals to his cause. By the autumn of 1917 Borden formed the Union Party, which he would lead into the election.

The new Union Party knew they would face a difficult election against Laurier's Liberal Party. To ensure a Union Party victory, and a victory for conscription, Borden introduced and passed several bills:
- The Military Voters Act **enfranchised** all members of the Canadian armed forces, including nurses and other women serving overseas.*
- The Wartime Elections Act enfranchised mothers, wives, daughters, and sisters of soldiers.

Members of the armed forces and their families were more likely to support a Union government and conscription.

Conscientious objectors and people born in enemy countries who were recent immigrants to Canada were disenfranchised. These groups would have been unlikely to support Borden's party.

This photograph of Canadian nurses voting in the 1917 federal election was taken in France.

All members of the Canadian armed forces were given the vote in the 1917 Election.

Election posters such as this encouraged troops to vote for conscription.

The Union Party passed the Military Service Act in August prior to the election. Then Borden called an election and the Union Party won a clear victory. After the election the act was enforced. In the months that followed, thousands were selected to report for military training. Those who refused were considered deserters and faced a prison term of five years of hard labour. Over 80% appealed to be made exempt under the rules of the Military Service Act. The most commonly used reason given was that it would create hardships for their families. A large number of those exemptions were approved. A few whose appeals were denied simply disappeared.

Of the 100 000 men conscripted, only 24 000 reached the battlefield in Europe before the war ended in November 1918.

For Your Notebook

1. a) What is conscription?
    b) Prime Minister Borden promised that his government would never introduce conscription. Did he keep this promise? Why?
    c) How did the Canadian public react to the Military Service Act (conscription)?
2. a) Provide several examples where Canadians had been divided over issues in the years prior to World War I.
    b) How did the issue of conscription (the Military Service Act) add to divisions between groups or regions?
3. 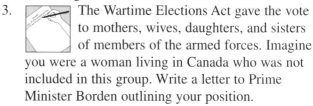 The Wartime Elections Act gave the vote to mothers, wives, daughters, and sisters of members of the armed forces. Imagine you were a woman living in Canada who was not included in this group. Write a letter to Prime Minister Borden outlining your position.

Enfranchise—to give the right to vote in elections
*Aboriginal members of the armed forces had the right to vote during the war but did not keep it (under the rules of the Indian Act) after they returned home.

Conclusion of World War I

The Treaty of Versailles

  World War I ended, but a peace treaty was not immediately signed. Peace talks took place months later in Versailles, France. At the peace talks, Borden insisted that the dominions in the British Empire be represented both as almost-independent countries and as part of the British Empire. This was rejected. A compromise was worked out. The dominions were allowed representation by non-voting delegates. Borden also insisted that Canada sign the peace treaty. This, too, was rejected. Again a compromise was worked out. The British delegates signed for the British Empire and each dominion signed below their signatures. The Dominion of Canada achieved increased status as an almost-independent country as a result of its participation in the peace talks.

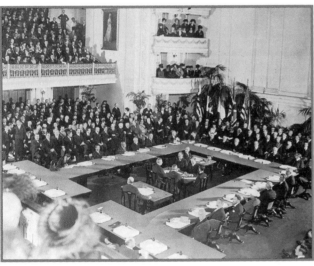

Representatives at the Peace Table in Paris in 1919 deciding on terms of the peace treaty

The Treaty of Versailles was signed on June 28, 1919, formally ending World War I. The terms affecting the former Central Powers included severe punishment for Germany.

- Germany was forced to accept blame for the war.
- Germany was forced to pay reparations (costs for damages caused by the war).
- Germany was forced to give up some territory.
- Germany was forced to substantially reduce its military strength of men, weapons, and supplies.
- Germany was to permit Allied troops to remain in Germany for a period of time.

Cost of World War I

Casualties

The cost of the war in human lives was enormous. Almost 15 000 000 persons, military and civilian, from both sides were killed. Another 7 000 000 were listed as prisoners or missing, and over 21 000 000 were wounded.

Canadian casualties included over 60 000 men and women who died, and over 173 000 who were wounded or gassed. Many would live in veterans' hospitals for years, some for the remainder of their lives.

Financial Costs

The total cost of the war on both sides was estimated to have reached over $200 billion. The almost $2 billion that Canada paid was staggering, considering Canada's population and stage of economic development. These costs included recruiting, training, and transporting men and women to Europe; providing for their daily needs; paying wages; and providing them with the supplies and equipment to fight the war. This sum also included financial support to Great Britain and donations given by a number of organizations to Canadian and British soldiers.

League of Nations

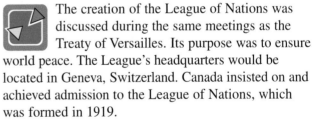 The creation of the League of Nations was discussed during the same meetings as the Treaty of Versailles. Its purpose was to ensure world peace. The League's headquarters would be located in Geneva, Switzerland. Canada insisted on and achieved admission to the League of Nations, which was formed in 1919.

Canada also insisted on admission to the International Labour Organization, also discussed in the Treaty of Versailles meetings. This was also granted. Canada's contributions during World War I were recognized. Canada was gaining respect from other countries as a country in its own right.

Review

The icons are your cue to refer to the Learning How to Learn Appendix (pages 348–371) for ideas on how to complete these activities.

1. Complete a self-assessment for one assignment from this chapter.

Understanding Concepts

2. At the beginning of the chapter, you created an overview/prediction chart. Fill out the "What I Learned" section.

3. Use one of the suggested methods for recording vocabulary (see page 369) to add any unfamiliar words from this chapter to the WordBook section of your notes.

4. Here are some of the main ideas from this chapter:
   - trench warfare
   - propaganda
   - homefront
   - conscription
   - enfranchise/disenfranchise

   Do either a) or b).

   a) Create a concept poster for one of these ideas. Present it to the class.

   b)   Use a web, mind map, outline, or chart to create a permanent set of notes about one of the ideas. Explain your work to a classmate.

5. a) Predict how countries in the world might have viewed and interacted with Canada differently following World War I. Why?

   b) The concepts of power, identity, and conflict have been the focus of this chapter. Create a web of examples in this chapter of these concepts.

   c) It has been said that as a result of World War I Canada had a new sense of itself as a nation. What does this mean? Which of the concepts (pages 24, 28, 29) used in this textbook best applies to this statement?

6. Add entries for this chapter to your timeline.

7. **Who Are We?** As a class discuss the three Section IV Focus questions on the easel on page 269 as they apply to Chapter 12 (the 1914–1918 time period).

Developing Research Skills

8.

   Section IV Activity

   Writing Historical Fiction

   1. In role, write an entry in your History Journal about Canadian identity and how you feel about Canada in 1918, after the war has ended.

   2. If you haven't done so already, complete the project you started on page 299.

9. Why was the victory at Vimy Ridge so important for Canada as a country? In what way did the battle focus attention on Canada's contributions to the war effort?

10. Research the accomplishments of women who were nurses, ambulance drivers, and otherwise served at the front.

11. The fear of war and the war itself resulted in technological advances. What technological advances preceded the war and occurred during the war?

   a) Some are mentioned in the text. Research others. How did *one* of these alter the war effort?

   b) Imagine the company you work for has been contracted to design some specialized equipment for soldiers in the trenches. Describe an item which would have improved comfort or offered better chances of survival to the soldiers.

Developing Communication Skills

Reading

12. Read "Over the Top" at http://www.civilization.ca/cwm/overtop/otopinte.html

Writing

13. For many of the soldiers, a comforting activity was writing letters home to loved ones. Their letters were carefully censored to ensure that no information was provided to the enemy.

    a) From the trenches at the Battle of Somme, write a letter to a friend or family member in Canada.

    b) Share your letter with a classmate. Her/his job is to censor your letter by using a black felt pen.

    c) When you receive your letter back, discuss with the censor the reason for making these deletions.

Listening and Speaking

14. Write and give a patriotic speech encouraging young men to enlist in the War.

15. Locate the words to the songs *La Marseillaise* or *Rule Britannia*. Why were these songs especially popular during the first few months of World War I? What does this music tell you about the feelings (mood) of the Canadian public?

16. Visit the Royal Canadian Legion building in your area and interview a member about the significance of Remembrance Day. Plan a Remembrance Day program that could be presented at your school. See page 355 in the Appendix for interviewing techniques.

Viewing and Representing

17. The cartoon to the right appeared during the election of 1917.

    a) In what way did war cartoons encourage people to support the war effort? What message is the cartoonist trying to get across?

    b) Is the cartoonist anti-conscription or pro-conscription?

HE'LL WANT TO KNOW

"Daddy, how did you vote in the Big War Election?"

"Daddy, how did you vote in the Big War Election?"

18. Using sand, plasticine, or papier-maché, build a model of the trench system.

Applying Concepts

19. Today the Canadian government decides for itself whether it will go to war or not and which countries it will support or form alliances with. If Canada declared war today in a situation similar to World War I, would you volunteer? Give your reasons.

20. Find examples in your newspaper of modern-day wars or military rivalry resulting from

    a) imperialism

    b) nationalism

    c) militarism (arms race)

21. How do we remember our war heroes today? What are memorials? Why are they important today? Should Canada continue to celebrate November 11? Why or why not? Interview five adults and share your results with your class.

National War Memorial in Ottawa with the Parliament Buildings in the background
(http://www.harrypalmergallery.ab.ca/galwartom/natwar.html)

Chapter 13

A Changed Canada

1914–1920

O v e r v i e w

Use this Overview to predict what you will read in this chapter.

3 The growth of labour unions led to better wages and working conditions. Some clashes between workers and employers led to violence, as in the 1919 Winnipeg General Strike.

1 Those involved in World War I returned home to a very changed Canada.

5 Due to the efforts of suffragists across the country, Canadian women earned the right to vote.

4 Farm and labour movements led to the development of new political parties in several provinces.

2 Canada was changing from a largely rural, agricultural country to an urban, industrial country.

Chapter 13 Focus

Chapter 12 dealt with World War I. There is some overlap between this chapter and Chapter 12. The years after the war were ones of unrest and discontent, resulting in major changes. Chapter 13 focuses on changes the soldiers returned to when they came home from World War I. While all the book's concepts will be examined, the focus of this chapter is on change, power, identity, and conflict.

Change   Regionalism   Power   Identity   Conflict

Other Concepts and Main Topics

- economic downturn
- flu epidemic
- growth of cities
- labour unrest
- labour unions
- agrarian discontent
- discrimination
- minorities
- enfranchisement
- suffragist

Learning How to Learn

 Research

 Writing

 Role-playing

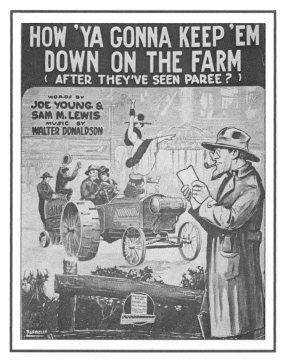

The popular song "How 'Ya Gonna Keep 'Em Down on the Farm" was a light-hearted treatment of a serious post-war issue. The lyrics are printed on page 332.

Chapter Preview/Prediction

Throughout your study of *Canada Revisited 8* you have been asked to use a variety of methods to preview the chapter and make predictions on the chapter's content. Select one of these methods and preview Chapter 13.

Chapter Activities

1. Do either a) or b).
   a) Brainstorm with a partner ways World War I changed Canada and its people. Make a list on a large wall chart and post it in the classroom to share your ideas with other students.
   b) Prepare a presentation on how Canada changed as a result of World War I. See the Appendix page 365 for presentation ideas.

2.  Add entries for this chapter to your timeline.

3. With a partner, interview your parents and other relatives, family friends, and people in your neighbourhood about how they think the Canadian nation will change in the future. Share your findings with your classmates. Ideas on interviewing techniques are found in the Appendix on page 355.

Section IV Activity

Continued from pages 271 and 272.

  Based on the information in this chapter, in the role you have created in this section, do number 1 and choose from 2 and 3.

1. Write a journal entry about your feelings on each of the following:
   - the soldiers coming home from the war
   - changes to Canada after the war

2. Write a conversation between soldiers coming home and Canadians who did not go to war.

3. In a format of your choice, re-create an experience from this chapter.

Coming Home

Canada was slow in bringing its soldiers home from Europe. Most were kept for months in Great Britain. Others were assigned tasks in Germany or in Russia to help keep the peace. In late 1918, soldiers began to return to Canada.

Economic Downturn

Tom

We were welcomed home with parades and ceremonies. After the celebrations we began trying to adjust to civilian life. We expected to go back to life as it was before the war. We found instead that Canada, like the rest of the world, had changed. To make matters worse, the world went into an economic slump. The munitions factories were closed. Wheat prices had fallen. We expected to return to the jobs we had before the war. Many of us have found ourselves without jobs right at a time when prices are rising! We fought and risked our lives for our country. We think our country should make sure we have secure jobs now.

Claudette

We women worked in the food industry, hotels, schools, offices—wherever we were needed. During the war over 100 000 of us moved into the jobs held by men. I drove a bus. Now that the war is over, I want to keep using the skills that I have learned. And I need to keep earning a living! I can't afford to give up my job to a returning soldier just because I am a woman. We knew when we took these jobs that when the war was over we were expected to return to our former roles working at home. But the situation has changed. I am as grateful as anybody else to the soldiers who fought for our country. But my boyfriend was killed in the war. I don't expect to marry soon. I have to support myself.

Below: Soldiers were welcomed home with great excitement. Soon, however, they found themselves competing for scarce jobs. Hours were long, pay was low, and many workers were unhappy.

The Flu Epidemic

Jeanette

We were so happy when the soldiers finally started coming home. Late in the fall of 1918 all over Canada we rushed to meet boats and trains. Our poor boys seemed tired and some were coughing. We didn't realize that they were carrying the virus that caused the Spanish flu.* Within a week my healthy neighbour was dead. It was that sudden. A cough, a temperature, then pneumonia set in.

The Spanish Flu

In 1918, thousands of soldiers arrived home from the war in Europe. Many had the Spanish flu. Within weeks, thousands of people all over Canada were deathly ill. The epidemic spread rapidly. Before it was over, about 50 000 Canadians had died. People between the ages of 20 and 40 were hit particularly hard. Most deaths resulted from the pneumonia that accompanied the flu.

The flu's early symptoms (fever, sore muscles, tiredness, and headache) were miserable but not alarming, and many victims got better. Others were less fortunate. As the disease progressed from the throat to the lungs, victims often became delirious. A blood-tinged froth sometimes gushed from their nose and throat, which they attempted to clear in their fight for oxygen. They turned purple from lack of oxygen as they neared death. For this reason, the Spanish flu also came to be known as Purple Death. The disease killed about one in 20 across Canada. In an attempt to control the disease, the nation's schools and other public places were closed. Public gatherings were cancelled. In some cities, authorities ordered people not to shake hands and stores not to hold sales.

The Spanish flu attacked people of all ages. In some cases it killed whole families. The flu claimed the lives of more people worldwide than any war, disease, or famine in history. It was responsible for the deaths of approximately 30 000 000 people around the world. Quebec and Labrador (in the colony of Newfoundland) experienced the greatest number of deaths, over 14 000 people. In Ontario, the flu claimed 8 700 lives.

As a result of the Spanish flu epidemic, the federal government took on the responsibility for the health of Canadians. The first federal department of health was created to co-ordinate health-care services throughout the country.

Different parts of Canada used different methods to try to control the Spanish flu epidemic. Some Prairie towns refused to allow trains to stop at their stations. The government of Alberta passed a law requiring everyone to wear a mask when in public.

Other Flu Epidemics

Scientists point to major flu epidemics in 1957 and 1968, which claimed the lives of 17 000 000 people around the world. They believe another deadly flu may occur in the future. Scientists are studying the genetic material of the virus, recovered from bodies of Spanish flu victims. They believe their research will save lives when another flu epidemic sweeps the world.

For Your Notebook

1. Make a bar graph comparing the number of Canadians who died in World War I with those who died from the Spanish Flu of 1918 (see page 361).

2.

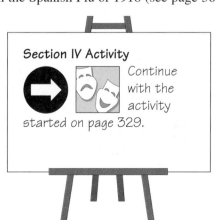

Section IV Activity

Continue with the activity started on page 329.

---

*Influenza, a highly contagious illness, is commonly called the flu.

Growth of Cities

 Canadian farmers were turning to new technologies in the second decade of the twentieth century. Gradually steam tractors (later, gasoline-driven tractors) were replacing horses. With the new technologies, farms could employ less labour and produce more crops. More sons and daughters of farmers moved to cities to look for jobs. The growing cities provided many jobs and a different lifestyle. They also had problems—slums, housing shortages, waste disposal problems, growing crime, and heavy traffic.

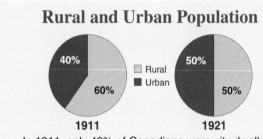

Rural and Urban Population

40% / 60% — 1911
50% / 50% — 1921

☐ Rural
■ Urban

In 1911, only 40% of Canadians were city dwellers. By 1921, half of Canadians lived in urban areas.

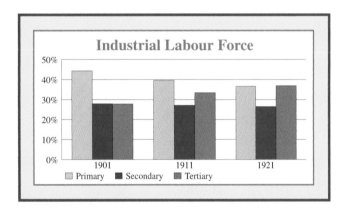

Industrial Labour Force

☐ Primary   ■ Secondary   ■ Tertiary

Many new factories had been built. Most had produced weapons and materials needed for the war. By 1920, most had been converted to other production. Some had been closed down.

For Your Notebook

1. Read the words of the popular World War I song, "How 'Ya Gonna Keep 'Em Down on the Farm (After They've Seen Paree?)."

   a) Discuss the words of the song with a friend. How do you think the experiences of the war changed the soldiers? Think of at least five situations where returning soldiers' lives would now be different from their pre-war lives.

   b) How does popular music reflect what was happening at the time the soldiers were coming back to Canada?

How 'Ya Gonna Keep 'Em Down on the Farm (After They've Seen Paree?)

How 'ya gonna keep'em down on the farm,
After they've seen Paree?
How 'ya gonna keep'em away from Broadway,
Jazzin' aroun,' and paintin' the town?
How 'ya gonna keep'em away from harm?
That's a mystery!
They'll never want to see a rake or plow,
And who the deuce can parley-vous a cow?
How 'ya gonna keep'em down on the farm,
After they've seen Paree?

The above photograph of many different types of transportation is authentic. No explanation is available for why a team of oxen and wagon is sharing a street with an automobile and a streetcar. However, horses would still have been commonly used for transportation at this time.

Discontent

Labour Unrest

  Government failure to deal with labour issues after the war was one cause of the labour unrest that resulted. The speakers below express their concerns.

Charlie

Where would Canada's 1500 factories have been without us? During the war, our manufactured exports increased enormously. Thank goodness for the women who filled in for the men who were at war!

Now that the war is over, Canada is no longer primarily a producer of raw materials. Our manufacturing and service industries produce a greater value of goods and employ more people. Politicians and businessmen need to realize that the well-being of Canada depends on its workers!

Bill

We would like to see laws that set the minimum wage that we can be paid. We also need laws that limit the number of hours we have to work each week. And there was talk of making a law about **collective bargaining**. If the government had made those laws, we might not have had the Winnipeg General Strike.

Marcel

Those of us who own businesses are very worried by the labour movement. It will be very expensive to pay our workers more and have them working fewer hours.

Some people are afraid that workers will start a revolution. There are some business owners who think that we must stop the labour unions before they get any stronger. Business owners think it is time for the government to step in and stop the workers' demands.

Collective bargaining—workers in a similar trade negotiating with employers as a group, seeking an agreement on wages and working conditions that would apply to all of them

Growth of Labour Unions

During World War I there was an increased demand for the products of Canadian industry. Many workers were serving overseas. This led to a shortage of workers. It put workers in a good position to demand better wages and working conditions. The next few pages will examine labour unions. Labour unions are workers' organizations that bargain for better wages or working conditions for their members.

Olaf

Canadian industry grew with all the new factories during the war years. The labour force grew too. But few employers have been willing to increase our salaries or improve our working conditions. This has led more of us to join labour unions.

Mary

Labour unions had a number of successes during and just after the war. Most of us worked fewer hours each week. On average, our wages rose by 18% during the war. However, the costs of food, fuel, rent, and clothing have risen even faster than our wages. Because our wages do not rise as fast as the cost of living, workers are actually becoming poorer. We think it is time for the government to step in and force business owners to pay us better wages.

Exploring Further

1. 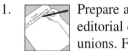 Prepare a speech or write a newspaper editorial explaining the need for trade unions. Focus especially on the effect trade unions had on working conditions.
2. Write a slogan for either Bill or Mary (shown on this page), who support trade unions. Create posters using this slogan and listing their demands.
3. Why do we celebrate Labour Day? Find out more about labour unions in Canada today.

Focus On: The Winnipeg General Strike

The Winnipeg General Strike of 1919 was one of the most important events in Canada's history. The strike seriously affected the city of Winnipeg, where unions were strong. As the strike spread, it affected other Canadian cities. Many Canadians even feared that a workers' revolution threatened the country's government.

The Winnipeg General Strike had its beginning outside Canada. The International Workers of the World believed the threat of a general strike would result in major gains for workers.

At the Western Labour Congress, held in Calgary in March 1919, labour delegates approved a Canadian One Big Union, OBU.

On May 1, before OBU could be established, the Building and Metal Trades Councils of Winnipeg voted to go on strike. They demanded a minimum wage of $0.85 an hour, a 48 hour work week, and collective bargaining (the right to bargain together for one agreement covering them all). Their employers rejected this.

The Building and Metal Trades Councils called on other Winnipeg workers to join them in a general sympathy strike. The strike was to begin on May 15. That day, over 27 000 workers left their jobs.

The city of Winnipeg, with a population of over 170 000, was brought to a standstill. Buses and street cars and the railways stopped. Mail, milk, and bread were not delivered. Newspapers were not published. Some city officials, including some firefighters and police officers, refused to work.

Soon the strike spread to other parts of Canada. A large number of workers in Toronto and Vancouver also left their jobs in support of the Winnipeg workers.

At first, the demonstrations in Winnipeg were peaceful. However, on June 4 a march by strike supporters was met by a march of anti-strike demonstrators organized by a group of citizens. The potential for violence caused the mayor to ban marches.

In mid-June, a riot broke out when special constables and Mounted Police attempted to stop a march. Shots were fired. Two men were killed and a number of others were injured.

On June 25, the Trades and Labour Council of Winnipeg announced the end of the Winnipeg General Strike. Strike leaders faced trials and a number were convicted and sentenced to jail terms.

The Winnipeg General Strike frightened most Canadians. Fewer workers chose to become members of unions. The powers of the unions were temporarily reduced.

Claris (Brownie) Freedman, ten years old at the time, witnessed the climax of the Bloody Saturday strike on June 21.

My father had a men's clothing store at the corner of Rupert and Main. We were standing, looking through the door window. I guess we must have been told something was happening. I remember seeing the streetcar overturned and a crowd of people. It turned over and then went on fire. I don't recall what happened after that.

When I look back on it, I think it was a pretty horrifying sight for young people to witness. Everybody was obviously very angry.

I was only 10 and I don't remember anything about the politics of the time. I know now that there were people out of work, that they didn't have enough to eat. I think the general strike created a strong labour movement here. I knew Gloria Queen, whose father, John Queen, was later mayor of Winnipeg. He went to jail because he was very active in the strike. So we heard a lot about that later on, about various people who went to jail. But I don't think we heard anything about the general strike in our schools or discussed it. Even in our history classes, I don't think we talked about it at all.

June 21, 1919: Bloody Saturday in Winnipeg

Agrarian Discontent

During the war, farmers made much greater profits than ever before. They were feeding not only their own country, but Great Britain as well, so exports were high. By 1916, their profits began to diminish, as the price of goods and farm equipment began to increase. Many farmers became dissatisfied and asked the government to take action to reduce tariffs on imports.

The growth of urban centres after the war was of concern to farmers. The political influence of farmers was reduced as cities became larger and more important. By 1920, rural and urban populations were evenly divided. Farmers were also dismayed by the fact that their sons and daughters often left for the city, where some were able to quickly gain employment. Many farmers viewed the cities as challenging rural values, traditions, and ways of life. Open distrust was building between the rural and urban populations.

The discontent of farmers resulted in distrust of traditional political parties—the Conservatives and the Liberals. Farmers throughout Canada felt they lacked the political power to force the government to address their concerns.

New Political Parties

During and after World War I, Canadians were often divided politically. Labourers and owners of businesses were suspicious of each other. Farmers also began to organize politically. They wanted reduced taxes on farm machinery and reduced freight rates when they sent their products to markets. These issues were not a concern to urban dwellers.

Many farmers chose to become politically active. Farmers' groups called for free trade in agricultural machinery and certain other goods to reduce their costs. They also wanted **nationalization** of railway companies so that freight rates could be reduced on grain shipments. Strict controls over resource development and changes to government were two other demands.

Labour and farm interests developed new political parties to try to get their goals met. In October 1919, the United Farmers of Ontario won the largest number of seats in the provincial election. With the support of elected labour movement representatives, they formed Ontario's provincial government.

Farm and labour interests were now established as significant new voices in Canadian politics. In the early 1920s, these farm movements and labour movements developed into political parties, both provincially and federally. They experienced considerable success.

Pierre

They say that an army moves on its stomach. Well, they couldn't have fought the war without the contributions of the farmers. Our wheat and flour were particularly in demand, as well as meat and dairy products. We worked hard during the war, increasing our production by 73%. We did what was needed then. Now we want the government to listen to us and address *our* needs!

Sarah

Our boys served in the war even though we needed them on the farm. We still managed to increase our production. We had to buy farm machinery to increase production when farm workers were hard to find, and we paid high tariffs on it. Sometimes we feel that the tax laws are made for city people, not for us. Now we have to pay heavy freight rates to ship our products to market. Farm people need somebody who will speak for us in parliament. Farm people need to get some laws changed.

It's no wonder that farmers are becoming politically active. I hear that the United Farmers of Ontario have actually formed the provincial government in Ontario. The new Ontario premier, Ernest Drury, is a farmer from Barrie. Now maybe our voices will be heard.

For Your Notebook

1. In what way was the Winnipeg General Strike an example of labour unrest?
2. What did the farmers and labour leaders have in common that led them to co-operate to achieve political change?

Exploring Further

3. Prepare a speech, write a newspaper editorial, or write a slogan for either Pierre or Sarah (shown above) on issues that the farmers believe need changing.

Nationalization—putting a business that is considered necessary for the public good under the ownership and control of the government

Discrimination Against Minorities

Racism and Ethnic Discrimination

Returning soldiers found that the **racism** and ethnic **discrimination** that had existed in Canada before the war had changed very little. Like most countries of the world at that time, officially and unofficially, Canada was a racist society. Many minorities experienced discrimination because of their origins. Their access to housing, employment, and services such as schools, theatres, hotels, and swimming pools was often limited. This was particularly true for visible minorities.

In 1911, people of German ancestry were the third largest ethnic group in Canada. During World War I, many felt the need to downplay their German roots. The Ontario city of Berlin rejected its German name in 1916. It was renamed Kitchener after a British military leader.

Today Canadian society recognizes the unfairness of racism. The government has officially apologized to Japanese-Canadians for internment during World War II and also to Chinese-Canadians for the head tax.

Canada's First Nations were a target of assimilation. Children were moved into residential schools, often far from their homes. Using their languages and celebrating their culture and religious beliefs were forbidden. Racism had a destructive effect on the families of these people, as well as on the families of many other Canadian minorities.

Racism—believing that a particular race is superior
Discrimination—an attitude of hostility directed against an individual, group, or race, which limits them unfairly compared with other groups

This tax certificate for Lau Shong (or Shing), 1912, shows that he paid $500, the amount of the "head tax" required to bring Chinese immigrants into Canada.

Many people living in Canada originated from countries considered enemies during World War I. Many lost their jobs or were interned during the war.

In 1914, the Canadian government ordered the steamer *Komagata Maru*, carrying 354 Sikhs who hoped to immigrate to Canada, to return to Asia.

Exploring Further

1. What efforts are being made in the present day to eliminate discrimination and promote understanding of minorities?

Women Get the Vote

New Roles for Women

  For Canadian women, the war meant rationing, shouldering new responsibilities, and facing hardships and sacrifices alone. In addition to their household duties, both rural and urban women undertook a variety of new tasks. During the war over 100 000 women moved into traditionally male jobs. Women were paid about half the salary of men. It was clearly understood that they would return to their former roles, primarily in the home, after the war.

Styles of clothing advertised for women reflected changes in women's roles.

Martha

 The war was an exhausting time for Canadian women. Most of us had at least one family member in the armed forces. We were worried all the time about whether they would come home safely. Many of our husbands were away. We had to run our homes alone. My sister's children were so young that they could hardly remember their father. Housekeeping was more difficult because we were short of some goods, and others were very expensive.

I saw many of my neighbours going to work in the factories. Now that the war is over, these women are expected to return to their homes. Some of them lost their husbands in the war. They will find it difficult to get along without the income from their jobs.

Johnson

 In my work, I am often called on to give advice to women who are dealing with family problems. The war has added new types of difficulties. Some husbands came home from the war with serious physical, mental, or emotional problems. They are not able to make good decisions regarding their families. However, Canadian law says that the husband is the head of the family. As long as the husband is alive, the law says he can make decisions regarding the children.

Some husbands are not able to work to support their families. However, there are fewer jobs for women now. Women without financial help are having a difficult time supporting their families.

Hilda

 I get very angry when I see women not allowed to make decisions regarding their own lives or the lives of their children. Canadian law must change. Women need to be given more freedom to manage their own lives and those of their dependents.

When I talk about these ideas to some people, they either disagree or just don't care. Some of them even laugh at the idea of women being able to vote. They say that women are too delicate to deal with the tough world of politics.

Women must be allowed to vote in all elections, not just in a few provinces. That is the only way that the laws of Canada will change to give women more rights. That is why I am a **suffragist**.

Suffragist—person who wants more people, especially women, to have the right to vote

Point of Contact

Fictional Narrative

—by Marilyn Scott

On a December afternoon in 1911, 20-year-old Violet Evans tucked the wisps of her brown hair under her fur hat and adjusted the wool scarf around her neck. She tried to open the front door quietly but the hinges squeaked.

"Violet! Is that you?"

Violet opened the door wider. She couldn't afford the time to get into an argument right now.

"Yes, Grandmother," she called. "I'm going out to see Evelyn. I left a note for Mother on the dining table. Bye."

Without waiting for a reply, Violet slipped out the door and closed it behind her. Lifting her long skirts she hurried out the gate and down the frosty wooden sidewalk.

Evelyn was at the corner, stamping her feet to keep warm.

"Did you have any trouble?" asked Evelyn when they met.

"Not much. I said I was going to see you. What about you?"

"I told mother I was going to meet you and then we were going to the university. We students have to study you know."

"Well, at least we told the truth. But I know our folks would be livid if they knew who we were going to see there today."

Evelyn laughed. "Father wouldn't care. He thinks it's all nonsense. Mother would think it was very unladylike to go to such an event."

"Do you really think she's as bad as some of the papers say?"

"I don't know. I've never gone to hear or see anyone who has been in prison before."

Violet and Evelyn arrived at the hall and found seats close to the front. There was a feeling of excitement in the room. The buzzing talk of the crowd suddenly faded to silence as two women appeared on the stage. The taller of the two introduced the second woman as Mrs. Emmeline Pankhurst, leader of the Women's Social and Political Union in Britain.

Was this tiny, elegant lady the one they had read about? The newspapers had talked about someone who threw stones at windows and attacked policemen, someone vicious and menacing. This small woman with the sweet smile couldn't be the same person.

Emmeline Pankhurst began speaking in a firm but gentle voice. She told how women had become militant only when other methods had failed. She told of the endless petitions and letters, and how men in power and members of parliament refused to even talk with the women. How women finally started to hold up banners saying "Votes for Women" at political rallies, and how they were thrown out of such meetings, arrested, and imprisoned.

Violet listened, fascinated. Could this delicate woman really have had her arms twisted by police, been pushed and slapped and called foul names by men? Is that what all this vote business would come to? Was it worth it?

Mrs. Pankhurst went on to tell of her hunger strike in prison and how she was force fed by having her hands and feet held down and a tube shoved down her throat. Many others were treated the same. Not just once but over and over.

Violet looked down at her clenched hands in her lap. Evelyn looked pale. It was almost too horrible to imagine.

The speech continued. Emmeline Pankhurst was sensitive and inspiring. "We are working for the vote as a preparation for a whole program of social legislation." Violet and Evelyn clapped long and hard at the end of the speech. They put all of the extra money they had into the donation box.

The two young women walked slowly towards the streetcar stop. Evelyn spoke first. "Well, what do you think?"

Violet answered softly. "She wasn't at all what I expected. It's hard to believe she's been through all that and is still alive."

"I don't think I could do it."

"Do you think it will ever get that bad here?"

"I hope not. All I know is that no matter what my mother and father think, I'm going to work toward women getting the vote."

Violet clasped her friend's hand. "Me too!"

338

Nellie McClung
1873–1951

Nellie McClung was born on a farm near Chatsworth, Ontario. As an adolescent she was often scolded by her mother for refusing to be restricted only to things expected of girls. She voiced her opinions, appeared in school plays, and played boys' games. Some people did not consider these proper activities for a young lady.

Nellie moved to Manitoba, where she experienced a pioneering life as a teacher and got married. When she married, she had to give up her teaching career. She eventually became a successful writer.

In 1911, the McClungs moved to Winnipeg. There Nellie began to come to the notice of the public. At first she spoke to promote her books. She began to include discussion of the abuse of alcohol in her speeches. Soon she was leading the fight for the right of women to vote.

In 1914, the McClung family moved to Edmonton. There she continued to campaign for the Women's Christian Temperance Union (WCTU). Many women of the WCTU became suffragists. They wanted the vote so they could change laws about alcohol.

Nellie McClung has been credited with leading the successful fight for the right of women to vote in provincial elections. In 1921, she

was elected to the Alberta Legislature. There she worked for women's property rights, **mothers' allowances**, and free medical and dental care for school children.

Nellie McClung was well known for her fight for women's rights. She insisted that women were as intelligent as men and should have as many rights. She said they were also as capable of serving in an elected office. Many of her goals were achieved in her lifetime. In her later years, she spoke to women's groups around the world.

Emily Murphy
1868–1933

Born at Cookstown, Ontario, Emily Murphy lived in Manitoba and England before she and her family settled in Edmonton in 1907. There she became a successful writer. She also worked for changes in city and provincial laws. She was particularly concerned with how these laws affected the rights of women and children. Like Nellie McClung, Emily Murphy believed women had the right to vote and hold office. They both believed that children had the right to a safe life, enough food, and education.

In 1916 Emily Murphy was appointed a police **magistrate**,

although she had no formal legal training. She was respected by many for her years as a social activist. She was the first woman in the British Empire appointed as a magistrate.

The Person's Case

At that time, women could not be appointed to the Senate. The regulations stated that only "persons" could be appointed, and this was interpreted to exclude women.

The issue of whether women were "persons" was fought and lost in the Supreme Court of Canada. It was then taken to the only higher court available at the time. Five Alberta women (Nellie McClung, Emily Murphy, Louise McKinney, Henrietta Muir Edwards, and Irene Parlby) known as "The Famous Five" took the case to the Judicial Committee of the Privy Council in England. In 1929, the Privy Council ruled "the word persons includes members of the male and female sex." Finally it was established that women could legally become members of the Senate of Canada.*

Exploring Further

1. Write a slogan for the women's suffrage movement and create a poster expressing the changes women wanted.

Mothers' allowances—money given by the government each month to mothers to buy necessities for their children

Magistrate—a government official who heard cases in a lower, provincial court
*They had gained the right to stand for election to the House of Commons in 1919, one year after achieving the vote in federal elections.

In the early years of the twentieth century, the struggle for women's rights was going on in many parts of the world. Many women admired Emmeline Pankhurst, who had suffered imprisonment and force-feeding in her attempts to win the vote for women in Great Britain. The above photograph shows Emmeline Pankhurst (on the left) with Nellie McClung.

Despite the many new roles they had taken on, women continued to have primary responsibility for care of homes and children. These women are ensuring that their babies' health is looked after at a baby clinic run by the Victorian Order of Nurses.

Enfranchisement (When Women Won the Vote)

1916 Women in Manitoba were first in Canada to win the vote and to run for provincial public office, although the candidate was not elected.

1917 Louise McKinney became a member of the Legislative Assembly for Alberta. She was the first woman elected to a government in Canada (and in the British Empire).

1917 In the Wartime Elections Act (see page 324), the federal government granted the right to vote to a select group of women: women with the armed forces and the wives, mothers, daughters, and sisters of soldiers.

1918 The right to vote in federal elections was extended to all women, except First Nations and Asian women. (First Nations and Asian men were not enfranchised either.) Women attained the right to be elected to Parliament in 1919 and to be appointed to the Senate in 1929.

Provinces granted the vote to women in different years:

Manitoba	January 28, 1916
Saskatchewan	March 14, 1916
Alberta	April 19, 1916
British Columbia	April 5, 1917
Ontario	April 12, 1917
Nova Scotia	April 26, 1918
New Brunswick	April 17, 1919
Prince Edward Island	May 3, 1922
Newfoundland	April 13, 1925
Quebec	April 25, 1940

For Your Notebook

1.

Section Activity

  In your role (see pages 271 and 272) pretend you have met either Nellie McClung or Emily Murphy. Write a story about this meeting. Include in it your personal beliefs about women getting the vote.

Exploring Further

2. What effect did the war have on the issue of votes for women?
3. How did Canadian women get the vote? How were Canadian methods different from those used by the British?
4. What does the term social reformers mean? How was Canada influenced by social reformers in Great Britain and the United States?

Arts and leisure in Canada between 1914 and 1920 were greatly influenced by cultural life in Great Britain and the United States. Reading material, fashion, and entertainment all showed these influences. However, there was a growing trend towards promoting Canadian national identity in art and literature.

Visual Arts

The National Gallery of Canada in Ottawa had been in operation since the 1880s. During World War I, the gallery's funding was limited but it continued to encourage and support Canadian talent.

Canadian art was greatly influenced by American and European art. Many Canadian artists went to Europe to study. For example, Emily Carr studied painting in San Francisco, England, and France. She produced many unique paintings of Canada's Pacific Coast.

The decade's most noted artist was Tom Thomson. Some of his co-workers were also artists. They

Tom Thomson's painting *Canoe Lake* features the place where he later drowned.

would form the Group of Seven in 1920. (The Group of Seven was a unique Canadian art movement. This group of painters developed new ways of painting the Canadian landscape.)

(For more information check: http://national.gallery.ca)

Leisure

The increase in numbers of working-class people in cities contributed to a change in leisure activities. Well-off Canadians were still attending the horse races and going to dances at luxury hotels. City planners developed more places for middle-class and working-class people to enjoy themselves, such as parks, baseball stadiums, and public beaches.

By 1914, for example, several of the private waterfront cottages on English Bay in Vancouver had been replaced by a bandstand, a dancehall, and a roller rink. The landscape now included advertisements for fish and chips and **vaudeville** theatres.

The public beach and boat dock at English Bay, Vancouver, about 1920

Vaudeville—theatre entertainment showing a variety of acts, such as singing, juggling, comedy

Entertainment

Travelling exhibits of Canadian paintings were organized by the National Gallery of Canada to help develop a Canadian identity. The Chautauqua movement was another way that the arts reached many parts of Canada.

Chautauqua was a travelling program of music, plays, speeches, and readings. This four-day festival toured across the country like a circus, setting up their distinctive brown tents in the towns and cities where they stopped. Chautauqua was entertainment for all the people. Prices were affordable for most: a season ticket was $2.50 and a single entrance was $0.50 or $0.75.

Between 1915 and 1919, wages increased 33%, but on average the cost of living had doubled. A greater proportion of salary had to be spent on necessities, leaving less money for leisure pursuits.

Movies were extremely popular during this time. Most movies shown in Canada were made in the United States. Several Canadians were involved in the film-making industry. The most famous woman from that era was a star of silent films, Mary Pickford. She got her start as a child actor on a Toronto stage. A Canadian film-maker, A.D. Kean, made cowboy and rodeo films. However, it was difficult for small Canadian film-making companies to compete with larger American companies.

In 1920, one of the first commercial radio stations in the world went on the air in Montreal. CFCF (Canada's First, Canada's Finest) had regular, scheduled broadcasts of musical and spoken programs. Radio used professional performers rather than amateurs. Canadians were no longer dependent on amusements organized in their own homes.

Above: Education, inspiration, and entertainment were the goals of Chautauqua.

Right: A 5-cent admission bought you a seat at the silent films.

Below: Mary Pickford was one of the best-known actors of the silent film era.

City of Toronto Archives, SC244-320

Section IV Review

This page will act as a combined Chapter 13 Review and the Section IV Review.

For Your Notebook

1.

The Section IV Activity Focused On

Change   Identity   Power

Writing Historical Fiction

 If you haven't done so already, complete the projects you started on page 329.

For Class Discussion

2. **Who Are We?** As a class, discuss the answers to the three questions on the easel on page 269.

For Your Notebook

3. a) Review pages 24 and 25 on change.

b) Use your History notes as a reference. Do a think-pair-share to identify examples in Chapters 11, 12, and 13 of changes brought about by the agents of change.

c) Fill in a chart similar to the following on changes in Canada from 1896–1920. Use the information from Chapters 11, 12, and 13 for this activity.

Canada 1896–1920

 Change
What was Canada like in 1896? In 1920?

Transition Describe what has changed between 1896 and 1920.	**Retention** Describe what has not changed (or is slow to change).	**Agents of Change** What caused the change?		
		External	Internal	Combination

 Identity
How did Canadians see and describe themselves between 1896 and 1920? How were we seen and described internationally?

Power
Who held the power? Did we as a country have control over our internal affairs? Our external affairs?

In 1920

 In 1920, Canadians still saluted the British flag (the Union Jack) and sang the British national anthem (God Save the King). During World War I, Canadian soldiers and others involved in the war were united under a common goal, although they came from many regions and walks of life. After the war, a new Canadian identity began to form. Canada's contributions in World War I had earned the Dominion respect, not only throughout the British Commonwealth, but throughout the world. Canadians began to see themselves as Canadians.

Identity issues:

- Should Canada become less British? more Canadian?
- How could a unique Canadian culture and identity grow when the political system was British, the economy was increasingly influenced by the USA, and the population came from many different cultural sources?
- How could Canada have a national identity when regional interests were getting stronger?
- How could relations between English Canadians and French Canadians be improved?
- How could issues creating divisions between urban and rural, labour and business be resolved?
- To what extent should women enter the workforce? Should they become politically active?

Economy

In 1920, more Canadians were still employed in primary industries (37%). Secondary industries employed 27% and service industries employed 36%.

 Employment of returning soldiers was an issue. Jobs had changed as new industries were developed. Mechanization had begun to take the place of many unskilled workers. Jobs had also been filled by women during the war. Although women were expected to leave the workforce, many could not afford to or did not wish to.

War-related industries needed to change from producing munitions to other products that could be marketed in Canada and exported. The worldwide economy experienced a downturn after World War I, so export markets were fewer. War-related debt also needed to be paid.

Economically, Canada's trading relationships were changing.

Canada was trading more with the USA and less with Great Britain. Americans were starting to invest more in Canada and British investors were spending less. Businesses in Canada were being bought by American firms.

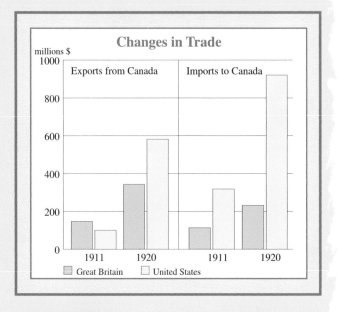

Changes in Trade

millions $

Exports from Canada | Imports to Canada

1911 | 1920 | 1911 | 1920

Great Britain   United States

Farmers in the grain-exporting provinces sought better rates shipping by railroad.

344

Society

Canada's population increased from 5 371 000 in 1910 to 8 788 000 in 1921. However, over 60 000 had been killed and over 173 000 injured in World War I. Most were men between 18 and 35. Some widows raised their children alone and many women did not marry.

The Spanish flu had killed about 50 000. Families lost children. Children lost parents. There came to be shortages of workers in some places. These losses and changes in communities changed Canada in many ways.

Rapid urbanization had led to social, economic, and political problems as well as advances.

Rural and Urban Population

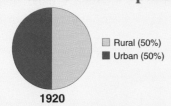

Rural (50%)
Urban (50%)

1920

Montreal was urban and international in 1920. Skirts were shorter, advertisements brighter, and the movie theatres offered inexpensive entertainment.

Relationships Between Groups

Canada was a British dominion, but it was also a country with many cultures. Two cultures were dominant, British and French. Large numbers from other immigrant groups were still attempting to be recognized as contributing members of Canadian society. The Prairie Region and the large cities had many cultural groups. This was a result of heavy immigration at the turn of the century, 20 years before. The next generation was gradually being assimilated into Canadian culture through schools and the workplace.

  Canadians continued to have strained relationships between groups, particularly English and French Canadians. Discrimination against visible and other minorities continued to be an issue. Many of Canada's First Nations people lived on reserves, separated from other Canadians. Their lives were regulated in many ways by the provisions of the Indian Act. They did not have the right to vote if they were Status Indians. If they wished to become enfranchised, they had to leave the reserve and lose any rights provided under a treaty.

Roles of Women

 The roles of women continued to change. Most women in Canada had achieved the right to vote in federal elections and in provincial elections everywhere except Quebec.

Women increasingly moved into jobs and professions that had formerly been done exclusively by men. Styles of dress, leisure activities, and social behaviour also changed.

Politics

 New political movements began after World War I. Both farmers and labour leaders began to demand an increasing role in Canadian politics. Women also became more politically active.

In 1920, Canada had nine provinces and two territories. Newfoundland was still a British colony.

Canada
Britain
United States of America
France (St. Pierre and Miquelon)

0   500 km

YUKON TERRITORY
NORTHWEST TERRITORIES
BRITISH COLUMBIA
ALBERTA
SASKATCHEWAN
MANITOBA
ONTARIO
QUEBEC
NEWFOUNDLAND
PRINCE EDWARD ISLAND
NOVA SCOTIA
NEW BRUNSWICK

Dominion of Canada, 1920

In Conclusion

· · · · · · · · · · · · · ·

As Haley and Jasmine said their last goodbyes to Chantal and thanked their hosts, they felt a little sad. "The time has gone by so fast," Jasmine said, "and we were becoming such great friends. I'll always remember my time here, getting to know you, the conference, seeing Anne of Green Gables' house."

By the time they got to the bus station for the four-hour trip back to Moncton, Antonio and the other returning delegates were assembling. "I seem to know everyone here," Haley said. "Isn't it weird that in such a short time you can come to know so many people."

"*Aprez-vous,*" said Jean, and directed Haley and Jasmine into the bus.

"*Merci,*" Haley responded, without hesitation. Jasmine and Haley sat beside each other and Antonio across from them. They had planned this beforehand so they could begin preparing for the presentation they would be making to their class when they got back to Lethburn.

As the bus left the depot, everyone began shouting and waving to those on the platform. Then the delegates became strangely quiet. They might have been reviewing their memories of the Conference. Or, perhaps they were looking forward with anticipation to returning to homes, schools, and friends. "It's been a wonderful experience!"

said Haley. Her remark broke the silence. Antonio began to share some of his thoughts and Jasmine followed. They chatted excitedly all the way to Moncton, where they boarded the train home.

As Antonio was finding his way to his seat, he turned his head to say, "I was really surprised by the first morning's session about Canada's identity. It really makes you think about how far our nation has come."

Haley nodded. "I think about that too. Our study of history this year has helped us see the changes in how Canadians have seen themselves, and how others have seen them."

"Do you think the Fathers of Confederation realized what kind of a country they were creating?" asked Antonio. "If they could have overheard our ideas, I think they would have been amazed!"

"Can you imagine students in 1867 being given the opportunity to shape Canada's future!" Jasmine exclaimed.

"No way," replied Antonio. "I was really excited by the seriousness with which each group undertook its job. There were some great recommendations. I guess my favourite was the recommendation that Canada needs to make every effort to share its resources with those who have fewer resources."

"I liked ours best," replied Jasmine. "Wouldn't you agree that Canada could best meet the needs of the world by continuing to serve as a peacekeeper? After all,

we're really good at it and many countries need our assistance."

Haley was reviewing the many excellent recommendations made. Finally she settled on the one she thought was the best. "I guess I like the idea of serving as a model society for the rest of the world, showing how a wide range of ethnic groups can live in harmony, each contributing to the nation, while retaining some of their ethnic identity."

"It's going to be great fun sharing our ideas from the conference with our class," Haley said. From time to time while the train sped through the countryside, towns, and cities, the group met to finalize their ideas.

"We need to do our best for Ms Pozzi and our class," Jasmine exclaimed. "After all, if it wasn't for each of them, we wouldn't have had this experience or made such connections with history."

Game Show

Canada Revisited Game Show

Your study of Canadian history has been divided into four sections: British North America Prior to Confederation, Confederation, Challenges to the New Dominion, and Emerging Canadian Identity. While working with these sections, you have been using five History concepts: change, regionalism, power, identity, and co-operation/conflict.

The following activity has been provided as an enjoyable way to conclude Grade 8 history. You will work together to review what you have learned in your class this year, then finish off by playing the game you create.

Your teacher will assign teams for doing Parts One and Two of this activity. The four sections are different lengths, so teams will be different sizes.

Part One: Synthesizing Information. Each section team makes a large graphic organizer (web or mind map) on a sheet of chart paper of the key information in their section. Use your History notes and the *Canada Revisited 8* textbook as reference.

Your web should include information for creating questions in the following five categories:
1. Vocabulary
2. Important people (their major accomplishments)
3. Key events (especially causes and effects)
4. Issues (points of view, results)
5. How the concepts of change, regionalism, power, identity, and co-operation/conflict apply to history

Part Two: Writing Game Questions. As a class, you will co-operate to create 140 game show questions (and their answers). Each section team writes two questions and answers for each chapter in their section, in each of the five categories above (a total of 10 per chapter). Use the graphic organizer you made in Part One, your History notes, and the textbook for reference when writing questions.

Questions may be true/false, multiple choice, or short answer. Each question should have an answer and specify the number of points it is worth.

Submit all questions, answers, and the points allotted, to the teacher to review. When the questions are all checked and approved, either the teacher or the appointed game show host will put all of the questions together, in random order. (All game show teams may be asked any of the questions on the whole text.)

Part Three: The Game Show. The whole class will be divided into game show teams (teams of either three or four, whichever works best for your class). Teams will play round-robin tournament style for team points, in timed games. After all teams have played, if there is no clear winner, play-off games can be played.

1. Set up the room: two opposing teams (A and B), a game show host, a scorekeeper, and a timer sit at the front. The scorekeeper records the points won by each team for each question. The timer has a bell to indicate when a player's or team's time on a question is up. All other class members are the audience.

2. Each team member receives a green card to signal when he or she has an answer to a question.

3. The host gives a brief introduction, introduces the teams, draws a question, and reads aloud the number of points to be gained. Then the host asks the question. For example, "For 2 points, Team A, a vocabulary question: What does *reciprocity* mean?"

4. The first member of Team A has 30 seconds to answer, for full points. If he or she cannot answer in that time, after the bell rings the member can consult the other Team A members. The team then earns half the points for a correct answer.

5. Each Team A player gets one question, then each Team B player gets one question. A second round of three more questions per team follows. In this second round, any team member can answer by putting up his or her green card and being recognized by the host.

6. An optional "scramble" round can be added, with all members of both teams competing to answer questions. Set the rules for time allotted and bonus points before beginning to play the game.

7. At the end of the game, the score-keeper totals the score, and the host announces both teams' scores and names the winner.

Appendix

Learning How to Learn
(SKIMM™)

On the following pages you will find a variety of ideas to help you with your assignments. Use these organizers as sample formats. Add to them or delete as needed.

NOTE: Registered™ 1996 Arnold Publishing Ltd. SKIMM™ (Skills, Models, and Methods) Learning How to Learn—the techniques of assigning questions/activities written in a textbook or digital presentation and referring users to an appendix or glossary (print or digital) for suggestions on how to carry it out—has been registered as a trademark by Arnold Publishing Ltd. All copy used in SKIMM™

Analysing

Analysing means separating a whole into parts or components in order to understand it.

 ## Brainstorming

Brainstorming is a strategy for coming up with as many ideas about a topic as possible, then choosing the best.

Suggestions for Brainstorming

1. Write down all ideas. Do not evaluate or criticize ideas as they are mentioned.
2. Quickly add ideas to the list. Don't reflect whether the idea is "good" or not. Unusual ideas should be included in your list.
3. Sometimes thinking about one idea leads to another. Add to, subtract from, join, and change ideas to come up with new ones— the more you have, the better.
4. Reflect about your ideas and choose the best.

Cause and Effect (Result)

A cause is something that makes an event or situation occur. The event or situation then leads to other results (effects).

- Use a diagram to help you understand cause and effect ideas.
- The words "reasons for" and "consequences" signal cause and effect.

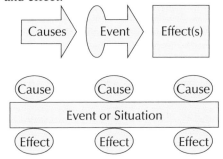

 An expansion of SKIMM™ (Learning How to Learn) is available on the Arnold Publishing website.

Charts and Graphic Organizers

Charts are ways to organize, record, and display information. They are also referred to as diagrams, tables, or graphs. (See also Graphic Notes, page 363.)

Retrieval Charts

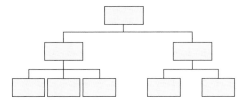

Title		
Criteria	A	B

List items or criteria you are describing.   Record important information as it relates to the criteria.

Flow Chart

Flow charts are diagrams of ideas in sequence (order). Flow charts can show classification, relationships, possibilities, or choices.

Classifying

To classify, you gather together ideas, events, or items and arrange them into groups that have common characteristics. Each of us thinks differently, so there are many ways to classify information. A flow chart (shown above) is one way to do this.

Steps for Classifying

1. List items or examples randomly.
2. Identify and label groups (categories) based on their characteristics.
3. Sort into groups based on similarities.
4. (Optional) Record information on a graphic organizer such as a flow chart.

Comparing

This thinking tool is used to show how something is similar to and different from something else.

Words Used in Making Comparisons

- although
- as well as
- but
- also
- either
- however
- like
- not only
- on the other hand
- or
- similarly
- unless
- unlike
- yet

Comparison Chart

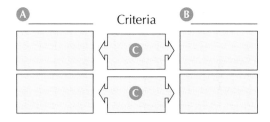

Steps for Comparing

1. Identify what you are comparing. Ⓐ Ⓑ
2. Identify what criteria you are going to use in comparing. The number of criteria will vary depending upon what you are comparing. Record in middle column of chart. Ⓒ
3. Show how the items you are comparing, Ⓐ and Ⓑ, are the same (or how they are different), based on the criteria you identified. Ⓒ

Venn Diagram

The Venn diagram is used for comparison, as the diagram following shows. (A variation of a Venn diagram is used on page 131, where the overlapping part shows shared responsibilities.)

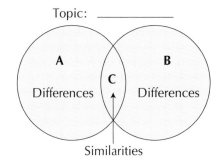

Concept Poster

A concept poster is an information display that is more than just visual. Concept posters are a fun way to learn, remember new information, and share what you've learned with your classmates. They may be done individually, in pairs, or as a small group.

Steps for Concept Posters

Step 1:
a) Review information about the concept in your textbook and your notebook.
b) List examples.
c) Brainstorm to decide what the examples have in common. Look for patterns, links, and connections.

Step 2: Plan and create a presentation to represent your ideas and examples about the concept. You could include any of the following:
- picture (photo, drawing, map, or diagram)
- skit or tableau
- music/song/sound effects
- words (spoken or on paper)
- objects/models

Step 3: Present your concept poster to your classmates. You may either tell them what concept you are presenting or have them guess.

Chronology

A chronology is a sequence of events as they occurred over time. When you put events in chronological order, you organize them according to when they happened.

Timeline

A timeline is a way to show events chronologically. It can include words, numerals, and pictures (see pages 2 and 8).

John's Life

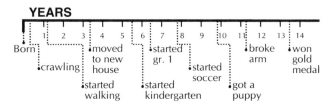

The timelines in this book use colour consistently as a way to organize and relate information. For example, time periods in timelines related to French colonization are always blue (see page 5).

How to Read a Timeline

- Timelines can be horizontal (across) or vertical (up and down).
- If a timeline is in scale, the years will be marked evenly along the line. If a timeline is not in scale, the specific dates are in sequence but not arranged in proportion. This usually occurs when some events shown were very far apart and others very close together in time.
- A sequence of events reads in one direction. However, dates of history read in two directions. In the system used in this book, events are either BCE (Before the Common Era) or CE (Common Era). On a horizontal timeline, the dates of events BCE read from right to left as the numbers get larger. Dates of CE read left to right as the numbers get larger.

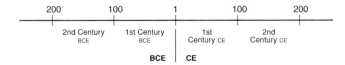

- Historical events are often referred to by century instead of specific dates. For example, the dates in the 1700s are in the eighteenth century.

Cartoon Analysis

Cartoons are drawings in which the artist exaggerates features to make a statement of opinion about the subject of the cartoon. (Cartoons appeal to the reader's emotions.)

- The purpose of a political cartoon is to get readers to look closely at the subject, question their views on it, and sometimes change their opinion about it.
- Political cartoons portray public figures, the general public, institutions (such as the government), and news events.
- Many cartoons use humour for a serious purpose (not just to be funny).
- Some of the information in cartoons is factual, and some information is symbolic. The reader's goal is to **interpret** the information shown and understand the cartoonist's message about the subject.

Example:

This cartoon appeared in the *Canadian Illustrated News* on January 29, 1870. What are the choices facing the Red River Settlement? What impression of the Red River Settlement does the cartoonist present to the viewer?

Interpret—understand or explain the meaning of a message that may be in a different form or language
Stereotype—an example with simplified characteristics used to represent a group; positive stereotypes show only the characteristics of the ideal person in a group; negative stereotypes show only negative characteristics, no individuality
Caricature—distortion or exaggeration

Steps for Interpreting Political Cartoons

Step 1: Examine what you see. Every detail has been included for a reason.
- the setting (public buildings, locations)
- the news story to which it relates
- the character(s): Who does the character represent? (A character may stand for the general public, a member of a specific group, or a well-known person.)
- symbols such as flags, logos, animals, or objects that represent something else (for example, the beaver is a symbol for Canada)

Step 2: Analyse what you see:
- What looks important or powerful? The foreground and the centre are important positions in a picture. The important parts of a picture are large, stand out, have more detail, or attract your attention in some way.
- What looks powerless? (may be small, in a low position, at the back, portrayed as weak)
- How does the cartoon make you feel? How do the characters make you feel?
- **Stereotypes** are often used to identify a character as belonging to a certain group. They may show negative bias. (See Bias on page 352.)
- **Caricature** of facial features may be used to identify public figures (for example, Macdonald's long curly hair and large nose).
- Words in cartoons give important information.
- When and where was the cartoon published? The common opinions and attitudes towards issues in the historical period can help you understand the intended message of the cartoon.

Step 3: Examine the cartoonist's attitude and purpose:
- Does the cartoonist praise or criticize the different characters or the event?
- Is something being made fun of? being explained? being revealed (made public)?
- Is a certain point of view given?
- Is something being distorted or made ugly or frightening?

Critical Thinking

![icon] Critical thinking means not accepting information just as it is presented to you, but questioning it to confirm its accuracy.

Facts and Opinion

The information that you receive was chosen by someone and gives that person's point of view.* Facts may be accurate or they may be wrong or confused. They involve the writer or speaker's opinion about facts. It is important to be able to distinguish between factual information and opinion.

- A fact is something that is supported by evidence and is not contradicted by other evidence. It can be checked and most people agree about it.
- An opinion is something believed to be so. Opinion may be based on fact. However, unless evidence is given to confirm or prove it, you must question it.

Example

Sir John A. Macdonald was Canada's first prime minister. (fact)

This can be verified (proven) using historical records.

Sir John A. Macdonald was Canada's most important prime minister. (opinion)

Bias

Learning to detect bias is an important part of critical thinking. Bias means showing a preference by portraying something positively or negatively. Bias shows the author/artist's opinion about the subject. Bias can distort the facts, so it is important to recognize when it occurs.

Examine images and text carefully.

- Do the photographs or illustrations portray the subject negatively or positively?
- What words are used? Are they negative or positive?
- What facts are given and what facts are left out?
- Are people, ideas, places, or events distorted in order to criticize or make fun of them?
- How do you think you were intended to feel about the subject?

*Points of view are represented throughout this textbook, in journal and diary excerpts, eyewitness accounts, quotations, role-plays, decision-making, and critical thinking activities.

**Issues involve a problem or question for debate. Issues are often written as a question that uses the word "should." There is often not a definite answer to an issue. Refer to pages 356 and 357 under Decision-making for more information about issues.

Critical Thinking Model 1

Steps for Critical Thinking

Step 1: Identify the issue and examine the information you already have about this issue.
- Are your facts accurate?
- Are there any ideas that do not relate or work together or ideas that contradict one another?
- How reliable is the information?

Step 2: Identify the various people who will have different points of view in a situation.
- Who are the various people who would have an interest in and opinion about this issue?

Step 3: Try "stepping out" of your own point of view and thinking about what one or more of the other people might think about this issue.
- Why does a person think the way s/he does?
- Why does a person think his or her way is best?
- Why does s/he choose to do things differently?
- What might a person be feeling to act the way he or she does?
- What might a person be thinking to have certain feelings?

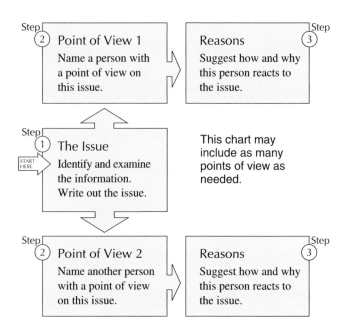

Step 2 — **Point of View 1** Name a person with a point of view on this issue.

Step 3 — **Reasons** Suggest how and why this person reacts to the issue.

Step 1 — **The Issue** START HERE Identify and examine the information. Write out the issue.

This chart may include as many points of view as needed.

Step 2 — **Point of View 2** Name another person with a point of view on this issue.

Step 3 — **Reasons** Suggest how and why this person reacts to the issue.

Critical Thinking Model 2

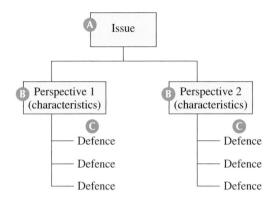

Steps for Critical Thinking

(A) Identify an issue or conflict and the points of view to be represented. Summarize the facts.

(B) Describe each person whose point of view is represented.

(C) Provide your defence. Use a graphic organizer such as the one above to diagram opposing points of view about the facts.

- Interpret how each character would view the facts.
- Defend the person's position, giving supporting evidence. Anticipate and understand the opposing point of view so that you can counter it effectively.

Thinking/Writing/Debating from Another's Point of View

Some questions require you to write or think from someone else's point of view; for example, *In role as a member of the Canadian Party, describe what happened in Red River before the Metis set up the provisional government.*

Understand the Person and the Issue

Ask yourself the following questions:

- Who is it? What background does the person have that is important to the issue? (e.g., country of origin, culture, politics, way of life, religion, age, gender)
- What are his/her values and beliefs?
- What is at stake for the person in this issue?
- Does the person understand the opposing viewpoints? What do his/her enemies say about the issue? How would the person counter these arguments?

Some Tips for Critical Thinking

- **Avoid oversimplifying.** It is possible that additional information could change how you think. Examples of oversimplifying follow.
  - It should always be this way.
  - It should *never* happen that way.
  - *Everyone* did it.
  - It was *completely* good.
  - It was *totally* wrong.
  - He/She is *always* right/wrong.
  - This factor is the *only* cause.

- **Use qualifiers like the ones below** to remind yourself that you may not have all the information you need to make a final judgement on an issue. Qualifiers help the reader to recognize that there is still some doubt. Examples of qualifiers follow.

  - highly likely
  - most
  - seldom
  - often
  - probably
  - many
  - some
  - sometimes
  - usually
  - I doubt
  - not very likely
  - I suspect

Example

Most people in Canada West were in favour of Confederation.

Because the word "most" is used instead of "all," the statement shows that there may also have been some people in Canada West who were opposed to Confederation.

353

Debates

Debates may be formal or informal, but they always have some rules. A debate has a purpose, a structure, and a conclusion.

Purpose

A debate is an organized way to discuss and come to a conclusion about an issue. The issue is stated at the beginning. All of the discussion must relate to it. Discussion may have two sides (as in a formal debate) or many different sides (as in a round-table debate with a chairperson).

Structure

In a debate, one person speaks at a time and the other participants listen. Either there is a particular order in which participants speak, or else someone acts as chairperson. In a chaired debate, speakers signal and are given permission to speak.

Conclusion

The last speakers in the debate sum up the discussion for their sides. There is more than one way to come to a conclusion on the issue. In a formal debate, a moderator may judge the points that have been made by each side and decide which side made the best arguments. In a round-table debate there may be a vote.

One Model for Formal Debating

Formal debates follow a set order of speakers and the time given to each speaker is arranged in advance. The following is one format for opposing three-person teams.

1. First Pro Speaker—introduction; define terms; give opening argument
2. First Con Speaker—summarize opposing argument; give rebuttal; give your team's first argument
3. Second Pro Speaker—summarize previous Pro argument; rebut Con argument; give your team's second argument
4. Second Con Speaker—summarize debate points; rebut pro argument; give your team's second argument
5. Third Pro Speaker—summarize previous points; rebut Con arguments; conclude your team's arguments
6. Third Con Speaker—summarize previous points; rebut Pro Arguments; conclude your team's argument

Games

1. Decide why players will be playing your history game (the game's **objective**).
   - to introduce new material
   - to review a chapter or section
   - to help them study
2. Decide the **topic/theme** that your history game will teach. Will it review a chapter or focus in depth on a certain topic (like the Canadian Pacific Railway or homesteading)?
3. Decide what **type** of history game you are going to create.
   - board game
   - card game
   - word game
   - game show
4. Will the game involve some or all of the following?
   - knowledge (questions and answers)
   - skill
   - chance (luck)
5. What will the game players have to do?
   - answer questions
   - match information
   - solve a problem (Will you provide alternatives and consequences?)
6. Prepare clear and concise **rules**.
7. Useful **materials** include: large pieces of cardboard, spinners, dice, index cards, tokens, felt pens, scissors
8. Consider
   - **number of players**
   - length of **time** to play
   - how the **winner** is decided (unless you are designing a co-operative game)
   - number of points a correct answer is worth

Some Tips

1. **De-bug** the game before playing. Play it with your family or friends. (Use their suggestions to improve the game.)
   - Does it teach what you want it to teach?
   - Does the game work?
   - Are your rules understandable?

   Test and re-test the game.
2. If your game has questions and answers, prepare an answer reference sheet. (If players question whether an answer is correct, refer to a reference, e.g., a page number in *Canada Revisited 8)*.
3. Name your history game.
4. Design a colourful, interesting game board or set of cards that reflects the game's theme, e.g., railway tracks in a game on the CPR, township and sections (as on page 177) for a homesteading game, a timeline shape for games involving dates. Include pictures.

Interviewing Techniques

An interview is used to gather information from a person.

1. Prepare yourself well for the interview. Find out about the person you are going to interview (e.g., from newspaper and magazine articles).
2. Set up an appointment ahead of time. Introduce yourself, tell where you are from, and give the reason for the interview.
3. Either tape the interview or take notes. Ask the person you are going to interview for their permission first.
4. Be friendly. Ask simple questions at first to put the person at ease.
5. Don't talk too much. Let the person you are interviewing do the talking.
6. Avoid questions that can be answered with just "yes" or "no."
7. Prepare about five questions ahead of time.

Sample questions to provide information about the person interviewed.
> "What is your name?"
> "Where do you work?"
> "Describe the type of work you do."

Sample questions to focus on how people feel about an issue or a problem.
> "How do you feel about . . . ?"
> "What do you think about . . . ?"
> "Do you agree with . . . ?"
> "Do you disagree with . . . ?"
> "How would you change . . . ?"
> "Do you think . . . is working?"
> "What needs to be changed?"
> "What are the problems?"
> "What do you like the best about your job?"
> "What do you like the least about your job?"

An interviewer usually summarizes the interview by asking a few summary questions.
These questions make sure the interviewer has understood what has been said by the person being interviewed.
> "You feel . . . ?"
> "You disagree with . . . because . . . ?"
> "You agree with . . . but think there are problems?"
> "You think . . . will work because . . . ?"

8. Write up your report as soon after the interview as possible.
9. Send a thank-you letter.

Interpreting Images

Photographs, paintings, illustrations, and drawings are excellent sources of information. You should "read" visuals for information as you would read words.

In your mind divide the photograph into parts.

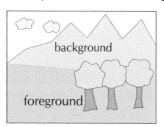 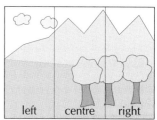

Look for details, then ask yourself the first set of questions. Not all questions will apply to all photographs.

Make a quick web or point form notes answering these five questions.

1. What do you see in this picture? Describe details in each part of the photo.
2. Who is in the photo? What are the people doing? What is happening?
3. Where do you think this picture was taken?
4. When? How can you tell?
5. Why do you think the photograph was taken or the picture drawn?

Other questions and activities.

1. How are people dressed? What does this tell about them?
2. Notice their facial expressions. What feelings do you think the people are expressing?
3. How do people seem to be relating to or interacting with each other?
4. Put yourself in the place of one of the people in the photo. How would you feel?
5. Locate buildings. Describe them. Are they old or new? Are they for living in or for work? What type of technology was used to build them?
6. Examine transportation and communication methods.
7. Examine the level of technology.
8. Examine the geographic features: landforms, climate, vegetation, rivers and other bodies of water. How do these features affect human activity?

Decision-making

![gear and head icon] Decision-making is a process used to resolve an issue. Issues are problems or questions for debate. They are often written as a question using the word "should." For example, Should students be allowed to wear whatever they like to school? There is often not a definite answer to an issue. A person must choose from several alternatives. As a result, opinions and emotions are often involved.

Decision-making Model 1

Steps for Decision-making

> **Step 1: Decide: What is the issue to be solved?**

> **Step 2: Brainstorm for alternatives (choices).**

> **Step 3: Analyse the alternatives.** List the consequences (results) of each. That is, list the pros (+) and the cons (−).

> **Step 4: Decide what options are best.** Try to select the alternative(s) with the most positive and the fewest negative consequences. Organize the alternatives in rank order, from the most desirable to the least desirable.

> **Step 5: What is your decision? Choose the "best" alternative.**

> **Step 6: Evaluate your results.** Ask yourself this:
> * Was this a fair and effective decision? Why?
> * What difficulties are expected from this decision?
> * What benefits are expected from this decision?
> * Faced with the same issue again, would I change my decision? Why?
> * What changes or improvements might be made to this method of decision-making?

Decision-making Chart 1

Issue: _____ Step①_____

Alternatives	Consequences	Step④ Priorities
1. Step②	+ Step③	
	−	
2.	+	
	−	
3.	+	Decision Step⑤
	−	Evaluation Step⑥

Decision-making Model 2

Steps for Decision-making

Step 1: Understand the Issue

a) **Brainstorming:** As a class, carry out a brainstorming activity focusing on these questions:
   - What is the issue?
   - Why is it important?
   - To whom is it important?
   - Who can do something about the issue?
   - What must be done to work towards a solution on the issue?

b) **Journal writing:** Analyse your own values and beliefs on the issue. Think about and then write about whether the issue is important to you. Provide reasons.

c) **Small group discussion, reporting to the class, and recording ideas:** In small groups of three or four students, discuss each member's feelings and beliefs on the issue (from Journal Writing above). Each group should take notes and report verbally to the class. The teacher should record the ideas on chart paper to be posted in the classroom for later reference.

Step 2: Study the Issue

a) **Research and record information on Decision-making Chart 2:** In original groups, classify and compare information on the issue to understand what **value conflicts** are involved in it.
   - How many sides (alternatives) are there? List these under Ⓐ on the chart.
   - What values are involved in each alternative? Ⓑ
   - What costs are involved in each alternative? Ⓒ

- What are the positive (+) and negative (–) consequences for each alternative? List these under Ⓓ .

b) **Individual journal writing:** Clarify your own position on the issue.
   - Read each side (alternative).
   - Think about each alternative and write in your journal how you view it. (Do you agree or disagree? Why?)

c) **Survey:** Survey your parents and/or several other adults about the issue.

d) **Small group discussion:** In original groups, share/discuss the results of the survey. Discuss any new ideas.

e) **Individual journal writing:** Think about new ideas on the issue. Write in your journal:
   - Have your values changed? If yes, in what ways? If no, why not?

Step 3: Make a Decision
Small group discussion:

a) If you were in a position to solve this issue, what would you do?

b) Who will make the final decision?
   - Are the decision-makers accountable to anyone?
   - Do you feel strongly enough on the issue to take action? What action can you take?

Step 4: Develop an action plan: (see page 365)

a) Record your plan on chart paper and post in the classroom.

b) Develop an assessment plan to evaluate the effectiveness of your action. (See page 368.)

Decision-making Chart 2

Issue							
Ⓐ Alternatives		Ⓑ Values involved in this alternative		Ⓒ Costs involved in this alternative		Ⓓ Consequences (+) (–)	
1.						(+)	
						(–)	
2. etc.						(+)	
						(–)	

Value conflict—choosing between competing beliefs

Essay Writing

Essays can also be called position papers.

An essay is a written composition on a certain subject. The purpose of an essay is to demonstrate that you understand a topic or to persuade a reader to share your point of view. An essay assignment often takes the form of a question beginning with "Why," "Should," or "To what extent."

Before Writing

- Read the topic or question carefully. (You cannot demonstrate your understanding if you don't understand the question.)
- Brainstorm ideas about a possible **thesis**, **arguments**, and supporting evidence.
- Make quick notes of ideas that occur to you. Use a web to show how ideas relate to each other.

Constructing an Essay

Regardless of length, an essay should include an introduction, a body, and a conclusion.

Introduction

To demonstrate understanding, you will need to introduce the topic. Write an overview about what your essay includes or the problem to be examined. Make a statement that answers the assigned question. This is your thesis.

Your thesis provides the focus of the essay and limits what you will write about. (For example, rather than writing everything about the government of the United Province of Canada, your essay might explain how forming the Great Coalition solved the problem of political deadlock.)

Recall your thesis regularly while writing your essay. It will help you

- avoid answering a different question than you started out to answer
- avoid adding extra details that don't support your argument (your thesis)

Body

Your essay needs to be well-organized and persuasive.

- Take the ideas and supporting evidence you came up with initially and begin to organize them. Use Charts and Graphic Organizers to organize your ideas (see pages 349 and 363), or make an outline of the order in which you will present your arguments and evidence.
- The length of an essay can vary. However, even in a short essay, you should support your thesis with a minimum of three important ideas. Present your arguments and evidence logically to support your thesis. (The diagram on page 353 may be helpful.)
- The simplest way is to present each argument as the topic sentence of a paragraph. Then support each argument with evidence in the same paragraph. Each point you make should lead to the next. All of the points should relate to the topic sentence. Do not include information that does not belong.
- Each paragraph in the body should also lead logically to the next. Use transition words and phrases to link ideas in your argument logically.

Examples of Transition Words

- with this in mind
- as a result
- later
- in a similar way
- however
- furthermore
- then
- therefore
- on the other hand
- as well
- so

Conclusion

Sum up your arguments by restating them. If possible, link them together in your final statement in order to persuade your reader that you are right about your thesis.

Thesis—a statement that is made about a topic and defended with evidence and logical argument

Argument—reasons that show your thesis is correct and reasons the opposite point of view is wrong

Propaganda

Propaganda is information designed to affect public opinion about an issue. It is created to persuade the public to do or believe something. It may be used in any mass-media form that reaches the general public: printed text or images, video, radio, or internet-based. For example, posters were used for propaganda by both sides during World War I.

- Propaganda usually does not give all of the important facts. It usually gives only one point of view on an issue. It is not balanced.
- The techniques used to get people to believe in or support one side of an issue often involve getting them to hate or oppose the other side. Propaganda appeals to people's emotions, both negative and positive. It uses a variety of means.
  - dramatic style of presentation, writing, or images (e.g., bright colour, large type, loud noises, fast-paced action or editing of film, exciting music)
  - emotional appeal (e.g., to love, hate, feel pride or loyalty)
  - disturbing or frightening images
  - sentimental, sweet, appealing images
- Advertising is propaganda directed at the public, encouraging them to buy one product and reject the competitor's product.

HE'LL WANT TO KNOW

"Daddy, how did you vote in the Big War Election?"

Techniques

Technique	Examples
Glittering generalities (Basket words) Using descriptions that are so broad that they are unclear Using slogans that capture attention and stick in the memory	"Live the Canadian dream. Let the majesty of the Rocky Mountains inspire you to greater heights." "Humanity's future rests in the arms of today's youth."
Transfer Transferring ideas and emotions from one idea to another	"Experience the woodsy fragrance of the northern forests in Muskoka air freshener."
Testimonial Using a well-known individual or organization to promote products	"Begin each morning with Champion cereal," says Mark Strong, 18-year-old Canadian swimming gold-medalist.
Plain folks Talking in words and phrases that appeal to ordinary people	"Round up the family and enjoy good times at Cowboy Bob's down-home barbeque grill."
Bandwagon Suggesting that everyone is doing it and, to be "in," so should you	"Well-informed people are joining the winner's circle. Vote for your local Nation Party candidate."
Card-stacking Strongly promoting favourable points while reducing or avoiding negative points	"Mistview Resorts, near Bluebird Falls, provides the holiday of your dreams: scenic walks, tours, free babysitting, and everything you need for a perfect week away."
Hidden fears Playing upon the individual's sense of insecurity	"Sleep well. Secure your home with Confidina locks."
Direct order Appealing to the desire in people to be told what to do	"Don't miss the deadline. Enrol today in Majesty Learning Centres, Canada's best home learning program."
Either-Or disease Suggesting there are only two possibilities, "right" and "wrong"	"A vote for me is a vote for progress; a vote for her is a vote for the past."
Name-calling Using "put down" words or phrases as labels for a person, group, or thing	

Sources

Historians obtain their information concerning Canada's past from three types of sources: primary, secondary, and objects from the past.

1. Primary Sources

Primary sources, also called eyewitness accounts, fall into three categories:
- those written *at the time* of the event by people who participated in or who witnessed the event described
- those written *a short time after* the event by people who participated in or who witnessed the event described
- those written *a long time after* the event by people who participated in or who witnessed the event described

Archives have collections of historical primary source material, especially photographs and documents like diaries and letters.* Individuals may also have family documents and photographs. Old paper is very fragile and must be handled carefully. Use only copies for your research.

Some Tips for Using Primary Sources
- When reading primary sources printed in a book, you may notice square brackets. This indicates that the author of the book has added or changed some words so you will find the excerpts easier to follow. The following example is repeated from page 100.

  . . . They [the United States] coveted Florida, and seized it; they coveted Louisiana, and purchased it; they coveted Texas . . .

- Periods (called ellipses) such as . . . and . . . . indicate that text has been left out. The person who selected the excerpts has chosen to include only those passages relevant to what you are studying.

  Three periods indicate text within a sentence has been deleted. Four periods indicate that the deleted text came at the end of a sentence, as in the quote below, repeated from page 174.

  . . . The only remedy for the evils which beset us, we believe to be in a close union with the adjoining States and Territories. . . .

2. Secondary Sources

Secondary sources are accounts recorded by people who were not present at the events described. They obtained their information by reading or talking with others who witnessed the events. They may contain primary source material if they use the words of an eyewitness to an event.

Examples of secondary sources that may contain primary source material:
- sagas
- legends
- most maps
- government reports
- religious records
- textbooks**
- storybooks, picture books
- audio recordings
- movies and videos that tell a story
- CD-ROMS

3. Objects from the Past

Objects from the past provide us with information of how people lived. They give information about technology, building materials, and styles of decoration. However, objects are only fragments from a culture. We don't always know how or why something was used, or what meaning it had for its owner. Objects and evidence from the past that tell how people long ago lived are called artifacts.

Pierre Descellier/National Archives of Canada/NMC 40461

The original of this map of North America is an artifact.

---

*Note: A visit to the website of the University of Saskatchewan Archives provides a list of various links to Canadian archives, museums, and special collections. The address is http://www.usask.ca/archives/menu.html

---

**While most textbooks are secondary sources, some textbooks also contain primary sources.

Graphs

Graphs are used to present numerical information visually. Three common kinds of graphs are used in this book: bar graphs, line graphs, and circle graphs.

Graph Grid

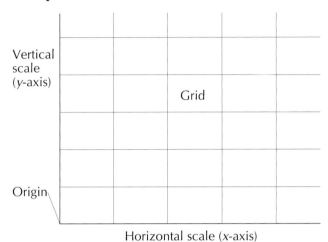

Bar Graphs

- used for comparison; may compare range in one or more items; for example, time, distance, quantity
- the vertical scale (y-axis) is marked in regular intervals (e.g., intervals of 10 percent) measuring the items being compared
- the unit of measurement is stated on the y-axis and the regular intervals shown
- the bottoms of the bars are placed on the horizontal base (x–axis)
- the bars are named or a colour-key used to identify them (e.g., Primary, Secondary, and Tertiary industry in the years 1901, 1911, and 1921)

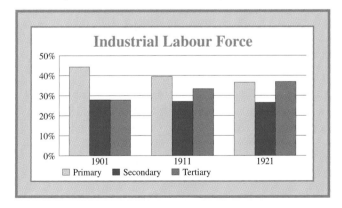

Line Graphs

- used to show trends over time
- the vertical (y-axis) line is marked at regular intervals; it shows changes that occur (e.g., intervals of $25 000 million)
- the horizontal (x-axis) line is marked in regular intervals; it is almost always labelled with units of time (e.g., yearly intervals)
- the unit of measurement on each axis is stated and the regular intervals shown

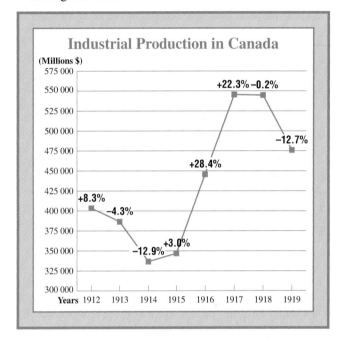

Circle Graphs

- also called "pie charts"
- used to compare the size of a part (or parts) to the whole amount or number
- usually created using percentages or fractions: the sum of the parts must equal 100% of something (e.g., population of a region)

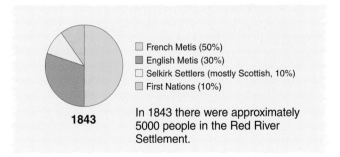

361

▦ Note Making

T-Notes

T-Notes combine written notes and drawings. Use the format below, or design your own.

Main title		
Write one or two sentences to describe what this section is about.		
Drawing or sketch	Sub-titles	• Write notes in point form here.

Point Form Notes (Rough Notes)

Writing point form notes involves reading a section, thinking about the main or most important ideas, and recording these ideas in your own words (paraphrasing). Your goal is to record only the most important ideas, using your own words.

Some ideas

• Use chapter and section headings.
• Under each heading, record only key words/ideas.
• Do not write in complete sentences. Use a dash (–) to begin new ideas.
• Use abbreviations.

Example
(Refer to page 34, Chapter 1)
Explorers and Fur Traders
–1778: Capt. Cook, Nuu-chah-nulth
  –already using iron
  –trade—Russian, Spanish explorers already here
  –area developed thru. fur trade (sea otter)
HBC
–George Simpson—duty to develop fur trade
–Ft. Vancouver
  –new post built when Ft. Astoria abandoned
  –became largest HBC fort on Pacific Coast
  –headquarters—HBC, McLoughlin

Outline Notes

Outline notes are also referred to as Outlining and Topical Outlines.

In this textbook titles are coded by size and colour in each section to help you create an outline or web. When a new idea is introduced the largest title size is used. Title size gets smaller as the idea is explained in greater detail.

Example

In Chapter 1, there are six *main ideas*—Nuu-chah-nulth (page 32), Explorers and Fur Traders (page 34), The British Colony of Vancouver Island (page 36), The British Territory of New Caledonia (page 40), The British Colony of British Columbia (page 42), and Change (page 48).

The six titles represent six main ideas, so they are each assigned a level one title in outline notes—a Roman numeral.

   I. Nuu-chah-nulth
   II. Explorers and Fur Traders
   III. The British Colony of Vancouver Island
   IV. The British Territory of New Caledonia
   V. The British Colony of British Columbia
   VI. Change

Under Explorers and Fur Traders (pages 34 and 35) there is one sub-title (level two title)—The Hudson's Bay Company—and two level three titles—HBC Post, Fort Vancouver and HBC Post, Fort Victoria. Sub-titles are smaller than the main idea title.

To make outline notes of pages 34–35, you could use a format similar to this one:

   I. Explorers and Fur Traders
     A. The Hudson's Bay Company
       1. HBC Post, Fort Vancouver
       2. HBC Post, Fort Victoria

When you have made an outline of all the titles, read the text and write brief notes under the appropriate titles. For example, under number 2. HBC Post, Fort Victoria, write the main details of the topic covered on page 35.

Graphic Notes

Graphic notes are also called graphic organizers.

- Create charts, diagrams, or timelines from the information in your notes.
- Add colour.
- Show comparisons visually (with little drawings and maps).
- Be creative in helping yourself see relationships between ideas; for example, use arrows, simple drawings, colour coding.
- If important material stands out on the page it will be recalled more easily.

Following are examples of different types of charts and graphic organizers. (See also page 349).

For organizing main ideas and supporting details:

a) **Webs**

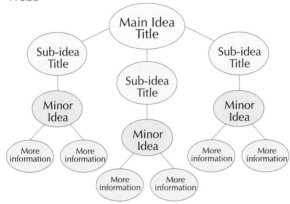

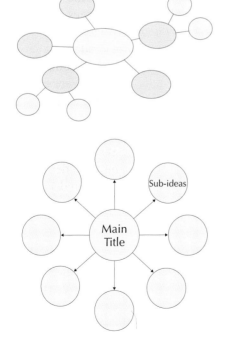

Write the title in the centre and notes in the "donut pieces," one idea per piece. Add to or take away partitions from the donut as needed.

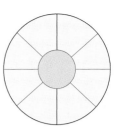

b) **Flow Chart**

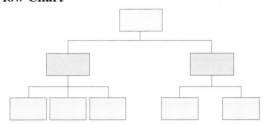

c) **Mind Map**

Mind maps work much like webs. Each idea is placed on a separate line. Each word or idea must be joined by a line to at least one other word or idea. Coloured sketches are often used to represent words or ideas. They help us remember.

The mind map shown below is based upon ideas and concepts covered in Section II.

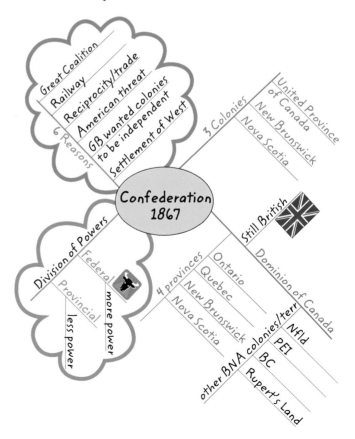

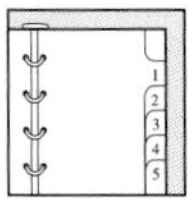

Notebook Organization

Your notebook is your record of the material you have studied. Your notes need to be easy to use and study from. One method of organizing your notes in four sections is outlined on page 23: Activities, WordBook, History Journal, and Learning How to Learn. Your teacher may tell you which categories to use, since she or he is familiar with what you will study. If you organize your notes by chapter, divide each chapter into the four sections.

Sample notebook page

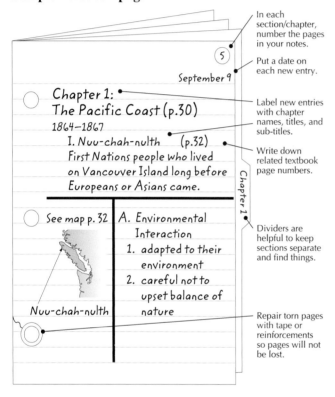

In each section/chapter, number the pages in your notes.

Put a date on each new entry.

Label new entries with chapter names, titles, and sub-titles.

Write down related textbook page numbers.

Dividers are helpful to keep sections separate and find things.

Repair torn pages with tape or reinforcements so pages will not be lost.

(notebook page contents:)

5

September 9

Chapter 1:
The Pacific Coast (p.30)
1864–1867
  I. Nuu-chah-nulth   (p.32)
  First Nations people who lived
  on Vancouver Island long before
  Europeans or Asians came.

See map p. 32 | A. Environmental
                 Interaction
              1. adapted to their
                 environment
Nuu-chah-nulth | 2. careful not to
                 upset balance of
                 nature

Chapter 1

Organization Suggestions

- Keep notes in sequence. Either date them and make them chronological or sort and organize them by topic using dividers in a binder.
- Create a table of contents for each section and chapter.
- Keep the pages in order. Add new information to the back of your old notes.
- Compare your notebook with that of a partner to check for items that are missing or out of order.
- Use colours to underline, highlight, illustrate, and code your notes. Colours help us to learn material.
- When you study, use the margins to add diagrams, list key words, write out definitions, refer to other sections of your notes, or connect to page numbers from the textbook.
- Develop a vocabulary of terms and unfamiliar words. (See Vocabulary, page 369.)

Study Skills

It is important to have good study skills and use them regularly. Study skills will help you learn new material, review, and prepare for exams.

Methods of Studying

- Learn by teaching to a friend or parent.
- Team study. Question each other. Read each other's notes—someone else's way of expressing an idea may stick with you. Get them to explain notes you do not understand. This will help you both.
- Use interviewing and role-playing to understand and be able to explain the point of view of important characters. You may need to write an assignment from someone's point of view.
- Use practice tests. Review old exams, predict the types of questions you may face, and practise sample answers. (Ideas follow.)

Test Questions

Make up your own exam questions and share them with others. For example, make the chapter headings into questions. Page 45 focuses on methods used to mine gold. Possible questions could be:

  –Name four methods of mining gold (or, What methods are used to mine gold? Describe each.)
  –Where is each mining method used?
  –What are the differences between the different methods?

Use the chapter headings to make up questions that ask the following:

- who
- why
- where
- contrast
- cause/effect
- when
- what
- compare
- describe
- classify

Visit Arnold Publishing's website for more details on studying and reviewing.

Presentations

In this book, presentation refers to communicating information in visual, oral, or written forms. To prepare and carry out a presentation, follow these steps:

Step 1: First, select one main topic or idea as a focus for your presentation. Everything you do must be related to or provide examples of this main idea.

Step 2: Select a method of presentation from the list that follows. Find out from your teacher or the library how you are to make or prepare it if you do not know.

Step 3: Read about your topic or idea in the textbook. Review any information you have about it in your research notes.

Step 4: Plan on paper how you are going to prepare the presentation you selected. Establish criteria for how to assess your presentation.

Step 5: Prepare the presentation on the topic or idea you selected.

Step 6: Present your topic or idea to your classmates. Assess your presentation based on the criteria from Step 4.

Some Presentation Ideas

advertisement	concept poster
banner	construction
booklet	cooking demonstration
cartoon	dance
charades	debate
chart	demonstration
collage	diagram
collection	diorama
comic strip	display

drawing	photographs
exhibition	picture
fact file	play
fairy tale	poem
flow chart	poster
game	project triangle
graph	puppet show
illustrated poem	puzzle
interview	questionnaire
job description	radio show
letter	rap
magazine	riddles
map	role-play/drama
mask	scrapbook
mime	scroll
mobile	sculpture
model	skit
mosaic	slide/tape show
multimedia presentation	song
mural	speech
music	story
newspaper	survey
newspaper article	tableau
oral report	talk show
painting	television show
pamphlet	timeline (illustrated)
panel discussion	top 10 list
papier-mâché	web page
photo album	written report

Action Plan

1. Date of Presentation _____

2. Describe what you want your part of the presentation to look like and/or sound like.

   _____
   _____
   _____

3. Plan on paper what tasks have to be done. Assign a completion date for each task.

	Task	Completion Date	Done
1.	_____	_____	_____
2.	_____	_____	_____
3.	_____	_____	_____

   (add to this list as needed)

Challenge yourself to complete a variety of presentations. Check the Arnold Publishing website for information about completing presentations.

Problem Solving

A problem is a difficult question that requires you to consider a number of possible solutions in order to choose the best. For certain kinds of problems (e.g., a math problem), there is one correct answer. However, there are many problems in life that have more than one solution.

Problems ask: Who? What? Where?
When? Why? How?

Steps for Problem Solving

Step 1: Define the problem. Decide what you want to find out.

Step 2: Come up with possible questions and a hypothesis to guide your research. (A hypothesis is a rough guess about the solution, based on what you know.)

Step 3: Do research to locate data (information) that relates to your hypothesis.

Step 4: Record the data (information) that relates to your hypothesis.

Step 5: Evaluate the information you have collected by thinking about whether it supports or disagrees with your hypothesis.

Step 6: Arrive at a conclusion by choosing what you think is the best solution—one that makes sense and solves the problem. Think about whether your conclusion agrees or disagrees with your hypothesis.

Step 7: Share your conclusion.

Problem Solving Chart

Problem	Step ①	
Hypothesis	Step ②	
Research Solution		**Data**
1.		
2.	Steps ③ ④	
3.		
4.		

I think #_____ is the best solution because
Steps ⑤ ⑥ ⑦

Problem: We don't have a lifeguard so the school swimming pool is closed except for classes.	
Hypothesis: If we can get a lifeguard, we will get more pool time.	
Research Solution	**Data**
1. Collect/earn money to pay lifeguard	—costs too much —not long-term solution
2. Find a qualified volunteer	—costs nothing —parents, older siblings —need more than 1, schedule
3. Best class swimmers take lifeguard test	—costs nothing — lifeguards don't get to swim —kids might not listen
4. Arrange to share costs with community	—have to share pool —school has no money to pay —school has the pool

I think #2 is the best solution because it doesn't cost anything and it will involve members of the community.

Role-playing

Role-playing is an opportunity to learn about a character and a situation using previous experience and knowledge and becoming involved in a lifelike situation.

This is an excellent activity for using critical thinking. When you place yourself in the situation of one of the individuals you are studying about, you experience an issue from their point of view.

Steps for Role-playing

Step 1: You will be assigned or you can choose a role-play scene. Research the historical time and the person you will be playing in advance.

Step 2: To begin a role-play, the people involved go into "freeze" positions, eyes closed. No one should be moving. Someone from the group (or the teacher) sets the scene by describing for the viewers the setting, the historical time period, and giving some background information on the issue.*

At the agreed-upon signal, the group "comes to life" and starts their planned conversation. Although characters are planned and researched ahead of time, you don't memorize lines as you would for a play. You speak and behave as the person you are playing might.

Step 3: After the role-play, discuss what happened. Think about what was learned from the activity by asking yourself the following:
- What did I learn about the issue?
- What did I learn about the points of view of the characters?
- How does this affect my viewpoint about the issue? (Has my viewpoint changed?)
- How can I relate this knowledge to what I am studying?
- Can I apply this information to other situations? How?

---

*Dressing in historical costumes or using suitable props may help to make role-play more authentic.

Researching Using the Internet

The internet is a network of computers around the world that are able to communicate with one another. When you go online to research a topic it means your computer is connected to this World Wide Web (the Web) of computers. The World Wide Web is made up of websites.

Anyone can publish anything they want on the internet. No one checks the information for accuracy. Websites can contain false and inaccurate information. It is always a good idea to ask, "Who produced this information?" when collecting information on the internet. Information posted on the internet by a government agency or an institution such as a university is likely to be more accurate than information created by an individual.

Avoid "cut + paste = plagiarize." When you find useful information on the internet, it is often tempting to just cut and copy sections from the website right into your own document. Copying other people's work without permission and calling it your own is called plagiarism. It is illegal. Record where information comes from and put quotation marks "—" around work you take directly from a website. Even if you use ideas from a website and write the information in your own words, you should record the online source you used.

Safe Surfing

When you are using the internet you need to be cautious about personal information you share. *Never* give out personal information (name, phone number, address, credit card numbers) over the internet. *Never* agree to meet someone you have met online. If you want to subscribe to an internet newsletter or register at a website, discuss this with your parents first. Have them check out the website.

Ad banners appear on nearly all of the commercial websites. They are the same as the advertisements you see on television. If you click on ad banners promising you prizes, free products, or chances to win money you will be linked to a website that will try to sell you something. *Never* buy anything on the internet until your parents have checked out the website.

Get your parents' or your teacher's permission before looking for information on the internet. Use only search engines and websites they have seen and approved. Tell your parents and/or teacher about unusual behaviour or objectionable material you encounter online.

Some useful websites on the internet are listed on page 390.

Self-assessment

Self-assessment means evaluating your work or performance to decide how well you have met the expectations of an activity. Check your own work against the ideas in Steps for Self-assessment below. Working with a partner, get him/her to also check your work, and you check his or her work. The goal is for both of you to improve the quality of your work.

Steps for Self-assessment

1. Review the expectations (criteria) for the assignment.
2. List the criteria you will use to assess your assignment.
3. Decide what you have to do to achieve Level 4 (highest rating) for each of the criteria. What would earn Level 3 (next highest rating) for each of the criteria? What would earn a Level 2? a Level 1?
4. Keep the criteria and rating descriptions in mind as you complete your assignment.
5. You may use the sample assessment format shown below. Change the criteria and descriptions to fit the assignment.

Three examples of self-assessment follow.

Self-assessment

Expectations (Criteria)
(Expectations to be decided by the teacher, the student, or both.)

1. _____
2. _____
3. _____

Personal Assessment   Level   1   2   3   4
                           (Circle one based on above criteria)

Reasons for circling the number I did: _____
_____

Next time, I would   _____
_____

This is what I learned about the way I think and work: __
_____
_____

Assessment by Teacher   Level   1   2   3   4
                            (Circle one based on above criteria)

Reasons for circling the number I did: _____
_____

Assessing a Group Activity

Performance Expectations (Criteria)

1. Started activity quickly and quietly
2. Demonstrated co-operative attitude
3. Worked quietly and effectively
4. Followed directions and stayed on task
5. Respected ideas, beliefs, and points of view of the other group members
6. Was sensitive to the feelings of others
7. Listened to others during discussion time
8. Everyone in group had opportunity to speak
9. All members of the group worked together to complete the task
10. Ideas/work from each member was included in final group activity

Evaluation of the Group: Level   1   2   3   4
                               (Circle one based on above criteria)

Reasons for circling the number I did:

What we learned about working together as a group:

What we would do differently next time:

Self Evaluation: Level   1   2   3   4
                        (Circle one based on above criteria)

Reasons for circling the number I did:

Teacher Evaluation: Level   1   2   3   4
                           (Circle one based on above criteria)

Reasons for circling the number I did:

Assessing a Project

Levels of Achievement

1	2	3	4
needs work	satisfactory	very good	excellent

Content

1. Effectiveness in accomplishing purpose (did what it was supposed to)
2. Amount and quality of ideas (enough ideas, good ideas)
3. Supporting detail (examples, evidence, or description)

Rating   1   2   3   4

Structure

4. Logical organization (sequence, order of ideas)
5. Coherence (hangs together as a whole)
6. Appropriate and correct format (as a letter, report, etc.)

Rating   1   2   3   4

Mechanics and Conventions

7. Spelling   9. Capitalization
8. Punctuation   10. Grammar

Rating   1   2   3   4

Presentation

11. Overall neatness
12. Special features (charts, drawings, graphs, title page)

Rating   1   2   3   4

Student Remarks

What I liked best . . . What I could do better next time

Vocabulary

Start a section in your notebook called WordBook. Record in it any new words you want to remember. Several strategies for recording vocabulary follow:

a)

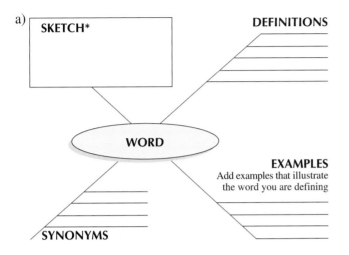

SKETCH*

DEFINITIONS

WORD

SYNONYMS

EXAMPLES
Add examples that illustrate the word you are defining

Example

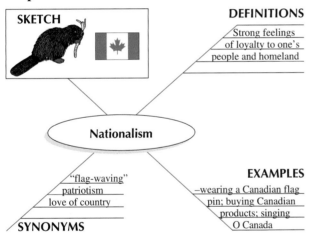

SKETCH

DEFINITIONS
Strong feelings of loyalty to one's people and homeland

Nationalism

SYNONYMS
"flag-waving"
patriotism
love of country

EXAMPLES
–wearing a Canadian flag pin; buying Canadian products; singing O Canada

b)

Word		Picture
		Draw a simple sketch of the word and colour it.* You are not expected to create something artistic. The activity of drawing aids memory.
Definition	**Example**	
Write a definition in your own words. Use the information in the textbook, the glossary, or from a dictionary.	Write examples using the word in context.	

Example

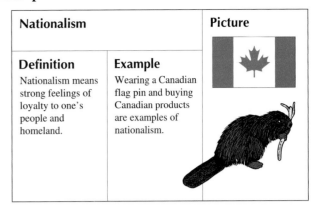

Nationalism		Picture
Definition	**Example**	
Nationalism means strong feelings of loyalty to one's people and homeland.	Wearing a Canadian flag pin and buying Canadian products are examples of nationalism.	

c)

Word
Definition
Coloured sketch*
Example

Word
Definition
Coloured sketch
Example

VOCABULARY

Word
Definition
Coloured sketch
Example

Word
Definition
Coloured sketch
Example

Example

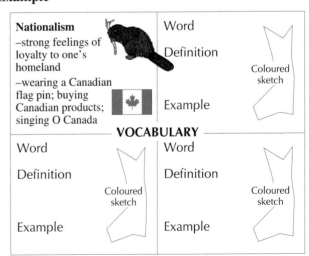

Nationalism
–strong feelings of loyalty to one's homeland
–wearing a Canadian flag pin; buying Canadian products; singing O Canada

Word
Definition
Coloured sketch
Example

VOCABULARY

Word
Definition
Coloured sketch
Example

Word
Definition
Coloured sketch
Example

*While drawing is preferred you could also use clip art or a photocopied image.

Writing

There are many types of writing. The form in which you write could include any of those described briefly on these two pages, or others. Your purpose for writing might include telling, persuading, explaining, reporting, describing. Think about your purpose and your audience so you can choose the most effective form and words. Challenge yourself by writing in a variety of forms.

Storytelling

There are many ways to tell a story about an incident or series of events. Stories may include your personal thoughts, feelings, and ideas. Stories are often meant to entertain.

1. **Biography**
   - Written account of someone's life
   - Includes information and events from the person's life so the reader can get to know that person
   - Will require research
   - An autobiography is a biography told by the person him/herself

2. **Diary or Journal**
   - Personal account (description) of daily activities and experiences
   - Each entry begins with the date
   - Includes thoughts, ideas, feelings

3. **Friendly Letter**
   - Tells about events/information of interest to the person who will receive the letter
   - Can also ask questions, congratulate, comment on events, tell entertaining stories
   - Intended for someone you know (e.g., friend)
   - Format includes writer's return address, the date, a greeting, and a closing

4. **Hard News Story**
   - Describes a current event of importance to the readers
   - Answers who, what, where, when, why, and how
   - Factual; may include quotations from people expressing opinions

5. **Historical Story**
   - Story based on historical fact (e.g., people, places, events) but may contain fictional parts (e.g., invented characters)
   - Requires research about people, events, and setting (description of place at the time)
   - See also Short Story (number 7)

6. **Play**
   - A story presented as a dramatic performance
   - Includes title, character and setting description, lines to be spoken by actors, direction about costumes, set/stage design, actions and expressions of the actors

7. **Short Story**
   - Includes title, description of characters and setting, conflict (problem)
   - Series of incidents or events take place as characters try to resolve conflicts
   - Climax or point of highest interest comes when the problem is solved. (Note: Problem may be solved in a positive or negative way.)
   - Conclusion

Persuading

Persuasive writing is intended to convince your reader to accept your point of view. Take care to use appropriate language and visuals. Hurting or insulting people will not change their viewpoints.

8. **Advertisement**
   - Announcement or written notice for the public
   - Provides information that is meant to persuade people to act in a certain way (e.g., buy a product, vote for a candidate)
   - Words and pictures should catch people's attention

9. **Brochure/Pamphlet/Flyer**
   - Usually a small booklet or folded sheet providing details (written and visual) that highlight the most appealing features of a place, person, event, idea

10. **Editorial**
    - An article (short essay) found in most newspapers that expresses an opinion on behalf of the newspaper about a current event or issue in the news
    - Includes facts that support a point of view and strengthen an argument

11. **Essay**
    - An essay is a written composition on a certain subject. See page 358 for details

12. **Letter to the Editor**
    - Letter written to a newspaper to express opinions about current events or issues
    - Includes facts that support a point of view and strengthen a position
    - May contain emotional and descriptive words

13. **Political Cartoon**
    * See page 351 for details

14. **Review or Critique**
    * An evaluation or judgement of a product or performance (e.g., play, movie, artwork, CD, book)
    * Gives information that supports the writer's claims and opinions
    * Can include emotional and descriptive words

15. **Speech**
    * May serve many different purposes (e.g., entertaining, paying tribute, congratulating); often intended to persuade or convince (e.g., campaign speech)
    * Intended to be spoken to an audience
    * Words should be appropriate for the audience and the situation
    * Planning and practising out loud are needed Volume, expression, pace, posture, and gestures give added meaning and impact to the words
    * Point-form notes (cue cards) may be used when presenting but should not be read

Explaining

This type of writing helps the reader understand how to do something and how/why something works as it does.

16. **Instructions/Directions/Manual**
    * Provide a step-by-step order
    * Use clear language that is easy to follow
    * Use special terms that relate to the topic and suit the audience (e.g., "sifting" is a suitable term in a recipe)

Reporting

Reports use knowledge gathered from a variety of sources and provide factual information.

17. **Census**
    * A specific count of the people living in an area
    * Might include information about ages, jobs, education, and religion

18. **News Report**
    * See Hard News Story (number 4)

19. **Newspaper**
    * Ideas for writing an historical newspaper found on page 137

20. **Magazine/Newspaper Feature Article**
    * Provides information about people, places, and events that are of interest to the readers
    * Usually requires an interview or other research
    * Includes visuals

21. **Research Report**
    * Provides detailed information on a specific topic or issue (see Research Model on pages x–xi)
    * Can be presented in a number of ways (see Presentations on page 365)

22. **Survey/Poll/Questionnaire**
    * An investigation about a situation or issue
    * Includes clear, specific questions intended for a certain group
    * Poll should allow for responses that are easily recorded and counted (e.g., Yes/No responses)
    * Results may be presented in graphs, charts, tables, or paragraphs
    * Polls should avoid bias; choose a large, random sample rather then just people you expect to answer a certain way

23. **Interview**
    * See page 355 for details

Describing

Describing can be a part of almost any form of writing.
* Includes details that appeal to the senses (sight, hearing, smell, taste, touch, and balance); these help the reader become involved in the subject
* Make careful word choices that are suitable to the form of writing (e.g., an instruction manual may need different descriptive detail than a brochure about a tropical resort)

Glossary

A

Absentee landlord—landowner who lives far from a property that is rented to tenant farmers, receiving revenue from the property but often not being responsible for costs

Accord—an agreement

Agents of change—causes of change

Alienated—isolated; feeling that laws and customs are foreign to them

Alliance—a group of nations that have agreed to co-operate

Ally—a person or nation agreeing to co-operate with another

Amnesty—a general pardon, usually for past political offences

Annex—join one territory to another; to take over neighbouring territory

Argument—reasons that show a statement (thesis) is correct and reasons the opposite point of view is wrong

Armistice—a formal agreement between countries to cease fighting

Arms race—a competition between countries to increase their weapons and fighting forces

Arsenal—a large collection of weapons

Artifact—an object or archaeological evidence of life from ancient times

Artillery barrage—an intense attack using many large weapons of war, often used to break down enemy defences before a ground attack by troops

Assassin—killer, especially one motivated by political or religious beliefs

Assimilation—the process through which one culture is absorbed into another

Autonomous—self-governing; able to act independently

B

Bannock—a flat, round bread made without yeast

Benevolent—wishing to help and do good for others; kind, caring

Biculturalism—two cultures existing side by side in the same country or province

BNA—British North America

Boers—descendants of Dutch settlers in South Africa

Bribe—a gift, usually money, given in order to get someone to do something wrong or against his or her intention

British Empire—all of the colonies, territories, and countries in the world that were ruled by England before 1931; a Commonwealth was formed in 1931 as a new political association among these countries

C

Canadiens—French-speaking people born in New France

Caricature—distortion or exaggeration

Cavalry—army units on horses

Censorship—examining communications and media for possibly offensive or dangerous material and removing it

Charter of rights—a written statement of legal and political rights

Chief factor—the Hudson's Bay Company employee in charge of a fur trade fort

Chinking—mud, often mixed with straw, forced between the logs of a log building to help make it weather-tight

Civilian—resident of a country who is not a member of the military

Claim—to mark out and then register a piece of land for the right to remove minerals from it

Clearances—the forced relocation or removal of small farmers from large estates owned by wealthy landowners; many immigrant families from Scotland lost their leased lands through clearances and sought new lands in North America that they could own

Coalition—a temporary joining together of two or more political parties

Collective bargaining—workers in similar trades negotiating with employers as a group, seeking an agreement on wages and working conditions that would apply to all of them

Colonial government—the government of a colony, usually led by a governor and other administrators who are appointed by the ruler or government of the parent country

Colonial secretary—the British Cabinet minister responsible for the colonies

Colonialism—a country's policy of seeking to rule over other territories as colonies

Commission—a group of people given specific tasks to perform or issues to consider; usually government-appointed

Compromise—an agreement in which each side gives up some of its demands

Compulsory—required

Concept—a general idea or thought

Concept poster—an information display that is more than just visual (See page 350.)

Confederation—the federal union of British North American colonies; the members retained some power over their own affairs and turned some powers over to a central government

Confiscate—to forcibly take away someone's property

Conscientious objectors—those who refuse to join the military because of their religious or moral beliefs

Conscription—the ability of a government to compel citizens by law to join the armed forces

Consensus—complete agreement among all

Constitution—the rules that govern a country; rules that define a country, the form of its governments, official language(s), and rights of citizens

Corn Laws—British laws that protected British agriculture by charging tariffs on the import of grain; grain from British colonies had lower tariffs than grain from other countries

Criteria—standards by which something is judged or categorized

Critical thinking—questioning information presented to you to confirm its accuracy (See page 352.)

Crofter—a Scottish person who cultivates a small farm

Crown lands—lands belonging to the government

Cultural distinctiveness—having unique cultural characteristics

Culture—a learned way of life shared by a group of people, including their shared knowledge, beliefs, attitudes, customs, traditions, laws, and roles

D

Dilemma—a difficult choice between equal options, each with good and bad consequences

Discrimination—an attitude of hostility directed against an individual, group, or race, which limits them unfairly compared with other groups

Disenfranchise—to take away someone's rights of citizenship, particularly the right to vote in elections

Diversity—differences, a variety

Dominions—the semi-autonomous major colonies of the British Empire

E

Economic change—change in the way a person or a community acquires the basic needs of life; for example, the discovery of gold in a region would introduce mining as a way of life, increase exports, change the population

Effigy—an imitation of a person

Emigrant—a person who leaves a country to go to live in another country

Emigrate—to leave one country for another

Employment insurance—money given by the government to assist people who have lost their jobs

Enfranchise—to give the right to vote in elections

Euro-Canadian—a person of European origin, whether from Great Britain, Europe, or the United States, who is living in Canada

Executive Branch—policy-making body of the Canadian government, headed by a governor general acting in the name of the British monarch (BNA Act, 1867); approves proposed legislation before it goes to the House of Commons and the Senate to be debated

F

Factory—a trading post where large quantities of food and trade goods were stored. The chief factor and the men of the Hudson's Bay Company lived at the factory.

Federal union—a political union with two levels of government in which the members (the colonies of British North America) have certain powers over their own affairs, and certain powers are turned over to a central government

Federalism—a system of two levels of government, a federal (national/central) government and provincial governments. The federal government has more power. Each level of government has responsibility for certain matters, and some matters are shared responsibility.

Fenians—a group of Irish Catholics in the United States who wanted to end British rule over Ireland

First Nation—a group that identifies itself as having been a nation living in Canada at the time Europeans came; a First Nation is a group of people with a shared language, territory, way of life, and government; today, may refer to a band (under the Indian Act) living on a certain reserve. The chart below lists a number of First Nations referred to in this book that may be found under different names in your research. This textbook has attempted to use the name the group chooses to call itself.

In this book	Other Names Used
Anishinabe	Ojibwa/Ojibway
Dakota	Sioux
Kainai	Blood
Mi'kmaq	Micmac
Nakoda	Stoney
Nakota	Assinaboine
Nuu-chah-nulth	Nootka
Pikuni	Peigan
Siksika	Blackfoot
Sto:lo	Coast Salish
Tsuu T'ina	Sarcee
Wendat	Huron

Free trade—trade between countries without taxes and tariffs on imports and exports

Free trader—person who believes in having no restrictions on what goods are sold or to whom they are sold, and no tariffs on goods being sold to another country

GH

HBC—Hudson's Bay Company

Homestead—a piece of unfarmed public land, granted to a settler by the federal government under certain conditions

Hundred-acre—describes a plot of land equal to about 4 hectares or 40 000 square meters

Hypothesis—a rough guess about the solution based on what you know (See page 366.)

I

Identity—the way you perceive yourself; the characteristics that make you distinctive

Immigrate—to move to a country from another one

Imperialism—building an empire by taking control of lands not part of the home country

Inauguration—official ceremonial beginning of something

Industrialization—the growth of large industries as an important part of a region, employing a large number of people

Intercolonial— joining the various colonies

Intern—to confine

Internment camp—place where people are confined, often placed in isolated regions

Interpret—understand or explain the meaning of a message that may be in a different form or language

Interpretation—trying to understand or explain information that is unclear

Inventory—the collection of unsold goods and other possessions belonging to a business

Issue—a problem or question for debate (See footnote page 352.)

J

Judiciary Branch—branch of the Canadian government comprised of the system of courts and the Supreme Court; interprets the law and carries out justice

Jurisdiction—area of authority and responsibility

K

Kinship—having some of the same ancestors or being related by marriage or adoption

L

Labour unions—workers' organizations that bargain for better wages or working conditions for their members

Land speculator—someone who buys land intending to sell it and make a quick profit, rather than to live on it

Legislate—make laws

Legislative Branch—Parliament; the branch of the Canadian government that makes laws and votes on taxes and sources of revenue

Loan guarantee—a promise to pay debts if the borrower is unable to

Lobby—represent a special interest to the government. A lobbyist tries to get lawmakers to introduce or vote for measures favourable to the lobbyist's special interest.

M

Magistrate—a government official who heard cases in a lower, provincial court of law

Mandatory—required

Manifest Destiny—an American policy of westward expansion based on the belief that all of the North American continent should become part of the United States

Maritime union—a proposed confederation of the Atlantic colonies based on their shared interests as a maritime (ocean) region

Mass production—producing many identical articles, usually in a factory

Mercantilism—economic theory that called for a country to accumulate wealth in gold and silver. This was done, in part, by developing colonies as sources of raw materials and markets for finished goods.

Metis—people of mixed First Nations and European ancestry; first referred to as a separate people in the Red River area

Metis Bill of Rights—a list of conditions the Metis demanded that the Canadian government recognize and abide by

Militarism—building up military strength through acquiring armies, navies, and arsenals (large collections of weapons)

Militia—citizens who are not regular soldiers but undergo training for emergency duty or local defence

Morale—mental attitude of courage, confidence, enthusiasm (can be positive or negative)

Mothers' allowances—money given by the government each month to mothers to buy necessities for their children

Multicultural—including cultural elements (language, religion, customs) from many different groups

Munitions—ammunition; shells, bombs, grenades

Muskeg—bog or marsh

N

Nationalism—strong feelings of loyalty to one's people and homeland

Nationalization—putting a business that is considered necessary for the public good under the ownership and control of the government

Navvy—a man who worked on the end of the railway line, laying tracks

Neutral—a government policy of not taking sides in conflicts between other countries

NWC—North West Company

NWMP—North West Mounted Police

O

Obituary—notice of a person's death

Optimistic—expecting the future to be positive

Order-in-council—a regulation passed by the Cabinet that does not require the approval of Parliament (the House of Commons and Senate)

PQ

Pagan—a person holding religious beliefs other than the major religions of the world

Palisade—a high fence or enclosure

Patriotism—love of one's country; loyalty and support for the country's interests

Patronage—the power to grant favours or give jobs in return for political advantage

Pay equity—equal pay for equal work

Paydirt—earth or ore that contains enough gold or valuable mineral to be worth mining

Pemmican—a food made of dried buffalo meat, buffalo fat, and berries. One kilogram of pemmican was considered equal to four kilograms of ordinary meat and would last for years. It was an ideal food for long journeys.

Petition—a formal request to a government or authority by a group of people, for a specific action

Piecework—pay for each item produced rather than a set wage

Placer—deposit of gravel or sand, usually in a stream bed, that contains valuable minerals such as gold

Political change—change in government or laws that affect a group; for example, the right to vote being given to a group that did not have it (enfranchisement)

Political deadlock—when government decisions (such as the passing of a bill) cannot be made because opposing sides have equal power

Population—the number of people living in a city, area, region, or country

Potlatch—large gathering or celebration where gifts are given, traditional to peoples of the Northwest Coast

Pre-Contact—before an Aboriginal group came into contact with European explorers. Contact happened sooner for groups nearer the oceans.

Primary industry—businesses that produce or extract natural resources and process them, such as agriculture, mining, fishing, forestry

Primary source—eyewitness accounts of the actual events, either in picture or text form

Proclamation—a formal announcement issued to the public by the government

Pro-manufacturing policy—a government policy to promote the development of Canadian manufacturing industries

Propaganda—information designed to affect public opinion about an issue

Protectionism—a government policy that protects the interests of groups within the country, particularly economic interests; for example, tariffs protect producers by adding taxes to the price of imports, making it possible for producers to compete successfully

Provisional government—a temporary government set up until a more permanent one can be established

R

Racism—believing that a particular race is superior

Radical—holding extreme opinions; wanting fundamental social, economic, and political changes

Rationing—controlling how much food or other products people can buy or use

Rebellion—a revolt or fight against a government that is legally in power

Rebuttal—argument that responds to and counters an opponent's argument

Recession—a sharp drop in levels of production and employment

Reciprocity—a mutual arrangement between two or more, in which each side gives the other similar advantages; an agreement for limited free trade between two countries

Red River cart—a strong, two-wheeled cart pulled by horses or oxen

Reform movement—group of people who want to change government and society

Repeal—to withdraw or abolish a law or regulation

Representation by population—the number of elected members in a Legislative Assembly (representatives) based on the number of voters (population); often shortened to "Rep by Pop"

Representative government—citizens elect people who represent them in their Legislative Assembly (decision-making body)

Resolution—a formal statement of intention

Responsible government—(United Province of Canada, 1849) members of the Executive Council were chosen from the group with the most elected members in the Legislative Assembly (rather than by the governor). If the Executive Council lost the confidence (or support) of the majority of the Legislative Assembly, it had to resign. The government was responsible to the Assembly.

Ruthless—merciless, without pity

S

Sacred—holy; having high spiritual value and given great respect

Satirical—holding someone or something up to ridicule in order to bring about change

Scrip—a certificate or coupon entitling the holder to either cash or land

Scurvy—a disease caused by a lack of Vitamin C

Secondary industry—businesses that manufacture goods

Self-government—the power of the members of a group to govern the group

Separate schools—publicly funded schools intended for Roman Catholic students (in most regions)

Separatist—trying to withdraw from a political union and set up a separate state

Significance—importance; making an important difference in a situation

Sinew—tough, strong fibres that connect muscle to bone

Slums—over-crowded, substandard urban housing lived in by the very poor

Social change—change in the relationships within a group or a community; for example, heavy immigration into a city might change the ratio between wealthy and poor, affect employment patterns, and affect the need for schools and services

Social issues—problems concerning groups or communities. Some social issues are inequality, racism, crime, violence, and neglect or abuse of people with less power by people with more power.

Social problems—problems concerning life in a community; problems that arise between people in day-to-day living

Social reform—improving the way people live by such means as education, health care, working conditions, wages, sanitation, and political power

Stereotype—an example with simplified characteristics used to represent a group; positive stereotypes show only the characteristics of the ideal person in a group; negative stereotypes show only negative characteristics, no individuality

Strategic—valuable for military or naval purposes

Subsidy—a grant; an amount of money that the government contributes or sets aside from a given year's budget, usually for a specific project

Suffrage—the right to vote

Suffragist—person who wants more people, especially women, to have the right to vote

T

Tableaux—participants represent a scene by taking a position and not moving. This can be based on a picture, story, or idea.

Tariff—tax paid on goods brought into a colony or country; tariffs protect internal production by raising the price of imported goods

Technology—using science to change raw materials for practical purposes; includes new skills, ideas, and tools for making life easier and more comfortable

Temperance—moderation in use or total avoidance of alcohol

Tenant farmers—farmers who rent, rather than own their land

Tertiary industry—businesses that provide services, such as transporting goods or building roads

Thatched—roof covering made from layers of straw or rushes tied together

Thesis—a statement that is made about a topic and defended with evidence and logical argument

Threshing machine—a harvesting machine used to separate grain from chaff and straw

Trade union movement—workers who are organized and working together to gain better working conditions and wages from their employers

Trading captains—leaders entrusted to carry on the fur trade

Transcontinental—across the continent

Travois—long poles with one end tied together and attached to a horse or dog and the other end dragging on the ground; used to move possessions

Treaty—an official agreement between nations

Typhus—a serious infectious disease that often occurred in epidemics in which many people died

UVW

U-boat—submarine (undersea boat)

Universal—for everyone

Urbanization—the growth of cities

Value conflict—choosing between competing beliefs

Vaudeville—theatre entertainment showing a variety of acts, such as singing, juggling, and comedy

Visible minorities—people whose appearance indicates they have a different ancestry from most people in their society

Winnow—to separate straw and chaff from grain by tossing it in the air so the heavier grain falls down and the chaff blows away in the wind

XYZ

York boat—a boat developed by the Hudson's Bay Company for transporting heavy freight by river

Other Contributions

Text Acknowledgements

24–25 BonBernard, Trudie, *Japan*. Edmonton, Arnold Publishing Ltd., 1997.

67 Cited from MacLeod, Margaret Arnett, ed., *Songs of old Manitoba*. Toronto: Ryerson Press, 1959.

119 Excerpt from Waite, P.B., ed., *Pre-Confederation*. Scarborough: Prentice-Hall of Canada, Ltd., 1965.

125 F 1075, the M.O. Hammond fonds, Archives of Ontario. Cited from Gwyn, Sandra, *The Private Capital*. Toronto: Harper & Collins Publishers Ltd., 1989.

126 Excerpt from Robertson, Heather, *More Than A Rose*. Toronto: Bantam-Seal, Inc., 1991.

133, 136 Excerpts from *Confederation*. Rolland Paper Company Limited.

183 From *Folk Songs of Canada*, Vol. 1 © 1954 Waterloo Music Co., Waterloo, ON, Canada, Used by permission.

196, 197 (bl), (mr), 199 (tl) Cited from Arnold, Phyllis A., *The Royal Canadian Mounted Police*. Edmonton: Canadian Social Sciences Services Ltd., 1974.

202, 203, 205 Excerpt from Denny, C.E., *The Law Marches West*. Toronto: J.M. Dent and Sons Ltd., 1939.

210 Cited from Ford, Clellan S., *Smoke from Their Fires: The Life of a Kwakiutl Chief*. New Haven: Yale University Press, 1941.

218 From Journal of Countess of Aberdeen.

222 Cited from *The Lounger*, July 1896 (Ottawa).

224 Excerpt from Wilson, Keith, "Making Tracks." *Horizon Canada*, Volume 6, Number 65.

228 Excerpt from Berton, Pierre, *The Great Railway*. Toronto: McClelland and Stewart Inc., 1992.

232 Questions adapted from R. Case and P. Clark, (eds.), *The Canadian Anthology of Social Studies and Issues and Strategies for Teachers*. Vancouver: Pacific Educational Press, 1999.

249 Excerpt from "The Spell of the Yukon" by Robert W. Service, © 1907.

250 Excerpt from "The Cremation of Sam McGee" by Robert W. Service, © 1907.

251 Cited from Morrison, William, "The Unsinkable Martha Black." *Horizon Canada*, Volume 7, Number 79.

290 Amaryllis, quoted in *The Private Capital* by Sandra Gwyn. Published by HarperCollinsPublishers Ltd. 1989.

332 How 'Ya Gonna Keep 'em Down On The Farm? (After They've Seen Paree). Words by Sam M. Lewis and Joe Young. Music by Walter Donaldson. Copyright © 1919 (Renewed) Donaldson Publishing Co., Warock Corp. and Mills Music, Inc., International Copyright Secured. All Rights Reserved.

334 Reprinted from "We Were There", *Maclean's*, January 1, 2000. Reprinted with permission.

368 (tr) Adapted from *Criterion-Referenced Evaluation: Getting Started* by Cathie Peters and Irene Rothenburger.

368 (br) Adapted from *Canada Revisited 7 Teacher's Resource Package*, Mary Sullivan and Sharon Smith, Arnold Publishing, 1999.

Picture Credits

The publisher gratefully acknowledges the assistance of the various public institutions, private firms, and individuals who provided material for use in this book. Every effort has been made to identify and credit all sources. The publisher would appreciate notification of any omissions or errors so that they may be corrected.

Legend

AO—Archives of Ontario
BCA—British Columbia Archives
CTA—City of Toronto Archives
GA—Glenbow Archives, Calgary, Canada
NAC—National Archives of Canada
NAL—National Library of Canada
PA—Phyllis A. Arnold
PAA—Provincial Archives of Alberta
PAM—Provincial Archives of Manitoba
SAB—Saskatchewan Archives Board
WCPI—Western Canada Pictorial Index

t	top	mc	middle center
tl	top left	mr	middle right
tc	top center	b	bottom
tr	top right	bl	bottom left
m	middle	bc	bottom center
ml	middle left	br	bottom right

2 tl Garry Andrashko for Plimouth Plantation, Box 1620, Plymouth, MA 02362; tc Photo: Parks Canada/Shane Kelly/1996; mr mc PA; br Photo: Brian Morin, Parks Canada, Ontario; bc ml Ted Curtin for Plimouth Plantation, Box 1620, Plymouth, MA 02362; **3** Courtesy of Arnold Jacobs **5** tl Ted Curtin for Plimouth Plantation, Box 1620, Plymouth, MA 02362; tr Photo: Parks Canada/Shane Kelly/1996; mc Photo Courtesy Tourism Newfoundland and Labrador; bl © NATIONAL WARTIME MUSEUM, London **6** (3) *First British Flag on North America*, by J. D. Kelly, by kind permission of Rogers Communications, Inc. **8** tl EDUTECH/ Arnold Publishing Ltd.; tc mc PA; tr Photo Courtesy of Sainte-Marie among the Hurons, Midland, ON, Canada; br Photo Courtesy of Lower Fort Garry National Historic Site; bl Photo Courtesy of Lower Fort Garry National Historic Site (W. Lynch) **10** (7) *Kelsey on the Plains*, by Rex Woods, by kind permission of Rogers Communications, Inc. **11** (9) PA **16** tl Photo Courtesy of Sainte-Marie among the Hurons, Midland, ON, Canada; tc bl ml PA; tr Photo Courtesy of Lower Fort Garry National Historic Site (LFG temp 1); mr mc Photo: Brian Morin, Parks Canada, Ontario **17** (4) *Emigrants' Arrival at Cork—A Scene on the Quay*, c.1830 (detail), IUV 10/5/ 1851, p.386, The Illustrated London News Picture Library **20** (11) *Canada's First Railway*, by J.D. Kelly, by kind permission of Rogers Communications, Inc.; (13) Reproduction of painting by Spencer Macky of *Market Day in Charlottetown*. Original painting currently hangs in the Council Chambers of City Hall in Charlottetown, PEI. This painting was presented to the city of Charlottetown in April, 1924 by Adam Andrew in memory of his early childhood days in Charlottetown. Courtesy of the Public Archives and Records Office of Prince Edward Island, Accession #2320/5-1 **24** mr (detail) NAC/PA-041359; br NAC/C-004988; (bottom row, left to right) (1) (3) (detail) NAC/C-004154; (2) (detail) NAC/C-010460; (4) (detail) NAC/C-000688; (5) (detail) Dupras & Solas/NAC/C-000694 **25** (top to bottom) (1) (detail) Jenny Russell Simpson/NAC/C-011246; (2) Massicotte, Edmond J., *L'Angélus*, 1921, Photolithographie, 22.6 x 31.4 cm, Collection: Musée du Québec, 69.515, Patrick Altman; (3) *The Taking of Vimy Ridge*, Richard Jack, 8178, © Canadian War Museum; (4) NAC/C-001173; (5) (detail) BCA/A-00937 **28** Reprinted with permission, Minneapolis Star Tribune. **29** Karen E. Bailey/ NAC/ C-143716 **32** tl PA; br Drawings by Gordon Miller **33** *Nootka Whalers*, reproduced with permission of Lewis Parker and Gerald Lazare/National Wildlife Federation; tr (detail) BCA/PDP02192 **34** (detail) Henry James Warre/NAC/C-001628 **35** ml *The Birth of Victoria, British Columbia*, by J.D. Kelly, by kind permission of Rogers Communications, Inc.; b (based on) Frederick Whymper/ NAC/C-001572 **36** tl BCA/ PDP00473; b (detail) Herman Otto Tiedemann/NAC/C-010379 **37** tl (detail) BCA/A-01112; mc (detail) BCA/A-01228; mr (detail) BCA/A-01679 **38** (detail) NAC/C-003101 **40** br Photo Courtesy Parks Canada, Langley National Historic Site; bl (detail) BCA/A-04313 **41** bl (detail) BCA/ PDP01898 **42** (detail) Hudson's Bay Company Archives, P-422, PAM **43** tr (detail) BCA/A-00937; bl BCA/A-00557 **44** tl (detail) BCA/A-01144; tr (detail) BCA/A-01100; bl BCA/A-03786 **46** br (detail) BCA/A-03081; bl (detail) BCA/A-00350 **47** ml (detail) BCA/A-03579; mr (detail) BCA/A-04915; br (detail) BCA/A-04046; bl (detail) BCA/A-03812 **48** ml GA (NA-674-66); bl (detail) BCA/C-09263 **51** PA **54** ml © Fred Cattroll; bl #S99-1130, © Canadian Museum of Civilization **56** tl PA; tr Illustration by Jan Sovak, © Jan Sovak; br *Moose Hunt*, Reproduced with permission of Lewis Parker and Gerald Lazare/ Sainte-Marie among the Hurons Historical Site **57** ml © 1999 Daniel Beatty Pawis; br Paul Kane (Canadian 1810-1871), *Indian Encampment on Lake Huron*, c.1845-50, Art Gallery of Ontario, Toronto, Purchase, 1932, Acc. no. 2121 **58** tl PA **61** tl (detail) C.W. Jefferys/NAC/C-073392; bl (detail) William George Richardson Hind/NAC/C-013965 **64** Manitoba Museum of Man and Nature **65** tl (detail) Henry Raeburn (attr.)/NAC/C-001346; br Sinclair, Caroline (Pruden), PAM, N8433 **67** John Kerr Collection, PAM, #5177 **69** bl © Fred Cattroll **77** ml Metropolitan Toronto Reference Library, J. Ross Robertson Collection, T12600; mr Photograph Courtesy of the Royal Ontario Museum, © ROM; br (detail) Benjamin Beaufoy/ NAC/C-002643; bl (detail) NAC/C-008166 **78** tl (detail) C.W. Jefferys/NAC/C-073395; tr Massicotte, Edmond J., *L'Angélus*, 1921, Photolithographie, 22.6 x 31.4 cm, Collection: Musée du Québec, 69.515, Patrick Altman; bl PA **80** tr Photograph Courtesy of the Royal Ontario Museum, © ROM **81** br PANB New Brunswick Museum Photographs P4-3-52 **82** br Fanny Bayfield (attr.)/NAC/C-005796; bl *View of Summerside, P.E.I., looking down Central Street from Willow Avenue, 1880*, (George Ackermann) (1803-1891), (watercolour on paper), Confederation Centre Art Gallery & Museum, Charlottetown, CAG 78.24 **83** ml Illustration by Francis Back from *Canada Rediscovered*, pg. 145. © Canadian Museum of Civilization; bl (detail) William Eager/NAC/C-041605 **85** (detail) John William Hill/NAC/ C-011239 **90** bl Digital imagery® copyright 1999 PhotoDisc, Inc. **97** Metropolitan Toronto Reference Library, JRR. 1456 T1B **98** Jenny Russell Simpson/NAC/C-011246 **99** (detail) NAC/C-018737 **105** (detail) Notman & Fraser Photographers. Copyright Toronto, Ont. To the Queen/NAC/C-006165 **106** tl (detail) NAC/C-004154 **108** tl (detail) Notman & Son/NAC/C-006166; tr (detail) William James Topley/NAC/PA-025477; bl (detail) William Notman/NAC/ C-016749 **110** tr (detail) NAC/C-022002; br (detail) NAC/C-006168 **112** bl (detail) NAC/C-018884; **113** tr (detail) Samuel Leonard Tilley, S1364, AO; mr (detail) William James Topley/NAC/ PA-025257 **118** *The Fathers of Confederation*, by Rex Woods, by kind permission of Rogers Communications, Inc. **119** tl Artist Dusan Kadlec; Commissioned by Parks Canada; br Barrett & MacKay, Courtesy of Parks Canada; bl Jamie Steeves, Courtesy of Parks Canada **120** tl Archives Nationales du Québec, Livernois (P560, S1, P200); b (detail) Jules-Isaiah Livernois/NAC/C-006350 **123** *All in the Family, Le Perroquet*. January 14, 1865. Courtesy Canadian Microfilming Company Limited **124** tr (detail) John William Bengough/NAL/C-078560; bl Election Banner. 1867. Artefact Collection. NSARM PANS N-4149 (Nova Scotia Archives and Records Management); tl (detail) Richard Short & Dominique

Serres/NAC/C-002482 **125** tl (detail) NAC/C-004154; ml (detail) Notman & Fraser Photographers. Copyright Toronto, Ont. To the Queen/NAC/C-006165; bc (detail) Notman & Son/NAC/C-006166 **126** tl (detail) William Notman/NAC/C-016749; tr (detail) AO, Samuel Leonard Tilley, S1364; br (detail) NAC/C-006168; mc (detail) NAL/C-007578 **127** tr (detail) William James Topley/NAC/ PA-028138; mr (detail) NAL/C-006186; mc (detail) William James Topley/NAC/PA-025477; ml (detail) NAC/C-022002 **128** *The London Conference*, by J.D. Kelly, by kind permission of Rogers Communications, Inc. **129** (detail) NAC/C-004154 **134** tr NAC/C-014989; mr NAC/POS-001434. © Canada Post Corporation, 1868. Reproduced with Permission.; br (detail) NAC/C-010813; bl *First Dominion*, Queen's University Archives, Kingston Picture Collection; ml The New Brunswick Museum, Saint John, N.B. **135** tl (detail) NAC/C-018292; mr GA (NA-1375-1); br (detail) S. McLaughlin/NAC/C-018371; bl Government of Canada/NAC/C-004393 **138** tr (detail) NAL/C-067619; mr (detail) NAC/C-003854; br (detail) McCord Museum of Canadian History, Montreal; bl Metropolitan Toronto Reference Library (E2-21B); ml PAA, H. Pollard Collection, P.1059 **139** tr Prince Edward Island Public Archives and Records Office, Acc. No. 2301-258; mr PAA, E. Brown Collection, B.37; bl GA (NA-1807-9) **140** br CP Picture Archive (Ken Gigliotti); bl CP Picture Archive (Ron Poling) **141** tr bl CP Picture Archive (Fred Chartrand) **151** (detail) NAL/C-050366 **152** tr *Completion of the Atlantic Telegraph Cable* (detail), The Illustrated London News Picture Library; ml *First Long Distance Telephone Call*, by Rex Woods, by kind permission of Rogers Communications, Inc.; br (detail) AO, Acc. 9434, S14861 **153** tr (detail) NAL/C-058477t; mr (detail) Notman & Son/NAC/C-017831; bc (detail) *Mr. Messiter's skating group, Montreal, QC*, 1869, I-37055.1, McCord Museum of Canadian History, Montreal; ml (detail) *Assorting the ore, Huntington Copper Mining Company's works, Bolton, QC*, 1867, N-0000.94.56, McCord Museum of Canadian History, Montreal **154** mc (detail) NAC/C-079643; mr (detail) NAC/PA-041359; br Hudson's Bay Company Archives, P-221, PAM **155** tr *Fort Garry*, 37-1878, PAM; mr Transportation - Boat - Dakota 1, PAM, N3440; ml Boundary Commission (1872-1874) 215, PAM, N14134 **156** (detail) NAL/C-048653 **157** bl HBCA Photograph Collection, 1987/363-C-43/6 Armorial Bearings of The Governor and Company of Adventurers of England Trading into Hudson's Bay, Hudson's Bay Company Archives, Provincial Archives of Manitoba. **158** GA (NA-1039-1) **162** tr (detail) NAC/C-018082; bl (detail) Frances Anne Hopkins/ NAC/C-002775 C-134840 (In memory of Viscount Wolsely) **169** bl (detail) BCA/C-04909; br (detail) E. Sandys/NAC/ C-011040 **170** Courtesy of the Historic O'Keefe Ranch **173** tl (detail) BCA/A-01350; tr (detail) BCA/A-01222 **175** (detail) NAC/C-012068 **176** tl (detail) BCA/A-04422; mr (digitally altered with permission) GA (NA-674-15); br BCA/B-03567; bl GA (NA-674-21); ml (detail) BCA/A-03033 **177** GA (NA-65-7) **179** PA **180** *Fanny Bailey*, ca.1858, J. Hunter (oil on canvas, 46.5 x 64.7 cm), Confederation Centre Art Gallery & Museum, Charlottetown, CAG 80.5 **181** NAC/C-046946 **182** Prince Edward Island Public Archives and Records Office, Acc. No. 2301-222 **183** PANL # B4-40, Provincial Archives of Newfoundland and Labrador **184** (detail) NAL/C-058640 **188** tl bl (detail) NAC/C-004154; ml (detail) NAC/C-010460 **189** (based on) NAC/C-008449 **190** (detail) NAC/C-010460 **191** ml PA; mr (detail) NAC/PA-028973 **192** NAL/C-063039 **193** tl (detail) NAC/C-010460 **194** tr (detail) NAC/PA-071697; br NAL/C-038966; bl GA (NA-1107-14); ml GA (NA-1966-20); tl (detail) Charles William Jefferys/NAC/C-073415 **195** Henri Julien/NAL/C-064551 **196** tl © Arnold Publishing Ltd.; ml PAA, H. Pollard Collection, P.126; br GA (NA-302-1) **197** GA (NA-550-18) **198** tr © Arnold Publishing Ltd.; mr GA (NA-23-1) **199** GA (NA-361-12) **200** tl GA (NA-23-2); mr GA (NA-1071-1) **201** tl GA (NA-2382-1); tr GA (NA-1237-1) **202** ml GA (NA-1060-2); bl GA (NA-2578-15) **203** tl GA (NA-

361-1); ml GA (NA-354-23); bl GA (NA-1241-99) **204** tl GA (NA-659-15); tc GA (NA-1771-1); mc GA (NA-23-2); bl GA (NA-40-1); ml GA (NA-29-1) **205** (top to bottom) (7) GA (NA-4809-3); (8) GA (NA-2054-6); (9a) GA (NA-716-19); (9b) GA (NA-25-9) **207** bl (detail) NAC/C-004154; bc (detail) NAC/C-010460 **210** Courtesy of the Royal British Columbia Museum, Victoria, British Columbia, PN 1499 **212** tr © Canada Post Corporation, 1999. Reproduced with Permission; br CP Picture Archive (Annette Bourgeois) **215** Steam train at Heritage Park Historical Village, Calgary, Alberta (www.heritagepark.ab.ca) **216** (detail) NAC/C-004154 **218** NAC/C-095466 **220** CTA, SC478-19 **221** tr © Bettmann/CORBIS; mr NAL/C-027839; br Digital imagery® copyright 1999 PhotoDisc, Inc. **222** tl (detail) William James Topley/NAC/PA-028026; bl (detail) William James Topley/ NAC/PA-028035 **224** NAC/C-001173 **225** tr J.F. Cooke/NAC/C-014114; br Courtesy Penney Clark; ml NAC/C-001602 **226** (top to bottom) (1) (detail) NAC/C-008549; (2) (detail) NAC/C-005489; (3) GA (NA-1375-4); (4) (detail) BCA/A-01321; (5) GA (NA-1949-1) **227** tl (detail) William James Topley/NAC/PA-026664; mc GA (NA-29-1); br (based on) Rev. Father Lacombe O.M.I., PAA, E. Brown Collection, B.9521; bl *The Birth of Standard Time*, by Rex Woods, by kind permission of Rogers Communications, Inc. **228** Vancouver Public Library, Special Collections, VPL 1773 **230** GA (NA-1494-5) **232** Ed Laugham/NAC/C-014115 **233** GA (NA-504-3) **236** (detail) Sergt. Grundy/NAC/C-002424 **237** tl (detail) Geraldine Moodie/NAC/PA-028853; tc (detail) Duffin & Co./NAC/ C-017430; tr SAB, Photograph No. R-A 6277; mc (detail) Major-General Frederick Middleton, Acc. 6876, #23, AO **238** tl GA (NA-1081-3); bl GA (NA-3012-4) **239** tr NAC/C-001173; br Glenbow Library (M1837f.22) **241** NAC/C-006536 **242** bl Hockey Hall of Fame; br NAC/PA-074583 **244** (based on) J.W. Bengough/NAC/C-013211 **247** Immigration 15, Stovel Advocate, PAM, N7934 **248** (detail) NAC/C-000688 **249** E.A. Hegg/NAC/C-005142 **250** tl Larss & Duclos/NAC/C-006648; br *Klondike Trail of '98*, by J.D. Kelly and Thomas Wilberforce Mitchell, by kind permission of Rogers Communications, Inc. **251** (detail) Yukon Archives, Martha Louise Black Collection, #3258 **252** tr bc GA (NA-2420-4); br Digital imagery® copyright 1999 PhotoDisc, Inc.; bl GA (NC-43-13) **253** ml (detail) William James Topley/NAC/PA-042183; mr br PA **254** NAL/C-030621 **255** tr Sifton, Clifford 1, PAM, N19973; bl NAC/C-063257 **256** tr (detail) William James Topley/NAC/C-010254; br PAA, E. Brown Collection, B.7235; ml GA (NA-984-2) **257** tr GA (NA-359-5); mr WCPI, #14; br GA (NA-695-1) **258** tr (detail) NAC/PA-066890; mr GA (NA-263-1); bc (detail) NAC/PA-125113; ml WCPI, A0273-08776 **259** (detail) NAC/C-065432 **260** tr PAA, E. Brown Collection, B.9945; mr GA (NA-303-158); br GA (NA-1262-5); bl GA (NA-1368-2); ml GA (NA-474-7) **261** tl PAA, H. Pollard Collection, P.226; tr GA (NA-4433-29); mr PAA, H. Pollard Collection, P.457; bl SAB, Photograph No. R-A4809 **262** tr PAA, E. Brown Collection, B.5050; br GA (NA-303-144); bl GA (NA-559-12); ml Winnipeg-Streets-Main 1905 #4, PAM, N10338 **264** tr PAA, E. Brown Collection, B.6661; mr GA (NA-2251-8); b PAA, E. Brown Collection, B.6635; ml PAA, Photograph Collection, A.439 **265** t SAB, Photograph No. R-B1095; mc SAB, Photograph No. R-A2470; br SAB, Photograph No. R-B930 **272** bc (detail) NAC/C-000688; br (detail) Dupras & Solas/NAC/C-000694 **273** tr GA (NA-1643-4); bl GA (NA-1640-2); mc CTA, SC478-19; ml PAA, H. Pollard Collection, P.226 **274** tl (detail) NAC/C-000688; mr PAA, E. Brown Collection, B.273 **275** mr Industry & Commerce, PAM, N231; br These illustrations within this book are reprinted by arrangement with Sears, Roebuck and Co. and are protected under copyright. No duplication is permitted (1905 Sears Catalog).; bc (detail) Illustrations by Grace H.H. Cochrane in Mrs. Ralston's "Little Men and Women in Their Spring Clothes", April 1905 Issue. © Copyright 1905, Meredith Corporation. All rights reserved. Used

with the permission of **Ladies' Home Journal®. 276** ml GA (NA-644-11); tr © 1999 Eyewire, Inc. **279** CTA, SC244-137 **280** mr NAL/C-030945; bl (detail) F1075-9-0-7, 88973, AO; ml (detail) NAC/PA-070057 **281** br (based on) NAL/C-030953; bl Foote 1491, PAM, N2438 **282** tr CTA, Board of Education, 92; mr (detail) James William/NAC/PA-126710 **283** tc WCPI, A 1311-39208; tr Canada's Sports Hall of Fame; br Canadian Football Hall of Fame Library; bl City of Vancouver Archives, BR.P.59, N.48 **284** tc (detail) NAC/C-011299; tr (detail) N.B. Henry/NAC/C-014141; ml (detail) NAL/C-029722 **287** tr PAA, E. Brown Collection, B.3955; c Kempthorne-Schools-1, PAM, N16510 **288** (detail) NAC/C-000688 **289** tl (based on) NAC/C-028727; br (based on) John Wilson Bengough/NAC/C-008427 **290** br (detail) NAC/C-024630; bl (detail) Steele & Co./NAC/PA-028911 **292** CTA SC244-585 **293** tl (detail) NAC/C-000688; br This publication includes images from *Corel Professional Photos* CD-ROMs which are protected by the copyright laws of the US, Canada, and elsewhere. Used under license. The photographic images may not be copied and are only to be used for viewing purposes. **294** (detail) Dupras & Solas/NAC/C-000694 **295** (detail) Sir Robert Borden/NAC/C-002082 **299** NAC/C-095392 **302** The Granger Collection, New York **303** tr (detail) William James Topley/NAC/PA-012223; mr CTA, SC244-824 **304** tl C273, Acc. 9164, S15159, AO; mr Kapuskasing internment camp, Acc. AO 9905, #27, AO; ml *Your Country Calls*, Paul Wickson, Metropolitan Toronto Reference Library **305** tr E. Henderson/NAC/C-095281; bl NAC/C-095730 **306** NAC/PA-001326 **307** (detail) NAC/PA-002855 **308** tr (detail) NAC/PA-002259; mc NAC/PA-000627; br William Ivor Castle/NAC/PA-000648; bl (based on) NAC/PA-002195 **309** mr NAC/PA-002946; br (based on) NAC/PA-000364; bl (based on) NAC/PA-001679 **310** William Ivor Castle/NAC/PA-001231 **311** t *The Taking of Vimy Ridge*, Richard Jack, 8178, © Canadian War Museum; br (detail) William Rider-Rider/NAC/PA-002162 **313** Glen BonBernard **314** bl *War in the Air*, Chistopher R.W. Nevinson, 8651, © Canadian War Museum; br NAC/PA-022731 **315** tl (detail) NAC/PA-001651; tc (detail) NAC/PA-002067; tr (detail) NAC/PA-001315; bc (detail) NAC/PA-002364; bl PANL #CI-23/a Provincial Archives of Newfoundland and Labrador; ml (detail) London Lafayette/NAC/C-088237 **316** br CTA, SC244-873; bl NAC/PA-024639; tl CTA, SC244-640 **317** t (detail) NAC/PA-024438; bl (detail) NAC/PA-005909 **318** CTA, SC244-2450 **319** tc Toronto Reference Library; br Judy Bauer/Arnold Publishing Ltd.; bl Trudie BonBernard **321** (detail) NAC/C-006859 **324** tr (detail) NAC/PA-008158; bl (based on) NAC/PA-002318; ml (detail) NAC/PA-002279 **325** Simmons/NAC/C-000242 **327** mr br PA; bl (based on) NAL/C-009021 **329** Toronto Reference Library **330** b GA (NB-16-609) **331** tr GA (NA-3452-2) **332** (detail) McDermid Studios/NAC/C-056695 **334** Foote 1696, PAM, N2762 **336** tr NAC/C-096443; mr GA (NA-1870-6); br (detail) BCA/D-09120; bl WCPI, A0195-06191 **337** Used with permission of Sears Canada Inc. ml NAL/C-100040 **339** tl GA (NA-1514-3); mc GA (NA-273-3) **340** tl GA (NC-6-1746); tr GA (NA-1068-2) **341** tr Tom Thomson, *Canoe Lake*, 1913, Collection of the Tom Thomson Memorial Art Gallery, Owen Sound, Ontario, Canada, Gift of Mrs. J.G. Henry, (www.tomthomson.org); bl City of Vancouver Archives, CVA-677-96 **342** tr GA (NA-2685-87); mr CTA, SC244-320; br Digital imagery® copyright 1999 PhotoDisc, Inc.; bc (detail), Mary Pickford, Acc. 2799, F2082-2-1-10, AO **344** br SAB, Photograph No. R-A2260-2 **345** bl Archives Nationales du Québec à Québec **351** (detail) NAL/C-048653 **359** (based on) NAL/C-009021 **360** Pierre Descellier/NAC/ NMC 40461 **369** Corel Corporation, Ottawa, Ontario, Canada. This publication includes images from *Corel Gallery 2* which are protected by the copyright laws of the U.S., Canada, and elsewhere. Used under license. **Back End Sheet** (1) tr (detail) NAC/C-004154; mr Government of Canada/NAC/C-004393

Index

```
_____KEY_____
● map   ■ picture   ▲ chart   ◆ biography
```

E

Eastern Townships 77
Eaton's catalogue 275
economic conditions 25, 277, 293, 330, 344
Edmonton 262■, 264■
education 20, 24, 25, 38, 39, 96, 131, 150, 152. *See also* schools
Edwards, Henrietta Muir (suffragist) 339
Elders 4, 57, 59
electricity 252, 274
electronic age 252
Elgin, Lord (governor) 19
employment insurance 153
energy sources. *See* power sources
enfranchisement. *See* right to vote
English–French conflict. *See* French–English relations
English–French relations. *See* French–English relations
entertainment 242, 283, 345
environmental interaction
    along the Pacific Coast 32–33
    in New Brunswick 81
    in Newfoundland 83
    in Nova Scotia 80
    in Prince Edward Island 82
    in Rupert's Land 56–57, 58–59
    in the United Province of Canada 78
epidemics 208, 331. *See also* cholera, diphtheria, flu epidemic, typhoid
ethnic diversity 72
Europeans 5, 6, 7, 55, 60, 68, 69
executive branch 132
exploration 2
    Asian 5, 6
    European 5●, 6
    French 6, 7, 9●
explorers 5, 6, 8, 30, 34, 55
    along the Pacific Coast 8, 30, 34
    from Britain 8, 30, 34
    from England 5, 6
    from France 5, 6
    from Russia 8, 34
    from Spain 6, 8, 34
    from the United States 8
exports 192, 253▲, 317▲, 333, 345. *See also* trade

F

factories 184, 192, 219, 252, 278, 279■, 280, 316, 317, 333
factory system 219■▲
Falcon, Pierre (song writer) 67◆
Family Compact 18
farm implements 194, 252■, 253■
farming 9, 20, 72, 78, 80, 81, 82, 105, 153, 169, 170, 177, 178, 192, 273, 335, 344
    in the West 177, 178, 254
    Metis 60, 61, 66
Fathers of Confederation 125–127
federal government 94, 130–131
federal union 96, 101, 108, 112, 113
federal/provincial conflict 28
    in Nova Scotia 150, 151
    in Quebec 141
federalism 130, 131
Fenians 92, 99■, 108, 110, 123, 126, 168, 201
First Nations 2–8, 10, 12, 17, 44, 46, 69, 211●. *See also* Aboriginal peoples, Anishinabe, Assiniboine, Cree, Dakota, Dene, Kainai, Kwakwaka'wakw, Maliseet, Mi'kmaq, Nakoda, Nakota, Nuu-chah-nulth, Pikuni, Saulteaux, Shuswap, Siksika, Sto:lo, Tlingit, Tsuu T'ina, Woodland Cree
    along the Pacific Coast 30, 32●–34, 42, 48■, 49
    and the North-West Resistance 234–237
    attempts to assimilate 17, 336
    culture 3, 4, 32, 33, 56–59
    definition 54
    discrimination against 239, 336, 345
    in British Columbia 170, 175, 176■, 210■
    in New Caledonia 40
    in Rupert's Land 16, 52, 55, 60, 66, 68, 148, 154, 163
    in the North-West Territories 179, 196■–200, 202–204, 207–209, 260■, 261■
    in the United Province of Canada 76
    location 3●, 32●, 56●, 58●, 196●, 199●, 200●
    self-government 212
    traditional ways of life 3
    treaties 8, 42, 48, 179, 186, 188, 201, 204, 207●–209, 211, 234
    values 3, 4
fishing 20, 72, 80, 81, 82, 83, 123, 153, 166, 168, 170, 171
fishing rights (American) 168
Fleming, Sandford (CPR engineer) 195, 227■
flu epidemic 331, 345
football 283
forestry 20, 48■, 76, 78, 80, 81, 123, 153, 169, 171
Fort Astoria 34●
Fort Benton (USA) 196, 199, 200●
Fort Calgary 202, 203●

Fort Douglas 66
Fort Edmonton (HBC post) 46, 199●
Fort Garry 46, 155, 159, 160
Fort Hamilton. *See* Fort Whoop-Up
Fort Kamloops (HBC post) 46
Fort Langley (HBC post) 36●, 40■, 41●, 42■
Fort Macleod 200, 201, 202, 203
Fort Vancouver (HBC post) 34●■, 35
Fort Victoria (HBC post) 34●, 35■, 36■●, 37–41●
Fort Walsh 202■
Fort Whoop-Up 196●■, 197■, 198–201
Fort William 13■
Foulis, Robert (inventor) 84–85
Fraser River 40, 46. *See* Lower Fraser River
Fraser Valley. *See* Lower Fraser River
free trade 74, 75, 79, 94, 95, 98, 106, 123, 193
    Metis 68
French Canadian nationalism 285, 288–292
French colonial rule (1663–1759) 2, 8, 9–11
French–English relations 12, 13, 20, 96, 122, 125, 127, 140–141, 239, 344, 345. *See also* Manitoba Schools Question, Struggle for Control
    at the Red River 159, 160
    during World War I 320–323
    in education 150
    regarding Riel 238, 239
    under Laurier 270, 285–290
French, George (NWMP Commissioner) 198, 199●, 201
French language 13, 60, 72, 96, 141, 150, 160, 285
Frobisher, Martin (explorer) 6
"From Sea to Sea" 156
Fubbister, John. *See* Gunn, Isabel
fur trade 7, 9, 10, 11, 17, 55
    in British Columbia 169
    in the North-West Territories 196
    in the Pacific region 34●, 36, 40
    in Rupert's Land 55, 57, 196
    rivalry 8, 54
fur traders 30, 34
    Aboriginal 34
    American 34, 40, 196–200
    British 40
    in Rupert's Land 52, 55
    on the Pacific Coast 30, 34●, 139■
    Russian 35, 40

KEY
● map　■ picture　▲ chart　◆ biography

KEY

● map   ■ picture   ▲ chart   ◆ biography

KEY
● map   ■ picture   ▲ chart   ◆ biography

KEY

● map   ■ picture   ▲ chart   ◆ biography

KEY
● map   ■ picture   ▲ chart   ◆ biography

Some Useful Websites

- SchoolNet
  www.schoolnet.ca/home/e/index.html

- Canadian Heritage (Parks Canada)
  http://www.pch.gc.ca
  (Ceremonial and Canadian Symbols and National Historical Sites)

- Canadian Museum of Civilization
  http://www.civilization.ca/

- CRB FoundationHeritage Project
  http://www.heritageproject.ca/

- National Archives of Canada
  http://www.archives.ca
  (The First Century of Confederation)

- National Library of Canada (Confederation)
  http://www.nlc-bnc.ca/confed/e-1867.htm
  (Mothers of Confederation)
  http://www.nlc-bnc.ca/confed/moc.htm

- BC Archives (Time Machine)
  http://www.bcarchives.gov.bc.ca/exhibits/timemach/galler09/frames/index.htm
  (First Nations Art in BC, The Caribou Gold Rush, First Nations in BC, Multiculturalism, and Economy and Technology)

- Canadian War Museum
  http://www.civilization.ca/cwm/cwmeng/cwmeng.html

- WW1 Trenches
  http://www.worldwar1.com/

- The National Gallery of Canada
  http://national.gallery.ca

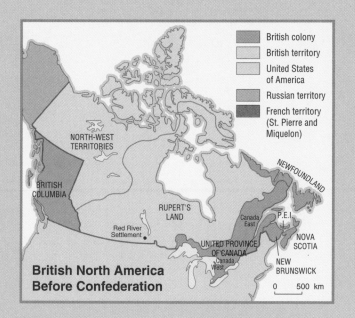

British colony
British territory
United States of America
Russian territory
French territory (St. Pierre and Miquelon)

NORTH-WEST TERRITORIES

BRITISH COLUMBIA

NEWFOUNDLAND

RUPERT'S LAND

Red River Settlement

Canada East

P.E.I

UNITED PROVINCE OF CANADA

Canada West

NOVA SCOTIA

NEW BRUNSWICK

British North America Before Confederation

0   500 km

Prime Ministers to 1920

□ Conservative Party   □ Liberal Party

Sir John A. Macdonald	1867–1873
Alexander Mackenzie	1873–1878
Sir John A. Macdonald	1878–1891
Sir John J. C. Abbott	1891–1892
Sir John S. D. Thompson	1892–1894
Sir Mackenzie Bowell	1894–1896
Sir Charles Tupper	1896
Sir Wilfrid Laurier	1896–1911
Sir Robert L. Borden	1911–1920

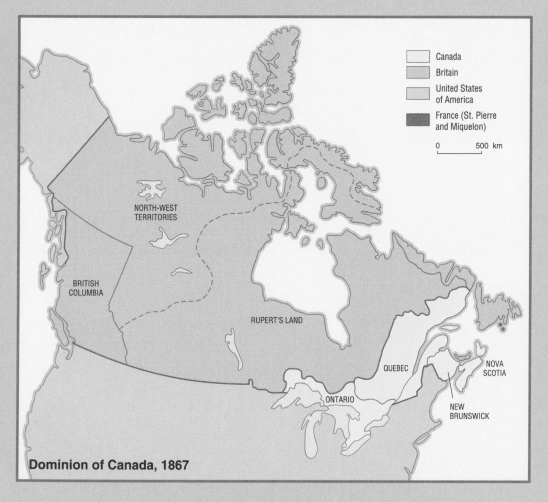

Canada
Britain
United States of America
France (St. Pierre and Miquelon)

0   500 km

NORTH-WEST TERRITORIES

BRITISH COLUMBIA

RUPERT'S LAND

QUEBEC

NOVA SCOTIA

ONTARIO

NEW BRUNSWICK

Dominion of Canada, 1867

Manitoba
Becomes a Province, 1870

Legend: Canada · Britain · United States of America · France (St. Pierre and Miquelon) · 0 500 km

NORTH-WEST TERRITORIES
MANITOBA
QUEBEC
ONTARIO
NOVA SCOTIA
NEW BRUNSWICK

Dominion of Canada, 1875

Legend: Canada · Britain · United States of America · France (St. Pierre and Miquelon) · 0 500 km

NORTH-WEST TERRITORIES
District of Keewatin
BRITISH COLUMBIA
MANITOBA
NORTH-WEST TERRITORIES
ONTARIO
QUEBEC
PRINCE EDWARD ISLAND
NOVA SCOTIA
NEW BRUNSWICK

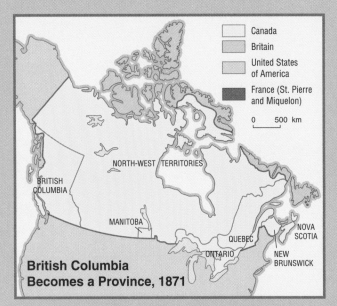

British Columbia
Becomes a Province, 1871

Legend: Canada · Britain · United States of America · France (St. Pierre and Miquelon) · 0 500 km

NORTH-WEST TERRITORIES
BRITISH COLUMBIA
MANITOBA
QUEBEC
ONTARIO
NOVA SCOTIA
NEW BRUNSWICK

Dominion of Canada, 1898

Legend: Canada · Britain · United States of America · France (St. Pierre and Miquelon) · 0 500 km

YUKON TERRITORY
NORTH-WEST TERRITORIES
BRITISH COLUMBIA
MANITOBA
QUEBEC
ONTARIO
PRINCE EDWARD ISLAND
NOVA SCOTIA
NEW BRUNSWICK

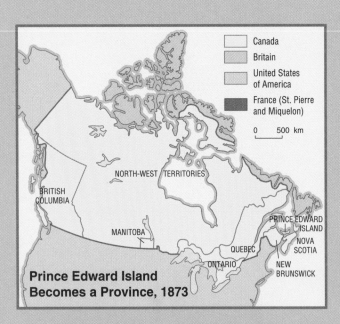

Prince Edward Island
Becomes a Province, 1873

Legend: Canada · Britain · United States of America · France (St. Pierre and Miquelon) · 0 500 km

NORTH-WEST TERRITORIES
BRITISH COLUMBIA
MANITOBA
QUEBEC
ONTARIO
PRINCE EDWARD ISLAND
NOVA SCOTIA
NEW BRUNSWICK

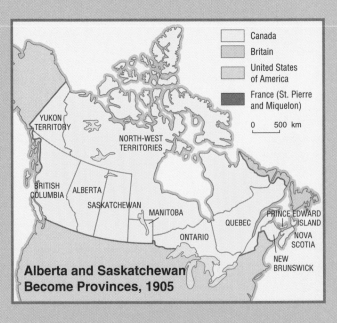

Alberta and Saskatchewan
Become Provinces, 1905

Legend: Canada · Britain · United States of America · France (St. Pierre and Miquelon) · 0 500 km

YUKON TERRITORY
NORTH-WEST TERRITORIES
BRITISH COLUMBIA
ALBERTA
SASKATCHEWAN
MANITOBA
QUEBEC
ONTARIO
PRINCE EDWARD ISLAND
NOVA SCOTIA
NEW BRUNSWICK